HISTORY AND RELATED DISCIPLINES
SELECT BIBLIOGRAPHIES
GENERAL EDITOR: R. C. RICHARDSON

WESTERN
POLITICAL THOUGHT

This is a comprehensive and accessible guide to the vast literature on the history of political thought which has appeared in English since 1945. The editors provide a brief annotation of the content of many entries and, where appropriate, indicate their significance and controversial nature.

This bibliography should become a standard reference work for students and scholars of political thought.

Robert Eccleshall is Professor of Politics at Queen's University, Belfast and Michael Kenny is Lecturer in Politics at the University of Sheffield.

HISTORY AND RELATED DISCIPLINES
SELECT BIBLIOGRAPHIES
GENERAL EDITOR: R. C. RICHARDSON

Bibliographical guides designed to meet the needs of under-graduates, postgraduates and their teachers in universities and colleges of higher education. All volumes in the series share a number of common characteristics. They are selective, manageable in size, and include those books and articles which are most impor-tant and useful. All volumes are edited by practising teachers of the subject and are based on their experience of the needs of students. The arrangement combines chronological with thematic divisions. Most of the items listed receive some descriptive comment.

Already published in the series:

BRITISH ECONOMIC AND SOCIAL HISTORY

EUROPEAN ECONOMIC AND SOCIAL HISTORY

RUSSIA AND EASTERN EUROPE, 1789–1985

THE STUDY OF HISTORY

SOCIETY AND ECONOMY
IN EARLY MODERN EUROPE

JAPANESE STUDIES FROM PRE-HISTORY TO 1990

BRITISH AND IRISH ARCHAEOLOGY

AFRICA, ASIA AND SOUTH AMERICA SINCE 1800

WESTERN
POLITICAL THOUGHT

A BIBLIOGRAPHICAL GUIDE
TO POST-WAR RESEARCH

COMPILED BY

ROBERT ECCLESHALL
AND MICHAEL KENNY

WITH THE ASSISTANCE OF MICHAEL DROLET,
GERARD FITZPATRICK AND GERARD McCANN

MANCHESTER UNIVERSITY PRESS
Manchester and New York

Distributed exclusively in the USA and Canada by St. Martin's Press

Published by
MANCHESTER UNIVERSITY PRESS
Oxford Road, Manchester M13 9PL, UK
and Room 400, 175 Fifth Avenue, New York
NY 10010, USA
Distributed exclusively in the USA and Canada by
St. Martin's Press, Inc., 175 Fifth Avenue, New York,
NY 10010, USA

British Library cataloguing-in-publication data
A catalogue record for this book is available from the
British Library

Library of Congress cataloging-in-publication data
Eccleshall, Robert.
  Western political thought : a bibliographical guide to post-war
research / compiled by Robert Eccleshall and Michael Kenny, with the
assistance of Michael Drolet, Gerard Fitzpatrick, and Gerard McCann.
      p.   cm. — (History and related disciplines select
bibliographies)
  ISBN 0-7190-3569-4
  1. Political science—History—Bibliography. I. Kenny, Michael.
II. Title. III. Series.
Z7161.E25   1995
[JA83]
016.32'001—dc20   94-26466
                                                              CIP

ISBN 0 7190 3569 4 *hardback*

Photoset in Linotron Plantin
by Northern Phototypesetting Co. Ltd, Bolton

Printed in Great Britain
by Cromwell Press Ltd, Melksham

CONTENTS

CONTENTS

GENERAL EDITOR'S PREFACE

History, to an even greater extent than most other academic disciplines, has developed at a prodigious pace in the twentieth century. Its scope has extended and diversified, its methodologies have been revolutionized, its philosophy has changed, and its relations with other disciplines have been transformed. The number of students and teachers of the subject in the different branches of higher education has vastly increased, and there is an ever-growing army of amateurs, many of them taking adult education courses. Academic and commercial publishers have produced a swelling stream of publications – both specialist and general – to cater for this large and expanding audience. Scholarly journals have proliferated. It is no easy matter even for specialists to keep abreast of the flow of publications in their particular field. For those with more general academic interests the task of finding what has been written on different subject areas can be time-consuming, perplexing, and often frustrating.

It is primarily to meet the needs of undergraduates, postgraduates and their teachers in universities and colleges of higher education, that this series of bibliographies is designed. It will be a no less valuable resource, however, to the reference collection of any public library, school or college.

Though common sense demands that each volume will be structured in the way which is most appropriate for the particular field in question, nonetheless all volumes in the series share a number of important common characteristics. First – quite deliberately – all are *select* bibliographies, manageable in size, and include those books and articles which in the editor's judgement are most important and useful. To attempt an uncritically comprehensive listing would needlessly dictate the inclusions of items which were frankly ephemeral, antiquarian, or discredited and result only in the production of a bulky and unwieldy volume. Like any select bibliography, however, this series will direct the reader where appropriate to other, more specialised and detailed sources of bibliographical information. That would be one of its functions. Second, all the volumes are edited not simply by specialists in the different fields but by practising teachers of the subject, and are based on their experience of the needs of students in higher education. Third, there are common features of arrangement and presentation. All volumes begin with listings of general works of a methodological or historiographical nature, and proceed within broad chronological divisions to arrange their material thematically. Most items will receive some descriptive comment. Each volume, for ease of reference, has an index of authors and editors.

R. C. RICHARDSON

EDITORIAL PREFACE

The literature on the history of political thought is now enormous, and even the specialist cannot keep abreast of the flow of books and articles on the subject. This bibliography is a reasonably comprehensive guide to the literature that has appeared since 1945, providing a brief annotation of the content of many entries and, where appropriate, indicating their significance, controversial nature and readability. As such it is intended to be useful to students and teachers of the history of political thought, as well as to researchers and specialists. The boundaries between the sub-disciplines of Politics are not precise, moreover, and those interested in public policy or international relations, for example, sometimes turn to political thought to elucidate problems that arise in the course of their research. The bibliography is intended to assist them as much as those with a direct interest in the subject.

The bibliography is arranged into eight sections. The first contains items on methodology, long- and shorter-span histories of political thought, and entries on works dealing with particular themes in the history of political thought – gender, contractarianism and the like. Following the general section are seven chronological ones, the first three covering the Western tradition until the sixteenth century and the next four each subsequent century. Each section begins with a sub-section on general works, followed by ones on geographical areas and specific thinkers. Many thinkers lived in more than one century, and in such cases – Bentham and Kautsky, for example – we have located them in the century in which they wrote most of their work.

In these ways the bibliography is intended to be both accessible and amenable to various users. There are sub-sections for those interested in particular thinkers or themes – Machiavelli, for example, or the British debate about the Revolution of 1688. Used in conjunction with the index the bibliography indicates the post-war contribution of specific scholars to aspects of political thought – Margaret Canovan on Arendt, for instance, or Quentin Skinner on both particular thinkers and methodological issues. In mapping the sometimes inaccessible terrain of secondary literature on political thought, finally, we hope to have given an overview of the directions in which the subject has moved in recent decades.

The bibliography, though in some respects fairly exhaustive, is necessarily restricted in scope. For practical reasons it is confined to the political thought of the British Isles, continental Europe and North America, even though there are rich traditions of political discourse beyond this geographical area. Excluded also are the primary writings of political thinkers, even those authors such as John Rawls whose corpus falls within the post-war period. This may seem a pity because some of the best work in political thought in recent decades has been editorial enterprises (Peter Laslett's edition of Locke's *Two Treatises of Government*, the Bentham project, Cambridge University Press's texts in the history of political thought, and so forth). Apart from constraints of space, however, our feeling is that anyone interested in the subject will probably discover primary material without assistance from a bibliographical guide.

Omitted from the bibliography, thirdly, is reference to much post-war political philosophy, apart from the secondary literature on particular thinkers such as Rawls and C. B. Macpherson. Since the 1970s there has been a deal of systematic reflection upon key political concepts such as liberty, justice and democracy. But an adequate directory to contemporary political philosophy would entail a separate volume – though at the end of the first section we have included about forty items on 'The nature of political theory' which give a flavour of the debates currently preoccupying political philosophers. We have, finally, excluded items dealing with political ideologies. Our intention was to include entries on the history of conservatism, liberalism and other doctrines, partly because of the growing number of university courses on the subject but also because of the post-war shift to a more contextual history of political thought – recognition that the subject-matter is constituted not so much by a few canonical texts as by rival traditions of political discourse to which numerous writers have contributed. But the inclusion of such items would have made the volume too bulky: indeed, there is now sufficient literature on ideologies to justify a separate bibliography on the subject.

One problem in deciding what to exclude from the bibliography was that of determining the conceptual scope of political thought. Political ideas have traditionally been expressed in religious and other language, which means that much of the secondary literature on Renaissance humanism, say, does not isolate the political thinking of the period from social, economic, legal, philosophical or theological notions. Until recently, moreover, there were no professional political philosophers. Many of the prominent figures in the history of political thought speculated about an impressive array of subjects, and again the secondary literature reflects the absence in their writings of a discrete 'political' category. These difficulties in drawing a boundary around political thought have increased because of post-war methodological developments in the subject, which have extended the range of authors deemed to be political thinkers as well as the kind of writings in which their ideas are to be found. In the first, 'General', section of the bibliography is a sub-section on 'Methods and purposes in the history of political thought', which contains entries by and about those intellectual historians – Quentin Skinner, J. G. A. Pocock and others – who have been responsible for this shift in our understanding of where political thought is to be discovered. No longer is political thought confined to classic texts containing ideas of a few individuals who reveal universal truths about the human condition; but is to be understood as a social activity undertaken by many people using various linguistic conventions. Political thought, according to the new methodology, is likely to be located as much in an ephemeral sermon or poem as in Hobbes's *Leviathan*. And this requires intellectual historians to cast their nets wide in searching for the appropriate context of political writings. The new contextualism has encouraged historians of political thought to extend the canon of political texts, and in doing so has compounded the problem of deciding what – given limits of space – ought to be included in a bibliography of the history of political thought.

To keep the bibliography within reasonable bounds we have excluded general histories, intellectual or otherwise, of particular periods unless they contain substantial commentary on political ideas. As far as specific thinkers are concerned we have included only the secondary literature which deals with their political thought. In the case of Hobbes, for example, the bulk of the literature does touch upon his political thinking, and we have therefore included nearly all the writings about him of which we are aware (excluding only those few articles and books which discuss his psychology or scientific method, for instance, in isolation from his political philosophy). For other thinkers – Calvin, Swift, Freud, and so on – our criteria of selection have excluded most of the scholarly work on them.

The numbering of entries is consecutive within each section and not through the volume as a whole. Cross-references are given where appropriate, and places of publication are given when these are outside Britain. Complementing the subject-cataloguing of the body of the bibliography is a separate index to the authors and editors named in the text.

Within the boundaries of what we take to constitute political thought we have sought to be fairly exhaustive, though some items will have been missed and others improperly omitted because of editorial stringency. The annotations are intended to be fair even when critical, though no doubt some authors will protest that their arguments have been misunderstood and distorted.

Our task was more demanding than we anticipated, and would not have been completed without far more than the usual clerical and library assistance as well as help from postgraduate students who for a pittance gladly checked references and brought us armfuls of books and periodicals. To these co-workers we acknowledge our gratitude: Kris Brown, Betty Donnelly, Stephen Farry, Gerard Gribben, John Gribben, Florence Gray, Marita Jaschob, Ellen Kruse, Eileen McNeil, Alan McMillan, Eileen Maguire, Suzanne Presland, Louise Seaye and Michael Smallman. We would also like to thank Richard English and Vincent Geoghegan for suggestions about particular thinkers.

Robert Eccleshall and Michael Kenny
January 1994

ABBREVIATIONS

Acta Polit. Acta Politica
Am. Econ. Rev. American Economic Review
Am. Hist. Rev. American Historical Review
Am. J. Econ. & Soc. American Journal of Economics and Sociology
Am. J. Leg. Hist. American Journal of Legal History
Am. J. Soc. American Journal of Sociology
Am. Phil. Q. American Philosophical Quarterly
Am. Phil. Soc. American Philosophical Society
Am. Pol. Sc. Rev. American Political Science Review
Am. Scholar American Scholar
Am. Soc. Rev. American Sociological Review
Ancient Phil. Ancient Philosophy
Augustinian Sts. Augustinian Studies
Aust. J. Phil. Australasian Journal of Philosophy
Aust. J. Pol. & Hist. Australian Journal of Politics and History
Aust. J. Pol. Sc. Australian Journal of Political Science
Berkeley J. Sociol. Berkeley Journal of Sociology
Brit. J. Int. Sts. British Journal of International Studies
Brit. J. Soc. British Journal of Sociology
Brit. J. Pol. Sc. British Journal of Political Science
Bull. N.Y. Pub. Lib. Bulletin of the New York

Public Library
Bull. Res. Hum. Bulletin of Research in the Humanities
Cambridge Hist. J. Cambridge Historical Journal
Cambridge J. Cambridge Journal
Cambridge Rev. Cambridge Review
Can. Hist. Assoc. Hist. Papers Canadian Historical Association Historical Papers
Can. J. Econ. & Pol. Sc. Canadian Journal of Economics and Political Science
Can. J. Phil. Canadian Journal of Philosophy
Can. J. Pol. Sc. Canadian Journal of Political Science
Can. J. Pol. & Soc. Theory Canadian Journal of Political and Social Theory
Cath. Hist. Rev. Catholic Historical Review
Church Hist. Church History
Class. J. Classical Journal
Class. Philol. Classical Philology
Class. Q. Classical Quarterly
Comp. Pol. Comparative Politics
Comp. Sts. Soc. & Hist. Comparative Studies in Society and History
Contemp. Rev. Contemporary Review
Crit. Rev. Critical Review
Durham Univ. J. Durham University Journal
Econ. J. Economic Journal
Eighteenth-Cent. Life Eighteenth-Century Life
Eighteenth-Cent. Sts. Eighteenth-Century Studies

Eng. Hist. Rev. English Historical Review
Eng. Lit. Ren. English Literary Renaissance
Eur. Hist. Q. European History Quarterly
Eur. J. Soc. European Journal of Sociology
Eur. Sts. Rev. European Studies Review
Franciscan Sts. Franciscan Studies
Govt. & Oppos. Government and Opposition
Harv. Theol. Rev. Harvard Theological Review
Hibbert J. Hibbert Journal
Hist. Euro. Ideas History of European Ideas
Hist. J. Historical Journal
Hist. & Theory History and Theory
Hist. Pol. Econ. History of Political Economy
Hist. Pol. Thought History of Political Thought
Hist. Today History Today
Hobbes Sts. Hobbes Studies
Huntington Libr. Q. Huntington Library Quarterly
Int. Rev. Soc. Hist. International Review of Social History
Int. Soc. Sc. J. International Social Science Journal
Int. Sts. Phil. International Studies in Philosophy
Italian Sts. Italian Studies
Ital. Q. Italian Quarterly
J. Brit. Sts. Journal of British Studies
J. Eccl. Hist. Journal of Ecclesiastical History
J. Engl. & Germ. Philol. Journal of English and Germanic Philology
J. Euro. Hist. Journal of European History
J. Euro. Ideas Journal of European Ideas
J. Gen. Ed. Journal of General Education
J. Hellenic Sts. Journal of Hellenic Studies
J. Hist. Ideas Journal of the History of Ideas
J. Hist. Phil. Journal of the History of Philosophy
J. Liber. Sts. Journal of Libertarian Studies
J. Med. & Ren. Sts. Journal of Medieval and Renaissance Studies
J. Mod. Hist. Journal of Modern History
J. Pol. Econ. Journal of Political Economy
J. Pol. Journal of Politics
J. Rel. Hist. Journal of Religious History
J. Rom. Sts. Journal of Roman Studies

J. Soc. Phil. Journal of Social Philosophy
J. Theol. Sts. Journal of Theological Studies
J. Thought Journal of Thought
J. Warburg & Courtauld Inst. Journal of the Warburg and Courtauld Institute
Law & Hist. Rev. Law and History Review
Law Q. Rev. Law Quarterly Review
Med. Sts. Mediaeval Studies
Mod. Lang. Q. Modern Language Quarterly
Mod. Philol. Modern Philology
New Germ. Crit. New German Critique
New Left Rev. New Left Review
New Lit. Hist. New Literary History
New Pol. New Politics
New Schol. New Scholasticism
Nottingham Med. Sts. Nottingham Medieval Studies
Pac. Soc. Rev. Pacific Sociological Review
Past & Pres. Past and Present
Phil. Philosophy
Phil. Forum Philosophical Forum
Phil. Inq. Philosophical Inquiry
Philos. & Phenom. Res. Philosophical and Phenomenological Research
Phil. & Pub. Affairs Philosophy and Public Affairs
Phil. Q. Philosophical Quarterly
Phil. Rev. Philosophical Review
Phil. & Rhet. Philosophy and Rhetoric
Phil. & Soc. Crit. Philosophy and Social Criticism
Phil. Soc. Scs. Philosophy of the Social Sciences
Phil. Sts. (Ireland) Philosophical Studies (Ireland)
Phil. Today Philosophy Today
Pol. Sc. Political Science
Pol. Sc. Q. Political Science Quarterly
Pol. Sc. Re-r Political Science Reviewer
Pol. Sts. Political Studies
Pol. & Soc. Politics and Society
Pol. Theory Political Theory
Procs. Am. Cath. Phil. Ass. Proceedings of the American Catholic Philosophical Association
Procs. Am. Phil. Soc. Proceedings of the American Philosophical Society

Procs. Aris. Soc. Proceedings of the Aristotelian Society

Procs. Brit. Acad. Proceedings of the British Academy

Rad. Am. Radical America

Rad. Phil. Radical Philosophy

Rel. Sts. Religious Studies

Ren. & Ref. Renaissance and Reformation

Ren. Q. Renaissance Quarterly

Rev. Metaph. Review of Metaphysics

Rev. Nat. Lit. Review of National Literatures

Rev. Pol. Review of Politics

Russ. Rev. Russian Review

Salisbury Rev. Salisbury Review

Scand. Pol. Sts. Scandinavian Political Studies

Scott. Hist. Rev. Scottish Historical Review

Sc. & Soc. Science and Society

Sixteenth Cent. J. Sixteenth Century Journal

Slavic Rev. Slavic Review

Social Res. Social Research

Sociol. Inq. Sociological Inquiry

Sociol. Q. Sociological Quarterly

Soc. Sc. Q. Social Science Quarterly

Soc. Theory & Pract. Social Theory and Practice

Southern Econ. J. Southern Economic Journal

Southwestern J. Phil. Southwestern Journal of Philosophy

Sov. Sts. Phil. Soviet Studies in Philosophy

Sts. Burke & Time Studies in Burke and his Time

Sts. Ch. Hist. Studies in Church History

Sts. in Philol. Studies in Philology

Sts. Pol. Thought Studies in Political Thought

Sts. Ren. Studies in the Renaissance

Sts. Voltaire Studies on Voltaire and the Eighteenth Century

Theory & Soc. Theory and Society

Trans. Am. Philol. Assoc. Transactions of the American Philological Association

Trans. Am. Phil. Soc. Transactions of the American Philosophical Society

Trans. Bibliographical Soc. Transactions of the Bibliographical Society

Trans. Royal Hist. Soc. Transactions of the Royal Historical Society

Westminster Theol. J. Westminster Theological Journal

West. Pol. Q. Western Political Quarterly

Wom. Sts. Int. For. Women's Studies International Forum

Wm. & Mary Q. William and Mary Quarterly

1

ANCIENT
HISTORY

(a) METHODS AND PURPOSES IN THE HISTORY OF POLITICAL THOUGHT

1.1 **Ashcraft**, R., 'On the problem of methodology and the nature of political theory', *Pol. Theory*, 3, 1975, 5–25. An effective critique of the stance of Q. Skinner and others with regard to the interpretation of historical texts, arguing for a more flexible approach than that demonstrated by purists on either side of the methodological debate.

1.2 **Boucher**, D., *Texts in Context: Revisionist Methods for Studying the History of Ideas*, 1985. A lucid and comprehensive discussion of recent methodological debates, focusing upon the approaches of W. H. Greenleaf, Q. Skinner and J. G. A. Pocock.

1.3 **Condren**, C., 'Ideas and the model of political events: a problem of historicity in the history of ideas', *Pol. Sc.*, 36, 1984, 53–66. Critique of the supposition that ideas can be studied as disembodied entities capable of transmission across the ages.

1.4 —— 'Radicals, conservatives and moderates in early modern political thought – a case of Sandwich Islands syndrome?', *Hist. Pol. Thought*, 10, 1989, 525–42. Analysis of the methodological problems involved in approaching texts from which we are historically separated.

1.5 —— *The Status and Appraisal of Classic Texts: An Essay on Political Theory, Its Inheritance and the History of Ideas*, Princeton, N.J., 1985. A dense and extensive argument for situating the writings of political thought in their appropriate contexts.

1.6 —— *Three Aspects of Political Theory: On Confusions and Reformation of an Expression*, Melbourne, 1979. Another warning against searching for timeless truths in historical texts.

1.7 **Drury**, S. B., 'The esoteric philosophy of Leo Strauss', *Pol. Theory*, 13, 1985, 315–38. Emphasises the influence of Machiavelli and Nietzsche on Strauss's approach to political thought.

1.8 —— *The Political Ideas of Leo Strauss*, New York, 1988. On the methodology of a twentieth-century scholar who insisted, against the fashion of the times, that the history of political thought is a means of apprehending eternal moral truths.

1.9 **Dunn**, J., 'The identity of the history of ideas', *Phil.*, 43, 1968, 85–104. Influential article urging intellectual historians to focus upon the intentions of those whom they study.

1.10 **Gunnell**, J. G., *Political Theory: Tradition and Interpretation*, Cambridge, Mass., 1979. Critical of historians such as Leo Strauss for succumbing to the myth of tradition – the supposition that the political ideas of the past belong to a coherent pattern of Western thought which can be used to highlight the deficiencies of the present age – and also those such as Q. Skinner for excessive historicity. For Gunner the political literature of the past is to be understood as 'a series of perspectives

1

on perennial and fundamental issues of political life which challenge and teach the reader to think about these issues'.

1.11 —— 'The myth of tradition', *Am. Pol. Sc. Rev.*, 72, 1978, 122–34.

1.12 **Gupta**, D., *Political Thought and Interpretation: The Linguistic Approach*, Jaipur, 1990. Accessible analysis of the methodologies of, for example, J. G. A. Pocock, Q. Skinner and J. Dunn.

1.13 **Höpfl**, H., 'John Pocock's new history of political thought', *Eur. Sts. Rev.*, 5, 1975, 193–206.

1.14 **Janssen**, P. L., 'Political thought as traditionary action: the critical response to Skinner and Pocock', *Hist. & Theory*, 24, 1985, 118–46. A kind of extended footnote on Pocock and Skinner in which he attempts to refine their characterisation of the appropriate context for understanding a political text.

1.15 **King**, P. and **Parekh**, B., ed., *Politics and Experience: Essays Presented to Michael Oakeshott*, 1968. Contains essays on methodology in the history of political thought by S. Wolin and J. G. A. Pocock.

1.16 **Lockyer**, A., ' "Traditions" as context in the history of political theory'. *Pol. Sts.*, 27, 1979, 201–17. Argues that locating historical texts in their appropriate intellectual context is not incompatible with the search for lessons of universal validity: we learn from past ideas as a traditional inheritance.

1.17 **Mulligan**, L., **Richards**, J., and **Graham**, J. K., 'Intentions and conventions: a critique of Quentin Skinner's method for the study of the history of ideas', *Pol. Sts.*, 27, 1979, 84–98.

1.18 **Nederman**, C. J., 'Quentin Skinner's state: historical method, and traditions of discourse', *Can. J. Pol. Sc.*, 18, 1985, 339–52. Argues that Skinner locates the texts of political thought in an inappropriate context because he understands history not as a continuous process, but as discrete ideological conflicts.

1.19 **Parekh**, B., and **Berki**, R. N., 'History of political ideas: a critique of Q. Skinner's methodology', *J. Hist. Ideas*, 34, 1973, 163–84. Argues that Skinner's notion of 'intention' is insufficient to unravel the complex process by which a text was created, and also that he is wrong to suppose that authors are incapable of

transcending the particularities of the historical context in which they write.

1.20 **Pocock**, J. G. A., 'Languages and their implications: the transformation of political thought', in *Politics, Language and Time: Essays on Political Thought and History*, 1974, 3–41. Classic essay on the shift to a more 'contextualised' account of the political ideas of the past.

1.21 —— 'The history of political thought: a methodological enquiry', in P. Laslett and W. G. Runciman, ed., *Philosophy, Politics and Society, Series II*, 1962, 183–202. Seminal article calling for a closer investigation of the languages of various political discourses through which thinking is conveyed.

1.22 —— 'Reconstructing the traditions: Quentin Skinner's historians' history of political thought', *Can. J. Pol. & Soc. Theory*, 3, 1979, 95–113.

1.23 —— 'Texts as events: reflections on the history of political thought', in K. Sharpe and S. Zwicker, ed., *Politics of Discourse: Literature and History in Seventeenth-Century England*, Berkeley, Calif., 1987.

1.24 **Sanderson**, J., 'The historian and the "masters" of political thought', *Pol. Sts.*, 16, 1968, 42–54. Urges historians of political thought to turn aside from the classic texts in search of writers who, though less talented, are more representative of the thinking of the age in which they lived.

1.25 **Schochet**, G. J., 'Quentin Skinner's method', *Pol. Theory*, 2, 1974, 261–76. Focusing on Skinner's interpretation of Hobbes, Schochet accuses him of methodological extremism in insisting upon 'the near-autonomy of historical periods'.

1.26 **Shapiro**, I., 'Realism in the study of the history of ideas', *Hist. Pol. Thought*, 3, 1982, 535–78. Accuses contextualists such as Q. Skinner, J. Dunn and J. G. A. Pocock of collapsing theoretical and ideological issues into questions about language.

1.27 **Skinner**, Q., 'Conventions and the understanding of speech acts', *Phil. Q.*, 20, 1970, 118–38.

1.28 —— 'Meaning and understanding in the history of ideas', *Hist. & Theory*, 8, 1968, 3–53. A seminal article urging historians of ideas to abandon the search for timeless truths by moving beyond the text to the linguistic context in which it was created; and doing so by treating a piece of writing as a set of utterances formulated by an author with the intention of communicating a certain meaning to the readers. The study of the ideas of the past, according to Skinner, is primarily a study of intentions.

1.29 —— 'Motives, intentions and the interpretation of texts', *New Lit. Hist.*, 3, 1972, 393–408. Chides 'New Literary Critics' for supposing that the meaning of a text can be derived without reference to the author's intentions in creating it.

1.30 —— 'Some problems in the analysis of political thought and action', *Pol. Theory*, 2, 1974, 277–303. Reply to various critics in which he refines rather than abandons the claim of his earlier articles that 'the key to understanding the actual historical meaning of a text must be in recovering the complex intentions of the author in writing it'.

1.31 **Tarlton**, C. D., 'Historicity, meaning and revisionism in the study of political thought', *Hist. & Theory*, 12, 1973, 307–28. Accuses Q. Skinner, J. G. A. Pocock and J. Dunn of an obsessive historicity causing them to confine the political ideas of the past within narrow interpretative frameworks.

1.32 **Tully**, J., ed., *Meaning and Context: Quentin Skinner and his Critics*, 1988. A representative sample of Skinner's articles and those of his critics, together with a new 'Afterword' by Skinner. No other book gives a better flavour of the methodological debates currently engaging historians of political thought.

1.33 —— 'Review article: "The pen is a mighty sword: Quentin Skinner's analysis of politics" ', *Brit. J. Pol. Sc.*, 13, 1983, 489–509. A careful exposition and defence of Skinner's approach to the history of political thought.

1.34 **Weiner**, J. M., 'Quentin Skinner's Hobbes', *Pol. Theory*, 2, 1974, 251–60. Focusing on Skinner's interpretation of Hobbes, Weiner argues that his conception of the appropriate context for understanding the political ideas of the past is too narrow: it should be broadened from a concern with the intentions of an author to the social milieu in which he wrote.

1.35 **Wood**, N., 'The social history of political theory', *Pol. Theory*, 6, 1978, 345–67.

Emphasises the need to relate the classic texts of political thought to their socio-political context, as well as their relevance to the modern world: 'in discovering and creating the past we are shaping the future by discovering and creating ourselves'.

(b) HISTORIES OF POLITICAL THOUGHT

General

1.36 **Ball**, T., **Farr**, J. and **Hanson**, R. L., ed., *Political Innovation and Conceptual Change*, 1989. This is not a standard history of political thought but an account of how some of the concepts of Western political discourse – the state, citizenship, ideology, rights, property, and so forth – have through time assumed different meanings. As such the book provides an interesting if unusual perspective on the subject.

1.37 **Ben-Amittay**, J., *The History of Political Thought from Ancient to Present Times*, New York, 1973. Broad historical perspective, though the accounts of the ideas of particular thinkers tend to be sketchy.

1.38 **Berki**, R. N., *The History of Political Thought: a Short Introduction*, 1977. Provides a clear and stimulating overview of political thinking from the ancient world to Marx by classifying the Western tradition into four roughly chronological 'visions' of the state: the philosophic vision of the Greek city-state; the medieval conception of a universal empire and church; the early modern civic vision of the nation state; and the modern social vision of the democratic and welfare state.

1.39 **Bowle**, J., *Western Political Thought: An Historical Introduction from the Origins to Rousseau*, 1947. Lively though not entirely reliable – many of the judgements on particular thinkers do not withstand the test of more recent scholarship.

1.40 **Cranston**, M., *Political Dialogues*, 1968. Unusual approach which presents some of the central themes of political thought through imaginary conversations between, for example, Savonarola and Machiavelli on the state, Diderot and Rousseau on progress, Burke, Paine and Mary Wollstonecraft on revolution, Marx and Bakunin on anarchism, Mill and James Stephen on liberty, and Locke and the third Earl of Shaftesbury on toleration.

1.41 —— ed., *Western Political Philosophers: A Background Book*, 1964. Short, snappy and – though outdated – enjoyable essays: Plato (A. Flew), Aristotle (K. Smellie), Aquinas (M. Cranston), Machiavelli (E. Landi), Hobbes (J. Watkins), Locke (R. Peters), Rousseau (B. De Jouvenel), Burke (J. Cameron), Marx (A. MacIntyre), and Mill (N. Annan).

1.42 **Dodge**, D., and **Baird**, D. H., ed., *Continuities and Discontinuities in Political Thought*, 1975.

1.43 **Faurot**, J. H., *The Philosopher and the State: From Hooker to Popper*, San Francisco, Calif., 1971. Considers thinkers from the perspective of what the author identifies as the four principal problems of political philosophy: order (Hobbes, Locke, Rousseau, Burke); justice (Hooker, Hume, Kant, Bentham); freedom (Spinoza, Mill, Green, Berdyaev); history (Hegel, Comte, Marx, Popper). This pedagogical scheme produces an accessible student text.

1.44 **Fitzgerald**, R., ed., *Comparing Political Thinkers*, 1980. Fifteen essays, most of them lucid and perceptive, on pairs of political theorists, including R. Fitzgerald on Socrates and Plato, W. Yao on Aristotle and Mencuis, D. Grace on Augustine and Hobbes, C. and A. Condren on More and Socrates, C. Condren on Marsilius of Padua and Machiavelli, R. Masters on Hobbes and Locke, J. MacAdam on Rousseau and Hobbes, P. Corcoran on Rousseau and Hume, W. Hudson on Hegel and Nietzsche, V. Di Norcia on Calvin and Kropotkin, P. Springborg on Rousseau and Marx, G. Duncan on Marx and Mill, R. Fitzgerald on Marcuse and Christian Bay, and M. Jackson on Rawls and Nozick.

1.45 **Forsyth**, M., and **Keens-Soper**, M., ed., *A Guide to the Political Classics: Plato to Rousseau*, 1988.

1.46 **Hallowell**, J. H., *Main Currents in Modern Political Thought*, New York, 1950. Less a comprehensive history than an analysis of the main currents in political philosophy since the seventeenth century. An ideologically loaded account urging the recovery of Christian values as a solution to the crisis of Western civilisation, but nevertheless more interesting and readable than many histories of political thought.

1.47 **Hampsher-Monk**, I., *A History of Modern Political Thought: Major Political Thinkers from Hobbes to Marx*, 1992. A reliable and accessible textbook which unravels the meaning of political texts by situating them in historical context. There are separate chapters on Hobbes, Locke, Hume, Rousseau, the 'Federalist', Burke, Bentham, J. S. Mill, Hegel and Marx.

1.48 **Harmon**, M. J., *Political Thought from Plato to the Present*, New York, 1964. Readable chapters on most of the principal figures.

1.49 **Jacobson**, N., *Pride and Solace: The Functions and Limits of Political Theory*, Berkeley, Calif., 1978.

1.50 **Lively**, J., and **Reeve**, A., ed., *Modern Political Theory from Hobbes to Marx: Key Debates*, 1988. Anthology of articles on Hobbes, Locke, Rousseau, Burke, J. S. Mill, and Marx.

1.51 **McCoy**, C. N. R., *The Structure of Political Thought: A Study in the History of Political Ideas*, New York, 1963.

1.52 **McDonald**, L. C., *Western Political Theory: From the Origins to the Present*, 1962. Discusses a vast number of thinkers and in doing so sacrifices depth for breadth.

1.53 **MacFarlane**, L. J., *Modern Political Theory*, 1970. Clear analysis of some of the concepts of modern political thought focusing on Hobbes, Locke, Rousseau, Bentham, J. S. Mill, Hegel, Marx and Engels.

1.54 **Miller**, D., ed., *The Blackwell Encyclopedia of Political Thought*, 1986. Over three hundred entries on the thinkers and concepts of Western political thought, and as such an invaluable handbook.

1.55 **Muschamp**, D., ed., *Political Thinkers*, 1986. Fifteen chapters, from Plato to 'Modern Political Ideas', by various contributors. A curate's egg of a textbook.

1.56 **Nelson**, R., *Western Political Thought: From Socrates to the Age of Ideology*, 1982. Very basic.

1.57 **Plamenatz**, J., *Man and Society: A Critical Examination of Some Important Social and Political Theories from Machiavelli to Marx*, 1963. This work in two volumes is a meticulous account and sharp critique of the ideas of particular thinkers.

1.58 **Redhead**, B., ed., *Political Thought from Plato to NATO*, 1990. Initially published to accompany a series of radio programmes, this book of essays by fourteen contributors is one of the more reliable and interesting introductions to the subject.

1.59 **Riley**, P., ed., *Essays on Political Philosophy*, New York, 1992. Two dozen essays collected from the *J. Hist. Ideas*, and covering the Western tradition from the ancient world.

1.60 **Sheldon**, G. W., *The History of Political Theory: Ancient Greece to Modern America*, New York, 1988. Trot through the ideas of thinkers from Plato to Rawls, aimed primarily at the American undergraduate market.

1.61 **Sibley**, M. Q., *Political Ideas and Ideologies: A History of Political Thought*, New York, 1976. Covers most of the principal thinkers since the ancient Hebrews and Greeks, and also contains chapters on the 'isms'. A clear and unpretentious student text.

1.62 **Strauss**, L., and **Cropsey**, J., ed., *History of Political Philosophy*, 2nd edn., 1972. Comprehensive selection of largely quality essays including L. Strauss, 'Plato', H. Jaffa, 'Aristotle', J. Holton, 'Cicero', E. Fortin, 'Augustine', E. Fortin, 'Aquinas', L. Strauss, 'Marilius of Padua', R. Cox, 'Grotius', L. Berns, 'Hobbes', W. Berns, 'Calvin', J. Rosen, 'Spinoza', R. Goldwin, 'Locke', D. Lowenthal, 'Montesquieu', R. Hill, 'Hume', A. Bloom, 'Rousseau', P. Hassner, 'Kant', H. Storing, 'Blackstone', J. Cropsey, 'Adam Smith', M. Diamond, 'The Federalist', F. Canavan, 'Paine', F. Canavan, 'Burke', H. Magid, 'Bentham and James Mill', P. Hassner, 'Hegel', M. Zetterbaum, 'Tocqueville', H. Magid, 'J. S. Mill', J. Cropsey, 'Marx' and W. Dannhauser, 'Nietzsche'.

1.63 **Thomson**, D., ed., *Political Ideas*, 1966. Short essays of uneven quality by different authors on most of the major political thinkers from Machiavelli.

1.64 **Vereker**, C., *The Development of Political Theory*, 1957. Textbook from Plato to the modern world that is organised around themes and concepts such as justice, freedom and progress.

1.65 **Ward**, S. G., *The History of Political Theory: Ancient Greece to Modern America*, New York, 1989.

1.66 **Williams**, G. L., *Political Theory in Retrospect: From the Ancient Greeks to the 20th Century*, 1991. Deals with eleven thinkers as well as liberalism, conservatism and socialism. The theme used for comparing the thinkers discussed is twofold: how did each conceive of political appearances in relation to some idea of an underlying reality, and how did each conceptualise the relation between politics and morality?

1.67 **Wolin**, S. S., *Politics and Vision: Continuity and Innovation in Western Political Thought*, 1960. Innovative attempt to conceptualise the Western tradition –focusing among others on Plato, Luther, Calvin, Machiavelli and Hobbes –which laments the reluctance of modern thinkers to engage in conventional political philosophy: the identification of the political with the welfare of society as a whole.

Shorter-span histories and those dealing with particular countries and/or a limited number of thinkers

1.68 **Beitzinger**, A. J., *A History of American Political Thought*, New York, 1972. Broad sweep from the Federalists to the New Left: interesting though partisan in assuming that authentic political thought takes its bearings from higher, natural law.

1.69 **Berlin**, W. S., *On the Edge of Politics: The Roots of Jewish Political Thought in America*, Westport, Conn., 1978.

1.70 **Colletti**, L., *From Rousseau to Lenin: Studies in Ideology and Society*, 1972. Interesting Marxist interpretation of among others Bernard Mandeville, Adam Smith and Rousseau.

1.71 **Collins**, S. L., *From Divine Cosmos to Sovereign State: An Intellectual History of Consciousness and the Idea of Order in Renaissance England*, 1989. Focuses on the shift from the Tudor to the Hobbesian idea of order with discussions of, for example, Shakespeare, Hooker, Sidney, Bacon, Filmer and Digges.

1.72 **Crowder**, G., *Classical Anarchism: The Political Thought of Godwin, Proudhon, Bakunin, and Kropotkin*, 1991. An analytically crisp and historically sensitive study, claiming that classical anarchism reveals a coherent and sophisticated theory of freedom.

1.73 **Elbow**, M. H., *French Corporative Theory, 1789–1948: A Chapter in the History of Ideas*, New York, 1953.

1.74 **Feinberg**, B. S., 'Creativity and the political community: the role of the law giver in the thought of Plato, Machiavelli, and Rousseau', *West. Pol. Q.*, 23, 1970, 471–85.

1.75 **Frisch**, M. J., and **Stevens**, R. G., ed., *American Political Thought: The Philosophical Dimension of American Statesmanship*, New York, 1971. Separate chapters on the political thinking of various statesmen, including Marshall, Story, Calhoun, Taney, Lincoln, Douglass, Root, Wilson, Holmes, Roosevelt and Frankfurter.

1.76 **Greenleaf**, W. H., *The British Political Tradition: Vol. Two, The Ideological Heritage*, 1983. Magisterial account of the development of liberalism, socialism and conservatism since the nineteenth century.

1.77 **Hanson**, D. W., *From Kingdom to Commonwealth: The Development of Civic Consciousness in English Political Thought*, Cambridge, Mass., 1970. Traces the continuities and discontinuities between medieval and early modern constitutional thinking, with interesting discussion of Bracton, Fortescue, Hooker, St. Germain and the Levellers.

1.78 **Hartz**, L., *The Liberal Tradition in America: An Interpretation of American Political Thought Since the Revolution*, New York, 1955. A readable and in some ways classic overview, emphasising that the United States lacks a genuine revolutionary tradition because of its non-feudal past.

1.79 **Horowitz**, A., and **Horowitz**, G., *Everywhere they are in Chains: Political Theory from Rousseau to Marx*, Ontario, 1988.

1.80 **Kahan**, A., *Aristocratic Liberalism: The Social and Political Thought of Jacob Burckhardt, John Stuart Mill, and Alexis de Tocqueville*, 1992.

1.81 **Keohane**, N. O., *Philosophy and the State in France: The Renaissance to the Enlightenment*, Princeton, N.J., 1980. Focuses on the articulation of three modes of discourse from Seyssel to Rousseau – absolutism, constitutionalism, and individualism.

1.82 **Krieger**, L., *The German Idea of Freedom: History of a Political Tradition*, Boston, Mass., 1957.

1.83 **Letwin**, S. R., *The Pursuit of Certainty: David Hume, Jeremy Bentham, John Stuart Mill, Beatrice Webb*, 1965. An ideologically loaded interpretation extolling the scepticism of Hume and lambasting the scientific rationalism of the other thinkers.

1.84 **Lynd**, S., *Intellectual Origins of American Radicalism*, 1969. Argues that modern radicals still use the revolutionary rhetoric of higher law and inalienable rights because of an unbroken continuity between the ideology of 1776 and the ideas of subsequent variants of radicalism.

1.85 **McCoy**, C. N. R., 'The logical and the real in political theory: Plato, Aristotle, and Marx', *Am. Pol. Sc. Rev.*, 48, 1954, 1058–66. Argues that, unlike Plato and Marx, Aristotle constructed a 'non-totalitarian political science' by clearly distinguishing the logical from the real order.

1.86 **Macpherson**, C. B., 'The false roots of Western democracy', in F. Dallmayr, ed., *From Contract to Community: Political Theory at the Crossroads*, New York, 1978, 17–27. On the inadequacies of traditional liberal theories of democracy, and as such a precis of the argument in his *The Life and Times of Liberal Democracy*.

1.87 —— *The Life and Times of Liberal Democracy*, 1977. Short, sharp, Marxist critique of liberal theories of democracy, focusing principally on Bentham, J. S. Mill and twentieth-century writers.

1.88 **Mayer**, J. P., *Political Thought in France from the Revolution to the Fifth Republic*, 1961.

1.89 **Pocock**, J. G. A., 'The history of British political thought: the creation of a center', *J. Brit. Sts.*, 24, 1985, 283–310. This article, written to mark the establishment of the Folger Center for the History of British Political thought, is a useful survey of the contours of political thinking from the sixteenth to eighteenth centuries and also of the methodological preoccupations of recent historiography.

1.90 —— *The Machiavellian Moment: Florentine Political Thought and the Atlantic Republican Tradition*, 1975. A seminal study of the revival among Renaissance thinkers of the ideal of the classical republic, tracing the influence of that ideal upon English and American political thought in the seventeenth and eighteenth centuries: among the thinkers considered are Machiavelli, Guicciardini, Harrington, and the American Federalists. An ambitious and brilliantly executed endeavour.

1.91 —— 'Transformations in British political thought', *Pol. Sc.*, 40, 1988, 160–78. Magisterial survey of the changes in British political discourse between 1640 and 1832.

1.92 **Rapaczynski**, A., *Nature and Politics: Liberalism in the Philosophies of Hobbes, Locke and Rousseau*, New York, 1987.

1.93 **Rauch**, L., *The Political Animal*, Amherst, Mass., 1981. Explores the idea of the state in the writings of Machiavelli, Hobbes, Locke, Rousseau, Hegel and Marx.

1.94 **Simmons**, E. J., ed., *Continuity and Change in Russian and Soviet Thought*, Cambridge, Mass., 1955. Includes essays on authoritarianism in Russian thought (Karpovich, Hammond, Ulam), Bakunin and Herzen on individual liberty (Berlin) and Russian messianism in post-war ideology (Barghoorn).

1.95 **Skidmore**, M. J., *American Political Thought*, New York, 1978. Introductory textbook from the seventeenth to twentieth centuries, brief on details but thematically more coherent than some accounts.

1.96 **Smith**, B. J., *Politics and Remembrance: Republican Themes in Machiavelli, Burke and Tocqueville*, Princeton, N.J., 1985.

1.97 **Soupios**, M. A., *European Political Theory: Plato to Machiavelli*, Lanham, M.D., 1986. Consists of readings from the writings of Plato, Aristotle, Aquinas and Machiavelli, prefaced by an introductory chapter which sketches the development of political thought from the classical to post-medieval periods.

1.98 **Stoner**, J. R., *Common Law and Liberal Theory and the Origins of American Constitutionalism*, Kansas, 1992. Argues that American constitutionalism and judicial review are rooted in English common and liberal political theory.

1.99 **Talmon**, J. L., *The Origins of Totalitarian Democracy: Political Theory and Practice During the French Revolution and Beyond*, 1951. A brilliant and provocative book, tracing the origins of modern totalitarianism to eighteenth-century thinkers such as Rousseau and the French revolutionaries. A good read, though the historical narrative rests upon dubious

ideological foundations.

1.100 **Tierney**, B., *Religion, Law and the Growth of Constitutional Thought, 1150–1650*, 1982. A scholarly and engaging account of the evolution of constitutional thought from Gratian to the English writer George Lawson. Far more reliable than older works on the subject such as J. N. Figgis, *Political Thought from Gerson to Grotius, 1414–1625*, (1907) and C. H. McIlwain, *Constitutionalism Ancient and Modern*, (1940).

1.101 **Vernon**, R., *Citizenship and Order: Studies in French Political Thought*, 1986. Chapters on Rousseau, Maistre, Proudhon, Tocqueville, Comte, Durkheim and Bergson.

1.102 **Wood**, E. M., *Mind and Politics: an approach to the meaning of liberal and socialist individualism*, 1972. Lively exploration of the relationship between theories of the mind and political doctrines from Locke to Marx.

Works dealing with particular themes and concepts

GENDER

1.103 **Bryson**, V., *Feminist Political Thought: An Introduction*, 1992. Admirably lucid account of feminist political thought from Mary Astell in the seventeenth century through nineteenth-century liberalism and Marxism to modern radical feminism.

1.104 **Charvet**, J., *Feminism*, 1982. Sharp and lucid account of the history of feminist thinking from Wollstonecraft to modern radicals and socialists –though as an introduction the book has been superseded by more recent works.

1.105 **Clark**, L. M. G. and **Lange**, L., ed., *The Sexism of Social and Political Theory: Women and Reproduction from Plato to Nietzsche*, Toronto, 1979. Articles devoted to a feminist critique of the Western philosophical tradition.

1.106 **Coole**, D., *Women in Political Theory: From Ancient Misogyny to Contemporary Feminism*, 1993. On the patriarchal assumptions of political thought since classical times, with a concluding chapter discussing contemporary feminist theory through post-structuralist and post-modernist themes.

1.107 **Elshtain**, J. B., *Meditations on Modern Political Thought: Masculine/Feminine Themes from Luther to Arendt*, New York, 1986. Illuminating chapters on Luther, Kant, Rousseau, Hegel, Freud and liberalism.

1.108 —— *Public Man and Private Woman: Women in Social and Political Thought*, Princeton, N.J., 1981. Sophisticated account of how political thinkers from the Greeks have supported or rationalised women's oppression, focusing on the public–private distinction and covering Plato, Aristotle, Rousseau, Augustine, Aquinas, Luther, Machiavelli, Hobbes and Locke, Hegel and Marx.

1.109 —— ed., *The Family in Political Thought*, 1982. Chapters by various contributors explore the treatment of the family by Plato, Aristotle, Montesquieu, Rousseau, Hegel, Mill and Nietzsche.

1.110 **Evans**, J., ed., *Feminism and Political Theory*, 1986. Includes two chapters with a historical perspective: one by U. Vogel on the liberal eighteenth-century debate about women's emancipation, and another by K. Hunt on the debate within the Social Democratic Federation, Britain's first Marxist party, in the late nineteenth and early twentieth centuries.

1.111 **Kennedy**, E. and **Mendus**, S., ed. *Women in Western Political Philosophy: Kant to Nietzsche*, 1987. Thinkers and topics covered include Adam Smith, Rousseau, Humboldt, utilitarianism and Hegelianism.

1.112 **Nichols**, M. P., 'Women in western political thought', *Pol. Sc. Re-r*, 13, 1983, 241–60.

1.113 **O'Brien**, M., *The Politics of Reproduction*, 1981. A critique of traditional political thought, focusing on conceptualisations of biological reproduction.

1.114 **Okin**, S. M., *Women in Western Political Thought*, Princeton, N.J., 1979. Focuses on the treatment of women in Plato, Aristotle, Rousseau and J. S. Mill.

1.115 **Pateman**, C., ed., *Feminist Interpretations and Political Theory*, 1991. Collection of essays previously published in journals including S. Okin, 'Philosopher queens and private wives: Plato on women and the family', A. Saxonhouse, 'Aristotle: defective males, hierarchy, and the limits of politics', C. Pateman, ' "God hath ordained to man a helper": Hobbes, patriarchy and conjugal right', M. Butler, 'Early liberal roots of feminism: John Locke and the attack on patriarchy', L. Lange, 'Rousseau and modern feminism', M. Gatens, ' "The oppressed state of my sex": Wollstonecraft on reason, feeling and equality', S. Berhabib, 'On Hegel, women and irony', C. Distefano, 'Masculine Marx', M. Shanley, 'Marital slavery and friendship: John Stuart Mill's *The Subjection of Women*', S. Okin, 'John Rawls: justice as fairness –for whom?', E. Spelman, 'Simone de Beauvoir and women: just who does she think "me" is?', J. Sawicki, 'Foucault and feminism: towards a politics of difference', M. G. Dietz, 'Hannah Arendt and feminist politics' and N. Fraser, 'What's critical about critical theory? the case of Habermas and gender'.

1.116 —— *The Disorder of Women: Democracy, Feminism and Political Theory*, 1989. Collection of her previously published articles, wide-ranging in scope, penetrating in analysis and with extensive reference to Rousseau, Locke, Hobbes, Mill and other political thinkers.

1.117 —— *The Sexual Contract*, 1988. Brilliantly teases out the patriarchal assumptions of social contract theory since the seventeenth century.

1.118 **Saxonhouse**, A. W., *Women in the History of Political Thought: Ancient Greece to Machiavelli*, New York, 1985.

1.119 **Shanley**, M. L., **Lyndon**, M., and **Tenenbaum**, S., 'Women through the prism of political thought', *Polity*, 15, 1982, 90–102.

PROPERTY

1.120 **Buckle**, S., *Natural Law and the Theory of Property: Grotius to Hume*, 1991. Includes discussions of Pufendorf, Locke and Hutcheson.

1.121 **Carter**, A. B., *The Philosophical Foundations of Property Rights*, 1989. A systematic introduction to the philosophical issues surrounding property rights, and a critique of the major philosophers of property from Locke to Nozick.

1.122 **Horne**, T. A., *Property Rights and Poverty: Political Argument in Britain, 1605–1834*, Chapel Hill, Car., 1990. Among writers

8

considered are Locke, Sidney, Smith, Paley, Paine and Bentham.

1.123 **Parel**, A. J. and **Flanagan**, T., ed., *Theories of Property: Aristotle to the Present*, Waterloo, 1979. Includes essays on Aquinas, Locke, Marx and Nozick.

1.124 **Reeve**, A., *Property*, 1986. Thinkers discussed include Connolly, Macpherson, Rawls, Nozick and Hayek.

1.125 **Ryan**, A., *Property*, 1987. Focuses on the connection between property and freedom in political and moral theories from Plato and Aristotle to Nozick.

1.126 —— *Property and Political Theory*, 1984. Sophisticated study of the 'career' of the idea of private property, beginning with Locke, including Rousseau, Kant, Hegel and the Utilitarians, and ending with a discussion of Marx and Mill.

SOCIAL CONTRACT

1.127 **Black**, A., 'The juristic origins of social contract theory', *Hist. Pol. Thought*, 14, 1993, 57–76. Careful examination of contractual thinking from the fourteenth to early seventeenth centuries, focusing on the formulations of constitutional lawyers.

1.128 **Hampton**, J., 'Contract and consent', in R. E. Goodin and P. Pettit, ed., *A Companion to Contemporary Political Philosophy*, 1993, 379–93. Short but clear historical overview of social contract theories.

1.129 **Herzog**, D., *Happy Slaves: A Critique of Consent Theory*, Chicago, Ill., 1989. Focuses on alleged contradictions in Hobbes, Locke and subsequent social contract theories in order to convince his intended American readers that they are 'happy slaves', socialised by their liberal institutions into the false belief that they are free.

1.130 **Höpfl**, H., and **Thompson**, M. P., 'The history of contract as a motif in political thought', *Am. Hist. Rev.*, 84, 1979, 919–44.

1.131 **Lessnoff**, M., *Social Contract: Issues in Political Theory*, 1986. Focuses on Hobbes, Locke, Hume, Hegel, Rawls and Nozick.

1.132 **Medina**, A., *Social Contract Theories: Political Obligation or Anarchy?*, Savage, Md., 1990. On the principal contractarian theorists – Hobbes, Locke, Rousseau, Kant and Rawls – and some of their critics including Hume, Hegel and T. H. Green.

1.133 **Riley**, P., 'How coherent is the social contract tradition?', *J. Hist. Ideas*, 34, 1973, 543–62. Claims to find coherence in the emphasis since the seventeenth century on voluntarism, the assent of individuals as the standard of political legitimacy.

1.134 —— *The General Will Before Rousseau: The Transformation of the Divine into the Civic*, Princeton, N.J., 1986. Traces the general will back to its (non-political) origins in the seventeenth century and demonstrates how this concept conveyed much of Rousseau's political and moral thought.

1.135 —— *Will and Political Legitimacy: A Critical Exposition of Social Contract Theory in Hobbes, Locke, Rousseau, Kant, and Hegel*, Harvard, Ill., 1982.

OTHER

1.136 **Black**, A., *Guilds and Civil Society in European Political Thought from the Twelfth Century to the Present*, 1984.

1.137 **Bolgar**, R. R., ed., *Classical Influences on Western Thought AD 1650–1870*, 1979. Of particular interest are essays by R. A. Leigh on Rousseau and the myth of antiquity, M. Reinhold on the classics in eighteenth-century American political thought, G. Costa on Vico, P. Stein on Adam Smith's theory of law and society, and H. Pappé on the Greek learning of the utilitarians.

1.138 **Botwinick**, A., *Participation and Tacit Knowledge in Plato, Machiavelli and Hobbes*, Lanham, M.D., 1986. Short book, more of an extended essay, on the status of tacit knowledge – that of the connoisseur acquired through participation in a form of life – in the three writers.

1.139 **Cassirer**, E., *The Myth of the State*, New Haven, Conn., 1946. A tract for the times in so far as his intention was to reveal how the myth of the state evolved from primitive times through Plato, the Middle Ages, Machiavelli, the Enlightenment, Carlyle and Hegel to Nazism. But the story is told with brilliance and panache, and the book remains one of the great surveys of Western political thinking.

1.140 **D'Entrèves**, A. P., *Natural Law*, 1951. Short, lucid account of the idea of natural law in Western political thought.

1.141 **Feaver**, G., and **Rosen**, F., ed., *Lives, Liberties and the Public Good: New Essays in Political Theory*, 1986. Essays on liberty by various contributors including discussions of Hobbes, Tocqueville, Bentham, Mill, Rousseau, the Webbs and Hayek.

1.142 **Hirschman**, A. O., *The Passions and the Interests: Political Arguments for Capitalism before its Triumph*, Princeton, N.J., 1977. Brilliant study demonstrating, contrary to other interpretations, the continuity of thinking in the seventeenth and eighteenth centuries from that of earlier periods, and focusing upon Montesquieu, Sir James Stewart, John Miller, the Physiocrats and Adam Smith.

1.143 **Lakoff**, S., *Equality in Political Philosophy*, Cambridge, Mass., 1964. Traces liberal, socialist and conservative conceptions of equality from classical times.

1.144 **Miller**, D., *Social Justice*, 1976. Contains much illuminating discussion on how the concept has been understood in political thought, with separate chapters on David Hume, Herbert Spencer and Peter Kropotkin.

1.145 **Oldfield**, A., *Citizenship and Community: Civic Republicanism and the Modern World*, 1990. Traces the ideal of the civic-republic from Greek thought to Machiavelli, Rousseau, Hegel and de Tocqueville.

1.146 **Pelczynski**, Z. A., and **Gray**, J. ed., *Conceptions of Liberty in Political Philosophy*, 1984. High quality essays discussing among others the ancient Greeks, Hobbes, Locke, Rousseau, Hegel, J. S. Mill, T. H. Green, Hayek, Oakeshott, Arendt and Rawls.

1.147 **Schwartz**, P. H., 'Equestrian imagery in European and American political thought: toward an understanding of symbols as political texts', *West. Pol. Q.*, 41, 1988, 653–73. On the horse and rider as symbols of political understanding.

1.148 **Sigmund**, P. E., *Natural Law in Political Thought*, Cambridge, Mass., 1971.

1.149 **Thompson**, M. P., 'The history of fundamental law in political thought from the French wars of religion to the American revolution', *Am. Hist. Rev.*, 91, 1986, 1103–28. Argues, contrary to most historians of constitutional theory, that the term fundamental law entered European political discourse in a relatively unconsidered way.

1.150 **Waldron**, J., *Nonsense upon Stilts: Bentham, Burke and Marx on the Rights of Man*, 1987. Anthology prefaced by an interesting overview of the doctrine of natural rights in the seventeenth and eighteenth centuries.

1.151 **Wilhelmsen**, F. D., *Christianity and Political Philosophy*, Athens, Ga., 1978. Includes discussions of St. Augustine, John Fortescue, Donoso Cortez and Thomas Aquinas.

1.152 **Zuckert**, C. H., ed., *Understanding the Political Spirit: Philosophical Investigations from Socrates to Nietzsche*, New Haven, Conn., 1988. Collection of uneven essays on 'spiritedness' – the psychological foundations of political life – in Plato, Aristotle, Machiavelli, Hobbes, Locke and Hegel.

(c) THE NATURE OF POLITICAL THEORY

1.153 **Almond**, G., 'Political theory and political science', *Am. Pol. Sc. Rev.*, 60, 1966, 869–79.

1.154 —— 'Political theory and the problem of ideology', *J. Pol.*, 42, 1980, 687–705. Charts the dominance of philosophy over the Anglo-American conception of political theory in the twentieth century, hence the disdain for ideology shown by many political thinkers.

1.155 **Ball**, T., *Transforming Political Discourse: Political Theory and Critical Conceptual History*, 1988. Argues that politics, understood as argumentation, is a linguistically and conceptually constituted activity; the task now facing political theorists is to construct 'critical conceptual histories' to show how changes actually occur in concrete political settings.

1.156 **Barber**, B. R., *The Conquest of Politics: Liberal Philosophy in Democratic Times*, Princeton, N.J., 1988. Challenging collection of essays on the state of contemporary political theory, which is criticised for its abstraction and refusal to engage with the political. This trend is countered with a celebration (sentimentalisation?) of citizenship within the political realm.

1.157 **Barry**, B., *Political Argument: A Reissue with a New Introduction*, 1990. An important contribution to the 1960s revival of Anglo-American political philosophy.

1.158 —— 'The strange death of political philosophy', *Govt. & Oppos.*, 15, 1980, 276–88. Story of the growth of political philosophy since 1961, mediated through the autobiographical ruminations of the author.

1.159   **Baumgold**, D., 'Political commentary on the history of political theory', *Am. Pol. Sc. Rev.*, 75, 1981, 928–40.

1.160   **Cobban**, A., 'The decline of political theory', in J. A. Gould and V. V. Thursby, ed., *Contemporary Political Thought*, New York, 1969, 289–303.

1.161   **Cohen**, J., 'Why more political theory?', *Telos*, 40, 1979, 70–94.

1.162   **Connolly**, W., *The Terms of Political Discourse*, Princeton, N.J., 1983. Sets out to analyse and categorise the often jargon-laden and obscure terminology of much contemporary political science and political theory.

1.163   **Cooper**, B., 'Reason and interpretation in contemporary political theory', *Polity*, 12, 1979, 387–99.

1.164   **Dahl**, R., 'Political theory: truth and consequences', *World Politics*, 11, 1958, 89–102.

1.165   **Easton**, D., 'The decline of modern political theory', *J. Pol*, 13, 1953, 36–58.

1.166   **Eckstein**, H., 'Political theory and the study of politics', *Am. Pol. Sc. Rev*, 50, 1956, 475–87.

1.167   **Gallie**, W. B., 'Essentially contested concepts', *Proc. Aris. Soc.*, 56, 1955–56, 167–98.

1.168   **Germino**, D., 'The revival of political theory', *J. Pol.*, 25, 1963, 437–60.

1.169   **Gray**, J., 'On the essential contestability of some social and political concepts', *Pol. Theory*, 5, 1977, 331–48.

1.170   **Gromez De Souza**, L. A., 'The future of ideologies and the ideologies of the future', *Anticipation*, 2, 1970, 10–26.

1.171   **Gunnell**, J. G., *Between Philosophy and Politics: The Alienation of Political Theory*, Amherst, Mass., 1976. Intellectual and lucid critique of the distorting illusions of the discourse of academic political theory which fosters a number of myths resulting in the 'alienation' of political theory. Illuminates the philosophical images of politics which political theory uncritically appropriates because of its dependence on the critical insights of other disciplines and readiness to borrow categories from metatheoretical realms of discourse.

1.172   —— 'Political theory: the evaluation of a "sub-field" ', in A. W. Finifler, ed., *Political Science: The State of the Discipline*, Washington, D.C., 1983, 3–45. Charts the development of this discipline, from the turn of the century until the 1980s in North America.

1.173   —— *Political Theory: Tradition and Interpretation*, Cambridge, Mass., 1979. Historical overview of the philosophical assumptions underpinning the practice of political theory.

1.174   **Havard**, W. C., *The Recovery of Political Theory: Limits and Possibilities*, Louisiana, Ill., 1984.

1.175   **Held**, D., ed., *Political Theory Today*, 1991. A series of essays on central themes within political thought, written in the context of recent intellectual and political upheavals. Particular focus is given to the key concepts in the analysis of modern political communities as well as the location of the individual within a wider framework of relations and forces, whilst Held's introduction to recent developments is illuminating. Includes Dunn on political obligation, Lukes on equality and liberty, Okin on gender, Reeve on property, Elster on rationality, Offe and Preuss on democratic institutions and moral resources, McLean on representation and voting, Held on democracy and globalism, Beitz on sovereignty and morality in international affairs, Cassese on violence and the rule of law in the international community, O'Neill on transnational justice, Amin on the state and development, and Heller on the concept of the political.

1.176   **Hiller**, A., and **Fehér**, F., *The Postmodern Political Condition*, 1991. Analysis of the causes of the recent changes in the vocabulary of modern political thought, examining the relevance of the modernity/postmodernity debate.

1.177   **Jaffa**, H., 'The case against political theory', *J. Pol.*, 22, 1960, 259–75.

1.178   **Kateb**, G., *Political Theory: Its Nature and Uses*, New York, 1968.

1.179   —— 'The condition of political theory', *American Behavioural Scientist*, 21, 1977, 135–79.

1.180   **Kleinberg**, S. S., *Politics and Philosophy: The Necessity and Limitations of Rational Argument*, 1991. Analyses the assumptions that political questions can be rationally resolved and our political beliefs can be morally justified.

1.181   **Landau**, M., *Political Theory and Political*

Science: Studies in the Methodology of Political Inquiry, 1972.

1.182 **McDonald**, N. A., and **Rosenau**, J. N., 'Political theory as an academic field and intellectual activity', *J. Pol.*, 30, 1968, 311–44.

1.183 **McShea**, R. J., 'Political philosophy, human nature, the passions', *Hist. Pol. Thought*, 7, 1986, 205–18. Discusses the role of political philosophy in contemporary life at a time when it seems to have been conquered by the logicians, scorned by the empiricists and exposed as crudely ideological. Perceives three dominant approaches in political philosophy: ahistorical, individualist 'reductionism'; historically relativist 'culturalism'; and classical, human nature discourses.

1.184 **Miller**, D., 'The resurgence of political theory', *Pol. Theory*, 38, 1990, 421–37. Skilful overview of recent trends in political theory, illustrating the importance of conceptual analysis and normative theory. Deals particularly with the tension between individualists and communitarians and the growth of political theory applied to public policy.

1.185 **Nelson**, J. S., *What Should Political Theory Be Now?*, Albany, N.Y., 1983.

1.186 **Raphael**, D. D., *Problems of Political Philosophy*, 1970.

1.187 **Riker**, W. H., 'Political theory and the art of heresthetics', in A. W. Finifler, ed., *Political Science: The State of the Discipline*, Washington, D.C., 1983, 47–67. Highly technical and offputting introduction to American analytical theory.

1.188 **Runciman**, W. G., *Social Science and Political Theory*, 1969.

1.189 **Spragens**, T. A., *The Dilemma of Contemporary Political Theory*, New York, 1973.

1.190 **White**, S. K., *Political Theory and Postmodernism*, 1991. Explores the thought of Heidegger, Foucault, Derrida, Lyotard and Habermas as well as 'difference' feminists, showing how postmodernism can inform ethical and political reflection.

1.191 **Wolin**, S. S., 'Political theory as a vocation', *Am. Pol. Sc. Rev.*, 63, 1969, 1062–82.

2

ANCIENT
POLITICAL THOUGHT

(a) GENERAL

2.1 **Finley**, M. I., *Politics in the Ancient World*, 1983. Contains a short but magisterial chapter on the ideology, especially the political ideas, of both the Greeks and Romans.

2.2 **Hammond**, M., *City and World State in Greek and Roman Political Theory until Augustus*, Cambridge, Mass., 1951.

2.3 **Hulter**, H., *Politics as Friendship: The origins of classical notions of politics in the theory and practice of friendship*, Waterloo, 1978. Traces the origins of Western political thought in the metaphor of friendship in both Greek and Roman writers.

2.4 **Kajanto**, I., ed., *Commentationes Humanarum Litterarum*, 75, 1984: *Equality and Inequality of Man in Ancient Thought*. The five essays in the volume are G. Kerford, 'The concept of equality in the thought of the Sophist movement', H. Thesleff, 'Plato and inequality', W. Kullman, 'Equality in Aristotle's political thought', J. Christensen, 'Equality of man and Stoic social thought', and D. Aalders, 'Ideas about human equality and inequality in the Roman Empire. Plutarch and some of his contemporaries'.

2.5 **Strauss**, L., 'The liberalism of classical political philosophy', *Rev. Metaph.*, 13, 1959, 390–439.

(b) GREECE

General

2.6 **Aalders**, G. J. D., *Political Thought in Hellenistic Times*, Amsterdam, 1975. Survey of the diverse patterns of Greek political thought between Alexander's death and about 30BC.

2.7 **Adkins**, A. W. H., '*Polupragmosune* and "minding one's own business": a study in Greek social and political values', *Class. Philol.*, 71, 1976, 301–27. On how the concept of meddlesomeness was used by many Greek thinkers to condemn political activism.

2.8 **Ball**, T., 'Plato and Aristotle: the unity versus the autonomy of theory and practice', in T. Ball, ed., *Political Theory and Praxis: New Perspectives*, Minneapolis, Minn., 1977, 57–69. Disputes 'the claim that Plato is the more "theoretical" and Aristotle the more "practical" thinker by showing how their respective conceptions of theoria and praxis differ'.

2.9 —— 'Theory and practice: an examination of the Platonic and Aristotelian conceptions of political theory', *West. Pol. Q.*, 25, 1972, 534–46.

2.10 **Campbell**, B., 'Constitutionalism, rights and religion: the Athenian example', *Hist. Pol. Thought*, 7, 1986, 239–73. Argues that the Athenians had an elementary but firm sense of constitutionalism – a legal framework safeguarding the rights of citizens and sanctioned by the city's gods.

2.11 —— 'Paradigms lost: classical Athenian

politics in modern myth', *Hist. Pol. Thought*, 10, 1989, 189–213. Wide-ranging and intelligent attempt to debunk the modern idea of the classical *polis* as a debating society in which citizens engaged in self-development through participation in public affairs; neither the institutions nor the political thought of Greece put such a premium on activism.

2.12 **Carter**, L. B., *The Quiet Athenian*, 1986. On the fifth century theory and practice of apragmosyne – the reaction against democracy – and of how quietism foreshadowed Plato's version of the contemplative life.

2.13 **Chestnut**, G. F., 'The ruler and the *logos* in Neo-Pythagorean, middle Platonic and late Stoic political philosophy', *Aufsteig und Niedergang der Römischen Welt II*, 16, 1978, 1310–32.

2.14 **Deane**, H. A., 'Classical and Christian political thought', *Pol. Theory*, 1, 1973, 415–25. Highlights the differences between the two modes of thought by focusing on Aristotle, Plato and Augustine.

2.15 **Donlon**, N., *The Aristocratic Ideal in Ancient Greece: Attitudes of Superiority from Homer to the End of the Fifth Century B.C.*, Lawrence, Kan., 1980.

2.16 **Euben**, J. P., ed., *Greek Tragedy and Political Theory*, Berkeley, Calif., 1986.

2.17 —— 'The battle of Salamis and the origins of political theory', *Pol. Theory*, 14, 1986, 359–90. The Athenian democratic ethos is said to have taken shape in the aftermath of the battle of 480BC.

2.18 **Farrar**, C., *The Origins of Democratic Thinking: The Invention of Politics in Classical Athens*, 1988. Carefully retrieves the democratic ideas of Protagoras, Thucydides, Democritus and other fifth-century thinkers.

2.19 **Fuks**, A., *The Ancestral Constitution, Four Studies in Athenian Party Politics at the End of the Fifth Century B.C.*, 1953. Explains how the concept of the ancestral constitution was used by the oligarchs, the democrats, and particularly by the moderates between 411 and 403BC.

2.20 **Greenhalgh**, P. A. L., 'Aristocracy and its advocates in archaic Greece', *Greece and Rome*, 19, 1972, 190–208. On the 'appearance in archaic Greek literature of the two basic principles of aristocracy – republicanism and noble rule – and how they were upheld, augmented, qualified, idealised, and justified against the alternatives of monarchy and the aspirations of non-nobles either to join or disestablish the nobility as the ruling class'.

2.21 **Grene**, D., *Greek Political Theory: The Image of Man in Thucydides and Plato*, Chicago, Ill., 1950.

2.22 **Havelock**, E. A., *The Greek Concept of Justice from its Shadow in Homer to its Substance in Plato*, Cambridge, Mass., 1978. Addresses the question of the origins and development of Greek conceptualisations of justice in the context of a culture which until the fifth century BC was basically oral and poetic. Analyses the moral function of the poets in archaic Greek culture before considering the justice of rational philosophy (and the written word) in Herodotus and Plato.

2.23 —— *The Liberal Temper in Greek Politics*, Yale, New Haven, 1957. Claims to detect the liberal temper in pre-Socratic and Sophist thinkers who, 'in contradiction to the formal, the teleological, and the authoritarian themes of Plato and Aristotle', were egalitarian and international in outlook. Havelock's scholarship has been severely criticised.

2.24 **Hintikka**, K. J. J., 'Some conceptual presuppositions of Greek political theory', *Scand. Pol. Sts.* 2, 1967, 11–25.

2.25 **Just**, R., 'Freedom, slavery and the female psyche', *Hist. Pol. Thought*, 6, 1985, 169–88. Notions integral to the Athenian conception of women are said to find their clearest expression in the context of freedom and slavery.

2.26 **Kagan**, D., *The Great Dialogue: History of Greek Political Thought from Homer to Polybius*, 1965. The dialogue on which he focuses is that between 'democratic' and 'aristocratic' traditions in ancient Greece; there are chapters on Homer, Theognis and Pindar, Aeschylus and Herodotus, Thucydides, the Sophists, Isocrates and Xenophon, Plato, Aristotle, the Hellenists and Polybius.

2.27 **Kahn**, C. H., 'The origins of social contract theory in the fifth century B.C.'. in G. B. Kerferd, ed., *The Sophists and their Legacy: Proceedings of the fourth International Colloquium on Ancient Philosophy*, Wiesbaden, 1981, 92–108.

2.28 **Loizou** A. and **Lesser**, H., ed., *Polis and Politics: Essays in Greek Moral and Political Philosophy*, 1990. Relevant essays are

S. Clark, 'Good and bad ethology and the decent *polis*', J. Creed, 'Aristotle and democracy', R. Stalley, 'The responsibility of Socrates', R. Chadwick, 'Feminism and eugenics: the politics of reproduction in Plato's *Republic*', N. Dent, 'Plato and social justice', A. Loizou, *Eikasia* and tyranny in Plato's *Republic*', and H. Lesser, 'Society and individual psychology in Plato's Republic'.

2.29 **McCoy**, C. N. R., 'On the revival of classical political philosophy', *Rev. Pol.*, 35, 1973, 161–79. Critique of Leo Strauss's interpretation of Plato and Aristotle.

2.30 **McKeon**, R., 'The interpretation of political theory and practice in ancient Athens', *J. Hist. Ideas*, 42, 1981, 3–12. Elusive discussion of the philosophical assumptions of Greek political thinking, particularly of Aristotle and Plato.

2.31 **Maguire**, J. P., 'Some Greek views of democracy and totalitarianism', *Ethics*, 56, 1946, 136–43. 'In many of the most important features which distinguish modern democracy from modern totalitarianism, the Greek tradition, including Plato, is emphatically on the side of democracy.'

2.32 **Manicas**, P. T., 'War, stasis, and Greek political thought', *Comp. Sts. Soc. & Hist.*, 24, 1982, 673–88. Addresses the question of why Greek thinkers focused on internal and constitutional issues rather than external conflict and foreign policy.

2.33 **Mion**, M., 'Athenian democracy: politicization and constitutional restraints', *Hist. Pol. Thought*, 7, 1986, 219–38. Argues that the Athenians had a rudimentary but nevertheless firm sense of constitutionalism.

2.34 **Mulgan**, R. G., 'Lycophron and Greek theories of social contract', *J. Hist. Ideas*, 40, 1979, 121–28. Argues that contract theorists did not intend to restrict the scope of government, but 'to justify the existence of law when it was thought to be contrary to natural impulse and desire'.

2.35 **Navone**, J. J., 'The division of parts in society according to Plato and Aristotle', *Phil. Sts.*, 6, 1956, 113–22. Portrays Aristotle as a pluralist and Plato as a kind of totalitarian.

2.36 **Nerseyants**, V. S., *Political thought of Ancient Greece*, Moscow, 1986. Originally published in Russia in 1979, the book is a clear and readable Marxist overview from

the ninth century BC to the Hellenistic period.

2.37 **Nichols**, M. P., *Socrates and the Political Community: An Ancient Debate*, Albany, N.Y., 1987. A study not only of Plato's *Republic* but of two works in which Socrates is criticised – Aristophanes' *Clouds* and Aristotle's *Politics* – emphasising their contribution to the debate on the relation between politics and philosophy.

2.38 **Ostwald**, M., *From Popular Sovereignty to the Sovereignty of Law: Law, Society and Politics in Fifth-Century Athens*, Berkeley, Calif., 1986. Traces the intellectual as well as the institutional development of Athenian democracy.

2.39 —— *Nomos and the Beginning of the Athenian Democracy*, 1969. Basically a philological study of two words, both meaning statute, 'which played a key role in Athenian political thought' by giving expression to democratic principles.

2.40 **Panagiotou**, S., ed., *Justice, Law and Method in Plato and Aristotle*, Edmonton, 1987. Includes B. Calvert, 'Plato's *Crito* and Richard Kraut', S. Panagiotou, 'Justified disobedience in the *Crito*?', R. Allen, 'The speech of Glaucon: on contract and the common good', T. Robinson, 'Professor Allen on Glaucon in the *Republic*', K. Dorter, 'Justice and method in the *Statesman*', and E. Weinrib, 'Aristotle's forms of justice'.

2.41 **Raaflaub**, K. A., 'Democracy, oligarchy, and the concept of the "free citizen" in late fifth-century Athens', *Pol. Theory*, 11, 1983, 517–44.

2.42 **de Romilly**, J., *The Rise and Fall of States According to Greek Authors*, Ann Arbor, Mich., 1977. On how the main Greek historians from Herodotus to Polybius characterised the rise and fall of states, arguing that the Greeks had no idea either of a continuous progress in history or of a general rhythm that would have commanded the rise and fall of states.

2.43 **Saxonhouse**, A. W., 'From tragedy to hierarchy and back again: women in Greek political thought', *Am. Pol. Sc. Rev.*, 80, 1986, 403–18. Focuses on Aeschylus's *The Seven Against Thebes* and Sophocles's *Antigone*, though also discusses Plato and Aristotle.

2.44 **Schlaifer**, R., 'Greek theories of slavery from Homer to Aristotle', in M. I. Finley, ed., *Slavery in Classical Antiquity*, 1960, 120–7.

2.45 **Sinclair**, T. A., *A History of Greek Political Thought*, 1951. A comprehensive account which situates Plato and Aristotle in a tradition of Greek thinking about politics – how to construct a state and how best to live in it – stretching from Homer to the Hellenists.

2.46 **Smith**, N. D., 'Plato and Aristotle on the nature of women', *J. Hist. Phil.*, 12, 1983, 467–78. Argues that the principal differences in their views about women derive from their theories of the soul: Plato is a 'feminist' because he sees male and female nature as essentially sexless souls incarnated temporarily in sexed bodies; Aristotle is a 'male chauvinist' because he makes the soul the form of the body and offers a biological account of reproduction that sharply distinguishes male and female psychology.

2.47 **Strauss**, L., *Studies in Platonic Political Philosophy*, Chicago, Ill., 1983. Includes 'On Plato's *Apology* of Socrates and *Crito*', 'On the *Euthydemus*', 'Preliminary observations on the Gods in Thucydides' work' and 'Xenophon's *Anabasis*'.

2.48 **Tuplin**, C. J., 'Imperial tyranny: some reflections on a classical Greek political metaphor', *Hist. Pol. Thought*, 6, 1985, 348–76.

2.49 **Vlastos**, G., 'Equality and justice in early Greek philosophy', *Class. Philol.*, 42, 1947, 156–78. Discusses justice in Empedocles, Parmenides, Heraclitus and Anaximander, arguing that their work reveals a transition in the conception of justice from a cosmic to a natural phenomenon – i.e. rooted in human nature and the product of civilisation.

2.50 **Voegelin**, E., *Order and Society, Vol. III: Plato and Aristotle*, Baton Rouge, La., 1957. Brilliant if tendentious study, focusing on their preoccupation with social disintegration and critical of Aristotle for proposing a solution to disorder that is less convincing than that of Plato.

2.51 **Wallach**, J. R., *Political Reason, Deliberation, and Democracy in Ancient Greek Political Theory*, Princeton, N.J., 1981.

2.52 **Winton**, R.I., and **Garnsey**, P., 'Political theory', in M. I. Finley, ed., *The Legacy of Greece: A New Appraisal*, 1981, 37–64. Neat overview of Greek political thinking.

2.53 **Wood**, E. M. and **Wood**, N., *Class, Ideology, and Ancient Political Theory: Socrates, Plato, and Aristotle in Social Context*, 1978. Stimulating though contentious study portraying their political thinking as the ideology of a declining aristocracy.

Plato

2.54 **Allen**. C. G., 'Plato on women', *Feminist Studies*, 2, 1975, 131–8.

2.55 **Allen**, R. E., 'Law and justice in Plato's *Crito*', J. Phil., 69, 1972, 547–67. Emphasises the dialectical nature of the argument in the *Crito*.

2.56 —— *Socrates and the Legal Obligation*, Minneapolis, Minn., 1980.

2.57 **Anastaplo**, G., 'Human being and citizen: a beginning to the study of Plato's *Apology of Socrates*', in J. Cropsey, ed., *Ancients and Moderns: Essays on the Tradition of Political Philosophy in Honor of Leo Strauss*, New York, 1964, 16–49.

2.58 **Andrew**, E., 'Descent to the cave', *Rev. Pol.*, 45, 1983, 510–35. On why the philosopher in Plato's *Republic* would condescend to participate in politics.

2.59 —— 'Equality of opportunity as the noble lie', *Hist. Pol. Thought*, 10, 1989, 577–95. 'No commentator has entertained the possibility that what Plato thought false in the noble lie was the central proposition of the myth of the metals, namely, that there are natural differences between human beings, which can be discerned prior to their education or cultivation. I wish to argue that Plato thought human differences to be manifest only after education.'

2.60 **Annas**, J., *An Introduction to Plato's Republic*, 1981. Clear companion emphasising the coherence of the moral argument throughout.

2.61 —— 'Plato's *Republic* and feminism', *Phil.*, 51, 1976, 307–21. 'Plato the feminist is a myth' because his concern was the stability of the state and not the rights of women.

2.62 **Ansbro**, J. J., 'Plato's just man: a re-examination', *New Schol.*, 44, 1970, 278–86. Critique of R. M. Hall for claiming that the ordinary citizen in Plato's state can be as just as the philosopher.

2.63 **Bambrough**, R., ed., *Plato, Popper and*

Politics: Some Contributions to a Modern Controversy, 1967. Useful collection on the debate as to whether Plato was totalitarian: R. Bambrough, 'Plato's modern friends and enemies', E. Unger, 'Contemporary anti-Platonism', J. Plamenatz, 'The open society and its enemies', E. Gombrich, 'The open society – a comment', J. Plamenatz, 'The open society – a rejoinder', R. Bambrough, 'Plato's political analogies', H. Meyerhoff, 'Plato among friends and enemies', and K. Popper, 'Reply to a critic'.

2.64 **Beatty**, J., 'Plato's happy philosopher and politics', *Rev. Pol.*, 38, 1976, 545–75. Argues that Plato's injunction on philosophers to engage in politics is logically incoherent without the assumption that in doing so they pursue truth and thereby promote their own happiness as well as that of the polis.

2.65 **Bertman**, M. A., 'Socrates' defence of civil disobedience', *Studium Generale*, 24, 1971, 576–82. Judges Socrates right in remaining in prison but wrong in claiming that every law is morally binding.

2.66 **Bloom**, A., 'Response to Hall', *Pol. Theory*, 5, 1977, 315–39. Defence of his view that the *Republic* was an exercise in irony.

2.67 **Bluck**, R. S., 'Is Plato's *Republic* a theocracy?', *Phil. Q.*, 5, 1955, 69–73. Defenders of Plato against K. Popper's accusation of totalitarianism forget, according to Bluck, that the state described in the *Republic* approximates to a theocracy.

2.68 **Bluestone**, N. H., 'Why women cannot rule: sexism in Plato scholarship', *Phil. Soc. Scs.*, 18, 1988, 41–60. On how through the centuries Plato's feminism 'has been largely dismissed, deplored, or ignored'.

2.69 —— *Women and the Ideal Society: Plato's Republic and Modern Myths of Gender*, 1987. An amusing analysis of anti-female bias in Plato scholarship, 1870–1970, and a close reading of Plato's texts on women in politics, philosophy and family life.

2.70 **Bookman**, J. T., 'Plato on political obligation', *West. Pol. Q.*, 25, 1972, 260–67. Concludes that there is no single Platonic teaching with regard to political obligation.

2.71 **Brown**, W., ' "Supposing truth were a woman . . ." Plato's subversion of masculine discourse', *Pol. Theory*, 16, 1988, 594–616. Gender in Plato's thought is examined in terms of his depiction of the nature of wisdom, the relation of philosophy to power, and the politics of the *Republic*, the guiding thread being Plato's personification of truth as female.

2.72 **Browning**, G. K. 'Plato and Hegel: reason, redemption and political theory', *Hist. Pol. Thought*, 8, 1987, 377–95. Focuses upon the specificity of Plato's and Hegel's approaches to what they took to be 'the task of political theory, the articulation of a political community resolving the problems and tensions of social practice'.

2.73 —— *Plato and Hegel: Two Modes of Philosophizing about Politics*, 1991. Short, careful comparison of their political theories.

2.74 —— 'The night in which all cows are black: ethical absolutism in Plato and Hegel', *Hist. Pol. Thought*, 12, 1991, 391–404. Both are said to wish to preserve political stability by eliminating ethical diversity.

2.75 **Bryant**, J. M., 'Enlightenment, psychology and political reaction in Plato's social philosophy: an ideological contradiction', *Hist. Pol. Thought*, 11, 1990, 377–95. Perceives a 'manifest inconsistency between the universalism inherent in Plato's apotheosis of the soul and his anti-humanitarian scorn and therapeutic neglect of the masses'.

2.76 **Calvert**, B., 'Plato and the equality of women', *Phoenix*, 29, 1975, 231–43. Suggests that he is a firmer feminist than some commentators contend.

2.77 —— 'Slavery in Plato's *Republic*', *Class. Q.*, 37, 1987, 367–72. Argues contrary to the standard view that the Republic could not contain slaves.

2.78 —— 'The politicians of Athens in the *Gorgias* and *Meno*', *Hist. Pol. Thought*, 5, 1984, 1–16. Examines Plato's epistemology to explain why the *Meno* is less hostile than the *Gorgias* to democratic institutions and politicians.

2.79 **Campbell**, B., 'Deity and human agency in Plato's *Laws*', *Hist. Pol. Thought*, 2, 1981, 417–47. Argues that Plato affords much greater independence from 'higher' forces in the *Laws* than in the *Republic*: the function of theology in the *Laws* does not deny the legitimacy of an autonomous human sphere but provides it with cosmological justification.

2.80 —— 'Intellect and the political order in Plato's *Republic*', *Hist. Pol. Thought*, 1, 1980, 361–89. The *Republic* 'is not, as often supposed, a political apotheosis of intellect. Rather Plato has here sought to achieve a mutual accommodation of intellect and politics, giving power to an intellectual class that has been stripped of the disruptive demand for *episteme* in political affairs which characterise the intellectual in the Socratic dialogues.'

2.81 **Coleman**, W. R., 'Knowledge and freedom in the political philosophy of Plato', *Ethics*, 71, 1960, 41–5. 'The hypothesis that the meaning of freedom shifts according to the frame of reference in which the nature, significance, and availability of knowledge appears constitutes the point of departure of this summary analysis of knowledge and freedom in Plato's political dialogues.'

2.82 **Congleton**, A., 'Two kinds of lawlessness: Plato's *Crito*', *Pol. Theory*, 2, 1974, 432–46. Emphasises that the *Crito* is to be read as a dialogue and not as a treatise.

2.83 **Cooper**, J. M., 'The psychology of justice in Plato', *Am. Phil. Q.*, 14, 1977, 151–7. On the Platonic conception of human perfection and the links between the psychology and metaphysics of the *Republic*.

2.84 **Crombie**, I. M., *An Examination of Plato on Man and Society*, 1962. Useful and interesting account of the political ideas of the *Republic*, *Statesman* and *Laws*.

2.85 —— *Plato: The Midwife's Apprentice*, 1964. The final chapter is a short but imaginative account of his political thought.

2.86 **Cross**, R. C. and **Woozley**, A. D., *Plato's Republic: A Philosophical Commentary*, 1964. Clearly dissects his logic with regard to justice and other political and moral issues.

2.87 **Davis**, L. P., 'The arguments of Thrasymachus in the first book of Plato's *Republic*', *Modern Schoolman*, 47, 1970, 423–32.

2.88 **Demos**, R., 'Paradoxes in Plato's doctrine of the ideal state', *Class. Q.*, 7, 1957, 164–74. Attempts to resolve some of the apparent contradictions in Plato's political views.

2.89 **Dent**, N.T., 'Common, civic and Platonic justice in the Republic', *Polis*, 5, 1983, 1–33.

2.90 **Dickason**, A., 'Anatomy and destiny: the role of biology in Plato's view of women', *Phil. Forum*, 5, 1973–4, 45–53. Argues that 'between the *Symposium* and the Timaeus, Plato's biological views of women change, and that this shift is then reflected in the respective political works'.

2.91 **Dreisbach**, D. F., 'Agreement and obligation in the *Crito*', *New Schol.*, 52, 1978, 168–86. The main point of the *Crito* is that 'the citizen must obey the laws because he depends upon them'.

2.92 **Euben**, J. P., 'Philosophy and politics in Plato's *Crito*', *Pol. Theory*, 6, 1978, 149–72. The inconsistency between Socrates' commitment to philosophy in the *Apology* and his equally firm commitment to the law of Athens in the *Crito* is explained less by the problem of civil disobedience than by the relationship between philosophy and politics.

2.93 **Dybikowski**, J., 'Socrates, disobedience and the law: Plato's *Crito*', *Dialogue*, 13, 1974, 518–35.

2.94 **Farrell**, D. M., 'Illegal actions, universal maxims, and the duty to disobey the law: the case for civil authority in the *Crito*', *Pol. Theory*, 6, 1978, 173–89. On why Socrates' arguments against escaping from prison are coherent and persuasive.

2.95 **Fortenbaugh**, W., 'On Plato's feminism in Republic V', *Apeiron*, 9, 1975, 1–4.

2.96 **Foster**, M. B., 'Plato's concept of justice in the *Republic*', *Phil. Q.*, 1, 1951, 206–17. Argues, contrary to K. Popper, that Plato did not hold a totalitarian view of justice: justice was essentially conformity to an objective standard, not conformity to the interests of the state.

2.97 **Fuks**, A., 'Plato and the social question: the problem of poverty and riches in the *Laws*', *Ancient Society*, 10, 1979, 33–78.

2.98 **Gavin**, B., 'A note on Socrates and "The Law" in the *Crito*', *Aitia*, 7, 1979, 26–28. Argues that Socrates did accept the reality of an unjust law, but that a person is never justified in opposing the nature of law in general.

2.99 **Gill**, C., 'Plato and politics; the *Critias* and the *Politicus*', *Phronesis*, 24, 1979, 148–67. On the relationship between the political thought underlying the Atlantis story and that found in the *Statesman*.

2.100 **Gouldner**, A. W., *Enter Plato: Classical Greece and the Origins of Social Theory*, 1967. Tantalising account of Plato as a theorist of social disunity, class conflict and other social issues.

2.101 **Greenberg**, N. A., 'Socrates' choice in the *Crito*', *Harvard Studies in Classical Philology*, 70, 1965, 45–82.

2.102 **Gulley**, N., *The Philosophy of Socrates*, 1968. A discussion of Socrates's moral paradoxes, his conception of the good society, and of Aristotle's critique of his methodology and conclusions.

2.103 **Hadgopoulos**, D. J., 'Thrasymachus and legalism', *Phronesis*, 18, 1973, 204–8. Argues that Thrasymachus is not a legalist equating justice merely with obedience to law.

2.104 **Hall**, D., 'The *Republic* and the "limits of politics" ', *Pol. Theory*, 5, 1977, 293–313. A critique of the suggestion of L. Strauss and A. Bloom that the *Republic* is an ironic book underlining the absurdity of striving for an ideal city.

2.105 **Hall**, R. W., 'Justice and the individual in the *Republic*', *Phronesis*, 4, 1959, 149–58. Argues that the justice of the individual and the state exhibit a relation of mutual dependence rather than ruthless subordination of the individual's welfare to the goal of the state.

2.106 —— *Plato*, 1981. A full-length study of Plato's political thought which discusses its evolution throughout the major dialogues within the context of developments in Athenian democracy. Intended primarily as an introductory work, especially for those seeking a companion piece for study of the *Republic*.

2.107 —— 'Plato – a minority report', *Southern Journal of Philosophy*, 2, 1964, 7–64. Argues that the division Plato makes between rulers and non-rulers is less hierarchical, more blurred, than most commentators acknowledge.

2.108 —— 'Plato and totalitarianism', *Polis*, 7, 1985, 105–15.

2.109 —— 'Plato's just man: thoughts on Strauss' Plato', *New Schol.*, 42, 1968, 202–25. Contends that in Plato's ideal state philosopher-kings and ordinary citizens would have an equal capacity for justice in their individual lives.

2.110 —— 'Plato's political analogy: fallacy or analogy?', *J. Hist. Phil.*, 12, 1974, 419–35. On the analogy between the state and the soul, and its relevance for Plato's understanding of justice.

2.111 —— 'The just and happy man of the *Republic*: fact or fallacy?' *J. Hist. Phil.*, 9, 1971, 146–58.

2.112 **Harlap**, S., 'Thrasymachus's justice', *Pol. Theory*, 7, 1979, 347–70. Thrasymachus is said to have 'the clear intention of supporting his political theory with a moral philosophy that is captured by an egoistic conception of self-interest'.

2.113 **Henderson**, T. Y., 'In defense of Thrasymachus', *Am. Phil. Q.*, 7, 1970, 218–28. His views on justice are said to be not only consistent but more persuasive than Socrates's counter-arguments.

2.114 **Hoerber**, R. G., 'More on justice in the *Republic*', *Phronesis*, 5, 1960, 32–4.

2.115 **Hourani**, G. F., 'Thrasymachus' definition of justice in Plato's "Republic" ', *Phronesis*, 7, 1962, 110–20. Justice for Thrasymachus is said to consist of obedience to the laws.

2.116 **Humphries**, S. C., 'Public and private interest in classical Athens', *Class. J.*, 73, 1977–78, 97–104. Fifth-century Athenians 'discovered two of the major problems of Western political theory: the relation between public and private interests, and the relation between politics and the economy'.

2.117 **Jackson**, M. W., 'Plato's political analogies', *Int. Sts. Phil.*, 20, 1988, 27–42. Critique of R. Bambrough's assessment of Plato's use of analogy.

2.118 **Jacobs**, W., 'Plato on female emancipation and the traditional family', *Apeiron*, 12, 1978, 29–31. Critique of S. Okin, 'Philosopher queens and private wives'.

2.119 **James**, G. G., 'Socrates on civil disobedience', *Southwestern J. Phil.*, 11, 1973, 119–27. Declares the Socrates of the *Crito* inconsistent with the Socrates of the *Apology*.

2.120 **Joshi**, N., *Political Ideals of Plato*, Bombay, 1965.

2.121 **Kahn**, C. H., 'Problems in the argument of Plato's *Crito*', *Apeiron*, 22, 1989, 29–43.

2.122 —— 'The meaning of "justice" and the theory of forms', *J. Hist. Phil.*, 69, 1972, 567–79. The moral and political arguments of the *Republic* are said to conceal the fact that Plato envisages justice as deriving from the more abstract pattern of the form.

2.123 **Kalla**, S., 'Plato's political thought: a critique of Popper's interpretation', *Indian Council of Philosophical Research*, 2, 1985, 77–88.

2.124 **Kayser**, J. R., 'Noble lies and justice: on reading Plato', *Polity*, 5, 1973, 489–517.

2.125 **Kerferd**, G. B., 'The doctrine of Thrasymachus in Plato's *Republic*', *Durham Univ. J.*, n.s.9, 1947, 19–27. Justice for Thrasymachus is said to consist in doing good for another.

2.126 —— 'Thrasymachus and justice: a reply', *Phronesis*, 9, 1964, 12–16.

2.127 **Klosko**, G., '*Demotike Arete* in the *Republic*', *Hist. Pol. Thought*, 3, 1982, 363–83. An analysis of a lacuna in Plato's *Republic* – how his theory of virtue and justice would affect the lowest, producing, class of the community.

2.128 —— 'Implementing the ideal state', *J. Pol.*, 43, 1981, 365–89. Plato believed that the founding of the ideal state was difficult but not impossible.

2.129 —— 'Plato's utopianism: the political content of the early dialogues', *Rev. Pol.*, 45, 1983, 483–509. Examination of the early dialogues and their relationship to the *Republic* suggests that the ideal state of the latter was designed with political reform in mind: Plato wished to bring it into existence and it was therefore not utopian in the usual sense of the word.

2.130 —— 'Provisionality in Plato's ideal state', *Hist. Pol. Thought*, 5, 1984, 171–93. Qualifies the common view that Plato's ideal state is authoritarian by emphasising that the philosophers are supposed to rule by discursive reason as well as intuitively perceived truth, maintaining an open, critical attitude towards the political structures they control: 'the ideal state is in a way an open society.'

2.131 —— 'Racism in Plato's *Republic*', *Hist. Pol. Thought*, 12, 1991, 1–14. Plato is a racist only in a limited sense, according to Klosko.

2.132 —— 'Rational persuasion in Plato's political theory', *Hist. Pol. Thought*, 7, 1986, 15–33. Argues that he came to similar conclusions as Aristotle regarding the limits of persuasion as a means of political reform.

2.133 —— *The Development of Plato's Political Theory*, 1986. Comprehensive introduction which also provides enough original analysis and commentary to interest more advanced students and specialist scholars.

2.134 —— 'The nocturnal council of Plato's *Laws*', *Pol. Sts.*, 36, 1988, 74–88. Repudiates the view of the role of the nocturnal council in G. Morrow, *Plato's Cretan City*.

2.135 —— 'The "rule" of reason in Plato's *Republic*', *Hist. of Phil. Q.*, 4, 1988, 341–56. On how different parts of the soul 'rule' in different people.

2.136 —— 'The "Straussian" interpretation of Plato's *Republic*', *Hist. Pol. Thought*, 7, 1986, 275–93. Critique of the view – propounded by L. Strauss, A. Bloom and others – that the Republic is a satirical work whose message is not that a perfect political order ruled by philosophers can be realised, but rather the impossibility of ideal political arrangements.

2.137 **Kraut**, R., 'Egoism, love, and political office in Plato', *Phil. Rev.*, 82, 1973, 330–44. Uses what Plato wrote about the philosophers' obligation to rule to argue that he was not an ethical egoist.

2.138 —— *Socrates and the State*, Princeton, N.J., 1984. Explains the political theory Socrates adopts when he refuses, in *Crito*, to escape from jail and puts the dialogue into broader context by examining the political orientation ascribed to him throughout Plato's early works.

2.139 —— 'The defense of justice in Plato's *Republic*', in R. Kraut, ed., *The Cambridge Companion to Plato*, 1992, 311–37.

2.140 **Lee**, E. N., **Mourelatos** A. P. D., and **Rorty**, R. M., ed., *Exegesis and Argument Studies in Greek Philosophy Presented to Gregory Vlastos*, Assen, 1973. Includes B. Williams, 'The analogy of city and soul in Plato's *Republic*' and R. Kraut, 'Reason and justice in Plato's *Republic*'.

2.141 **Lesser**, H., 'Plato's feminism', *Phil.*, 54, 1979, 113–17. Defence of Plato against the charge of J. Annas that he was not a feminist.

2.142 **Levinson**, R. B., *In Defence of Plato*, Cambridge, Mass., 1953. Repudiates the accusation of Popper and others that Plato was totalitarian in an enormous monograph that provides a detailed and engaging account of his political ideas.

2.143 **Leys**, A. R., 'Was Plato non-political?', *Ethics*, 75, 1965, 272–76. Plato is said to have had an aversion to politics and cannot therefore be considered to be a political philosopher in the usual sense.

2.144 **Lycos**, K., *Plato on Justice and Power: Reading Book I of Plato's Republic*, 1987. The central theme of Book I is said to be the relation of justice to human power.

2.145 **McLauglin**, R. J., 'Socrates on political disobedience: a reply to Gary Young', *Phronesis*, 21, 1976, 185–97. Argues, contrary to Young, that Socrates does not restrict the right to disobey philosophers who are forbidden to philosophise.

2.146 **Maguire**, J. P., 'Plato's theory of natural law', *Yale Classical Studies*, 10, 1947, 151–78.

2.147 —— 'Thrasymachus . . . or Plato?', *Phronesis*, 16, 1971, 142–63. Defends the view that no coherent position can be attributed to Thrasymachus on the ground that Plato is mixing up the views of the historical Thrasymachus with his own.

2.148 **Mara**, G. M., 'Constitution, virtue and philosophy in Plato's *Statesman* and *Republic*', *Polity*, 13, 1982, 355–82.

2.149 —— 'Socrates and liberal toleration', *Pol. Theory*, 16, 1988, 468–95. 'Plato's Socrates is not a contemporary liberal, but his alternative to political liberalism is not an authoritarianism justified by the certain knowledge possessed by gifted holders of power; the necessity and importance of individual intellectual and moral choices within a fluid and imperfect political horizon are more significant to him than his liberal critics believe.'

2.150 **Martin**, R., 'Socrates on disobedience to law', *Rev. Metaph.*, 24, 1970, 21–38. Interprets the *Crito* as teaching that justice or injustice is irrelevant to the question of obedience.

2.151 —— 'The ideal state in Plato's *Republic*', *Hist. Pol. Thought*, 2, 1981, 1–31. Analyses the *Republic* in the light of its fundamental concern with rightness in the arrangements of parts of the *polis*, and concludes that Plato's treatise is not so much a body of solved doctrine but a work of exploration and reflection.

2.152 **Melling**, D. J., *Understanding Plato*, 1987. Contains an economical but sensible discussion of his political ideas.

2.153 **Moors**, K. F., *Glaucon and Adeimantus on Justice: The Structure of Argument in Book II of Plato's Republic*, Washington, D.C., 1981.

2.154 **Moravesik**, J. M. E., 'Plato and Pericles on freedom and politics', *Can. J. Phil.*, 9, Supp., 1983, 1–18.

2.155 **Morrison**, J. S., 'The origins of Plato's philosopher-statesman', *Class. Q.*, 8, 1958, 198–218. Traces how Plato's thinking on the relation of philosophy to politics evolved until 388 BC.

2.156 **Morrow**, G. R., 'Plato and the law of nature', in M. R. Konvitz and A. E. Murphy, ed., *Essays in Political Theory Presented to George H. Sabine*, Ithaca, N.Y., 1948, 17–44. On the extent to which Plato's philosophy was a factor in the formulation of the Stoic doctrine of natural law.

2.157 —— *Plato's Cretan City*, Princeton, N.J., 1960. A new look at the *Laws* demonstrating Plato's blending of his knowledge of political history with his own principles in legislating for a new colony – the principles being the mixed constitution, the rule of law and the rule of philosophy.

2.158 **Mulgan**, R. G., 'Individual and collective virtues in the *Republic*', *Phronesis*, 13, 1968, 84–7. Reaffirms, against recent scholarship, the traditional view that there are inconsistencies in Plato's account of the virtues in the tripartite state and individual.

2.159 —— 'Socrates and authority', *Greece and Rome*, 19, 1972, 208–12. Socrates does not, as some commentators argue on the basis of passages in the *Apology*, believe in freedom of conscience as a general right of the individual to resist the state when it interferes with this freedom.

2.160 **Murphy**, N. R., *The Interpretation of Plato's Republic*, 1951. Dated but solid interpretation.

2.161 **Nederman**, C. J., 'Thrasymachus and Athenian politics: ideology and political thought in the late fifth century B.C.', *Historical Reflections*, 8, 1981, 143–68.

2.162 **Neu**, J., 'Plato's analogy of the state and the individual: the *Republic* and the organic theory of the state', *Phil.*, 46, 1971, 238–54. Plato did not, contrary to the suggestion of K. Popper and others, derive from analogy the image of a monster organic state that lived by devouring individual rights.

2.163 **Nichols**, M. P., 'The Republic's two alternatives: philosopher-kings and Socrates', *Pol. Theory*, 12, 1984, 252–74. 'Mathematics is at the heart of the city's philosophy, for mathematics promises the intelligibility and power that men seek through politics. Socrates's philosophy, in contrast, is erotic . . . While philosopher-kings discover and impose unity, Socrates makes men aware of the diversity that makes community problematic.'

2.164 **Nicholson**, P. P., 'Unravelling Thrasymachus' arguments in "The Republic" ', *Phronesis*, 19, 1974, 210–37. Thrasymachus is said to have conceived justice to be of advantage to another rather than, as scholars usually claim, to the ruler.

2.165 **Okin**, S. M., 'Philosopher queens and private wives: Plato on women and the family', *Phil. & Pub. Affairs*, 6, 1977, 344–68. Argues that the inconsistencies between the *Republic* and the *Laws* are not due to a change in Plato's beliefs about the potential of women, but to the reinstatement of private property and the family in the *Laws* – with the consequence that women are again perceived as the privately owned appendages of their husbands.

2.166 **Ophir**, A., *Plato's Invisible Cities: Discourse and Power in the Republic*, Savage, Md., 1991. Explores the relationship between philosophy and politics in the *Republic*, arguing that the book was 'a political act in the way it created a possibility for a discourse that understood itself as dissociated from the practical realm, immune to its requirements and constraints, and which could be translated back into practice only with the miraculous presence of a philosopher-king'.

2.167 **Osborne**, M. L., 'Plato's unchanging view of women: a denial that anatomy spells destiny', *Phil. Forum*, 6, 1975, 447–52.

2.168 **Ostwald**, M., 'The two states in Plato's *Republic*', in J. P. Anton and G. L. Kustas, ed., *Essays in Ancient Greek Philosophy*, Albany, N.Y., 1972, 316–27. Argues that he 'maintains a clear distinction between Guardians and Philosophers throughout the *Republic* and that his political doctrine in the *Republic* involves not one kind of state but two, which, although they are not mutually exclusive, are still sufficiently distinct from one another to justify our taking Plato at his word when he speaks of them as separate entities, the state of the Guardians and the state of the Philosopher'.

2.169 **Pierce**, C., 'Equality: *Republic* V', *Monist*, 57, 1973, 1–11.

2.170 **Popper**, K. R., *The Open Society and its Enemies: Vol. I: The Spell of Plato*, 1945. Brilliant though tendentious argument that Plato favoured a totalitarian society – a thesis which provoked a deal of subsequent commentary.

2.171 **Reeve**, C. D. C., *Philosopher-Kings: The Argument of Plato's 'Republic'*, Princeton, N.J., 1988. Important study claiming that Plato broke decisively with Socraticism, with a chapter on politics vigorously defending him against the accusation of being totalitarian.

2.172 **Rice**, D. H., 'Plato on force: the conflict between his psychology and political sociology and his definition of temperance in the *Republic*', *Hist. Pol. Thought*, 10, 1989, 565–76.

2.173 **Rosen**, F., 'Obligation and friendship in Plato's *Crito*', *Pol. Theory*, 1, 1973, 307–16. Argues that the *Crito* is concerned not only with political obligation but with the claims of friendship.

2.174 **Rowe**, C. J., 'Plato on the sophists as teachers of virtue', *Hist. Pol. Thought*, 4, 1983, 409–27.

2.175 **Sachs**, D., 'A fallacy in Plato's *Republic*', *Phil. Rev.*, 72, 1963, 141–58. Influential article suggesting that Plato's argument in defence of justice cannot count as a valid answer to Glaucon and Adeimantus unless a close connection is established between the Platonic conception of justice defended as an intrinsic good for the soul, and the ordinary behavioural notion of justice for which the challenge was raised.

2.176 **Santas**, G. X., *Socrates: Philosophy in Plato's Early Dialogues*, 1979. Part I is a discussion of Socrates and political obligation.

2.177 **Sartorius**, R., 'Fallacy and political radicalism in Plato's *Republic*', *Can. J. Phil.*, 3, 1974, 349–63. 'That one can not give men motivating reasons for acting justly in a given society is, for Plato, not a reason for adopting moral scepticism, but rather the very best of reasons for radically restructuring that society so as to bring about those conditions under which rational morality will be possible.'

2.178 **Saunders**, T. J., 'Plato's later political thought', in R. Kraut, ed., *The Cambridge Companion to Plato*, 1992, 464–92. Excellent discussion of the *Laws*, claiming that it contains Plato's 'blueprint for a second-best ideal state, which would foster the demotic virtues to the greatest extent he deemed practical'.

2.179 **Saxonhouse**, A. W., 'Eros and the female in Greek political thought: an interpretation of Plato's Symposium', *Pol*

Theory, 12, 1984, 5–27. 'The brilliance of Plato via Socrates is that despite the misogyny of the grown polis he has been able to incorporate the female into his thinking, far more so than many of the commentators on his works have been able to do.'

2.180 —— 'The philosopher and the female in the political thought of Plato', *Pol. Theory*, 4, 1976, 195–212. 'As Socrates attempts to turn women into men by making them equal participants in the political community, he ignores the peculiar natures of each and thus undermines the perfection of the political society in the *Republic*.'

2.181 **Schiller**, J., 'Just man and just acts in Plato's *Republic*', *J. Hist. Phil.*, 6, 1968, 1–14.

2.182 **Seery**, J. E., 'Politics as ironic community: on the themes of descent and return in Plato's *Republic*', *Pol. Theory*, 16, 1988, 229–56. The *Republic* is said to be profoundly ironic not only in its strategy of presentation but also in its philosophical spirit.

2.183 **Sesonske**, A., ed., *Plato's Republic: Interpretations and Criticism*, Belmont, Calif., 1966. Includes A. Sesonske, 'Plato's apology: *Republic I*', H. A. Pritchard, 'Justice in the *Republic*' and D. Sachs, 'A fallacy in Plato's *Republic*'.

2.184 **Shiell**, T. C., 'The unity of Plato's political thought', *Hist. Pol. Thought*, 12, 1991, 337–98. Plato's two conflicting accounts of the ideal state in the *Republic* and *Laws* are said to be not radically inconsistent.

2.185 **Siemsen**, T., ' "Radical persuasion in Plato's political theory": a reconsideration', *Hist. Pol. Thought*, 9, 1988, 1–18. Analyses critically Klosko's arguments that in rejecting the primacy of rational persuasion Plato adopted alternative approaches to extend philosophy into the realm of politics.

2.186 —— 'Thrasymachus' challenge', *Hist. Pol. Thought*, 8, 1987, 1–19. Plato is said to fail in Book I of the *Republic* to provide a viable mechanism by which philosophy can become politically operative.

2.187 **Skemp**, J. B., 'Comment on communal and individual justice in the *Republic*', *Phronesis*, 5, 1960, 35–8.

2.188 —— 'How political is the *Republic*?', *Hist. Pol. Thought*, 1, 1980, 1–7. Discusses whether the *Republic* is primarily an enquiry into the nature of the good society or a prescription for an actual political system.

2.189 —— *Plato*, 1976. Literature review with a section on 'Plato and politics'.

2.190 —— 'The causes of decadence in Plato's Republic', *Govt. & Oppos.*, 17, 1982, 80–93.

2.191 —— 'The development of Plato's political thought', in *Plato's Statesman: A Translation of the Politicus of Plato with Introductory Essays and Footnotes*, 1952, 26–66.

2.192 **Smith**, N. D., 'The logic of Plato's feminism', *J. Soc. Phil.*, 11, 1980, 5–11. His views on women in the *Republic* are said to be 'generated on grounds independent of his general views on the nature of virtue or justice'.

2.193 **Sparshott**, F. E., 'Plato as anti-political thinker', *Ethics*, 77, 1967, 214–19. Response to W. Leys.

2.194 —— 'Socrates and Thrasymachus', *Monist*, 50, 1966, 412–59. Useful extended discussion of Book I of the *Republic*.

2.195 **Spencer**, M. E., 'Plato and the autonomy of constitutions', *Soc. Theory & Pract.*, 5, 1978, 95–130.

2.196 **Sprague**, R. K., *Plato's Philosopher-King: A Study of the Theoretical Background*, Columbia, S.C., 1976. A study of the philosopher-king as a person of art or science rather than as a head of state.

2.197 **Stalley**, R. F., *An Introduction to Plato's Laws*, 1983. Discusses the relationship of the *Laws*, Plato's longest treatise on politics, to the *Republic*.

2.198 **Strauss**, L., *The Argument and Action of Plato's Laws*, Chicago, Ill., 1975. An examination of the *Laws*, a chapter being devoted to discussion of each book of Plato's work. Engages with the major issue of whether the Laws represent an intentionally pragmatic recantation of the idealism of the *Republic*.

2.199 **Taylor**, C. W., 'Plato's totalitarianism', *Polis*, 2, 1986, 4–29. Plato is said not to put the happiness of the state over and above that of its citizens.

2.200 **Thorson**, T. H., ed., *Plato: Totalitarian or Democrat?*, Englewood Cliffs, N.J., 1963. Collection of readings from the writings of some of the principal protagonists in the debate: R. H. S. Crossman, K. R. Popper, J. Wild, J. H. Hallowell, L. Strauss, and B. Russell.

2.201 **Tigerstedt**, E. N., *Interpreting Plato*,

Uppsala, 1977. Excellent overview of the various interpretations of Plato as totalitarian, liberal and so forth.

2.202 **Versenyi**, L. G., 'Plato and his liberal opponents', *Phil.*, 46, 1971, 222–37. Philosophically, Plato is said to be 'a better friend of democracy than democracy's would be defenders, his avowed critics, could ever hope to be'.

2.203 **Vlastos** G., 'Justice and psychic harmony in the Republic', *J. Phil.*, 66, 1969, 505–21.

2.204 —— ed., *Plato: A Collection of Critical Essays II: Ethics, Politics, and Philosophy of Art and Religion*, New York, 1971. Includes D. Sachs, 'A fallacy in Plato's *Republic*', R. Demos, 'A fallacy in Plato's *Republic?*', J. D. Mabbot, 'Is Plato's *Republic* utilitarian?', G. Vlastos, 'Justice and happiness in the *Republic*', G. Morrow, 'Plato and the rule of law', W. Leys, 'Was Plato non-political?' and F. Sparshott, 'Plato as anti-political thinker'.

2.205 —— *Platonic Studies*, Princeton, N.J., 1973. Includes most of his previously published articles on Plato's political thought: 'Justice and happiness in the *Republic*', 'Does slavery exist in Plato's *Republic?*', 'Slavery in Plato's political thought' and 'Isonomia Politike'.

2.206 —— *Socrates, Ironist and Moral Philosopher*, Ithaca, N.Y., 1991. Excellent book by the doyen of Socratic studies.

2.207 —— 'Socrates on political obedience and disobedience', *Yale Review*, 63, 1974, 517–34. Tries to reconcile the *Apology* and *Crito* by distinguishing between the abstract and general obligation of obedience and – given circumstances of overriding importance – the concrete and particular duty of disobedience to *this* law.

2.208 —— 'The argument in the *Republic* that "justice pays" ', *J. Phil.*, 65, 1968, 665–74.

2.209 —— *The Philosophy of Socrates*, Garden City, Mich., 1971.

2.210 —— 'The theory of social justice in the *Polis* in Plato's Republic', in H. North, ed., *Interpretations of Plato*, Leiden, 1977, 1–40. Generally regarded as one of the most lucid accounts of the topic.

2.211 **Vogelin**, E., *Plato*, Baton Rouge, La, 1957. Emphasises Plato's preoccupation with moral and political disorder and his efforts to restore the order of Hellenic civilisation through the love of wisdom, tracing this concern from the *Gorgias*

through the *Republic* to the *Laws*.

2.212 **de Vries**, G. J., *Antisthenes Redivivus: Popper's Attack on Plato*, Amsterdam, 1952. Careful refutation of the charge that Plato was totalitarian.

2.213 **Wade**, F., 'In defense of Socrates', *Rev. Metaph.*, 25, 1971, 311–26. Argues, contrary to R. Martin, that Socrates's arguments do not lead to the conclusion that unjust laws should never be disobeyed.

2.214 **Weingartner**, R., 'Vulgar justice and Platonic justice', *Philos. and Phenom. Res.*, 25, 1964–65, 248–52.

2.215 **Wender**, D., 'Plato. Misogynist, paedophile and feminist', *Arthusa*, 6, 1973, 75–90.

2.216 **Whelan**, F. G., 'Socrates and the "meddlesomeness" of the Athenians', *Hist. Pol. Thought*, 4, 1983, 1–29. Argues that although Socrates's definitions of justice and injustice in the *Republic* contain an implicit condemnation of Athenian institutions and policies, his affinities to the party of conservative opposition to democracy are limited – the philosophical life that he defends resembling the active quality that his city characteristically encouraged.

2.217 **White**, N. P., *A Companion to Plato's Republic*, 1979. Introductory overview followed by a section-by-section summary of, and commentary on, Plato's work.

2.218 **Wild**, J., *Plato's Modern Enemies and the Theory of Natural Law*, Chicago, Ill., 1953. Argues, contrary to Popper and others, that Plato was an intellectual ancestor of modern democracy rather than totalitarianism.

2.219 **Williams**, B., 'The analogy of city and soul in Plato's *Republic*', *Phronesis*, Supp. I, 1973, 196–206. Argues that the analogy is not wholly satisfactory.

2.220 **Wilson**, J. F., *The Politics of Moderation: An Interpretation of Plato's Republic*, Lanham, 1984. Attempts to tease out the dialectic of the *Republic*, arguing that the fundamental problem of the work is the relationship between justice and moderation.

2.221 **Wilson**, J. R. S., 'The basis of Plato's society', *Phil.*, 52, 1977, 281–300.

2.222 **Woozley**, A. D., *An Introduction to Plato's Republic*, 1964.

2.223 —— *Law and Obedience: The Arguments of Plato's Crito*, 1979.

2.224 —— 'Socrates on disobeying law', in G. Vlastos, ed., *The Philosophy of Socrates: A Collection of Critical Essays*, New York, 1971, 299–318. 'Once we see that it is not the doctrine of the *Crito* that a man must always, and no matter what, obey the laws of his state, the supposed conflict between that dialogue and the *Apology* disappears.'

2.225 **Yonezawa**, S., 'Socrates' two concepts of the polis', *Hist. Pol. Thought*, 12, 1991, 565–76. Explains the apparent inconsistencies in Socrates's views of political obligation by suggesting he used the word 'state' in two different senses in the *Apology* and *Crito*.

2.226 **Young**, C. M., 'Polemarchus' and Thrasymachus' definition of justice', *Phil. Inq.*, 2, 1980, 404–19.

2.227 **Young**, G., 'Socrates and obedience', *Phronesis*, 19, 1974, 1–29. Startling argument that Socrates restricted the right to disobey to philosophers not entitled to philosophise.

Aristotle

2.228 **Adkins**, A. W., 'The connection between Aristotle's *Ethics* and *Politics*', *Pol. Theory*, 12, 1984, 29–49. Emphasises the essentially moral dimension of his political thinking.

2.229 **Allan**, D. J., 'Individual and state in the *Ethics* and *Politics*', in *Entretiens sur l'Antiquité: Classique XI: La 'Politique' d'Aristotle*, Geneva, 1965, 55–95.

2.230 **Ambler**, W., 'Aristotle on nature and politics: the case of slavery', *Pol. Theory*, 15, 1987, 390–410. 'His reflections on slavery are an indirect but concise introduction to the general problem of whether and how rule can be defended as natural and just. By showing us the natural rule of soul over body and of godlike men over imperfect men, Aristotle does not defend natural slavery; he shows us what we lack.'

2.231 —— 'Aristotle's understanding of the naturalness of the city', *Rev. Pol.*, 47, 1985, 163–85. The relationship between nature and city is more complex than is implied in the doctrine that the city is natural.

2.232 **Arnhart**, L., *Aristotle on Political Reasoning*, Delkalb, Ill., 1981.

2.233 —— 'Aristotle's biopolitics: a defense of biological teleology against biological nihilism', *Politics and the Life Sciences*, 6, 1988, 173–228.

2.234 —— 'Darwin, Aristotle, and the biology of human rights', *Social Science Information*, 23, 1984, 493–521.

2.235 **Bakshi**, O. P., *Politics and Prejudice: Notes on Aristotle's Political Theory*, Delhi, 1975.

2.236 **Barnes**, J., **Schofield**, M. and **Sorabji**, R., ed., *Articles on Aristotle: 2. Ethics and Politics*, 1977. Includes K. von Fritz and E. Kapp, 'The development of Aristotle's political philosophy and the concept of nature', W. Fortenbaugh, 'Aristotle on slaves and women', M. Wheeler, 'Aristotle's analysis of the nature of political struggle', H. Kelsen, 'Aristotle and Hellenic-Macedonian policy', M. Defourny, 'The aim of the state: peace', and R. Weil, 'Aristotle's view of history'.

2.237 **Berns**, L., 'Spiritedness in ethics and politics: a study in Aristotelian psychology', *Interpretation*, 12, 1984, 335–48.

2.238 **Bluhm**, W. T., 'The place of the "polity" in Aristotle's theory of the ideal state', *J. Pol.*, 24, 1962, 743–53.

2.239 **Boesche**, R., 'Aristotle's "science" of tyranny', *Hist. Pol. Thought*, 14, 1993, 1–25. Distills the analysis of tyranny scattered through his writings.

2.240 **Bookman**, J. T., 'The wisdom of the many: an analysis of the arguments of Books III and IV of Aristotle's *Politics*', *Hist. Pol. Thought*, 13, 1992, 1–12. Examines Aristotle's arguments in favour of according a role to the many in governing.

2.241 **Booth**, W. J., 'Politics and the household: a commentary on Aristotle's *Politics* Book One', *Hist. Pol. Thought*, 2, 1981, 203–26. Addresses the question of whether he considered political rule to be natural or conventional.

2.242 **Cashdallar**, S., 'Aristotle's politics of morals', *J. Hist. Phil.*, 11, 1973, 145–60. Disproves the idea that Aristotle treated politics as a field of inquiry distinct from the science of ethics.

2.243 **Chambers**, N., 'Aristotle's "forms of democracy" ', *Trans. Am. Philol. Assoc.*, 92, 1961, 20–30. On how he used his classification of types of democracy to trace the history of the Athenian constitution.

2.244 **Chan**, J., 'Does Aristotle's political theory rest on a "blunder"?', *Hist. Pol. Thought*,

13, 1992, 189–202. Claims, contrary to D. Keyt in *Phronesis*, 32, 1987, that Aristotle is not inconsistent in contending that the polis is both natural and a product of statesmanship.

2.245 **Clark**, S. R. L., 'Aristotle's woman', *Hist. Pol. Thought*, 3, 1982, 177–92. If man is a political animal, what is woman?

2.246 **Coby**, P., 'Aristotle's four conceptions of politics', *West. Pol. Q.*, 39, 1986, 480–503. The four conceptions in the *Polis* are said to be politics as art, education, law and reward.

2.247 **Day**, J. and **Chambers**, M., *Aristotle's History of Athenian Democracy*, Berkeley, Calif., 1962. Examines what they contend to be Aristotle's quasi-biological approach to the historical development of democracy by analysing how he applied his doctrines to a specific body of historical data in his *Constitution of the Athenians*.

2.248 **De Laix**, R. A., 'Aristotle's conception of the Spartan constitution', *J. Hist. Phil.*, 12, 1974, 21–30. His changing views about Sparta are said to illustrate Aristotle's empiricism, a readiness to allow data to shape his thinking.

2.249 **Develin**, R., 'The good man and the good citizen in Aristotle's *Politics*', *Phronesis*, 18, 1973, 71–9. Adopts a philological approach to unravel the distinction.

2.250 **Drury**, S., 'Aristotle on the inferiority of women', *Women and Politics*, 7, 1987, 51–65.

2.251 **Everson**, S., 'Aristotle on the foundations of the state', *Pol. Sts.*, 36, 1988, 89–101. Attempts to resolve the apparent tension in the *Politics* between a recognition of the desirability of individual liberty and the claim that 'none of the citizens belongs to himself but all belong to the state'.

2.252 **Ferguson**, J., 'Teleology in Aristotle's *Politics*,' in A. Gotthelf, ed., *Aristotle on Nature and Living Things: Philosophical and Historical Studies Presented to David M. Balman on his Seventieth Birthday*, Pittsburgh, Penn., 1985, 259–73. 'Aristotle's political thought is governed by the principles which he lays down at the outset of his *Nicomachean Ethics*. Every action we take is directed to some good or evil. This is relative teleology. But there is a master-end, which is the cause of our desiring other ends, and this is the Good or the *summum bonum*. The science which identifies this end, which spells out the absolute teleology, is politics.'

2.253 **Frank**, D. H., 'Aristotle on freedom in the *Politics*', *Prudentia*, 15, 1983, 108–16.

2.254 **Goedecke**, W. R., 'Aristotle's search for the perfect state: the methodology of the *Politics*', *Southwestern J. Phil.*, 1, 1970, 58–64.

2.255 **Hamburger**, M., *Morals and Law: The Growth of Aristotle's Legal Theory*, New Haven, Conn., 1951.

2.256 **Hantz**, H., 'Justice and equality in Aristotle's *Niomachean Ethics* and *Politics*', *Diotima*, 3, 1975, 85–94.

2.257 **Huxley**, G., 'Crete in Aristotle's politics', *Greek, Roman and Byzantine Studies*, 12, 1971, 505–15. On his critical examination of Cretan polity.

2.258 —— 'On Aristotle's best state', *Hist. Pol. Thought*, 6, 1985, 139–49. Argues that Aristotle's best state was the one which was most stable and avoided both civil disorder (stasis) and incessant constitutional change (metabole): laws that are obeyed are the necessary prerequisite for the emergence of good laws.

2.259 **Irwin**, T. H., 'Moral science and political theory in Aristotle', *Hist. Pol. Thought*, 6, 1985, 150–68. On how he attempts to unify his ethical theory with his empirical study of politics.

2.260 **Johnson**, C. N., 'Aristotle's polity; mixed or middle constitution?', *Hist. Pol. Thought*, 9, 1988, 189–204. Attempts to resolve the confusion surrounding Aristotle's discussion of the form of constitution called polity and assesses the significance of this issue for his political thought as a whole.

2.261 —— *Aristotle's Theory of the State*, 1990. Argues that Aristotle's *Politics* as a whole issued from his answer to the 'first question of politics': what is the state, or constitution?

2.262 —— 'The Hobbesian conception of sovereignty and Aristotle's *Politics*', *J. Hist. Ideas*, 46, 1985, 327–47. Notwithstanding the accusation of Hobbes, Aristotle is said to have grasped the true nature of sovereignty.

2.263 —— 'Who is Aristotle's citizen?', *Phronesis*, 29, 1984, 73–90. Attempts to illuminate various obscurities in Book III of the *Politics*.

2.264 **Keaney**, J. J., 'The structure of Aristotle's *Athenaion Politea*', *Harvard Studies in Classical Philology*, 67, 1963, 115–46. On the philosophical pattern to be discerned in his constitutional history of Athens.

2.265 **Keyt**, D., 'Distributive justice in Aristotle's *Ethics* and *Politics*', *Topoi*, 4, 1985, 23–45.

2.266 —— and **Miller**, F. D., ed., *A Companion to Aristotle's Politics*, Cambridge, Mass., 1991. Useful sourcebook of fifteen essays, some written for the volume and many of the others updated for republication: C. Rowe, 'Aims and methods in Aristotle's politics', A. Adkins, 'The connection between Aristotle's *Ethics* and *Politics*', W. Kullmann, 'Man as a political animal in Aristotle', D. Keyt, 'Three basic theorems in Aristotle's *Politics*', N. Smith, 'Aristotle's theory of natural slavery', S. Meikle, 'Aristotle and exchange value', T. Irwin, 'Aristotle's defense of private property', W. Fortenbaugh, 'Aristotle on prior and posterior, correct and mistaken constitutions', D. Keyt, 'Aristotle's theory of distributive justice', F. Miller, 'Aristotle on natural law and justice', R. Mulgan, 'Aristotle's analysis of oligarchy and democracy', R. Polansky, 'Aristotle on political change', and D. Depew, 'Politics, music and contemplation in Aristotle's ideal state'.

2.267 **Klein**, J., 'Aristotle, an introduction', in J. Cropsey, ed., *Ancients and Moderns: Essays on the Tradition of Political Philosophy in Honor of Leo Strauss*, New York, 1964, 50–69. Brief but magisterial consideration of the principal features of Aristotle's philosophy.

2.268 **Lewis**, T. J., 'Acquisition and anxiety: Aristotle's case against the market', *Can. J. Econ.*, 11, 1978, 69–90. Market exchange and human virtue are represented as incompatible in Aristotle's writings, because the market generates anxiety about livelihood leading to the destruction of the possibility of friendship and citizenship.

2.269 **Lloyd**, G. E. R., *Aristotle: the Growth and Structure of his Thought*, 1968. Contains a short chapter on his political ideas.

2.270 **Lord**, C., *Education and Culture in the Political Thought of Aristotle*, Ithaca, N.Y., 1982. On the significance for Aristotle of literature and the arts in educating good citizens.

2.271 —— 'Politics and philosophy in Aristotle's *Politics*', *Hermes*, 106, 1978, 33–57. Argues that Book VII of the *Politics* 'does not directly pose the issue of the superiority of the philosophic life – and that the question of philosophy is actually introduced by Aristotle with a view to resolving the practical question of the best way of life for the city'.

2.272 —— 'The character and composition of Aristotle's *Politics*', *Pol. Theory*, 9, 1981, 459–79. Defends the old view that Books VII and VIII properly belong between Books III and IV.

2.274 **Mara**, G. M., 'The role of philosophy in Aristotle's political science', *Polity*, 19, 1987, 375–401.

2.275 **Masters**, R. D., 'The case of Aristotle's missing dialogues: who wrote the *Sophist*, the *Statesman*, and the *Politics*?', *Pol. Theory*, 5, 1977, 31–60. Suggests that Theophrastus wrote Books IV–VI of the *Politics* and that Aristotle is the author of the Platonic dialogues known as the *Sophist* and *Statesman*.

2.276 **Mathie**, W., 'Justice and the question of regimes in ancient and modern political philosophy: Aristotle and Hobbes', *Can. J. Pol. Sc.*, 9, 1976, 449–63. Whereas Aristotle understands the conflicting claims to rule associated with the various regimes to pose a question of justice, Hobbes provides an account of justice that precludes any consideration of the merit of those claims as a question of justice.

2.277 **Meikle**, S., 'Aristotle and the political economy of the polis', *J. Hellenic Sts.*, 99, 1979, 57–73. Argues that he not only condemned certain civil practices damaging to the polis, but provided an extensive and acute analysis of the process of social and economic change – including the development of a market economy – in fourth-century Athens.

2.278 **Miller**, F. D., 'Aristotle and the natural rights tradition', *Reason Papers*, 15, 1988, 166–81.

2.279 —— 'Aristotle on property rights', in J. P. Anton and A. Preus, ed., *Essays in Ancient Greek Philosophy 4: Aristotle's Ethics*, Albany, N.Y., 1991, 227–48. Argues that scattered through his works are the elements of a coherent justification of the right to private property.

2.280 —— 'Aristotle's political naturalism', *Apeiron*, 22, 1989, 195–218.

2.281 **Meikle**, S., 'The state and the community in Aristotle's *Politics*', *Reason Papers*, 1,

1974, 61–9.

2.282 **Mingay**, J., 'How should a philosopher live?: two Aristotelian views', *Hist. Pol. Thought*, 8, 1987, 21–32. Aristotle 'thrashed about with an insoluble problem' – the kind of life intellectuals should lead to become good rulers – 'and produced two unsatisfactory solutions'.

2.283 **Morrall**, J. B., *Aristotle*, 1977. Neat introduction to his political thinking.

2.284 **Morrow**, G. R., 'Aristotle's comments on Plato's *Laws*', in G. E. L. Owen, ed., *Aristotle and Plato in the mid-Fourth Century. Papers of the Symposium Aristotelicum held at Oxford in August, 1957*, Göteborg, 1969, 144–63. The comments are said to be less superficial than is usually suggested.

2.285 **Mulgan**, R. G., 'Aristotle and absolute rule', *Antichthon*, 8, 1974, 21–8. Deals with the extent of his debt to Plato, the qualities which fit a person for rule, and the relevance of the account of absolute rule to Aristotle's general principles.

2.286 —— 'Aristotle and the democratic conception of freedom', in B. F. Harris, ed., *Auckland Classical Essays Presented to E. M. Blaiklock*, Auckland, 1970, 95–111.

2.287 —— 'Aristotle and the value of political participation', *Pol. Theory*, 18, 1990, 187–215. Aristotle is said to be less than a wholehearted advocate of political participation as essential for happiness.

2.288 —— 'Aristotle's doctrine that man is a political animal', *Hermes*, 102, 1974, 438–45. Aristotle is said to use the phrase 'political animal' in three different though related senses.

2.289 —— *Aristotle's Political Theory: An Introduction for Students of Political Theory*, 1977. Clear and lucid overview focusing on the *Politics*.

2.290 —— 'Aristotle's sovereign', *Pol. Sts.*, 18, 1970, 518–22. On the differences from modern doctrines of sovereignty.

2.291 **Newell**, W. R., 'Superlative virtue: the problem of monarchy in Aristotle's "politics" ', *West. Pol. Q.*, 40, 1987, 159–78.

2.292 **Nichols**, M. P., 'Aristotle's defense of rhetoric', *J. Pol.*, 49, 1987, 657–77. On his rhetoric as a bridge between private and public, passion and reason, individual interest and common good, and equity and law.

2.293 —— 'The good life, slavery, and acquisition: Aristotle's introduction to politics', *Interpretation*, 2, 1983, 171–83.

2.294 **Nussbaum**, M. C., 'Shame, separateness and political unity: Aristotle's criticism of Plato', in A. O. Rorty, ed., *Essays on Aristotle's Ethics*, Berkeley, Calif., 1980, 395–435. On Aristotle's criticism of Plato's defence of paternalistic coercion as a necessary condition of self-respecting life for the majority, and why this is not conducive to the kind of unity proper for a rational community.

2.295 **Papageorgiou**, C. I., 'Four or five types of democracy in Aristotle?', *Hist. Pol. Thought*, 11, 1990, 1–8.

2.296 **Patzig**, G., ed., *XI. Symposium Aristotelicum: Studien zur Politik des Aristoteles*, Gottingen, 1989. Papers in English are J. Barnes, 'Aristotle and political liberty', J. Cooper, 'Political animals and civic friendship', T. Irwin, 'The good of political activity', C. Kahn, 'The normative structure of Aristotle's *Politics*', and M. Schofield, 'Ideology and philosophy in Aristotle's theory of slavery'.

2.297 **Polansky**, R., 'The dominance of polis for Aristotle', *Dialogos*, 14, 43–56.

2.298 **Richter**, M., 'Aristotle and the classical Greek concept of despotism', *Hist. Euro. Ideas*, 12, 1990, 175–87.

2.299 **Rosen**, F. 'The political context of Aristotle's categories of justice', *Phronesis*, 20, 1975, 228–40. Focuses on the connection between his four categories of justice (universal, distributive, corrective and reciprocity) and political themes in the *Ethics* and *Politics*.

2.300 **Rowe**, C. J., 'Aims and methods in Aristotle's *Politics*', *Class. Q.*, 27, 1977, 159–72. Tries to explain the apparent contradiction between the empirical and theoretical aspects of the work.

2.301 —— 'Reality and utopia', *Elenchos*, 10, 1989, 317–36. On the tension between the scientific and normative aspects of the *Politics*.

2.302 **Salkever**, S. G., 'Aristotle's social science', *Pol. Theory*, 9, 1981, 479–508. Argues that for Aristotle the study of politics was a kind of natural science.

2.303 —— *Finding the Mean: Theory and Practice in Aristotelian Political Philosophy*, Princeton, N.J., 1990. Both a clarification of Aristotle's political thinking and an attempt to use it to shed light on the problems of liberal democracy – on the assumption that he 'exemplifies a theoretical tone that avoids treating politics either as a perfectly soluble problem or as a tragic dilemma or paradox'.

2.304 —— 'Women, soldiers, citizens: Plato and Aristotle on the politics of virility', *Polity*, 18, 1986, 232–53.

2.305 **Saxonhouse**, A. W., 'Family, polity, and unity: Aristotle on Socrates' community of wives', *Polity*, 15, 1982, 202–19.

2.306 **Schmid**, W. T., 'Aristotle on choice: liberty and the *Polis*', *Paideia*, 2, 1978, 182–85.

2.307 **Schmidt**, J., 'A raven with a halo: the translation of Aristotle's *Politics*', *Hist. Pol. Thought*, 7, 1986, 295–319. Analyses the importance of textual translation and linguistic reception for the *Politics*' influence on Western political thought – especially the identification of 'civil society', 'political community' and 'state', an identification not ruptured until Hegel's time.

2.308 **Schott**, R., 'Aristotle on women', *Kinesis*, 11, 1982, 69–84.

2.309 **Schroeder**, D. N., 'Aristotle on law', *Polis*, 4, 1981, 17–31.

2.310 **Shellens**, M. S., 'Aristotle on natural law', *Natural Law Forum*, 4, 1959, 72–100. Careful exposition of what he meant by the concept.

2.311 **Smith**, S. B., 'Goodness, nobility, and virtue in Aristotle's political science', *Polity*, 19, 1986, 5–26.

2.312 **Solmsen**, F., 'Leisure and play in Aristotle's ideal state', *Rheinische Museum für Philologie*, 107, 1964, 193–220.

2.313 **Sparshott**, F. F., 'Aristotle on women', *Phil. Inq.*, 7, 1985, 177–200.

2.314 **Spelman**, E. V., 'Aristotle and the politicization of the soul', in S. Harding and M. B., Hintikka, ed., *Discovering Reality: Feminist Perspectives on Epistemology, Metaphysics, Methodology, and Philosophy of Science*, Dordrecht, 1983, 17–30.

2.315 **Springborg**, P., 'Aristotle and the problem of needs', *Hist. Pol. Thought*, 5, 1984, 393–425. Argues that he steers a way between an *a priori* conceptualisation of needs as metaphysical requirements and the libertarian view of needs as nothing but an empirical category of expressed demands.

2.316 **Stern**, S. M., *Aristotle on the World State*, 1968. Primarily a discussion of a purported letter from Aristotle to Alexander the Great.

2.317 **Swanson**, J. A., *The Public and the Private in Aristotle's Political Philosophy*, Ithaca, N.Y., 1992. Argues, contrary to the standard interpretation, that Aristotle did not equate the private with the household and, further, that public and private exist not in opposition but in dynamic equilibrium to one another.

2.318 **Swazo**, N. K., 'The authentic tele of politics: a reading of Aristotle', *Hist. Pol. Thought*, 12, 1991, 405–20. Uses Heidegger to clarify the bond between Aristotle's metaphysics and his ethical and political doctrines.

2.319 **Tumulty**, P., 'Aristotle, feminism and natural law theory', *New Schol.*, 55, 1981, 450–64. Argues that although Aristotle was 'wrong about women', his moral philosophy contains the potential for treating them as equal to men.

2.320 **Vander Waerdt**, P. A., 'Kingship and philosophy in Aristotle's best regime', *Phronesis*, 30, 1985, 249–73. On the apparent contradiction between the readiness to countenance a monarch's permanent role and his doctrine that it is just for natural freemen to share in ruling through rotation of office.

2.321 —— 'The political intention of Aristotle's moral philosophy', *Ancient Phil.*, 5, 1985, 77–89.

2.322 **von Fritz**, K., 'Aristotle's contribution to the practice and theory of historiography', *University of California Publications in Philosophy*, 28, 1958, 113–38. Argues that he applied the concept of biological evolution to society.

2.323 —— 'The composition of Aristotle's *Constitution of Athens* and the so-called Dracontian constitution', *Class. Philol.*, 49, 1954, 73–93. Argues contrary to some interpreters that chapter 4 of the *Constitution* is neither an interpolation nor an insertion into a previously completed work.

2.324 **von Leyden**, W., 'Aristotle and the concept of law', *Phil.*, 42, 1967, 1–19. Clear guide to his complex analysis of the concept of law, arguing that its merit is the recognition of the need for a multiple definition.

2.325 —— *Aristotle on Equality and Justice: His*

Political Argument, New York, 1985.
Discusses the Aristotelian, as well as
modern, answer to the question of how to
render the principle of equality compatible
with the idea of fairness; and how to
combine the facts of individual as well as
social diversity in civil life with the
demands for political justice.

2.326 **Wilson**, J. F., 'Power, rule and politics:
the Aristotelian view', *Polity*, 13, 1980,
80–96.

2.327 **Winthrop**, D., 'Aristotle and political
responsibility', *Pol. Theory*, 3, 1975,
406–22. Argues that Aristotle's political
science rested upon the premise that the
common sense of the good citizen was
responsible.

2.328 —— 'Aristotle and theories of justice',
Am. Pol. Sc. Rev., 72, 1978, 1201–16.
Aristotle is said to have considered all
theories of justice, including his own, to be
unsatisfactory. 'In his opinion, a politics
that understands its highest purpose as
justice and a political science that attempts
to comprehend all political phenomena
within a theory of justice are practically all
theoretically unsound.'

2.329 —— 'Aristotle on participatory
democracy', *Polity*, 11, 1978, 151–71.

2.330 **Wormuth**, F. D, 'Aristotle on law', in
M. R. Konvitz and A. E. Murphy, ed.,
*Essays in Political Theory Presented to
George H. Sabine*, Ithaca, N.Y., 1948,
45–61. His attitude to law is said to be
thoroughly pragmatic.

2.331 **Yack**, B., 'A reinterpretation of Aristotle's
political teleology', *Hist. Pol. Thought*, 12,
1991, 15–33. Addresses the apparent
contradiction between his empirical and
teleological approaches, claiming the
contradiction disappears when Aristotle is
understood not to have treated the polis as a
natural substance with its own internal
principle of motion.

2.332 —— 'Community and conflict in
Aristotle's political philosophy', *Rev. Pol.*,
47, 1985, 92–112. Cautions against a
Rousseaunian interpretation of
Aristotelian community: trust among the
citizens of the polis cannot be expected to
eliminate disagreement and conflict.

2.333 —— 'Natural right and Aristotle's
understanding of justice', *Pol. Theory*, 18,
1990, 216–37. Aristotelian natural right is
said to refer not to a higher, absolutely
correct, standard of justice, but rather to a

kind of judgement about justice that
develops naturally in political
communities.

2.334 **Zuckert**, C. H., 'Aristotle on the limits and
satisfactions of political life', *Interpretation*,
2, 1983, 185–206. Argues that the
economic and educational requirements of
Aristotle's politics exclude the bulk of
people from participation.

Thucydides

2.335 **Bluhm**, W. T., 'Causal theory in
Thucydides' Peloponnesian war', *Pol.
Sts.*, 10, 1962, 15–35. Depicts the *History*
as a forerunner of modern concepts of
international politics.

2.336 **Brown**, C. W., 'Thucydides, Hobbes, and
the derivation of anarchy', *Hist. Pol.
Thought*, 8, 1987, 33–63. Argues that they
share similar views about how the
calculations of rational decision-makers
produce conflict, war and anarchy under
certain conditions.

2.337 **Bruell**, C., 'Thucydides' view of Athenian
imperialism', *Am. Pol. Sc. Rev.*, 68, 1974,
11–17. Warns against interpreting him as a
forerunner of modern behavioural science.

2.338 **de Romilly**, J., *Thucydides and Athenian
Imperialism*, 1963.

2.339 **Euben**, J. P., 'Creatures of a day: thought
and action in Thucydides', in T. Ball, ed.,
*Political Theory and Praxis: New
Perspectives*, Minneapolis, Minn., 1977,
28–56. Subtle analysis of political themes
in the *History*.

2.340 **Fleiss**, P. J., 'Political disorder and
constitutional forms: Thucydides' critique
of contemporary politics', *J. Pol.*, 21,
1959, 592–673.

2.341 —— *Thucydides and the Politics of
Bipolarity*, Baton Rouge, La., 1966.

2.342 **French**, A., 'Thucydides and the power
syndrome', *Greece and Rome*, 27, 1980,
22–30. What Herodotus emphasised
allegorically, Thucydides did by explicit
analysis – that power is basically
dangerous.

2.343 **Hussey**, E., 'Thucydidean history and
Democritean theory', *Hist. Pol. Thought*,
6, 1985, 118–38. Traces the influence of
Democritus' moral and political writings
on Thucydides.

2.344 **McGregor**, M. F., 'The politics of the
historian Thucydides', *Phoenix*, 10, 1956,

93–102.

2.345 **Neumann**, H., 'The philosophy of individualism: an interpretation of Thucydides', *J. Hist. Phil.*, 3, 1969, 234–46.

2.346 **Palmer**, M., 'Thucydides' "History" as political theory', *Teaching Political Science*, 15, 1988, 108–14.

2.347 **Pouncey**, P. R., 'Disorder and defeat in Thucydides, and some alternatives', *Hist. Pol. Thought*, 7, 1986, 1–14. On the parallels Thucydides finds between politics and military action.

2.348 —— *The Necessities of War: A Study of Thucydides' Pessimism*, New York, 1980. On how he substitutes for an epic view of history one in which concerted action and civic unanimity lead to national prosperity, whilst internal discord leads to a war of all against all.

2.349 **Sears**, C. D., 'Thucydides and the scientific approach to international politics', *Aust. J. Pol. & Hist.*, 23, 1977, 28–40. To depict Thucydides' methodology as scientific in the modern sense is to misrepresent his thought.

2.350 **Wasserman**, F. M., 'Post-Periclean democracy in action: the Mytilenean debate (Thuc. III, 37–48)', *Trans. Am. Philol. Assoc.*, 87, 1956, 27–41. 'Despite his insight into the failures of a democracy lacking a leadership both dynamic and self-restrained, Thucydides keeps his belief in the *polis* as the natural political form of the Greek world.'

2.351 **Whitehead**, D., 'Thucydides: fact-grabber or philosopher?', *Greece and Rome*, 27, 1980, 158–65. He was concerned throughout his life to chronicle events in order to understand both the universal features of human nature and the general origins of political conflict.

2.352 **Woodhead**, A. G., *Thucydides on the Nature of Power*, Cambridge, Mass., 1970. Clear and insightful guide to his political thinking.

Other thinkers

2.353 **Aalders**, G. J. D., 'The political faith of Democritus', *Mnemosyne*, 3, 1951, 302–13.

2.354 **Baldry**, H. C., 'Zeno's ideal state', *J. Hellenic Sts.*, 79, 1959, 3–15. On the *Politeia*, a short work probably intended as a reply to Plato's *Republic*, in which Zeno outlines his own version of a utopia peopled by citizens of moral excellence.

2.355 **Cole**, A. T., 'The Anonymous Iamblichi and his place in Greek political theory', *Harvard Studies in Classical Philology*, 65, 1961, 127–63. In part an attempt to identify the work, but also an argument to the effect that the Anonymous Iamblichi was no less a political thinker than Democritus.

2.356 **Devine**, F. E., 'Stoicism on the best regime', *J. Hist. Ideas*, 31, 1970, 323–36. Although the Stoics were usually considered to have favoured mixed government, only the thinkers of the Middle Stoa did so without qualification.

2.357 **Furley**, D. J., 'Antiphon's case against justice', in G. B. Kerferd, ed., *The Sophists and their Legacy: Proceedings of the Fourth International Colloquium on Ancient Philosophy*, Wiesbaden, 1981, 81–91. Argues that he 'rejects justice on the grounds that to be just is to damage or neglect one's own natural interest. Antiphon's position is thus similar to that of Thrasymachus in Plato, Republic I, although Thrasymachus differs in making no explicit appeal to nature.'

2.358 **Higgins**, W. E., *Xenophon the Athenian: The Problem of the Individual and the Society of the Polis*, Albany, N.Y., 1977. Straussian reading which emphasises the irony of Xenophon's treatment of the relation between the individual and the polis.

2.359 **Kerferd**, G. B., 'The moral and political doctrines of Antiphon the Sophist: a reconsideration', *Proceedings of the Cambridge Philological Society*, 184, 1956–57, 26–32.

2.360 **Larsen**, J. A. O., 'Cleisthenes and the development of the theory of democracy at Athens', in M. R. Konvitz and A. E. Murphy, ed., *Essays in Political Theory Presented to George H. Sabine*, Ithaca, N.Y., 1948, 1–16. Speculates as to why Cleisthenes, supposed founder of democratic institutions in the sixth century BC, was neither widely nor long perceived as such within Athens.

2.361 **Moulton**, C., 'Antiphon the Sophist and Democritus', *Museum Helveticum*, 31, 1974, 129–39. The political and ethical doctrines of the two are depicted as less incompatible than is usually suggested.

2.362 **Nicholson**, P. P., 'Protagoras and the

justification of Athenian democracy',
Polis, 3, 1980–81, 14–24.

2.363 **Procope**, J. F., 'Democritus on politics
and the soul', *Class. Q.*, 39, 1989, 307–31.
Excellent account of the political thinking
scattered through a number of
Democritean fragments.

2.364 **Reesor**, M. E., *The Political Thought of the
Old and Middle Stoa*, New York, 1951.

2.365 **Saunders**, T. J., 'Antiphon the Sophist on
natural laws', *Procs. Aris. Soc.*, 78, 1978,
216–35. Speculates that he was 'a kind of
conservative fundamentalist (perhaps
unique in ancient Greek thought),
impatient of general concepts, and intent,
possibly in a reformist spirit, on
simplifying assimilation of the workings of
society to those of nature'.

2.366 **Saxonhouse**, A. W., 'Men, women, and
politics: family and polis in Aristophanes
and Euripides', *Pol. Theory*, 8, 1980,
65–81. On three plays in which the rule of
women illuminates the tension between the
public and private spheres.

2.367 **Schofield**, M., *The Stoic Idea of the City*,
1991. On the political thought of Zeno,
Chrysippus and others, illustrating the
transition from a republican to natural law
style of thinking.

2.368 **Vlastos**, G., 'Solonian justice', *Class.
Philol.*, 41, 1946, 65–83. On Solon's
Fragment 4, 'a document of the highest
importance in the development of Greek
political ideas' because it presented justice
as a natural, self-regulating order. The
'naturalization of justice meant its
socialization: it became the common
possession of the *polis*, for it defined the
common peace and the common freedom
of all'.

2.369 **Walbank**, F. W., 'Political morality and
the friends of Scipio', *J. Rom. Sts.*, 55,
1965, 1–16. On the views of two Greeks,
Panaetius and Polybius, about the
Roman state and empire.

2.370 **Winton**, R. I., *The Political Thought of
Protagoras*, 1974. On a Sophist who was
sceptical about claims to absolute
knowledge.

(c) ROME

General

2.371 **Adcock**, F. E., *Roman Political Ideas and
Practice*, Ann Arbor, Mich., 1959. Brief
but magisterial overview from the early
Republic to the degeneration of the
Augustan Principate into autocracy.

2.372 **Brunt**, P. A., 'Laus Imperii', in
P. Garnsey and C. R. Whittaker, ed.,
Imperialism in the Ancient World, 1978,
159–91. Explores conceptions of empire in
the writings of, among others, Cicero and
Caesar.

2.373 —— *The Fall of the Roman Republic and
Related Essays*, 1988. Includes much
discussion of Roman political concepts,
with a particularly illuminating chapter on
libertas.

2.374 **Dickinson**, J., *Death of a Republic: Politics
and Political Thought at Rome, 59–44 B.C.*,
New York, 1963. Analyses the reasons
underlying the demise of Roman
republicanism, particularly from the
perspective of the basis of, and relationship
between, law and political authority.
Depicts two rival political philosophies in
Cicero's 'institutionalism' and Caesar's
'instrumentalism'.

2.375 **Dunkle**, J. R., 'The Greek tyrant and
Roman political invective of the late
Republic', *Trans. Am. Philol. Assoc.*, 98,
1967, 51–71. On how images of Greek
despotism featured in oratory and the
writings of, among others, Cicero.

2.376 —— 'The rhetorical tyrant in Roman
historiography: Sallust, Livy, and
Tacitus', *Classical World*, 65, 1971, 12–20.

2.377 **Earl**, D., *The Moral and Political Tradition
of Rome*, 1967. Essentially a study of the
ideals of the Roman nobility including a
sharp examination of political concepts.

2.378 **Griffin**, M., 'Philosophy, politics, and
politicians at Rome', in M. Griffin and J.
Barnes, ed., *Philophia Togata: Essays on
Philosophy and Roman Society*, 1989, 1–37.
Authoritative overview of how the Romans
perceived the relation between philosophy
and politics.

2.379 **Lind**, L. R., 'The idea of the Republic and
the foundation of Roman political liberty',
in C. Deroux, ed., *Studies in Latin
Literature and Roman History IV*, Brussels,
1986, 44–108. Analyses the use of political

concepts such as *res publica*, *imperium* and *princeps*, illustrating the tendency of Cicero and others to identify moral and political values.

2.380 —— 'The tradition of Roman moral conservatism', in C. Deroux, ed., *Studies in Latin Literature and Roman History I*, Brussels, 1979, 7–58. Excellent examination of Roman political as well as moral ideas, including concepts such as *gloria*, *dignitas*, *auctoritas*, and *honos*.

2.381 **Wirszubski**, C., *Libertas as a Political Idea at Rome during the Late Republic and Early Principate*, 1950.

Cicero

2.382 **Annas**, J., 'Cicero on Stoic moral philosophy and private property', in M. Griffin and J. Barnes, ed., *Philosophia Fogata, Essays on Philosophy and Roman Society*, 1989, 151–73. Explores how Cicero attempted to resolve the contradiction between the realism of pursuing politico-material advantage and the asceticism of Stoicism.

2.383 **Mitchell**, T. N., 'Cicero on the moral crisis of the late Republic', *Hemathena*, 186, 1984, 21–41. Clear and extensive account of the links he thought existed between ethics and politics.

2.384 **Morrall**, J. B., 'Cicero as a political thinker', *Hist. Today*, 33, 1982, 33–7.

2.385 **Nicgorski**, W., 'Cicero's paradoxes and his idea of utility', *Pol. Theory*, 12, 1984, 557–78. Argues that he achieved a coherent philosophy which, grounded in the inclinations and needs of human nature, was intended to inform the life of the statesman-orator.

2.386 **Rawson**, E., 'The interpretation of Cicero's *De Legibus*', *Aufsteig und Niedergang der romaischen Weld I*, 1973, 334–56.

2.387 **Seager**, R., 'Cicero and the word *Popularis*', *Classical Q.*, 22, 1972, 328–38. He used the word loosely to mean sovereignty of the people, a concept to which he was opposed.

2.388 **Wirszubski**, C., 'Cicero's *Cum Dignitate Otium*: a reconsideration', *J. Rom. Sts.*, 44, 1954, 1–13. For Cicero the phrase is said to have meant tranquillity with dignity in the state.

2.389 **Wood**, N., *Cicero's Social and Political Thought*, Berkeley, Calif., 1988. The only full-scale study in English, arguing that more than any other ancient thinker he foreshadowed modern conceptions of the state.

2.390 —— '*Populares* and *Circumcelliones*: the vocabulary of "fallen man" in Cicero and St. Augustine', *Hist. Pol. Thought*, 7, 1986, 33–51. Compares the way in which they denounced those they regarded as irrational disturbers of political order.

2.391 —— 'The economic dimension of Cicero's political thought: property and state', *Can. J. Pol. Sc.*, 16, 1983, 739–56. Claims that as an economic individualist who recommended the enlightened pursuit of self-interest, he was the first major political thinker to make the protection of private property the primary purpose of the state.

Lucretius

2.392 **Fowler**, D. P., 'Lucretius and politics', in M. Griffin and J. Barnes, ed., *Philosophia Fogata: Essays on Philosophy and Roman Society*, 1989, 120–50. Particularly useful on the concordances between Lucretius' language and that of contemporary political discourse of among others Cicero and Sallust.

2.393 **Minyard**, J. D., *Lucretius and the Late Republic*, *Mnemosyne*, supp. 90, Leiden, 1985. Makes a fervent case for treating the *De Rerum Natura* as a political work.

2.394 **Monti**, R. C., 'Lucretius on greed, political ambition, and society: *de rer. nat. 3. 59–86*', *Latomus*, 40, 1981, 48–66. Useful account of the Lucretian doctrine on the value of political society.

2.395 **Nichols**, J. H., *Epicurean Political Philosophy: the De Rerum Natura of Lucretius*, Ithaca, N.Y., 1976. A Straussian reading of Lucretius in which he searches for the essence of Epicurean philosophy in a poem whose political character is not immediately apparent – the essence being a mistrust of political projects for transforming the human condition.

Polybius

2.396 **Alonso-Numez**, J. M., 'The anacyclosis in Polybius', *Eranos*, 84, 1986, 17–22. On his deterministic account of constitutional change.

2.397 **Brink**, C. O., and **Walbank**, F. W., 'The construction of the sixth book of Polybius', *Class. Q.*, 4, 1954, 97–122. What lends a certain unity to the book – in which he advocates a mixed constitution as a partial antidote to the natural decay of political structures – is a determination to base the writing of Roman history on fundamental principles, and to use Greek political theory to supply them.

2.398 **Fontana**, B., 'Tacitus on empire and republic', *Hist. Pol. Thought*, 14, 1993, 27–40.

2.399 **Podes**, S., 'Polybius and his theory of *anacyclosis*: problems of not just ancient political theory', *Hist. Pol. Thought*, 12, 1991, 577–87. On his theory of constitutional change.

2.400 **von Fritz**, K., *The Theory of the Mixed Constitution in Antiquity: A Critical Analysis of Polybius' Political Ideas*, New York, 1954. Comprehensive study which compares him with other ancient political theorists.

2.401 **Walbank**, F. W., *Polybius*, Berkeley, Calif., 1972. Includes extensive discussion of his constitutional thinking.

2.402 —— 'The idea of decline in Polybius', in R. Koselleck and P. Widmer, ed., *Niedergang. Studien zu einem geschlichtlichen Thema*, Stuttgart, 1980, 41–58.

Tacitus

2.403 **Bernario**, H. W., *An Introduction to Tacitus*, Athens, Ga., 1975. Includes a chapter on his political thought.

2.404 **Boesche**, R., 'The politics of pretence: Tacitus and the political theory of despotism', *Hist. Pol. Thought*, 8, 1987, 189–210. Argues that, in spite of its shortcomings, Tacitus's characterisation of despotism provided – more than did Plato or Aristotle – the theoretical framework of subsequent political writers.

2.405 **Percival**, J., 'Tacitus and the Principate', *Greece and Rome*, 27, 1980, 119–33. Reveals what Tacitus meant by *libertas* in condemning the *servitus* existing from the reign of Augustus.

2.406 **Saxonhouse**, A. W., 'Tacitus' dialogue on oratory: political activity under a tyrant', *Pol. Theory*, 3, 1975, 53–68. Interprets the *Dialogue* less as a simple treatise on oratory than a consideration of the way of life individuals must lead if they are to perform a significant political function under tyranny.

2.407 **Syme**, R., *Tacitus*, vol. II, 1958. Contains a section on his doctrines of government.

2.408 —— *Ten Studies in Tacitus*, 1970. The final chapter, 'The political opinions of Tacitus', contains some interesting comments about Roman political theory in general – or rather its paucity.

Other thinkers

2.409 **Earl**, D., *The Political Thought of Sallust*, 1961.

2.410 **Griffin**, M., *Seneca: A Philosopher in Politics*, 1976. Relates his political career to his general philosophical position and to his particular writings on politics and society.

2.411 **Rainage**, E. S., *The Nature and Purpose of Augustus' "Res Gestae"*, Stuttgart, 1987. Careful examination of 'the single most important historical document of the Augustan period', a narrative on government in which Augustus reveals his political philosophy.

3

MEDIEVAL
POLITICAL THOUGHT

(a) GENERAL

3.1 **Burns**, J. H., ed., *The Cambridge History of Medieval Political Thought c.350–c.1450*, 1988. The most comprehensive and authoritative survey available.

3.2 **Chroust**, A. H., 'The corporate idea and the body politic in the middle ages', *Rev. Pol.*, 9, 1947, 423–52.

3.3 **Folz**, R., *The Concept of Empire in Western Europe from the Fifth to the Fourteenth Century*, 1969.

3.4 **Harding**, A. L., 'Political liberty in the Middle Ages', *Speculum*, 40, 1980, 423–43. Argues that territorial immunity – the lord's power to act in the affairs of the community free from the interference of the sovereign government – was the oldest and most persistent meaning of liberty throughout the medieval period.

3.5 **Ladner**, G. B., 'Aspects of medieval thought on church and state', *Rev. Pol.*, 9, 1947, 403–22.

3.6 **Morrall**, J. B., *Political Thought in Medieval Times*, 1958. Brief but authoritative survey from the fifth to the fifteenth centuries.

3.7 **Oakley**, F., 'Celestial hierarchies revisited: Walter Ullmann's vision of medieval politics', *Past & Pres.*, 60, 1973, 3–48. Sustained critique of the conceptual framework used by Ullmann in most of his books – the conflict between descending and ascending theories of government – claiming that it obscures the intricacies of medieval political thought.

3.8 **Ullmann**, W., *Law and Politics in the Middle Ages: Introduction to the Sources of Medieval Political Ideas*, 1955. Claims to be 'one of the first attempts to present the principal sources' – legal, literary, annalistic and so forth – 'of medieval political ideas in an integrated and coherent manner'.

3.9 —— *The Growth of Papal Government in the Middle Ages*, 1955. Traces late medieval papal ideology into the Dark Ages, focusing upon the conflict between the papal claim of supremacy in temporal affairs and the Caesaro-papist claim of secular Christian authority.

3.10 —— *Principles of Government and Politics in the Middle Ages*, 1961. Structured – like so many of Ullmann's books – around the conflict between descending and ascending conceptions of political authority.

3.11 —— *A History of Political Thought: The Middle Ages*, 1965. Argues that the history of medieval political thought is largely a history of the conflict between an 'ascending' theory of government – in which power is located in the community – and a 'descending' one in which rulers are responsible to God from whom their authority is delegated; and, further, that from the Christianisation of the Germanic peoples in the fifth century until the revival of classical learning in the thirteenth century the descending conception of authority held sway. A scholarly and readable introduction.

3.12 —— *The Individual and Society in the Middle Ages*, 1967. Exploration of how the individual gradually came to be perceived as a citizen rather than a subject.

3.13 **Wilhelmsen**, F. D., *Christianity and Political Philosophy*, Athens, 1978. On various Christian interpretations of political power, including those of Augustine, Sir John Fortescue and Thomas Aquinas.

(b) THE EARLY MIDDLE AGES

General

3.14 **Dvornik**, F., *Early Christian and Byzantine Political Philosophy: Origins and Background*, 2 vols., Washington, D.C., 1966. Comprehensive and authoritative account through to the sixth century.

3.15 **Finlay**, R., 'Early Christian political philosophy', *Il Pensiero Politico*, 3, 1970, 264–67.

3.16 **Morrison**, K. F., *The Two Kingdoms: Ecclesiology in Carolingian Political Thought*, Princeton, N.J., 1964.

3.17 **Nelson**, J. L., 'Not bishops' bailiffs but lords of the earth: Charles the Bald and the problem of sovereignty', in D. Wood, ed., *Sts. Ch. Hist.*, 9, *The Church and Sovereignty, c.590–1918*, 1991, 23–34. Some of the theoretical disputes of the late Middle Ages are said to have been foreshadowed in the reign of Charles.

3.18 **Ullmann**, W., *The Carolingian Renaissance and the Idea of Kingship*, 1969.

3.19 **Wallace-Hadrill**, J. M., 'The *via regia* of the Carolingian age', in B. Smalley, ed., *Trends in Medieval Political Thought*, 1965, 22–41. On ninth-century conceptions of monarchy.

Augustine

3.20 **Adams**, J. du Q., *The Populus of Augustine and Jerome: A Study in the Patristic Sense of Community*, New Haven, Conn., 1971.

3.21 **Bathory**, P. D., *Political Theory as Public Confession: The Social and Political Thought of St. Augustine of Hippo*, 1981. Interesting analysis of the *Confessions* and the *City of God*, claiming that throughout his writings there is a concern – often latent and

expressed in non-political language – with creating a just world.

3.22 **Bourke**, V. J., 'Saint Augustine', in B. Smalley, ed., *Trends in Medieval Political Thought*, 1965, 1–21. Neat introduction to Augustine's political thinking, emphasising that he never overcame the dichotomy between an awareness of the human condition in the *saeculum* and a yearning for the heavenly city.

3.23 —— 'Voluntarism in Augustine's ethico-legal thought', *Augustinian Sts.*, 5, 1970, 3–19.

3.24 **Brown**, P. R., *Augustine of Hippo: a Biography*, 1967.

3.25 **Buckenmeyer**, R., 'The meaning of *judicium* and its relation to illumination in the *Dialogues* of Augustine', *Augustinian Sts.*, 5, 1970, 89–133.

3.26 **Burnell**, P. J., 'The status of politics in St. Augustine's *City of God*', *Hist. Pol. Thought*, 13, 1992, 13–29. Argues that for Augustine the civil state is the chief natural means of justice; it is not merely, as most commentators suggest, a coercive corrective to sin.

3.27 **Carlson**, C. P., 'The natural order and historical explanation in St. Augustine's *City of God*', *Augustiniana*, 21, 1971, 417–47.

3.28 **Caton**, H., 'St. Augustine's critique of politics', *New Schol.*, 47, 1973, 433–57.

3.29 **Deane**, H. A., *The Political and Social Ideas of St. Augustine*, New York, 1963.

3.30 —— 'Classical and Christian political thought', *Pol. Theory*, 1, 1973, 415–25. Brief but clear account of how Augustine's doctrine of the state differed from that of Plato and Aristotle.

3.31 **Ferrari**, L. C., 'Background to Augustine's *City of God*', *Class. J.*, 67, 1972, 198–208.

3.32 **Fortnin**, E. L., *Political Idealism and Christianity in the Thought of St. Augustine*, Villanova, Pa., 1972.

3.33 —— 'Augustine's *City of God* and the modern historical consciousness', *Rev. Pol.*, 41, 1979, 323–43.

3.34 **Hartigan**, R. S., 'Saint Augustine on war and killing: the problem of the innocent', *J. Hist. Ideas*, 27, 1966, 195–204. Claims that Augustine's doctrine of the just war is ambivalent, resulting in an apparent indifference to the killing of innocent victims.

3.35 **Kirwan**, C., *Augustine*, 1991. Focuses on

Augustine's philosophy, though with a useful chapter on his idea of a Christian society.

3.36 **Markus**, R. A., ed., *Augustine: A Collection of Critical Essays*, New York, 1972. Collection of some of the better essays on Augustine including two by F. E. Crantz, '*De Civitate Dei* XV.2 and Augustine's idea of a Christian society' and 'The development of Augustine's ideas on society before the Donatist controversy'.

3.37 —— *Saeculum: History and Society in the Theology of Saint Augustine*, 1970. Focuses on Augustine's concern with human achievement within the *saeculum*.

3.38 —— 'The sacred and the secular: from Augustine to Gregory the Great', *J. Theol. Sts.*, 36, 1955, 84–96.

3.39 **Martin**, R., 'The two cities in Augustine's political philosophy', *J. Hist. Ideas*, 33, 1972, 195–216. Argues that Augustine did not identify either of the two cities with earthly institutions, and emphasises his radical discontinuity from classical political philosophy.

3.40 **Meynell**, H. A., ed., *Grace, Politics and Desire. Essays on Augustine*, Calgary, 1990.

3.41 **Mommsen**, T. F., 'St. Augustine and the Christian idea of progress: the background of the *City of God*', in E. G. Rice, ed., *Medieval and Renaissance Studies*, Ithaca, N.Y., 1959, 265–98.

3.42 **O'Donovan**, O., 'Augustine's *City of God* XIX and Western political thought', *Dionysius*, 11, 1987, 89–110. Broadly agrees with most other commentators on Augustine that because political institutions are a necessary corrective to sin, they are not something natural in the full sense.

3.43 **Parel**, A. J., 'Justice and love in the political thought of St. Augustine', in H. A., Meynell, ed., *Grace, Politics and Desire: Essays on Augustine*, Calgary, 1990, 71–84. On how he thought that love, not justice, was the foundation of civil society.

3.44 **Wilks**, M. J., 'Roman Empire and Christian state in the "De civitate Dei" ', *Augustinus*, 12, 1967, 489–510.

3.45 **Wood**, N., '*Populares* and *Circumcelliones*: the vocabulary of fallen man in Cicero and St. Augustine', *Hist. Pol. Thought*, 7, 1986, 33–53. Compares the way in which Cicero and Augustine denounced those they regarded as irrational disturbers of political and social order.

3.46 —— 'African peasant terrorism and Augustine's political thought', in F. Krantz, ed., *History from Below: Studies in Popular Protest and Popular Ideology in Honour of George Rudé*, Montreal, 1985, 279–99.

Other thinkers

3.47 **Barnes**, T. D., *Constantine and Eusebius*, Cambridge, Mass., 1981. Interesting on the ideas of Eusebius (263–339), the first apologist of the Christian Roman Empire.

3.48 **Cranz**, F. E., 'Kingdom and polity in Eusebius of Caesarea', *Harvard Theol. Rev.*, 45, 1952, 47–66.

3.49 **Dvornik**, F., 'The Emperor Julian's "reactionary" ideas on kingship', in *Late Classical and Medieval Studies in Honor of A. M. Friend*, Princeton, N.J., 1955. On a fourth century emperor who embraced the concept of absolute monarchy.

3.50 **Markus**, R. A., 'Gregory the Great on kings: rulers and preachers in the *Commentary on I Kings*', in D. Wood, ed., *Sts. Ch. Hist.*, 9, *The Church and Sovereignty*, *c.590–1918*, 1991, 7–21. Gregory is said to illustrate the transition to a style of thinking in which 'secular' rulership was understood within an essentially religious dimension.

3.51 **Nelson**, J. L., 'Kingship, law and liturgy in the political thought of Hincmar of Rheims' *Eng. Hist. Rev.*, 92, 1975, 241–79. On a ninth century writer who provided an early formulation of the theory of the jurisdiction of the church over secular rulers.

3.52 **Morino**, C., *Church and State in the Teaching of St. Ambrose*, Washington, D.C., 1969.

(c) THE ELEVENTH CENTURY ONWARDS

General

3.53 **Black**, A., 'Classical Islam and medieval Europe: a comparison of political philosophies and cultures', *Pol. Sts.*, 41, 1993, 58–69. Brief but illuminating account of the salient differences, arguing that Europe, being open to Greco-Roman influences, developed, as Islam did not, a notion of the legitimate secular state.

3.54 —— *Council and Commune: The Conciliar Movement and the Fifteenth Century Heritage*, 1979. Focuses on the political ideas of mid-fifteenth century conciliarists, especially Juan de Segovia and Heimrich Van de Velde.

3.55 —— *Monarchy and Community: Political Ideas in the Later Conciliar Controversy 1430–1450*, 1970. Authoritative study of Baslean conciliarism and of mid-fifteenth century papal political theory, with particular attention to the ideas of John of Segovia and John Turrecremata.

3.56 —— 'Political languages in later medieval Europe', in D. Wood, ed., *Sts. Ch. Hist.*, 9, *The Church and Sovereignty, c.590–1918*, 1991, 313–28. Applies the methodological insights of Q. Skinner and J. G. Pocock – that the study of particular ideas is primarily an examination of appropriate linguistic contexts – to the period.

3.57 —— *Political Thought in Europe, 1250–1450*, 1992. The most accessible introduction to the political thought of the later middle ages, covering major thinkers such as Aquinas, Marsilius, William of Ockham and Nicholas of Cusa, and also prevalent notions of church and state, kingship, parliament and the law.

3.58 —— 'The political ideas of conciliarism and papalism 1430–50', *J. Euro. Hist.*, 20, 1969, 45–65.

3.59 —— 'What was conciliarism? Conciliar theory in historical perspective', in B. Tierney and P. Linehan, ed., *Authority and Power: Studies on Medieval Law and Government Presented to Walter Ullmann on his Seventieth Birthday*, 1980, 213–24. Brief but masterly survey, critical of other interpretations and arguing that conciliarism gained a momentum which 'both separated it from the Marsilian-secularist heritage and made it independent of canonist doctrine'.

3.60 **Blythe**, J. M., 'Family, government and the medieval Aristotelians', *Hist. Pol. Thought*, 10, 1989, 1–16.

3.61 —— *Ideal Government and the Mixed Constitution in the Middle Ages*, Princeton, N.J., 1992.

3.62 **Burns**, J. H., *Lordship, Kingship and Empire: the Idea of Monarchy 1400–1525*, 1992. Subtle and authoritative account of fifteenth-century political thought.

3.63 **Canning**, J. P., 'A state like any other? The fourteenth century papal patrimony through the eyes of Roman law jurists', in D. Wood, ed., *Sts. Ch. Hist.*, 9, *The Church and Sovereignty, c.590–1918*, 1991, 245–60.

3.64 —— 'Ideas of the state of thirteenth and fourteenth-century commentators on the Roman law', *Trans. Royal Hist. Soc.*, 33, 1983, 1–27.

3.65 **Dunbabin**, J., 'Aristotle in the schools', in B. Smalley, ed., *Trends in Medieval Political Thought*, 1965, 65–85. On the uses made of Aristotle by Giles of Rome, Aquinas and others.

3.66 —— 'The reception and interpretation of Aristotle's *Politics*', in N. Kretzmann, ed., *Cambridge History of Later Medieval Philosophy*, 1982, 723–37.

3.67 **Gewirth**, A., 'Philosophy and political thought in the fourteenth century', in F. Utley, ed., *The Forward Movement of the Fourteenth Century*, Columbus, Ohio, 1961.

3.68 **Johnson**, H. J., ed., *The Medieval Tradition of Natural Law*, Kalamazoo, Mich., 1987.

3.69 **Kantorowicz**, E. H., *The King's Two Bodies: A Study in Medieval Political Theology*, Princeton, N.J., 1957. Classic exploration of the late medieval fiction of the king's two bodies – the private body that was subject to law and his public body that was not – and the transmission of the idea into the early modern period.

3.70 **Keen**, M. H., 'The political thought of the fourteenth-century civilians', in B. Smalley, ed., *Trends in Medieval Political Thought*, 1965, 105–26. Illustrates how Bartolus and others shaped a doctrine of legal sovereignty from Roman law.

3.71 **Leyser**, K. J., 'The polemics of the papal revolution', in B. Smalley, ed., *Trends in Medieval Political Thought*, 1965, 42–64. On the political ideas of Gregory VII and his circle in the late eleventh century.

3.72 **Lewis**, E., *Medieval Political Ideas*, 2 vols., 1954. Comprehensive survey from the eleventh to the fifteenth centuries.

3.73 **McCready**, W. D., 'Papal *plenitudo potestatis* and the source of temporal authority in late medieval hierocratic theory', *Speculum*, 48, 1973, 654–74. Argues that though papal theorists emphasised the constitutive role of the papacy in the process whereby the temporal ruler is created, they also attributed a role to the people through their customary elective or hereditary procedures.

3.74 —— 'Papalists and anti-papalists: aspects of the church-state controversy in the late middle ages', *Viator*, 6, 1975, 241–73.

3.75 —— *The Theory of Papal Monarchy in the Fourteenth Century*, Toronto, 1982.

3.76 **Marongiu**, A., 'The theory of democracy and consent in the fourteenth century', in F. L. Cheyette, ed., *Lordship and Community in Medieval Europe*, 1968, 404–21.

3.77 **Martin**, C., 'Some medieval commentaries on Aristotle's *Politics*', *History*, 36, 1951, 29–44. Focus is the reception of Aristotle in the late thirteenth and early fourteenth centuries.

3.78 **Nederman**, C. J., 'Aristotelianism and the origins of "political science" in the twelfth century', *J. Hist. Ideas*, 52, 1991, 179–94.

3.79 —— 'Aristotle as authority: alternative Aristotelian sources of late medieval political theory', *Hist. Euro. Ideas*, 8, 1987, 31–44. Includes discussion of Pierre Dubois, Marsiglio of Padua and Sir John Fortescue.

3.80 —— 'Nature, sin and the origins of society: the Ciceronian tradition in medieval political thought', *J. Hist. Ideas.*, 49, 1988, 3–26. Identifies a coherent tradition of thought, taking its substance from Cicero and connecting it with the doctrine of original sin, in the ideas of John of Salisbury, John of Paris and Marsilius of Padua.

3.81 **Oakley**, F., 'Natural Law, the *Corpus Mysticuum* and consent in conciliar thought from John of Paris to Matthias Ugonius', *Speculum*, 56, 1981, 786–810.

3.82 —— 'Legitimation by consent: the question of the medieval roots', *Viator*, 14, 1983, 303–35.

3.83 —— *The Western Church in the later Middle Ages*, Ithaca, N.Y., 1979. Rich on the strands of political thinking within the church.

3.84 **Parker**, T. M., 'The conciliar movement', in B. Smalley, ed., *Trends in Medieval Political Thought*, 1965, 127–39. A rather slight piece.

3.85 **Petry**, R. C., 'Unitive reform principles of the late medieval conciliarists', *Church Hist.*, 31, 1962, 164–81. Emphasises the common consent of the governed as the fundamental doctrine of the conciliar movement.

3.86 **Post**, G., *Studies in Medieval Legal Thought: Public Law and the State*, 1100–1322, Princeton, N.J., 1964. Focus is the legal thought resulting from the revival of Roman Law, and its influence on the ideas of the late medieval and early modern state.

3.87 —— 'The theory of public law and the state in the thirteenth century', *Seminar*, 6, 1948, 42–59.

3.88 **Riesenberg**, P., *Inalienability of Sovereignty in Medieval Political Thought*, New York, 1956.

3.89 **Tierney**, B., 'A conciliar theory of the thirteenth century', *Cath. Hist. Rev.*, 36, 1951, 415–40.

3.90 —— *Church, Law and Constitutional Thought in the Middle Ages*. Collection of fifteen of his essays, many of them dealing with political ideas.

3.91 —— ' "Divided Sovereignty" at Constance: A problem of medieval and early modern political theory', *Annuarium Historiae Conciliorum*, 7, 1975, 238–56. Demonstrates how the fifteenth-century debates at the Council of Constance as to whether sovereignty is divisible were reflected in later political theory, particularly that of Bodin.

3.92 —— *Foundations of the Conciliar Theory: the Contribution of the Medieval Canonists from Gratian to the Great Schism*, 1955. Classic account of how jurists shaped the idea that the pope was servant rather than master of the church, demonstrating the extent to which conciliar thinking drew upon ideas of collective government embedded within medieval canon law.

3.93 —— 'Origins of natural rights language: texts and contexts, 1150–1250', *Hist. Pol. Thought*, 10, 1989, 615–46. Excellent article arguing that 'the humanistic jurisprudence of the twelfth century, especially the writings of the medieval Decretists, may provide a better starting point for investigating the origins of natural rights theories than either fourteenth-century nominalism or the nascent capitalism of the seventeenth century'.

3.94 —— *Origins of Papal Infallibility 1150–1350. A study on the Concepts of Infallibility, Sovereignty and Tradition in the Middle Ages*, Leiden, 1972. Includes chapters on the canonists, St. Bonaventure, Pietro Olivi, Guido Terreni and William of Ockham.

3.95 —— *Religion, Law and the Growth of Constitutional Thought, 1150–1650*, 1982. Excellent account of the medieval roots of early modern political thought.

3.96 —— 'Some recent works on the political theories of the medieval canonists', *Traditio*, 10, 1954, 594–625.

3.97 —— 'The canonists and the medieval state', *Rev. Pol.*, 15, 1953, 378–88.

3.98 —— 'The continuity of papal political theory in the thirteenth century. Some methodological considerations', *Med. Sts.*, 27, 1965, 227–45. A critique of recent historiography on the subject, claiming that the political doctrines of Innocent III and Innocent IV have been distorted because of the super-imposition of modern connotations on their concepts.

3.99 —— 'Tuck on rights: some *medieval problems*', *Hist. Pol. Thought*, 4, 1983, 429–41. A critique of R. Tuck's *Natural Rights Theories* which illuminates the late medieval discourse of rights.

3.100 **Ullmann**, W., *Medieval Foundations of Renaissance Humanism*, Ithaca, N.Y., 1977.

3.101 —— *Medieval Papalism: the Political Theories of the Medieval Canonists*, 1949. Seminal study focusing upon the thirteenth and fourteenth centuries, and claiming that the Canonist tradition supported a theory of direct papal intervention in temporal affairs.

3.102 —— 'The development of the medieval idea of sovereignty', *Eng. Hist. Rev.*, 64, 1949, 1–33. *Tour de force* focusing on the ideological differences between those who defended the juristic universality of the Holy Roman Empire and those who affirmed the sovereignty of regional kingdoms.

3.103 **Watanabe**, M., 'Authority and consent in church government: Panormitanus, Aeneas Sylvius, Cusanus', *J. Hist. Ideas*, 33, 1972, 217–36. Shows how the Council of Basel (1431–49) frightened some conciliarists into abandoning their principle of consent and become supporters of papal authoritarianism.

3.104 **Watt**, J. A., 'The theory of papal monarchy in the thirteenth century: the contribution of the canonists', *Traditio*, 20, 1964, 179–317.

3.105 —— *The Theory of Papal Monarchy in the Thirteenth Century*, 1965.

3.106 **Wilks**, M. J., *The Problem of Sovereignty in the Later Middle Ages: The Papal Monarchy with Augustinus Triumphus and the Publicists*, 1963. Magisterial study of the papal theory of divine-right monarchy, particularly through the political ideas of Augustinus, and the assault upon the concept by conciliarists and others.

3.107 **Witt**, R., 'The rebirth of the concept of republican liberty in Italy', in A. Molho and J. A. Tedeschi, ed., *Renaissance Studies in Honor of Hans Baron*, Dekalb, Ill., 1971, 173–200. Focuses on the writings of the fourteenth-century canonist, Giovanni da Legnano, but also finds evidence for the birth of the republican concept of liberty in the writings of Leonardo Bruni and others.

St. Thomas Aquinas

3.108 **Blythe**, J. M., 'The mixed constitution and the distinction between regal and political power in the work of Thomas Aquinas', *J. Hist. Ideas*, 47, 1986, 547–65. Argues that he created a synthesis of Greek and medieval thinking to provide an original conception of the mixed constitution.

3.109 **Catto**, J., 'Ideas and experience in the political thought of Aquinas', *Past & Pres.*, 71, 1976, 3–21. Demonstrates how he derived his political views not only from philosophical considerations, but from his social and professional position as a friar close to Urban IV, frequently asked to comment on public affairs.

3.110 **Cranston**, M., 'St. Thomas Aquinas as a political philosopher', *Hist. Today*, 14, 1964, 313–17. Brief but clear introduction.

3.111 **Crofts**, R., 'The common good in the political theory of Thomas Aquinas', *Thomist*, 37, 1973, 155–74.

3.112 **Eschmann**, I. T., 'St. Thomas Aquinas on the two powers', *Med. Sts.*, 20, 1958, 177–205. Close analysis of Aquinas's apparently contradictory views about the relationship of spiritual and temporal authority.

3.113 —— 'Studies on the notion of society in St.

Thomas Aquinas: I. St. Thomas and the Decretal of Innocent IV *Romanae Ecclesiae*', *Med. Sts.*, 8, 1946, 1–42.

3.114 —— 'Studies on the notion of society in St. Thomas Aquinas: II. Thomistic social philosophy and the theology of original sin', *Med. Sts.*, 9, 1947, 19–55.

3.115 **Fay**, T. A., 'Thomas Aquinas on the justification of revolution', *Hist. Euro. Ideas*, 16, 1993, 501–6. Detects a shift from his earlier writings, in which a right of rebellion is readily conceded, to a more cautious position in his later writings.

3.116 **Fitzgerald**, L. P., 'St. Thomas Aquinas and the two powers', *Angelicum*, 36, 1979, 515–56.

3.117 **Gilby**, T., *Between Community and Society: A Philosophy and Theology of the State*, 1953. A detailed, though partisan, study of Aquinas's political theology.

3.118 —— *Principality and Polity: Aquinas and the Rise of State Theory in the West*, 1958. Outlines the intellectual background of Aquinas's political thought.

3.119 **Goerner**, E. A., 'On Thomistic natural law: the bad man's view of Thomistic natural right', *Pol. Theory*, 7, 1979, 101–22. Argues that Aquinas treats natural law as an imperfect and supplementary standard for right action and that the perfect standard is natural right, understood from the perspective of virtue rather than that of one subject to a law.

3.120 —— 'Thomistic natural right: the good man's view of Thomistic natural law', *Pol. Theory*, 11, 1983, 393–418. Advances the radical proposition that 'Thomas's moral and political doctrine is not *fundamentally* a natural law teaching at all, and that in his teaching the morality of a natural law is crucially different from (and subordinate to) the morality of natural virtue, both in the mode of its coming to be known *and in its content*'.

3.121 **Hutchins**, R. M., *St. Thomas and the World State*, Milwaukee, Wis., 1949.

3.122 **Kayser**, J. R., and Lettieri, R. J., 'Aquinas's *Regimene bene commixtum* and the medieval critique of classical republicanism', *Thomist*, 46, 1982, 195–220.

3.123 **Kries**, D., 'Thomas Aquinas and the politics of Moses', *Rev. Pol.*, 52, 1990, 84–104. Demonstrates how he believed that the Mosaic regime was relevant to Christian political theology.

3.124 **O'Connor**, D. J., *Aquinas and Natural Law*, 1967.

3.125 **Regan**, R. J., 'Aquinas on political obedience and disobedience', *Thought*, 56, 1981, 77–88.

3.126 **Riedl**, J. O., 'Thomas Aquinas on citizenship', *Procs. Cath. Phil. Ass.*, 37, 1963, 159–66.

3.127 **Scully**, F., 'The place of the state in society according to Aquinas', *Thomist*, 45, 1981, 407–429.

Dante Alighieri

3.128 **Davis**, C. T., *Dante and the idea of Rome*, 1957.

3.129 **D'Entrèves**, A. P., *Dante as a political thinker*, 1952. Traces the evolution of Dante's political thought in three phases, symbolised by the concepts of *civitas*, *imperium* and *ecclesia*.

3.130 **Gilbert**, A. H., *Dante's Conception of Justice*, 1971.

3.131 **Limentani**, U., 'Dante's political thought', in U. Limentani, ed., *The Mind of Dante*, 1965, 113–37.

3.132 **Losoncy**, T. A., 'Good citizen and government in Dante's "De Monarchia": to what extent an echo of Aristotle?', *Diotima*, 13, 1985, 50–2.

3.133 **Peters**, E. M., '*Pars parte*: Dante and an urban contribution to political thought', in H. Miskimin, D. Herlihy and A. Udovitch, ed., *The Medieval City*, New Haven, Conn., 1977.

John of Paris

3.134 **Coleman**, J., '*Dominium* in thirteenth- and fourteenth-century political thought and its seventeenth-century heirs: John of Paris and Locke', *Pol. Sts.*, 33, 1985, 73–100.

3.135 —— 'Medieval discussion of property: *ratio* and *dominium* according to John of Paris and Marsilius of Padua', *Hist. Pol. Thought*, 4, 1983, 209–28. Compares the two and claims that it was John who 'should be far better known for providing the early modern and modern world, with the defence of private property as a man's natural and inalienable right'.

3.136 —— 'The Dominican political theory of John of Paris in its context', in D. Wood, ed., *Sts. Ch. Hist.*, 9, *The Church and*

Sovereignty, c.590–1918, 1991, 187–223.
Argues that *De potestate regia et papali* was a
series of tracts written over several years in
response to various events 'to defend a
Dominican thesis on the relationship
between all ecclesiastics and collective
Church property, and to defend the natural
origins of lay property . . . In defending
individual and collective ownership, John
denies to *both* kings *and* popes the power to
true *dominium*.'

3.137 **Griesbach**, M. F., 'John of Paris as a
representative of Thomistic political
philosophy', in C. J. O'Neill, ed., *An
Etienne Gibson Tribute*, Milwaukee, Wis.,
1959.

3.138 **Heiman**, G., 'John of Paris and the theory
of the two swords', *Classica et Mediaevalia*,
32, 1980, 324–47.

3.139 **Renna**, T. J., 'The populus in John of
Paris' theory of monarchy', *Revue d'histoire
du droit*, 42, 1974, 243–68. Stresses the
restricted manner in which John applied
consent theory to the secular polity.

3.140 **Saenger**, P., 'John of Paris, principal
author of the *Quaestio de potestate papae*',
Speculum, 56, 1981, 41–55. Marshalls
evidence to suggest that John largely wrote
an 'important document in the history of
political thought' whose authorship was
previously shrouded in mystery.

Marsilius of Padua

3.141 **Condren**, C., 'Democracy and the *Defensor
Pacis*: On the English language tradition of
Marsilian interpretation', *Il Pensiero
Politico*, 13, 1980, 301–16.

3.142 —— 'Marsilius of Padua's argument from
authority: a survey of its significance in the
Defensor Pacis', *Pol. Theory*, 5, 1977,
205–18. Urges a contextual reading of the
Defensor which avoids both the search for
philosophical coherence and the
temptation to derive lessons for the modern
world.

3.143 —— 'On interpreting Marsilius of Padua's
use of St. Augustine', *Augustiniana*, 25,
1975.

3.144 **Gewirth**, A., *Marsilius of Padua*, New
York, N.Y., 1951. Magisterial study which
identifies three intellectual sources for the
secular doctrines of the *Defensor Pacis*:
Aristotelianism, Augustinianism and
Averrorism.

3.145 **Lewis**, E., 'The positivism of Marsiglio of
Padua', *Speculum*, 38, 1963, 541–82.
Argues, unlike some historians, that
Marsilius's concepts of law 'were taken
directly from well-established medieval
traditions and that, in the light of these
traditions, it is clear that they became in his
hands no more "positivist" or "voluntarist"
in definition or application than they had
been before'.

3.146 **Mulcahy**, D. G., 'The hands of Augustine
but the voice of Marsilius', *Augustiana*, 21,
1971, 457–66.

3.147 **Nederman**, C. J., 'Character and
community in the *Defensor Pacis*:
Marsiglio of Padua's adaptation of
Aristotelian moral psychology', *Hist. Pol.
Thought*, 13, 1992, 377–90.

3.148 —— 'Knowledge, consent and the critique
of political representation in Marsiglio of
Padua's *Defensor Pacis*', *Pol. Sts.*, 39,
1991, 19–35. Argues that Marsilius is
critical of representative institutions
because they erode the responsibility of
citizens to be directly involved in public
affairs.

3.149 —— 'Nature, justice, and duty in the
Defensor Pacis: Marsiglio of Padua's
Ciceronian impulse', *Pol. Theory*, 18,
1990, 615–37. Detailed examination of
how the political teachings of Cicero
provided raw material for Marsilius. 'In as
much as Marsiglio's central lesson – that
nature, sociability, and justice impose an
inescapable duty to act against papal
interference with tranquil human relations
– has its origins in Cicero, we may begin to
view the *Defensor* less as a radical departure
from the tradition as of medieval political
writing and more as an extension to new
problems and issues'.

3.150 —— 'Marsiglio of Padua as political
theorist: ideology and middle class politics
in the early fourteenth century', *University
of Ottawa Quarterly*, 51, 1981, 197–209.

3.151 —— 'Private will, public justice:
household, community and consent in
Marsiglio of Padua's *Defensor Pacis*', *West.
Pol. Q.*, 43, 1990, 699–717. Characterises
Marsilius's thought as a form of civic
patriarchalism that rigorously
distinguishes the rule of the household and
that of the community, and in doing so
anticipates some of the arguments of liberal
individualists.

3.152 **Reeves**, M., 'Marsiglio of Padua and

Dante Alighieri', in B. Smalley, ed., *Trends in Medieval Political Thought*, 1965, 86–104.

3.153 **Rubinstein**, N., 'Marsilius of Padua and Italian political thought of his time', in J. R. Hale, J. R. L. Highfield and B. Smalley, ed., *Europe in the Late Middle Ages*, 1965, 44–75.

3.154 **Scott**, J. V., 'Influence or manipulation? The rule of Augustinianism in the *Defensor Pacis* of Marsiglio of Padua', *Augustinian Sts.*, 9, 1978, 59–79.

3.155 **Sigmund**, P. E., 'The influence of Marsilius of Padua on fifteenth century conciliarism', *J. Hist. Ideas*, 23, 1962, 392–402. Traces his influence on Dietrich of Neim and Nicholas of Cusa, arguing that both consciously disguised their debt because of Marsilius's reputation as an heretical writer.

3.156 **Tierney**, B., 'Marsilius on rights', *J. Hist. Ideas*, 52, 1991, 3–17.

3.157 **Wilks**, M. J., 'Corporation and representation in the *Defensor Pacis*', *Studia Gratiana*, 15, 1972, 251–92.

Nicholas of Cusa

3.158 **Sigmund**, P. E., 'Cusanus' *Concordantia*, a re-interpretation', *Pol. Sts.*, 10, 1962, 180–97. Neat introduction to his political thought, depicting it as reasonably consistent.

3.159 —— *Nicholas of Cusa and Medieval Political Thought*, Cambridge, Mass., 1963.

3.160 **Watanabe**, M., 'Nicholas of Cusa and the Tyrolese Monasteries: reform and resistance', *Hist. Pol. Thought*, 7, 1986, 53–73. Reveals the limitations of Nicholas of Cusa as a church reformer attempting to practise what he believed in, and assesses him as theorist, administrator and reformer.

3.161 —— 'The episcopal election of 1430 in Triev and Nicholas of Cusa', *Church Hist.*, 39, 1970, 299–316. Shows how his conciliarism was shaped in part by the anti-papal cause of his patron, Count Ulrich.

3.162 —— *The Political Ideas of Nicholas of Cusa, with Special Reference to his 'De concordantia catholica'*, Geneva, 1963.

Other thinkers

3.163 **Black**, R., 'The political thought of the Florentine chancellors', *Hist. J.*, 29, 1986, 991–1003. Useful survey of recent historiography on the subject, particularly on the ideas of Coluccio Salutati in the late fourteenth century.

3.164 **Brabant**, M., ed., *Politics, gender, and genre: the Political Thought of Christine de Pisan*, 1992. Fifteen essays on a Venetian writer (d. 1429) who depicted the body politic as an integrated hierarchy of functions.

3.165 **Canning**, J. P., 'A fourteenth-century contribution to the theory of citizenship: political man and the problem of created citizenship in the thought of Baldus de Ubaldis', in B. Tierney and P. Linehan, ed., *Authority and Power: Studies on Medieval Law and Government Presented to Walter Ullmann on his Seventieth Birthday*, 1980, 197–212.

3.166 —— 'The corporation in the political thought of the Italian jurists of the thirteenth and fourteenth centuries', *Hist. Pol. Thought*, 1, 1980, 9–31. Focuses on the political ideas of Baldus de Ubaldis.

3.167 —— *The Political Thought of Baldus de Ubaldis*, 1987. On a fourteenth-century Italian jurist (d. 1400) who developed a theory of government by popular consent.

3.168 **Chodorow**, S., *Christian Political Theory and Church Politics in the Mid Twelfth Century: The Ecclesiology of Gratian's 'Decretium'*, Los Angeles, Calif., 1972. On a canonist who asserted the judicial supremacy of the papacy.

3.169 **Davis**, C. T., 'An early Florentine political theorist: Fra Remigio De' Girolami', *Am. Phil. Soc.*, 104, 1960, 662–76. Remigio (d. 1319), though a Thomist, was more hierocratic than Aquinas and therefore less inclined firmly to distinguish secular from spiritual authority.

3.170 **Fasolt**, C., *Council and Hierarchy. The Political Thought of William Durant the Younger*, 1991. On Durant's (d. 1330) project to turn the church into a constitutional commonwealth, and of the reasons for its ultimate failure.

3.171 **Lerner**, R., 'Natural law in Albo's *Book of Roots*', in J. Cropsey, ed., *Ancients and Moderns: Essays on the Tradition of Political Philosophy in Honor of Leo Strauss*, New York, 1964, 132–47. On the political theory of a Spanish writer (c.1380–1444) who was almost alone among medieval Jews in using the term 'natural law'.

3.172 **McCready**, W. D., 'The problem of empire in Augustinus Triumphus and late medieval papal hierocratic theory', *Traditio*, 30, 1975, 325–49. On the recrudescence of hierocratic theory in the early fourteenth century. Augustinus (d. 1328) was a major proponent of the doctrine of universal papal monarchy.

3.173 **Morrall**, J. B., *Gerson and the Great Schism*, 1960. A study of Gerson's ecclesiology.

3.174 **Oakley**, F., *The Political Thought of Pierre d'Ailly. The Voluntarist Tradition*, New Haven, Conn., 1964. Excellent account of the political ideas of the French theologian who in the late fourteenth and early fifteenth centuries elaborated a conciliar theory – the insistence that the authority of the Church lay not with the Pope but with the whole body of the faithful – and explored its implications for temporal as well as spiritual society. The penultimate chapter demonstrates the transmission of conciliarist ideas into Reformation political thought.

3.175 **Robey**, D., 'P. P. Vergerio the Elder: republicanism and civic values in the work of an early humanist', *Past & Pres.*, 58, 1973, 3–37. Emphasises the traditional aspects of the humanism of Vergerio, a Florentine writer at the end of the fourteenth and beginning of the fifteenth centuries.

3.176 **Rueger**, Z., 'Gerson, the conciliar movement and the right of resistance (1642–1644)', *J. Hist. Ideas*, 25, 1964, 467–86. Shows how Gerson's theory of the legality of conciliar action against the Pope was used by English parliamentarians to demonstrate a right of resistance against Charles I.

3.177 **Rupp**, T., ' "Common" = "of the commune": private property and individualism in Remigio dei Girolami's *De Bono Paris*', *Hist. Pol. Thought*, 14, 1993, 41–56. On how, in response to the political problems of Florence in 1304, he argued that for the good of peace individuals could be compelled to surrender their claims to property damages.

3.178 **Tierney**, B., 'Public expediency and natural law: a fourteenth-century discussion on the origins of governmental property', in B. Tierney and P. Linehan, ed., *Authority and Power: Studies on Medieval Law and Government Presented to Walter Ullmann on his Seventieth Birthday*, 1980, 167–82. Focusing on the fourteenth-century *Tractatus de legibus*, attributed to Durandus of St. Pourcain, Tierney identifies the emergence of various strands of argument that were to be woven into more coherent patterns of political thinking by Locke and other seventeenth-century writers.

3.179 —— ' "The prince is not bound by the laws": Accursius and the origins of the modern state', *Comp. Sts. Soc. & Hist.*, 5, 1963, 378–400. Demonstrates that Accursius, the thirteenth-century glossator on Roman law, extracted 'a constitutionalist doctrine from a structure of texts that was originally intended to buttress Justinian's theocratic absolutism'

3.180 **Ullmann**, W., *The Medieval Idea of Law as Represented by Lucas de Penna*, 1946.

British Isles

HENRY de BRACTON

3.181 **Lapsley**, G., 'Bracton and the authorship of the *Addicio de cartis*', *Eng. Hist. Rev.*, 62, 1947, 1–19.

3.182 **Lewis**, E., 'King above the law? "Quod Principi Placuit" in Bracton', *Speculum*, 39, 1964, 240–69. Close textual analysis suggests that Bracton did not set the monarch above the law.

3.183 **Miller**, S. J. T., 'The position of the king in Bracton and Beaumanoir', *Speculum*, 31, 1956, 263–96.

3.184 **Nederman**, C. J., 'Bracton on kingship revisited', *Hist. Pol. Thought*, 5, 1984, 61–78. Attempt to demonstrate the consistency of his doctrine of monarchy by revealing his use of Aristotelian principles.

3.185 —— 'The royal will and the baronial bridle: the place of the *addicio de cartis* in Bractonian political thought', *Hist. Pol. Thought*, 9, 1988, 415–29. Argues that Bracton's defence of the occasional legitimacy of the restraint of kings by inferior magistrates is not inconsistent with his assertion elsewhere in *De Legibus* that the monarch is subject to God and law, but not to man.

3.186 **Post**, G., 'A Romano-canonical maxim "quod omnes tangit" in Bracton', *Traditio*, 4, 1946, 197–251.

3.187 —— 'Bracton on kingship', *Tulane Law Review*, 42, 1968, 519–54. Argues that Bracton supposed the ruler to be morally bound to obey the statutes of the realm.

3.188 **Radding**, C. M., 'The origins of Bracton's *Addicio de cartis*', *Speculum*, 44, 1969, 239–46.

3.189 **Richardson**, H. G., *Bracton: the Problem of his Text*, 1965. Detailed examination of the intellectual sources of *De Legibus*.

3.190 —— 'Studies in Bracton', *Traditio*, 6, 1948, 61–104.

3.191 **Tierney**, B., 'Bracton on Government', *Speculum*, 38, 1963, 295–317. Magisterial warning against treating Bracton as the self-conscious godfather of modern constitutionalism. 'His work was essentially an attempt to fit a massive structure of English private law into a rather flimsy framework of Romanesque public law and naturally there are signs of strain. The figure of a king, half feudal lord half divine ruler, that he found in his plea rolls could not easily have been transformed into the first magistrate of a constitutional government even if Bracton had had any such conscious intention'.

3.192 **Yale**, D. E. C., 'Of no mean authority: some later uses of Bracton', in M. S. Arnold, T. A. Green, S. A. Scolly and S. D. White, ed., *On the Laws and Customs of England*, Chapel Hill, 1981, 383–96.

JOHN OF SALISBURY

3.193 **Forham**, K. L., 'Salisburian stakes: the uses of "tyranny", in John of Salisbury's *Policraticus*', *Hist. Pol. Thought*, 11, 1990, 397–408. 'The *Policraticus* is unique in its recognition that tyranny is something that happens when a society is not ruled polycratically, and when rulers and ruled forget their purpose, the quest for wisdom and virtue'.

3.194 **Liebeschütz**, H., *Medieval Humanism in the Life and Writings of John of Salisbury*, 1950.

3.195 **Linder**, A., 'John of Salisbury's *Policraticus* in thirteenth-century England: the evidence of MS Cambridge Corpus Christi College 469', *J. Warburg & Courtauld Inst.*, 40, 1977, 276–82.

3.196 —— 'The knowledge of John of Salisbury in the Late Middle Ages', *Studi Medievali*, 18, 1977, 315–66.

3.197 **Massey**, H. J., 'John of Salisbury: some aspects of his political philosophy', *Classica et Mediaevalia*, 28, 1967, 357–72.

3.198 **Nederman**, C. J., and **Brückmann**, J., 'Aristotelianism in John of Salisbury's *Policraticus*', *J. Hist. Phil.*, 21, 1983, 203–24. Argues that his use of *habitus* and other Aristotelian ideas reflects his familiarity with the Latin translations of Aristotle's *Categories* and *Topics*.

3.199 **Nederman**, C. J., 'A duty to kill: John of Salisbury's theory of tyrannicide', *Rev. Pol.*, 1988, 365–89.

3.200 —— 'The Aristotelian doctrine of the mean and John of Salisbury's concept of liberty', *Vivarium*, 24, 1986, 128–42.

3.201 —— 'The changing face of tyranny: the reign of King Stephen in John of Salisbury's political thought', *Nottingham Med. Sts.*, 33, 1989, 1–20.

3.202 —— 'The physiological significance of the organic metaphor in John of Salisbury', *Hist. Pol. Thought*, 8, 1987, 211–25. Argues that an anatomic interpretation of the metaphor of the body politic should be displaced by a physiological one which conveys John's concern with the health of the polity.

3.203 **Rouse**, R. H., and Rouse, M., 'John of Salisbury and the doctrine of tyrannicide', *Speculum*, 42, 1967, 693–709. Exposes the inconsistencies in his advocacy of tyrannicide.

3.204 **Ullmann**, W., 'John of Salisbury's *Policraticus* in the late Middle Ages', in K. Hauck and M. Nordele, ed., *Geschichtsschreibung und geistiges Leben im Mittelalter. Festschrift für Heinz Löwe zum 65. Geburtstag*, 1978.

3.205 **Wilks**, M. J., ed., *The World of John of Salisbury*, 1984. Fifteen essays including T. Struve, 'The importance of the organism in the political theory of John of Salisbury' and J. Van Laurhoven, 'Thou shalt *not* slay a tyrant! The so-called theory of John of Salisbury'.

WILLIAM OF OCKHAM

3.206 **Bayley**, C. C., 'Pivotal concepts in the political philosophy of William of Ockham', *J. Hist. Ideas*, 10, 1949, 199–218.

3.207 **Leff**, G., *William of Ockham: The Metamorphosis of Scholastic Discourse*, 1975.

3.208 **McDonnell**, K., 'Does William of Ockham have a theory of natural law?', *Franciscan Sts.*, 34, 1974, 383–92.

3.209 **McGrade**, A. S., 'Ockham and the birth of individual rights', in B. Tierney and P. Linehan, ed., *Authority and Power: Studies on Medieval Law and Government Presented to Walter Ullmann on his Seventieth Birthday*, 1980, 149–65. Demonstrates how Ockham's logical nominalism is reflected in his subjective conception of rights.

3.210 —— *The Political Thought of William Ockham: Personal and Institutional Principles*, 1974. The fullest and clearest account of his political ideas.

3.211 **Maurer**, A., 'Ockham on the possibility of a better world', *Med. Sts.*, 38, 1976, 291–312.

3.212 **Moody**, E. A., 'Ockham and Aegidius of Rome', *Franciscan Sts.*, 9, 1949, 417–42.

3.213 **Morrall**, J. B., 'Some notes on a recent interpretation of Ockham's political philosophy', *Franciscan Sts.*, 9, 1949, 335–69.

3.214 **Nederman**, C. J., 'Royal education and the English church: the origins of William of Ockham's *An princeps*', *J. Eccl. Hist.*, 37, 1986, 377–88. Argues that *An princeps*, the first of his writings to discuss the relationship between secular and ecclesiastical authority, was shaped by the church-state conflict of fourteenth-century England.

3.215 **Oakley**, F., 'Medieval theories of natural law: William of Ockham and the significance of the voluntarist tradition', *Natural Law Forum*, 6, 1961, 65–83.

3.216 **Tierney**, B., 'Ockham, the conciliar theory, and the canonists', *J. Hist. Ideas*, 15, 1954, 40–70. Seminal study of the relationship between Ockham's theories on church government and the doctrines of earlier canonistic writers, claiming that later conciliarists ignored what was original in his thinking and preferred instead to build their systems around doctrines that Ockham himself had borrowed from earlier writers.

OTHER THINKERS

3.217 **Daly**, L. J., *The Political Thought of John Wyclif*, Chicago, Ill., 1962.

3.218 **Haahr**, J. G., 'The concept of kingship in William of Malmesbury's *Gesta regum* and *Historia novella*', *Med. Sts.*, 38, 1976, 351–71. On Malmesbury's preference for absolute monarchy beyond the control of spiritual authority.

3.219 **Kaminsky**, H., 'Wyclifism as ideology of revolution', *Church Hist.*, 32, 1963, 57–74.

3.220 **McGrade**, A. S., 'Somersaulting sovereignty: a note on reciprocal lordship and servitude in Wyclif', in D. Wood, ed., *Sts. Ch. Hist.*, 9, *The Church and Sovereignty, c.590–1918*, 1991, 261–68. On his attempts to reconcile the claims of authority and subordination.

3.221 **Tierney**, B., 'Grosseteste and the theory of papal sovereignty', *J. Eccl. Hist.*, 6, 1955, 1–17. Demonstrates that in defying the Pope he was acting in accordance with canonistic theory.

3.222 **Wilks**, M. J., 'Predestination, property and power: Wyclif's theory of dominion and grace', *Sts. Ch. Hist.*, 2, 1965, 220–36.

4

EARLY MODERN POLITICAL
THOUGHT c.1450–1600

(a) GENERAL

4.1 **Archambault**, P., 'The analogy of the "body" in renaissance political thought', *Bibliothèque d'Humanisme et Renaissance*, 29, 1967, 21–52. Excellent guide to the vast literature on the body politic image.

4.2 **Burns**, J. H., 'Conciliarism, papalism, and power, 1511–1518', in D. Wood., ed., *Sts. Ch. Hist.*, 9, *The Church and Sovereignty, c.590–1918*, 1991, 409–28. On one of the last intellectual episodes in the conciliar controversy.

4.3 —— ed., *The Cambridge History of Political Thought 1450–1700*, 1991. The most comprehensive account available of the development of European political thinking through the Renaissance and the Reformation to the upheavals of the seventeenth century.

4.4 **Donaldson**, P. S., *Machiavelli and Mystery of State*, 1988. A study of six figures – Cardinal Pole, Stephen Gardiner, John Wolfe, Arnold Clapman, Gabriel Naude and Louis Machon – for whom Machiavelli was associated with *arcana imperic* or mysteries of state. A fascinating exploration of one aspect of Renaissance political discourse.

4.5 **Eliav-Feldon**, M., *Realistic Utopias: The Ideal Imaginary Societies of the Renaissance, 1516–1630*, 1982. Focuses on More, Eberlin, Rabelais, Patizi da Cherso, Doni, Stiblinus, Agostini, Campanella, Andreae, Burton, Bacon and Zuccolo.

4.6 **Heller**, A., *Renaissance Man*, 1978. A Marxist interpretation of the Renaissance including a consideration of Machiavelli and More.

4.7 **Hexter**, J. H., *The Vision of Politics on the Eve of the Reformation: More, Machiavelli and Seyssel*, Princeton, N.J., 1972.

4.8 **Kelley**, D. R., 'Civil science in the Renaissance: the problem of interpretation', in A. Pagden, ed., *The Languages of Political Theory in Early-Modern Europe*, 1987, 57–78. Considers how Roman law was shaped by Renaissance humanism.

4.9 —— *History, Law and the Human Sciences: Medieval and Renaissance Perspectives*, 1984. Contains essays previously published on, for example, 'History, English law and the Renaissance' and French and Italian jurisprudence.

4.10 **McKenzie**, L. A., 'Natural rights and the emergence of the idea of interest in early modern political thought: Francesco Guicciardini and Jean de Silhon', *Hist. Euro. Ideas*, 2, 1981, 277–98.

4.11 **Major**, J. R., 'The Renaissance monarchy as seen by Erasmus, More, Seyssel, and Machiavelli', in J. Siegel and T. K. Rabb, ed., *Action and Conviction in Early Modern Europe: Essays in Memory of E. H. Harbison*, Princeton, N.J., 1969, 17–31. Focusing on books written between 1513 and 1517, he claims that the 'dynastic, decentralized, constitutional, aristocratic monarchy', as the four authors saw it, was neither medieval nor modern: 'it was the monarchy of the Renaissance, a monarchy whose power rested neither on its army nor on its bureaucracy but on the degree of support it received from the people'.

4.12 **Oakley**, F., 'Natural law, the *corpus mysticum*, and consent in conciliar thought from John of Paris to Matthias Ugonius', *Speculum*, 56, 1981, 786–810. Wide-ranging essay on intellectual developments within conciliarism from the fourteenth to the sixteenth centuries, emphasising the marginal role of natural law and a tendency to designate the general council of the Church as its sovereign authority.

4.13 **Rubinstein**, N., 'Political theories in the Renaissance', in A. Chastel, ed., *The Renaissance: Essays in Interpretation*, 1982, 153–200. Useful introductory overview.

4.14 **Schellhase**, K. C., *Tacitus in Renaissance Political Thought*, Chicago, Ill., 1976.

4.15 **Schmitt**, C. B., *Aristotle and the Renaissance*, Cambridge, Mass., 1983. Excellent study of the influence of Aristotle's writings on Renaissance political thought.

4.16 **Skinner**, Q., 'Political philosophy', in C. B. Schmitt and Q. Skinner, ed., *The Cambridge History of Renaissance Philosophy*, 1988, 389–452. Masterly survey covering Italy and Northern Europe.

4.17 —— *The Foundations of Modern Political Thought: Vol. one: The Renaissance*, 1978. Superbly lucid and comprehensive account of the period.

4.18 —— *The Foundations of Modern Political Thought: Vol. two: The Age of Reformation*, 1978. By far the most intelligent and comprehensive account of the political thinking of the period.

4.19 **Tonkin**, J., *The Church and the Secular Order in Reformation Thought*, 1971. A comparative study of the ecclesiology of Calvin, Luther and Menno Simons.

4.20 **Tuck**, R., 'Humanism and political thought', in A. Goodman and A. MacKay, ed., *The Impact of Humanism on Western Europe*, 1990. On Renaissance uses of classical Greek and particularly Roman political ideas.

4.21 **Yates**, F., *Astrae: The Imperial Theme in the Sixteenth Century*, 1975. Brilliant exploration of the revival of the medieval idea of empire.

(b) ITALY

General

4.22 **Baron**, H., *Humanistic and Political Literature in Florence and Venice*, Cambridge, Mass., 1955.

4.23 —— *In Search of Florentine Civic Humanism*, 2 vols., Princeton, N.J., 1988. For Baron, the leading authority on the Renaissance, the Florentines were the first thinkers to break with the medieval world by adopting a secular and civic view of politics.

4.24 —— 'New light on the political writers of the Florentine renaissance', *J. Hist. Ideas*, 8, 1947, 241–8.

4.25 —— 'Root problems of Renaissance interpretation: an answer to Wallace K. Ferguson', *J. Hist. Ideas*, 19, 1958, 26–34. Defends his thesis that the emergence of a concept of civic humanism in the Florentine Republic of the early fifteenth century marked a dramatic break with medieval patterns of thinking.

4.26 —— *The Crisis of the Early Italian Renaissance: Civic Humanism and Republican Liberty in an Age of Classicism and Tyranny*, Princeton, N.J., 2nd edn., 1966. A classic study, though tends to overstate the discontinuity of Renaissance thought with earlier political discourse.

4.27 **Bouwsma**, W. J., *Venice and the Defense of Republican Liberty: Renaissance Values in the Age of the Counter-Reformation*, Berkeley, Calif., 1968. Detailed exploration of the formation and development of the powerful myth of Venice as the ideal combination of liberty and order from the Renaissance to the early seventeenth century, paying particular attention to the ideas of Paolo Sarpi.

4.28 **Brown**, A., 'Platonism in fifteenth-century Florence and its contribution to early modern political thought', *J. Mod. Hist.*, 58, 1986, 383–413.

4.29 **Ferguson**, W. K., 'The interpretation of Italian humanism: the contribution of Hans Baron', *J. Hist. Ideas*, 19, 1958, 14–25. Questions Baron's assumption that the Venetian concept of civic humanism in the first half of the fifteenth century marked a decisive break between medieval and Renaissance styles of thinking.

4.30 **Gilbert**, F., 'Florentine political

assumptions in the period of Savonarola and Soderini', *J. Warburg & Courtauld Inst.*, 20, 1957, 187–214.

4.31 —— *History: Choice and Commitment*, 1977. Contains an essay on an Italian intellectual circle at the beginning of the sixteenth century, 'Bernardo Rucellai and Orti Oricellari: a study on the origin of modern political thought', another on the intellectual background to Machiavelli's thought, 'The humanist concept of the Prince and *The Prince* of Machiavelli', as well as 'Machiavelli's *Istorie Fiorentine*: an essay in interpretation'.

4.32 —— *Machiavelli and Guicciardini: Politics and History in Sixteenth-Century Florence*, Princeton, N.J., 1965. Classic study which roams freely through the political thinking of Renaissance Italy.

4.33 —— 'The Venetian constitution in Florentine political thought', in N. Rubinstein, ed., *Florentine Studies*, 1, 968, 463–500.

4.34 **Gilmore**, M. P., 'Myth and reality in Venetian political theory', in J. R. Hale, ed., *Renaissance Venice*, 1973, 431–444.

4.35 **Holmes**, G., *The Florentine Enlightenment, 1400–1450*, 1969. Account of the emergence of what the author describes as a 'self-confident expression of republican and bourgeois attitudes' in the early Renaissance.

4.36 **Libby**, L. J., 'Venetian history and political thought after 1509', *Sts. Ren.*, 20, 1973, 7–46.

Machiavelli

4.37 **Andrew**, E., 'The foxy prophet: Machiavelli versus Machiavelli on Ferdinand the Catholic', *Hist. Pol. Thought*, 11, 1990, 409–22. Argues that Machiavelli's ambivalence towards Ferdinand reflects his incompatible expectations of great statesmen – that they be fox-like prophets combining low cunning and lofty inspiration.

4.38 **Anglo**, S., *Machiavelli: A Dissection*, 1969. Comprehensive and acute analysis of Machiavelli's writings.

4.39 **Balaban**, O., 'The human origins of *fortuna* in Machiavelli's thought', *Hist. Pol. Thought*, 11, 1990, 21–36. Argues that Machiavelli conceived of *fortuna* as both belonging to the realm of circumstance

beyond human will and a consequence of human action.

4.40 **Ball**, T., 'The picaresque prince: reflections on Machiavelli and moral change', *Pol. Theory*, 12, 1984, 521–36. Machiavelli can be considered a moralist because he stipulated criteria of virtuous conduct for princes.

4.41 **Baron**, H., 'Machiavelli: the republican citizen and the author of 'The Prince', *Eng. Hist. Rev.*, 76, 1961, 217–53. Classic article suggesting that scholars have misunderstood Machiavelli by falsely supposing that the *Discourses* was written before the *Prince*.

4.42 **Basu**, S., 'In a crazy time the crazy come out well: Machiavelli and the cosmology of his day', *Hist. Pol. Thought*, 11, 1990, 213–41. Situates his political views within prevailing cosmological assumptions to highlight the extent to which he was grappling with the possibilities for human action (*virtù*) given the occult nature of the world (*fortuna*).

4.43 **Belliotti**, R. R., 'Machiavelli and Machiavellianism', *J. Thought*, 13, 1978, 293–300.

4.44 **Berlin**, I., 'The originality of Machiavelli', in his *Against the current: essays in the history of ideas*, 1979, 25–79. Magisterial survey of the various interpretations of Machiavelli, concluding that he was – in spite of himself – an originator of liberal pluralism.

4.45 **Black**, R., 'Florentine political traditions and Machiavelli's election to the chancery', *Italian Sts.*, 41, 1985, 1–16.

4.46 **Bock**, G., **Skinner**, Q., and **Viroli**, M., ed., *Machiavelli and Republicanism*, 1990. Includes N. Rubinstein, 'Machiavelli and Florentine republican experience', E. Guarini, 'Machiavelli and the crisis of the Italian republics', R. Black, 'Machiavelli, servant of the Florentine republic', Q. Skinner, 'Machiavelli's *Discorsi* and the pre-humanist origins of republican ideas', M. Viroli, 'Machiavelli and the republican idea of politics', M. Mallet, 'The theory and practice of warfare in Machiavelli's republic', G. Bock, 'Civil discord in Machiavelli's *Istorie Florentine*'.

4.47 **Bonadeo**, A., *Corruption, conflict, and power in the works and times of Niccoli Machiavelli*, Berkeley, Calif., 1973. Demonstrates Machiavelli's aversion to political absolutism.

4.48 —— 'The role of "Grandi" in the political

world of Machiavelli', *Sts. Ren.*, 16, 1969, 9–29.

4.49 —— 'The role of the people in the works and times of Machiavelli', *Bibliothèque d'Humanisme et Renaissance*, 32, 1970, 351–77.

4.50 **Bookman**, J. T., 'Utility, coercion and the public interest: Machiavelli's politics', *J. Thought*, 18, 1983, 54–64.

4.51 **Brudney**, K. M., 'Machiavelli on social class and class conflict', *Pol. Theory*, 12, 1984, 507–19. Suggests that for Machiavelli 'the logic of class-based politics engendered a political vigilance and a public orientation that were essential to the maintenance of republican institutions and republican liberty'.

4.52 **Butters**, H., 'Good government and the limitations of power in the writings of Niccolo Machiavelli', *Hist. Pol. Thought*, 7, 1986, 411–19. Argues that Machiavelli saw rulers' freedom of action limited by fortune, social structure, human nature and the desires and beliefs of their subjects.

4.53 **Campbell**, W. R., *Machiavelli: An Anti-Study*, Rhode Island, N.Y., 1968. Short study claiming that he anticipated the fundamental problem of liberal political philosophy: that of defining the consensual foundations of political obligation in a society where the majority obey laws out of fear rather than allegiance.

4.54 —— 'Machiavelli's anthropology of obligation: the politics of morality', *Polity*, 4, 1972, 449–79.

4.55 **Chabod**, F., *Machiavelli and the Renaissance*, 1958. Collection of essays, originally published between 1924 and 1955, by a leading authority on the Renaissance.

4.56 **Cochrane**, E., 'Machiavelli: 1940–1960', *J. Mod. Hist.*, 33, 1961, 113–36. Survey of the literature about Machiavelli.

4.57 **Colish**, M. L., 'The idea of liberty in Machiavelli', *J. Hist. Ideas*, 32, 1971, 323–50. Detailed textual and contextual analysis of the different meanings of *libertà* in Machiavelli's writings.

4.58 **de Grazia**, S., *Machiavelli in Hell*, 1988. A major intellectual biography.

4.59 **Drury**, S. B., 'The hidden meaning of Strauss's *Thoughts on Machiavelli*', *Hist. Pol. Thought*, 6, 1985, 575–91. Argues that Leo Strauss's condemnation of Machiavelli was really a criticism of his imprudent honesty in expressing anti-Christian sentiments and revolting against the tradition of Greek philosophy which ostensibly bound politics to morality.

4.60 **Eldar**, D., 'Glory and the boundaries of public morality in Machiavelli's thought', *Hist. Pol. Thought*, 7, 1986, 419–39. Demonstrates how Machiavelli uses the concept of *gloria* to 'define the borders of public morality, or rather to advise rulers about setting the limits to prudent villainy in the sphere of politics'.

4.61 **Fiore**, S. R., *Niccolo Machiavelli: An annotated Bibliography of Modern Criticism and Scholarship*, 1990. A comprehensive catalogue of all the writings on Machiavelli between 1935–85.

4.62 **Flaumenhaft**, M. J., 'The comic remedy: Machiavelli's "Mandragola" ', *Interpretation*, 7, 1978, 33–74. Assesses the relationship between the plays of Machiavelli and his political works.

4.63 **Fleisher**, M., ed., *Machiavelli and the Nature of Political Thought*, 1972. Collection of sharp essays including M. Fleisher, 'A passion for politics: the vital core of the world of Machiavelli', J. G. A. Pocock, 'Custom and grace, form and matter: an approach to Machiavelli's concept of innovation', R. Orr, 'The time motif in Machiavelli', H. Mansfield, 'Party and sect in Machiavelli's *Florentine Histories*' and N. Wood, 'The value of asocial sociability: contributions of Machiavelli, Sidney, and Montesquieu'.

4.64 —— 'Trust and deceit in Machiavelli's comedies', *J. Hist. Ideas*, 27, 1966, 365–380. The private world of Machiavelli's comedies is revealed as amoral, characterised by the rule of will and desire using force and fraud in a situation of continuous flux.

4.65 **Garver**, E., *Machiavelli and the History of Prudence*, Madison, 1987.

4.66 **Geerken**, J., 'Machiavelli studies since 1969', *J. Hist. Ideas*, 37, 1976, 351–68. Survey of the literature about Machiavelli.

4.67 **Gilbert**, F., 'Machiavelli in modern historical scholarship', *Ital. Q.*, 14, 1970, 9–26.

4.68 —— 'Review discussion: the composition and structure of Machiavelli's *Discourses*', *J. Hist. Ideas*, 14, 1953, 36–56. Dismisses the traditional view that the *Discourses* were composed as a single work between 1513 and 1519.

4.69 —— 'The concept of nationalism in

Machiavelli's *Prince*', *Sts. Ren.*, 1, 1954, 38–48.

4.70 **Gilmore**, M. P., ed., *Studies in Machiavelli*, Florence, 1972. Includes N. Rubinstein, 'Machiavelli and the world of Florentine politics', I. Berlin, 'The originality of Machiavelli', D. Weinstein, 'Machiavelli and Savonarola' and R. Hatfield, 'A source for Machiavelli's account of the regime of Pero de 'Medici'.

4.71 **Hale**, J. R., *Machiavelli and Renaissance Italy*, 1961. Rich in biographical detail.

4.72 —— 'To fortify or not to fortify? Machiavelli's contribution to a Renaissance debate', in H. C. Davis, ed., *Essays in honour of John Humphreys Whitfield*, 1975. In the *Prince* Machiavelli accepts that a well-fortified city can be secure, but suggests that is is better for a prince to rely upon the loyalty of his subjects; in the *Discourses* he argues more vehemently that strong walls tend to weaken the resolve of citizens to defend themselves.

4.73 **Hannaford**, I., 'Machiavelli's concept of virtù in the *Prince* and the *Discourses* reconsidered', *Pol. Sts.*, 20, 1972, 185–9. Response to Wood in *Pol. Sts.*, 15, 1967.

4.74 **Hariman**, R., 'Composing modernity in Machiavelli's *Prince*', *J. Hist. Ideas*, 50, 1989, 3–29. Argues that Machiavelli was able to depict power as an autonomous, material force by breaking with rhetorical tradition.

4.75 **Hexter**, J. H., ' "Il Principe" and "lo stato" ', *Sts. Ren.*, 4, 1957, 113–38. Argues that the *Prince* does not contain a conception of the state as an abstract political body which transcends the individuals who compose it.

4.76 **Hulliung**, M., *Citizen Machiavelli*, Princeton, N.J., 1984. Rejects the view that Machiavelli was fundamentally a republican democrat preoccupied with political liberty. His only concerns were conquest and glory.

4.77 **Ionescu**, G., 'Responsible government and responsible citizens: six variations on a theme by Machiavelli', *Pol. Sts.*, 23, 1975, 255–70. Reflections on Machiavelli's maxim that to avoid corruption 'well-ordered republics have to keep the public rich but their citizens poor'.

4.78 **Leonard**, J., 'Public versus private claims: Machiavellianism from another perspective', *Pol. Theory*, 12, 1984, 491–506. 'The absence of virtue in Machiavelli's political thought is not the result of shallow and unprincipled cynicism but of a deeply rooted pessimism concerning the ability of most men to internalize a code of conduct that clashes with immediate self-interest combined with an exaltation of the public sphere as an arena of conflict in which the practice of Christian virtue would amount to self-martyrdom'.

4.79 **Lord**, C., 'On Machiavelli's *Mandragola*', *J. Pol.*, 41, 1979, 806–27. The allegory of the play is said to take us to the heart of Machiavelli's political thinking by documenting the projected overthrow of the political order by a prince acting in the service not of classical republicanism but of a wholly new regime.

4.80 **McIntosh**, D., 'The modernity of Machiavelli', *Pol. Theory*, 12, 1984, 184–203. Argues that his thinking enables us to understand such issues as the nation state, capitalism and gender.

4.81 **Mansfield**, H. C., *Machiavelli's New Modes and Orders: A Study of the Discourses in Livy*, Berkeley, Calif., 1980.

4.82 —— 'Machiavelli's political science', *Am. Pol. Sc. Rev.*, 75, 1981, 293–305. Argues that he broke with classical thinking by inaugurating 'a political science that routinely excludes soul from what it calls "behavior" and flutters at the mention of virtue'.

4.83 —— 'Strauss's Machiavelli', *Pol. Theory*, 3, 1975, 372–84. Essentially a defence of Strauss's interpretation against its many critics.

4.84 **Mattingly**, G., 'Machiavelli's Prince: political science or political satire?', *Am. Schol.*, 27, 1957/58, 482–91.

4.85 **Mazzeo**, J., 'The poetry and power: Machiavelli's literary vision', *Rev. Nat. Lit.*, 7, 1970, 38–62.

4.86 **Mindle**, G. B., 'Machiavelli's realism', *Rev. Pol.*, 47, 1985, 212–30. Depicted as an extremist rather than a realist.

4.87 **Newell**, W. R., 'How original is Machiavelli? A consideration of Skinner's interpretation of virtue and fortune', *Pol. Theory*, 15, 1987, 612–34. Questions Skinner's suggestion in *The Foundations of Modern Political Thought* that the context for Machiavelli's understanding of virtue and fortune is provided by the Italian humanists of the fourteenth and fifteenth centuries, arguing that he conceived the two concepts in a radically different way from classical Christian or humanist writers.

4.88 **Norton**, P. E., 'Machiavelli's road to paradise: "The Exhortation to Penitence" ', *Hist. Pol. Thought*, 4, 1983, 31-42. Argues that Machiavelli's idea of repentance demonstrates his break from Christian orthodoxy.

4.89 **Orwin**, C., 'Machiavelli's unchristian charity', *Am. Pol. Sc. Rev.*, 72, 1978, 1217–28. In his treatment of virtue Machiavelli is said to prefigure economic liberalism.

4.90 **Parel**, A. J., 'Machiavelli's notions of justice: text and analysis', *Pol. Theory*, 18, 1990, 528–44. Analysis of Machiavelli's 'Allocution Made to a Magistrate'.

4.91 —— 'Ptolemy as a source of *The Prince* 25', *Hist. Pol. Thought*, 14, 1993, 77–83. Argues that Machiavelli subscribed to the heterodox view that the things of this world are governed by fate and fortune, a view derived from Ptolemaic astrology.

4.92 —— *The Machiavellian Cosmos*, 1992.

4.93 —— ed., *The Political Calculus: Essays on Machiavelli's Philosophy*, Toronto, 1972. Includes N. Wood, 'Machiavelli's humanism of action', T. Flanagan, 'The concept of *Fortuna* in Machiavelli, and A. Plamenatz, 'In search of Machiavellian *Virtù*'.

4.94 —— 'The question of Machiavelli's modernity', *Rev. Pol.*, 53, 1991, 320–39. Argues that Machiavelli is not a modern political theorist as is Hobbes, for instance, because the former's argument derived from a pre-modern cosmology and anthropology.

4.95 **Pitkin**, H. F., *Fortune Is a Woman: Gender and Politics in the Thought of Niccolo Machiavelli*, Berkeley, 1984.

4.96 **Pocock**, J. G. A., 'Machiavelli in the liberal cosmos', *Pol. Theory*, 13, 1985, 559–74. Critique of the interpretations by Hulliung, *Citizen Machiavelli*, and Pitkin, *Fortune is a Woman*.

4.97 —— 'Prophet and inquisitor: or, a church built upon bayonets cannot stand: a comment on Mansfield's "Strauss's Machiavelli" ', *Pol. Theory*, 3, 1975, 385–401. Brilliant demolition of Mansfield's defence – in the same issue of the journal – of Strauss's interpretation of Machiavelli.

4.98 **Preus**, J. S., 'Machiavelli's functional analysis of religion: context and object', *J Hist. Ideas*, 40, 1979, 167–90. Explains why he supposed that Christianity was a political failure.

4.99 **Prezzoline**, G., *Machiavelli*, 1967. Not only a study of his ideas but also of his adversaries, adherents and interpreters through to the twentieth century.

4.100 —— 'The Christian roots of Machiavelli' moral pessimism', *Rev. Nat. Lit.*, 7, 1970 26–37. Politics in Machiavelli's understanding is 'separated not from morality but only from the morality of optimistic Christianity'.

4.101 **Price**, R., 'Ambizione in Machiavelli's thought', *Hist. Pol. Thought*, 3, 1983, 383–447. Argues that Machiavelli usually deprecated internal ambition, striving for personal gain, power and riches, but lauded external ambition, seeking to further the interests of one's country, as a essential aspect of *virtù* in the citizen.

4.102 —— 'Machiavelli quincentenary studies' *Eur. Sts. Rev.*, 5, 1975, 313–35. Useful review article.

4.103 —— 'The sense of virtù in Machiavelli', *Eur. Sts. Rev.*, 3, 1973, 315–45. Demonstrates that he did not invent the wide range of meanings he gives to the concept, nor did he change virtue from a moral to an amoral or immoral concept.

4.104 —— 'The theme of *Gloria* in Machiavelli' *Ren. Q.*, 30, 1977, 588–631. Close textua analysis demonstrating that 'he expressed common ideas about fame or glory explicitly and vividly'.

4.105 —— 'Self-love, "egoism" and *ambizione* i Machiavelli's thought', *Hist. Pol. Though* 9, 1988, 237–63.

4.106 **Rebhorn**, W. A., *Foxes and Lions: Machiavelli's Confidence Men*, Ithaca, N.Y., 1988. Focuses on Machiavelli's ambivalence towards statesmen.

4.107 **Richardson**, B., 'Notes on Machiavelli's sources and his treatment of the rhetorica tradition', *Italian Sts.*, 26, 1971, 24–48.

4.108 —— 'The structure of Machiavelli's *Discorsi*', *Italica*, 49, 1972, 46–71.

4.109 **Rousseau**, G. S., 'The *Discorsi* of Machiavelli in history and theory', *Cahie d'histoire mondiale*, 9, 1965–6, 143–61.

4.110 **Santi**, V. A., 'Religion and politics in Machiavelli', *Machiavelli Studies*, 1, 1987 17–24.

4.111 **Schellhase**, K. C., 'Tacitus in the politica

thought of Machiavelli', *Il Pensiero Politico*, 4, 1971, 381–93.

4.112 **Shumer**, S. M., 'Machiavelli: Republican politics and its corruption', *Pol. Theory*, 7, 1979, 5–34. Uses Machiavelli's theory of republican politics and its corruption as presented in the *Discourses* to reflect on contemporary American politics.

4.113 **Skinner**, Q., *Machiavelli*, 1981. Probably the best brief survey of his life and writings, portraying Machiavelli 'as an exponent of a distinctive humanist tradition of classical republicanism'.

4.114 **Stephens**, J., and **Butters**, H., 'New light on Machiavelli', *Eng. Hist. Rev.*, 97, 1982, 54–69. Unearths fresh biographical detail from archival material.

4.115 **Stephens**, S. N., 'Machiavelli's Prince and the Florentine revolution of 1512', *Italian Sts.*, 41, 1986, 45–61. Interesting observations on the relationship between the Medici and Machiavelli after 1512.

4.116 **Strauss**, L., 'Machiavelli and classical literature', *Rev. Nat. Lit.*, 1, 1970, 7–25. Largely a reworking of ideas in *Thoughts on Machiavelli*.

4.117 —— 'Machiavelli's intention: *The Prince*', *Am. Pol. Sc. Rev.*, 51, 1957, 13–40. Brilliant exegesis demonstrating that the text is both a treatise and a tract for the times, and also that in being apparently deferential to 'the Great Tradition' of political thought Machiavelli uproots it.

4.118 —— *Thoughts on Machiavelli*, Glencoe, Ill., 1968. Classic portrayal of Machiavelli as a teacher of evil.

4.119 **Tarcov**, N., 'Quentin Skinner's method and Machiavelli's *Prince*', *Ethics*, 92, 1982, 692–709. Accuses Skinner, in a sustained critique of his methodology, of concealing Machiavelli's originality through a 'superficial, confused and poorly documented interpretation'.

4.120 **Tarlton**, C. D., 'The symbolism of redemption and the exorcism of fortune in Machiavelli's *Prince*', *Rev. Pol.*, 30, 1968, 332–48. Analyses the *Prince* as a poetic structure, casting the prince in the role of both saviour of Italy and sacrificial scapegoat who makes himself superfluous by creating a state ruled by good laws.

4.121 **Viroli**, M., 'Republic and politics in Machiavelli and Rousseau', *Hist. Pol. Thought*, 9, 1989, 405–21. Argues that the differences emerging from the comparison between Machiavelli's and Rousseau's

political language reveal crucial shifts within the republican tradition and illuminate the dilemmas of a republican politics.

4.122 **Whitfield**, J. H., *Discourses on Machiavelli*, 1969.

4.123 —— *Machiavelli*, 1947. A brief survey of his ideas.

4.124 —— 'On Machiavelli's use of *ordini*', *Italian Sts.*, 10, 1955, 19–39.

4.125 **Wood**, N., 'Machiavelli's concept of virtù reconsidered', *Pol. Sts.*, 15, 1967, 159–72. Close textual analysis of the various uses of the concept.

Other thinkers

4.126 **Gilbert**, F., 'Religion and politics in the thought of Gasparo Contarini', in T. K. Rabb and J. E. Seigel, ed., *Action and Conviction in Early Modern Europe: Essays in Memory of E. H. Harbison*, Princeton, N.J., 1969, 90–116. Discusses Contarini's *De magistratibus et republica Venetorum* (first published in 1543) which idealised Venetian political institutions as a means of demonstrating how government can lead people to perfection.

4.127 **Perry**, D., 'Paridis de Puteo: a fifteenth-century civilian's concept of papal sovereignty', in D. Wood, ed., *Sts. Ch. Hist.*, 9, *The Church and Sovereignty, c.590–1918*, 1991, 369–92. On the political thought of one of the last representatives of the Neapolitan law school.

(c) BRITISH ISLES

General

4.128 **Adams**, R. P., *The Better Part of Valor: More, Erasmus, Colet and Vives, on Humanism, War and Peace, 1496–1535*, Seattle, Wash., 1962. Substantial account of the ideas of the leading humanists of early Tudor England.

4.129 **Bowler**, G., ' "An axe or an acte": the parliament of 1572 and resistance theory in early Elizabethan England', *Canadian*

Journal of History, 19, 1984, 349–59. Demonstrates the persistence of Marian theories of resistance.

4.130 —— 'Marian Protestants and the idea of violent resistance to tyranny', in P. Lake and M. Dowling, ed., *Protestantism and the National Church in Sixteenth-Century England*, 1987, 124–43. Argues that English protestants under Mary went far beyond their continental forebears in developing theories of resistance.

4.131 **Burns**, J. H., 'The conciliarist tradition in Scotland', *Scott. Hist. Rev.*, 42, 1963, 89–104. Demonstrates the continuing influence of conciliarism on fifteenth- and sixteenth-century Scottish political thought.

4.132 —— 'The political ideas of the Scottish Reformation', *Aberdeen University Review*, 36, 1955–6, 251–68.

4.133 **Caspari**, F., *Humanism and the Social Order in Tudor England*, Chicago, Ill., 1954. Traces the revival of classical ideals in the writings of More, Sir Thomas Elyot, Thomas Starkey, Sir Philip Sidney and Edmund Spenser.

4.134 **Clancy**, T. H., *Papist Pamphleteers: The Allen-Persons Party and the Political Thought of the Counter-Reformation in England, 1572–1615*, Chicago, Ill., 1964. Close analysis of Catholic political thought.

4.135 **Davis**, J. C., *Utopia and the Ideal Society: A Study of English Utopian Writing, 1516–1700*, 1981.

4.136 **Dawson**, J. E. A., 'Revolutionary conclusions: the case of the Marian exiles', *Hist. Pol. Thought*, 11, 1990, 257–73. Account of how the Protestant exiles during Mary's reign espoused a theory of resistance and of how their radical political ideas survived the accession of Elizabeth.

4.137 **Eccleshall**, R. R., *Order and Reason in Politics: Theories of Absolute and Limited Monarchy in Early Modern England*, 1978. Explores the medieval antecedents of the theories of absolute and limited monarchy in the fifteenth and sixteenth centuries.

4.138 **Ferguson**, A. B., 'Renaissance realism in the "Commonwealth" literature of early Tudor England', *J. Hist. Ideas*, 16, 1955, 287–305. Illustrates how the social criticism of writers such as Robert Crowley and Thomas Starkey typify the transition from medieval to modern styles of thinking.

4.139 —— *The Articulate Citizen and the English Renaissance*, Durham, N.C., 1965. After surveying the late medieval literature of social criticism the author focuses on the ideas of Tudor humanists, particularly those of More, Starkey and Sir Thomas Smith.

4.140 **Fideler**, P. A., and **Mayer**, T. F., ed., *Political Thought and the Tudor Commonwealth: Deep Structure, Discourse and Disguise*, 1992. Essays include D. Woolf, 'The power of the past: history, ritual and political authority in Tudor England', T. Mayer, 'Nursery of resistance: Reginald Pole and his friends', F. Conrad, 'The problem of counsel reconsidered: the case of Sir Thomas Elyot', N. Wood, 'Foundations of political economy: the new moral philosophy of Sir Thomas Smith', P. Fideler, 'Poverty, policy and providence: the Tudors and the poor', and A. Slavin, 'The Tudor state, reformation and understanding change: through the looking glass'.

4.142 **Fox**, A., and **Guy**, J. A., *Reassessing the Henrician Age: Humanism, Politics and Reform, 1500–1550*, 1986. Discussion of More, Elyot, St. German, and Starkey, the argument being that Tudor humanism – including its political ideas – 'was not monolithic as is usually depicted, but a multifarious phenomenon'.

4.143 **Genet**, J. P., 'Ecclesiastics and political theory in late medieval England: the end of a monopoly', in R. B. Dobson, ed., *The Church, Politics and Patronage in the Fifteenth Century*, 1984, 23–44. Argues that nowhere else in Europe was the abandonment of the monopoly of the church so complete as in fifteenth-century England.

4.144 **Greaves**, R. L., 'Concepts of political obedience in late Tudor England: conflicting perspectives', *J. Brit. Sts.*, 22, 1982, 23–34. Deals with the doctrines of Puritans and Roman Catholics as well as the standard Anglican position.

4.145 **Greenleaf**, W. H., *Order, Empiricism and Politics: Two Traditions of English Political Thought 1500–1700*, 1964. An excellent study, Oakeshottian in conception, which explores two traditions of political thought those of order and empiricism, through the writings of James I, Edward Forset, Filmer, Bacon, Harrington and Petty as well as a host of other figures.

4.146 **Hanson**, D. W., *From Kingdom to Commonwealth: The Development of Civic Consciousness in English Political Thought*, Cambridge, Mass., 1970. Traces the continuity and discontinuity of constitutional thinking from Bracton to the Levellers.

4.147 **Hinton**, R. W. K., 'English constitutional theories from Sir John Fortescue to Sir John Eliot', *Eng. Hist. Rev.*, 75, 1960, 410–25. A masterly survey suggesting that in constitutional thinking from the fifteenth century to the eve of Civil War 'we may observe a switch from the theory of mixed government to the theory of absolute government under the rule of law'.

4.148 **Holmes**, P., *Resistance and Compromise: The Political Thought of the Elizabethan Catholics*, 1982. Analysis of the numerous tracts of the period in which Roman Catholics debated whether resistance to a Protestant sovereign was legitimate.

4.149 **Jones**, W. R. D., *The Tudor Commonwealth 1529–1559: A study of the impact of the social and economic developments of mid-Tudor England upon contemporary concepts of the nature and duties of the commonwealth*, 1970. Traces a growing concern with the economic and social aspects of governance in mid-Tudor England through the ideas of Thomas Starkey, Sir Thomas Smith, Henry Brinklow, Robert Crowley and others.

4.150 **Jordan**, C., 'Woman's rule in sixteenth-century British political thought', *Ren. Q.*, 40, 1987, 421–51. Interesting survey of the arguments against female rule – principally by the Marian exiles – and of the justifications – by John Aylmer, John Leslie and David Chambers – on behalf of women exercising political authority.

4.151 **Kelley**, D. R., 'History, English law and the Renaissance', *Past & Pres.*, 65, 1974, 24–51. Emphasises the insularity of English legal scholarship.

4.152 —— 'Ideas of resistance before Elizabeth', in H. Dubrow and R. Strier, ed., *The Historical Renaissance: New Essays on Tudor and Stuart Literature and Culture*, Chicago, Ill., 1988, 48–76. Focuses on the Marian exiles, emphasising the eclectic character of the discourse of resistance.

4.153 **Lehmberg**, S. E., 'English humanists, the Reformation and the problem of counsel', *Archiv für Reformationgeschichte*, 52, 1961, 74–90. Basic article on the influence of humanism on Tudor political thought.

4.154 **Levack**, B. P., 'Law and ideology: the civil law and theories of absolutism in Elizabethan and Jacobean England', in H. Dubrow and R. Strier, ed., *The Historical Renaissance: New Essays on Tudor and Stuart Literature and Culture*, Chicago, Ill., 1988, 220–41. Argues, contrary to some historians, that civil law was an important source of new constitutional ideas that began to circulate at the end of Elizabeth's reign; and, further, that these ideas were less absolutist than is usually suggested.

4.155 **McConica**, J. K., *English Humanists and Reformation Politics under Henry VIII and Edward VI*, 1965. Emphasises the influence of Erasmus upon the intellectual milieu of Reformation England.

4.156 **Mason**, R. A., 'Kingship, tyranny and the right to resist in fifteenth century Scotland', *Scott. Hist. Rev.*, 66, 1987, 125–51. Argues that the radicalism of sixteenth-century Scottish political theory, with its emphasis on the accountability of kings, had no precedent in the previous century, 'when the idea of resisting the crown . . . was stated . . . in only the most hesitant and ambiguous terms'.

4.157 **Mayer**, T. F., 'Tournai and tyranny: imperial kingship and critical humanism', *Hist. J.*, 34, 1991, 257–77. On the emergence of a doctrine of imperial monarchy during Henry's occupation of Tournai between 1513 and 1519, and its influence on More's meditations on tyranny in *Utopia*.

4.158 **Morris**, C., *Political Thought in England: Tyndale to Hooker*, 1953. A dated but nevertheless accessible and readable overview of the period.

4.159 **Pritchard**, A., *Catholic Loyalism in Elizabethan England*, 1979. Detailed study of the political ideas of Elizabethan Catholics.

4.160 **Raab**, F., *The English Face of Machiavelli: A Changing Interpretation 1500–1700*, 1964. Seminal study of the reception of Machiavelli in England which focuses on Hobbes, Harrington and many other figures.

4.161 **Salmon**, J. H. M., *The French Religious Wars in English Political Thought*, 1959. Interesting study of how thinkers from the Elizabethan age to the late seventeenth century used the experiences of France in thinking about English politics.

4.162 **Skinner**, Q., 'The origins of the Calvinist theory of revolution', in B. C. Malament, ed., *After the Reformation: Essays in Honor of J. H. Hexter*, 1980, 309–30. Perceptive analysis of the emergence of a Protestant theory of revolution, focusing on the Scottish writers John Mair and George Buchanan.

4.163 **Wood**, N., 'Cicero and the political thought of the early English renaissance', *Mod. Lang. Q.*, 51, 1990, 185–207. Argues that, notwithstanding the paucity of references to his works, Cicero may 'very well have been an intellectual touchstone for speculation about the state' in the sixteenth century, especially for Thomas Starkey, John Ponet and Thomas Smith.

4.164 **Zeeveld**, W. G., *Foundations of Tudor Policy*, Cambridge, Mass., 1948. Still useful on the continental influences upon English political ideas.

More

4.165 **Allen**, W., 'The tone of More's farewell to *Utopia*: a reply to J. H. Hexter', *Moreana*, 51, 1976, 108–18.

4.166 **Ames**, R. A., *Citizen More and his Utopia*, Princeton, N.J., 1949. Portrays *Utopia* as an exercise in the literature of social protest.

4.167 **Avineri**, S., 'War and slavery in More's *Utopia*', *Int. Rev. Soc. Hist.*, 7, 1962, 260–90.

4.168 **Baker-Smith**, D., *More's Utopia*, 1991. Excellent textual analysis which is also a clear guide through the maze of conflicting interpretations of *Utopia*.

4.169 —— 'The escape from the cave: Thomas More and the vision of Utopia', in D. Baker-Smith and C. C. Barfoot, ed., *Between Dream and Nature. Essays on Utopia and Dystopia*, Amsterdam, 1987, 5–19.

4.170 **Blockmans**, W. P., *Thomas More, 'Utopia', and the Aspirations of the Early Capitalist Bourgeoisie*, Rotterdam, 1978.

4.171 **Bradshaw**, B., 'More on Utopia', *Hist. J.*, 24, 1981, 1–27. Brilliant critique of the interpretations of Hexter, Skinner and others.

4.172 —— 'The controversial Sir Thomas More', *J. Eccl. Hist.*, 36, 1985, 535–69. Vigorous repudiation of the contention of some recent historians that More was a reactionary masquerading as a humanist.

4.173 **Caspari**, F., 'Sir Thomas More and *Justum Bellum*', *Ethics*, 56, 1946, 303–8. More was not an ideologue of emerging English imperialism in elaborating a doctrine of the just war; he was articulating the teachings of the medieval Aristotelians.

4.174 **Caudle**, M. W., 'Sir Thomas More's *Utopia*: origins and purposes', *Soc. Sc.*, 45, 1970, 163–69.

4.175 **Coles**, P., 'The interpretation of More's *Utopia*', *Hibbert J.*, 56, 1958, 365–70.

4.176 **Davis**, J. C., 'More, Morton and the politics of accommodation', *J. Brit. Sts.*, 9, 1970, 27–49. Argues that the whole of *Utopia* is preoccupied with means and that the problem of how the ideal society is to be achieved is never finally resolved.

4.177 —— *Utopia and the Ideal Society: A Study of English Utopian Writing, 1516–1700*, 1981. Includes a chapter on More.

4.178 **Duhamel**, P. A., 'The medievalism of More's *Utopia*', *Sts. in Philol.*, 52, 1955, 234–50.

4.179 **Fenlon**, D., 'England and Europe: Utopia and its aftermath', *Trans. Royal Hist. Soc.*, 25, 1975, 115–35. Depicts *Utopia* as a critique of the humanist strategy of using secular government as an instrument of Christian renewal.

4.180 **Fleisher**, M., *Radical Reform and Political Persuasion in the Life and Writings of Thomas More*, Geneva, 1973. More is depicted as a social reformer intent on humanising and christianising everyday life: 'social justice, defined as radical equality, must constitute the basic principle of social life if that life is ever to be thoroughly spiritualized. Furthermore, spirituality is not primarily a personal and private experience [but] is achieved in carefree industry willingly expended in the joyous service of the common good'.

4.181 **Fox**, A., *Thomas More: History and Providence*, 1982. An acclaimed intellectual biography which locates *Utopia* within the context of More's belief in a providentially directed history, working by means of ambiguity towards consensus.

4.182 **Gogan**, B., *The Common Corps of*

Christendom: Ecclesiological Themes in the Writings of Sir Thomas More, Leiden, 1982. Sets More in the context of late medieval and Reformation ecclesiology.

4.183 **Guegen**, J. A., 'Reading More's *Utopia* as a criticism of Plato', *Albion*, 10, 1978, 43–54.

4.184 **Guy**, J. A., *The Public Career of Sir Thomas More*, New Haven, Conn., 1980. The basic work for More as a common lawyer and useful on his political ideas.

4.185 **Hay**, D., 'Sir Thomas More's *Utopia*: literature or politics?', *Rendiconti dell'Academia Nazionale dei Lincei*, 175, 1972, 3–17; repr. in Hay, *Renaissance Essays*, 1988, 249–63. In his social and economic thought More was 'old fashioned and somewhat impractical, though much of his approach derives ultimately from bedrock Christian doctrine. In his explicitly moral and educational works he is much nearer to the heart of Renaissance theory'.

4.186 **Hexter**, J. H., 'Intention, words and meaning: the case of Thomas More's *Utopia*', *New Lit. Hist.*, 6, 1975, 529–41.

4.187 —— *More's Utopia: The Biography of an Idea*, Princeton, N.J., 1952. A brilliant and pathbreaking analysis, depicting *Utopia* as a scheme for radical social reform: that of establishing communal ownership as a means of curbing pride.

4.188 —— 'Thomas More and the problem of counsel', *Albion*, 10, 1978, 55–66.

4.189 —— 'Thomas More: on the margins of modernity', *J. Brit. Sts.*, 1, 1961, 20–37. Original and influential article arguing that in his commitment to utopian communism More was neither a medieval nor a Renaissance thinker, but a modern radical whose *Utopia* was the first post-medieval attempt 'to envisage the specific public conditions of a decently ordered civil life for all'.

4.190 **Johnson**, R. S., *More's Utopia: Ideal and Illusion*, New Haven, Conn., 1969. Portrays More as a political realist more concerned with defining the proper stance towards the illusions of a utopian myth than with presenting to society a perfected vision of itself.

4.191 **Jones**, E., 'Commoners and kings: book one of More's *Utopia*', in D. L. Heyworth, ed., *Medieval Studies for J. A. W. Bennett*, 1981, 255–72.

4.192 **Kenny**, A., *Thomas More*, 1983. Readable and authoritative.

4.193 **Kenyon**, T. A., 'The problem of freedom and moral behavior in Thomas More's *Utopia*', *J. Hist. Phil.*, 21, 1983, 349–73. Emphasises More's eclecticism and his debt to both Augustinian and Thomist patterns of thought: the (Thomist) theme of *Utopia* was that people could live rationally and virtuously, but More's Augustinian pessimism led him to emphasise the need for institutional constraints upon the human propensity to human wickedness.

4.194 **Kristeller**, P. O., 'Thomas More as a Renaissance humanist', *Moreana*, 65–66, 1980, 5–22.

4.195 **Logan**, G. M., *The Meaning of More's 'Utopia'*, Princeton, N.J., 1983. Among the finest of the numerous books about More.

4.196 **Moulakis**, A., 'Pride and the meaning of *Utopia*', *Hist. Pol. Thought*, 11, 1990, 241–57. Attempts to discover More's intentions in writing his notoriously elusive work.

4.197 **Nendza**, J., 'Religion and republicanism in More's Utopia', *West. Pol. Q.*, 37, 1984, 189–211.

4.198 **Neumann**, H., 'On the Platonism of More's *Utopia*', *Social Res.*, 33, 1966, 495–512.

4.199 **Raitiere**, M. N., 'More's *Utopia* and *The City of God*', *Sts. Ren.*, 20, 1973, 144–68.

4.200 **Rebhorn**, W. A., 'Thomas More's enclosed garden: Utopia and Renaissance Humanism', *Eng. Lit. Ren.*, 6, 1976, 140–55. More is said to perceive human nature and the natural world through a few key images: 'both are *terrain* to be *cultivated* or *farmed*, transformed by the human art of *agriculture* into a perfect, almost paradisical *garden*'. *Utopia* is a walled garden, a rigidly controlled environment insulating those within against worldly corruption.

4.201 **Sargent**, L. T., 'More's *Utopia*: an interpretation of its social theory', *Hist. Pol. Thought*, 5, 1984, 195–210. Close textual analysis claiming that the interesting features of More's political theory have been buried by recent scholarship.

4.202 **Skinner**, Q., 'More's *Utopia*', *Past & Pres.*, 38, 1967, 153–68. Review article which usefully surveys some recent interpretations.

4.203 —— 'Sir Thomas More's *Utopia* and the

language of Renaissance humanism', in A. Pagden, ed., *The Languages of Political Theory in Early-Modern Europe*, 1987, 123–57. Careful and perceptive analysis repudiating the view that More was equivocal about the desirability of the ideal society he depicted: 'for all the ironies and ambiguities in More's text, his main aim was to challenge his readers at least to consider seriously whether utopia may not represent the best state of a commonwealth'.

4.204 **Starnes**, C., *The New Republic: A Commentary on Book 1 of More's Utopia Showing its Relation to Plato's Republic*, Waterloo, 1990.

4.205 **Surtz**, E., 'Interpretations of *Utopia*', *Cath. Hist. Rev.*, 38, 1952, 156–74.

4.206 —— *The Praise of Pleasure: Philosophy, Education, and Communism in More's Utopia*, Cambridge, Mass., 1957. A racy account depicting *Utopia* as 'a cry of distress over the exploited poor and a call to reform in every department of human endeavour'.

4.207 —— *The Praise of Wisdom: A Commentary on the Religious and Moral Problems and Backgrounds of St. Thomas More's Utopia*, Chicago, Ill., 1957. Depicts *Utopia* as a humanistic document intended to reform Christendom: its description of an ideal commonwealth was a reminder to Christians that their institutions should outstrip the practices of rational pagans.

4.208 **Sylvester**, R. S., ed., *Sir Thomas More: Contemplation and Action*, New Haven, Conn., 1972.

4.209 **Thompson**, C. R., 'The humanism of More reappraised', *Thought*, 52, 1977, 231–48.

4.210 **Tinckler**, J. F., 'Praise and advice: rhetorical approaches in More's *Utopia* and Machiavelli's *The Prince*', *Sixteenth Cent. J.*, 19, 1988, 187–207.

4.211 **Trinkaus**, C., 'Thomas More and the humanist tradition', in his *The Scope of Renaissance Humanism*, Michigan, 1983.

4.212 **White**, T. I., 'Pride and the public good: Thomas More's use of Plato in *Utopia*', *J. Hist. Phil.*, 20, 1982, 329–54. The argument is that More used Plato principally to demonstrate the need for institutional constraints to the destructive effects of pride.

Hooker

4.213 **Almasy**, R., 'The purpose of Richard Hooker's polemic', *J. Hist. Ideas*, 39, 1978, 251–70. Argues that the *Polity* was a polemical response to the Puritan Thomas Cartwright.

4.214 **Bradshaw**, B., 'Richard Hooker's ecclesiastical polity', *J. Eccl. Hist.*, 34, 1983, 438–44.

4.215 **Cargill Thompson**, W. D. J., 'The philosopher of the "politic society": Richard Hooker as a political thinker', in W. S. Hill, ed., *Studies in Richard Hooker: Essays Preliminary to an Edition of His Works*, Cleveland, Ohio, 1972, 279–320. Brilliant and influential article, firmly establishing the ideological context of Hooker's *Polity*.

4.216 —— 'The source of Hooker's knowledge of Marsilius of Padua', *J. Eccl. Hist.*, 25, 1974, 75–81.

4.217 **Davies**, E. T., *The Political Ideas of Richard Hooker*, 1946. Short and readable.

4.218 **Eccleshall**, R. R., 'Richard Hooker and the peculiarities of the English: the reception of the *Ecclesiastical Polity* in the seventeenth and eighteenth centuries', *Hist. Pol. Thought*, 2, 1981, 63–118. Traces the varied uses made of Hooker's political ideas by subsequent writers.

4.219 —— 'Richard Hooker's synthesis and the problem of allegiance', *J. Hist. Ideas*, 37, 1976, 111–24. Argues that Hooker's political thought was coherent.

4.220 **Faulkner**, R. K., *Richard Hooker and the Politics of a Christian England*, Berkeley, Calif., 1981. Sympathetic and informative, though Faulkner is more concerned to derive lessons for the modern world from Hooker's thinking than to establish its historical context.

4.221 **Ferguson**, A. B., 'The historical perspective of Richard Hooker: a Renaissance paradox', *J. Med. & Ren. Sts.*, 3, 1973, 17–49. Argues that Hooker 'backed into modernity', expressing Thomist ideas in the context of Renaissance society.

4.222 **Forte**, P. E., 'Richard Hooker's theory of law', *J. Med. & Ren. Sts.*, 12, 1982, 133–57. Argues that Hooker formulated a coherent legal philosophy.

4.223 **Hill**, W. S., 'Doctrine and polity in Hooker's *Laws*', *Eng. Lit. Ren.*, 2, 1972, 173–93. Teases out the political implications of Hooker's theology.

4.224 —— 'Hooker's *Polity*: the problem of the "Three Last Books" ', *Huntington Libr. Q.*, 34, 1971, 317–36. Convincing attempt to establish their authenticity.

4.225 **Hillerdal**, G., *Reason and Revelation in Richard Hooker*, Lund, 1962. Argues that Hooker fails to reconcile his Aristotelian-Thomist philosophy of reason and his Protestant theology of grace.

4.226 **Kearney**, H. F., 'Richard Hooker: a reconstruction', *Cambridge Hist. J.*, 5, 1952, 300–11. Portrays Hooker's *Polity* as incoherent, arguing that it opens with a Thomist vindication of reason and concludes with a pre-Hobbesian assertion that might is right.

4.227 **Lake**, P., *Anglicans and Puritans? Presbyterianism and English Conformist Thought from Whitgift to Hooker*, 1988. Substantial discussion of Hooker which sets his *Laws of Ecclesiastical Polity* into the ideological context in which it was written.

4.228 **McGrade**, A. S., 'Richard Hooker and the medieval resistance to modern politics', in G. C. Simmons, ed., *Paideia 1980: the Intellectual and Cultural Life of the Middle Ages*, New York, 1985. On Hooker's use of medieval legal sources.

4.229 —— 'The coherence of Hooker's polity: the books on power', *J. Hist. Ideas*, 24, 1963, 163–82. Excellent analysis of Hooker's political ideas.

4.230 —— 'The public and the religious in Hooker's *Polity*', *Church Hist.*, 38, 1968, 404–22. Focuses on the structure of argument in the fifth book of the *Polity*.

4.231 **Marshall**, J. S., *Hooker and the Anglican Tradition: An Historical and Theological Study of Hooker's Ecclesiastical Polity*, 1963. An Anglo-Catholic interpretation of Hooker as a systematic thinker in the manner of Aquinas.

4.232 **Munz**, P., *The Place of Hooker in the History of Thought*, 1952. Argues that Hooker began as a Thomist but ended by using Marsilian arguments to justify the Tudor state as a secular institution, and that this ideological incoherence explains his failure to complete the last three books of the *Polity*. An ingenious argument unsupported by more recent scholarship.

4.233 **Nyman**, M., *Bentham and Hooker*, 1973.

4.234 **Porter**, H. C., 'Hooker, the Tudor constitution, and the via media', in W. S. Hill, ed., *Studies in Richard Hooker: Essays Preliminary to an Edition of His Works*, Cleveland, Ohio, 77–116. Useful on Hooker's common-law heritage.

4.235 **Shirley**, F. J. J., *Richard Hooker and Contemporary Political Ideas*, 1949. Readable but derivative.

4.236 **Sommerville**, J. P., 'Richard Hooker, Hadrian Saravia, and the advent of the divine right of kings', *Hist. Pol. Thought*, 4, 1983, 229–47. Argues that Hooker's constitutionalism was less typical of official opinion than the absolutist doctrine of his friend, the Dutch Calvinist Saravia.

4.237 **Wolin**, S. S., 'Richard Hooker and English conservatism', *West. Pol. Q.*, 6, 1953, 28–47. Illuminating account depicting Hooker, not Burke, as the grandparent of conservatism.

Other thinkers

4.238 **Abrams**, M. C., 'Equity and natural law in Christopher St. German', in M. D. Forkosch, ed., *Essays in Legal History in Honor of Felix Frankfurter*, Indianapolis, 1966.

4.239 **Burns**, J. H., 'Fortescue and the political theory of *dominium*', *Hist. J.*, 28, 777–97. Perceptive article on a leading fifteenth-century thinker.

4.240 —— 'George Buchanan and the anti-monarchomachs', in N. Phillipson and Q. Skinner, ed., *Political Discourse in Early Modern Britain*, 1993, 3–22. On the debate triggered by his *De jure regni apud Scotos*.

4.241 —— 'John Knox and Revolution, 1558', *Hist. Today*, 8, 1958, 565–73. Argues that he developed a Calvinist theory of resistance with reluctance.

4.242 —— '*Politia regalis et optima*: the political ideas of John Mair', *Hist. Pol. Thought*, 2, 1981, 31–61. The best analysis of the political thought of a Scots theologian whose doctrine of the consensual foundation of legitimate government derived from a conciliar theory of ecclesiastical authority.

4.243 —— 'St. German, Gerson, Aquinas, and Ulpian', *Hist. Pol. Thought*, 4, 1983, 443–49. Critique of Z. Rueger's article, 'Gerson's concept of equity and Christopher St. German', *Hist. Pol. Thought*, 4, 1983, 1–30. Burns argues that St. German was an eclectic thinker who took the doctrine of equity from various intellectual sources, including Aquinas, and not merely from Gerson.

4.244 —— 'The political ideas of George Buchanan', *Scott. Hist. Rev.*, 30, 1951, 60–8.

4.245 **Dawson**, J. E. A., 'The two John Knoxes: England, Scotland and the 1558 tracts', *J. Eccl. Hist.*, 42, 1991, 555–76. Analysis of the writings of a leading Marian exile who proffered different advice to the Scots and the English, urging the former to establish Protestant worship and the latter to depose their ungodly ruler.

4.246 **Dewar**, M., *Sir Thomas Smith: a Tudor Intellectual in Office*, 1964. Study of a diplomat whose *De Republica Anglorum* (1565) celebrated England's limited monarchy.

4.247 **Doe**, N., 'Fifteenth-century concepts of law: Fortescue and Pecock', *Hist. Pol. Thought*, 10, 1989, 257–80. Argues that the similarity of their legal and political views derived from a common grounding in Thomist philosophy.

4.248 **Elton**, G. R., 'Reform by statute: Thomas Starkey's *Dialogue* and Thomas Cromwell's policy', *Procs. Brit. Acad.*, 54, 1968, 165–88. Uses the proposals of Starkey's *Dialogue* to explore the intellectual foundations of Cromwell's reforms.

4.249 —— 'The political creed of Thomas Cromwell', in *Studies in Tudor and Stuart Politics and Government*, 3 vols., 1974–84, vol. II, 215–35.

4.250 **Gill**, P. E., 'Politics and propaganda in fifteenth-century England: the polemical writings of Sir John Fortescue', *Speculum*, 46, 1971, 333–47. Focuses on Fortescue's views about the succession question which arose between the Lancastrian and Yorkist factions in the 1450s.

4.251 **Gillespie**, J. L., 'Sir John Fortescue's concept of royal will', *Nottingham Med. Sts.*, 23, 1979. Fortescue is said to have presented a doctrine of limited but not constitutionally controlled royal will.

4.252 **Guy**, J. A., *Christopher St. German on Chancery and Statute*, 1985. The best treatment of a lawyer and political pamphleteer who during the Henrician Reformation justified the regal assumption of papal jurisdiction.

4.254 **Hogrefe**, P., *The Life and Times of Sir*

Thomas Elyot, Englishman, Ames, Iowa, 1967. On a humanist whose treatise on monarchy was an early justification of the Reformation.

4.255 **Kingdon**, R. M., 'William Allen's use of Protestant political argument', in C. H. Carter, ed., *From the Renaissance to the Counter-Reformation*, 1966, 164–78. Argues that Allen, an Elizabethan Catholic polemicist, poached his resistance theory from Calvinist monarchomachs.

4.256 **Lehmberg**, S. E., *Sir Thomas Elyot, Tudor Humanist*, Austin, Texas, 1960. Biography of a writer whose praise of monarchy in *The Book Named the Gouvernour* 'stands as one of the earliest implicit justifications of the English Reformation'.

4.257 **Major**, J. M., *Sir Thomas Elyot and Renaissance Humanism*, Lincoln, Nebr., 1964. Explores the Renaissance setting of Elyot's principal work, *The Book Named the Gouvernour* (1531).

4.258 **Mason**, R. A., 'Knox, resistance and the moral imperative', *Hist. Pol. Thought*, 1980, 411–37. Analyses the contradiction involved in Knox's simultaneously wanting to establish a godly commonwealth on earth whose absence led him to develop a theory of resistance for the righteous and to affirm an overriding obligation to obey the powers that be.

4.259 —— 'Rex Stoicus: George Buchanan, James VI and the Scottish Polity', in J. Dwyer, R. A. Mason and A. Murdoch, ed., *New Perspectives on the Politics and Culture of Early Modern Scotland*, 1982, 9–33. On Buchanan's resistance theory.

4.260 **Mayer**, T. F., 'Faction and ideology: Thomas Starkey's *Dialogue*', *Hist. J.*, 28, 1985, 1–25. Attempt to recover Starkey's intentions in writing his *Dialogue between Reginald Pole and Thomas Lupset* which, according to Mayer, 'represents one of the first attempts to blend continental humanism . . . with native English traditions in the creation of a theoretical justification for . . . a "mixed state". In this and in the practical reform proposals which issued from it, Starkey went beyond Thomas More, however superior *Utopia* may be as a work of literature'.

4.261 —— *Thomas Starkey and the Commonwealth: Humanist Politics and Religion in the Reign of Henry VIII*, 1989.

Best treatment of an English humanist who vindicated the Henrician Reformation and advocated a programme of reform for both church and state.

4.262 —— 'Thomas Starkey, an unknown conciliarist at the court of Henry VIII', *J. Hist. Ideas*, 49, 1988, 207–27. Traces Starkey's belief in government by general council, whether ecclesiastical or secular, not to his reading of Marsilius of Padua – as is usually contended – but to his exposure to the ideas of conciliarists in contemporary Italy.

4.263 —— 'Thomas Starkey's aristocratic reform programme', *Hist. Pol. Thought*, 7, 1986, 439–63. Argues that Starkey, an 'oligarchical republican', a supporter of the aristocracy in English terms, successfully fitted much of his constitutional programme to their needs, to the goal of making the nobility responsible for its actions.

4.264 **Oakley**, F., 'On the road from Constance to 1688: the political thought of John Major and George Buchanan', *J. Brit. Sts.*, 2, 1962, 1–31. Demonstrates the affinity between Catholic conciliarism (represented by Major) and those sixteenth-century Protestant theories of resistance (of which Buchanan was an exponent) which were to become influential in seventeenth-century English thought.

4.265 **Peardon**, B., 'The politics of polemic: John Ponet's *Short Treatise of Politic Power* and contemporary circumstance, 1553–6', *J. Brit. Sts.*, 22, 1982, 35–49. On the ideas of a Marian exile who developed a Calvinist theory of popular revolution and tyrannicide.

4.266 **Rueger**, Z., 'Gerson's concept of equity and Christopher St. German', *Hist. Pol. Thought*, 3, 1982, 1–30. Argues that the Henrician juristic theorist took the doctrine of equity from the conciliarist Gerson.

4.267 **Shephard**, A., 'Henry Howard and the lawful regiment of women', *Hist. Pol. Thought*, 12, 1991, 589–603. Discusses the ideas of a Catholic aristocrat whose *A dutiful defense of the lawful regiment of weomen* repudiated patriarchy.

4.268 **Wollman**, D., 'The biblical justification for resistance to authority in Ponet's and Goodman's polemics', *Sixteenth Cent. J.*, 13, 1982, 29–41. Account of the ideas of

two Marian exiles who elaborated a Calvinist theory of resistance to tyranny.

(d) OTHER EUROPEAN COUNTRIES

General

4.269 **Baumgartner**, F. J., *Radical Reactionaries: The Political Thought of the French Catholic League*, Geneva, 1975. Study of a group of thinkers in the second half of the sixteenth century who asserted the authority of the papacy to depose heretical (i.e. Protestant) sovereigns.

4.270 **Beame**, E. M., 'The use and abuse of Machiavelli: the sixteenth century French adaptation', *J. Hist. Ideas*, 43, 1982, 33–54. Suggests that, though the attacks on Machiavelli were too widespread during the sixteenth century to label anti-Machiavellism a French phenomenon, there is nevertheless 'much truth to the notion that anti-Machiavellism, as a conscious political weapon, was forged in the fires of French political and religious conflict'.

4.271 **Bleznick**, D. W., 'Spanish reaction to Machiavelli in the sixteenth and seventeenth centuries', *J. Hist. Ideas*, 19, 1958, 542–50. Demonstrates that not all Spanish political writers were rabidly anti-Machiavellian.

4.272 **Church**, W. F., *Constitutional Thought in Sixteenth-Century France*, New York, 1969.

4.273 **Fernández-Santamaria**, J. A., *The State, War and Peace: Spanish Political Thought in the Renaissance, 1516–1559*, 1977. Demonstrates how 'the themes which the age inherited from the medieval tradition and which constitute the composite heart of Renaissance political theory' were extensively studied by Spanish writers such as Alonso de Castrillo, Francisco de Vitoria, Juan Gine's de Sepúlveda and Furió Ceriol.

4.274 **Giesey**, R. E., 'The monarchomach triumvirs: Hotman, Beza and Mornay', *Bibliothèque d'Humanisme et Renaissance*,

32, 1970, 41–56. On the architects of French Huguenot resistance theory.

4.275 **Griffiths**, G., 'Democratic ideas in the revolt of the Netherlands', *Archiv für Reformationsgeschichte*, 50, 1959, 50–63.

4.276 **Hamilton**, B., *Political Thought in Sixteenth-Century Spain. A Study of the Political Ideas of Vitoria, De Soto, Suarez and Molina*, 1963. Lucid survey of the political thought of four theologians who, in a country largely untouched by the ideas of the Protestant Reformation, refined Thomist philosophy.

4.277 **Hanley**, S., 'The *Discours politique* in monarchomaque ideology: resistance right in sixteenth century France', in *Assemblea di stati e istituzioni rappresentative nella storia del pensiero politico moderno*, Rimini, 1983, 121–34.

4.278 **Kelley**, D. R., 'Murd'rous Machiavelli in France: a post mortem', *Pol. Sc. Q.*, 85, 1970, 545–59. On the sixteenth-century reception of Machiavelli.

4.279 —— *The Beginning of Ideology: Consciousness and Society in the French Reformation*, 1981. Richly textured study of Theodore Beza, Peter Ramus and many other figures.

4.280 **Oakley**, F., 'Figgis, Constance, and the divines of Paris', *Am. Hist. Rev.*, 75, 1969, 368–86. Emphasises that the conciliarism of Pierre d'Ailly and Jean Gerson in the fifteenth century and John Major and Jacques Almain in the sixteenth century was less ambiguous than is sometimes contended.

4.281 **Salmon**, J. H. F., 'Cicero and Tacitus in sixteenth-century France', *Am. Hist. Rev.*, 85, 1980, 307–31.

4.282 —— *Society in Crisis: France in the Sixteenth Century*, 1975. Useful on Bodin, Huguenot ideas of popular sovereignty and other themes in French political thought.

4.283 **Van Gelderen**, M., 'A political theory of the Dutch Revolt and the *Vindiciae contra tyrannos*', *Il Pensiero Politico*, 19, 1986, 163–82.

4.284 —— 'Conceptions of liberty during the Dutch Revolt (1555–1590)', *Parliaments, Estates and Representation*, 7, 1987, 163–76.

4.285 —— 'The Machiavellian moment and the Dutch revolt: the rise of Neostoicism and Dutch republicanism', in G. Bock, Q. Skinner and M. Viroli, ed., *Machiavelli and Republicanism*, 1990, 205–23. On the Roman sources of republican ideas in the latter half of the sixteenth century.

4.286 —— *The Political Thought of the Dutch Revolt 1555–1590*, 1992. The only comprehensive study of the ideas used to justify resistance against Spanish rule.

4.287 **Yardeni**, M., 'French Calvinist political thought, 1534–1715', in M. Prestwich, ed., *International Calvinism, 1541–1715*, 1985, 315–38. The only comprehensive account of the period, emphasising two apparently opposed tendencies. 'On the one hand, there was fidelity to Calvin's ideas, and on the other hand, there was an unfailing pragmatism.'

Calvin

4.288 **Höpfl**, H., *The Christian Polity of John Calvin*, 1982. Comprehensive account of his political theology.

4.289 **Kingdon**, R. M., 'John Calvin's contribution to representative government', in R. Mack and M. C. Jacob, ed., *Politics and Culture in Early Modern Europe*, in *Essays in Honour of H. G. Koenigsberger*, 1987, 183–98.

4.290 **Lloyd**, H. A., 'Calvin and the duty of guardians to resist', *J. Eccl. Hist.*, 32, 1981, 65–7. Argues that for Calvin the authority of magistrates to resist tyranny derived from God rather than the will of the people.

4.291 **McNeill**, J. T., 'The democratic element in Calvin's thought', *Church Hist.*, 18, 1949, 153–71.

4.292 **Mueller**, W. A., *Church and State in Luther and Calvin: A Comparative Study*, Nashville, 1954.

4.293 **Ullmann**, W., 'Calvin and the duty of the guardians to resist: a further comment', *J. Eccl. Hist.*, 32, 1981, 499–501. Argues that Calvin's concept of sovereignty was both traditional and novel.

4.294 **Walzer**, M., *The Revolution of the Saints: A Study in the Origins of Radical Politics*, 1966. Primarily a study of seventeenth-century Puritanism, but with a brilliant chapter on Calvin's political thought.

4.295 **Wolin**, S. S., 'Calvin and the Reformation: the political education of Protestantism', *Am. Pol. Sc. Rev.*, 51, 1957, 428–53. Clear and penetrating account of his political thought.

Luther

4.296 **Benert**, R. R., 'Lutheran resistance theory and the imperial constitution', *Il Pensiero Politico*, 6, 1973, 17–36.

4.297 **Cargill Thompson**, W. D. J., *Studies in the Reformation: Luther to Hooker*, 1980. Includes an essay on 'Luther and the right of resistance to the Emperor' and a brilliant account of Luther's theology of the spiritual and temporal orders of government, 'The "Two Kingdoms" and the "Two Regiments": some problems of Luther's *zwei-Reiche, Lehre*.

4.298 —— *The Political Thought of Martin Luther*, 1984. The best introduction to the subject, arguing that Luther was a major political thinker whose ideas were the principal source of various divergent streams in later Protestant thought.

4.299 **Carlson**, E., 'Luther's conception of government', *Church Hist.*, 15, 1946, 257–70.

4.300 **Cranz**, F. E., *An Essay on the Development of Luther's Thought on Justice, Law and Society*, Cambridge, Mass., 1959. Careful analysis emphasising 1518 as a watershed in Luther's thinking, for it was then that he began to distinguish the two realms of Christian existence: the spiritual and temporal. Cranz illuminates the complex evolution of Luther's thought after 1518.

4.301 **Grimm**, H. J., 'Luther's conception of territorial and national loyalty', *Church Hist.*, 17, 1948, 79–94.

4.302 **Gritsch**, E., 'Martin Luther and violence: a reappraisal of a neuralgic theme', *Sixteenth Cent. J.*, 3, 1972, 37–56.

4.303 **Porter**, J. M., 'Luther and political millenarianism', *J. Hist. Ideas*, 42, 1981, 389–406. Not only an account of his response to political millenarianism, but a clear outline of his political thought generally.

4.304 **Rotstein**, A., 'Lordship and bondage in Luther and Marx', *Interpretation*, 8, 1979, 75–102.

4.305 **Shoenberger**, C. G., 'Luther and the justifiability of resistance to legitimate authority', *J. Hist. Ideas*, 40, 1979, 3–20. Traces the evolution of Luther's political thought from the 1520s to the 1540s to counter the common assumption that he never condoned any form of active resistance to oppressive political authority – though Shoenberger concedes that

Luther 'shied away from the democratic implications of resistance theories, upholding the right of the princes to resist the Emperor but denying a similar right to the princes' subjects'.

4.306 —— 'The development of the Lutheran theory of resistance: 1523–30', *Sixteenth Cent. J.*, 8, 1977, 61–76.

4.307 **Spitz**, L. W., 'Luther's ecclesiology and his concept of the Prince as *Notbischof*', *Church Hist.*, 22, 1953, 113–41.

4.308 **Wolin**, S. S., 'Politics and religion: Luther's simplistic imperative', *Am. Pol. Sc. Rev.*, 50, 1956, 24–42.

Bodin

4.309 **Bonney**, R., 'Bodin and the development of the French monarchy', *Trans. Royal Hist. Soc.*, 5th series, 40, 1990, 43–61.

4.310 **Burns**, J. H., 'Sovereignty and constitutional law in Bodin', *Pol. Sts.*, 7, 1959, 174–7. Argues that Bodin saw the necessity of basic norms of the political system, which he confusingly described as constitutional law.

4.311 **Denzer**, H., ed., *Jean Bodin: Proceedings of the International Conference on Bodin in Munich*, Munich, 1973. Collection of essays including R. E. Geisey, 'Medieval jurisprudence in Bodin's concept of sovereignty', W. H. Greenleaf, 'Bodin and the idea of order', R. W. K. Hinton, 'Bodin and the retreat into loyalism', D. R. Kelley, ' The development and context of Bodin's method', J. H. Franklin, 'Jean Bodin and the end of medieval constitutionalism', R. J. Schoeck, 'Bodin's opposition to the mixed state and to Thomas More' and H. D. McRae, 'Bodin and the development of empirical political science'.

4.312 **Franklin**, J. H., *Jean Bodin and the Rise of Absolutist Theory*, 1973. A short, sharp analysis, claiming that the absolutism of Bodin's *République* marked an abrupt departure from both his earlier views and the constitutionalism characteristic of French political thinking.

4.313 —— *Jean Bodin and the sixteenth-century revolution in the methodology of law and history*, New York, 1963. Uses Bodin to illustrate how the medieval exegesis of Roman law was undermined by Renaissance ideals, and of how this juristic revolution was related to the emergence of a general theory of historical criticism.

4.314 **King**, P., *The Ideology of Order: a Comparative Analysis of Jean Bodin and Thomas Hobbes*, 1974. Argues that Bodin's theory of absolutism is contradictory, whereas that of Hobbes is incomplete.

4.315 **Lewis**, J. W., 'Jean Bodin's "Logic of Sovereignty" ', *Pol. Sts.*, 26, 1968, 206–22. Emphasises Bodin's continuing preoccupation with just rule.

4.316 **Mosse**, G. L., 'The influence of Jean Bodin's *République* on English political thought', *Medievala et Humanistica*, 5, 1948, 73–83.

4.317 **Parker**, D., 'Law, society and the state in the thought of Jean Bodin', *Hist. Pol. Thought*, 2, 1981, 253–85. Critical of other scholars for 'treating Bodin as a primer for Hobbes which follows from laying undue stress on the novel and secular elements in his thought'. Bodin's political thinking is an aspect of his belief in a divinely regulated, hierarchical universe.

4.318 **Rose**, P. L., *Bodin and the Great God of Nature. The Moral and Religious Universe of a Judaiser*, Geneva, 1980. Claims that a 'religious aura' permeates all his writings with Judaistic influences becoming increasingly evident in his intellectual development.

4.319 —— 'Bodin's universe and its paradoxes: some problems in the intellectual biography of Jean Bodin', in E. I. Kouri and T. Scott, ed., *Politics and Society in Reformation Europe*, 1987, 266–88.

4.320 **Tentler**, T. N., 'The meaning of prudence in Bodin', *Traditio*, 15, 1959, 365–84.

4.321 **Wolfe**, M., 'Jean Bodin on taxes: the sovereignty-taxes paradox', *Pol. Sc. Q.*, 83, 1968, 268–84.

Montaigne

4.322 **Brown**, F. S., *Religious and Political Conservatism in the Essays of Montaigne*, Geneva, 1963. Demonstrates that his conservatism arose not only from the French civil and religious wars of the sixteenth century but from his scepticism and his conviction that the preservation of established institutions was essential to public order and individual liberty.

4.323 **Burke**, P., *Montaigne*, 1981. Reliable intellectual biography of the French essayist who, influenced by Stoicism, took a sceptical view of politics, arguing that disputes about the best form of government were fruitless.

4.324 **Clark**, C. E., 'Montaigne and the imagery of political discourse in sixteenth-century France', *French Studies*, 24, 1970, 337–54.

4.325 **Keohane**, N. O., 'Montaigne's individualism', *Pol. Theory*, 5, 1977, 363–90. Mines the political themes in Montaigne's *Essays*.

4.326 **Schaefer**, D. L., 'Montaigne's political reformation', *J. Pol.*, 42, 1980, 766–91.

4.327 —— 'Montaigne's political skepticism', *Polity*, 11, 1979, 512–41.

4.328 —— 'Of cannibals and kings: Montaigne' egalitarianism', *Rev. Pol.*, 43, 1981, 43–74. Claims that Montaigne's political thought was fundamentally more radical than is usually acknowledged, and that hi professed conservatism was a device to protect himself against the charge of heterodoxy.

4.329 —— *The Political Philosophy of Montaigne* Ithaca, N.Y., 1990. Comprehensive account portraying him as more consisten and systematic than is usually acknowledged, and as an early philosophi architect of modern liberalism.

Other thinkers

4.330 **Burns**, J. H., '*Jus gladii* and *jurisdictio*: Jacques Almain and John Locke', *Hist. J.* 26, 1983, 369–74. Argues that Almain, who is sometimes said to have influenced Locke, failed to 'integrate the potentially radical individualism of his theory of rights with the "communitarian" radicalism which characterises his theory of political society'.

4.331 **Carro**, V., 'The Spanish theological – juridical Renaissance and the ideology of Bartolomé de las Casas', in J. Friede and B. Keen, ed., *Bartolomé de las Casas*, De Kalb, Ill., 1971, 236–75.

4.332 **Costello**, F. B., *The Political Philosophy of Luis de Molina, SJ. (1535–1600)*, Rome, 1974.

4.333 **D'Andrea**, A., 'The political context of Innocent Gentillet's Anti-Machiavel', *Ren. Q.*, 23, 1970, 397–411. On Gentillet's debt to the *Monarchomachi* in writing his *Contre-Machiavel* (1576), the prototype of the anti-Machiavellian treatise.

4.334 **Echard**, G., 'The Erasmian ideal of kingship, as reflected in the work of Ronsard and d'Aubigne', *Renaissance and Reformation*, 5, 1981, 26–39.

4.335 **Fernández**, J. A., 'Erasmus on the just war', *J. Hist. Ideas*, 34, 1973, 209–26. Locates Erasmus's discussion of the problem of war within the context of his general political theory.

4.336 **Franklin**, J. H., 'Constitutionalism in the sixteenth century: the Protestant Monarchomachs', in D. Spitz, ed., *Political Theory and Social Change*, New York, 1967, 117–32.

4.337 **Gamble**, R. C., 'The Christian and the tyrant: Beza and Knox on political resistance theory', *Westminster Theol. J.*, 46, 1984, 125–39.

4.338 **Kelley**, D. R., *François Hotman: A Revolutionary's Ordeal*, Princeton, N.J., 1973. Study of the leading proponent in late sixteenth-century France of a Calvinist theory of resistance to Catholic tyranny.

4.339 **Kingdon**, R. M., 'The first expression of Theodore Beza's political ideas', *Archiv für Reformationsgeschichte*, 46, 1955, 88–100.

4.340 **Lewy**, G., *Constitutionalism and Statecraft during the Golden Age of Spain: a Study of the Political Philosophy of Juan de Mariana, SJ.*, Geneva, 1960. Study of a leading Jesuit political thinker whose *De rege et egis institutione* (1599) justified tyrannicide.

4.341 **Linder**, R. D., 'Pierre Viret and the sixteenth century French Protestant revolutionary tradition', *J. Mod. Hist.*, 38, 1966, 125–37.

4.342 —— *The Political Ideas of Pierre Viret*, Geneva, 1964. Study of a Swiss theologian who shaped the Calvinist theory of resistance to tyranny.

4.343 **Lloyd**, H. A., 'The political thought of Charles Loyseau (1564–1627)', *Eur. Sts. Rev.*, 11, 1981, 53–82. Account of the ideas of a French proponent of political absolutism.

4.344 **Oakley**, F., 'Almain and Major: conciliar theory on the eve of the Reformation, *Am. Hist. Rev.*, 70, 1965, 673–90. Demonstrates through these two writers, one French and the other Scottish, that the medieval theory of ecclesiastical constitutionalism was still vibrant in the early sixteenth century.

4.345 —— 'Disobedience, consent, political obligation: the witness of Wessel Gansfort (c.1419–1489)', *Hist. Pol. Thought*, 9, 1988, 211–21. Considers the political ideas of a Dutch theologian who, according to Oakley, 'came closer' than any other medieval thinker to applying a 'contractarian model to secular political society'.

4.346 **Pagden**, A., 'Dispossessing the barbarian: the language of Spanish Thomism and the debate over the property rights of the American Indians', in A. Pagden, ed., *The Languages of Political Theory in Early-Modern Europe*, 1987, 79–98.

4.347 **Perry**, D., ' "Catholicum opus imperiale regiminis mundi". An early sixteenth-century restatement of empire', *Hist. Pol. Thought*, 2, 1981, 227–52. Analysis of a tract by a Spanish writer, Michael de Ulcurrunus, who revived the medieval idea of imperial absolutism.

4.348 **Southgate**, W. M., 'Erasmus: Christian humanism and political theory', *History*, 40, 1955, 240–54. Neat exposition of Erasmus's political thought arguing that, though he was neither original nor systematic, his writings nevertheless convey in a particularly clear manner the transition from medieval to modern political thinking.

4.349 **Tracy**, J. D., *The Politics of Erasmus: A Pacifist Intellectual and His Political Milieu*, Toronto, 1978. A study of the political commentary scattered through his writings.

4.350 **Wilenius**, R., *The Social and Political Theory of Francisco Suarez*, Helsinki, 1963.

5

SEVENTEENTH CENTURY

(a) GENERAL

5.1 **Holstoun**, J., *A Rational Millenium: Puritan Utopias of Seventeenth-Century England and America*, New York, 1987. Considers, among others, John Eliot and James Harrington.

5.2 **Tuck**, R., *Natural Rights Theories: Their Origin and Development*, 1979. Sophisticated and influential analysis of the emergence of the discourse of natural rights, with chapters on the Middle Ages and the Renaissance, but paying particular attention to seventeenth-century thinkers such as Grotius, Selden and Hobbes.

5.3 —— *Philosophy and Government 1572–1651*, 1993. Charts the formation of a modern political vocabulary, based upon arguments of political necessity and 'raison d'état' in the work of thinkers such as Hobbes, Grotius and Montaigne.

(b) BRITISH ISLES

General

5.4 **Appleby**, J., 'Ideology and theory: the tension between political and economic liberalism in seventeenth-century England', *Am. Hist. Rev.*, 81, 1976, 499–515. Argues that new ideas of universal economic rationality were not reflected in political theory because they challenged the ideological imperatives of a hierarchical and paternalistic society.

5.5 **Aylmer**, G. E., 'The meaning and definition of "property" in seventeenth-century England', *Past & Pres.*, 86, 1980, 87–97.

5.6 **Bradford**, A. T., 'Stuart absolutism and the "utility" of Tacitus', *Huntington Libr. Q.*, 46, 1983, 127–55.

5.7 **Brenman**, T and **Pateman**, C., ' "Mere auxiliaries to the commonwealth": women and the origins of liberalism', *Pol. Sts.*, 27, 1979, 183–200. Critique of early social contract theorists, particularly Hobbes and Locke, for compromising with patriarchal assumptions.

5.8 **Burgess**, G., 'Common law and political theory in early Stuart England', *Pol. Sc.*, 40, 1988, 4–17. On the widespread assumption that the principles of common law were sufficient to deal with all national political issues.

5.9 —— 'The divine right of kings reconsidered', *Eng. Hist. Rev.*, 107, 1992, 837–61. Argues that the doctrine of the divine right of kings in early Stuart discourse was neither necessarily absolutist in its implications nor essentially a doctrine of sovereignty: 'rather it was a theory of *obligation*, concerned primarily with the need to demonstrate to both rulers and subjects their duties to God'.

5.10 —— *The Politics of the Ancient Constitution, an Introduction to English Political Thought, 1603–1642*, 1992. Primarily a study of the political ideas of the common lawyers, including Coke and Selden, but perceptive on early Stuart thought in general.

5.11 **Burtt**, S., *Virtue Transformed: Political Argument in England, 1688–1740*, 1992. Traces the evolution of a privately orientated conception of civic virtue.

5.12 **Christianson**, P., 'Political thought in early Stuart England', *Hist. J.*, 30, 1987, 955–71.

5.13 —— 'Royal parliamentary voices on the ancient constitution, c.1604–1621', in L. L. Peck, ed., *The Mental World of the Jacobean Court*, 1991, 71–95. Challenges the assumption that for the early Stuarts, divine right meant absolutism, which in turn meant arbitrary rule by the crown, arguing that constitutional debates 'more often pitted rival versions of the ancient constitution against each other than theories of absolutism versus constitutionalism'.

5.14 **Daly**, J., 'Cosmic harmony and political thinking in early Stuart England', *Trans. Am. Phil. Soc.*, 69, pt.7, 1979, 3–41. Explores the impact upon political thought of the prevalent belief that the universe assumed the form of a Great Chain of Being, and is critical of Greenleaf, *Order, Empiricism and Politics*, for suggesting that the principle of cosmic harmony was used to advocate arbitrary monarchy.

5.15 —— 'The idea of absolute monarchy in seventeenth-century England', *Hist. J.*, 21, 1978, 227–50.

5.16 **Davis**, J. C., *Utopia and the ideal society: A study of English utopian writing 1516–1700*, 1981. Chapters on Robert Burton, Francis Bacon, Samuel Gott, Gerrard Winstanley and James Harrington.

5.17 **Edie**, C. A., 'Succession and monarchy: the controversy of 1679–1681', *Am. Hist. Rev.*, 70, 1964, 350–70. Useful survey of the pamphlet literature accompanying the Exclusion crisis.

5.18 **Furley**, O. W., 'The Whig Exclusionists: pamphlet literature in the Exclusionist campaign, 1679–81', *Cambridge Hist. J.*, 13, 1957, 19–36.

5.19 **Goldie**, M., 'Priestcraft and the birth of Whiggism', in N. Phillipson and Q. Skinner, ed., *Political Discourse in Early Modern Britain*, 1993, 209–31. Sharp account of Whig ecclesiology in the later seventeenth century.

5.20 **Goodale**, J. R., 'J. G. A. Pocock's neo-Harringtonians: a re-consideration', *Hist.*

Pol. Thought, 1, 1980, 237–59. Critique of Pocock's interpretation of those seventeenth- and eighteenth-century thinkers who, like Harrington, used the tenets of civic humanism in commenting upon English society and government.

5.21 **Gough**, J. W., *Fundamental Law in English Constitutional Thought*, 1955. Principal focus of the book is the seventeenth century.

5.22 **Greenberg**, J. R., 'Our grand maxim of state, "the king can do no wrong" ', *Hist. Pol. Thought*, 12, 1991, 209–28. On seventeenth-century interpretations of the maxim.

5.23 —— 'The Confessor's laws and the radical face of the ancient constitution', *Eng. Hist. Rev.*, 104, 1989, 611–37. Demonstrates how opponents of Stuart kingship frequently forged their radical versions of the ancient constitution from the so-called laws of Edward the Confessor and other medieval sources.

5.24 **Greenleaf**, W. H., 'James I and the divine right of kings', *Pol. Sts.*, 5, 1957, 36–48. Crisp account of the doctrine of regal absolutism.

5.25 —— *Order, Empiricism and Politics: Two Traditions of English political thought, 1500–1700*, 1964. Excellent account of the thinking of the period with chapters on James I, Edward Forset, Filmer, Francis Bacon, James Harrington and William Petty.

5.26 **Gunn**, J. A. W., *Politics and the Public Interest in the Seventeenth Century*, 1969. Illuminating account of conceptions of the public interest, focusing on the growth of a philosophy of individualism.

5.27 **Harris**, T., ' "Lives, liberties and estates": rhetorics of liberty in the reign of Charles II', in T. Harris, P. Seaward, and M. Goldie, ed., *The Politics of Religion in Restoration England*, 1990, 217–41.

5.28 **Harvey**, R., 'The problem of social–political obligation for the Church of England in the seventeenth century', *Church Hist.*, 40, 1971, 156–69. On the preoccupation in clerical writings with social hierarchy and religious uniformity.

5.29 **Hill**, C., *Intellectual Origins of the English Revolution*, 1965. Lively account of the ideological background of the Revolution with chapters on 'Francis Bacon and the parliamentarians', 'Ralegh, science, history, and politics' and 'Sir Edward

Coke – myth-maker'.

5.30 —— 'The Norman Yoke', in *Puritanism and Revolution*, 1968, 58–125. Brilliant exploration of the belief of the Levellers and others that the Norman Conquest had deprived the English of their ancient liberties by subjecting them to the tyranny of an alien monarchy and to the oppression of landowners.

5.31 **Judson**, M. A., *The Crisis of the Constitution: an essay in constitutional and political thought, 1603–45*, New Brunswick, N.J., 1949. Probably still one of the best general accounts of early Stuart political ideas, though she exaggerates the extent to which the Civil War period secularised political discourse.

5.32 **Klein**, W., 'The ancient constitution revisited', in N. Phillipson and Q. Skinner, ed., *Political Discourse in Early Modern Britain*, 1993, 23–44. Critical of J. G. A. Pocock for probing pre-Restoration constitutional debate for signs of a prefiguration of Whig and Tory arguments.

5.33 **Levack**, B. P., 'Law and ideology: the civil law and theories of absolutism in Elizabethan and Jacobean England', in H. Dubrow and R. Strier, ed., *The Historical Renaissance: New Essays on Tudor and Stuart Literature and Culture*, Chicago, Ill., 1988, 220–41. Argues that civil law was a more important source than is usually acknowledged of new constitutional ideas, and that it played a part in the transition from the Tudor celebration of mixed government to the Stuart emphasis upon the power of monarchy.

5.34 **Macpherson**, C. B., *The Political Theory of Possessive Individualism, Hobbes to Locke*, 1962. Brilliant and controversial study suggesting that Hobbes, Locke, the Levellers and Harrington were laying the philosophical foundations of a market society.

5.35 **Nederman**, C. J., 'Bracton on kingship first visited: the idea of sovereignty and Bractonian political thought in seventeenth-century England', *Pol. Sc.*, 40, 1988, 49–66. On the ways in which Filmer, Hobbes, Milton and Sidney reconstructed 'the conception of kingship and government in *De Legibus* with reference to a distinctively modern theory of sovereignty (construed as inalienable, and indivisible)'.

5.36 **O'Buachalla**, B., 'James our true king: the ideology of Irish royalism in the seventeenth century', in D. G. Boyce, R. R. Eccleshall and V. Geoghegan, ed., *Irish Political Thought Since the Seventeenth Century*, 1993, 7–35.

5.37 **Oakley**, F., 'From Constance to 1688 revisited', *J. Hist. Ideas*, 27, 1966, 429–32. Stresses the widespread influence of conciliar ideas upon seventeenth-century English political thought.

5.38 —— 'Jacobean political theology: the absolute and ordinary powers of the king', *J. Hist. Ideas*, 29, 1968, 323–46. Traces the medieval origins of the early seventeenth-century distinction between absolute power – in which the king is not bound by the laws of the land – and ordinary power in which the king is bound by common law and parliament, arguing that the distinction was essentially an exercise in political theology with a more intricate history than is usually recognised.

5.39 —— 'The "hidden" and "revealed" wills of James I: more political theology', *Studia Gratiana*, 41, 1972, 365–75.

5.40 **Pocock**, J. G. A., 'Authority and property: the question of liberal origins', in B. C. Malament, ed., *After the Reformation: Essays in Honor of J. H. Hexter*, 1980, 331–51. A sharp critique, elaborated more fully in Pocock's other writings, of historians who identify in seventeenth-century English political thought the origins of liberal or bourgeois ideology.

5.41 —— *The Ancient Constitution and the Feudal Law: A Study of English Historical Thought in the Seventeenth Century*, 1957. Classic study arguing that there was an insular, a-historical common law tradition of thinking.

5.42 **Salmon**, J. H. M., *The French Religious Wars in English Political Thought*, 1959. Illustrates how during moments of turmoil – the Civil War, the Exclusion crisis and the Revolution of 1688 – thinkers drew analogies between the upheavals of their own country and those of France in the sixteenth century.

5.43 **Sampson**, M., 'Laxity and liberty in seventeenth-century English political thought', in E. Leites, ed., *Conscience and Casuistry in Early Modern Europe*, 1988, 72–118. Argues that Protestant casuistry, by popularising juristic concepts, alerted the laity to rights against government.

5.44 **Sanderson**, J., 'Conrad Russell's ideas', *Hist. Pol. Thought*, 14, 1993, 85–102. Takes issue with Russell's revisionist thesis that there were no deep ideological divisions in the first half of the seventeenth century.

5.45 **Schochet**, G. J., *Patriarchalism in Political Thought: the authoritarian family and political speculation in seventeenth-century England*, 1975. Authoritative account, particularly of Filmer.

5.46 —— 'Patriarchalism, politics and mass attitudes in Stuart England', *Hist. J.*, 12, 1969, 413–41.

5.47 **Scott**, J., 'The law of war: Grotius, Sidney, Locke and the political theory of rebellion', *Hist. Pol. Thought*, 13, 1992, 565–85. Argues that Locke and Sidney are much closer than is usually assumed in justifying resistance, because both drew on Grotius's *The Laws of War and Peace*.

5.48 **Shanley**, M. L., 'Marriage contract and social contract in seventeenth century English political thought', *West. Pol. Q.*, 32, 1979, 79–91. Whereas in the 1640s nearly all writers spoke of the contractual element in marriage as the consent to a status which was hierarchical and unalterable, by 1690 Locke suggested that there was nothing inherent in the contracting of marriage which dictated women's subordination to men.

5.49 **Sommerville**, J. P., 'From Suarez to Filmer: a reappraisal', *Hist. J.*, 25, 1982, 525–40. Suggests that Catholic political theory was more radically constitutionalist than is usually supposed, which was why English royalists generally, not merely Filmer, were provoked into repudiating contractualism with a patriarchal political theory.

5.50 —— 'History and theory: the Norman Conquest in early Stuart political thought', *Pol. Sts.*, 34, 1986, 249–61. Critical of the orthodox view that political thought before 1640 was characteristically historical rather than philosophical, demonstrating through an examination of conceptions of the ancient constitution that theory frequently took precedence over history.

5.51 —— 'Ideology, property and constitution', in R. Cust and A. Hughes, ed., *Conflict in Early Stuart England 1603–1642*, 1989, 47–71. Challenges recent suggestions that there was broad unity on constitutional issues, arguing that there was an ideological rift on the question of whether kings derived their powers from God or the people.

5.52 —— 'James I and the divine right of kings: English politics and continental theory', in L. L. Peck, ed., *The Mental World of the Jacobean Court*, 1991, 55–70. Excellent account of his political ideas and their relation to continental controversies.

5.53 —— *Politics and Ideology in England, 1603–40*, 1986. Readable and perhaps the best account of the political ideas of the early Stuart period.

5.54 **Straka**, G. M., 'Revolutionary ideology in Stuart England', in P. J. Korshin, ed., *Studies in Change and Revolution*, 1971, 3–17.

5.55 **Taft**, B., 'That lusty puss, the good old cause', *Hist. Pol. Thought*, 5, 1984, 447–69. Analysis of radical politics in England between the end of the Civil Wars and the "Glorious Revolution", of the catch-phrase which became the common cry of those who rejected the regal rule of the Cromwellian Protectorate and concluded that their rights and liberties could only be secured by a supreme legislator elected by the people untrammelled by lords, kings or any single executive.

5.56 **Thompson**, M. P., 'A note on "reason" and "history" in late seventeenth century political thought', *Pol. Theory*, 4, 1976, 491–504. Argues that historical and philosophical styles of argument were not mutually exclusive; in Whig arguments of the period history and reason were usually interwoven.

5.57 **Tuck**, R., '*Power* and *authority* in seventeenth-century England', *Hist. J.*, 17, 1974, 43–61. Traces the dissolution of the old terminology of power in political thinking.

5.58 **Walzer**, M., *The Revolution of the Saints: A Study in the Origins of Radical Politics*, 1966. Brilliant study of the ideology of seventeenth-century Puritanism.

5.59 **Weston**, C. C., 'Concepts of estates in Stuart political thought', *Studies Presented to the International Commission for the History of Representative and Parliamentary Institutions*, 39, 1970, 87–130.

5.60 —— 'Legal sovereignty in the Brady controversy', *Hist. J.*, 15, 1972, 409–31. On the differences in the 1680s between the Tory assertion of indivisible regal authority and the Whig contention that the monarch shared a co-ordinate authority with the two houses of parliament.

5.61 —— 'The theory of mixed monarchy under Charles I and after', *Eng. Hist. Rev.*, 75, 1960, 426–43.

5.62 —— and **Greenberg**, J. R., *Subjects and Sovereigns: The Grand Controversy over Legal Sovereignty in Stuart England*, 1981. Comprehensive account of political thinking from the 1640s until the Revolution of 1688, focusing on the divergences between proponents of royal absolutism and those who argued that the monarch exercised a co-ordinate authority in conjunction with the two houses of parliament.

5.63 **Willman**, R., 'The origins of "Whig" and "Tory" in English political language', *Hist. J.*, 17, 1974, 247–64. Traces the emergence of the concepts during the Exclusion crisis.

5.64 **Wootton**, D, ed., *Divine Right and Democracy: An Anthology of Political Writings in Stuart England*, 1986. Contains a long and useful introductory essay.

5.65 **Wormald**, J., 'James VI and I, *Basilikon Doron* and the Trew Law of Free Monarchies: the Scottish context and the English translation', in L. L. Peck, ed., *The Mental World of the Jacobean Court*, 1991, 36–54. Compelling account of James's political theory, and also of its varied reception in England and Scotland.

Civil War and Commonwealth

5.66 **Baskerville**, S., *Not Peace but a Sword: The Political Theology of the English Revolution*, 1993. Explores the link between Calvinism and political radicalism, primarily through a reading of the sermons preached during the Long Parliament.

5.67 **Burgess**, G., 'The impact on political thought: rhetorics for troubled times', in J. S. Morrill, ed., *The Impact of the English Civil War*, 1991.

5.68 —— 'Usurpation, obligation and obedience in the thought of the Engagement controversy', *Hist. J.*, 29, 1986, 515–36. Analysis of the *de facto* arguments in favour of allegiance to the Commonwealth, and of the Presbyterian counter-arguments of Edward Gee.

5.69 **Capp**, B., 'The Fifth Monarchists and popular millenarianism', in J. F.

McGregor and B. Reay, *Radical Religion in the English Revolution*, 1984, 165–89.

5.70 —— *The Fifth Monarchy Men: A Study in Seventeenth-century English millenarianism*, 1972. Account of a movement of the 1650s claiming the right to overthrow existing regimes in order to establish a godly discipline.

5.71 **Coltman**, I., *Private Men and Public Causes: Philosophy and Politics in the English Civil War*, 1962. Focuses on the Tew Circle (particularly Clarendon) and Anthony Ascham.

5.72 **Davis**, J. C., 'Radicalism in a traditional society: the evaluation of radical thought in the English commonwealth 1649–60', *Hist. Pol. Thought*, 3, 1982, 193–215.

5.73 **Dow**, F. D., *Radicalism in the English Revolution, 1640–1660*, 1985. Short, readable and reliable introduction with chapters on parliamentarians, the Levellers and the Diggers.

5.74 **Goldsmith**, M. M., 'Levelling by sword, spade and word: radical egalitarianism in the English Revolution', in C. Jones, M. Newitt and S. Roberts, ed., *Politics and People in Revolutionary England*, 1986, 65–80.

5.75 **Hill**, C., *The World Turned Upside Down: Radical Ideas During the English Revolution*, 1975. Magisterial account of the political ideas of radical groups and sects in the 1640s and 1650s, including the Levellers, Diggers, Fifth Monarchists, Seekers, Ranters and Quakers.

5.76 **Judson**, M. A., *From Tradition to Political Reality: A Study of the Ideas set forth in support of the Commonwealth Government in England, 1649–1653*, Hamden, Conn., 1980.

5.77 **Kishlansky**, M. A., 'Ideology and politics in the parliamentary armies, 1645–9', in J. S. Morrill, ed., *Reactions to the English Civil War, 1642–1649*, 1982, 163–84. Demonstrates from a survey of public manifestos that there were three elements in the army's ideology: all Englishmen had inherent liberties and birthrights; the authority of government resided in parliament; and private interest ought to be subordinated to the common good.

5.78 **Manning**, B. S., 'Puritanism and democracy 1640–1642', in D. Pennington and K. Thomas, ed., *Puritans and Revolutionaries: Essays in Seventeenth-century History presented to Christopher Hill*,

1978, 139–60. On the democratic ideas of religious sects that bubbled to the surface on the eve of Civil War.

5.79 **Mendle**, M., *Dangerous Positions: Mixed Government, The Estates of the Realm, and the Answer to the XIX Propositions*, Alabama, Ala., 1985. Account of the background to Charles I's admission in 1642 that English government consisted of a mixture of monarchy, aristocracy and democracy, a concession that encouraged a flurry of radical constitutional ideas in the civil war period.

5.80 —— 'Parliamentary sovereignty: a very English absolutism', in N. Phillipson and Q. Skinner, ed., *Political Discourse in Early Modern Britain*, 1993, 97–119. On the doctrine of parliamentary sovereignty that emerged on the eve of Civil War, a mirror image, according to Mendle, of the theory of royal absolutism.

5.81 —— 'Politics and political thought 1640–1642', in C. Russell, ed., *The Origins of the English Civil War*, 1973, 219–45. On the emergence of the idea that sovereignty lay with the king-in-parliament.

5.82 **Pocock**, J. G. A., 'Political thought in the Cromwellian interregnum', in G. A. Wood and P. S. O'Connor, ed., *W. P. Morrell: A Tribute*, Dunedin, 1973, 21–36. Highlights the 'conceptual breakthroughs' of the period.

5.83 **Sanderson**, J., *'But the people's creatures': The Philosophical Basis of the English Civil War*, 1989. Crisp and readable – probably the best introduction to the period – with chapters on parliamentarian and royalist theories, Dudley Digges, Hobbes, the Levellers and Milton.

5.84 —— 'The *Answer to the Nineteen Propositions* Revisited', *Pol. Sts.*, 32, 1984, 627–36. On royalist polemics on the eve of Civil War, and in particular a critique of the interpretation by C. C. Weston and J. R. Greenberg, in *Subjects and Sovereigns*, of the concession by Charles I that his legislative authority was shared with the other two estates of the realm.

5.85 **Sharp**, A., *Political ideas of the English Civil Wars 1641–1649*, 1983. Collection of extracts prefaced by an introductory essay.

5.86 **Wallace**, J. M., 'The engagement controversy 1649–1652: an annotated list of pamphlets', *Bull. N.Y. Pub. Lib.*, 68, 1964, 384–405. Useful compilation with brief summaries of the contents of each tract.

5.87 **Weston**, C. C., 'Co-ordination: a radicalising principle in Stuart politics', in M. C. Jacob and J. Jacob, ed., *The Origins of Anglo-American Radicalism*, 1984, 85–104. On the emergence in the 1640s of the idea that sovereignty was exercised by the co-ordinate authority of the three estates of the realm.

5.88 **Woolrych**, A., 'Political theory and political practice', in C. A. Patrides and R. B. Waddington, ed., *The Age of Milton: Backgrounds to Seventeenth-Century Literature*, 1980, 34–71.

5.89 **Wootton**, D., 'The crisis of the winter of 1642/3 and the origins of civil war radicalism', *Eng. Hist. Rev.*, 105, 1990, 654–69. Whereas most historians identify 1646 as the year in which novel ideas appeared during the civil war period, Wootton argues that the winter of 1642/3 saw a dress rehearsal for the Leveller radicalism of four years later; the willingness of pamphleteers in 1642 to contemplate the destruction of the ancient constitution paved the way, in an ideological sense, from rebellion to revolution.

5.90 **Worden**, B., 'Classical republicanism and the Puritan Revolution', in H. Lloyd-Jones, V. Pearl and B. Worden, ed., *History and Imagination: Essays in Honour of H. R. Trevor Roper*, 1981, 182–200. Lucid survey of republicanism up to the Restoration.

5.91 **Zagorin**, P., *A History of Political Thought in the English Revolution*, 1954. Dated and sometimes perfunctory in its treatment of particular thinkers, but still a useful comprehensive survey of political thinking between 1640 and 1660.

The Revolution of 1688

5.92 **Eccleshall**, R. R., 'Anglican political thought in the century after the revolution of 1688', in D. G. Boyce, R. R. Eccleshall and V. Geoghegan, ed., *Political Thought in Ireland Since the Seventeenth Century*, 1993, 36–72. Shows how the Irish establishment was more inclined than English thinkers to characterise the Revolution in Lockean terms as a dissolution of government.

5.93 **Goldie**, M., 'Edmund Bohun and *Jus Gentium* in the Revolution debate', *Hist.*

J., 20, 1977, 569–86. Sophisticated analysis of how from 1688 to 1693 some writers, particularly Bohun, contended that William's title to the throne was conferred by just conquest.

5.94 —— 'The political thought of the Anglican Revolution', in R. Beddard, ed., *The Revolutions of 1688*, 1991, 102–36. Perceptive analysis not of the allegiance debate that followed the Glorious Revolution, but of the political theology of Anglican opposition to James in the preceding three years – demonstrating in particular the Church's recourse to the traditional doctrine of passive resistance.

5.95 —— 'The Revolution of 1689 and the structure of political argument: An essay and an annotated bibliography of pamphlets on the allegiance controversy', *Bulletin of Research in the Humanities*, 83, 1980, 473–564. Indispensable bibliography and guide to the various political arguments.

5.96 —— 'The roots of true whiggism 1688–94', *Hist. Pol. Thought*, 1, 1980, 195–236. Exploration of the ideas of a group of agitators, active in the Revolution, through whom radical and commonwealth whiggism was transmitted to the eighteenth century.

5.97 **Kenyon**, J. P., *Revolution Principles: The Politics of Party, 1689–1720*, 1977. Wide-ranging and sophisticated account of Whig and Tory political ideas from the Revolution to the Hanoverian succession.

5.98 —— 'The Revolution of 1688: resistance and contract', in N. McKendrick, ed., *Historical Perspectives: Studies in English Thought and Society, in honour of J. H. Plumb*, 1974, 43–69. On Whig and Tory explanations of the events of 1688 in the decades before the Hanoverian succession.

5.99 **Lenman**, B. P., 'The poverty of political theory in the Scottish Revolution of 1688–90', in L. G. Schwoerer, ed., *The Revolution of 1688–1689: Changing perspectives*, 1992, 244–59.

5.100 **McGuire**, J. I., 'The Church of Ireland and the "Glorious Revolution" of 1688', in A. Cosgrove and D. McCartney, ed., *Studies in Irish History presented to R. Dudley Edwards*, Dublin, 1979, 137–49. Analysis of the way in which Irish churchmen justified allegiance to the new regime, focusing on the political arguments of Edward Wetenhall and William King.

5.101 **Miller**, J., 'The Glorious Revolution: "contract" and "abdication" reconsidered', *Hist. J.*, 25, 1982, 541–55. Criticism of the argument of T. P. Slaughter, ' "Abdicate" and "contract" in the Glorious Revolution', *Hist. J.*, 24, 1981, 323–37, that both lords and commons understood James's 'abdication' as implying his deposition for breaking the original contract and deserting his kingdom.

5.102 **Monod**, P. K., *Jacobitism and the English people, 1688–1788*, 1989. Demonstrates how political arguments in favour of the exiled Stuarts assumed various ideological forms, not merely nonjuring absolutism.

5.103 **Pocock**, J. G. A., 'The fourth English civil war: dissolution, desertion and alternative histories in the Glorious Revolution', *Govt & Oppos.*, 23, 1988, 151–66. Imaginative construction of the ideological responses which the Revolution of 1688 might have generated had it been similar to the bloody conflict of the 1640s.

5.104 **Schwoerer**, L. G., *The Declaration of Rights, 1689*, Baltimore, Md. 1981. Includes a useful discussion of the political debates accompanying the Revolution.

5.105 —— ed., *The Revolution of 1688–1689: Changing Perspectives*, 1992. Includes J. G. A. Pocock, 'The fourth English civil war: dissolution, desertion, and alternative histories in the Glorious Revolution', G. Schochet, 'John Locke and religious toleration' and B. P. Lenman, 'The poverty of political theory in the Scottish Revolution of 1688–1690'.

5.106 —— 'The right to resist: Whig resistance theory, 1688 to 1694', in N. Phillipson and Q. Skinner ed., *Political Discourse in Early Modern Britain*, 1993, 232–52.

5.107 **Slaughter**, T. P., ' "Abdicate" and "contract" in the Glorious Revolution', *Hist. J.*, 24, 1981, 323–37. Argues, contrary to other historians, that 'abdicate' was interpreted in parliamentary debates as the forcible deposition of James.

5.108 —— ' "Abdicate" and "contract" restored', *Hist. J.*, 28, 1985, 399–403.

5.109 **Straka**, G. M., *Anglican Reaction to the Revolution of 1688*. Madison, Wis., 1962. A dated but still valuable guide to the political doctrines of the period.

5.110 —— 'The final phase of divine right theory in England, 1688–1702', *Eng. Hist. Rev.*, 77, 1962, 638–58. Slightly misleading title because the article is primarily a study of how the Revolution of 1688 was interpreted as a providential intervention in human affairs – nevertheless a seminal and still useful study.

5.111 **Thompson**, M. P., 'The idea of conquest in controversies over the 1688 Revolution', *J. Hist. Ideas*, 38, 1977. Highlights how from 1688 to 1693 both supporters and opponents of the Revolution depicted William as conqueror.

Filmer

5.112 **Daly**, J., *Sir Robert Filmer and English Political Thought*, Toronto, 1979. Comprehensive and perceptive, though he exaggerates Filmer's originality.

5.113 —— 'Some problems in the authorship of Sir Robert Filmer's works', *Eng. Hist. Rev.*, 98, 1983, 737–47. Argues, contrary to Weston, that Filmer rather than Holbourne wrote *The Freeholders Grand Inquest*.

5.114 **Geisst**, C. R., 'The Aristotelian motif in Filmer's *Patriarcha*', *Pol. Sts.*, 21, 1973, 490–99.

5.115 **Greenleaf**, W. H., 'Filmer's patriarchal history', *Hist. J.*, 9, 1966, 157–71. Neat exposition, setting Filmer's genealogical argument in its historical context to illustrate that it was neither foolish nor unusual.

5.116 **Hardie**, I., 'The Aristotelian motif in Filmer's *Patriarcha*: a second look', *Pol. Sts.*, 22, 1974, 479–84. Accuses Geisst, probably correctly, of exaggerating the Aristotelian influence on Filmer's patriarchalism in his 'The Aristotelian motif in Filmer's *Patriarcha*', *Pol. Sts.*, 21, 1973.

5.117 **Hinton**, R. W. K., 'Husbands, fathers and conquerors', *Pol. Sts.*, 15, 1967, 291–300. Comparison of Filmer and Bodin.

5.118 **Laslett**, P., 'Sir Robert Filmer: the man versus the whig myth', *Wm. & Mary Q.*, 5, 1948, 523–46. Still the best biographical guide.

5.119 **Schochet**, G. J., 'Sir Robert Filmer: some new bibliographical discoveries', *Trans. Bibliographical Soc.*, June, 1971, 135–160. Shows how *Patriarcha* was published during the Exclusion crisis with the intention of making it the ideological flagship of Toryism.

5.120 **Smith**, C. I., 'Filmer, and the Knolles

translation of Bodin', *Phil. Q.*, 13, 1963, 248–52. Demonstrates Filmer's detailed use, sometimes unacknowledged, of Bodin.

5.121 **Tuck**, R, 'A new date for Filmer's *Patriarcha*', *Hist. J.*, 29, 1986, 183–6. Argues that *Patriarcha* was written in the 1620s or earlier.

5.122 **Wallace**, J. M., 'The date of Sir Robert Filmer's *Patriarcha*', *Hist. J.*, 23, 1980. Argues that *Patriarcha* was possibly written in 1648, though most scholars favour a dating sometime before the Civil War.

5.123 **Weston**, C. C., 'The authorship of the *Freeholders grand inquest*', *Eng. Hist. Rev.*, 95, 1980, 74–98. Makes the case that Sir Robert Holbourne authored *The Freeholders Grand Inquest*, though the work is usually attributed to Filmer.

5.124 —— 'The case for Sir Robert Holbourne reasserted', *Hist. Pol. Thought*, 8, 1987, 435–60. Restates her argument, first made in 1980, that Holbourne rather than Filmer wrote the anonymous royalist work *The Freeholders Grand Inquest*.

The Levellers

5.125 **Aylmer**, G. E., 'Gentlemen Levellers?', *Past & Pres.*, 49, 1970, 120–5. On the social origins of the Levellers.

5.126 —— ed., *The Levellers in the English Revolution*, 1975. Collection of Leveller writings prefaced by a long and perceptive introduction.

5.127 **Brailsford**, H. N., *The Levellers and the English Revolution*, 1961. A lively and extensive study arguing that at key moments in the Revolution the intellectual and political initiative lay with the Levellers.

5.128 **Davis**, J. C., 'The Levellers and Christianity', in B. S. Manning, ed., *Politics, Religion, and the English Civil War*, 1973, 225–50. Suggests that the Christian doctrines of equity and stewardship were at the heart of Leveller political thinking.

5.129 —— 'The Levellers and democracy', *Past & Pres.*, 40, 1968, 174–80. Argues that the Levellers were not so consistent that they can be characterised as either unqualified proponents of a restricted franchise (as does C. B. Macpherson) or as fervent democrats (as does H. N. Brailsford): they adopted a democratic stance when it was tactically convenient.

5.130 **Diethe**, J., 'The Moderate: politics and allegiances of a revolutionary newspaper', Hist. Pol. Thought, 4, 1983, 247–79. On a newspaper with strong sympathies for the Levellers.

5.131 **Frank**, J, The Levellers: A History of the Writings of Three Seventeenth-century Social Democrats: John Lilburne, Richard Overton, William Walwyn, Cambridge, Mass., 1955. Argues that Leveller genealogy consists primarily of 'the iconoclasm inherent in militant Calvinism and, to a much lesser degree, of the utopian potential in the belief in the supremacy of natural law'.

5.132 **Gleissner**, R. A., 'The Levellers and natural law: the Putney debates of 1647', J. Brit. Sts., 20, 1980, 74–89. Emphasises the traditional roots of Leveller thinking.

5.133 **Gregg**, P., Free-Born John: A Biography of John Lilburne, 1961.

5.134 **Hampsher-Monk**, I., 'The political theory of the Levellers: Putney, property, and Professor Macpherson', Pol. Sts., 24, 1976, 397–422. Sharp critique of Macpherson's depiction of the Levellers as possessive individualists.

5.135 **Howell**, R., and **Brewster**, D. E., 'Reconsidering the Levellers: the evidence of The Moderate', Past & Pres., 46, 1970, 68–86. Emphasises the heterogeneity of Leveller thinking on the franchise and religious toleration.

5.136 **Kishlansky**, M. A., 'Consensus politics and the structure of debate at Putney', J. Brit. Sts., 20, 1981, 50–69. Attempt to demonstrate the context as well as the content of the Putney debates, arguing that they were intended by the Army Council to resolve conflicts – though their effect was to highlight ideological differences.

5.137 —— 'The army and the Levellers: the roads to Putney', Hist. J., 22, 1979, 795–824. Contends that 'the equation of the New Model Army with the Levellers can no longer be supported': the army had its own grievances and was insulated from the Leveller programme by its reluctance to interfere in matters of state.

5.138 **Levy**, M., 'Freedom, property and the Levellers: the case of John Lilburne', West. Pol. Q., 36, 1983, 116–133. Argues, contrary to C. B. Macpherson, that Lilburne was not a 'possessive individualist' articulating the ideology of emerging capitalism, but an egalitarian agitator intent on defending a dissident religious minority from political absolutism.

5.139 **Macpherson**, C. B., 'Hampsher-Monk's Levellers', Pol. Sts., 25, 1977, 571–6. Response to Hampsher-Monk in Pol. Sts. 24, 1976.

5.140 **Manning**, B. S., 'The Levellers and religion', in J. F. McGregor and B. Reay, ed., Radical Religion in the English Revolution, 1984, 65–89. 'The interrelation between their religion and their politics was determined by their recognition . . . o the fact that both the church and the state were instruments of class'.

5.141 **Mulligan**, L., 'The religious roots of William Walwyn's radicalism', J. Rel. Hist., 12, 1982, 162–79. Claims that Walwyn's political radicalism derived from antinomianism (a theology of free grace).

5.142 **Parking-Speers**, D., 'John Lilburne: a revolutionary interprets statutes and common law due process', Law & Hist. Rev., 1, 1983, 276–96. Demonstrates how Lilburne attempted to defend himself by appeal to the existing law of the land.

5.143 **Robertson**, D. B., The Religious Foundations of Leveller Democracy, New York, 1951.

5.144 **Seaberg**, R. B., 'The Norman Conquest and the common law: the Levellers and th argument from continuity', Hist. J., 24, 1981, 791–806. Suggests that the Leveller had a more complex understanding than other scholars acknowledge of the rhythm of English history.

5.145 **Sharp**, A., 'John Lilburne and the long parliament's Book of Declarations: a radical's exploitation of the words of authorities', Hist. Pol. Thought, 9, 1988, 19–45.

5.146 —— 'John Lilburne's discourse of law', Pol. Sc., 40, 1988, 18–33. Lilburne is attributed with a consistent conception of law, even though on most issues he was ideologically incoherent.

5.147 **Thomas**, K., 'The Levellers and the franchise', in G. E. Aylmer, ed., The Interregnum: The Quest for Settlement, 1646–60, 1972, 57–78. Judicious assessment, emphasising the ideal of a modest economic self-sufficiency for all and repudiating the charge that they were prophets of nascent capitalism and wage-labour: 'whether they would have excluded wage-labourers and alms-takers from the franchise [is] debatable. What is certain is that they hoped that these classes would wither away to the absolute minimum'.

5.148 **Thompson**, C., 'Maximillian Petty and the Putney debate on the franchise', *Past & Pres.*, 88, 1980, 63–9. Portrays Petty as a representative spokesman for the Levellers in the franchise debate: his shift from support of manhood suffrage to a more restricted franchise, excluding beggars, apprentices and servants, was the first sign of the movement the Levellers subsequently made for tactical rather than ideological reasons.

Winstanley and the Diggers

5.149 **Alsop**, J. D., 'Gerrard Winstanley: religion and respectability', *Hist. J.*, 28, 1985, 705–9. Presents fresh biographical evidence to suggest that from the late 1650s Winstanley's radicalism evaporated as he became moderately prosperous and increasingly conventional.

5.150 —— 'Gerrard Winstanley's later life', *Past & Pres.*, 82, 1979, 73–81.

5.151 **Aylmer**, G. E., 'The religion of Gerrard Winstanley', in J. F. McGregor and B. Reay, ed., *Radical Religion in the English Revolution*, 1984, 91–139. A perceptive account of the evolution of his political thinking.

5.152 **Davis**, J. C., 'Gerrard Winstanley and the restoration of true magistracy', *Past & Pres.*, 70, 1976, 76–93. Detects a shift in his writings from an optimistic belief in the moral perfectibility of every individual to 'an acceptance of the repressive functioning of the state, transforming men from without through an apparatus of totalitarian discipline'.

5.153 **Elmen**, P., 'The theological basis of Digger communism', *Church Hist.*, 23, 1954, 207–18.

5.154 **George**, C. H., 'Gerrard Winstanley, a critical retrospect', in C. R. Cole and M. E. Moody, ed., *The Dissenting Tradition: Essays for Leland H. Carlson*, Athens, Ga., 1975, 191–225.

5.155 **Hayes**, T. W., *Winstanley the Digger: A Literary Analysis of Radical Ideas in the English Revolution*. Cambridge, Mass., 1979. The first full-scale study, depicting Winstanley as a 'poet-prophet'.

5.156 **Hill**, C., 'Forerunners of socialism in the 17th century English Revolution', *Marxism Today*, Sept. 1977, 270–77. Short, clear exposition of Winstanley's ideas.

5.157 **Hudson**, W. S., 'Economic and social thought of Gerrard Winstanley: was he a seventeenth-century Marxist?', *J. Mod. Hist.*, 18, 1946, 1–21. Characterises him as a left-wing Puritan but not a communist.

5.158 **Juretic**, G., 'Digger no millenarian: the revolutionizing of Gerrard Winstanley', *J. Hist. Ideas*, 36, 1975, 263–80. Detects a sharp break between his pre-Digger millenarian tracts and his Digger writings: 'the latter were increasingly secularized, rationalized critiques, bereft of mysticism, culminating in his communist utopia, *The Law of Freedom*'.

5.159 **Kenyon**, T., *Utopian Communism and Political Thought in Early Modern England*, 1989. Principally a comparison of Winstanley and Thomas More.

5.160 **Mulligan**, L., **Graham**, J. K., and **Richards**, J., 'Winstanley: a case for the man he said he was', *J. Eccl. Hist.*, 28, 1977, 57–75. Critical of recent scholarship for overplaying the modern aspects of his thought while minimising the theological element. Winstanley was not a simple economic determinist who believed that sin and disorder would be eradicated with the abolition of private property: the spirit of his writings 'had more in common with the apocalyptic visions of his puritan contemporaries than with modern socialist and communist ideologies'.

5.161 **Sanderson**, J., 'The Digger's apprenticeship: Winstanley's early writings', *Pol. Sts.*, 22, 1974, 453–62.

Milton

5.162 **Hill**, C., *Milton and the English Revolution*, 1977. Brilliant portrayal of Milton as a Protestant heretic which sets his political ideas in the context of the radical thinking of the period.

5.163 **Davies**, S., *Images of Kingship in 'Paradise Lost': Milton's Politics and Christian Liberty*, Columbia, Miss., 1983. Unravels the layers of meaning in the poem, warning against a simplistic assimilation of its image of the good to the image of republican liberty, and evil to the corrupted monarchy, as characterised in Milton's prose writings.

5.164 **Geisst**, C. R., *The Political Thought of John Milton*, 1984. Charts the development of Milton's republican views.

5.165 **Kendrick**, C., *Milton: A Study in Ideology and Form*, 1986. A Marxist interpretation of *Aeropagitica* and *Paradise Lost*, purporting to demonstrate the links between revolutionary Protestantism and capitalist individualism.

5.166 **Sirluck**, E., 'Milton's political thought: the first cycle', *Mod. Philol.*, 61, 1964, 209–24. The best short survey of his political ideas.

5.167 **Worden**, B., 'Milton's republicanism and the tyranny of heaven', in G. Bock, Q. Skinner, and M. Viroli, ed., *Machiavelli and Republicanism*, 1990, 225–45. Sharp comparison of Milton and other English republicans of the period.

Harrington

5.168 **Cotton**, J., 'James Harrington as Aristotelian', *Pol. Theory*, 7, 1979, 371–89.

5.169 —— 'James Harrington and Thomas Hobbes', *J. Hist. Ideas*, 42, 1981, 407–21. Emphasises Harrington's divergence from Hobbes in significant aspects of his political thought.

5.170 —— 'The Harringtonian "party" (1659–1660) and Harrington's political thought', *Hist. Pol. Thought*, 1, 1980, 51–67. On the ideological uses of Harrington's political thought in the final eighteen months of the Interregnum.

5.171 **Davis**, J. C., 'Pocock's Harrington: grace, nature, and art in the classical republicanism of James Harrington', *Hist. J.*, 24, 1981, 683–97. Claims that there is an unresolved tension in Harrington's writings between a belief in the capacity of citizens to govern themselves and scepticism about their potential for virtue.

5.172 **Diamond**, W. C., 'Natural philosophy in Harrington's political thought', *J. Hist. Ideas*, 16, 1978, 387–98. Demonstrates how he used various strands of natural philosophy to depict the millennial character of *Oceana*.

5.173 **Downs**, M., *James Harrington*, Boston, Mass., 1977.

5.174 **Goldie**, M., 'The civil religion of James Harrington', in A. Pagden, ed., *The Languages of Political Theory in Early-Modern Europe*, 1987, 197–222. Demonstrates how a Christian Reformist vision was integral to his construction of a just polity.

5.175 **Lockyer**, A., 'Pocock's Harrington', *Pol. Sts.*, 26, 1980, 458–64. Endorses, with some reservations, J. G. A. Pocock's view of Harrington as primarily a civic humanist.

5.176 **MacPherson**, C. B., 'Harrington's "opportunity state" ', *Past & Pres.*, 17, 1960, 45–69. Brilliant, if flawed, attempt to portray Harrington as a realistic analyst of an emerging bourgeois society.

5.177 **Pocock**, J. G. A., 'James Harrington and the Good Old Cause: a study of the ideological context of his writings', *J. Brit. Sts.*, 10, 1970, 30–48. Argues that *Oceana*, with its attack upon the House of Lords, was read in the late 1650s in the context of an impending return to government by the three estates.

5.178 **Scott**, J., 'The rapture of motion: James Harrington's republicanism', in N. Phillipson and Q. Skinner, ed., *Political Discourse in Early Modern Britain*, 139–63. Harrington is said to be 'the most idiosyncratic member of the republican intellectual flock'.

5.179 **Shklar**, J. N., 'Ideology hunting: the case of James Harrington', *Am. Pol. Sc. Rev.*, 53, 1959, 662–92. Partly an exposition of his ideas, but more interestingly a survey of subsequent interpretations of his thinking.

5.180 **Toth**, K., 'Interpretation in political theory: the case of Harrington', *Rev. Pol.*, 37, 1975, 317–39.

Hobbes

5.181 **Abbott**, P., 'The three families of Thomas Hobbes', *Rev. Pol.*, 43, 1981, 242–58. Identifies three conceptions of the family as an institution in Hobbes, concluding that the sovereign is created in the image not of a strong father but of 'an insurance agent with a gun'.

5.182 **Ake**, C., 'Social contract theory and the problem of politicization: the case of Hobbes', *West. Pol. Q.*, 23, 1970, 463–71

5.183 **Albritton**, R. R., 'Hobbes on political science and political order', *Can. J. Pol. Sc.*, 9, 1976, 464–72. On the similarity between the way he supposes both knowledge and politics should be organised.

5.184 **Ashcraft**, R., 'Hobbes's natural man', *J. Pol.*, 33, 1971, 1076–1117. Demonstrates how Hobbes blends philosophical abstraction and anthropological evidence in his depiction of the state of nature as savage and anarchic.

5.185 —— 'Ideology and class in Hobbes's political theory', *Pol. Theory*, 6, 1978, 27–54. Argues that Hobbes's scientific political theory was an attempt to overcome the class and ideological divisions that had precipitated civil war.

5.186 —— 'Leviathan triumphant: Thomas Hobbes and the politics of wild men', in E. Dudley and M. E. Novak, ed., *The Wild Man Within: An Image of Western Thought from the Renaissance to Romanticism*, Pittsburgh, Pa., 1972, 141–82. Fascinating exploration of how fears of savagery and anarchy were fused in Hobbes's idea of the state of nature, and of how this image of barbarism became a potent weapon in subsequent liberal defences of English civilisation.

5.187 —— 'Political theory and practical action: a reconsideration of Hobbes's state of nature doctrine', *Hobbes Sts.*, 1, 1988, 63–88.

5.188 **Barnouw**, J., 'Hobbes's psychology of thought: endeavours, purpose and curiosity', *Hist. Euro. Ideas*, 10, 1989, 519–45.

5.189 —— 'Persuasion in Hobbes's Leviathan', *Hobbes Sts.*, 1, 1988, 3–25.

5.190 **Baumgold**, D., *Hobbes's Political Theory*, 1988. Argues that Hobbes was not an individualistic political thinker, but rather was concerned with the varying roles and duties of sovereign and subjects – she even denies, contrary to conventional interpretations, that Hobbes was a natural rights theorist.

5.191 —— 'Subjects and soldiers: Hobbes on military service', *Hist. Pol. Thought*, 4, 1983, 43–65.

5.192 **Baumrin**, B. H., ed., *Hobbes's Leviathan: Interpretation and Criticism*, Calif., 1969.

5.193 **Bertman**, M. A., 'Equality in Hobbes, with reference to Aristotle', *Rev. Pol.*, 38, 1976, 534–44.

5.194 —— 'Hobbes and Xenophon's Tyrannicus', *Hist. Euro. Ideas*, 10, 1989, 507–17. On why Hobbes, unlike the ancient Greeks, had no need to conceptualise forms of government in terms of degrees of excellence.

5.195 —— *Hobbes: The Natural and the Artifacted Good*, Bern, 1981.

5.196 **Blits**, J. H., 'Hobbesian fear', *Pol. Theory* 17, 1989, 416–31. Horror of violent death is not the primary fear in Hobbes's account: 'Hobbesian fear is best understood as a primal, indeterminate fear of the unknown'.

5.197 **Botwinick**, A., *Hobbes and Modernity*, Washington, D.C., 1983.

5.198 **Bowles**, J., *Hobbes and his Critics. A Study in Seventeenth-Century Constitutionalism*, 1951. Considers the criticisms made of Hobbes by his contemporaries – Rosse, Bramhall, Clarendon – with only perfunctory attention to Hobbes himself.

5.199 **Brown**, C. W., 'Thucydides, Hobbes, and the derivation of anarchy', *Hist. Pol. Thought*, 8, 1987, 33–63. Argues that Hobbes was indebted to Thucydides for some of his observations about conflict, and that they share similar views about how the calculations of rational decision-makers produce conflict, war and anarchy under certain conditions.

5.200 —— 'Thucydides, Hobbes and the linear causal perspective', *Hist. Pol. Thought*, 10, 1989, 215–56. Attempts to unravel the influence of Thucydides on Hobbes's views about motion, sequence, time, cause and, hence, power.

5.201 **Brown**, K. C., ed., *Hobbes Studies*, 1965. Collection of some of the influential essays on Hobbes, including C. B. MacPherson, 'Hobbes's bourgeois man', J. Plamenatz, 'Mr. Warrender's Hobbes', H. Warrender, 'A reply to Mr. Plamenatz', L. Strauss, 'On the spirit of Hobbes's political philosophy', A. F. Taylor, 'The ethical doctrine of Hobbes', S. M. Brown, 'The Taylor thesis', J. R. Pennock, 'Hobbes's confusing "clarity" – the case of "liberty" ', A. G. Wernham, 'Liberty and obligation in Hobbes', W. B. Glover, 'God and Thomas Hobbes', K. Thomas, 'The social origins of Hobbes's political thought' and J. W. N. Watkins, 'Philosophy and politics in Hobbes'.

5.202 **Brown**, S. M., 'Hobbes: the Taylor thesis', *Phil. Rev.*, 68, 1959, 303–25. Argues, contrary to Taylor, that Hobbes's egoistic psychology is indispensable to his political philosophy: 'what is completely dispensable in Hobbes are prudential maxims and the commands of God'.

5.203 **Burgess**, G., 'Contexts for the writing and publication of Hobbes's *Leviathan*', *Hist. Pol. Thought*, 11, 1990, 675–702. Suggests that though *Leviathan* was used in the Engagement controversy as a justification of the *de facto* theory of political obligation, it was conceived as a defence of monarchy, and, further, that Hobbes's intentions raise fresh questions as to whether or not his theory is one of prudential self-interest.

5.204 **Campbell**, B., 'Prescription and description in political thought: the case for Hobbes', *Am. Pol. Sc. Rev.*, 65, 1971, 376–89.

5.205 **Carmichael**, D. J. C., 'C. B. Macpherson's "Hobbes", a critique', *Can. J. Pol. Sc.*, 16, 1983, 61–80. Argues that the depiction of Hobbes as a possessive individualist is without foundation.

5.206 —— 'Hobbes on natural rights in society: the *Leviathan* account', *Can. J. Pol. Sc.*, 23, 1990, 3–21. Although Hobbesian authority is absolute, the account of natural rights is said significantly to limit its proper scope.

5.207 —— 'Reply: Macpherson versus the text of *Leviathan*', *Can. J. Pol. Sc.*, 16, 1983, 807–9.

5.208 **Caton** H., 'On the basis of Hobbes' political philosophy', *Pol. Sts.*, 22, 1974, 414–31.

5.209 **Chapman**, R. A., '*Leviathan* writ small: Thomas Hobbes on the family', *Am. Pol. Sc. Rev.*, 69, 1975, 76–90. Suggests that unlike Filmer, who saw the state as the family writ large, Hobbes saw the family as a diminutive state – as an artificial institution rather than a natural one.

5.210 **Coleman**, F. M., *Hobbes and America: Exploring the Constitutional Foundations*, 1977. Depicts Hobbes as the theorist of bourgeois protestantism and the ideological progenitor of liberal constitutionalism, and attributes the failures of modern American liberal democracy to its foundations in Hobbesian principles. A reading which distorts both Hobbes and American history.

5.211 **Condren**, C., 'On the rhetorical foundations of Leviathan', *Hist. Pol. Thought*, 11, 1990, 703–20. Questions the emphasis of recent scholarship on rhetoric as the key to unlocking the secrets of Hobbes.

5.212 **Cranston**, M., and **Peters**, R. S., ed., *Hobbes and Rousseau: A Collection of Critical Essays*, New York, 1972. Includes W. H. Greenleaf, 'Hobbes: the problem of interpretation', B. Barry, 'Warrender and his critics', K. R. Minogue, 'Hobbes and the just man', Q. Skinner, 'The context of Hobbes's theory of political obligation', W. Letwin, 'The economic foundations of Hobbes' politics', S. I. Benn, 'Hobbes on power'. J. W. N. Watkins, 'Liberty', and P. Winch, 'Man and society in Hobbes and Rousseau'.

5.213 **Cropsey**, J., 'Hobbes and the transition to modernity', in J. Cropsey, ed., *Ancients and Moderns: Essays on the Tradition of Political Philosophy in Honor of Leo Strauss*, New York, 1964, 213–37.

5.214 **Dalgarno**, M. T., 'Analysing Hobbes's Contract', *Procs. Aris. Soc.*, 76, 1976, 2019–26.

5.215 **Damrosh**, L., 'Hobbes as Reformation theologian: implications of the free-will controversy', *J. Hist. Ideas*, 40, 1979, 339–52.

5.216 **Danford**, J. W., 'The problem of language in Hobbes's political science', *J. Pol.*, 42, 1980, 102–34.

5.217 **Devine**, F. E., 'Hobbes: the theoretical basis of political compromise', *Polity*, 5, 1972, 55–77.

5.218 **Dietz**, M. G., ed., *Thomas Hobbes and Political Theory*, Lawrence, Kan., 1990. Includes S. Wolin, 'Hobbes and the culture of despotism', D. Johnston, 'Plato, Hobbes, and the science of practical reasoning', G. Schochet, 'Intending (political) obligation: Hobbes and the voluntary basis of society', D. Baumgold, 'Hobbes's political sensibility: the menace of political ambition', M. Dietz, 'Hobbes's subject as citizen', S. Holmes, 'Political psychology in Hobbes's *Behemoth*', R. Tuck, 'Hobbes and Locke on toleration', and J. Farr, 'Atomes of scripture: Hobbes and the politics of biblical interpretation'.

5.219 **Distephano**, C., 'Masculinity as ideology in political theory: Hobbesian man considered', *Wom. Sts. Int. For.*, 6, 1983, 633–44. Characterises Hobbes as a masculine theorist. 'His image of natural, atomised individuals, springing up like mushrooms, denies any significance to the mother–child relationship and the dependence on the mother that provides the first intersubjective context for the development of human capacities.'

5.220 **Dzelzainis**, M., 'Edward Hyde and Thomas Hobbes's *Elements of Law, Natural and Politic*', *Hist. J.*, 32, 1989, 303–17.

5.221 **Eisenach**, E. J., 'Hobbes on church, state and religion', *Hist. Pol. Thought*, 3, 1982, 215–43. Detects in Hobbes's theory of church–state relations both the genesis and ambivalence of modern liberalism.

5.222 **Flathman**, R. E., 'Absolutism, individuality and politics: Hobbes and a little beyond', *Hist. Euro. Ideas*, 10, 1989, 547–68. Suggests that for Hobbes absolutism and individuality are not incompatible.

5.223 —— *Thomas Hobbes: Skepticism, Individuality and Chastened Politics*, Newbury Park, Calif., 1993. Claims that 'the primary objective of his political and moral thinking is to promote and protect each person's pursuit of her own felicity as she herself sees it', and attempts – intelligently if at times pretentiously and impenetrably – to assess the relevance of the Hobbesian project for the modern world.

5.224 **Flinker**, N., 'The view from the Devil's Mountain': dramatic tension in Hobbes's *Behemoth*', *Hobbes Sts.*, 2, 1989, 10–22.

5.225 **Forsyth**, M., 'Thomas Hobbes and the constituent power of the people', *Pol. Sts.*, 29, 1981, 191–203. Argues that implicit in Hobbes's doctrine of representation is the modern notion of the people as the constituent power of the state.

5.226 —— 'Thomas Hobbes and the external relations of states', *Brit. J. Int. Sts.*, 5, 1979, 196–209.

5.227 **Fuller**, T., 'Compatibilities on the idea of law in Thomas Aquinas amd Thomas Hobbes', *Hobbes Sts.*, 3, 1990, 112–34.

5.228 **Gauthier**, D., *The Logic of Leviathan: The Moral and Political Theory of Thomas Hobbes*, 1969. Analyses Hobbes's thought in terms of game theory, arguing that the state of nature can be represented as a kind of 'prisoners' dilemma'.

5.229 **Geach**, P., 'The religion of Thomas Hobbes', *Rel. Sts.*, 17, 1981, 549–58.

5.230 **Gent**, B., 'Hobbes and psychological egoism', *J. Hist. Ideas*, 28, 1967, 503–20. Repudiates the common assumption that Hobbes was a psychological egoist, claiming that his political theory depends upon the human capacity to do what is right and just – i.e. to keep promises – rather than an incapacity to act other than from self-interest.

5.231 —— 'Hobbes, mechanism, and egoism', *Phil. Q.*, 15, 1965, 341–9.

5.232 **Glass**, J. M., 'Hobbes and narcissism: pathology in the state of nature', *Pol. Theory*, 8, 1980, 335–63. Suggests that his description of a psychological war of all against all serves as a theoretical metaphor for the human condition in the modern world.

5.233 **Glover**, W. B., 'Human nature and the state in Hobbes', *J. Hist. Phil.*, 5, 1966, 293–311.

5.234 **Goldsmith**, M. M., 'Hobbes's ambiguous politics', *Hist. Pol. Thought*, 11, 1990, 639–73. Focuses on his political position in 1651, neither unambiguously royalist nor republican.

5.235 —— 'Hobbes on liberty', *Hobbes Sts.*, 2, 1989, 23–39.

5.236 —— 'Hobbes's "mortal God": is there a fallacy in Hobbes's theory of sovereignty?', *Hist. Pol. Thought*, 1, 1980, 33–50.

5.237 —— *Hobbes's Science of Politics*, 1966. Comprehensive, readable and shrewd account.

5.238 —— 'The Hobbes industry', *Pol. Sts.*, 39, 1991, 135–47. Useful survey of recent literature on Hobbes.

5.239 **Grover**, R. A., 'Individualism, absolutism, and contract in Thomas Hobbes' political theory', *Hobbes Sts.*, 3, 1990, 89–111. Legal concepts of contract and agency are said to reconcile individualism and absolutism.

5.240 —— 'The legal origin of Thomas Hobbes's doctrine of consent', *J. Hist. Phil.*, 18, 1980, 177–94.

5.241 **Halliday**, R. J., **Kenyon**, T., and **Reeve**, A., 'Hobbes's belief in God', *Pol. Sts.*, 31, 1983, 418–33. Interesting suggestion that for him the art of politics consists in imitating the commands of an omnipotent God. 'Just as the *Book of Job* revealed the irresistible power of an omnipotent God, *Leviathan* demonstrated the irresistible power of God's personator, the mortal sovereign'.

5.242 **Hampton**, J. *Hobbes and the Social Contract Tradition*, 1986. Original claim that Hobbes appealed not to a contract but to a self-interested agreement or convention – in doing so she uses game theory and other analytical techniques to resolve what she considers to be flaws in Hobbes's own theory.

5.243 **Hanson**, D. W., 'The meaning of "demonstration" in Hobbes's science', *Hist. Pol. Thought*, 11, 1990, 587–626. Argues that Hobbes demonstrated the conclusions of his political theory by deploying 'a connected series of little steps', not by using the deductive method usually attributed to him.

5.244 **Hartman**, M., 'Hobbes's concept of revolution', *J. Hist. Ideas*, 47, 1986, 487–95. Claims that he revolutionised the concept of revolution by conceptualising it as a process of usurpation which followed an invariable six-stage pattern.

5.245 **Hinton**, R. W. K., 'Husbands, fathers and conquerors', *Pol. Sts.*, 16, 1968, 55–67. Primarily a discussion of Hobbes's patriarchalism with some attention to Locke.

5.246 **Hood**, F. C., *The Divine Politics of Thomas Hobbes*, 1957. A contentious reading, arguing that in his political philosophy the laws of nature oblige only because they are the commands of God revealed with certainty in scripture.

5.247 **Johnson**, C., 'The Hobbesian conception of sovereignty and Aristotle's politics', *J. Hist. Ideas*, 46, 1985, 327–348. Argues that they held a similar view of sovereignty, though Hobbes was unaware that this was so because of his careless reading of Aristotle.

5.248 **Johnson**, P. J., 'Deduction and dialectic in Hobbes's theory of civility', *Hobbes Sts.*, 4, 199, 96–114. Hobbes's commitment to understanding all things as dynamic systems is said to take precedence over any commitment he had to geometising deduction.

5.249 **Johnston**, D., 'Hobbes's mortalism', *Hist. Pol. Thought*, 10, 1989, 647–65. Contends that mortalism, the denial that the soul is an incorporeal substance that outlives the body, was as central to the design of Hobbes's theological argument in *Leviathan* as it was to the reception of that argument.

5.250 —— *The Rhetoric of Leviathan: Thomas Hobbes and the Politics of Cultural Transformation*, Princeton, N.J., 1986. Claims that in *Leviathan* Hobbes was engaged in a project of cultural transformation: the task of ridding people of those Christian superstitions which lay behind the political conflicts of the 1640s.

5.251 **Kateb**, G., 'Hobbes and the irrationality of politics', *Pol. Theory*, 17, 1989, 355–91. On his preoccupation with civil war and his commitment to individuality.

5.252 **Kavka**, G. S., *Hobbesian Moral and Political Theory*, Princeton, N.J., 1986. Discards those aspects of Hobbes's thinking he finds distasteful in order to fashion a purified Hobbesian theory relevant to the modern world.

5.253 —— 'Some neglected liberal aspects of Hobbes's philosophy', *Hobbes Sts.*, 1, 1988, 89–108.

5.254 **Klosko**, G., and **Rice**, D. H., 'Thucydides and Hobbes's state of nature', *Hist. Pol. Thought*, 6, 1985, 405–9. Seeks to demonstrate that Hobbes's characterisation of life in the state of nature is influenced by a description of life among the earliest inhabitants of Hellas in Book I of Thucydides's *History*.

5.255 **Kraynak**, R. P., *History and Modernity in the Thought of Thomas Hobbes*, Ithaca, N.Y., 1990. Focuses on Hobbes's interest in history, portraying him as an early representative of enlightenment thinking. Uses Hobbes – in the manner of Leo Strauss – as a peg on which to hang a condemnation of modernism.

5.256 **Kronman**, A., 'The idea of an author and the unity of the commonwealth in Hobbes' *Leviathan*', *J. Hist. Phil.*, 18, 1980, 159–76.

5.257 **Letwin**, S. R., 'Hobbes and Christianity', *Daedalus*, 105, 1976, 1–21.

5.258 **Lloyd**, S. A., *Ideals as Interests in Hobbes's Leviathan*, 1992. Fresh interpretation arguing that religious and moral interests, not merely the fear of death, were crucial to Hobbes's analysis of social disorder and his proposed remedy.

5.259 **Lund**, W. R., 'Hobbes on opinion, private judgement and civil war', *Hist. Pol. Thought*, 13, 1992, 51–72. Argues that Hobbes used *Behemoth* to provide historical illustrations of a principal assumption of his political philosophy: that the preservation of public order is incompatible with an unlimited right to private judgement.

5.260 —— 'The historical and "political" origins of civil society: Hobbes on presumption and certainty', *Hist. Pol. Thought*, 9, 1988, 223–35.

5.261 —— 'The use and abuse of the past:

Hobbes on the study of history', *Hobbes Sts.*, 5, 1992, 3–22. Hobbes is said gradually to feel 'his way toward an account of history which denied its current utility but left it as an autonomous discipline for reconstructing causal knowledge about the past'.

5.262 **MacGillivray**, H., 'Thomas Hobbes's history of the English civil war: a study of *Behemoth*', *J. Hist. Ideas*, 31, 1970, 179–98. Characterises *Behemoth* as a brilliant historical essay distorted by a defect fundamental to Hobbes's political philosophy – a failure to comprehend minds radically different from his own.

5.263 **McLean**, I., 'The social contract in Leviathan and the prisoner's dilemma Supergame', *Pol. Sts.*, 29, 1981, 339–51. Application of the game theory approach to the study of Hobbes.

5.264 **McNeilly**, F. S., 'Egoism in Hobbes', *Phil. Q.*, 16, 1966, 193–206. The egoism of earlier works is discarded in *Leviathan*, according to McNeilly, where political conclusions are derived from largely non-egoistic arguments.

5.265 —— *The Anatomy of Leviathan*, 1968. Carefully sustained argument that the political doctrine of *Leviathan* is presented as a deductive system which has logical affinities with mathematics rather than science. Written with verve, though rather difficult for those not versed in philosophical concepts.

5.266 **Macpherson**, C. B., '*Leviathan* restored: reply to Carmichael', *Can. J. Pol. Sc.*, 16, 1983, 795–809. Spirited defence of his reading of Hobbes as a possessive individualist.

5.267 **Mansfield**, H. C., 'Hobbes and the science of indirect government', *Am. Pol. Sc. Rev.*, 65, 1971, 97–110. Portrays Hobbes as the founder of political science because he was the first writer to substitute the indirect political question of whether government is representative of the people for the direct question of whether what government does is good or useful.

5.268 **Martinich**, A. D., *The Two Gods of Leviathan: Thomas Hobbes on Religion and Politics*, 1992.

5.269 **Mathie**, W., 'Justice and the question of regimes in ancient and modern political philosophy: Aristotle and Hobbes', *Can. J. Pol. Sc.*, 9, 1976, 449–72. Demonstrates how Hobbes broke the link with classical

political philosophy by removing the controversy about the best form of government from the domain of justice.

5.270 —— 'Reason and rhetoric in Hobbes's *Leviathan*', *Interpretation*, 14, 1986, 281–98.

5.271 **May**, L., 'Hobbes on fidelity to law', *Hobbes Sts.*, 5, 1992, 77–89.

5.272 —— 'Hobbes's contract theory', *J. Hist. Phil.*, 18, 1980, 195–208.

5.273 **Milner**, B., 'Hobbes on religion', *Pol. Theory*, 16, 1988, 400–25. Argues that, to effect the political control of religion, Hobbes attempts a synthesis of natural and biblical theology.

5.274 **Minogue**, T., 'From precision to peace: Hobbes and political language', *Hobbes Sts.*, 3, 1990, 75–88.

5.275 **Mintz**, S. I., 'Leviathan as metaphor', *Hobbes Sts.*, 2, 1989, 3–9.

5.276 —— *The Hunting of Leviathan. Seventeenth Century Reactions to the Materialism and Moral Philosophy of Hobbes*, 1962.

5.277 **Missner**, M., 'Hobbes's method in *Leviathan*', *J. Hist. Ideas*, 38, 1977, 607–21. Fundamentally a formal, quasi-geometrical method, according to Missner, supplemented by other types of argument such as qualified introspection to persuade people unable to follow his scientific reasoning.

5.278 —— 'Skepticism and Hobbes's political philosophy', *J. Hist. Ideas*, 44, 1983, 407–27. Claims that Hobbes became increasingly sceptical concerning the ability of people to know what the passions of others are, and that as a consequence *Leviathan* is logically flawed: its bold claim of a universal desire for power is undermined by his skepticism about gaining knowledge of the specific aims of other people.

5.279 **Morgan**, G., 'Hobbes and the right of self-defence', *Pol. Sts.*, 30, 1982, 413–25. Examines Hobbes's reasons as to why individuals should be cautious in exercising their right of self-defence against the sovereign.

5.280 **Nagel**, T., 'Hobbes's concept of obligation', *Phil. Rev.*, 68, 1950, 68–83. Argues, contrary to Warrender, that moral obligation plays no part in *Leviathan*, but that what Hobbes calls moral obligation is based exclusively on considerations of self-interest.

5.281 **Nerney**, G., 'Homo notans: marks, signs,

and imagination in Hobbes's conception of human nature', *Hobbes Sts.*, 4, 1991, 53–75.

5.282 **Nunan**, R., 'Hobbes on morality, rationality and foolishness', *Hobbes Sts.*, 2, 1989, 40–64.

5.283 **Oakeshott**, M., *Hobbes on Civil Association*, 1975. A collection of his earlier essays, including his influential introduction to *Leviathan*.

5.284 **Okin**, S. M., ' "The sovereign and his counsellours": Hobbes's re-evaluation of parliament', *Pol. Theory*, 10, 1982, 49–75. Analysis of Hobbes's late book, *A Dialogue between a Philosopher and a Student of the Common Law of England*.

5.285 **Orr**, R., 'Thomas Hobbes on the regulation of voluntary motion', in G. Feaver and F. Rosen, ed., *Lives, Liberties and the Public Good*, 1987, 45–60.

5.286 **Orwin**, C., 'On the sovereign authorisation', *Pol. Theory*, 3, 1975, 26–44. Sharp analysis of Hobbes's concept of authorisation – 'the words, or actions of one man being taken to represent those of another' – 'which is the substance of the original contract, where each contracts with each save one, to grant that particular one an unlimited authorization to act for him'.

5.287 **Pasqualucci**, P., 'Hobbes and the myth of "final war" ', *J. Hist. Ideas*, 51, 1990, 647–57. On his prediction of a merciless war as a response to overpopulation.

5.288 **Pateman**, C., ' "God hath ordained to man a helper": Hobbes, patriarchy and conjugal right', *Brit. J. Pol. Sc.*, 19, 1989, 445–64. Original claim that Hobbes was a patriarchalist who rejected paternal right, demonstrating how he turns 'mother right' in the state of nature into a non-paternal form of patriarchy.

5.289 **Patton**, P., 'Politics and the concept of power in Hobbes and Nietzsche', in P. Patton, ed., *Nietzsche, Feminism and Political Theory*, 1993, 144–61.

5.290 **Peters**, R. S., *Hobbes*, 1956. Argues that Hobbes's political theory was intimately connected with his general scientific philosophy. Comprehensive and illuminating.

5.291 **Pitkin**, H. F., 'Hobbes's concept of representation', *Am. Pol. Sc. Rev.*, 58, 1964, 328–40, 902–18. Sharp two-part article, contending that Hobbes's account is plausible but incorrect.

5.292 **Plamenatz**, J., 'Mr. Warrender's Hobbes', *Pol. Sts.*, 5, 1957, 295–308. Critique of Warrender's *The Political Philosophy of Hobbes*.

5.293 **Pocock**, J. G. A., 'Thomas Hobbes: atheist or enthusiast? His place in a Restoration debate', *Hist. Pol. Thought*, 11, 1990, 737–51. An analysis of his theology and metaphysical beliefs and their reception in the Restoration.

5.294 —— 'Time, history and eschatology in the thought of Thomas Hobbes', in *Politics, Language and Time: Essays on Political Thought*, 1972, 148–201

5.295 **Polansky**, R. and **Torrell**, K., 'Power, liberty, and counter factual conditionals in Hobbes' thought', *Hobbes Sts.*, 3, 1990, 3–17.

5.296 **Popkin**, R. H., 'Hobbes and skepticism', in L. J. Thro, ed., *History of Philosophy in the Making*, Washington, D.C., 1982, 133–48.

5.297 **Prokhovnik**, R., *Rhetoric and Philosophy in Hobbes's Leviathan*, New York, 1991. A rather unsatisfactory study of Hobbes's rhetorical practice.

5.298 **Raphael**, D. D., 'Hobbes', in Z. A. Pelczynski and J. Gray, ed., *Conceptions of Liberty in Political Philosophy*, 1984, 27–38.

5.299 —— *Hobbes. Morals and Politics*, 1977. Meticulous and reliable analysis which subjects other interpretations of Hobbes to judicious scrutiny.

5.300 **Rayner**, J., 'Hobbes and the rhetoricians', *Hobbes Sts.*, 4, 76–95. Hobbes is said to regard the classical tradition in rhetoric and its revival in humanistic scholarship as an impediment to political stability.

5.301 **Reik**, M., *The Golden Lands of Thomas Hobbes*, Detroit, Mich., 1977. General survey of his life and philosophy.

5.302 **Reiner**, G., 'Hobbes, the rhetorical tradition, and toleration', *Rev. Pol.*, 54, 1992, 5–35. Argues that there is nothing in the logic of Hobbes's argument precluding a greater degree of toleration, based on the sovereign's prudential assessment of the existing circumstances.

5.303 **Riley**, P., 'Will and legitimacy in the philosophy of Hobbes: is he a contract theorist', *Pol. Sts.*, 21, 1973, 500–22. Suggests that Hobbes's voluntaristic doctrine of consent fails to cohere with his deterministic account of the will.

5.304 **Rogers**, C. A. J., and **Ryan**, A., ed.,

Perspectives on Thomas Hobbes, 1988. Includes R. Tuck, 'Hobbes and Descartes', T. Sorrell 'The science in Hobbes's politics', A. Ryan, 'Hobbes and individualism', F. Tricaud, 'Hobbes's conception of the state of nature from 1640 to 1651', D. Gauthier, 'Hobbes's social contract' and D. Raphael, 'Hobbes on Justice'.

5.305 **Rogou**, A., *Thomas Hobbes: Radical in the Service of Reaction*, New York, 1986. The only extensive modern biography of Hobbes.

5.306 **Ross**, R., **Schneider**, H. W., and **Waldman**, T., ed., *Thomas Hobbes in His Times*, Minneapolis, Minn., 1974.

5.307 **Rossini**, G., 'The criticism of rhetorical historiography and the ideal of scientific method: history, nature and science in the political language of Thomas Hobbes', in A. Pagden, ed., *The Languages of Political Theory in Early Modern Europe*, 1987, 303–24.

5.308 **Rudolph**, R., 'Conflict, egoism and power in Hobbes', *Hist. Pol. Thought*, 7, 1986, 73–89. Contends that Hobbes shifted from a psychological explanation of conflict to one emphasising false belief and inadequate knowledge.

5.309 —— 'The micro-foundations of Hobbes's political theory: appetites, emotions, dispositions, and manners', *Hobbes Sts.*, 4, 1991, 34–52. Although in 1640 Hobbes 'treated passions as the passive effects of external stimuli, and the drive for power as a passion, after 1650 he explicitly allowed for active judgement in the formation of passions, in his introduction of dispositions and manners, and his analysis of power as a manner'.

5.310 **Ryan**, A., 'A more tolerant Hobbes?', in S. Mendus, ed., *Essays on Toleration*, 1988.

5.311 —— 'Hobbes, toleration and the inner life', in D. Miller and L. A. Siedentop, ed., *The Nature of Political Theory*, 1981, 197–218. Persuasively argues that he was less obsessed with intellectual orthodoxy and social conformity than appears in the usual illiberal portraits of him.

5.312 **Sacksteder**, W., 'Hobbes: philosophical and rhetorical artifice', *Phil. & Rhet.*, 17, 1984, 30–46.

5.313 —— 'Hobbes's science of human nature', *Hobbes Sts.*, 3, 1990, 35–53. Argues that his solution to the human desire for honour and glory is logical and plausible.

5.314 —— *Hobbes Studies 1879–1979: A Bibliography*, Bowling Green, Ohio, 1982. Contains more than fifteen hundred items, as well as an introductory essay sketching the shifting tendencies in Hobbes scholarship.

5.315 **Sampson**, M., ' "Will you hear what a casuist he is?": Thomas Hobbes as director of conscience', *Hist. Pol. Thought*, 11, 1990, 721–36. Demonstrates how he sought to secularise the science of casuistry as part of his anti-clerical polemic.

5.316 **Sanderson**, J., 'Murray Forsyth on Hobbes: a note', *Pol. Sts.*, 30, 1982, 553–6. A response to M. Forsyth, 'Thomas Hobbes and the constituent power of the people', *Pol. Sts.*, 29, 1981. Sanderson deals not with Hobbes but rather with the widespread belief in popular sovereignty among the various anti-royalists of the 1640s.

5.317 **Schochet**, G. J., 'Thomas Hobbes on the family and the state of nature', *Pol. Sc. Q.*, 82, 1967, 427–45.

5.318 **Schwartz**, J., 'Hobbes and the two kingdoms of God', *Polity*, 18, 1985, 7–24.

5.319 **Shaver**, R., 'Leviathan, king of the proud', *Hobbes Sts.*, 3, 1990, 54–74.

5.320 **Sherlock**, R., 'The theology of *Leviathan*: Hobbes on religion', *Interpretation*, 10, 1982, 43–60.

5.321 **Shulman**, G., 'Hobbes, Puritans, and Promethean politics', *Pol. Theory*, 16, 1988, 426–43. Argues that *Leviathan* 'did not simply discredit Puritanism but also assimilated Puritan commitments to the market and the patriarchal family'.

5.322 —— 'Metaphor and modernization in the political thought of Thomas Hobbes', *Pol. Theory*, 1989, 392–416.

5.323 **Skinner**, Q., 'Conquest and consent: Thomas Hobbes and the engagement controversy', in G. E. Aylmer, ed., *The Interregnum: the Quest for Settlement 1646–1660*, 1972, 79–98. Brilliant exploration of *de facto* justifications of obedience to the new Commonwealth of 1649, arguing that *Leviathan* was intended as a contribution to the engagement debate. Hobbes's political beliefs were commonplace, and his originality lies rather in the reasons he advanced for holding those beliefs.

5.324 —— 'Liberty and legal obligation in Hobbes's *Leviathan*', in H. Gross and R. Harrison, ed., *Jurisprudence: Cambridge*

Essays, 1992, 231–56. Argues that the apparent confusions in his analysis of legal obligation and liberty dissolve on close inspection.

5.325 —— ' "Scientia Civilis" in classical rhetoric and in the early Hobbes', in N. Phillipson and Q. Skinner, ed., Political Discourse in Early Modern Britain, 1993, 67–93.

5.326 —— 'The ideological context of Hobbes's political thought', Hist. J., 9, 1966, 286–317. Seminal article suggesting that the intention of his political theory was the same as that of other writers who defended allegiance to the republic established in 1649: the argument being that a ruler in possession of power ought to be obeyed, irrespective of the means by which he had assumed power. Recent scholarship has followed Skinner's lead in examining the ideological context of Hobbes's thought.

5.327 —— 'Thomas Hobbes on the proper signification of liberty', Trans. Royal Hist. Soc., 5th ser., 40, 1990, 121–51. Brilliant exposition of what Hobbes understood by liberty and of his intended ideological uses of the concept.

5.328 —— 'Thomas Hobbes: rhetoric and the construction of morality', Procs. Brit. Acad., 76, 1991, 1–61. Hobbes's moral theory was intended to overcome a particular form of rhetorical scepticism.

5.329 —— 'Warrender and Skinner on Hobbes: a reply', Pol. Sts., 38, 1988, 692–5. Response to B. Trainor in the same volume of Pol. Sts., defending his claim that Hobbes analysed the concept of political obligation in terms of protection.

5.330 Slomp, G., 'Hobbes, Thucydides and the three greatest things', Hist. Pol. Thought, 11, 1990, 565–86. Suggest that Hobbes attempted to find an escape from the dilemmas raised by Thucydides regarding the conditions under which fear and ambition can sustain or subvert civilisation.

5.331 Sommerville, J. P., Thomas Hobbes: Political Ideas in Historical Context, 1992. Lucid exposition of Hobbes's arguments, setting them against a background of the ideas of his contemporaries and of the political events of his lifetime.

5.332 Sorrell, T., Hobbes, 1986. A reliable account that sets Hobbes's political theory within the context of his general philosophy; though, unlike some scholars, Sorrell finds little correspondence between Hobbes's natural and civil philosophy.

5.333 —— 'Hobbes's UnAristotelian political rhetoric', Phil. & Rhet., 23, 1990, 96–10

5.334 —— 'Hobbes's persuasive civil science' Phil. Q., 40, 1990, 342–51.

5.335 Spragens, T. A., The Politics of Motion: The World of Thomas Hobbes, Lexington Ky., 1973. Argues, not wholly persuasively, that Aristotelian thinking was a paradigm for Hobbes which he proceeded to transform.

5.336 Springborg, P., 'Leviathan and the problem of ecclesiastical authority', Pol. Theory, 3, 1975, 289–303. Focuses on th difficulties Hobbes encountered in tryin to integrate theology with philosophy.

5.337 —— 'Leviathan, the Christian commonwealth incorporated', Pol. Sts., 24, 1976, 171–83. Demonstrates the significance of the Roman Law concept the corporation for Hobbes's theory of authority.

5.338 State, S., 'Hobbes and Hooker: politics and religion: a note on the structuring of Leviathan', Can. J. Pol. Sc., 20, 1987, 79–96. Compares the way in which each conceives religious practice to be a matter of public policy, and reaches the unusual conclusion that the first part of Leviathan is a conceptual primer – a guide to scriptural exegesis – lending coherenc to the work as a whole.

5.339 —— 'Text and context: Skinner, Hobbe and theistic natural law', Hist. J., 28, 198 27–50. Argues, contrary to Skinner, that the interpretation by seventeenth-centur 'Hobbists' of the ideas of their mentor we too heterogeneous to be a reliable guide to what Hobbes actually thought; and, further, that Hobbes's recourse to divine natural law terminology cannot be dismissed in the manner of Skinner as me window-dressing for a secular theory of obligation.

5.340 —— 'The religious and the secular in the work of Thomas Hobbes', in J. E. Crimmins, ed., Religious Secularization an Political Thought: Thomas Hobbes to J. S Mill, 1989, 17–38.

5.341 Sutherland, S., 'God and religion in "Leviathan" ', J. Theol. Sts., 25, 1974, 373–80.

5.342 Tarlton, C. D., 'Levitating Leviathan: glosses on a theme in Hobbes', Ethics, 88 1978, 1–19. On Hobbes's use of imagery and symbolism, particularly in his depiction of the world in its two aspects of reality and appearance.

343 —— 'The creation and maintenance of government: a neglected dimension of Hobbes's Leviathan', *Pol. Sts.*, 26, 1978, 307–27. Argues that philosophical preoccupation with moral, legal and hypothetical problems have led us to neglect those practical dimensions of *Leviathan* in which Hobbes confronts the problems of how order can actually be created from disorder and how, once begun, the germ of order can be perpetuated in stable political society.

344 **Trainor**, B. T., 'The politics of peace: the role of the political covenant in Hobbes's *Leviathan*', *Rev. Pol.*, 47, 1985, 347–69.

345 —— 'Hobbes' sovereign and the right of self-defence', *Pol. Sts.*, 32, 1984, 280–287. Repudiates G. Morgan's charge, 'Hobbes and the right of self-defence', *Pol. Sts.*, 30, 1982, that Hobbes's theory is centrally defective because he allows subjects an inalienable right to self-defence.

346 —— 'Warrender and Skinner on Hobbes', *Pol. Sts.*, 38, 1988, 680–91. Defence of Warrender against Skinner's critique of his interpretation of Hobbes.

347 **Tuck**, R., *Hobbes*, 1989. Lucid and perceptive account of his life and thinking which locates him firmly within the debates of his age.

348 —— 'Optics and sceptics: the philosophical foundations of Hobbes's political thought', in E. Leites, ed., *Conscience and Casuistry in Early Modern Europe*, 1988, 235–63. Restores 'the seventeenth-century view of Hobbes as, to some extent, a philosophical associate of Grotius. Both were members of a group whose common concern was a philosophically sensitive response to the scepticism of both classical antiquity and modern Europe'.

349 —— 'The civil religion of Thomas Hobbes', in N. Phillipson and Q. Skinner, ed., *Political Discourse in Early Modern Britain*, 1993, 120–38.

350 **von Leyden**, W., *Hobbes and Locke*, 1982. Focuses on Hobbes's notion of freedom and its implications for scientific determinism.

351 **Walton**, C., and **Johnson**, P. J., ed., *Hobbes's Science of Natural Justice*, Dordrecht, 1987.

5.352 **Warrender**, H., 'Hobbes's conception of morality', *Rivista critica di storia della filosofia*, 17, 1962, 433–49. Defence of the thesis of his book on Hobbes.

5.353 —— 'Obligation and right in Hobbes', *Phil.*, 37, 1962, 352–7.

5.354 —— 'Political theory and historiography: a reply to Professor Skinner on Hobbes', *Hist. J.*, 22, 1979, 931–40. Defends his thesis that Hobbes was essentially a natural law philosopher, and takes a swipe at Skinner for treating political texts as little more than tracts for the times: 'to consign them to their contemporary milieu, with whatever honours, is to bury them. Hobbes more than most has preserved his relevance and justified his own claim not to be placed on a limited historical stage, but to be regarded as writing for all time'.

5.355 —— ' "The place of God in Hobbes's philosophy": a reply to Mr. Plamenatz', *Pol. Sts.*, 8, 48–57, 1960. Spirited defence of his book on Hobbes.

5.356 —— *The Political Philosophy of Hobbes: His Theory of Obligation*, 1957. A seminal and controversial interpretation, arguing that for Hobbes we are obliged to obey the laws of nature because they are God's commands, not out of considerations about self-preservation.

5.357 **Watkins**, J. W. N., *Hobbes's System of Ideas: A Study in the Political Significance of Philosophical Theories*, 1965. Influential book arguing that Hobbes's political philosophy is scientific because it extends to bodies politic a scientific method whose primary application is to natural phenomena: throughout his system of ideas there is evidence of the resolutive-composite method associated with Galileo and the new science.

5.358 —— 'Philosophy and politics in Hobbes', *Phil. Q.*, 5, 1955, 125–46. Emphasises the systematic nature of Hobbes's thinking by demonstrating how his political doctrines are drawn from the whole of his philosophy.

5.359 **Weinberger**, J., 'Hobbes's doctrine of method', *Am. Pol. Sc. Rev.*, 69, 1975, 1336–53. Argues that Hobbes links political and natural science by use of a subtle rhetoric.

5.360 **Whelan**, F. G., 'Language and its abuses in Hobbes's political philosophy', *Am. Pol. Sc. Rev.*, 75, 1981, 59–75. On Hobbes's project, flawed according to Whelan, to devise a political discourse that will do away with doctrinal controversies.

5.361 **Whitaker**, M., 'Hobbes's view of the Reformation', *Hist. Pol. Thought*, 9, 1988, 45–59.

5.362 **Willms**, B., 'Leviathan and the post-modern', *Hist. Euro. Ideas*, 10, 1989, 569–76. Argues that Hobbes's depiction of the human condition is not dissimilar from that of post-modernists such as Lyotard.

5.363 **Wood**, N., 'Thomas Hobbes and the crisis of the English aristocracy', *Hist. Pol. Thought*, 1, 1980, 437–53. Argues that the Hobbesian absolutist state was a masterful project designed to salvage, rejuvenate and contain a disorderly peerage and gentry, rather than a design to prevent the self-destruction of bourgeois man.

5.364 **Zagorin**, P., 'Hobbes on our mind', *J. Hist. Ideas*, 51, 1990, 317–35. Not an essay on his conception of mental functioning but a perceptive survey of the tendencies and themes in recent Hobbes studies.

5.365 **Zaitchik**, A., 'Hobbes and hypothetical consent', *Pol. Sts.*, 23, 1975, 475–85. Attempt to demonstrate how Hobbes's emphasis on covenanting and consent coheres with his deterministic account of the will.

5.366 —— 'Hobbes's reply to the fool: the problem of consent and obligation', *Pol. Theory*, 10, 1982, 245–66.

5.367 **Zvesper**, J., 'Hobbes's individualistic analysis of the family', *Politics*, 5, 1985, 28–33.

Locke

5.368 **Albritton**, R. R., 'The politics of Locke's philosophy', *Pol. Sts.*, 24, 1976, 253–67. Attempts to tease out the links between Locke's politics and his epistemology, psychology and religion.

5.369 **Anderson**, C., ' "Safe enough in his honesty and prudence": the ordinary conduct of government in the thought of John Locke', *Hist. Pol. Thought*, 13, 1992, 605–30. On the qualities of the people Locke presumed would govern in a well-ordered nation.

5.370 **Andrew**, E., 'Inalienable right, alienable property and freedom of choice: Locke, Nozick and Marx on the alienability of labour', *Can. J. Pol. Sc.*, 18, 1985, 529–50.

5.371 **Anglim**, J., 'On Locke's state of nature', *Pol. Sts.*, 26, 1978, 78–90. Emphasises th[a]t for Locke only obedience to natural law prevents communities lapsing into a state of nature.

5.372 **Appleby**, J., 'Locke, liberalism and the natural law of money', *Past & Pres.*, 71, 1976, 43–69. Focuses on the debate of 169[0] over recoinage, arguing that in it Locke 'forged the link between political and economic liberalism by removing money from the realm of politics and making it a creature of nature' – thereby prefiguring Adam Smith.

5.373 **Arenilla**, L., 'The notion of civil disobedience according to Locke's *Diogenes*', 35, 1986, 109–35.

5.374 **Arneil**, B., 'John Locke, natural law and colonialism', *Hist. Pol. Thought*, 13, 199[2], 587–603. Suggests that the *Two Treatises* was an attempt to undermine the America[n] Indians' claims to land by creating a new definition of property.

5.375 **Arneson**, R. J., 'Lockean self-ownership towards a demolition', *Pol. Sts.*, 39, 199[1], 36–54. An attempt to clarify and refute th[e] principle of self-ownership running from Locke to Nozick: the idea that one ought t[o] be left free to do whatever one chooses so long as other persons are not thereby harmed.

5.376 **Ashcraft**, R., 'John Locke belimed: the case of political philosophy', *Pol. Sts.*, 20 1972, 190–4.

5.377 —— ed., *John Locke: Critical Assessment[s] Volumes I–IV*, 1991. Collection of over a hundred articles on Locke published between 1904 and 1989.

5.378 —— 'Locke's state of nature: historical fact or moral fiction?', *Am. Pol. Sc. Rev.* 62, 1968, 898–915. Locke is said to have used both moral criteria and historical information in constructing his image of the state of nature.

5.379 —— *Locke's Two Treatises of Government* 1987. A close analysis of the text revealin[g] him as a political radical.

5.380 —— *Revolutionary Politics and Locke's Tw[o] Treatises of Government*, Princeton, N.J., 1986. No other book so thoroughly locate[s] Locke within the context of Restoration political opposition to an increasingly authoritarian state and church on the bas[is] of which Ashcraft persuasively highlight[s] the radicalism of his political ideas.

5.381 —— 'Revolutionary politics and Locke's *Two Treatises of Government*: radicalism and Lockean political theory', *Pol. Theory*, 8, 1980, 429–86. Highlights his place among a small group of radicals at the time of the Exclusion crisis, persuasively repudiating images of the moderate and conservative Locke by showing how the ideas of the *Two Treatises* were formulated in the context of a revolutionary conspiracy.

5.382 —— 'Simple objections and complex reality: theorizing political radicalism in seventeenth-century England', *Pol. Sts.*, 40, 1992, 99–115. Response to various critics of his depiction in *Revolutionary Politics and Locke's Two Treatises of Government* of a politically radical Locke.

5.383 —— 'The radical dimensions of Locke's political thought: a dialogic essay on some problems of interpretation', *Hist. Pol. Thought*, 13, 1992, 703–72. Defends his portrayal of a radical Locke against critics.

5.384 —— 'The *Two Treatises* and the exclusion crisis: the problem of Lockean political theory as bourgeois ideology', in J. G. A. Pocock and R. Aschcraft, ed., *John Locke: Papers read at a Clark Library Seminar 10 December 1977*, Los Angeles, Calif., 1980, 25–113. Persuasive depiction of Locke as a radical political thinker rather than a bourgeois ideologue, with close attention to the historical context from which the *Two Treatises* emerged.

5.385 —— and **Goldsmith**, M. M., 'Locke, revolution principles, and the formation of Whig ideology', *Hist. J.*, 6, 1983, 773–800. Demonstrates how radical Lockean ideas gained currency through a popular political manifesto, the anonymous *Political aphorisms* of 1690, which plagiarised the *Two Treatises of Government*.

5.386 **Batz**, W. G., 'The historical anthropology of John Locke', *J. Hist. Ideas*, 35, 1974, 663–70.

5.387 **Becker**, R., 'The ideological commitment of Locke: freemen and servants in the *Two Treatises of Government*', *Hist. Pol. Thought*, 13, 1992, 631–56. His apparently radical arguments 'were designed to reinforce socially conservative beliefs'.

5.388 **Beier**, A. L., ' "Utter strangers to industry, morality and religion": John Locke on the poor', *Eighteenth-Cent. Life*, 12, 1988, 28–41.

5.389 **Bennett**, J., 'A note on Locke's theory of tacit consent', *Phil. Rev.*, 88, 1979, 224–34. Accuses Locke of grounding his theory of tacit consent in an implausible account of property.

5.390 **Blum**, W. T., **Winfield**, N., and **Teger**, S. H., 'Locke's idea of God: rational or political myth?', *J. Pols.*, 42, 1980, 414–38.

5.391 **Brandt**, R., ed., *John Locke: Symposium Wolfenbüttel 1979*, Berlin, 1981. Includes J. Dunn, 'Individuality and clientage in the formation of Locke's social imagination', E. Leites, 'Locke's liberal theory of parenthood', and other essays principally on Locke's philosophy.

5.392 **Caffentzis**, C. G., *Clipped Coins, Abused Words and Civil Government: John Locke's Philosophy of Money*, Brooklyn, N.Y., 1989.

5.393 **Clark**, L. M. G., 'Woman and John Locke, or who owns the apples in the Garden of Eden?', *Can. J. Phil.*, 7, 1977, 699–724.

5.394 **Coby**, P., 'The law of nature in Locke's *Second Treatise*: is Locke a Hobbesian?', *Rev. Pol.*, 49, 1987, 3–28. To some extent, says Coby, because Locke adapts the principle of "might makes right" almost as thoroughly as Hobbes, though the former makes more effort to conceal the grim reality of power with a theory of justice. A contentious reading of Locke which accords more with that of Leo Strauss than with recent scholarship.

5.395 **Cohen**, J. G. A., 'Marx and Locke on land and labour', *Procs. Brit. Acad.*, 71, 1985, 357–88.

5.396 —— 'Structure choice and legitimacy: John Locke's theory of the state', *Phil. & Pub. Affairs*, 15, 1986, 301–24. Sophisticated analysis suggesting that Locke's belief in equal human freedom and rationality is not incompatible with his defence of a property owner's state.

5.397 **Colella**, E. P., 'The commodity form and socialization in Locke's state of nature', *Int. Sts. Phil.*, 16, 1984, 1–13.

5.398 **Coleman**, J., *John Locke's Moral Philosophy*, 1983.

5.399 **Cox**, R. H., *Locke on War and Peace*, 1966.

5.400 **Cranston**, M., *John Locke: A Biography*, 1957.

5.401 —— 'John Locke and the case for toleration', in S. Mendus and D. Edwards, ed., *On Toleration*, 1987, 101–21.

5.402 **Day**, J. P., 'Locke on property', *Phil. Q.*, 16, 1966, 207–20. Exposition and critique of Locke's justification of private property.

5.403 **den Hartogh**, G. A., 'Express consent and

full membership in Locke', *Pol. Sts.*, 38, 1990, 105–15. Argues that Locke slotted the passage on express consent into the *Two Treatises* in 1689 in order to legitimate William's accession.

5.404 **Dunn**, J., 'Consent in the political theory of John Locke', *Hist. J.*, 10, 1967, 153–82. Claims that consent for Locke is not, contrary to the usual view, a theory of how government should be organised, but a theory of how individuals become subject to political obligation and how legitimate political societies can arise.

5.405 —— 'Justice and the interpretation of Locke's political theory', *Pol. Sts.*, 16, 1968, 68–87. Demonstrates the ambivalent meaning of justice in Locke's thought, arguing that he ultimately gave it a more unitary meaning as the fundamental rule by which a Christian should live.

5.406 —— *Locke*, 1984. Short but authoritative account of his life and ideas, emphasising trust as the key concept in his understanding of politics.

5.407 —— 'The concept of "trust" in the politics of John Locke', in R. Rorty, J. B. Schneewind, and Q. Skinner, ed., *Philosophy in History: Essays on the historiography of philosophy*, 1984, 279–301.

5.408 —— *The Political Thought of John Locke: An Historical Account of the 'Two Treatises of Government'*, 1969. Sets his political thought firmly within its historical context and emphasises its foundation in Calvinist theology.

5.409 —— 'What is living and what is dead in the political philosophy of John Locke?', in *Interpreting Political Responsibility*, 1990, 9–25.

5.410 **Edwards**, S., 'Political philosophy belimed: the case of Locke', *Pol. Sts.*, 17, 1969, 273–93.

5.411 **Farr**, J., ' "So Vile and Miserable an Estate": the problem of slavery in Locke's political thought', *Pol. Theory*, 14, 1986, 263–89. Argues that though Locke's just-war theory of slavery is consistent with his account of natural rights, it is inadequate as an account of Afro-American slavery.

5.412 **Farr**, J., and **Roberts**, C., 'John Locke on the Glorious Revolution: a rediscovered document', *Hist. J.*, 28, 1985, 385–98. Discussion of a short manuscript in which Locke comments on the Revolution and the Williamite Settlement, the only document which contains his thoughts on these issues.

5.413 **Franklin**, J. H., *John Locke and the Theory of Sovereignty: Mixed Monarchy and the Right of Resistance in the Political Thought of the English Revolution*, 1978. Traces Locke's claim that sovereignty reverted to the people when government dissolved to the ideas of George Lawson in the 1650s.

5.414 **Friedman**, J., 'Locke as politician', *Crit. Rev.*, 2, 1988, 64–101.

5.415 **Gale**, G., 'John Locke on territoriality: an unnoticed aspect of the *Second Treatise*', *Pol. Theory*, 1, 1973, 472–85.

5.416 **Gauthier**, D., 'The role of inheritance in Locke's political theory', *Can. J. Econ. & Pol. Sc.*, 32, 1966, 38–45.

5.417 **Glat**, M., 'John Locke's historical sense', *Rev. Pol.*, 43, 1981, 3–21. Suggests that although Locke rejected English historical thought, he appreciated the more sophisticated form of historical political analysis taking shape on the continent in the writings of Bodin and others.

5.418 **Glausser**, W., 'Three approaches to Locke and the slave trade', *J. Hist. Ideas*, 51, 1990, 199–216. Tries to make sense of the conflicting ways in which Locke scholars have explained how the pre-eminent theorist of natural rights and liberties participated in the slave trade.

5.419 **Glenn**, G. D., 'Inalienable rights and Locke's argument for limited government: political implications of a right to suicide', *J. Pols.*, 46, 1984, 80–105.

5.420 **Goldie**, M., 'John Locke and Anglican Royalism', *Pol. Sts.*, 31, 1983, 61–85. Demonstrates that Locke's target in the *Two Treatises* was not merely Filmer but a whole generation of Anglican ideologues who embraced authoritarian conceptions of church and state. An excellent overview of Restoration political thought.

5.421 **Goldwin**, R. A., 'Locke's state of nature in political society', *West. Pol. Q.*, 29, 1976, 126–35. Argues that for Locke a remnant of the state of nature – the vestiges of natural liberty – is a feature of civil society, which has the potential of reverting to an unadulterated state of nature in the form of either tyranny or anarchy.

5.422 **Gough**, J. W., *John Locke's Political Philosophy: Eight Studies*, 1950. Dated but still readable account of the main aspects of Locke's political thought.

5.423 **Grady**, R. C., 'Obligation, consent and Locke's right to revolution: "Who is to judge?" ', *Can. J. Pol. Sc.*, 9, 1976, 277–92. Claims that in conceding a popular right to revolt against tyranny Locke nevertheless subordinates individual rights to the majority-rule procedure.

5.424 —— 'Property and 'natural political virtue': the implications of Locke as a "Liberal" ', *Polity*, 10, 1977, 86–103.

5.425 **Grant**, R. W., *John Locke's Liberalism*, Chicago, Ill., 1987. Depicts Locke's ideas as internally consistent and also as an example of liberal political theory, to be assessed partly on the basis of whether it offers an adequate solution to the doctrine's perennial problems.

5.426 —— 'Locke's political anthropology and Lockean individualism', *J. Pols.*, 50, 1988, 42–63.

5.427 **Hampsher-Monk**, I., 'Resistance and economy in Dr. Anglim's Locke', *Pol. Sts.*, 26, 1978, 91–98. Rejoinder to Anglim in the same volume.

5.428 —— 'Tacit concept of consent in Locke's *Two Treatises of Government*: a note on citizens, travellers, and patriarchalism', *J. Hist. Ideas*, 40, 1979, 135–39. Contends that Locke failed to escape from the patriarchal assumptions he set out to demolish.

5.429 **Hancey**, J. D., 'Class, commerce and the state: economic discourse and Lockean liberalism in the seventeenth century', *West. Pol. Q.*, 38, 1985, 565–821.

5.430 —— 'John Locke and the law of nature', *Pol. Theory*, 4, 1976, 439–54.

5.431 **Harpham**, E. J., ed., *John Locke's Two Treatises of Government: New Interpretations*, Lawrence, Kan., 1992. Collection of six essays demonstrating how interpretations of the *Two Treatises* have changed in recent decades: R. Ashcraft on Locke's conception of politics, E. Eisenach on his religious assumptions, D. Resnick on his rationalism, K. Vaughan on the economic background to the *Two Treatises*, and R. Hamowy and S. Newman on the impact of modern Locke scholarship on understandings of the Anglo-American liberal tradition.

5.432 —— 'Natural law and early liberal economic thought: a reconsideration of Locke's theories of value', *Soc. Sc. Q.*, 65, 1984, 966–74.

5.433 **Heyd**, T., 'Some remarks on science, method and nationalism in John Locke', *Hist. Euro. Ideas*, 16, 1993, 97–102.

Critical of Locke for justifying territorial annexation.

5.434 **Hinton**, R. W. K., 'A note on the dating of Locke's *Second Treatise*', *Pol. Sts.*, 22, 1974, 471–8. Suggests 1673–5 as a possible dating, which does not accord with the evidence of more recent scholarship.

5.435 **Hoffheimer**, M. H., 'Locke, Spinoza, and the idea of political equality', *Hist. Pol. Thought*, 7, 1986, 341–60. Demonstrates the similarities in the political thinking of the two writers and challenges the conventional assumption that Locke was not influenced by Spinoza.

5.436 **Hughes**, M., 'Locke on taxation and suffrage', *Hist. Pol. Thought*, 11, 1990, 423–43. Depicts Locke as a radical democrat, not an apologist for a property-based oligarchy.

5.437 —— 'Locke, taxation and reform: a reply to Wood', *Hist. Pol. Thought*, 13, 1992, 691–702. Stands by his claim that Locke was a radical democrat.

5.438 **Hundert**, E. J., 'Market society and meaning in Locke's political philosophy', *J. Hist. Phil.*, 15, 1977, 33–44. Repudiates the claim that Locke's theory was essentially bourgeois.

5.439 —— 'The making of *homo-faber*: John Locke between ideology and history', *J. Hist. Ideas*, 33, 1972, 3–22. Seeks to demonstrate how Locke, partly through his own ambiguities on the subject, 'established labor as a prime ingredient of social philosophy'.

5.440 **Isaac**, J. C., 'Was John Locke a bourgeois theorist?: a critical appraisal of Macpherson and Tully', *Can. J. Pol. & Soc. Theory*, 11, 1987, 107–29. Yes, says Isaac, defending C. B. Macpherson's depiction of Locke as a possessive individualist against the criticisms of James Tully, *A Discourse of Property: John Locke and his Adversaries*.

5.441 **Kato**, T., 'On the "complexity" of Locke's thought: a methodological sketch', *Hist. Pol. Thought*, 2, 1981, 287–313. Claims that an understanding of Locke's religious conviction must be the corner-stone of any attempt to identify his thought.

5.442 **Kelly**, P., ' "All things richly to enjoy" ': economics and politics in Locke's *Two Treatises of Government*', *Pol. Sts.*, 36, 1988, 273–93. Illuminating account of Locke's understanding of money, and of its relevance for his theory of labour in the

Two Treatises of Government.

5.443 **Kilcullen**, J., 'Locke on political obligation', *Rev. Pol.*, 45, 1983, 323–44. Argues that Locke's intention was not to demonstrate that political obligation rests upon consent, but rather that there are certain limits to political obligation which not even consent can set aside.

5.444 **Kraynak**, R. P., 'John Locke: from absolutism to toleration', *Am. Pol. Sc. Rev.*, 74, 1980, 53–69. Argues that the authoritarian stance of the young Locke in his *Two Tracts in Government* is not incompatible with his subsequent defence of religious toleration.

5.445 **Lebovics**, H., 'The uses of America in Locke's *Second Treatise of Government*', *J. Hist. Ideas*, 47, 1986, 567–81. Boldly contends that 'Locke employed the vast unexploited resources of the New World to supply the key premise of his political philosophy', namely the right to private property.

5.446 **Lemos**, R. M., 'Locke's theory of property', *Interpretation*, 5, 1975, 226–44.

5.447 **Letwin**, S. R., 'John Locke: liberalism and natural law', in K. Haakonssen, *Traditions of Liberalism: Essays on John Locke, Adam Smith and John Stuart Mill*, St. Leonards, 1988, 3–32. Argues that Locke's lack of commitment to pluralism makes him at best a half-hearted liberal.

5.448 **Lowenthal**, D., 'Locke on conquest' in C. H. Zuckert, ed., *Understanding the Political Spirit*, New Haven, Conn., 1988.

5.449 **McDonald**, V., 'A guide to the interpretation of Locke as political theorist', *Can. J. Pol. Sc.*, 6, 1973, 602–23.

5.450 **McNally**, D., 'Locke, Levellers and liberty: property and democracy in the thought of the first Whigs', *Hist. Pol. Thought*, 10, 1989, 17–41. Argues, against some recent interpretations, that the more we probe the depths of Locke's debt to Shaftesbury, the more we are forced to recognise the gulf that separates his political thought from that of the Levellers.

5.451 **Macpherson**, C. B., 'Locke on capitalist appropriation', *West. Pol. Q.*, 4, 1951, 550–66.

5.452 —— 'The social bearing of Locke's political theory', *West. Pol. Q.*, 7, 1954, 1–22.

5.453 **Mansfield**, H. C., 'On the political character of property in Locke', in

A. Kontos, ed., *Powers, Possessions and Freedom: Essays in Honor of C. B. MacPherson*, Toronto, 1979, 23–8.

5.454 **Marini**, F., 'John Locke and the revision of classical democratic theory', *West. Pol. Q.*, 22, 1969, 5–18.

5.455 **Marshall**, P., 'John Locke: between God and Mammon', *Can. J. Pol. Sc.*, 12, 1979 73–96.

5.456 **Mautner**, T., 'Locke on original appropriation', *Am. Phil. Q.*, 19, 1982, 259–70. Careful exposition of his account of the origins of private property.

5.457 **Mehta**, U. S., *The Anxiety of Freedom: Imagination and Individuality in Locke's Political Thought*, Ithaca, N.Y., 1992. Provocative interpretation arguing that for Locke the imagination is a potential threat to political stability, which made him preoccupied with social mechanisms for moulding individuality into the requirements of a liberal political order.

5.458 **Menake**, G. T., 'A research note and query on the dating of Locke's *Two Treatises*', *Pol. Theory*, 9, 1981, 547–8.

5.459 —— 'Research note and query on the dating of Locke's *Two Treatises*. A Sequel', *Pol. Theory*, 10, 1982, 609–11.

5.460 **Milam**, M., 'The epistemological basis of Locke's idea of property', *West. Pol. Q.*, 20, 1967, 16–30.

5.461 **Mitchell**, J., 'John Locke and the theological foundation of liberal toleration: A Christian dialectic of history', *Rev. Pol.*, 52, 1990, 64–83. His doctrine of toleration is to be understood in the context of his argument about the political significance of Christ who, according to Locke, separated the spiritual and political realms.

5.462 **Moulds**, H., 'John Locke's four freedoms seen in a new light', *Ethics*, 71, 1961, 121–26. His apparently inconsistent accounts of freedom are said to be relatively coherent.

5.463 —— 'Private property in John Locke's state of nature', *Am. J. Econ. & Soc.*, 23, 1964, 179–88.

5.464 —— 'John Locke and rugged individualism', *Am. J. Econ. & Soc.*, 24, 1965, 97–109.

5.465 **Mulligan**, L., **Richards**, J., and **Graham**, J. K., 'A concern for understanding: a case of Locke's precepts and practice', *Hist. J.*, 25, 1982, 841–57. Focuses on Locke's attempt to communicate with his audience by using familiar words in an innovative manner.

5.466 **Nelson**, J. M., 'Unlocking Locke's legacy: a comment', *Pol. Sts.* 26, 1978, 101–8. Rejoinder to M. Thompson, 'The reception of Locke's *Two Treatises of Government* 1690–1705', *Pol. Sts.*, 24, 1976.

5.467 **Oakley**, F., and **Urdang**, E., 'Locke, natural law and God', *Natural Law Forum*, 11, 1966, 102–9.

5.468 **Olivecrona**, K., 'Appropriation in the state of nature: Locke on the origin of property', *J. Hist. Ideas*, 35, 1974, 211–30.

5.469 —— 'Locke's theory of appropriation', *Phil. Q.*, 24, 1974, 220–34. Close textual analysis of Locke's account of the origin of private property.

5.470 **Parry**, G., 'Individuality, politics and the critique of paternalism in John Locke', *Pol. Sts.*, 12, 1964, 163–77.

5.471 —— *Locke*, 1978. One of the better introductions to his political thought.

5.472 —— 'Locke and representation in politics', *Hist. Euro. Ideas*, 3, 1982, 403–14.

4.473 **Pocock**, J. G. A., 'The myth of John Locke and the obsession with liberalism', in J. G. A. Pocock and R. Ashcraft, ed., *John Locke: Papers read at a Clark Library Seminar 10 December 1977*, Los Angeles, Calif., 1980, 3–24. Uses a blunderbuss against Marxists and non-Marxists who slot Locke into a liberal paradigm.

5.474 **Poole**, R, 'Locke and the bourgeois state', *Pol. Sts.*, 28, 1980, 222–37. Argues that the concept of class, which is absent from Locke's analysis in the *Second Treatise*, provides the key to its interpretation.

5.475 **Rapaczynski**, A., 'Locke's conception of property and the principle of sufficient reason', *J. Hist. Ideas*, 42, 1981, 305–16.

5.476 **Rea**, B., 'John Locke: between charity and welfare rights', *J. Soc. Phil.*, 18, 1987, 13–26.

5.477 **Resnick**, D., 'John Locke and the problem of naturalization', *Rev. Pol.*, 49, 1987, 368–88. Uses an unpublished manuscript of Locke on immigration to suggest that his mature political thought relied upon the model of an expanding commercial society based upon trade and economic competition.

5.478 —— 'Locke and the rejection of the ancient constitution', *Pol. Theory*, 12, 1984, 97–114. Claims that Locke eschewed an historical in favour of a philosophical mode of argument because he found Whig constitutional history defective – an odd claim given that Locke was one of the first Whigs.

5.479 **Richards**, J.; **Mulligan**, L., and **Graham**, J. K., ' "Property" and "People": political usages of Locke and some contemporaries', *J. Hist. Ideas*, 42, 1981, 29–51. Argues that by using the term property in a particular way Locke arrived at a political definition of the people radically different from that of his contemporaries.

5.480 **Riley**, P., 'Locke on "voluntary agreement" and political power', *West. Pol. Q.*, 29, 1976, 136–45.

5.481 —— 'On finding an equilibrium between consent and natural law in Locke's political philosophy', *Pol. Sts.*, 22, 1974, 632–52.

5.482 **Rohbeck**, J., 'Property and labour in the social philosophy of John Locke', *Hist. Euro. Ideas*, 5, 1984, 65–7.

5.483 **Russell**, P., 'Locke on express and tacit consent: misinterpretations and inconsistencies', *Pol. Theory*, 14, 1968, 291–306.

5.484 **Ryan**, A., 'Locke and the dictatorship of the bourgeoisie', *Pol. Sts.*, 13, 1965, 219–30. Critique of C. B. Macpherson's suggestion that the *Two Treatises* justify class rule, though Ryan concedes that 'it is beyond doubt a bourgeois mind which envisages all rights as property rights'.

5.485 —— 'Locke on freedom: some second thoughts', in K. Haakonssen, ed., *Traditions of Liberalism: Essays on John Locke, Adam Smith and John Stuart Mill*, St. Leonards, N.S.W., 1988, 33–58. Subtle on what Locke has to say about the connection between freedom and property, and generally persuasive in repudiating the claim that Lockean liberalism is an essentially 'privatised view of the world'.

5.486 **Sandoz**, E., 'The civil theology of liberal democracy. Locke and his predecessors', *J. Pols.*, 34, 1972, 2–37.

5.487 **Schochet**, G. J., 'John Locke and religious toleration', in L. G. Schwoerer, ed., *The Revolution of 1688–1689: Changing Perspectives*, 1992, 147–64.

5.488 —— ed., *Life, Liberty and Property: Essays on Locke's Political Ideas*, Belmont, Calif., 1971.

5.489 —— 'Radical politics and Ashcraft's treatise on Locke', *J. Hist. Ideas*, 50, 1989, 491–510. Questions aspects of R. Ashcraft's reading of Locke, in

Revolutionary Politics and Locke's "Two Treatises of Government", as a radical political egalitarian.

5.490 —— 'Toleration, revolution, and judgment in the development of Locke's political thought', *Pol. Sc.*, 40, 1988, 84–96. Suggests that the gap between his early tracts and later writings was not as great as is sometimes contended, the constant theme being Locke's attempt to reconcile the conflict between religious nonconformity and political order.

5.491 **Schwarzenbach**, S. A., 'Locke's two conceptions of property', *Soc. Theory & Pract.*, 14, 1988, 141–72.

5.492 **Schwoerer**, L. G., 'Locke, Lockean ideas, and the Glorious Revolution', *J. Hist. Ideas*, 51, 1990, 531–48. Uses papers that Locke wrote between 1690 and 1695 to throw light on his response to the Revolution.

5.493 **Seliger**, M., 'Locke's natural law and the foundation of politics', *J. Hist. Ideas*, 24, 1963, 337–54. Depicts Locke as a kind of liberal pluralist whose natural law doctrine justified 'a view of politics as a continuously competitive process of maintaining or re-establishing, by reference to rational criteria, a tolerable balance between powers which represent individual and collective rights and capacities'.

5.494 —— 'Locke's theory of revolutionary action', *West. Pol. Q.*, 16, 1963, 548–68.

5.495 —— *The Liberal Politics of John Locke*, 1968. Close textual analysis of the *Two Treatises*, though he tries too hard to depict Locke as a founder of modern liberalism.

5.496 **Simmons**, A. J., 'Locke's state of nature', *Pol. Theory*, 17, 1989, 449–70.

5.497 —— *The Lockean Theory of Rights*, Princeton, N.J., 1992. Attempts to detach Locke's theory of rights from its theological foundations in order to make it relevant to contemporary moral and political debates.

5.498 **Singh**, R., 'John Locke and the theory of natural law', *Pol. Sts.*, 9, 1961, 105–18.

5.499 **Snare**, F., 'Consent and conventional acts in John Locke', *J. Hist. Phil.*, 13, 1975, 27–36.

5.500 **Snyder**, D. C., 'Locke on natural law and property rights', *Can. J. Phil.*, 16, 1986, 723–50.

5.501 **Soles**, D. E., 'Intellectualism and natural law in Locke's *Second Treatise*', *Hist. Pol.*

Thought, 8, 1987, 63–82. Claims that the work 'provides a brief but philosophically interesting derivation of natural law which is independent of theological commitments'.

5.502 **Sparks**, A. W., 'Trust and teleology: Locke's politics and his doctrine of creation', *Can. J. Phil.*, 3, 1973, 263–73.

5.503 **Steinberg**, J., *Locke, Rousseau and the Idea of Consent: An Inquiry into the Liberal-Democratic Theory of Political Obligation*, Westport, Conn., 1978.

5.504 **Strauss**, L., 'Locke's doctrine of natural law', *Am. Pol. Sc. Rev.*, 52, 1958, 490–501. A contentious interpretation portraying Locke as quasi-Hobbesian.

5.505 **Tarcov**, N., *Locke's Education for Liberty*, Chicago, Ill., 1984.

5.506 —— 'Locke's *Second Treatise* and "the best fence against rebellion" ', *Rev. Pol.*, 43, 1981, 198–217. Thorough analysis of Locke's argument for a right of resistance.

5.507 **Tarlton**, C. D., 'A rope of sand: interpreting Locke's *First Treatise of Government*', *Hist. J.* 21, 1978, 43–73.

5.508 —— 'The Exclusion controversy, pamphleteering, and Locke's *Two Treatises*', *Hist. J.*, 24, 1981, 49–68. Argues that the *Two Treatises* was a strategic communication written to warn Charles II of the dangers of absolutism and of the likelihood of resistance should he persist in his absolutist claims.

5.509 —— 'The rulers now on earth: Locke's *Two Treatises* and the Revolution of 1688', *Hist. J.*, 28, 1985, 279–98. Argues that Locke published his book in late 1689 because, having written it during the Exclusion crisis to warn Charles II of the dangers of absolutism, he feared that William III showed signs of succumbing to the same temptations of power.

5.510 **Thompson**, M. P., 'Significant silences in Locke's *Two Treatises of Government*: constitutional history, contract and law', *Hist. J.*, 31, 1988, 275–94. Detailed survey of the diverse uses of contractual language in the 1680s and 1690s, from which he concludes that Locke avoided the discourse of constitutional contract favoured by his radical Whig contemporaries: 'And precisely because of these differences, Locke was not the covert, radical revolutionary that he has been painted in some recent historical research'.

5.511 —— 'The reception of Locke's *Two Treatises of Government*, 1690–1705', *Pol. Sts.* 24, 1976, 184–91. Demonstrates how infrequently the book was used by Locke's contemporaries to justify the Revolution of 1688.

5.512 **Tully**, J., *A Discourse on Property: John Locke and his Adversaries*, 1980. Dense analysis which surveys the theories of Suarez, Hobbes, Filmer and Pufendorf, treating Locke's doctrine not as a justification for private property but within the context of his belief that human beings are the 'workmanship' of God.

5.513 —— *An Approach to Political Philosophy: Locke in Contexts*, 1993. Collection of his essays written between 1979 and 1990.

5.514 —— 'Governing conduct', in E. Leites, ed., *Conscience and Casuistry in Early Modern Europe*, 1988, 12–71. Attempt to demonstrate by focusing on Locke that 'a new practice of governing conduct was assembled in the period from the Reformation to the Enlightenment': one which did not celebrate the sovereignty of individual conscience – as is often contended – but was rather 'an effort to create habits that would replace the conscience and guide conduct'.

5.515 —— 'Placing the Two Treatises', in N. Phillipson and Q. Skinner, ed., *Political Discourse in Early Modern Britain*, 1993, 253–80. On the similarities of Locke's political arguments with those of theories of the ancient constitution and of republicanism.

5.516 **von Leyden**, W., 'John Locke and natural law', *Phil.*, 31, 1956, 23–35. Clear exposition of Locke's doctrine of natural law and its importance within his moral and political philosophy.

5.517 **Waldron**, J., 'John Locke: social contract versus political anthropology', *Rev. Pol.*, 51, 1989, 3–28. Argues that Locke's gradualist account of the evolution of political society from the state of nature was intended to be historically accurate, but that he depicted it in contractural terms to accommodate historical events in a moral framework.

5.518 —— 'Locke, Tully and the regulation of property', *Pol. Sts.*, 32, 1984. Effective critique of J. Tully's argument, in *A Discourse on Property: John Locke and his Adversaries*, that for Locke property rights are conventional rather than natural.

5.519 —— 'Locke's account of inheritance and bequest', *J. Hist. Phil.*, 19, 1981, 39–51.

5.520 **Warner**, S. D., 'Anarchical snares: a reading of Locke's "Second Treatises" ', *Reason Papers*, 14, 1989, 1–24. Demonstrates how Locke repudiates Filmer's allegation that the doctrine of natural rights underpins anarchism.

5.521 **Weynark**, J. A., 'Money and Locke's theory of property', *Hist. Pol. Econ.*, 12, 1980.

5.522 **Williams**, A., 'Cohen on Locke, land and labour', *Pol. Sts.*, 40, 1992, 51–66. Challenges G. A. Cohen's contention, 'Marx and Locke on land and labour', *Procs. Brit. Acad.*, 71, 1985, that Locke's remarks on the value-creating capacity of labour are incoherent.

5.523 **Winfrey**, J. C., 'Charity versus justice in Locke's theory of property', *J. Hist. Ideas*, 42, 1981, 423–38.

5.524 **Wood**, E. M., 'Locke against democracy: consent, representation and suffrage in the *Two Treatises*', *Hist. Pol. Thought*, 13, 1992, 657–89. Argues against recent scholarship that he was not remotely a radical democrat, even by the standards of his day.

5.525 **Wood**, N., *John Locke and Agrarian Capitalism*, Los Angeles, Calif., 1984. Argues that Locke was an early theorist of agrarian capitalism and that his views on property and his economic ideas reflect contemporary agrarian changes.

5.526 —— *The Politics of Locke's Philosophy: A Social Study of 'An Essay Concerning Human Understanding'*, Berkeley, Calif., 1983. A Marxian critique of Locke's metaphysics and epistemology, which characterises Lockean philosophy as representative of a nascent bourgeoisie preparing to sever the traditional bonds of society.

5.527 **Wootton**, D., 'John Locke and Richard Ashcraft's *Revolutionary Politics*', *Pol. Sts.*, 40, 1992, 79–98. Challenges Ashcraft's portrayal of an ultra-radical Locke by examining the latter's views on colonization, poverty, the franchise, and the ancient constitution.

5.528 —— 'John Locke: Socinian or natural law theorist?', in J. E. Crimmins, ed., *Religion, Secularization and Political Thought: Thomas Hobbes to J. S. Mill*, 1989, 39–67.

5.529 **Yolton**, J. W., *A Locke Dictionary*, 1993. A survey of Locke's thinking through over

130 alphabetically organized entries.

5.530 —— *John Locke: Problems and Perspectives: A Collection of New Essays*, 1969. Includes R. Polin, 'John Locke's conception of freedom', M. Seliger, 'Locke, liberalism and nationalism', E. de Beer, 'Locke and English liberalism: the *Second Treatise of Government* in its contemporary setting', J. Dunn, 'The politics of Locke in England and America in the eighteenth century', G. J. Schochet, 'The family and the origins of the state in Locke's political philosophy', H. Aarsleff, 'The state of nature and the nature of man in Locke', and other essays on Locke's economics, theology and philosophy.

5.531 —— *Locke: An Introduction*, 1985. Principally an exposition of his ideas about morality, religion, education, and metaphysics, though including a short but perceptive account of the arguments of the *Two Treatises*.

5.532 —— 'Locke on the law of nature', *Phil. Rev.*, 67, 1958, 477–98. Reliable if dated analysis emphasising natural law as the moral underpinning of his political theory.

5.533 **Zvesper**, J., 'The utility of consent in John Locke's political philosophy', *Pol. Sts.*, 32, 1984, 55–67. Focuses on Locke's views about religious toleration and property to argue that his doctrine of consent combines aspects of voluntarism and utilitarianism.

Sidney

5.534 **Brown**, I. C., 'Algernon Sidney, the noble republican', *Hist. Today*, 34, Feb. 1984, 11–17.

5.535 **Conniff**, J., 'Reason and history in early Whig thought: the case of Algernon Sidney', *J. Hist. Ideas*, 43, 1982, 397–416. Argues that Sidney, in combining the historical discourse of the ancient constitution with the abstract language of contract, typified – in a way that Locke did not – common Whig arguments.

5.536 **Houston**, A. C., *Algernon Sidney and the Republican Heritage in England and America*, Princeton, N.J., 1991. Close analysis not only of Sidney's writings but of seventeenth-century republicanism, arguing that its complexity is captured neither by Machiavellian notions of virtue and corruption (J. G. A. Pocock) nor by C. B. Macpherson's concept of possessive individualism.

5.537 **Scott**, J., *Algernon Sidney and the English Republic, 1623–1677*, 1988. First part of Scott's intellectual biography of a leading republican, which is also an excellent guide to the political thought of the period as a whole.

5.538 —— *Algernon Sidney and the Restoration Crisis, 1677–1683*, 1991. Final part of Scott's intellectual biography of this influential republican activist and theorist, which sheds much light on the political thought of the 'Exclusion Crisis' of 1678–1683.

5.539 **Worden**, B., 'The Commonwealth kidney of Algernon Sidney', *J. Brit. Sts.*, 24, 1985, 1–40. Neat guide to the life and political ideas of a radical Whig.

Other thinkers

5.540 **Bywaters**, D., 'Dryden and the Revolution of 1688: political parallel 12 *Don Sabastian*', *J. Engl. & Germ. Philol.*, 85, 1986, 346–65. Contends that Dryden was a Jacobite.

5.541 **Christianson**, P., 'Young John Selden and the ancient constitution, ca. 1610–18', *Procs. Am. Phil. Soc.*, 128, 1984, 271–315.

5.542 **Condren**, C., 'Confronting the monster: George Lawson's reactions to Hobbes's *Leviathan*', *Pol. Sc.*, 40, 1988, 67–83. Suggests that Lawson's *Politica* owes much to his earlier confrontation with Hobbes, and that the book has a good deal in common with *Leviathan*.

5.543 —— 'George Lawson and the *Defensor Pacis*: reflections on the use of Marsilius in seventeenth-century England', *Medioevo*, 6, 1980, 595–618. Argues that Lawson was a Marsilian rather than a proto-Lockean.

5.544 —— *George Lawson's Politics and the English Revolution*, 1989. First full-scale study of his political ideas and of the ideological uses made of the *Politica* in the seventeenth century.

5.545 —— 'Resistance and sovereignty in Lawson's *Politica*: an examination of a part of Professor Franklin, his chimera', *Hist. J.*, 24, 1981, 673–81. Critical of J. H. Franklin's interpretation of Lawson in *John Locke and the theory of sovereignty*, particularly of his failure to grasp the influence on Lawson's thinking of

Marsilius of Padua.

5.546 —— '*Saca* before *civilis*: understanding the ecclesiastical politics of George Lawson', *J. Rel. Hist.*, 11, 1981, 524–35. Sets Lawson's political theory within the context of his ecclesiology.

5.547 —— 'The image of utopia in the political writings of Lawson', *Moreana*, 69, 1980, 1901–5. On Lawson's treatment of More.

5.548 **Conlon**, M. J., 'The passage on government in Dryden's *Absalom and Achitophel*', *J. Engl. & Germ. Philol.*, 78, 1979, 17–32. Argues that Dryden's work is a defence of kingship and an attack on Whiggism as a form of republicanism.

5.549 **Daly**, J., 'John Bramhall and the theoretical problems of royalist moderation', *J. Brit. Sts.*, 11, 1971, 26–44. On the political thought of an Anglican bishop whose numerous writings included several repudiating Hobbes.

5.550 **Frank**, J., *Cromwell's Press Agent: A Critical Biography of Marchamont Nedham 1620–1678*, Latham, Md., 1980. Story of a trimmer who was a royalist in the 1640s, subsequently defended the Cromwellian regime in *The Case of the Commonwealth of England* (1650), and then reverted to royalism after the Restoration.

5.551 **Gough**, J. W., 'James Tyrrell, Whig historian and friend of John Locke', *Hist. J.*, 19, 1976, 581–610. Combines biographical detail with an account of his ideas and his influence upon Locke.

5.552 **Harris**, P., 'Young Sir Henry Vane's arguments for freedom of conscience', *Pol. Sc.*, 40, 1988, 34–48. Account of Vane's theological arguments for freedom of conscience which demonstrates the connections between his theology and constitutional theory.

5.553 **Jones**, D. M., 'Sir Edward Coke and the interpretation of lawful allegiance in seventeenth-century England', *Hist. Pol. Thought*, 7, 1986, 321–41. On the uses made of Coke's doctrine of the common law and ancient constitution.

5.554 **MacLean**, A. H., 'George Lawson and John Locke', *Cambridge Hist. J.*, 9, 1947, 69–77. The first study to identify the similarities in the political thinking of the two.

5.555 **Mendle**, M., 'The ship money case, *The Case of Shipmony*, and the development of Henry Parker's parliamentary absolutism', *Hist. J.*, 32, 1989, 513–36. On how a leading parliamentary pamphleteer in the early 1640s developed a theory of parliamentary absolutism which echoed the arguments of his royalist opponents.

5.556 **Nicholls**, D., 'Divine analogy: the theological politics of John Donne', *Pol. Sts.*, 32, 1984, 570–80.

5.557 **Patterson**, A., 'John Donne, kingsman?', in L. L. Peck, ed., *The Mental World of the Jacobean Court*, 1991, 251–72. On his political ideas.

5.558 **Pawlisch**, H. S., *Sir John Davies and the Conquest of Ireland: A study in legal imperialism*, 1985. Deals with Davies's recourse to Roman law as Irish Attorney-General, questioning the argument of J. G. A. Pocock that English common lawyers constructed a mythical ancient constitution in ignorance of continental legal scholarship.

5.559 —— 'Sir John Davies, the ancient constitution and civil law', *Hist. J.*, 23, 1980, 689–702. Uses Davies's legal eclecticism and frequent recourse to civil law, particularly during his period as Attorney-General for Ireland, to question the proposition – advanced by J. G. A. Pocock and others – that English common lawyers were ignorant of continental law.

5.560 **Sanderson**, J., 'Philip Hunton's "appeasement": moderation and extremism in the English civil war', *Hist. Pol. Thought*, 3, 1982, 447–65. On Hunton's doctrine of mixed monarchy.

5.561 —— '*Serpent-salve*, 1643: the royalism of John Bramhall', *J. Eccl. Hist.*, 25, 1974, 1–14. On the moderate royalism of an Anglican bishop who was a fairly sophisticated political theorist.

5.562 **Schochet**, G. J., 'Between Lambeth and Leviathan: Samuel Parker on the Church of England and political order', in N. Phillipson and Q. Skinner, ed., *Political Discourse in Early Modern Britain*, 1993, 189–208. On a Restoration polemicist who argued for religious uniformity and political absolutism.

5.563 **Schonhorn**, M., *Defoe's Politics: Parliament, Power, Kingship, and 'Robinson Crusoe'*, 1991. Challenges the view that he was a possessive individualist or some other form of 'modern' thinker, arguing that his was a traditional 'royalism that retained its scriptural, medieval and English antecedents and never forgot that the people shared in the activating power of government'.

5.564 **Smart**, I. M., 'The political ideas of the Scottish covenanters, 1638–88', *Hist. Pol. Thought*, 1, 1980, 167–95. An analysis of the thought of the covenanters on obedience, legitimate resistance and the role of monarchy in the early modern state, which claims that their political philosophy rested on scripture and reason rather than historical precedent.

5.565 **Sommerville**, J. P., 'John Selden, the law of nature, and the origins of government', *Hist. J.*, 27, 1984, 437–47.

5.566 —— 'Oliver Cromwell and English political thought', in J. Morrill, ed., *Oliver Cromwell and the English Revolution*, 1990, 234–58. Careful analysis revealing the diverse roots of Cromwell's political thinking.

5.567 **Tuck**, R., ' "The Ancient Law of Freedom": John Selden and the civil war', in J. Morrill, ed., *Reactions to the English Civil War, 1642–1649*, 1982, 137–61. Demonstrates how Selden's support of the parliamentary cause in the 1640s was consistent with the political theory he had elaborated in *De Iure Naturali et Gentium juxtu Disciplinam Ebraeorum* and elsewhere.

5.568 **Wallace**, J. M., *Destiny His Choice: The Loyalism of Andrew Marvell*, 1968. Includes a useful exposition of the civil war debates and also an excellent account of the political ideas of the Engagement controversy of 1649–52.

5.569 **White**, S. D., *Sir Edward Coke and 'the Grievances of the Commonwealth'*, 1979. Focuses on his career and constitutional thinking in the 1620s.

5.570 **Ziskind**, M. A., 'John Selden: criticism and affirmation of the common law tradition', *Am. J. Leg. Hist.*, 19, 1975, 22–39.

(c) OTHER COUNTRIES

General

5.571 **Kossmann**, E. H., 'The devolopment of Dutch political theory in the seventeenth-century', in J. S. Bromley and E. H. Kossmann, ed., *Britain and the Netherlands*, Vol. 1, 1960, 91–110.

5.572 **Lovejoy**, D. S., *The Glorious Revolution i America*, New York, 1972. On the ideas c colonial rebels in the latter half of the seventeenth century, focusing on their exploitation of the Glorious Revolution fc their own purposes.

5.573 **Mulier**, E. H., 'A controversial republican: Dutch views on Machiavelli i the seventeenth and eighteenth centuries' in G. Bock, Q. Skinner and M. Viroli, ed. *Machiavelli and Republicanism*, 1990, 247–63.

5.574 —— 'The language of seventeenth-centur republicanism in the United Provinces: Dutch or European?', in A. Pagden, ed., *The Languages of Political Theory in Early Modern Europe*, 1987, 179–95.

5.575 —— *The Myth of Venice and Dutch Republican Thought*, Assen, 1980.

5.576 **Sargent**, L. T., 'Utopianism in colonial America', *Hist. Pol. Thought*, 4, 1983, 483–523. Looks at the earliest period of utopianism in America under four headings: the image of the native America as a noble savage, the literature depicting America in terms of an earthly paradise/ golden age, the millennial writings, and th often utopian foundations of the colonies.

5.577 **Van de Klashorst**, G. O., **Blom**, H. W., and **Haitsma Mulier**, E. O. G., *A Bibliography of Dutch Seventeenth-Century Political Thought: An Annotated Inventory*, Amsterdam, 1986.

Leibniz

5.578 **den Vyl**, D. J., 'The aristocratic principle in the political philosophy of Leibniz', *J. Hist. Phil.*, 15, 1977, 281–92. Contends that he saw monarchs and aristocrats as having to support scientific endeavours and welfare projects that advance the public good.

5.579 —— 'Science and justice in Leibniz', *New Schol.*, 52, 1978, 317–42.

5.580 **Friedrich**, C. J., 'Philosophical reflections of Leibniz on law, politics and the state', *Natural Law Forum*, 11, 1966, 79–91. One of the best accounts of Leibniz's political thought.

5.581 **Jolley**, N., *Leibniz and Locke: A Study of the New Essays on Human Understanding*,

1984. Contends that Leibniz was a conservative thinker whose political ideas were governed by a number of religious assumptions.

5.582 —— 'Leibniz on Hobbes, Locke's *Two Treatises*, and Sherlock's *Case of Allegiance*', *Hist. J.*, 18, 1975, 22–35. Argues that Leibniz's conservatism made him strongly opposed to the views expressed in Locke's *Two Treatises*.

5.583 **Meyer** , R. W., *Leibniz and the Seventeenth-Century Revolution*, 1952. Sketches a number of parallels between Leibniz's philosophical doctrines and his political ideas.

5.584 **Rescher**, N., *The Philosophy of Leibniz*, Pittsburgh, Penn., 1967. Contains a useful chapter on his ethical and political thought.

5.585 **Schrecker**, P., 'Leibniz's principles of international justice', *J. Hist. Ideas*, 7, 1946, 484–98. Sketches affinities between Leibniz's politico-juridical theories and his ideas on logic and metaphysics.

Pufendorf

5.586 **Hont**, I., 'The language of sociability and commerce: Samuel Pufendorf and the theoretical foundations of the "four-stages theory" ', in A. Pagden, ed., *The Languages of Political Theory in Early-Modern Europe*, 1987, 253–276. Argues that his theory of sociability 'was the result of Pufendorf's attempt to reconstruct Grotius's jurisprudence by applying the intellectual method of Thomas Hobbes'.

5.587 **Kreiger**, L., 'History and law in the seventeenth century: Pufendorf', *J. Hist. Ideas*, 21, 1960, 198–210. Argues that for Pufendorf politics was the meeting-ground of law and history: 'through politics the "moral science" of law was sufficiently loosened for history to have a place in the nature of human things'.

5.588 —— *The Politics of Discretion: Pufendorf and the Acceptance of Natural Law*, Chicago, Ill., 1965.

5.589 **Nutkiewz**, M., 'Samuel Pufendorf: obligation as the basis of the state', *J. Hist. Phil.*, 21, 1983, 15–29. Contrasts Pufendorf with Hobbes and Spinoza for whom 'mechanistic principles provided scientific, self-evident laws for the construction of a rational political theory. Pufendorf, by contrast, finds these self-evident principles neither in the mechanistic theory of nature nor in traditional divine theories of law but . . . in the working legal system itself'.

Spinoza

5.590 **Battisti**, G. S., 'Democracy in Spinoza's unfinished *Tractatus Politicus*', *J. Hist. Ideas*, 38, 1977, 623–34.

5.591 **Blom**, H. W., 'Virtue and republicanism: Spinoza's political philosophy in the context of the Dutch Republic', in H. G. Koenigsberger, ed., *Republiken und Republikanismus im Europa der fruhen Neuzeit*, Munich, 1988, 195–213.

5.592 **Dunner**, J., *Baruch Spinoza and Western Democracy: An Interpretation of his Philosophical, Religious, and Political Thought*, New York, 1955.

5.593 **Feuer**, L., *Spinoza and the Rise of Liberalism*, Boston, Mass., 1962.

5.594 **Geismann**, G., 'Spinoza: beyond Hobbes and Rousseau', *J. Hist. Ideas*, 1991, 35–53.

5.595 **Greene**, M., ed., *Spinoza: A Collection of Critical Essays*, New York, 1973. Only one of the essays deals directly with his political philosophy: H. Gildin, 'Spinoza and the political problem'.

5.596 **McShea**, R.J., *The Political Philosophy of Spinoza*, New York, 1968. Clear exposition linking his political thinking to his metaphysics and ethics.

5.597 **Mandelbaum**, M., and **Freeman**, E., ed., *Spinoza: Essays in Interpretation*, La Salle, Ill., 1975. Includes W. Sacksteder, 'Spinoza and democracy' and R. J. McShea, 'Spinoza: human nature and history'.

5.598 **Mara**, G. M., 'Liberal politics and moral excellence in Spinoza's political philosophy', *J. Hist. Phil.*, 20, 1982, 129–50. Exposition and critique of how he combines the claim that the morally superior way of life can be rationally reconciled with a liberal endorsement of democracy and the sanctity of private judgement.

5.599 **Pacchi**, A., '*Leviathan* and Spinoza's *Tractatus* on revelation: some elements for comparison', *Hist. Euro. Ideas*, 10, 1989, 577–93. Spinoza did not 'think, as Hobbes did, that religion, accepted by the subjects because of tradition, but made to fit the political needs of the state, had to be

conceived exclusively in terms of
preserving the power of the sovereign'.

5.600 **Pocock**, J. G. A., 'Spinoza and
Harrington: an exercise in comparison:
*Bijdragen en Mededelingen betreffende de
Geschiedenis der Nederlanden*, 102, 1987,
435–9.

5.601 **Sacksteder**, W., 'How much of Hobbes
might Spinoza have read?', *Southwestern J.
Phil.*, 11, 1980, 25–39.

5.602 **West**, D., 'Spinoza on positive freedom',
Pol. Sts., 41, 1993, 284–96. Spirited
defence of Spinoza's philosophy, arguing
that the concept of positive freedom
enables him to reconcile liberal toleration
with Hobbesian assumptions.

Other thinkers

5.603 **Cochrane**, E., 'The failure of political
philosophy in seventeenth-century
Florence: Lorenzo Magalotti's "Concordia
della Religione e del Principato" ', in A.
Molho and J. A. Tedeschi, ed.,
*Renaissance Studies in Honor of Hans
Baron*, Dekalb, Ill., 1971, 557–76.
Attributes Magalotti's flawed attempt at
political philosophy to unpropitious
historical circumstances.

5.604 **Dodge**, G. H., *The Political Theory of the
Huguenots of the Dispersion with Special
Reference to the Thought and Influence of
Pierre Jurieu*, New York, 1947. Detailed
study of Jurieu, the principal political
theorist of late seventeenth-century French
Calvinism.

5.605 **Edwards**, C. S., *Hugo Grotius: the miracle
of Holland*, Chicago, Ill., 1981.
Emphasises the constitutional elements in

his thought.

5.606 —— 'The law of nature in the thought of
Grotius', *J. Pol.*, 32, 1970, 784–807.
Although Grotius freed natural law from its
medieval moorings, he retained a belief in a
transcendental moral order: he was
neither a rationalist nor a secularist in the
modern sense.

5.607 **Haakonssen**, K., 'Hugo Grotius and the
history of political thought', *Pol. Theory*,
13, 1985, 239–65. Examines his influence
on the way subsequent writers understood
rights and natural law.

5.608 **Herman**, A., 'The Huguenot republic and
anti-republicanism in seventeenth-century
France', *J. Hist. Ideas*, 53, 1992, 249–69.
On the anti-republican language of
Catholic political thought.

5.609 **Hueglin**, T., 'Have we studied the wrong
authors? On the relevance of Johannes
Althusius', *Sts. Pol. Thought*, 1, 1992,
75–93.

5.610 **Labrousse**, E., 'The political ideas of the
Huguenot Diaspora (Bayle and Jurieu)', in
R. M. Golden, ed., *Church, State and
Society under the Bourbon Kings of France*,
Lawrence, Kan., 1982, 222–83.

5.611 **Sarashon**, L. T., 'The ethical and political
philosophy of Pierre Gassendi', *J. Hist.
Phil.*, 20, 1982, 239–60. Exposition of the
ideas of an early seventeenth-century
French social contract theorist.

5.612 **Whaley**, J., 'Obedient servants? Lutheran
attitudes to authority and society in the first
half of the seventeenth century: the case of
Johann Balthasa Schupp', *Hist. J.*, 35,
1992, 27–42. A scrutiny of the ideas of a
German writer suggests that Lutheranism
was less politically conservative than is
usually suggested.

6

EIGHTEENTH CENTURY

(a) GENERAL

6.1 **Brown**, S. C., ed., *Philosophers of the Enlightenment*, 1979. Includes D. D. Raphael, 'Adam Smith, philosophy, science, social science', D. Forbes, 'Hume and the Scottish Enlightenment', I. White, 'Condorcet: politics and reason', J. F. Brumfitt, 'Diderot: man and society', R. Grimsley, 'Jean-Jacques Rousseau, philosopher of nature' and B. Harrison, 'Kant and the sincere fanatic'.

6.2 **Cranston**, M., *Philosophers and Pamphleteers: Political Theorists of the Enlightenment*, 1986. Explores the central themes of the Enlightenment through a study of Montesquieu, Voltaire, Rousseau, Diderot, Holbach and Condorcet.

6.3 **Dunn**, J., 'The politics of Locke in England and America in the eighteenth century', in J. W. Yolton, ed., *John Locke: Problems and Perspectives*, 1969, 45–80. Standard account of the diverse uses to which his thought was put.

6.4 **Godechot**, J., *The Counter-Revolution: Doctrine and Action, 1789–1804*, New York, 1971. Detailed examination of Burke, Mallet, du Pan, de Maistre, de Bonald and Chateaubriand.

6.5 **Hellmuth**, E., ed., *The Transformation of Political Culture: England and Germany in the Late Eighteenth Century*, 1990. Twenty-two essays including D. Klippel, 'The true concept of liberty: political theory in Germany in the second half of the eighteenth century', J. Dinwiddy, 'Conceptions of revolution in English

radicalism of the 1790s', and R. Vierhaus, 'The revolutionizing of consciousness: a German utopia?'.

6.6 **Hirschman**, A. O., *The Passions and the Interests: Political Arguments for Capitalism before its Triumph*, 1978. Brilliantly reveals how the ideas of capitalism did not mark a radical disjuncture with existing styles of thinking, with separate sections on Montesquieu, Stewart, Millar, the Physiocrats and Smith.

6.7 **Kramnick**, I., *Republicanism and Bourgeois Radicalism: Political Ideology in Late Eighteenth-Century England and America*, Ithaca, N.Y., 1991. Argues, contrary to recent scholarship, that the dominant thought of the period was essentially liberal capitalist, and considers, among others, Priestley, Price, Burgh, Madison and Hamilton.

6.8 —— 'Republicanism revisionism revisited', *Am. Hist. Rev.*, 87, 1982, 629–64. Argues that J. G. A. Pocock and other revisionists, in conceptualising eighteenth-century political thought as civic humanism, underestimate Locke's 'influence on the entire century including the radicalism of post-Wilkes England and the ideology of the American founding'.

6.9 **Krieger**, L., *An Essay on the Theory of Enlightened Despotism*, Chicago, Ill., 1975. A short and elusive account of the concept in the eighteenth century.

6.10 **Lucas**, F. L., *The Art of Living: Four Eighteenth-Century Minds: Hume, Horace Walpole, Burke, Benjamin Franklin*, 1959. Attempts to reconstruct the mindset of this period in the form of four separate essays.

An insightful introduction, flawed by its ahistorical and opinionated approach.

6.11 **Pocock**, J. G. A., 'Conservative Enlightenment and democratic revolutions: the American and French cases in British perspective', *Govt. & Oppos.*, 24, 1989, 81–105. Argues that some Enlightenment thinkers were less concerned to emancipate individuals from tradition than with protecting sovereign authority and personal security against religious fanaticism and civil war. A typically brilliant overview of the period.

6.12 —— 'The problem of political thought in the eighteenth century: patriotism and politeness', *Theoretische Geschiedenis*, 9, 1982, 3–36.

6.13 **Richter**, M., 'Toward a concept of political illegitimacy: Bonapartist dictatorship and democratic legitimacy', *Pol. Theory*, 10, 185–214. Wide-ranging essay explaining how Montesquieu, Tocqueville, Guizot and Constant distinguished between legitimate and illegitimate regimes in Europe and America.

6.14 **Ripley**, R. B., 'Adams, Burke, and eighteenth-century conservatism', *Pol. Sc. Q.*, 80, 1965, 216–35. On the similarities and dissimilarities between the two, explaining the latter in terms of the differences between English and American society.

6.15 **Schlereth**, T. J., *The Cosmopolitan Ideal in Enlightenment Thought: Its Form and Function in the Ideas of Franklin, Hume, and Voltaire, 1694–1790*, 1977. Traces the impact of this ideal on 'Enlightenment intellectual life throughout the trans-Atlantic community' in an ambitious study of intellectual trends, relating to science, history, religion and politics in this period.

6.16 **Sher**, R. B. and **Smitten**, J. R., *Scotland and America in the Age of Enlightenment*, 1990. Includes T. P. Miller, 'Witherspoon, Blair and the rhetoric of civic humanism', D. W. Livingston, 'Hume, English barbarism and American independence', A. S. Skinner, 'Adam Smith and America: the political economy of conflict', and B. P. Lenman, 'Aristocratic "country" Whiggery in Scotland and the American Revolution'.

6.17 **Vogel**, U., 'When the earth belonged to all: the land question in eighteenth-century justifications of private property', *Pol. Sts.*, 36, 1988, 102–22. Examines the

tension betwen the libertarian and egalitarian premises of liberalism by focusing upon Smith's and Kant's views on property.

(b) BRITISH ISLES

General

6.18 **Barnard**, T. C., 'The uses of 23 October 1641 and Irish Protestant celebrations', *Eng. Hist. Rev.*, 106, 1991, 889–920. Excellent account of the ideology of Irish Anglicans as revealed in political sermons.

6.19 **Black**, J., 'The European idea and Britain, 1688–1815', *Hist. Euro. Ideas*, 17, 1993, 439–60. On how the peculiarities of Britain set its thinkers apart from the European Enlightenment.

6.20 **Bland**, D. E., 'Population and liberalism, 1770–1817', *J. Hist. Ideas*, 34, 1973, 113–22. On how the Physiocrats, Burke, Smith, Paley and Malthus conceived of the relationship between property and population.

6.21 **Bonwick**, C., *English Radicals and the American Revolution*, Chapel Hill, N.C., 1979. Focuses upon four types of radicalism: utilitarianism, natural rights theory, the commonwealth or real Whig tradition and the Wilkite movement.

6.22 **Boulton**, J. T., 'Arbitrary power: an eighteenth-century obsession', *Sts. Burke & Time*, 9, 1968, 905–26. On the treatment of the concept in the fiction of the 1740s and 50s, especially in Fielding, Smollett and Richardson.

6.23 —— *The Language of Politics in the Age of Wilkes and Burke*, 1963. Thorough survey of the ideological response both to Wilkes's movement and the French Revolution.

6.24 **Brewer**, J., 'English radicalism in the age of George III', in J. G. A. Pocock, ed., *Three British Revolutions: 1641, 1688, 1776*, Princeton, N.J., 1980, 323–67. Strong on the antecedents of radicalism in Country ideology.

6.25 —— *Party Ideology and Popular Politics at the Accession of George III*, 1976. Magisterial account of the interplay between popular and parliamentary politics in an attempt to explain the transformation of party politics. Examines Burke's conception of party, and how Wilkes, his followers and other radicals contributed to parliamentary reform.

6.26 —— 'The Wilkites and the law, 1763–74: a study of radical notions of government', in J. Brewer and J. Styles, ed., *An Ungovernable People. The English and their Law in the Seventeenth and Eighteenth Centuries*, 1980, 128–71.

6.27 **Browning**, R., *Political and Constitutional Ideas of the Court Whigs*, Baton Rouge, La., 1982. Analysis of the politico-constitutional arguments put forward by the Whigs in office from 1720–58. Includes chapters on John Hervey, Benjamin Hoadly, Thomas Herring, Samuel Squire and Philip Yorke.

6.28 **Burtt**, S., *Virtue Transformed: Political Argument in England, 1688–1740*, 1992. Carefully traces the emergence of a privately oriented conception of civic virtue, with perceptive chapters on *Cato's Letters*, *Bolingbroke*, the Society for Reformation of Manners, Mandeville, and the Court Whigs.

6.29 **Clark**, J. C. D., *English Society, 1688–1832*, 1985. Major exercise in revisionism, claiming that England remained an *ancien régime*, and doing so through an extensive survey of conservative and radical political ideas. Particularly illuminating on Anglican political theology, but perceptive about all aspects of the political thought of the period.

6.30 —— *Revolution and Rebellion: State and Society in England in the Seventeenth and Eighteenth Centuries*, 1986. Contains a chapter on political ideology, which provides a critique of historians who conceptualise the ideas of post-revolutionary England as a form of bourgeois political discourse.

6.31 **Creasey**, J., 'Some dissenting attitudes towards the French Revolution', *Transactions of the Unitarian Historical Society*, 13, 1966, 155–67.

6.32 **Dickinson**, H. T., *Liberty and Property: Political Ideology in Eighteenth-Century Britain*, 1977. Comprehensive account of Whig, Tory and radical thinking, and as such an indispensable guide to the ideas of the period.

6.33 —— 'Radicals and reformers in the age of Wilkes and Wyvill', in J. Black, ed., *British Politics and Society from Walpole to Pitt, 1742–1789*, 1990, 123–46. Includes a discussion of the ideological context of their activities.

6.34 —— 'The eighteenth-century debate on the "Glorious Revolution" ', *History*, 61, 1976, 28–45. Focuses upon Tory and Whig interpretations, culminating in the orthodox Whig view, advanced by Hume, that the Revolution had established liberty in Britain for the first time. Also examines radical interpretations of the Revolution and Burke's response to them.

6.35 —— 'The eighteenth-century debate on the sovereignty of parliament', *Trans. Royal Hist. Soc.*, 5th ser., 26, 1976, 189–210.

6.36 —— 'The rights of man: from John Locke to Tom Paine', in O. D. Edwards and G. A. Shepperson, ed., *Scotland, Europe and the American Revolution*, 1976, 38–58.

6.37 **Eayrs**, J., 'The political ideas of the English agrarians, 1775–1815', *Can. J. Econ. & Pol. Sc.*, 18, 1952, 287–302. On the proposals of Paine, Thomas Spence and William Ogilvie for eliminating rural poverty.

6.38 **Francis**, M. and **Morrow**, T., 'After the ancient constitution: political theory and English constitutional writings, 1765–1832', *Hist. Pol. Thought*, 9, 1988, 283–302. Examines the constitutional thought of Blackstone, Millar and Hallam, revealing how the discourse of the balanced constitution was displaced by the ideas of strong sovereignty and individual rights.

6.39 **Gascoigne**, J., 'Anglican latitudinarianism and political radicalism in the late eighteenth century', *History*, 71, 1986, 22–38. Challenges the view that Anglicans invariably supported the *status quo*, demonstrating the support of some Whig churchmen for civil and political liberties.

6.40 **Goldsmith**, M. M., 'Faction detected: ideological consequences of Robert Walpole's decline and fall', *History*, 64, 1979, 1–19. Careful examination of the nuances of political thought expressed in newspapers, poetry and the writings of Spelman and Hume, arguing that what emerged was a more sceptical, disillusioned view of politics.

6.41 —— 'Liberty, luxury and the pursuit of

happiness', in A. Pagden, ed., *The Languages of Political Theory in Early-Modern Europe*, 1987, 225–51. Examines the role of civic humanism as an ideological framework for discussing politics in eighteenth-century Britain.

6.42 **Goodale**, J. R., 'J. G. A. Pocock's neo-Harringtonians: a reconsideration', *Hist. Pol. Thought*, 1, 1980, 237–61. Argues that Pocock's placing of the work of neo-Harringtonians from Henry Neville to Bolingbroke within the intellectual tradition of civic humanism is misplaced insofar as it overstates both their attachment to the past and their antipathy towards contemporary social and economic developments. Among writers considered are John Trenchard and Bolingbroke.

6.43 **Gunn**, J. A. W., *Beyond Liberty and Property: The Process of Self-Recognition in Eighteenth-Century Political Thought*, Kingston and Montreal, 1983. Collection of perceptive essays on 'legal tyranny' in political rhetoric, Mandeville, the persistence of high-Tory ideas, the political thought of David Williams, and ideas of liberty and patriotism.

6.44 —— 'Opinion in eighteenth-century thought: what did the concept purport to explain?', *Utilitas*, 5, 1993, 17–33. Carefully traces the evolution of the idea of public opinion.

6.45 **Hamowy**, R., 'Cato's Letters, John Locke, and the republican paradigm', *Hist. Pol. Thought*, 11, 1990, 273–94. Takes issue with J. G. A. Pocock's claim that the political thought of the period can best be analysed not in terms of a concern for natural rights, but as a product of Renaissance humanism, arguing that the Lockean themes of *Cato's Letters* show the strength of a radical Whig paradigm.

6.46 **Hill**, J. R., 'Popery and protestantism, civil and religious liberty: the disputed lessons of Irish history, 1690–1812', *Past. & Pres.*, 118, 1988, 96–129. Illuminating account of the conflicting political arguments to be found in the Irish historiography of the period.

6.47 **Hole**, R., *Pulpits, Politics and Public Order in England, 1760–1832*, 1989. Extensive examination of Christian political argument, focusing on Anglican divines but including the whole spectrum of opinion – Roman Catholics, Methodists, Old Dissenters, Unitarians – and discussing Paine, Godwin, Wollstonecraft, Price, Hume and many others. The French Revolution, according to Hole, prompted Anglican writers to abandon the constitutional arguments used since 1689 in favour of 'social theory' which emphasised the need for inequality and subordination, instead of considering the origin of political society and nature of government authority.

6.48 **Kelley**, J., 'The origins of the act of union: an examination of unionist opinion in Britain and Ireland, 1650–1800', *Irish Historical Studies*, 25, 1987, 236–63. Perceptive account of the political arguments for a closer union of Ireland and Britain.

6.49 **Kelly**, P., 'Perceptions of Locke in eighteenth-century Ireland', *Proceedings of the Royal Irish Academy*, 89, 1989, 17–35. Excellent account of the uses made of Locke, from Molyneux to the United Irishmen, and of how conservative writers attempted to reconstruct a less radical version of his ideas.

6.50 —— 'William Molyneux and the spirit of liberty in eighteenth-century Ireland', *Eighteeth Century Ireland*, 3, 1988, 133–48. On the use of his *The Case of Ireland* in Irish political discourse.

6.51 **Kirk**, R., 'Three pillars of order: Edmund Burke, Samuel Johnson, Adam Smith', *Modern Age*, 25, 1981, 226–33. Compares their views on the relationship between freedom and authority.

6.52 **Kramnick**, I., 'Augustan politics and English historiography: the debate on the English past, 1730–35', *Hist. & Theory*, 6, 1967, 35–56. Argues that although Walpole was a Whig in politics, his historiography follows Tory traditions. Also suggests that the Tory Bolingbroke held a Whig view of history.

6.53 —— *Bolingbroke and his Circle: The Politics of Nostalgia in the Age of Walpole*, Cambridge, Mass., 1968. Comprehensive account of the political ideas of the period – including those of Commonwealth men such as Trenchard, Molesworth and Toland, as well as Walpole and Bolingbroke – in which Bolingbroke and others are said to have developed a coherent oppositional ideology to finance capitalism.

6.54 —— 'English middle-class radicalism in the eighteenth century', *Literature of*

Liberty, 3, 1980, 5–48.

6.55 —— 'Religion and radicalism: English political theory in the age of revolution', *Pol. Theory*, 5, 1977, 505–30. On Priestley, Paine and other radicals, presenting their ideas as a form of 'bourgeois ideology'.

6.56 **Langford**, P., 'Old Whigs, old Tories and the American Revolution', *Journal of Imperial and Commonwealth History*, 8, 1979–80, 106–30. Excellent account of the political thinking of the period; useful in demonstrating the persistence – contrary to the suggestion of some commentators – of a Tory ideology.

6.57 **Lee**, J., 'Political antiquarianism unmasked: the conservative attack on the myth of the ancient constitution', *Bulletin of the Institute of Historical Research*, 55, 1982, 166–79. On how John Reeves and other anti-Jacobin writers countered the argument of radicals that enshrined in the Anglo-Saxon constitution were democratic principles.

6.58 **Lincoln**, A., *Some Political and Social Ideas of English Dissent, 1763–1800*, 1971. Classic study portraying the variety and complexity of dissenting political theory, with discussion of Priestley, Price and many other writers.

6.59 **Loftis**, J., 'Political and social thought in drama', in R. D. Hume, ed., *The London Theatre World, 1660–1800*, Carbondale, Ill., 1980, 253–85. Argues that 'the tragedies more than the comedies reveal changing patterns of political thought'.

6.60 **Monod**, P. K., *Jacobitism and the English People, 1688–1788*, 1989. Excellent survey, illustrating that Jacobites were not merely reactionaries yearning for a restoration of divine right monarchy, but that among them were Whigs opposed to the establishment.

6.61 **Peters**, M., 'The "Monitor" on the constitution, 1755–65: new light on the ideological origins of English radicalism', *Eng. Hist. Rev.*, 86, 1971, 706–25. On a weekly political essay paper which pressed the traditional concept of mixed government into service on behalf of 'country ideology'.

6.62 **Pocock**, J. G. A., *Virtue, Commerce and History: Essays on Political Thought and History Chiefly in the Eighteenth Century*, 1985. Collection of essays by the most influential historian of eighteenth-century political thought on modes of historical

time, Hume, conservatism, Whiggism, 1776, Gibbon, Tucker and Burke.

6.63 **Robbins**, C., *The Eighteenth Century Commonwealth-Man: Studies in the Transmission, Development and Circumstance of English Liberal Thought from the Restoration of Charles II until the War with the Thirteen Colonies*, Cambridge, Mass., 1959. Classic study of eighteenth-century radical Whig and republican thought in England, Ireland and Scotland.

6.64 **Sack**, J. J., *From Jacobite to Conservative: Reaction and Orthodoxy in Britain, c.1760–1832*, 1993. The most thorough and reliable account of right-wing ideology in the period, arguing that at its heart lay neither nationalism nor monarchism but a defence of the Church of England.

6.65 **Simms**, J. G., *Colonial Nationalism, 1698–1776*, Cork, 1976. Standard account of the arguments of Swift, William Molyneux and others for the right of Ireland's protestant colonists to exercise 'domestic self-government within an imperial framework'.

6.66 **Stafford**, W., *Socialism, Radicalism and Nostalgia. Social Criticism in Britain, 1775–1830*, 1987. Views all the major forms of non-liberal social and political thought as united by anti-industrial and anti-commercial assumptions – and thus as less disparate than political preferences alone might have indicated.

6.67 **Stromberg**, R., *Religious Liberalism in Eighteenth-Century England*, 1954. Readable account of the political, as well as the religious, debates of the century.

6.68 **Zaller**, M., 'The continuity of British radicalism in the seventeenth and eighteenth centuries', *Eighteenth-Cent. Life*, 6, 1981, 17–38.

The Scottish Enlightenment

6.69 **Bowles**, P., 'The origin of property and the development of historical science', *J. Hist. Ideas*, 76, 1985, 197–209. Examines the views of Smith, Hutcheson and Millar on property, arguing that Smith and Hutcheson sought to arrive at a universal doctrine of property whilst Millar was more concerned with its anthropological dimension.

6.70 **Campbell**, R. H. and **Skinner**, A. S., ed., *The Origins and Nature of the Scottish*

Enlightenment, 1982. Includes N. MacCormick, 'Law and Enlightenment', T. D. Campbell, 'Francis Hutcheson: "Father" of the Scottish Enlightenment', D. Forbes, 'Natural law and the Scottish Enlightenment', and K. Haakonssen, 'What might properly be called natural jurisprudence?'.

6.71 **Haakonssen**, K., 'Moral philosophy and natural law: from the Cambridge Platonists to the Scottish Enlightenment', *Pol. Sc.*, 40, 97–110. Examines the influence of the Cambridge Platonists on the thought of Richard Cumberland and Francis Hutcheson, and argues that the ideas of the Platonists shaped Scottish conceptions of civic moralism and legalism.

6.72 **Hamowy**, R., *The Scottish Enlightenment and the Theory of Spontaneous Order*, Carbondale, Ill., 1987. Reveals the Scottish Enlightenment contribution to the theory of spontaneously generated orders by focusing on Hume's analysis of justice, Smith's economic writings, and Ferguson's sociological works.

6.73 **Hont**, I. and **Ignatieff**, M., ed., *Wealth and Virtue: The Shaping of Political Economy in the Scottish Enlightenment*, 1983. The 'jewel in the crown' of much recent work on the Scottish Enlightenment. Essays focusing on political ideas include I. Hont and M. Ignatieff, 'Needs and justice in *The Wealth of Nations*', J. Dunn, 'From applied to social analysis: the break between John Locke and the Scottish Enlightenment', J. Robertson, 'The Scottish Enlightenment and the limits of the civic tradition', N. Phillipson, 'Adam Smith as civic moralist', J. G. A. Pocock, 'Cambridge paradigms and Scottish philosophers: a study of the relations between the civic humanist and the civic jurisprudential interpretation of eighteenth-century social thought', D. Winch, 'Adam Smith's "enduring particular result": a political and cosmopolitan perspective', I. Hont, 'The "rich country–poor country" debate in Scottish classical political economy', and M. Ignatieff, 'John Millar and individualism'.

6.74 **Hope**, V., ed., *Philosophers of the Scottish Enlightenment*, 1989. Includes M. Dalgarne, 'Reid's natural jurisprudence: the language of rights and duties', J. Jenkins, 'Hume's account of sympathy – some difficulties', K. Haakonssen,

'From moral philosophy to political economy: the contribution of Dugald Stewart', and N. MacCormick, 'The idea of liberty: some reflections on Lorimer's institutes'.

6.75 **McBride**, I., 'The school of virtue: Francis Hutcheson, Irish Presbyterians and the Scottish Enlightenment', in D. G. Boyce, R. R. Eccleshall and V. Geoghegan, ed., *Irish Political Thought since the Seventeenth Century*, 1993, 73–99. Innovative exploration of civic humanism in Irish political discourse, and of the influence of Hutcheson in linking Ireland to the Scottish Enlightenment.

6.76 **Mizuta**, H., 'Two Adams in the Scottish Enlightenment: Adam Smith and Adam Ferguson on progress', *Sts. Voltaire*, 191, 1980, 812–19. Examines their views on the economic division of labour and a standing army.

6.77 **Sher**, R. B., 'Adam Ferguson, Adam Smith, and the problem of national defence', *J. Mod. Hist.*, 61, 1989, 240–89. Examines the debate between Ferguson and Smith on the need for a standing army and demonstrates how defence was linked to issues of moral philosophy and political economy.

6.78 **Stein**, P. G., 'Law and society in eighteenth-century Scottish thought', in N. T. Phillipson and R. Mitchison, ed., *Scotland and the Age of Improvement*, 1970, 148–68. An informative survey of the development of Scottish legal thinking.

6.79 —— 'The general notions of contract and property in eighteenth-century Scottish thought', *Juridical Review*, 8, 1963, 1–13. Examines the ideas of Hutcheson, Reid, Stair, Hume, Smith and Millar on property, natural law and contract.

6.80 **Trevor-Roper**, H., 'The Scottish Enlightenment', *Sts. Voltaire*, 58, 1967, 1635–58. Fine analysis of the ideas of Hutcheson, Hume, Ferguson, Robertson Smith and Millar.

The French Revolution

6.81 **Bernstein**, S., 'English reactions to the French Revolution: the division of public opinion between the Burkeites and the Paineites', *Sc. & Soc.*, 9, 1945, 147–71.

6.82 **Butler**, M., *Romantics, Rebels and*

Revolutionaries, 1981. Standard account of the political ideas of romantic writers such as Wordsworth who supported the French Revolution.

6.83 **Canavan**, F. P., 'The Burke–Paine controversy', *Pol. Sc. Re-r*, 6, 1976, 389–420.

6.84 **Claeys**, G., 'Republicanism versus commercial society: Paine, Burke and the French Revolution debate', *Hist. Euro. Ideas*, 11, 1989, 313–24.

6.85 —— 'The French Revolution debate and British political thought', *Hist. Pol. Thought*, 11, 1990, 59–80. Excellent survey of a wide range of pamphlet literature, arguing that much of the controversy was waged in terms not immediately given in the writings of Burke and Paine.

6.86 **Cone**, C. B., 'English reform ideas during the French Revolution', *Southwestern Social Science Quarterly*, 27, 1947, 368–84.

6.87 —— 'Pamphlet replies to Burke's *Reflections*', *Southwestern Social Science Quarterly*, 26, 1945, 22–34.

6.88 —— *The English Jacobins: Reformers in Late Eighteenth-Century England*, New York, 1968.

6.89 **Cookson**, J. E., *The Friends of Peace: Anti-War Liberalism in England, 1793–1815*, 1982. Thorough account of an anti-aristocratic ideology, grounded in religious dissent, of which anti-war rhetoric was part.

6.90 **Crossley**, C. and **Small**, I., ed., *The French Revolution and British Culture*, 1989. Essays touching on political ideas include G. Woodcock, 'The meaning of revolution in Britain, 1770–1800', B. Rigby, 'Radical spectators of the Revolution: the case of the *Analytical Review*', and R. Scruton, 'Man's second disobedience: a vindication of Burke'.

6.91 **Dickinson**, H. T., ed., *Britain and the French Revolution, 1789–1815*, 1989. Includes J. O'Gorman, 'Pitt and the "Tory" reaction to the French Revolution', J. Derry, 'The opposition Whigs and the French Revolution, 1789–1815', H. T. Dickinson, 'Popular conservatism and militant loyalism, 1789–1815', M. Elliott, 'Ireland and the French Revolution' and I. Robertson Scott, ' "Things as they are": the literary response to the French Revolution, 1789–1815', all of which consider the political ideas of the period.

6.92 —— *British Radicalism and the French Revolution, 1789–1815*, 1985. Excellent, brief survey of the activities and ideas of English Jacobins and their successors.

6.93 —— with **Keogh**, D. and **Whelan**, K., ed., *The United Irishmen: Republicanism, Radicalism and Rebellion*, Dublin, 1993. Includes R. B. McDowell, 'Burke and Ireland', D. Dickson, 'Paine and Ireland', J. Brims, 'Scottish radicalism and the United Irishmen' and K. Whelan, 'The United Irishmen, the Enlightenment and popular culture'.

6.94 **Elliott**, M., *Partners in Revolution: The United Irishmen and France*, 1982. Standard account of the Irish Jacobins.

6.95 —— 'The origins and transformation of early Irish republicanism', *Int. Rev. Soc. Hist.*, 23, 1978, 405–28. Illuminating account of the ideas of the United Irishmen.

6.96 **Fennessy**, R. R., *Burke, Paine, and the Rights of Man: A Difference of Political Opinion*, The Hague, 1963. A clear and thorough exposition not only of their ideas, but also of how the Burke–Paine controversy was treated by public opinion in the 1790s, arguing that 'Burke's attack on the French Revolution and its English admirers was generally considered to be exaggerated', and that Paine's views were 'too radical and republican for most readers'.

6.97 **Goodwin**, A., *The Friends of Liberty: The English Democratic Movement in the Age of the French Revolution*, 1979. Standard account of English radicalism from Wilkes to 1799 which, though not primarily concerned with political ideas, is excellent in establishing their historical context.

6.98 **Hampsher-Monk**, I., 'Civic humanism and parliamentary reform: the case of the Society of the Friends of the People', *J. Brit. Sts.*, 18, 1978, 70–89. On the arguments for an extended franchise by Francis, Wyvill and others in the 1790s, demonstrating the neo-Harrington nature of their arguments.

6.99 **Hole**, R., 'British counter-revolutionary popular propaganda in the 1790s', in C. Jones, ed., *Britain and Revolutionary France: Conflict, Subversion and Propaganda*, 1983, 53–69. On the flood of propaganda from right-wing organisations such as the Association for Preserving

Liberty and Property against Republicans and Levellers.

6.100 **Kelly**, G., *The English Jacobin Novel, 1780–1805*, 1976. Standard account of the political ideas of radical novelists of the period.

6.101 **Pendleton**, G. T., 'The English pamphlet literature of the age of the French Revolution anatomized', *Eighteenth-Cent. Life*, 5, 1978, 29–37.

6.102 —— 'Towards a bibliography of the *Reflections* and *Rights of Man* controversy', *Bull. Res. Hum.*, 85, 1982, 65–103. Describes about 350 titles belonging to the Burke–Paine debate.

6.103 **Schofield**, T. P., 'Conservative political thought in Britain in response to the French Revolution', *Hist. J.*, 29, 1986, 601–22. Examines the response of a number of British conservative thinkers to the French Revolution, including Burke, Pitt, Paley, Ferguson and Drummond.

6.104 **Smyth**, J., *The Men of No Property: Irish Radicals and Popular Politics in the Late Eighteenth Century*, 1992. Includes perceptive discussion of the ideological context of the United Irishmen.

6.105 **Stevenson**, J., 'Paineites to a man? The English popular radical societies in the 1790s', *Society for the Study of Labour History Bulletin*, 54, 1989, 14–25. Examines the influence of Paine's work, especially *The Rights of Man*, on the development of British radicalism.

6.106 **Walvin**, J., 'The English Jacobins, 1789–1799', *Historical Reflections*, 4, 1977, 91–110.

6.107 **Whale**, J. C., 'Literal and symbolic representation: Burke, Paine and the French Revolution', *Hist. Euro. Ideas*, 16, 1993, 343–9. Contends that in Burke's *Reflections* 'the organism of the state depends upon difference on all levels', whereas Paine uses a geometrical model to conceptualise society.

6.108 **Winkler**, H. R., 'The pamphlet campaign against political reform in Great Britain, 1790–95', *Historian*, 15, 1952, 23–40.

Burke

6.109 **Adams**, L. L., 'Edmund Burke: the psychology of citizenship', *Interpretation*, 3, 1974, 191–204.

6.110 **Archibald**, D. N., 'Edmund Burke and the conservative imagination', *Colby Library Quarterly*, 12, 1976, 191–204 and 13, 1977, 19–41. Part one is an ideologically charged attack upon twentieth-century conservative assessment and appropriation of Burke's thought. Part two is a psychological analysis of his work and political career.

6.111 **Ayling**, S., *Edmund Burke: His Life and Opinions*, 1988. Sets Burke against the background of contemporary events and his personal and family circumstances to reveal a man of principle and theory who regarded politics as theatre.

6.112 **Baldaschino**, J., 'The value-centred historicism of Edmund Burke', *Modern Age*, 27, 1983, 139–45. Takes issue with the Straussian argument that Burke's political and historical thought is uniquely modern, contending that this gives a disproportionate emphasis to utilitarianism and a subjectivist ethics.

6.113 **Bevan**, R. A., *Marx and Burke: A Revisionist View*, La Salle, Ill., 1973. Unusual and unconvincing exploration of their theoretical similarities as 'historical empiricists', leading both to reject the abstractions of rationalism.

6.114 **Black**, J., 'Edmund Burke: history, politics and polemic', *Hist. Today*, 37, 1987, 42–7.

6.115 **Blakemore**, S., *Burke and the Fall of Language. The French Revolution as Linguistic Event*, Hanover, N.H., 1988.

6.116 **Boucher**, D., 'The character of the history of the philosophy of international relations and the case of Edmund Burke', *Rev. Int. Sts.*, 17, 1991, 127–48. Analyses Burke's contribution to international relations theory, emphasising his empirical realism and conception of universal moral order.

6.117 **Boulton**, J. T., 'Exposition and proof: the apostrophe in Burke's *Reflections*', *Renaissance and Modern Studies*, 2, 1958, 38–65. On the literary techniques Burke uses to express his political views.

6.118 —— 'The *Reflections*: Burke's preliminary draft and methods of composition', *Durham Univ. J.*, 45, 1953, 114–19.

6.119 **Brewer**, J., 'Party and the double cabinet: two facets of Burke's *Thoughts*', *Hist. J.*, 14, 1971, 479–501. Elucidates Burke's intention in writing *Thoughts on the Cause of the Present Discontents* by examining the immediate historical context of the pamphlet – the disunity of the parliamentary opposition.

6.120 **Bridge**, C., 'Burke and the conservative tradition', in D. Close and C. Bridge, ed., *Revolution: A History of the Idea*, 1985, 75–88.

6.121 **Browning**, R., 'The origin of Burke's ideas revisited', *Eighteenth-Cent. Sts.*, 18, 1984, 57–71. Traces the origins of his social and political thought to Cicero and Lord Hardwick.

6.122 **Bryant**, D. C., 'Burke's *Present Discontents*: the rhetorical genesis of a party testament', *Quarterly Journal of Speech*, 42, 1956, 115–26.

6.123 **Cameron**, D. R., *The Social Thought of Rousseau and Burke: A Comparative Study*, Toronto, 1973. Contends that profound similarities exist between the two thinkers, particularly in their responses to empiricism and rationalism.

6.124 **Campbell**, J. A., 'Edmund Burke: argument from circumstance in *Reflections on the Revolution in France*', *Sts. Burke & Time*, 12, 1970–71, 1764–83.

6.125 **Canovan**, F. P., 'Burke as a reformer', *Burke Newsletter*, 5, 1964, 300–11. Examines his conceptions of society and social reform.

6.126 —— 'Burke on prescription of government', *Rev. Pol.*, 35, 1973, 454–75. Explores the theoretical foundations underpinning the doctrine of prescription.

6.127 —— *Edmund Burke: Prescription and Providence*, Durham, N.C., 1987. Focuses on the relationship between Burke's political thought and his relativist and historical thinking.

6.128 —— 'Edmund Burke's conception of the role of reason in politics', *J. Pol.*, 21, 1959, 60–79. Examination of the concepts of reason, nature and prudence.

6.129 —— *The Political Reason of Edmund Burke*, Durham, N.C., 1960. Unusual, and unconvincing, challenge to the notion that Burke was an empiricist, setting out to reconstruct his non-rationalist conception of reason, and presenting him 'as a Christian humanist who has something significant to say to those of us in the twentieth century who are still concerned with the perennial problem of reconciling political necessity with moral principles'.

6.130 **Carnall**, G., 'Burke as modern Cicero', in G. Carnall and C. Nicholson, ed., *The Impeachment of Warren Hastings: Papers from a Bicentenary Commemoration*, 1989, 79–90.

6.131 **Chapman**, G. W., *Edmund Burke: The Practical Imagination*, Cambridge, Mass., 1967. Argues that the complexities of his thought prevent a rigid categorisation of his politics as either conservative or liberal.

6.132 **Cone**, C. B., 'Burke and the European social order', *Thought*, 39, 1964, 273–88. A blow-by-blow account of his reaction to the French Revolution.

6.133 —— *Burke and the Nature of Politics: The Age of American Revolution*, Lexington, Ky., 1957–64. Whilst largely a political biography, the second volume analyses his thought in detail, especially with regard to the French Revolution.

6.134 **Conniff**, J., 'Burke on political economy: the nature and extent of state authority', *Rev. Pol.*, 49, 1987, 490–514. Argues against free market interpretations of Burke: he is best seen as a moderate Whig, strongly influenced by Scottish moral theory.

6.135 —— 'Edmund Burke's reflections on the coming revolution in Ireland', *J. Hist. Ideas*, 47, 1986, 37–61. Careful examination of his views on Ireland in the 1790s, claiming that 'any interpretation which makes Burke, even the late Burke, into an unregenerate defender of political reaction ignores important elements of his thought'.

6.136 **Courtney**, C. P., 'Edmund Burke and the Enlightenment', in A. Whiteman, J. S. Bromley and P. G. M. Dickson, ed., *Statesmen, Scholars and Merchants. Essays in Eighteenth-Century History Presented to Dame Lucy Sutherland*, 1973, 304–22. Sharp critique of the then orthodox view that Burke denounced the Enlightenment, and turned instead to natural law thinking. 'He is a man whose affinities are with the early Enlightenment, so that by the end of the century he becomes something of an anachronism, defending an old-fashioned constitution, with old-fashioned arguments.'

6.137 **Courtney**, C. P., *Montesquieu and Burke*, 1963.

6.138 **Crosland**, M., 'The image of science as a threat: Burke versus Priestley and the "philosophic revolution" ', *British Journal for the History of Science*, 20, 1987, 277–307. Examines their reactions to the French Revolution, contending that

Priestley applauded its thinkers for applying the 'spirit' of scientific research to society, whilst Burke condemned it because of the rational principles it embodied.

6.139 **Davidson**, J. F., 'Natural law and international law in Edmund Burke', *Rev. Pol.*, 21, 1959, 483–94. Contends that Burke's conception of international law was derived from a Lockean conception of natural law.

6.140 **Deane**, S. F., 'Burke and the French *Philosophes*', *Sts. Burke & Time*, 10, 1968–69, 113–37. Examines his antipathy to the rationalism of Voltaire and the *Philosophes*.

6.141 **Devine**, F. E., 'Ostracism in popular government: Burke and Adams', *Southern Quarterly*, 14, 1975, 17–20. Compares their political thought, focusing on how they view the problem of individuality and its relation to political power.

6.142 **Dinwiddy**, J. R., 'Burke and the utilitarians: a rejoinder', *Sts. Burke & Time*, 19, 1978, 119–26. Argues against P. J. Stanlis's 'Reflections on Dinwiddy on Mill on Burke on prescription', contending that Burke adhered to a form of utilitarianism in arguing for social reform.

6.143 —— 'Utility and natural law in Burke's thought: a reconsideration', *Sts. Burke & Time*, 16, 1974–75, 105–28. Contends that his political thought was grounded in the utilitarian tradition of Morley and Stephen rather than that of natural law.

6.144 **Dreyer**, F. A., *Burke's Politics: A Study in Whig Orthodoxy*, Waterloo, 1979. A short work which argues that his thought was coherent because it fell within the tradition of Whig political orthodoxy derived from the work of Locke – though Dreyer's account of Lockean political theory is not sustained by recent historiography.

6.145 —— 'Edmund Burke: the philosopher in action', *Sts. Burke & Time*, 15, 1975–75, 121–40. Portrays him as a natural law thinker.

6.146 —— 'Legitimacy and usurpation in the thought of Edmund Burke', *Albion*, 12, 1980, 257–67. Argues that his political thought is grounded in a commitment to the rule of law, and that most modern interpreters of Burke fail to recognise this point.

6.147 —— 'The genesis of Burke's reflections', *J. Mod. Hist.*, 50, 1978, 462–79. Analyses the book as a response to Richard Price's *Discourse on the Love of Our Country*.

6.148 **Durant**, J. D., 'Sheridan, Burke and revolution', *Eighteenth-Cent. Life*, 6, 1981, 103–13. Compares their views on the French Revolution.

6.149 **Eagleton**, T.., 'Aesthetics and politics in Edmund Burke', *History Workshop Journal*, 28, 1989, 53–62.

6.150 **Eaves**, R. G., 'Edmund Burke; his enduring influence on political thought', *J. Thought*, 14, 1979, 122–31.

6.151 **Eulau**, H., **Walker**, J. C., **Buchanan**, W. and **Ferguson**, L. C., 'Role of the representative: some empirical observations on the theory of Edmund Burke', *Am. Pol. Sc. Rev.*, 53, 1959, 742–56. Uses his theory of representation as the basis for an empirical study of 'the relationship between public expectations and legislative decisions'.

6.152 **Fasel**, G., *Edmund Burke*, Boston, Mass. 1983. A handy introduction to his thought and principal works.

6.153 —— ' "The soul that animated": the role of property in Burke's thought', *Sts. Burke & Time*, 17, 1976, 27–41. A rigorous analysis of his conception of private property.

6.154 **Freeman**, M., *Edmund Burke and the Critique of Political Radicalism*, 1980. Carefully dissects his hostility to revolution and political radicalism.

6.155 —— 'Edmund Burke and the sociology of revolution', *Pol. St.*, 25, 1977, 458–73. Contends that despite a number of inconsistencies, his sociology of revolution was founded upon the premises of classical political theory.

6.156 —— 'Edmund Burke and the theory of revolution', *Pol. Theory*, 6, 1978, 277–97. Defends his theory as superior to recent empirical discussion because of his sensitivity to questions of progress and historical significance.

6.157 **Gardy**, C. I. and **Stanlis**, P. J., *Edmund Burke. A Bibliography of Secondary Studies to 1982*, New York, 1983.

6.158 **Garnett**, M. A., 'Hazlitt against Burke: radical versus conservative?', *Durham Univ. J.*, 81, 1989, 229–39. Contends that their opinions on reform were not as diametrically opposed as commonly thought.

6.159 **Goodwin**, A., 'The political genesis of Edmund Burke's *Reflections on the*

Revolution in France', *Bulletin of the John Rylands Library*, 50, 1968, 336–74.

6.160 **Gottfried**, P. E., 'Romanticism and natural law', *Studies in Romanticism*, 7, 1968, 231–42. Argues that his political philosophy was founded on the idea of natural rights.

6.161 **Gottschalk**, L., 'Reflections on Edmund Burke's *Reflections on the French Revolution*', *Procs. Am. Phil. Soc.*, 100, 1956, 417–29. Suggests that Burke became a 'metaphysical doctrinaire in his persuasion that only evil could come from [the] doctrinaire principles' of the Revolution.

6.162 **Graham**, G. J., 'Edmund Burke's "developmental consensus" ', *Midwest Journal of Political Science*, 14, 1972, 29–46.

6.163 **Greenleaf**, W. H., 'Burke and state necessity: the case of Warren Hastings', in R. Schnur, ed., *Staatsrason: Studien zur Geschichte eines Politischen Begriffs*, Berlin, 1975, 549–67. Demonstrates that Burke had an elaborate doctrine of 'reason of state'.

6.164 **Gunter**, B., 'Burke's philosophy of organic reform', *Queen's Quarterly*, 77, 1970, 368–73.

6.165 **Guroian**, V., 'Natural law and historicity: Burke and Niebuhr', *Modern Age*, 25, 1981, 162–72. Argues that Burke adhered to a conception of natural law whilst avoiding both moral absolutism and relativism.

6.166 **Gurr**, T. R., 'Burke and the modern theory of revolution. A reply to Freeman', *Pol. Theory*, 6, 1978, 299–311. Defends empiricist theorising as compatible with Burke's views on revolution.

6.167 **Hampsher-Monk**, I., 'Rhetoric and opinion in the politics of Edmund Burke', *Hist. Pol. Thought*, 9, 1988, 455–84. Evokes the salience and meaning of rhetoric in his intellectual background and shows how the political writings of his final years were preoccupied with the rhetorician's task of guarding against the destruction of opinion by rationalism.

6.168 **Hart**, J., 'Bentham and Burke', *Burke Newsletter*, 6, 1964, 347–59.

6.169 —— 'Burke and radical freedom', *Rev. Pol.*, 29, 1967, 221–38. Argues that for Burke freedom was not an abstract, *a priori*, concept, but rather a reality with deep, social and religious roots.

6.170 **Himmelfarb**, G., 'Edmund Burke: the politician as philosopher', in *Victorian Minds*, New York, 1968, 14–31. Contrasts his conception of natural law with the eighteenth-century notion of natural rights.

6.171 —— 'The hero as politician', *Twentieth Century*, 153, 1953, 356–61. Explores his opposition to theories of 'the rights of man' and political reform.

6.172 **Hindson**, P. and **Gray**, T., *Burke's Dramatic Theory of Politics*, 1988. Argues that drama was integral to his political theory. Through it he elevated politics into a semi-divine form, depicting the statesman as a beleaguered actor holding centre-stage in a battle with the forces of adversity.

6.173 **Kiernan**, C., 'Edmund Burke and the science of politics', *University of Newcastle Historical Journal*, 2, 1973, 5–16.

6.174 **Kilcup**, R. W., 'Burke's historicism', *J. Mod. Hist.*, 39, 1977, 394–410. Contends that for Burke the will of God was expressed through human nature and the state in the temporal order of things, leading him to reject the French Revolution as a direct challenge to God.

6.175 —— 'Reason and the basis of morality in Burke', *J. Hist. Phil.*, 17, 1979, 271–84.

6.176 **Kirk**, R., 'Burke and natural rights', *Rev. Pol.*, 13, 1951, 441–56. Contends that he adhered to a classical conception of natural rights derived from natural law.

6.177 —— 'Burke and the philosophy of prescription', *J. Hist. Ideas*, 14, 1953, 365–80.

6.178 —— 'Burke and the principle of order', *Sewanee Review*, 60, 1952, 187–201.

6.179 —— *Edmund Burke: A Genius Reconsidered*, New Rochelle, N.Y., 1967.

6.180 **Kramnick**, I, 'The left and Edmund Burke', *Pol. Theory*, 11, 1983, 198–214. On the reception given to Burke on the left, from Goodwin to C. B. Macpherson, claiming that his 'genius' was 'in sensing that *in the future*, capitalist market society would require internalized status differentiation'.

6.181 —— *The Rage of Edmund Burke: Portrait of an Ambivalent Conservative*, New York, 1977. Makes extensive use of his correspondence, suggesting that he offers 'a pivotal insight into that great turning point in our history – the transformation from the aristocratic to the bourgeois world. He does this not only in his ideas, but also in himself. He personifies the transformation.'

6.182 **Kriegel**, A. D., 'Edmund Burke and the quality of honor', *Albion*, 12, 1980, 337–49. Demonstrates how, for Burke, honour was connected to property rights and individual liberty.

6.183 **Laskowsky**, H. J., 'In praise of ignorance: Burke on nature and human nature', *Studies in the Humanities*, 5, 1976, 26–31.

6.184 **Livingston**, D. W., 'Burke, Marcuse, and the historical justification for revolution', *Sts. Burke & Time*, 14, 1972–73, 119–31. Contrasts Marcuse's abstract historical method with Burke's, which is lauded for its concrete nature.

5.185 **Lock**, F. P., *Burke's Reflections on the Revolution in France*, 1985. Careful exposition of his ideas as well as a substantial section on the reception of the *Reflections* by his contemporaries and subsequent generations.

6.186 **Love**, W. D., 'Edmund Burke's idea of the body corporate: a study in imagery', *Rev. Pol.*, 27, 1965, 184–97.

6.187 —— ' "Meaning" in the history of conflicting interpretations of Burke', *Burke Newsletter*, 7, 1965–66, 526–38. Questions the orthodox view that his theory constituted a fundamental rejection of Lockean politics.

6.188 **Lucas**, P., 'On Edmund Burke's doctrine of prescription; or, an appeal from the new to the old lawyers', *Hist. J.*, 11, 1968, 35–63. Careful exposition of his traditionalism, claiming that he 'revolutionized the meaning of prescription' and moved far beyond the thinking of the common and natural lawyers.

6.189 **MacCunn**, J., *The Political Philosophy of Burke*, New York, 1965. Examines his rejection of abstract reasoning and provides a thorough account of the central concepts of his political thought.

6.190 **McGoldrick**, J. E., 'Edmund Burke as Christian activist', *Modern Age*, 17, 1973, 275–86. Superficial and ideologically charged survey of his principal writings.

6.191 **Macpherson**, C. B., 'Edmund Burke', *Transactions of the Royal Society of Canada*, 52, 1959, 19–26. A Marxist critique of the 'traditional and capitalist moralities' in his economic and political thought.

6.192 —— 'Edmund Burke and the new conservatism', *Sc. & Soc.*, 22, 1958, 231–39. A review article of C. Parkin, *The Moral Basis of Burke's Political Thought*, P. J. Stanlis, *Edmund Burke and the Natural Law*, C. B. Cane, *Burke and the Nature of Politics*, which is in itself a significant contribution to Burke scholarship – questioning the extent to which he was a natural law thinker and demonstrating his commitment to the free market.

6.193 —— *Burke*, 1981. Short, sharp Marxist interpretation showing how his thinking is a blend of aristocratic and bourgeois elements.

6.194 **McLoughlin**, T. O., 'Edmund Burke's *Abridgement of English History*', *Eighteenth Century Ireland*, 5, 1990, 45–59. On an unfinished early work illustrating 'that several years before his involvement with the Rockington Whigs Burke had drafted for himself a decidedly Whig version of the history of the early stages of the country or his adoption.'

6.195 **Mahoney**, T. H. D., 'Edmund Burke, 1729–1797: a portrait and an appraisal', *Hist. Today*, 6, 1956, 727–34. Short but useful introduction to his life and thought.

6.196 —— *Edmund Burke and Ireland*, Cambridge, Mass., 1960. Whilst primarily an historical text, the book provides insight into his political reflections on Ireland and how these stand in relation to his wider political thought.

6.197 —— 'Edmund Burke and the American Revolution', in J. Browning and R. Morton, ed., *1776*, Toronto, 1976, 53–73. Pays attention to Burke's views on taxation and its relation to individual liberty.

6.198 **Mansfield**, H. C., *Statesmanship and Party Government: A Study of Burke and Bolingbroke*, Chicago, Ill., 1965.

6.199 **Mazlish**, B., 'The conservative revolution of Edmund Burke', *Rev. Pol.*, 20, 1958, 21–33. Finds the key to his conservatism in his rejection of *a priori* rationalism.

6.200 **Melvin**, P. H., 'Burke on theatricality and revolution', *J. Hist. Ideas*, 36, 1975, 447–68. Shows how he deployed a theatrical discourse to interpret and criticise the deeds of the French Revolution. In particular, he saw in the Revolution the signs of a neo-classical understanding of the theatre which he vehemently opposed.

6.201 **Miller**, A. P., *Edmund Burke and his World*, Old Greenwich, Conn., 1979.

Straightforward intellectual and political biography.

6.202 **Murphy**, D. D., *Burkean Conservatism and Classical Liberalism*, Wichita, Kan., 1979.

6.203 **O'Brien**, C. C., 'Burke and Marx', *New American Review*, 1, 1967, 243–58. Argues that there is much in common between the two thinkers.

6.204 —— *The Great Melody: A Thematic Biography and Commented Anthology of Edmund Burke*, 1992. A massive and impressive account of his life and ideas, regarded by some as one of the best books about Burke ever written.

6.205 **O'Gorman**, F., 'Edmund Burke and the idea of party', *Sts. Burke & Time*, 11, 1969–70, 1428–41.

6.206 —— *Edmund Burke: His Political Philosophy*, 1973. Sound introduction which argues that his political thinking was shaped more by events than the tradition of natural law, and that it is vain to search for a systematic philosophy in his writings.

6.207 —— 'Party and Burke: the Rockingham Whigs', *Govt. & Oppos.*, 3, 1968, 92–110. Focuses on *Thoughts on the Causes of the Present Discontents* and provides a thorough examination of Burke's theoretical formulation of the nature and role of the political party.

6.208 **Osborn**, A. M., *Rousseau and Burke: A Study of the Idea of Liberty in Eighteenth-Century Political Thought*, New York, 1964. Unusual and unconvincing comparison of these thinkers, attempting to synthesise their conclusions, so that 'Rousseau bequeathed to posterity the constructive principles upon which a free society must be based; while Burke gave warning of the dangers that surrounded a democratic constitution'.

6.209 **Pagano**, F. N., 'Burke's view of the evils of political theory: or, a vindication of natural society', *Polity*, 17, 1985, 446–62. Examines his critique of rationalist theorising in his early work, *A Vindication of Natural Society*.

6.210 **Palmer**, W., 'Edmund Burke and the French Revolution: notes on the genesis of the *Reflections*', *Colby Library Quarterly*, 20, 1984, 181–90. Argues that the *Reflections* is based on a number of fundamental theoretical errors.

6.211 **Parkin**, C., *The Moral Basis of Burke's Political Thought*, 1956. Contends that much of this thinking rests on religious premisses and that this distinguishes his conception of human nature and the individual in society.

6.212 **Paulson**, R., 'Burke's sublime and the representation of revolution', in P. Zagorin, ed., *Culture and Politics: From Puritanism to the Enlightenment*, Berkeley and Los Angeles, Calif., 1980, 241–69. Burke's characterisation in the *Philosophical Enquiry* of the terrible as the defining feature of sublimity is said to be the source of his imagery of revolution.

6.213 **Petrella**, F., 'Edmund Burke: a liberal practitioner of political economy', *Modern Age*, 8, 1963–64, 52–60. Demonstrates that he was strongly influenced by Adam Smith, hence his beliefs in free trade and minimal government.

6.214 **Pocock**, J. G. A., 'Burke and the ancient constitution – a problem in the history of ideas', *Hist. J.*, 3, 1960, 125–43. Influential article, challenging the orthodox view that Burke was primarily a natural law thinker.

6.215 —— 'The political economy of Burke's analysis of the French Revolution', *Hist. J.*, 25, 1982, 331–49. Situates his response to the Revolution in the traditions of commercial humanism and the defence of the Whig regime in England.

6.216 **Preece**, R., 'Edmund Burke and his European reception', *Eighteenth Century: Theory and Interpretation*, 21, 1980, 255–73. Particular attention is paid to his influence on French and German conservatives.

6.217 —— 'The political economy of Edmund Burke', *Modern Age*, 24, 1980, 266–73. Argues that there is no contradiction between his *laissez-faire* economics and political thought. Burke held a theory of 'discriminatory interventionism' in relation to the preservation of the rule of law, limited government, social order, and individual liberty.

6.218 **Priestly**, F. E. C., 'Reflections on Burke', *Dalhousie Review*, 63, 1983, 13–21. Cursory survey of his major political writings.

6.219 **Rashid**, S., 'Forum: economists and the age of chivalry: notes on a passage in Burke's *Reflections*', *Eighteenth-Cent. Sts.*, 20, 1986, 56–61. Examines his hostility towards Physiocratic doctrines and the thought of Condorcet and Turgot.

6.220 **Reedy**, W. J., 'Burke and Bonald:

paradigms of late eighteenth-century conservatism', *Historical Reflections*, 8, 1981, 69–93. Bonald is said to be more rationalistic in his political arguments than Burke who eschewed rationalism for traditionalism.

6.221 **Reid**, C., *Edmund Burke and the Practice of Political Writing*, New York, 1986. Examines the literary form of Burke's writings – especially his reliance on rhetoric – and its implications for his politics.

6.222 —— 'Language and practice in Burke's political writing', *Literature and History*, 6, 1977, 203–18.

6.223 **Rose**, S. D., 'Edmund Burke: an introduction', *Catholic University of America Law Review*, 7, 1958, 61–90.

6.224 **Rothbard**, M., 'A note on Burke's *Vindication of Natural Society*', *J. Hist. Ideas*, 19, 1958, 114–8. Argues that the book is a critique of civil society rather than a sustained ironical argument and satire on 'natural society'.

6.225 **Sarason**, B. D., 'The legend of Edmund Burke', *Dissent*, 2, 1955, 275–63.

6.226 **Sharma**, G. N., 'Samuel Butler and Edmund Burke: a comparative study in British conservatism', *Dalhousie Review*, 53, 1973, 5–29.

6.227 **Stanlis**, P. J., 'A preposterous way of reasoning: Frederick Dreyer's "Edmund Burke: the philosopher in action" ', *Sts. Burke & Time*, 15, 1974, 265–75. Argues that Dreyer badly distorts the tradition of natural law in Burke's thought by exaggerating the influence on him of Hobbes and Locke.

6.228 —— 'Burke and the sensibility of Rousseau', *Thought*, 36, 1961, 246–76. On Burke's criticisms of Rousseau's sentimental view of human nature.

6.229 —— 'Edmund Burke and revolution', *Intercollegiate Review*, 7, 1971, 215–25. Contends that he was the first political thinker to deal consciously with the problem of modern political and social revolution, examining his views on the English, American and French Revolutions.

6.230 —— 'Edmund Burke and the law of nations', *American Journal of International Law*, 47, 1953, 397–413. Argues that his philosophy of history and political thought were strongly influenced by the works of Suarez and Grotius.

6.231 —— 'Edmund Burke and the natural law', *University of Detroit Law Journal*, 33, 1956, 150–90. Portrays him as a natural law thinker, rather than a utilitarian.

6.232 —— *Edmund Burke and the Natural Law*, Ann Arbor, Mich., 1959. Presents him as a defender of natural law morality and politics, and places him within the classical tradition of Aristotle and Cicero.

6.233 —— ed., *Edmund Burke: The Enlightenment and the Modern World*, Detroit, Mich., 1967. A collection of eight articles which examine the principal aspects of his thought.

6.234 —— 'Edmund Burke, the perennial political philosopher', *Modern Age*, 26, 1982, 325–9.

6.235 —— 'Reflections on Dinwiddy on Mill on Burke on prescription', *Sts. Burke & Time*, 18, 1977, 191–8. Challenges Dinwiddy's thesis that Burke was a utilitarian in the tradition of Bentham and Mill, contending that their utilitarianism was marked by the kind of *a priori*, speculative, and abstract reasoning that Burke despised.

6.236 —— 'The basis of Burke's political conservatism', *Modern Age*, 1961, 263–74. Contends that his conservatism was marked by the fundamental principles of natural law and political prudence.

6.237 —— ed., *The Relevance of Edmund Burke*, New York, 1964. Six articles attempting to demonstrate the relevance of his ideas for the twentieth century.

6.238 —— 'The role of prudence in Burke's politics', *Religion and Society*, 1, 1968, 13–29.

6.239 **Suter**, J. F., 'Burke, Hegel, and the French Revolution', in Z. A. Pelczynski, ed., *Hegel's Political Philosophy: Problems and Perspectives*, Cambridge, Mass., 1971, 52–72. Emphasises the coincidence of their views on state and society, while acknowledging significant differences. 'Against the French Revolution Burke sets up *political action*, the practical wisdom of the statesman; Hegel, on the other hand, elaborates a *political theory* which takes account at the same time of the possibility of the Revolution and the necessity of maintaining the state.'

6.240 **Vincent**, R. J., 'Edmund Burke and the theory of international relations', *Review of International Studies*, 10, 1984, 205–18. Examines the relevance of his political thought for international relations theory.

6.241 **Weiser**, D. K., 'The imagery of Burke's *Reflections*', *Sts. Burke & Time*, 16, 1975, 213–33.

6.242 **Weston**, J. C., 'Edmund Burke's view of history', *Rev. Pol.*, 23, 1961, 203–29. Analyses the significance of the concepts of 'abstract rights' and 'historical development' in his political thought.

6.243 —— 'The ironic purpose of Burke's *Vindication* vindicated', *J. Hist. Ideas*, 19, 1958, 435–41. A refutation of Rothbard's 'A note on Burke's *Vindication of Natural Society*'.

6.244 **White**, H. B., 'Edmund Burke on political theory and practice', *Social Res.*, 17, 1950, 106–27.

6.245 **White**, S. K., 'Burke on politics, aesthetics, and the dangers of modernity', *Pol. Theory*, 21, 1993, 507–27. Argues that he saw aesthetics as not only resisting 'the grasping, obliterating, levelling gestures of modern thought', but as cultivating political and ethical sensitivity and care.

6.246 **Wilkins**, B. T., *The Problem of Burke's Political Philosophy*, 1967. Suggests that his political thought lies within the natural law tradition, and that 'any resemblances between Burke and the utilitarians appear ultimately superficial'.

6.247 **Willis**, R. E., 'Some further reflections on Burke's *Discontents*', *Sts. Burke & Time*, 11, 1969–70, 1417–27. Asserts that he failed to integrate his view of party government within a coherent theory of state and society because the very constitutional system that he accepted would not permit it.

6.248 **Winch**, D., 'The Burke–Smith problem and late eighteenth-century political and economic thought', *Hist. J.*, 28, 1985, 231–47. Careful comparison of their views on political economy, as well as an assessment of the extent to which they influenced one another.

6.249 **Wood**, N., 'Burke on power', *Burke Newsletter*, 5, 1964, 311–26.

6.250 —— 'The aesthetic dimension of Burke's political thought', *J. Brit. Sts.*, 4, 1964, 41–64. Examines his conception of the sublime and the beautiful, and demonstrates how these categories informed his political thought.

Godwin

6.251 **Bellamy**, R., 'Godwin and the development of "The New Man of Feeling" ', *Hist. Pol. Thought*, 6, 1985, 411–31. Argues that his philosophy was more a programme for the ethical regeneration of the individual than the mechanical restructuring of society, and that, as a consequence, he gradually shifted from utilitarianism to a romanticism which emphasised individual self-development.

6.252 **Claeys**, G., 'The concept of "political justice" in Godwin's *Political Justice*: a reconsideration', *Pol. Theory*, 11, 1983, 565–84. A meticulous study of the changing conception of justice in the 1793, 1796 and 1798 editions of *An Enquiry Concerning Political Justice*.

6.253 —— 'The effect of property on Godwin's theory of justice', *J. Hist. Phil.*, 22, 1984, 81–101.

6.254 —— 'William Godwin's critique of democracy and republicanism and its sources', *Hist. Euro. Ideas*, 7, 1986, 253–69. Rigorous analysis of his critique of large-scale republicanism and democracy, contending that he viewed them as inimical to individual and civic virtue.

6.255 **Clark**, J., 'On anarchism in an unreal world: Kramnick's view of Godwin and the anarchists', *Am. Pol. Sc. Rev.*, 69, 1975, 162–7. Reply to Kramnick's 'On anarchism in the real world: William Godwin and radical England', *Am. Pol. Sc. Rev.*, 66, 1972, 114–28, arguing that Godwin opposed violence, was an ardent defender of freedom of thought and expression, and saw decentralised democracy as a transition to an anarchist utopia.

6.256 —— *The Philosophical Anarchism of William Godwin*, Princeton, N.J., 1977. Thorough treatment of his political thought, demonstrating how it is grounded in a hedonistic utilitarianism, and arguing that his contribution to political theory was his 'demonstration of the inseparable connection between individual freedom and human happiness, rationality and self-realization'.

6.257 **Fearn**, M., 'William Godwin and the "wilds of literature" ', *British Journal of Education Studies*, 29, 1981, 247–57. Demonstrates that he incorporated Lockean and Rousseaunian ideas in his writings for children.

6.258 **Fleischer**, D., *William Godwin: A Study in Liberalism*, 1951. Short, readable analysis of *Political Justice*, which accuses him of naïve faith in human perfectibility.

6.259 **Garret**, R., 'Anarchism or political democracy: the case of William Godwin', *Soc. Theory & Pract.*, 1, 1971, 111–20.

6.260 **Grylls**, R. G., *William Godwin and his World*, 1953. Enjoyable biographical study which, despite its often anecdotal tone, conveys the atmosphere of his milieu.

6.261 **Knapp**, E. F., 'William Godwin's *Caleb Williams* and the origins of revolution', *Consortium on Revolutionary Europe, 1750–1850: Proceedings*, 19, 1989, 189–200.

6.262 **Kramnick**, I., 'On anarchism and the real world: William Godwin and radical England', *Am. Pol. Sc. Rev.*, 6, 1972, 114–28. Lively account of his ideas, as well as a discussion of the divisions among English Jacobins arising from his arguments with John Thelwall and other members of the London Corresponding Society.

6.263 **Locke**, D., *A Fantasy of Reason: The Life and Thought of William Godwin*, 1980. Biographical approach, with close attention to his political ideas, though tends to neglect the historical context.

6.264 **McCrocken**, D., 'Godwin's literary theory: the alliance between fiction and political philosophy', *Phil. Q.*, 49, 1970, 113–33. Examines his social and political ideas in *Political Justice* and their relation to his perception of literature as a vehicle to stimulate revolutionary social change.

6.265 **Marshall**, P., *William Godwin*, 1984. Argues that his ideas were rooted in the English dissenting tradition rather than the Enlightenment, and that his fundamental beliefs were developed long before the publication of *Political Justice*.

6.266 **Monro**, D. H., *Godwin's Moral Philosophy: An Interpretation of William Godwin*, 1953.

6.267 **Morrow**, J., 'Republicanism and public virtue: William Godwin's *History of the Commonwealth of England*', *Hist. J.*, 34, 1991, 645–64. Suggests that his study of the revolutionary period of the seventeenth century was intended as a case-study yielding principles of radical reform.

6.268 **Philp**, M., *Godwin's Political Justice*, Ithaca, N.Y., 1985. Examines the three

editions of his *Enquiry Concerning Political Justice* in their intellectual, political and social context, suggesting that his conception of political justice was perfectionist rather than utilitarian.

6.269 **Pollin**, B. R., *Education and Enlightenment in the Works of William Godwin*, New York, 1962.

6.270 —— *Godwin Criticism: A Synoptic Bibliography*, Toronto, 1967. Contains over 3000 entries.

6.271 —— 'Godwin's "letters of Verax" ', *J. Hist. Ideas*, 25, 1984, 353–73. Reveals his opposition to British attempts to unseat Bonaparte, and examines his relations with other Bonapartists: Capel Lofft, John Thelwall and Hazlitt.

6.272 **Preu**, J. A., *Antimonarchism in Swift and Godwin*, Tallahassee, Fla., 1955.

6.273 —— 'Swift's influence on Godwin's doctrine of anarchism', *J. Hist. Ideas*, 15, 1954, 371–83. Argues that Godwin interpreted the fourth book of Swift's *Gulliver's Travels*, 'a voyage to the Houyhnhnms', as an anarchist manifesto and Swift's description of Houyhnhnm society as a portrait of utopia.

6.274 **Ritter**, A., 'Godwin, Proudhon and the anarchist justification of punishment', *Pol Theory*, 3, 1975, 69–87. Repudiates the conventional belief that anarchists cannot believe in punishment, emphasising the role of rebuke and disapproval, as well as the belief in restraint, in their thought.

6.275 **Rodway**, A. E., *Godwin and the Age of Transition*, 1952. A survey of his political and literary writings, together with an evaluation of his influence.

6.276 **Rosen**, F., 'The principle of population as political theory: Godwin's *Of Population* and the Malthusian controversy', *J. Hist. Ideas*, 31, 1970, 33–48. On how he challenged the science of political economy with a political theory intended to demonstrate that population was determined in large part by the institutions of government.

6.277 **Scrivener**, M. H., 'Godwin's philosophy: a reevaluation', *J. Hist. Ideas*, 39, 1978, 615–26. On his understanding of necessity and perfectibility, as well as his influence on romantic thought.

6.278 **Stafford**, W., 'Dissenting religion translated into politics: Godwin's *Political Justice*', *Hist. Pol. Thought*, 1, 1980, 279–99. Suggests that *Political Justice* was the product of his Congregationalist background, and should be read therefore as 'an imperfect synthesis of dissenting culture and philosophical radicalism'.

6.279 **Watkins**, F. M., 'Godwin's *Enquiry Concerning Political Justice*', *Can. J. Econ. & Pol. Sc.*, 141, 1948, 107–12.

6.280 **Wekmeister**, L., 'Coleridge and Godwin on the communication of truth', *Mod. Philol.*, 55, 1958, 170–7. Compares their views on freedom of the press.

6.281 **Woodcock**, G., 'Ancestors, party', *Politics*, 3, 1946, 260–7. Examines Godwin's radicalism, his distrust of political institutions, attacks on property, and defence of reason and freedom of education.

6.282 —— *William Godwin: A Biographical Study*, 1946. Standard biography with an excellent account of the arguments of *Political Justice*.

Hume

6.283 **Adair**, D., ' "That politics may be reduced to a science": David Hume, James Madison, and the tenth *Federalist*', in D. W. Livingston and J. T. King, ed., *Hume: A Re-Evaluation*, New York, 1976, 404–17. Develops an interesting philosophical connection between American Revolutionary thought and Scottish philosophy, especially Hume.

6.284 **Aitken**, H. D., 'An interpretation of Hume's theory of the place of reason in ethics and politics', *Ethics*, 90, 1979, 66–80. Although 'Hume's argument in book three of the *Treatise* is tortuous, a strong case can be made for contending that there is a sense in which reason plays a guiding role both in our ethics and in our political deliberations and judgements, and that they are corrigible and hence true or false'.

6.285 —— *Hume's Moral and Political Philosophy*, New York, 1948. Clear, if dated, survey of his ideas.

6.286 **Ardal**, P. S., *Passion and Value in Hume's Treatise*, 1966. Stresses his discussion of the passions in this text as the key to many of his ideas, including his notions of justice and liberty.

6.287 **Ayer**, A. J., *Hume*, 1980. Excellent account of his thought.

6.288 **Bagolini**, L., 'On Hume's theory of justice in the *Treatise* and *Original Contract*', *Archiv für Rechts Soziologie*, 63, 1977, 557–66.

6.289 **Baier**, A., 'Good men's women: Hume on chastity and trust', *Hume Studies*, 5, 1979, 1–19. Examines his conception of artificial virtues in the context of the role he projects for women.

6.290 —— 'Hume on women's complexion', in P. Jones, ed., *The 'Science of Man' in the Scottish Enlightenment*, 1989, 33–53. Argues that Hume's thought on women is radical for the age because he identifies the roots of women's unequal social status to men, and focuses on sexual desire as a means by which that status can be improved.

6.291 **Barker**, J. H., 'Hume on the pre-social state', *Auslegung*, 10, 1983, 185–93.

6.292 **Battersby**, C., 'An enquiry concerning Humean woman', *Sts. Voltaire*, 193, 1980, 1964–7. Contends that although Hume was a strong advocate of sexual equality, he attributed women's social inferiority to their violent passions which led to 'mental slavery'.

6.293 **Baxter**, I. F. G., 'David Hume and justice', *Revue Internationale de Philosophie*, 13, 1959, 112–31. Examines the reflections on justice in the *Enquiry Concerning the Principles of Morals*.

6.294 **Beitzinger**, A. J., 'Hume's aristocratic preference', *Rev. Pol.*, 28, 1966, 154–71.

6.295 **Berman**, D., 'David Hume on the 1641 rebellion in Ireland', *Studies: An Irish Quarterly Review*, 65, 1976, 101–12.

6.296 **Berry**, C. J., 'From Hume to Hegel: the case of the social contract', *J. Hist. Ideas*, 38, 1977, 691–703. Compares their rejection of the contractarian justification of political allegiance because of their views of human nature which differed markedly.

6.297 **Bongie**, L. L., *David Hume, Prophet of the Counter-Revolution*, 1965. Argues that his history of the Stuarts and other historical works strongly influenced counter-revolutionary French thinkers.

6.298 **Botwinick**, A., *Ethics, Politics and Epistemology: A Study in the Unity of Hume's Thought*, Washington, D.C., 1980. Includes an examination of his theory of justice and a brief assessment of his notion of political obligation, comparing his ideas with those of Hobbes.

6.299 **Brownsey**, P., 'Hume and the social

contract', *Phil. Q.*, 28, 1978, 132–48. Argues not only that Hume failed convincingly to refute social contract theory, but that his political principles are compatible with a contractual justification of political obligation.

6.300 **Buckle**, S. and **Castiglione**, D., 'Hume's critique of the contract theory', *Hist. Pol. Thought*, 12, 1991, 457–96. Careful analysis of his opposition to contractualism, emphasising his central argument – that the ultimate foundation of authority lies in opinion.

6.301 **Burns**, S., 'The Humean female', *Dialogue*, 15, 1976, 415–24. Dissects his sexism.

6.302 **Capaldi**, N., 'Hume as social scientist', *Rev. Metaph.*, 32, 1978, 99–123.

6.303 —— and **Livingston**, D. W., ed., *Liberty in Hume's History of England*, 1990.

6.304 **Chappell**, V. C., *Hume: A Collection of Critical Essays*, 1968. Includes F. A. Hayek, 'The legal and political philosophy of David Hume'.

6.305 **Charron**, W. C., 'Convention, games of strategy, and Hume's philosophy of law and government', *Am. Phil. Q.*, 17, 1980, 327–34. Provides a game model of his explanatory and normative account of rules of justice and legitimate government.

6.306 **Conniff**, J., 'Hume on political parties: the case for Hume as a Whig', *Eighteenth-Cent. Sts.*, 12, 1978–79, 150–73. Emphasises his freethinking views on religion, epistemological scepticism, and adherence to Enlightenment values, in order to challenge the view that he was a conservative political thinker.

6.307 —— 'Hume's political methodology: a reconsideration of "That politics may be reduced to a science" ', *Rev. Pol.*, 38, 1976, 88–108. Argues that there is no break in the development of his thought because his methodological reliance on history unifies his earlier moral and later political writings.

6.308 **Cook**, T. I., 'Reflections on the moral and political philosophy of David Hume: a review article', *Sts. Burke & Time*, 9, 1968, 949–58. Argues that his thorough-going rationalism and distrust of the 'common man' led him to espouse a conservative political doctrine.

6.309 **Cottle**, C. E., 'Justice as artificial virtue in Hume's *Treatise*', *J. Hist. Ideas*, 40, 1979, 457–66.

6.310 **Cummins**, P. D., 'Hume's disavowal of the *Treatise*', *Phil. Rev.*, 82, 1973, 371–9 Examines the various suggestions as to wh in 1775 he publicly disowned his *Treatise e Human Nature*.

6.311 **Day**, J., 'Hume on justice and allegiance *Phil.*, 40, 1965, 35–56. Intelligent exposition and critique of his theory of political obligation.

6.312 **Ellin**, J., 'Hume on the morality of princes', *Hume Studies*, 14, 1988, 111–60

6.313 **Forbes**, D., *Hume's Philosophical Politic* 1975. A rigorous study of his political thought which demonstrates its groundir in the modern natural law tradition of Grotius, Pufendorf, Heineccius and Hutcheson.

6.314 —— 'Politics and history in David Hume *Cambridge Hist. J.*, 6, 1963, 280–95.

6.315 **Gauthier**, D., 'David Hume, contractarian', *Phil. Rev.*, 88, 1979, 3–3 Argues that his theory of property, justic government and obedience are contractarian. An ahistorical reading which makes a too rigid distinction between his general theory of morals and specific analysis of justice.

6.316 **Ginsberg**, R., 'David Hume versus the Enlightenment', *Sts. Voltaire*, 88, 1972, 599–650. Thorough assessment of the differences between the thought of Hume and that of the *philosophes*, focusing on th former's political theory, philosophy of religion and theory of knowledge.

6.317 **Glossop**, R. J., 'Hume and the future of society of nations', *Hume Studies*, 10, 198 46–58. Considers his views on the origin o government and the light they shed on th problem of creating a 'world community o nations'.

6.318 —— 'Is Hume a "classical utilitarian"?', *Hume Studies*, 2, 1976, 1–16. Disentangle five possible interpretations of his utilitarianism, emphasising that which maximises equality and justice.

6.319 **Harrison**, J., *Hume's Theory of Justice*, 1981. Close analysis of Book III, Part II o his *Treatise*.

6.320 **Hiskes**, R. P., 'Has Hume a theory of social justice?', *Hume Studies*, 3, 1977, 72–93.

6.321 **Hoffert**, R. W., 'Religion and public life David Hume's dialogue with liberalism', *Social Science Journal*, 18, 1980, 1–18.

6.322 **King**, J. T., 'Hume's classical theory of justice', *Hume Studies*, 7, 1981, 32–54.

6.323 **Kuhns**, R., 'Hume's republic and the universe of Newton', in P. Gay, ed., *Eighteenth Century Studies Presented to Arthur M. Wilson*, New York, 1972, 73–95. Examines the influence of the Newtonian concepts of space and time on his moral and political thought.

6.324 **Lacoste**, L. M., 'The consistency of Hume's position concerning women', *Dialogue*, 15, 1976, 425–40. Examines his sexism in relation to his moral thought.

6.325 **Lawrence**, R., 'Hume's theory of social and political order', *South African Journal of Philosophy*, 4, 1985, 137–42. On his critique of contractarianism.

6.326 **Letwin**, S. R., 'Hume: inventor of a new task for philosophy', *Pol. Theory*, 3, 1975, 134–58. Celebration of his philosophical scepticism.

6.327 **Livingston**, D. W., 'Time and value in Hume's social and political philosophy', in D. F. Norton, N. Capaldi and W. L. Robinson, ed., *McGill Hume Studies*, San Diego, Calif., 1979, 181–201. Dissects his perception of the social and political order as shaped by history, comparing him with the doctrines of Cartesian rationalism in which social and political order is without temporal content, and with 'providential narrative' accounts in which the political and social are understood as part of some teleological purpose.

6.328 —— and **Martin**, M., ed., *Hume as Philosopher of Society, Politics and History*, Rochester, N.Y., 1991. A collection of thirteen articles, all appearing previously in *J. Hist. Ideas*, examining his political thought and reflections on society, political economy, history and the American Revolution.

6.329 **Lyon**, R., 'Notes on Hume's philosophy of political economy', *J. Hist. Ideas*, 31, 1970, 457–61. Examines his ideas on money and trade, and his rejection of collectivism and egalitarianism in favour of the utility of private property. Concludes that whilst his philosophical and religious ideas are clearly liberal, his conceptions of politics and economics are a mixture of liberal and conservative assumptions.

6.330 **Mackie**, J. L., *Hume's Moral Theory*, 1980. Important reconstruction of this area of his thought, drawing upon close textual discussion of his *Treatise*, and highlighting a number of its overtly political passages.

6.331 **Macleod**, A., 'Rule-utilitarianism and Hume's theory of justice', *Hume Studies*, 7, 1981, 74–87. Argues that even though he made a distinction between justice and utility, his theory of justice is utilitarian.

6.332 **McLynn**, F. J., 'Jacobitism and David Hume: the ideological backlash foiled', *Hume Studies*, 9, 1983, 171–99. Argues that in addressing the question of Jacobitism, he succeeded in giving both the Revolution settlement and the Hanoverian succession a respectable intellectual base.

6.333 **MacNabb**, D. G. C., *David Hume: His Theory of Knowledge and Morality*, 1966. Basic, and somewhat dated, introduction to his ideas, with a chapter on his theory of justice.

6.334 **McRae**, R., 'Hume as a political philosopher', *J. Hist. Ideas*, 12, 1951, 285–90. A short, though interesting, account of the tension between the psychological and scientific basis of his political thought and its literary and historical foundation.

6.335 **Marshall**, G., 'David Hume and political scepticism', *Phil. Q.*, 4, 1953, 247–57. Examines his conception of justice, political change and political parties in the light of his general philosophical outlook.

6.336 **Mertill**, K. R. and **Shahan**, R. W., ed., *David Hume: Many-Sided Genius*, Norman, Okla., 1976. Includes chapters on his conceptions of justice, virtue, history and property.

6.337 **Miller**, D., 'Hume and possessive individualism', *Hist. Pol. Thought*, 1, 1980, 261–78. Challenges C. B. Macpherson's account of Hume as a possessive individualist and, consequently, of England in 1750 as a market society. In fact, Hume talks of an open and progressive aristocracy and deploys a powerful sense of social duty and virtue.

6.338 —— *Philosophy and Ideology in Hume's Political Thought*, 1981. Astute, important treatment of his ideas, demonstrating why he cannot be easily labelled as either conservative or liberal.

6.339 **Moore**, J., 'Hume's political science and the classical republican tradition', *Can. J. Pol. Sc.*, 10, 1977, 809–39. Argues that his political science can best be understood as a challenge to the classical republican tradition.

6.340 —— 'Hume's theory of justice and property', *Pol. Sts.*, 24, 1979, 104–19. Careful explanation of how in his account of the origins of justice and property he tried to avoid what he regarded as the pitfalls of other juridical theories.

6.341 **Morice**, G. P., *David Hume: Bicentenary Papers*, 1977. A collection of nineteen essays examining all aspects of Hume's thought, including D. D. Raphael on Hume's influence on Adam Smith, D. Forbes, 'Hume's science of politics', and I. Berlin, 'Hume and the sources of German anti-rationalism'.

6.342 **Moses**, G. J., 'David Hume as philosophical historian', *Aust. J. Pol. & Hist.*, 35, 1989, 80–91. Examines his philosophy of history with a view to illuminating his moral theory and conception of the individual in society.

6.343 **Mossner**, E. C., 'Hume and the French men of letters', *Revue Internationale de Philosophie*, 6, 1952, 222–35. Considers his intellectual and personal relationship with d'Alembert, Voltaire, Diderot and the Physiocrats.

6.344 —— 'The Enlightenment of David Hume', *Rivista Critica di Storia della Filosofia*, 22, 1967, 388–99. Examines his views on economics and politics, in relation to his philosophical scepticism.

6.345 —— *The Life of David Hume*, 1970. Standard intellectual biography which considers *Essays Moral and Political*, *Political Discourses* and his *A History of England*.

6.346 **Murphy**, J. G., 'Hume and Kant on social contract', *Phil. Sts.*, 33, 1978, 65–79. Careful comparison of their views on social contract and of how their differences emanate from their moral philosophies.

6.347 **Nuyen**, A. T., 'Hume's justice as a collective good', *Hume Studies*, 12, 1986, 39–56. Focuses upon the distinction between private and public goods to elucidate his conception of justice as an artificial virtue.

6.348 **Pence**, G. E., 'Can Hume answer Cromwell?', *Can. J. Phil.*, 11, 1981, 505–24. Re-examines Hume's conceptions of justice and sympathy in the light of his assessment of Cromwell in *The History of England*.

6.349 **Penelhum**, T., *Hume*, 1975. Includes a chapter on his moral and political views in this penetrating study of his philosophy.

6.350 **Phillipson**, N., *Hume*, 1989. Accessible survey of his thought, especially strong on his historiographical concerns, placing him in his contemporary British context.

6.351 **Pocock**, J. G. A., 'Hume and the American Revolution: the dying thoughts of a north Briton', in D. F. Norton, N. Capaldi and W. L. Robinson, ed., *McGill Hume Studies*, San Diego, Calif., 1979, 325–44. Places Hume's historical writing within a tradition of discourse descending from Machiavelli through Harrington to Montesquieu.

6.352 **Pomeroy**, R. S., 'Hume's proposed league of the learned and conversible worlds', *Eighteenth-Cent. Sts.*, 19, 1986, 373–94. Suggests that his essays are crucial to an understanding of his political, social and philosophical thought.

6.353 **Ponko**, T. A., 'Artificial virtue, self-interest, and acquired social concern', *Hume Studies*, 9, 1983, 46–58. Examines his distinction between natural and artificial virtue, contending that although both yield individual pleasure, natural virtue is a crude form of self-interest and pre-social action, whilst artificial virtue is social in nature.

6.354 **Price**, J. V., 'Hume's concept of liberty and *The History of England*', *Studies in Romanticism*, 5, 1966, 139–57. Focuses upon his distinction between an ideal and potentially real state, and examines his conceptions of political and religious liberty.

6.355 **Raphael**, D. D., 'Hume and Adam Smith on justice and utility', *Procs. Aris. Soc.*, 73, 1973, 87–103. A cogent presentation of Hume's rule-utilitarianism and Smith's empiricist, natural-law theory.

6.356 **Raynor**, D., 'Hume's abstract of Adam Smith's "Theory of Moral Sentiments" ', *J. Hist. Phil.*, 22, 1984, 51–80. A reprint of a review of Adam Smith's *Theory of Moral Sentiments*, allegedly by Hume, together with an analysis of the latter's critique, particularly of Smith's concept of sympathy.

6.357 **Robinson**, W. L., 'Hume and the constitution', in A. S. Rosenbaum, ed., *Constitutionalism: The Philosophical Dimension*, New York, 1988, 31–53. Argues that Hume, in disregarding Lockean social contract theory, grounds political legitimacy in mutual advantage and security.

6.358 **Scaff**, L. A., 'Hume on justice and the original contract', *Phil. Sts.*, 33, 1978,

101–8. Believes that his political theory is flawed because of an inadequate understanding of both citizenship and shared political experience within a constitutional order.

6.359 **Stewart**, J. B., *Opinion and Reform in Hume's Political Philosophy*, Princeton, N.J., 1992. Presents him as a more self-confident liberal philosopher than has been conventional.

6.360 —— *The Moral and Political Philosophy of David Hume*, Columbia, N.Y., 1963.

6.361 **Stockton**, C. N., 'David Hume among the historiographers', *Studies in History and Society*, 3, 1971, 14–25.

6.362 —— 'Hume – historian of the English constitution', *Eighteenth-Cent. Sts.*, 44, 1971, 277–93. On his refutation of the Whig myth of the ancient constitution.

6.363 **Stroud**, B., *Hume*, 1981. Includes a chapter on his theory of society and government in which the ideas of virtue and justice, and their relationship to social convention, are systematically scrutinised.

6.364 **Thompson**, M. P., 'Hume's critique of Locke and the "original contract" ', *Il Pensiero Politico*, 10, 1977, 189–201. Maintains that Locke's theory of political obligation was not dented by Hume because it is not based on consent, as the latter believed, but on God's command.

6.365 **Venning**, C., 'Hume on property, commerce, and empire in the good society: the role of historical necessity', *J. Hist. Ideas*, 37, 1976, 79–92. Argues that for Hume the good society is one dominated by private property and commercial activity.

6.366 **Wallech**, S., 'The elements of social status in Hume's "Treatise of human nature" ', *J. Hist. Ideas*, 45, 1984, 207–18.

6.367 **Walton**, C., 'Hume and Jefferson on the uses of history', in D. W. Livingston and J. T. King, ed., *Hume: A Re-Evaluation*, New York, 1976, 389–403. Sets out to explain why Jefferson, once a fan of Hume's *History*, set out to prevent its popularisation after 1807, providing an insightful glimpse into the political considerations and tensions of the United States in the early nineteenth century.

6.368 **Werner**, J. M., 'David Hume and America', *J. Hist. Ideas*, 33, 1972, 439–56. Examines the influence that his writings, especially about the social contract, had on Americans at the time of the Revolution.

6.369 **Wexler**, V. G., *David Hume and the History of England*, Philadelphia, Penn., 1979. Careful analysis of the *History*.

6.370 **Whelan**, F. G., *Order and Artifice in Hume's Political Philosophy*, Princeton, N.J., 1985.

6.372 **Wolff**, J., 'Hume, Bentham, and the social contract', *Utilitas*, 5, 1993, 87–90. A suggestive account of their rejection of social contract theories.

6.373 **Wolin**, S. S., 'Hume and conservatism', *Am. Pol. Sc. Rev.*, 48, 1954, 999–1016. An influential reconstruction of his ambiguous political theory, which stresses his conservative inclinations in the face of Enlightenment ideals.

6.374 **Woozley**, A. D., 'Hume on justice', *Phil. Sts.*, 33, 1978, 81–99.

Mandeville

6.375 **Castiglione**, D., 'Considering things minutely: reflections on Mandeville and the eighteenth-century science of man', *Hist. Pol. Thought*, 7, 1986, 463–88. Sharp, if elusive, account of his thought with close attention to its ideological and historical context.

6.376 —— 'Mandeville moralized', *Annali della Fondazione Luigi Einaudi*, 17, 1983, 239–90.

6.377 **Chalk**, A., 'Mandeville's fable of the bees: a reappraisal', *Southern Econ. J.*, 33, 1966, 1–16.

6.378 **Chiasson**, E. J., 'Bernard Mandeville: a reappraisal', *Philological Quarterly*, 49, 1970, 489–519.

6.379 **Coleman**, J., 'Bernard Mandeville and the reality of virtue', *Phil.*, 47, 1972, 125–39.

6.380 **Cook**, R. I., *Bernard Mandeville*, New York, 1974. Useful introduction to his thought.

6.381 **Dickinson**, H. T., 'Bernard Mandeville: an independent Whig', *Sts. Voltaire*, 152, 1976, 559–70. Examines his ideas on the origin and development of civil society and reflections on court and country life, especially in relation to the problem of corruption.

6.382 **Goldsmith**, M. M., 'Mandeville and the spirit of capitalism', *J. Brit. Sts.*, 17, 1977, 62–81.

6.383 —— *Private Vices, Public Benefits: Bernard Mandeville's Social and Political Thought*,

1985. Provides not only an excellent account of his ideas, but, more than any other book, sets them in their appropriate ideological context.

6.384 —— 'Public virtues and private vices: Bernard Mandeville and English political ideologies in the early eighteenth century', *Eighteenth-Cent. Sts.*, 9, 1975–76, 477–510. Interesting account of the Augustan ideology of public virtue, arguing that Mandeville's ideas were less a response to prevalent ideas and more a specific attack on Isaac Bickerstaff – Richard Steele's *persona* as author of the *Tatler*.

6.385 —— 'Regulating anew the moral and political sentiments of mankind: Bernard Mandeville and the Scottish Enlightenment', *J. Hist. Ideas*, 49, 1988, 587–606. A rigorously structured and systematic account of the influence of the civic humanist and natural law traditions on the thought of Hutcheson, Hume and Smith. Argues that although Mandeville's ideas conflicted with civic humanist and natural law traditions, aspects of his conception of society and morality were incorporated in the ideas of Smith, Hume and Hutcheson.

6.386 —— ' "The treacherous arts of mankind": Bernard Mandeville and female virtue', *Hist. Pol. Thought*, 7, 1986, 93–114. Interesting account of his rejection of both patriarchalism and civic humanism. 'Against the ideal life of the male landowner-citizen proposed by civic humanism, Mandeville was prepared to argue for the idle hedonist and the dedicated capitalist; but he was also prepared to argue a case for women and not just women as daughters, sisters, wives and mothers.'

6.387 **Hayek**, F. A., 'Dr. Bernard Mandeville', *Procs. Brit. Acad.*, 52, 1966, 125–41. Argues that he was one of the first social thinkers to make a serious contribution to the ideas of evolution and a self-regulating social system.

6.388 **Horne**, T. A., *The Social Thought of Bernard Mandeville: Virtue and Commerce in Early Eighteenth-Century England*, 1978. Reliable account which discusses Societies for the Reformation of Manners, antecedents of Mandeville's thought in French moral discourse, and the reception of Mandeville by Hume, Hutcheson and lesser writers.

6.389 **Jack**, M., *The Social and Political Thought of Bernard Mandeville*, New York, 1987. Examines his conception of human nature and its social, political and economic implications.

6.390 **Malcolm**, J., 'One state of nature: Mandeville and Rousseau', *J. Hist. Ideas*, 39, 1978, 119–24. Contends that they held similar views about the state of nature and the evolution of society.

6.391 **Maxwell**, J. C , 'Ethics and politics in Mandeville', *Phil.*, 26, 1951, 242–52. Claims that he had a utilitarian view of politics, logically independent of any individual ethics.

6.392 **Monro**, H., *The Ambivalence of Bernard Mandeville*, 1975.

6.393 **Primer**, I., ed., *Mandeville Studies: New Explorations in the Art and Thought of Bernard Mandeville*, The Hague, 1975. Includes H. T. Dickinson, 'The politics of Bernard Mandeville', R. Cook, ' "The great Leviathan of lechery": Mandeville's *Modest Defence of Public Stews (1724)*', J. Gunn, 'Mandeville and Wither: individualism and the workings of providence', R. Hopkins, 'The cant of social compromise: some observations on Mandeville's satire', M. Jack, 'Religion and ethics in Mandeville', P. Pinkus, 'Mandeville's paradox', I. Primer, 'Mandeville and Shaftesbury: some facts and problems', W. Speck, 'Mandeville and the Eutopia seated in the brain', G. S. Vichert, 'Bernard Mandeville's *The Virgin Unmask'd*'.

6.394 **Rosenberg**, N., 'Mandeville and laissez-faire', *J. Hist. Ideas*, 29, 1963, 183–96.

6.395 **Schneider**, L. C., 'Mandeville as forerunner of modern sociology', *Journal of History and Behavioral Sciences*, 10, 1964, 25–37.

6.396 **Scott-Taggart**, M. J., 'Mandeville: cynic or fool?', *Phil. Q.*, 16, 1966, 221–32. Argues that he was sceptical of naturalistic explanations of morality.

Paine

6.397 **Aldridge**, A. O., *Man of Reason: The Life of Thomas Paine*, 1960. A standard, if romantic, intellectual biography.

6.398 —— 'The influence of Thomas Paine in the United States, England, France, Germany

120

and South America', in W. P. Friedrich, ed., *Comparative Literature. Proceedings of the Second Congress at the University of North Carolina, 1958*, Chapel Hill, N.C., 1959, 369–83.

6.399 —— 'The problem of Thomas Paine', *Sts. Burke & Time*, 19, 1978, 127–43. Through an analysis of E. Foner, *Tom Paine and Revolutionary America*, Aldridge examines the relationship between political ideology and social status in Paine's work.

6.400 —— 'Thomas Paine and the classics', *Eighteenth-Cent. Sts.*, 1, 1968, 370–80. Contrasts his favourable readings of classical civilisation with his more critical comments.

6.401 —— 'Thomas Paine and the *Ideologues*', *Sts. Voltaire*, 151, 1976, 109–17. Examines the overlap between their ideas, focusing on André Morellet's influence on Paine.

6.402 —— *Thomas Paine's American Ideology*, Newark, N.J., 1984. A thorough examination of his American writings.

6.403 —— 'Why did Thomas Paine write on the bank?', *Procs. Am. Phil. Soc.*, 93, 1949, 309–15.

6.404 **Andrews**, S., 'Paine's American pamphlets', *Hist. Today*, 31, 1981, 7–11.

6.405 —— 'Tom Paine in France', *Hist. Today*, 33, 1983, 5–11.

6.406 **Ayer**, A. J., *Thomas Paine*, 1988. A clear and engaging biography which places his thought within its intellectual context through an examination of the seventeenth- and eighteenth-century distinction between natural and civil rights as revealed in the works of Hobbes, Locke, Hume and Rousseau, and provides a sharp analysis of his ideas, especially his dispute with Burke.

6.407 **Bailyn**, B., 'The most uncommon pamphlet of the revolution, *Common Sense*', *American Heritage*, 25, 1973, 36–41, 91–3.

6.408 —— 'Thomas Paine', *UNESCO Courier*, 29, 1976, 20–8. On the rhetorical qualities of *Common Sense* and its contention, contrary to opinion of the day, that simplicity in government is a good thing.

9.409 **Chase**, M., 'Paine, Spence and the "Real Rights of Man" ', *Bulletin of the Society for the Study of Labour History*, 52, 1988, 32–9. Demonstrates that Thomas Spence advanced some radical political ideas normally attributed to Thomas Paine.

6.410 **Christian**, W., 'The moral economics of Tom Paine', *J. Hist. Ideas*, 34, 1973, 367–80. Argues that what is original in Paine was the 'suggestion that social amelioration should follow rather than precede revolution'.

6.411 **Claeys**, G., 'Thomas Paine's *Agrarian Justice* (1976) and the secularization of natural jurisprudence', *Bulletin of the Society for the Study of Labour History*, 52, 1988, 21–31.

6.412 —— *Thomas Paine. Social and Political Thought*, 1989. Excellent account of his political theory, demonstrating its consistency and sophistication as well as the controversy it generated among contemporaries.

6.413 **Coolidge**, O. E., *Tom Paine, Revolutionary*, New York, 1960.

6.414 **Dickinson**, H. T., 'Thomas Paine's Rights of Man, 1791–92: a bi-centenary assessment', *Historian*, 32, 1991, 18–21.

6.415 **Dyck**, I., ed., *Citizen of the World. Essays on Thomas Paine*, New York, 1988. Includes G. Spater, 'The legacy of Thomas Paine', J. Wiener, 'Collaborators of a sort: Thomas Paine and Richard Carlisle', and J. F. C. Harrison, 'Thomas Paine and millenarian radicalism'.

6.416 **Edwards**, S., *Rebel. A Biography of Thomas Paine*, 1974.

6.417 **Elder**, D., *The Common Man Philosophy of Thomas Paine: A Study of the Political Ideas of Paine*, South Bend, Ind., 1951.

6.418 **Essiek**, R. N., 'William Blake, Thomas Paine, and biblical revolution', *Studies in Romanticism*, 30, 1991, 189–212. Argues that parallels can be drawn between Paine's *The Rights of Man* and Blake's attempt to combine radical politics with an apocalyptic Christianity.

6.419 **Foner**, E., *Tom Paine and Revolutionary America*, 1976. Attempts to make sense of his ideas by relating them to key moments of Paine's career in America.

6.420 **Fruchtman**, J., 'Nature and revolution in Paine's *Common Sense*', *Hist. Pol. Thought*, 10, 1989, 421–38. Asserts that what makes the book remarkable is the way Paine located his radical egalitarianism within prevailing views of nature and common sense.

6.422 —— 'The revolutionary millennialism of Thomas Paine', *Studies in Eighteenth-Century Culture*, 13, 1984, 65–77. Compares his secular millennialism, grounded in the language of 'the coming republican apocalypse', with the more traditional version of Joseph Priestley.

6.423 **Gabrieli**, V., 'Tom Paine between Europe and America: a re-consideration', *European Contributions to American Studies*, 14, 1988, 167–83.

6.424 **Gimbel**, R., 'Thomas Paine fights for freedom in three worlds: the new, the old, the next', *Proceedings of the American Antiquarian Society*, 70, 1960, 397–492.

6.425 **Greene**, J. P., 'Paine, America, and the "modernization" of political consciousness', *Pol. Sc. Q.*, 93, 1978, 73–92. Claims that he played a major role in propagating the principles of Enlightenment – equivalent, for Greene, to modernity.

6.426 **Gummere**, R., 'Thomas Paine: was he really anticlassical?', *Proceedings of the American Antiquarian Society*, 75, 1965, 253–69.

6.427 **Hawke**, D. F., *Paine*, New York, 1974. A thorough and rigorous intellectual biography which carefully analyses the intellectual sources of his political ideas.

6.428 **Iude**, H., 'Thomas Paine and his influence on the democratic tradition', in T. Frank, ed., *The Origins and Originality of American Culture*, Budapest, 1984. A Marxist interpretation which portrays him as a 'sincere bourgeois revolutionary'.

6.429 **Jordan**, W. D., 'Familial politics: Thomas Paine and the killing of the king, 1776', *Journal of American History*, 60, 1973, 294–308. On why *Common Sense* was so successful among its American readers in symbolically destroying royal authority.

6.430 **Kashatus**, W. C., 'Thomas Paine: a Quaker revolutionary', *Quaker History*, 73, 1984, 38–61. Argues that his Quakerism was manifested in his public stances against slavery and duelling, as well as his proto-feminism, and that his views on loyalty to legitimate government, pacifism and millennialism were strongly influenced by William Penn.

6.431 **Kates**, G., 'From liberalism to radicalism: Tom Paine's *Rights of Man*', *J. Hist. Ideas*, 50, 1989, 569–87. Presents a complex picture of his ideological development, in which his thought is interpreted in a developmental fashion because of the key influence of French radicals.

6.432 **Keane**, J., 'Democracy, war and the rights of man', *Thomas Paine Society Bulletin*, 3, 1992, 7–12. Examines Paine's views on the relation between war and despotic government, arguing that the *Rights of Man* was a call to establish democratic institutions in order to end war.

6.433 **Kenyon**, C., 'Where Paine went wrong', *Am. Pol. Sc. Rev.*, 45, 1951, 1086–99. Paine is said to be a 'novice in the politics of republicanism' because his commitment to logical deduction (natural rights theory) made him oblivious to the contingencies of political life.

6.434 **Kistler**, M., 'German-American liberalism and Thomas Paine', *American Quarterly*, 14, 1962, 81–91.

6.435 **Kramnick**, I., 'Tommy Paine and the idea of America', in P. J. Korshin, ed., *The American Revolution and Eighteenth-Century Culture*, New York, 1986, 75–91.

6.436 **Meng**, J. J., 'The constitutional theories of Thomas Paine', *Rev. Pol.*, 8, 1946, 283–306.

6.437 **Newman**, S., 'A note on *Common Sense* and Christian eschatology', *Pol. Theory*, 6, 1978, 101–8. Argues that Paine drew from the language of radical Calvinism, especially in his conception of independence and virtue.

6.438 **Nursey-Bray**, P. F., 'Thomas Paine and the concept of alienation', *Pol. Sts.*, 16, 1968, 223–42. Examines the weaknesses in his theory of natural rights and his consequently ambivalent understanding of alienation.

6.439 **Philp**, M., *Paine*, 1989. Short, but authoritative, account of his ideas and activities.

6.440 **Powell**, D., *Tom Paine: The Greatest Exile*, 1985. A biography which places his ideas in intellectual and historical context.

6.441 **Prochaska**, F. K., 'Thomas Paine's "the age of reason" revisited', *J. Hist. Ideas*, 33, 1972, 561–76.

6.442 **Robbins**, C., 'The lifelong education of Thomas Paine (1737–1809): some reflections upon his acquaintance among books', *Procs. Am. Phil. Soc.*, 127, 1983, 135–42. Consideration of the sources cited by Paine, including Rousseau and James Burgh, concluding that he tended to avoid speculative and philosophical discussion, using books primarily as sources of information.

6.443 **Royle**, E., 'The reception of Paine', *Bulletin of the Society for the Study of Labour History*, 52, 1988, 14–20. On the reception of *Rights of Man*.

6.444 **Seaman**, J. W., 'Thomas Paine: ransom, civil peace, and the natural right to welfare', *Pol. Theory*, 16, 1988, 120–42. Argues that he not only advanced a radical doctrine of natural rights but through his call for economic assistance for the poor, defended a natural right, rather than a utilitarian injunction, to welfare.

6.445 **Stevenson**, J., 'Reflections on William Blake and Thomas Paine', *San José Studies*, 15, 1989, 62–70. Compares their critical stance toward repressive, socio-political institutions.

6.446 **Williamson**, A., *Thomas Paine. His Life, Work and Times*, New York, 1973. Interesting intellectual biography, although journalistic in style.

6.447 **Wilson**, D. A., *Paine and Cobbett: The Transatlantic Connection*, Montreal, 1988. Focuses upon the transformation of British radical ideas into a republican and democratic American ideology, and the impact the American and French Revolutions had upon British radicalism.

6.448 **Wilson**, J. D. and **Ricketson**, W. F., *Thomas Paine*, Boston, Mass., 1978. Introduction to his life and ideas, with a useful annotated bibliography.

Price

6.449 **Agnew**, J. P., *Richard Price and the American Revolution*, Urbana, Ill., 1949.

6.450 **Andrews**, S., ' "Insects of the hour"?: Dr. Price's "Revolutions" ', *Hist. Today*, 41, 1991, 48–53. On his defence of the American and French Revolutions.

6.451 **Cone**, C. B., 'Richard Price and the constitution of the United States', *Am. Hist. Rev.*, 53, 1948, 726–47.

6.452 —— *Torchbearer of Freedom, The Influence of Richard Price on Eighteenth-Century Thought*, Lexington, Ky., 1952.

6.453 **Fruchtman**, J., 'The apocalyptic politics of Richard Price and Joseph Priestley: a study in late eighteenth-century English republican millenarianism', *Trans. Am. Phil. Soc.*, 73, 1983, 1–125. On their political theology generally, but focusing specifically on how they linked millenarian views with ideas of progress and perfectibility.

6.454 **Laboucheix**, H., *Richard Price as Moral Philosopher and Political Theorist*, 1982.

6.455 **Lippy**, C. H., 'Trans-Atlantic dissent and the Revolution: Richard Price and Charles Chauncy', *Eighteenth-Cent. Life*, 4, 1977, 31–7. Argues that whereas Price looked favourably upon the American Revolution, Chauncy was less sanguine about the new republic because of its treatment of slaves and dissenters.

6.456 **Peach**, B., ed., *Richard Price and the Ethical Foundations of the American Revolution*, Durham, N.C., 1979.

6.457 **Peterson**, S. R., 'The compatibility of Richard Price's politics and his ethics', *J. Hist. Ideas*, 45, 1984, 537–48. Examines the deontological and rationalist basis of his ethics, and argues that his *Review of the Principal Questions in Morals* provided the philosophical foundation for his political ideas.

6.458 **Thomas**, D. O., 'Richard Price and Edmund Burke: the duty to participate in government', *Phil.*, 34, 1959, 308–22.

6.459 —— *The Honest Mind: The Thought and Work of Richard Price*, 1977. The best survey of his thought, illustrating how his political philosophy was firmly grounded in his theology and moral theory, and dealing with Burke's attack upon his liberalism.

Smith

6.460 **Anderson**, G. M., 'The butcher, the baker and the policy-maker: Adam Smith on public choice', *Hist. Pol. Econ.*, 21, 1989, 631–60. Examines his application of economic ideas to political behaviour.

6.461 **Anspach**, R., 'The implications of the *Theory of Moral Sentiments* for Adam Smith's economic thought', *Hist. Pol. Econ.*, 4, 1972, 176–206. Stresses his belief that the conditions for a successful *laissez-faire* economy lie in individual conscience, a moral code and a system of justice. This well-presented interpretation undermines the appropriation of Smith for simple, private enterprise politics.

6.462 **Billet**, L., 'Political order and economic development: reflections on Adam Smith's

Wealth of Nations', *Pol. Sts.*, 23, 1975, 430–41. Argues for a greater understanding of the relationship between political institutions and behaviour and the process of economic development. Smith's discussion of the character of a nation's administration of justice, the type of political authority and the coherence of authority systems provide a starting point for understanding this relationship.

6.463 —— 'The just economy: the moral basis of the wealth of nations', *Review of Social Economics*, 34, 295–315. Examines Smith's ideas on justice, liberty, human nature and morality as portrayed in *The Wealth of Nations*.

6.464 **Bowles**, P., 'Adam Smith and the "natural progress of opulence" ', *Economica*, 53, 1986, 109–18. Examines *The Wealth of Nations*, specifically his discussion on the 'natural progress of opulence' and how it relates to social and political development.

6.465 **Brau**, M., *Adam Smith's Economics and its Place in the Development of Political Thought*, 1988.

6.466 **Campbell**, R. H. and **Skinner**, A. S., *Adam Smith*, 1982. A thorough, intellectual biography, providing important insights into his political and philosophical thought.

6.467 **Campbell**, T. D. 'Adam Smith and natural liberty', *Pol. Sts.*, 25, 1977, 523–34. Examines *The Wealth of Nations* and *Theory of Moral Sentiments* with a view to establishing that he presented a system of natural liberty in utilitarian terms. Argues that Smith's utilitarianism, when viewed in relation to his theory of political obligation and natural theology, is conservative.

6.468 —— *Adam Smith's Science of Morals*, 1971. Contains a short but perceptive chapter on his politics.

6.469 —— and **Ross**, A. S., 'The utilitarianism of Adam Smith's policy advice', *J. Hist. Ideas*, 42, 1981, 73–92. Argues that his views on the union of Scotland and England, the rebellion of the American colonies and monopolies suggest that he was in fact a utilitarian despite his explicit rejection of the principle of utility in the *Theory of Moral Sentiments*.

6.470 **Chisick**, H., 'The wealth of nations and the poverty of the people in the thought of Adam Smith', *Canadian Journal of History*, 25, 1990, 325–44. Explores Smith's reflections on mercantilism and liberalism and their relationship to working-class poverty.

6.471 **Coase**, R. H., 'Adam Smith's view of man', *Journal of Law and Economics*, 19, 1976, 529–46. Focusing on the *Theory of Moral Sentiments* and *The Wealth of Nations*, Coase argues that Smith saw human nature as being motivated by self-interest.

6.472 **Coats**, A. W., 'Adam Smith's conception of self-interest in economic and political affairs', *Hist. Pol. Econ.*, 7, 1975, 132–6.

6.473 **Coker**, E. W., 'Adam Smith's concept of the social system', *Business and Professional Ethics Journal*, 9, 1990, 139–42. A superficial examination of how his economic thought was grounded in his conception of individual liberty and psychology of sympathy and self-interest.

6.474 **Cole**, A. H., 'Puzzles of the *Wealth of Nations*', *Can. J. Econ. & Pol. Sc.*, 24, 1958, 1–8. Surveys Smith's attitude toward politicians, members of the clergy, merchants and bankers.

6.475 **Collins**, D., 'Adam Smith's social contract: The proper role of individual liberty and government intervention', *Business and Professional Ethics Journal*, 7, 1988, 119–46.

6.476 **Cremaschi**, S., 'Adam Smith: skeptical Newtonianism, disenchanted republicanism', in D. Macelo, ed., *Knowledge and Politics*, Boulder, Calif., 1988, 83–110. Charts the tension between his epistemology and his political philosophy, highlighting the influences of essentialism and the natural law tradition.

6.477 **Cropsey**, J., *Polity and Economy: An Interpretation of the Principles of Adam Smith*, The Hague, 1957. Argues that his views in *Theory of Moral Sentiments* and *The Wealth of Nations* are not inconsistent, because of his determinist, psychological understanding of human conduct in both the personal and social spheres.

6.478 **Danford**, J. W., 'Adam Smith, equality and the wealth of sympathy', *Am. J. Pol. Sc.*, 24, 1980, 674–95. Scrutinising *The Wealth of Nations* and *Theory of Moral Sentiments*, Danford argues that his theories of historical progress and moral transactions suggest that he understood that a society's morality evolves in response to changing economic circumstances.

6.479 **Danner**, P. L., 'Sympathy and

exchangeable values: keys to Adam Smith's social philosophy', *Review of Social Economics*, 34, 1976, 317–31.

6.480 **de Vries**, P. H., 'Adam Smith's "theory of justice" ', *Business and Professional Ethics Journal*, 8, 1989, 37–56.

6.481 **Evensky**, J., 'The voices of Adam Smith: moral philosopher and social critic', *Hist. Pol. Econ.*, 19, 1987, 447–68. Argues that his *Theory of Moral Sentiments* advocates a theory of *laissez-faire* based on a divine regulative principle, whilst *The Wealth of Nations* offers scope for state intervention.

6.482 **Forbes**, D., ' "Scientific" Whiggism: Adam Smith and John Millar', *Cambridge J.*, 7, 1954, 643–70. Sharp and detailed analysis, tracing an intellectual lineage from Smith through Millar to utilitarianism.

6.483 **Freeman**, R. D., 'Adam Smith, education and laissez-faire', *Hist. Pol. Econ.*, 1, 1969, 173–86. Argues that for Smith the free market could not operate effectively without efficient government, and that he viewed education as a means of improving the standards of government.

6.484 **Freudenthal**, G., 'Adam Smith's analytic-synthetic method and the "system of natural liberty" ', *Hist. Euro. Ideas*, 2, 1981, 135–54. Examines his conception of society through a rigorous scrutiny of his philosophical method.

6.485 **Gill**, E. R., 'Justice in Adam Smith: the right and the good', *Review of Social Economics*, 34, 1976, 275–96. Argues that his theory of social justice surpasses simple utilitarianism.

6.486 **Grampp**, W. D., 'Adam Smith and the American revolutionists', *Hist. Pol. Econ.*, 11, 1979, 179–91. Examines the importance of nationalism and utilitarianism in Smith's political and economic thought, drawing a number of parallels between his ideas and those of the American revolutionists, particularly Thomas Jefferson.

6.487 **Haakonssen**, K., *The Science of a Legislator: The Natural Jurisprudence of David Hume and Adam Smith*, 1981. Important examination of Smith's appropriation of the Humean theory of justice as he developed his natural jurisprudence. Masterful account of the interrelations between Smith's legal and political ideas.

6.488 **Harpham**, E. J., 'Liberalism, civic humanism, and the case of Adam Smith', *Am. Pol. Sc. Rev.*, 78, 1984, 764–74. Places his political liberalism within the context of his moral and economic writings, especially their treatment of the idea of commercial society.

6.489 **Heilbroner**, R. L., 'The paradox of progress. Decline and decay in *The Wealth of Nations*', *J. Hist. Ideas*, 4, 1973, 243–62. Argues that the message of this text is profoundly pessimistic – economic development terminates in a stagnant state in which there is also moral decay.

6.490 —— 'The socialization of the individual in Adam Smith', *Hist. Pol. Econ.*, 14, 1982, 427–39. Demonstrates that the economically astute person of the *Wealth* is the prudent person of the *Theory*, but that Smith's theory does not resolve the paradox of how private vice is supposed to result in public virtue.

6.491 **Hetherington**, N. S., 'Issac Newton's influence on Adam Smith's natural laws in economics', *J. Hist. Ideas*, 44, 1983, 497–505. Contends that Newtonian physics was the methodological model for Smith's *The Wealth of Nations*.

6.492 **Hont**, I. and **Ignatieff**, M., 'Needs and justice in *The Wealth of Nations*: an introductory essay', in I. Hont and M. Ignatieff, ed., *Wealth and Virtue: The Shaping of Political Economy in the Scottish Enlightenment*, 1983, 1–44. *The Wealth of Nations* is said to be centrally concerned with 'finding a market mechanism capable of reconciling inequality of property with adequate provision for the excluded'.

6.493 **Horne**, T. A., 'Envy and commercial society: Mandeville and Smith on "private vices, public benefits" ', *Pol. Theory*, 9, 1981, 551–69. Examines their views on the tension between private interest and public good within commercial society.

6.494 **Hutchinson**, T. W., 'Adam Smith and the wealth of nations', *Journal of Law and Economics*, 19, 1976, 507–28. Argues that Smith saw *The Wealth of Nations* as part of a much larger philosophical enterprise that he was unable to complete.

6.495 **Lamb**, R. B., 'Adam Smith's system: sympathy not self-interest', *J. Hist. Ideas*, 35, 1974, 671–82.

6.496 **Letwin**, W., 'Adam Smith: re-reading *The Wealth of Nations*', *Encounter*, 46, 1976, 45–53. Examines his ideas of justice, order, liberty and wealth in this text.

6.497 —— 'Was Adam Smith a liberal?', in K. Haakonssen, ed., *Traditions of Liberalism: Essays on John Locke, Adam Smith and John Stuart Mill*, St. Leonards, N.S.W., 1988, 63–80.

6.498 **Levy**, D., 'Adam Smith's "natural law" and contractual society', *J. Hist. Ideas*, 39, 1978, 665–74. Considers Smith's idea of a free and pleasant society in the light of Hume's transformation of natural law theory and his reaction to Hobbes's conception of absolute freedom as a state of war.

6.499 **Lindgren**, J. R., *The Social Philosophy of Adam Smith*, The Hague, 1973. Preceptive and meticulous study, including a chapter on his political ideas.

6.500 **Long**, D., 'Adam Smith's "two cities" ', *Sts. Pol. Thought*, 1, 1992, 43–59.

6.501 **Meek**, R. L., *Smith, Marx and After: Ten Essays in the Development of Economic Thought*, 1977. Contains three essays relevant to the history of political thought: 'Smith and Marx', 'Smith, Turgot, and the "four stages" theory', and 'New light on Adam Smith's Glasgow lectures on jurisprudence'.

6.502 **O'Driscoll**, P., ed., *Adam Smith and Modern Political Economy*, Iowa, 1979. Includes K. J. Arrow, 'The division of labor in the economy, the polity, and society', J. Buchanan, 'The justice of natural liberty', L. Schneider, 'Adam Smith on human nature and social circumstance', and E. G. West, 'Adam Smith's economics and politics'.

6.503 **Pesciarelli**, E., 'On Adam Smith's lectures on jurisprudence', *Scottish Journal of Political Economy*, 33, 1986, 74–85. Contends that Pufendorf and Hutcheson exercised a greater influence on Smith's juristic ideas than is usually acknowledged.

6.504 **Phillipson**, N., 'Adam Smith as civil moralist', in I. Hont and M. Ignatieff, ed., *Wealth and Virtue: The Shaping of Political Economy in the Scottish Enlightenment*, 1983, 179–202. Smith is portrayed as 'a practical moralist who thought that his account of the principles of morals and social organization would be of use to responsibly-minded men of middling rank, living in a modern, commercial society'.

6.505 **Raphael**, D. D., *Adam Smith*, 1985. Clearly written and concise account of his economic, moral and political ideas.

6.506 —— 'Adam Smith and "the interpretation of David Hume's society" ', *J. Hist. Ideas*, 30, 1969, 225–48. Examines Smith's indebtedness to Hume's thought through the analysis of an unknown manuscript.

6.507 **Rendall**, J., 'Virtue and commerce: women in the making of Adam Smith's political economy', in E. Kennedy and S. Mendus, ed., *Women in Western Political Philosophy*, 1987, 44–77.

6.508 **Rimlinger**, G. V., 'Smith and the merits of the poor', *Review of Social Economics*, 34, 1976, 333–44. Suggests that he advocated a policy of state intervention for the very poor.

6.509 **Robertson**, J., 'Scottish political economy beyond the civic tradition: government and economic development in *The Wealth of Nations*', *Hist. Pol. Thought*, 4, 1983, 451–83. The book's originality is said to lie in 'the assimilation of the indigenous British constitutional principles of parliamentary sovereignty into political economy'.

6.510 **Samuels**, W. J., 'The political economy of Adam Smith', *Ethics*, 87, 1976–77, 189–207. Argues that he viewed the economy as a system of power as well as an arena of voluntary exchange, with the result that he possessed a complex theory of policy formulation.

6.511 **Skinner**, A. S., 'Adam Smith and the American Revolution', *Presidential Studies Quarterly*, 7, 1977, 75–87. Suggests that although he favoured taxation of the colonies, he nevertheless argued for their representation in parliament, and for free trade to be established within the empire.

6.512 —— *Adam Smith and the Role of the State*, 1974. A paper published as a pamphlet which persuasively argues that the functions which he ascribed to the state are more extensive than is commonly supposed.

6.513 —— 'Adam Smith: the devlopment of a system', *Scottish Journal of Political Economy*, 23, 1976, 111–32. Assesses the influence that the Physiocrats, Hutcheson and Hume had on the development of Smith's thought.

6.514 —— *A System of Social Science: Papers Relating to Adam Smith*, 1979. A collection of his previously published essays including 'Moral philosophy and civil society' and 'The functions of government'.

6.515 —— and **Wilson**, T., ed., *Essays on Adam*

Smith, 1975. A collection of twenty-six essays examining his moral, political and economic thought. Includes W. P. D. Wrightman, 'Adam Smith and the history of ideas', H. Mizuta, 'Moral philosophy and civil society', J. Cropsey, 'Adam Smith and political philosophy', D. Forbes, 'Sceptical Whiggism, commerce, and liberty' and P. E. Charnley, 'The conflict between Montesquieu and Hume: a study of the origins of Adam Smith's universalism'.

6.516 **Spiegel**, H. W., 'Adam Smith's heavenly city', *Hist. Pol. Econ.*, 8, 1976, 478–93. Argues that although he was an Enlightenment thinker, his belief in the divine order of the universe was at odds with his progressive views.

6.517 **Stein**, P. G., 'Adam Smith's theory of law and society', in R. R. Bolgar, ed., *Classical Influences on Western Thought, 1650–1870*, 1979, 263–73. Examines such classical influences on Smith's views of law and society as the works of Grotius, Pufendorf and Montesquieu.

6.518 **Stigler**, G. J., 'Adam Smith and public choice: a reply to Anderson', *Hist. Pol. Econ.*, 21, 1989, 641–60. Argues against G. M. Anderson, 'The butcher, the baker and the policy-maker', *Hist. Pol. Econ.*, 21, 1989, that Smith could not have developed a systematic theory of rational political behaviour because of the specificity of his economic thinking.

6.519 —— 'Smith's travels on the ship of state', *Hist. Pol. Econ.*, 3, 1971, 265–77. Suggests that he failed to apply the principle of self-interest to political behaviour, unlike economic actions.

6.520 **Teichgraeber**, R., ' "Less abused than I had reason to expect": the reception of *The Wealth of Nations* in Britain, 1776–90', *Hist. J.*, 30, 1987, 337–66.

6.521 —— 'Rethinking *Das Adam Smith Problem*', in J. Dwyer, R. A Mason and A. Murdoch, ed., *New Perspectives on the Politics and Culture of Early Modern Scotland*, 1982. Sharp reading of the *Theory*, arguing that it is rooted in the concepts of Renaissance humanism. In the book 'individual morality was depoliticized and politics demoralized'. Interesting commentary on the late nineteenth-century debate about a possible rupture in his moral thought.

6.522 **Werhane**, P. H., *Adam Smith and his* *Legacy for Modern Capitalism*, 1991. Full of insight on his political views.

6.523 —— 'The role of self-interest in Adam Smith's *Wealth of Nations*', *J. Phil.*, 86, 1989, 669–80.

6.524 **West**, E. G., 'Adam Smith and Rousseau's *Discourse on Inequality*: inspiration or provocation', *Journal of Economics Issues*, 5, 1971, 56–70.

6.525 —— 'Adam Smith's economics of politics', *Hist. Pol. Econ.*, 8, 1976, 515–39. Pieces together from his writings a coherent account of his political views, arguing that of the three dimensions of politics – pre-constitutional, constitution-making and post-constitutional – Smith was predominantly concerned with the second.

6.526 —— 'The political economy of alienation: Karl Marx and Adam Smith', *Oxford Economic Papers*, 21, 1969, 1–23. Clear account of the similarities and dissimilarities in their treatment of alienation.

6.527 **Willis**, K., 'The role in parliament of the economic ideas of Adam Smith, 1776–1800', *Hist. Pol. Econ.*, 11, 1979, 505–44. Examines the influence that Smith's political and economic ideas had on North, Shelbourne and Pitt the Younger.

6.528 **Winch**, D., 'Adam Smith and the liberal tradition', in K. Haakonssen, ed., *Traditions of Liberalism: Essays on John Locke, Adam Smith and John Stuart Mill*, St. Leonards, N.S.W., 1988, 83–106. Provides further evidence to substantiate his argument, in *Adam Smith's Politics*, that his ideas belong to a humanist rather than liberal capitalist tradition.

6.529 —— 'Adam Smith's "enduring particular result": a political and cosmopolitan perspective', in I. Hont and M. Ignatieff, ed., *Wealth and Virtue: The Shaping of Political Economy in the Scottish Enlightenment*, 1983, 253–70. Subtly locates *The Wealth of Nations* in the context of Scottish civic moralism.

6.530 —— *Adam Smith's Politics: An Essay in Historiographic Revision*, 1978. Brilliant, if contentious, interpretation, suggesting that he belonged to a civic-humanist rather than liberal-capitalist ideological tradition.

6.531 —— 'Science and the legislator: Adam Smith and after', *Econ. J.*, 93, 1983, 501–20. Contends that his ideas were intended to furnish legislators with guidelines for creating a just society.

6.532 —— 'The Burke-Smith problem and late eighteenth-century political and economic thought', *Hist. J.*, 28, 1985, 231–47. Careful comparison of their views on political economy, and an assessment of the extent to which they influenced one another.

Swift

6.533 **Cook**, R. I., *Jonathan Swift as a Tory Pamphleteer*, Seattle, Wash., 1967. Examines his early political views, conversion to Toryism and role in the Harley-St. John ministry.

6.534 **Downie**, J. A., *Jonathan Swift: Political Writer*, 1984. Extensive, chronological biography, illuminating a number of his moral and political concerns.

6.535 **Ehrenpreis**, I., 'Swift on liberty', *J. Hist. Ideas*, 13, 1953, 131–46.

6.536 —— *Swift: The Man, his Works, and the Age*, 1962–83. The definitive intellectual biography in three volumes, including his political ideas with regard to Ireland, England and the relationship of church and politics.

6.537 **Eilon**, D., 'Private spirit: the prosecution of self-interest and faction in Swift's satire', *Hist. Pol. Thought*, 5, 1984, 79–89.

6.538 **Ferguson**, O. W., *Jonathan Swift and Ireland*, Urbana, Ill., 1982. Historically informed study of his Irish writings, which charts his 'gradual and reluctant' involvement with Anglo-Irish politics, and explores his belief that 'patriotism is a virtue and a duty'.

6.539 **Fink**, Z. S., 'Political theory in *Gulliver's Travels*', *English Literary History*, 14, 1947, 151–61. Argues that Swift's political thought emerges from the classical republican and civic humanist traditions, and that he was not therefore a typical Tory.

6.540 **Fitzgerald**, R. P., 'Science and politics in Swift's voyage to Laputa', *J. Engl. & Germ. Philol.*, 87, 1988, 213–29. Argues that Swift's work was motivated by his rejection of absolutist government as portrayed in the writings of Bodin, Filmer and Hobbes.

6.541 **Halewood**, W. H., 'Plutarch in Houyhnhnmland: a neglected source for Gulliver's fourth voyage', *Philological Quarterly*, 44, 1965, 185–94. Notes the similarity between Houyhnhnmland

society and the Spartan institutions described in Plutarch's *Life of Lycurgus*.

6.542 **Jeffares**, A. N., ed., *Swift: Modern Judgements*, 1968. Includes J. W. Johnson 'Swift's historical outlook', and I. Ehrenpreis, 'Swift on liberty' – the latter providing a succinct account of his political theory.

6.543 **Lock**, F. P., *Swift's Tory Politics*, 1983. Thorough exposition of his ideas in their appropriate intellectual context. 'By temperament and conviction he was conservative and authoritarian; an accident of history made him a patron and champion of liberty.'

6.544 —— *The Politics of Gulliver's Travels*, 1980. Comprehensive account of his political ideas and their intellectual context.

6.545 **McDowell**, R. B., 'Swift as a political thinker', in R. McHugh and P. Edwards, ed., *Jonathan Swift, 1667–1967, A Dublin Tercentenary Tribute*, Dublin, 1967, 176–86. Accessible introduction to his major political concerns, which stresses the theological and Irish 'dimensions of his thought'.

6.546 **McMinn**, J., 'A weary patriot: Swift and the formation of an Anglo-Irish identity', *Eighteenth-Century Ireland*, 2, 1987, 103–13. His pamphlets on constitutional and other issues are said to express a 'transitional national sense from English to Irish citizenship'.

6.547 **Mezciems**, J., 'The unity of Swift's "voyage to Laputa": structure and meaning in utopian fiction', *Modern Language Review*, 72, 1977, 1–21. Subtle reading, charting the influence of Plato and More on Swift.

6.548 **Reichert**, J. F., 'Plato, Swift, and the Houyhnhnms', *Philological Quarterly*, 47, 1968, 179–92. On what he found sympathetic in Plato's politics – the sense of corruption of contemporary society, the insistence on ethics as the basis of politics, the admiration for the Spartan way of life, and the aristocratic and authoritarian bias.

6.549 **Rodino**, R. H. and **Read**, H. J., ed., *Reading Swift: Papers for the Second Münster Symposium on Jonathan Swift*, Munchen, 1993. Includes J. Black, 'Swift and foreign policy revisited', W. Zack, 'Jonathan Swift and colonialism' and H.-Z. Müllenbrock, 'Swift as a political essayist'.

6.550 **Rogers**, P., 'Swift and Bolingbroke on

faction', *J. Brit. Sts.*, 9, 1970, 71–101. On the Augustan obsession with political discord.

6.551 **Rosenheim**, E. W., 'Swift and the martyred monarch', *Philological Quarterly*, 54, 1975, 178–94. Excellent account of his political views as revealed in a sermon he delivered, 30th January, 1726.

6.552 **Speck**, W., 'The *Examiner* examined: Swift's Tory pamphleteering', in C. J. Rawson, ed., *Focus: Swift*, 1971, 138–54. On his political writing during the crisis years 1710–14.

6.553 **Vickers**, B., ed., *The World of Jonathan Swift*, 1968. Includes P. Rogers, 'Swift and the idea of authority', W. A. Speck, 'From principles to practice: Swift and party politics', and B. Vickers, 'The satiric structure of *Gulliver's Travels* and More's *Utopia*'.

Wollstonecraft

6.554 **Barker-Benfield**, G. J., 'Mary Wollstonecraft: eighteenth-century commonwealthwoman', *J. Hist. Ideas*, 50, 1989, 95–115. Demonstrates how her critique of the political system, in particular her response to Burke, drew upon this earlier tradition of thought.

6.555 **Ferguson** M. and **Todd**, J., *Mary Wollstonecraft*, Boston, Mass., 1984. Useful introduction to her life and work.

6.556 **Gatens**, M., 'Rousseau and Wollstonecraft: nature vs reason', *Aust. J. Phil.*, supp. 64, 1986, 1–15. Examines their conceptions of nature and culture, reason and passion, and the relationship between politics and morality.

6.557 —— ' "The oppressed state of my sex": Wollstonecraft on reason, feeling and equality', in M. L. Shanley and C. Pateman, ed., *Feminist Interpretations and Political Theory*, 1991, 112–28. Careful analysis of her account of the private and public spheres, arguing that the questions she leaves unanswered constitute the most important legacy of her work.

6.558 **George**, M., *One Woman's 'Situation': A Study of Mary Wollstonecraft*, Urbana, Ill., 1970. Interesting biography, suggesting that she failed, in her life and ideas, to transcend a 'middle-class female "situation" '.

6.559 **Grimshaw**, J., 'Mary Wollstonecraft and

the tensions in feminist philosophy', *Rad. Phil.*, 52, 1989, 11–17.

6.560 **Guralnick**, E. S., 'Radical politics in Mary Wollstonecraft's *A Vindication of the Rights of Woman*', *Sts. Burke & Time*, 18, 1977, 155–66. Argues that she drew upon the condition of women to advocate a wider programme of radical reform.

6.561 **Hughes**, P., 'Mary Wollstonecraft: stoic liberal-democrat', *Can. J. Pol. & Soc. Theory*, 1, 1977, 59–74. Presents her as a flawed radical because of her failure to tackle the inequalities of private property.

6.562 **Janes**, R. M., 'Mary, Mary, quite contrary, or Mary Astell and Mary Wollstonecraft compared', in R. C. Rosbottom, ed., *Studies in Eighteenth-Century Culture*, Madison, Wis., 1976, 121–39. Argues that the language of natural rights provides Wollstonecraft 'with something Astell did not want – an argument for change not only in women, but also in the world'.

6.563 —— 'On the reception of Mary Wollstonecraft's *A Vindication of the Rights of Woman*', *J. Hist. Ideas*, 39, 1978, 293–302. Suggests that initial scholarly evaluation of the work was favourable and focused primarily on her ideas on education.

6.564 **Kelly**, G., 'Expressive style and "the female mind": Mary Wollstonecraft's *Vindication of the Rights of Woman*', *Sts. Voltaire*, 193, 1980, 1942–49. Examines her *Vindications* in the light of eighteenth-century social politics.

6.565 —— *Revolutionary Feminism: The Mind and Career of Mary Wollstonecraft*, 1992. A vigorously modern reading of Mary Wollstonecraft's 'mind' and career in relation to the cultural revolution that founded the modern state in late eighteenth-century Britain, connecting her work to more recent feminist concerns with subjectivity, ideology and culture. A stark counterpiece to interpretations of her as a bourgeois feminist.

6.566 **Korsmeyer**, C. W., 'Reason and morals in the early feminist movement: Mary Wollstonecraft', *Phil. Forum*, 5, 1973–74, 97–111.

6.567 **Larson**, E., 'Mary Wollstonecraft and women's rights', *Free Inquiry*, 12, 1992, 45–8.

6.568 **Myers**, M., 'Politics from the outside: Mary Wollstonecraft's first *Vindication*', in

R. C. Rosbottom, ed., *Studies in Eighteenth-Century Culture*, 6, Madison, Wis., 1977, 113–32. On her *Vindication of the Rights of Men* and its vehement attack on Burke.

6.569 —— 'Reform or ruin: "a revolution in female manners" ', *Studies in Eighteenth-Century Culture*, 11, 1982, 199–216. Examines the work of Wollstonecraft and Hannah More on female reform and the transformation of social mores. Contends that Wollstonecraft's radical feminism was less successful in triggering reform than More's 'evangelical femininity'.

6.570 **Poovey**, M., *The Proper Lady and the Woman Writer: Ideology as Style in the Works of Mary Wollstonecraft, Mary Shelley, and Jane Austen*, 1984. Includes an interesting chapter on Wollstonecraft's ideas on gender, set in the context of the sexism of contemporary advocates of the 'rights of man', and an assessment of her appropriation of romantic ideals and sentiments.

6.571 **Ravetz**, A., 'The trivialisation of Mary Wollstonecraft: a personal and professional career re-vindicated', *Wom. Sts. Int. For.*, 6, 1983, 491–9. A re-evaluation of her life and work.

6.572 **Rosalind**, S., 'From liberal to radical: the work and life of Mary Wollstonecraft', *Atlantis*, 17, 1991, 36–51. Traces her intellectual development from *Thoughts on the Education of Daughters* to *A Vindication of the Rights of Woman* in the light of her role in promoting women's education.

6.573 **Sepiro**, V., *A Vindication of Political Virtue: The Political Theory of Mary Wollstonecraft*, Chiacago, Ill., 1992. Examines her work in relation to the idea of masculinity, characterised by the concepts of rationality, independence and strength, arguing that she saw these as something to which women should aspire.

6.574 —— 'Feminist studies and the discipline: a study of Mary Wollstonecraft', *University of Michigan Papers in Women's Studies*, 1, 1974, 178–200. Places her firmly in her intellectual and political context, concluding that *A Vindication of the Rights of Woman* is a clear expression of late eighteenth-century radicalism and utilitarianism.

6.575 **Stuart**, C. L., 'Mary Wollstonecraft's *A Vindication of the Rights of Men*: a rhetorical assessment', *Western Journal of Speech Communication*, 42, 1978, 83–92.

6.576 **Theriot**, N. M., 'Mary Wollstonecraft and Margaret Fuller: a theoretical comparison', *International Journal of Women's Studies*, 2, 1979, 560–74. Comparison of Wollstonecraft's *A Vindication of the Rights of Woman* and Fuller's *Woman in the Nineteenth Century*.

6.577 **Todd**, J., *Mary Wollstonecraft: An Annotated Bibliography*, 1976.

6.578 —— 'Reason and sensibility in Mary Wollstonecraft's the wrongs of woman', *Frontiers*, 5, 1980, 17–20. Argues that the apparent contradiction between *A Vindication of the Rights of Woman* and *Maria* is unfounded because she allots a central position to reason in both.

6.579 **Vlasopolos**, A., 'Mary Wollstonecraft's mask of reason in *A Vindication of the Rights of Woman*', *Dalhousie Review*, 60, 1980, 462–71.

6.580 **Wardle**, R., *Mary Wollstonecraft: A Critical Biography*, Lincoln, Mich., 1966.

Other thinkers

6.581 **Aers**, D., 'Coleridge and the egg that Burke laid: ideological collusion and opposition in the 1790s', *Literature and History*, 9, 1983, 152–63. On why Coleridge believed that Burke and Paine were not ideologically apart on some issues, and what it meant for romantics such as Coleridge to be 'converted' to Burkean conservatism.

6.582 **Allen**, R. J., 'William Oldisworth: "the author of the Examiner" ', *Philological Quarterly*, 26, 1947, 159–80. On a Tory propagandist during the crisis years of 1710–14.

6.583 **Berman**, D., 'The Jacobitism of Berkeley's *Passive Obedience*', *J. Hist. Ideas*, 47, 1986, 310–19. Unconvincing attempt to demonstrate that he was a Jacobite during the political crisis of 1710–14.

6.584 **Bernstein**, J. A., 'Adam Ferguson and the idea of progress', *Sts. Burke & Time*, 19, 1978, 99–118. Examines the central question in Ferguson's thought of the relation between the imperfection of humanity and divine goodness.

6.585 —— 'Shaftesbury's optimism and eighteenth-century social thought', in A. C. Kors and P. J. Korshin, ed., *Anticipations of the Enlightenment in*

England, France, and Germany,
Philadelphia, Penn., 1987, 86–101.
Focuses in part on his response to Locke's
political theory.

6.586 **Boulton**, J. T., 'James Mackintosh:
"Vindiciae Gallicae" ', *Renaissance and
Modern Studies*, 21, 1977, 106–18.
Thorough study of his rebuttal of Burke's
Reflections.

6.587 **Bowles**, P., 'John Millar, the four-stages
and women's position in society', *Hist. Pol.
Econ.*, 16, 1984, 619–38. Examines his use
of the 'four-stages' theory in his analysis of
the social advancement of women.

6.588 —— 'John Millar, the legislator and the
mode of subsistence', *Hist. Euro. Ideas*, 7,
1986, 237–51. Considers the limits and
potential of legislative action in the light of
his 'four-stages' theory of social
development.

6.589 **Browning**, R., 'Samuel Squire:
pamphleteering churchman', *Eighteenth-
Cent. Life*, 5, 1978, 12–20. Among Squire's
publications defending the Whig order was
*Enquiry into the Foundations of the English
Constitution* (1753).

6.590 **Burns**, J. H., 'Bolingbroke and the
concept of constitutional government',
Pol. Sts., 10, 1962, 264–76.

6.591 **Burrows**, B. M., 'Whig versus Tory – a
genuine difference?', *Pol. Theory*, 4, 1976,
455–70. On Shaftesbury's political
thought, comparing it with that of
Bolingbroke, and arguing that,
notwithstanding party labels, their
doctrines were essentially similar.

6.592 **Canovan**, M., 'Paternalistic liberalism:
Joseph Priestley on rank and inequality',
Enlightenment and Dissent, 2, 1983, 23–37.

6.593 —— 'The un-Benthamite utilitarianism of
Joseph Priestley', *J. Hist. Ideas*, 45, 1984,
435–50. Rejection of the claim that he was a
pseudo-Benthamite.

6.594 **Chard**, L. F., *Dissenting Republican:
Wordsworth's Early Life and Thought in their
Political Context*, The Hague, 1972.
Contains a chapter on the political theory
he developed in response to the French
Revolution, tracing its roots to the English
'commonwealth' tradition as well as
French Enlightenment thinking.

6.595 **Christian**, W., 'James Mackintosh, Burke,
and the case of reform', *Eighteenth-Cent.
Sts.*, 7, 1973–74, 193–206. Argues that
Mackintosh was never as radical as his
Vindiciae Gallicae may suggest, and that

his apparent shift to a conservative position
had more to do with his earlier principles
than the influence of Burke.

6.596 **Conroy**, G. P., 'George Berkeley and the
Jacobite heresy: some comments on Irish
Augustian politics', *Albion*, 3, 1971,
82–91.

6.597 **Crimmins**, J., ' "The study of true
politics": John Brown on manners and
liberty', *Sts. Voltaire*, 241, 1986, 65–86.
Scrutinises his ideas on civic virtue and
public welfare, and reveals the influence of
Montesquieu and Machiavelli.

6.598 **Dybikowski**, J., 'David Williams and the
eighteenth-century distinction between
civil and political liberty', *Enlightenment
and Dissent*, 3, 1984, 15–35.

6.599 **Elliot**, M., *Wolfe Tone. Prophet of British
Independence*, 1989. The best biography of
Tone so far, which, while primarily a
narrative history, helps to set the radical
liberal ideas of the United Irishmen in their
historical and intellectual context,
debunking contemporary nationalist
myths about him.

6.600 **Erskine-Hill**, H., 'Alexander Pope: the
political poet in his time', *Eighteenth-Cent.
Sts.*, 15, 1981–82, 123–48. Interesting not
only on Pope's political views but on the
Toryism of the period generally.

6.601 **Garrett**, C., 'Joseph Priestley, the
millenium, and the French Revolution',
J. Hist. Ideas, 34, 1972, 51–66. Examines
the connections between his political and
religious thought, revealing the link
between the French Revolution – a symbol
of the fall of the papacy and the European
monarchies – and the ushering in of
popular government founded on principles
of rational Christianity.

6.602 **Gassman**, B., 'Alexander Pope as utopian:
Arcadia to apocalypse', *Sts. Voltaire*, 191,
1980, 672–78. Interesting analysis of
Pope's *Pastorals, Messiah, Windsor Forest,
Essay on Man* and *The Dunciad*, intended to
reveal the utopian vision in his writings.

6.603 **Geoghegan**, V., 'A Jacobite history: the
Abbey MacGeoghegan's *History of
Ireland*', *Eighteenth-Century Ireland*, 6,
1991, 37–56. Reconstructs the political
theory underpinning a text that was co-
opted by Irish nationalism.

6.604 **Haakonssen**, K., 'Science of a legislator in
James Mackintosh's moral philosophy',
Hist. Pol. Thought, 5, 1984, 245–81. Sharp
discussion of his political ideas, claiming

that he was less consistent than his mentor, Dugald Stewart.

6.605 **Hampsher-Monk**, I., 'John Thelwall and the eighteenth-century radical response to political economy', *Hist. J.*, 34, 1991, 1–20. On the radical uses he made of the doctrine of natural rights.

6.606 **Hart**, J., *Viscount Bolingbroke: Tory Humanist*, 1965. Interprets his views as a repudiation of Machiavelli's immoral political thought.

6.607 **Horne**, T. A., 'Moral and economic improvement: Francis Hutcheson on property', *Hist. Pol. Thought*, 7, 1986, 115–30. Demonstrates how he used natural law theory to charge the propertied classes to seek the common good, and in doing so to create a more 'polite' Scotland.

6.608 —— 'Politics in a corrupt society: Williamson Arnall's defense of Robert Walpole', *J. Hist. Ideas*, 41, 1980, 601–14. On the political ideas of a propagandist for the court Whigs.

6.609 **Kelly**, P., 'William Molyneux and the spirit of liberty in eighteenth-century Ireland', *Eighteenth-Century Ireland*, 3, 1988, 133–48. Excellent discussion of the reception of his *The Case of Ireland* (1698), which used Lockean arguments on behalf of an independent Irish parliament, in the later decades of the century.

6.610 **Kettler**, D., 'History and theory in Ferguson's essay on the history of civil society: a reconsideration', *Pol. Theory*, 5, 1977, 437–60. On the role of politics in dealing with the defects of commercial society.

6.611 —— 'The political vision of Adam Ferguson', *Sts. Burke & Time*, 9, 1967, 773–8. Suggests that his thought is difficult to classify because it contained both radical and conservative elements.

6.612 —— *The Social and Political Thought of Adam Ferguson*, Columbus, Ohio, 1965.

6.613 **Klein**, L. E., 'Liberty, manners, and politeness in early eighteenth-century England', *Hist. J.*, 32, 1989, 583–605. On how Shaftesbury and others assimilated 'politeness' into Whig political discourse in order to refine the civic humanist meaning of liberty.

6.614 —— 'The third earl of Shaftesbury and the progress of politeness', *Eighteenth-Cent. Sts.*, 18, 1984–85, 185–214. On how the concept of politeness in Whig discourse came to signify virtue in a commercial society.

6.615 **Knox**, T. R., 'Thomas Spence. The trumpet of jubilee', *Past & Pres.*, 76, 1977, 75–98. On Jacobinism in the 1790s.

6.616 **Kramnick**, I., 'An Augustan reply to Locke: Bolingbroke on natural law and the origin of government', *Pol. Sc. Q.*, 82, 1967, 571–94.

6.617 **Leary**, D. E., 'Berkeley's social theory: context and development', *J. Hist. Ideas*, 38, 1977, 635–49. On his *The Bond of Society* (1713) which used Newtonian principles to analyse society.

6.618 **McDowell**, G. L., 'Commerce, virtue and politics: Adam Ferguson's constitutionalism', *Rev. Pol.*, 45, 1983, 536–52. Suggests that Ferguson's theory of politics was the precursor of Tocqueville's *Democracy in America*, in particular through his critique of commercialism for which he advocated a properly constituted polity as the remedy.

6.619 **McKenzie**, L. A., 'The French Revolution and English parliamentary reform: James Mackintosh and the *Vindiciae Gallicae*', *Eighteenth-Cent. Sts.*, 14, 1981, 264–82. Contends that his political principles, derived from the commonwealth tradition, prompted him, in response to the French Revolution, to embrace some of Burke's views.

6.620 **Parssinen**, T. M., 'Thomas Spence and the origins of English land nationalization', *J. Hist. Ideas*, 34, 1973, 135–41. A short, but thorough, examination of his revolutionary ideas on land reform.

6.621 **Rudé**, G., 'John Wilkes and the re-birth of British radicalism', *Pol. Sc.*, 14, 1962, 11–29.

6.622 **Schonhorn**, M., *Defoe's Politics: Parliament, Power, Kingship and Robinson Crusoe*, 1991. Careful exposition of his political ideas, which is also illuminating on the ideas of the period generally.

6.623 **Shelton**, G., *Dean Tucker: Eighteenth-Century Economic and Political Thought*, 1981. On the author of a *Treatise Concerning Civil Government* who repudiated Locke, defended American independence and was an early proponent of a free-market economy.

6.624 **Skinner**, Q., 'The principles and practice of opposition: the case of Bolingbroke versus Walpole', in N. McKendrick, ed., *Historical Perspectives*, 1974, 93–128. Innovative account of the connection between his conduct and political principles.

6.625 **Wells**, D., 'Resurrecting the dismal parson: Malthus, ecology and political thought', *Pol. Sts.*, 30, 1982, 1–15. Argues, against the dismissal of Malthus as a political thinker, for the relevance of his ecological perspective and for a reassessment of his rich and complex thought.

6.626 **Williams**, J., *Wordsworth: Romantic Poetry and Revolutionary Politics*, 1989. Suggests that his republican views of the French Revolutionary period were rooted more in a native discourse of dissidence than in the ideas of continental writers such as Rousseau.

(c) EUROPE

General

6.627 **Abray**, J., 'Feminism in the French Revolution', *Am. Hist. Rev.*, 80, 1975, 43–62. On Condorcet and others who advocated women's rights.

6.628 **Acomb**, F. D., *Anglophobia in France, 1763–1789: An Essay in the History of Constitutionalism and Nationalism*, Durham, N.C., 1950. Analyses the decline of the ideas of Anglophile liberalism in French political discourse.

6.629 **Adams**, H. P., 'Political and historical thought in the French Revolution', *University of Birmingham Historical Review*, 1, 1948, 288–322.

6.630 **Appleby**, J., 'America as a model for the radical French reformers of 1789', *Wm. & Mary Q.*, 28, 1971, 267–86. On how some French reformers cited the American experience and pamphleteers such as John Stevens in favour of a unicameral legislature, whereas others used the English model to argue for a bicameral legislature.

6.631 **Artz**, F. B., *The Enlightenment in France*, Kent, Ohio, 1968. Brief introduction to the principal thinkers of the French Enlightenment, including Montesquieu, Voltaire, Diderot, the Physiocrats, L'Abbé de Saint Pierre, Holbach, Helvetius, La Mettrie, L'Abbé Mably, and Rousseau.

6.632 **Baker**, K. M., 'French political thought at the accession of Louis XVI', *J. Mod. Hist.*, 50, 1978, 279–303. Examines the formation of French Revolutionary thought.

6.633 —— 'On the problem of the ideological origins of the French Revolution', in D. La Capra and S. L. Kaplan, ed., *Modern European Intellectual History: Reappraisals and New Perspectives*, Ithaca, N.Y., 1982, 197–219. Argues that the political discourse of the Revolution emerged from a blend of three modes of political argument based on reason, justice and will.

6.634 **Barnard**, F. M., 'Self-direction: Thomasius, Kant, and Herder', *Pol. Theory*, 11, 1983, 343–68. A thorough analysis of the notion of 'Mündigkeit' ('coming of age') in their thought.

6.635 **Beik**, P. H., 'The French Revolution seen from the right: social theories in motion, 1789–99', *Trans. Am. Phil. Soc.*, 46, 1–122, 1956. Comprehensive account of the ideas of de Maistre, Bonald, Chateaubriand and other counter-revolutionaries.

6.636 **Berdahl**, R. M., 'The Stände and the origins of conservatism in Prussia', *Eighteenth-Cent. Sts.*, 6, 1973, 298–321. Examines the influence of the aristocratic resurgence on the development of German conservatism.

6.637 **Church**, W. F., 'The decline of the French jurists as political theorists, 1660–1789', *French Historical Studies*, 5, 1967, 1–40. Examines the transition from divine right theory to natural rights discourse, focusing on the ideas of jurists such as Fleury and Domat.

6.638 **Epstein**, A., *Genesis of German Conservatism*, Princeton, N.J., 1966. A social and political history of German conservatism from about 1770 to the fall of the Holy Roman Empire, with insights into the thought of Möser, J. A. Stark, L. A. Hoffmannan, and August Rehberg.

6.639 **Furet**, F., and **Ozouf**, M., ed., *A Critical Dictionary of the French Revolution*, 1989. Includes a section on the different concepts which emerged within the revolutionary period as well as a selection of historical responses to and interpretations of the Revolution.

6.640 **Gay**, P., *The Party of Humanity: Studies in*

the *French Enlightenment*, 1964. Essays dealing with the work of Voltaire and Rousseau, the relation between rhetoric and politics during the French Revolution, and the ideas of the *philosophes*.

6.641 **Goldstein**, M. A., *The People in French Counter-Revolutionary Thought*, N.Y., 1988. Discussion of, among others, Mallet du Pan, Rivarol, de Maistre, de Bonald, the Abbés Maury and Barruel.

6.642 **Greenleaf**, W. H. 'Hume, Burke and the general will', *Pol. Sts.*, 20, 1972, 131–40. Argues that Rousseau, along with Burke and Hume, saw laws being sustained by social practices and customs, and that the general will – the basis of these laws – is tied to a standard of conduct 'that is more than merely personal and yet not merely suprahuman'.

6.643 **Hampson**, N., *Will and Circumstance: Montesquieu, Rousseau and the French Revolution*, 1983. Examines the influence of Rousseau and Montesquieu on the ideas of Brissot, Marat, Mercier, Robespierre and Saint-Just.

6.644 **Head**, B. W., 'The idéologues revisited: ideology, science and perfectibility', *Can. J. Pol. & Soc. Theory*, 8, 1984, 163–78. On the original uses of the concept of ideology, particularly by Destutt de Tracy.

6.645 **Herr**, R., and **Parker**, H. T., ed., *Ideas in History: Essays Presented to Louis Gottschalk by his Former Students*, Durham, N.C., 1965. Includes K. J. Weintraub, 'Towards the history of the common man: Voltaire and Condorcet', R. O. Rockwood, 'The legend of Voltaire and the cult of revolution, 1791', and G. H. McNeil, 'Robespierre, Rousseau, and representation'.

6.646 **Hoffmeister**, G., *The French Revolution and the Age of Goethe*, Hildesheim, 1989. Includes A. A. Kuzniar, 'Kant and Herder on the French Revolution', D. Pugh, 'Schiller and revolution', H. Reiss, 'The French Revolution and the "Aufklärung". Two perspectives: Kant and Goethe', K. Mueller-Vollmer, 'The abstractness of reason and real life of individuals and institutions: Humboldt's educational politics and the French Revolution'.

6.647 **Jacob**, M. C., *The Radical Enlightenment: Pantheists, Freemasons and Republicans*, 1981. Fascinating study of eighteenth-century republicans, many of whom were radical Whig emigrants who left England for the Netherlands and other continental countries, who formed an international social network espousing heretical political and scientific ideas.

6.648 **Jacobs**, E., **Barber**, W. H., **Bloch**, J. H., **Leakey**, F. W. and **Le Breton**, E., *Women and Society in Eighteenth-Century France: Essays in Honour of John Stephenson Spink*, 1979. Includes P. D. Jimack, 'The paradox of Sophie and Julie: contemporary response to Rousseau's ideal wife and ideal mother', E. J. Gardner, 'The *philosophes* and women: sensationalism and sentiment', and R. Niklaus, 'Diderot and women'.

6.649 **Kelly**, G. A., 'From Lèse-Majesty to Lèse-Nation: treason in eighteenth-century France', *J. Hist. Ideas*, 4, 1981, 269–86. Argues that the Enlightenment critique of monarchy, the development of a conception of fraternal and patriotic unity within the wider idea of nation, and the 'evolution of a *representative* rather than omnipotent notion of kingship' explain the rise of the idea of *Lèse-Nation*.

6.650 —— *Idealism, Politics and History: Sources of Hegelian Thought*, 1969. Focuses upon four thinkers: Rousseau, Kant, Fichte, and Hegel.

6.651 **Kramer**, L. S. and **Ramsey**, M., 'Liberal theory and the critique of Bonapartism: Lafayette, Destutt de Tracy, and Benjamin Constant', *Consortium on Revolutionary Europe, 1750–1850: Proceedings*, 19, 1989, 495–508.

6.652 **Leeb**, I. L., *The Ideological Origins of the Batavian Revolution: History and Politics in the Dutch Republic, 1747–1800*, 1973. Detailed and careful account of the political thought of the period, tracing the shift from a historical discourse to one of natural rights, and suggesting that the ideological differences between Patriots and Orangists were not as great as is usually suggested.

6.653 **Loubère**, L. A., 'The intellectual origins of French Jacobin socialism', *Int. Rev. Soc. Hist.*, 4, 1959, 415–39.

6.654 **Lough**, J., *The Philosophes and Post-Revolutionary France*, 1982. Examines the ideas of the *philosophes* and their influence on French social and political thought until 1879.

6.655 **Margerison**, K. and **Roederer**, P. L., *Political Thought and Practice during the French Revolution*, Philadelphia, Penn.,

1983.

6.656 **Martin**, K., *French Liberal Thought in the Eighteenth Century*, 1962. A longstanding textbook on this subject, tracing the intellectual influences and political context of a number of French theorists, highlighting the purchase of the key concepts of the French Revolution. Lucid and elegant in style, the book's interpretations have been supplanted by work on these various thinkers.

6.657 **Moore**, J. M., *The Roots of French Republicanism: The Evolution of the Republican Ideal in French Revolutionary France and its Culmination in the Constitution of 1793*, New York, 1973.

6.658 **Osen**, J. L., 'French absolutist political thought, 1789–1791', *Consortium on Revolutionary Europe, 1750–1850: Proceedings*, 16, 1986, 21–34. Discusses Baptiste du Voisin, de Barruel and Royou.

6.659 **Pappas**, J. N., 'Individual rights and general welfare in eighteenth-century French thought', *Romanic Review*, 60, 1969, 5–22. Examines conceptions of human nature in the thought of Rousseau, Voltaire and Diderot, stressing the anti-libertarian conclusions implied by their theories of individual rights.

6.660 **Peyre**, H., 'The influence of eighteenth-century ideas on the French Revolution', *J. Hist. Ideas*, 10, 1949, 63–87. Examines the influence of Rousseau and other thinkers on the Revolution.

6.661 **Popkin**, J. D., 'The newspaper press in French political thought, 1789–99', *Studies in Eighteenth-Century Culture*, 10, 1981, 113–33.

6.662 **Roberts**, J. M., 'The French origins of the "right" ', *Trans. Royal Hist. Soc.*, 5th series, 23, 1973, 27–53. Careful analysis of the emergence of a conservative discourse before and during the Revolution.

6.663 **Rolland**, R., **Maurois**, A., and **Herriot**, E., *French Thought in the Eighteenth Century: Rousseau, Voltaire, Diderot*, 1953.

6.664 **Rose**, R. B., 'Socialism and the French Revolution: the Cercle social and the Enragés', *Bulletin of the John Rylands Library*, 41, 1958, 39–66.

6.665 —— *The Enragés: Socialists of the French Revolution?*, 1965. Surveys the life and work of the principal figures in this group: Jean-François Varlet, Jacques Roux, Théophile Leclerc, Pauline Léon and Claire Lacambe.

6.666 **Sa'adah**, A., *The Shaping of Liberal Politics in Revolutionary France*, Princeton, N.J., 1990.

6.667 **Seidler**, G. L., 'The concept of "reason of state" and the Polish Enlightenment', *Sts. Voltaire*, 155, 1976, 2015–32. Survey of the development of this idea from Machiavelli to the works of Hugo Kottataj and Stanislaw Staszic.

6.668 **Souleyman**, E. V., *The Vision of World Peace in Seventeenth- and Eighteenth-Century France*, Kennikat, Mass., 1971.

6.669 **Stricklen**, C. G., 'The *philosophes*' political mission: the creation of an idea, 1750–1789', *Sts. Voltaire*, 86, 1971, 137–228. Argues that whilst the initial work of the *philosophes* was not expressly pre-occupied with issues of political theory, in the 1770s and 1780s these questions became crucial.

6.670 **Suckling**, N., 'The unfulfilled Renaissance: an essay on the fortunes of enlightened humanism in the eighteenth century', *Sts. Voltaire*, 89, 1971, 25–136. Focuses upon the political, moral and religious dimensions of Enlightenment thought, particularly in the works of Diderot.

6.671 **Tenenbaum**, S., 'The Coppet circle: literary criticism as political discourse', *Hist. Pol. Thought*, 1, 1980, 753–73. Examines this group's contribution to the development of French liberalism, focusing upon the relationship between aesthetics and politics in their thought.

6.672 **Vartanian**, A., 'Necessity or freedom? The politics of an eighteenth-century meta-physical debate', *Studies in Eighteenth-Century Culture*, 7, 1978, 153–74. Explores the paradox that some thinkers of the French Enlightenment who advocated freedom as a political goal – La Meltrie, Diderot, D'Holbach – spurned it as a metaphysical and moral concept.

6.673 **Wasberg**, G. C., 'The influence of the "enlightened" philosophy of history on Scandinavian political thought', *Sts. Voltaire*, 27, 1963, 1775–85. Contends that for Sweden and Denmark it is difficult to establish any direct influence, whilst in the case of Norway, French Enlightenment thought had a significant influence.

6.674 **Welch**, C. B., *The French Idéologues and the Transformation of Liberalism*, New York, 1984.

6.675 **Williams**, D., 'The politics of feminism in

the French Enlightenment', in P. Hughes and D. Williams, ed., *The Varied Pattern: Studies in the Eighteenth Century*, Toronto, 1971, 333–51. Discusses the idea of sexual equality in the writings of Diderot, Condorcet and others.

6.676 **Wilson**, I. M., 'The influence of Hobbes and Locke in the shaping of the concept of sovereignty in eighteenth-century France', *Sts. Voltaire*, 101, 1973, 1–290. Thorough and perceptive survey including discussions of Montesquieu, the *Encyclopédie*, Réal de Curban and Rousseau.

6.677 **Wokler**, R., '*La Querelle des Bouffons* and the Italian liberation of France: a study in revolutionary foreplay', *Studies in the Eighteenth Century*, 6, 1987, 95–116. Interesting analysis of the musical and literary controversy that was the *Querelle des Bouffons*, seeking to reveal links between music and politics and how both influenced the French Revolution.

Condorcet

6.678 **Aldridge**, A. O., 'Condorcet, Paine, and historical method', *Condorcet Studies*, 1, 1984, 49–60. Comparison of Paine's *Rights of Man* and Condorcet's *Réflections sur la révolution de 1688, et sur celle de 10 août, 1792.*

6.679 **Baker**, K. M., *Condorcet: From Natural Philosophy to Social Mathematics*, Chicago, Ill., 1974. Contends that the Enlightenment conception of social science was central to Condorcet's thought and examines in detail how he applied this model to politics.

6.680 ——— 'Scientism, elitism and liberalism: the case of Condorcet', *Sts. Voltaire*, 55, 1967, 129–65. Analyses Condorcet's belief that the physical sciences could positively transform the moral and political sciences.

6.681 **Brookes**, B., 'The feminism of Condorcet and Sophie de Grouchy', *Sts. Voltaire*, 189, 1980, 297–361. Teases out Condorcet's feminist principles from his *Sur l'admission des femmes au droit de eité* to *Fragment sur l'Atlantide* and reveals the influence of Sophie de Grouchy's thought.

6.682 **Lewis**, T. T., 'Condorcet, the heavenly city, and the French Revolution', in *The Consortium on Revolutionary Europe, 1750–1850: Proceedings 1981*, Athens, Ga.,

1981, 160–6.

6.683 **Niklaus**, R., 'Condorcet's feminism: a reappraisal', *Condorcet Studies*, 2, 1987, 119–40.

6.684 **Popkin**, R. H., 'Condorcet, abolitionist', *Condorcet Studies*, 1, 1984, 35–48. Examines in detail Condorcet's *Reflexions on the Enslavement of Blacks* of 1781.

6.685 **Rosenblum**, V. C., 'Condorcet as constitutional draftsman: dimensions of substantive commitment and procedural implementation', *Condorcet Studies*, 1, 1984, 187–205. Examines his constitutional thought, especially in relation to his proposed constitution of 1793, comparing it with the ideas of the framers of the American constitution.

6.686 **Schapiro**, J. S., *Condorcet and the Rise of Liberalism*, New York, 1978. Compact study of his ideas as indicative of the emergence of liberal doctrines, examining, among other themes, his economic liberalism and proto-feminism.

6.687 **Verger**, M. C., 'Condorcet and the inherent contradictions in the American affirmation of natural rights and slave holding', *Sts. Voltaire*, 191, 1980, 768–74. Demonstrates that his understanding of natural rights, universal equality and a universally acceptable code of ethics, was instrumental in his stance against slavery in America as early as 1776.

6.688 **Williams**, D., 'Condorcet, feminism and the egalitarian principle', *Studies in Eighteenth-Century Culture*, 5, 1976, 151–63.

Constant

6.689 **Cappadocia**, E., 'Benjamin Constant and Restoration liberalism', in P. Fritz and D. Williams, ed., *The Triumph of Culture: Eighteenth-Century Perspectives*, Toronto, 1972, 244–59. On the pamphlets he wrote in the latter part of his political career (1814–30) which 'were responses to day-to-day issues and they elaborated his essentially middle-class, Natural Rights liberalism, the credo that feared the despotism of both the absolute monarch and of the masses'.

6.690 **Cruickshank**, J., *Benjamin Constant*, New York, 1974. Brief and lucid presentation of his interconnected ideas and career; a good starting point for the uninitiated.

6.691 **Dodge**, G. H., *Benjamin Constant's Philosophy of Liberalism*, Chapel Hill, N.C., 1980. Rescues Constant from his critics, sympathetically presenting his concepts of liberty, popular sovereignty and political economy and comparing his ideas with other nineteenth-century liberals. Clear discussion which overestimates his coherence and underplays internal tensions within his thought.

6.692 **Fink**, B. C., 'Benjamin Constant and the Enlightenment', in H. E. Pagliaro, ed., *Studies in Eighteenth-Century Culture: Racism in the Eighteenth Century*, Cleveland, Ohio, 1973, 67–81. Examines the influence of Montesquieu, Herder, Rousseau, Condorcet, and Godwin on Constant's social and political thought.

6.693 —— 'Benjamin Constant on equality', *J. Hist. Ideas*, 33, 1972, 307–14. Exposes the tension between his utilitarianism and teleological conception of human history based on the idea of perfectibility.

6.694 **Fontana**, B., *Benjamin Constant and the Post-Revolutionary Mind*, New Haven, Conn., 1991. Places Constant's political thought within its historical context, and examines its relation to his ideas on morality, religion and aesthetics.

6.695 —— 'The shaping of modern liberty: commerce and civilization in the writings of Benjamin Constant', *Annales Benjamin Constant*, 5, 1985, 3–15.

6.696 **Holdheim**, W. W., *Benjamin Constant*, 1961. Brief, introductory survey of his thought, including a truncated discussion of his liberalism and political career.

6.697 **Holmes**, S., *Benjamin Constant and the Making of Modern Liberalism*, New Haven, Conn., 1984. Constant's thought is said to focus on the problem that private rights and individual independence cannot be assured without some form of active citizen political participation.

6.698 —— 'Liberal users of Bourbon legitimism', *J. Hist. Ideas*, 43, 1982, 229–48. On Constant's use of Bourbon legitimism.

6.699 **Lowe**, D. K., *Benjamin Constant, an Annotated Bibliography of Critical Editions and Studies, 1946–1978*, 1979.

6.700 **Nicolson**, H., *Benjamin Constant*, 1949.

De Staël

6.701 **Golin**, S., 'Madame de Staël: culture as social control', *Rev. Pol.*, 33, 1971, 342–59.

6.702 **Hamilton**, J. F., 'Mme de Staël, partisan of Rousseau or Voltaire?', *Sts. Voltaire*, 106, 1973, 253–65. Contrasts her ideas on art, literature and politics with those of Rousseau and Voltaire.

6.703 **Hartman**, E., 'Mme de Staël, the continuing quarrel of the ancients and the moderns, and the idea of progress', *Research Studies*, 5, 1982, 33–45.

6.704 **Herold**, C. J., *Mistress to an Age: A Life of Madame de Staël*, Indianapolis, Ind., 1958. A lengthy biography, examining her influence on Constant and vice versa.

6.705 **Sydenham**, M. J. and **Montgomery**, F. S., 'Madame de Staël and the French Revolution', *Hist. Today*, 21, 1971, 89–98. Exposes the republican and liberal basis of her thought.

6.706 **Tenenbaum**, S., 'Montesquieu and Mme de Staël: the woman as a factor in political analysis', *Pol. Theory*, 1, 1973, 92–103. Contends that her perception of the role of women in socio-political arrangements was strongly influenced by Montesquieu.

6.707 **Weightman**, J., 'Madam de Staël', *Encounter*, 5, 1973, 45–62. Examines de Staël's *Dix années d'exil* and *Considérations sur la Révolution Française* as expressions of an Enlightenment political perspective.

6.708 **Winegarten**, R., *Madame de Staël*, 1985. A thorough and succinct introduction to her ideas.

Diderot

6.709 **Bremner**, G., *Order and Chance: The Pattern of Diderot's Thought*, 1983. Extensive survey of his ideas, stressing the centrality of the concept of order, which elucidates his conception of society, state and the body politic.

6.710 **Crocker**, L. G., 'Diderot as political philosopher', *Revue Internationale de Philosophie*, 38, 1984, 120–39.

6.711 —— *Diderot's Chaotic Order: Approach to Synthesis*, Princeton, N.J., 1974. Includes a section on his analysis of the problem of political order and disorder.

6.712 **France**, P., *Diderot*, 1983. Brief introduction to his ideas, including a chapter ('The free thinker') on his understanding of social and political order.

6.713 **Goodman**, D., 'The structure of political argument in Diderot's *Supplément au voyage de Bougainville*', *Diderot Studies*, 21, 1983, 123–37.

6.714 **McDonald**, C. V., 'The utopia of the text: Diderot's "Encyclopédie" ', *The Eighteenth Century: Theory and Interpretation*, 21, 1980, 128–44.

6.715 **Mason**, J. H., *The Irresistible Diderot*, 1982. Examines in detail various aspects of his thought from his contributions to the Encyclopedia to his political writings.

6.716 **Meyer**, P. H., 'Diderot's *Prince*: the "Principes de Politique des Souverains" ', in J. N. Pappas, ed., *Essays on Diderot and the Enlightenment in Honor of Ottis Fellows*, Geneva, 1974, 162–81.

6.717 **Perkins**, M. L., *Diderot and the Time–Space Continuum: His Philosophy, Aesthetics and Politics*, 1982. Argues that his political thought, especially his ideas on the individual, citizenship, and nation, stem from his philosophy of science and aesthetics.

6.718 **Proust**, J., 'Diderot and legal theories of antiquity', in P. Gay, ed., *Eighteenth Century Studies Presented to Arthur M. Wilson*, New York, 1972, 117–30. A systematic account of how ancient thinkers and schools of thought influenced Diderot's thinking on social morality and political philosophy.

6.719 **Strenski**, E. M., 'Diderot, for and against the physiocrats', *Sts. Voltaire*, 57, 1967, 1435–55. Examines the influence that physiocratic writers had on Diderot's theory of property and liberty.

6.720 —— 'The problem of inconsistency, illustrated in Diderot's social and political thought', *Diderot Studies*, 14, 1971, 197–216. Examines his political and social thought in the light of his personal psychology, his literary and narrative technique, and his methodology.

6.721 **Strugnell**, A., 'Diderot on luxury, commerce and the merchant', *Sts. Voltaire*, 217, 1983, 83–93. Argues that Diderot, especially in viewing the Dutch, came to see commerce as undermining political virtue and liberty.

6.722 —— *Diderot's Politics: A Study of the Evolution of Diderot's Political Thought after the Encyclopédie*, The Hague, 1973. Clear and perceptive attempt 'to elucidate the complexity and at times apparent incoherence' of his political thought, claiming that its evolution illustrates that Enlightenment thinkers were not naïve optimists with an unqualified belief in social progress.

6.723 **Suckling**, N., 'Diderot's politics', *Diderot Studies*, 16, 1973, 275–93.

6.724 **Wilson**, A. M., *Diderot: The Testing Years 1713–1759*, New York, 1957.

6.725 —— 'The concept of moeurs in Diderot's social and political thought', in W. H. Barber, et al., ed., *The Age of Enlightenment: Studies Presented to Theodore Besterman*, 1967, 188–99. Teases out the various meanings of this notion, illustrating how it underpinned his conception of law and politics.

6.726 —— 'The development and scope of Diderot's political thought', *Sts. Voltaire*, 27, 1963, 1871–1900. Examines the influence of Locke, Montesquieu and Rousseau on Diderot's political thought.

Kant

6.727 **Anderson-Gold**, S., 'Kant's ethical commonwealth: the highest good as a social goal', *International Philosophical Quarterly*, 26, 1986, 23–32.

6.728 **Ansbro**, J. J., 'Kant's limitations on individual freedom', *New Schol.*, 47, 1973, 88–99. Examines his ideas of liberty, equality and independence, contending that they are not as radical as they first appear.

6.729 **Arendt**, H., *Lectures on Kant's Political Philosophy*, Chicago, Ill., 1982. Brilliant examination of the relationship between the *Critique of Judgement* and his political writings.

6.730 **Axinn**, S., 'Kant, authority, and the French Revolution', *J. Hist. Ideas*, 32, 1971, 423–32. Views Kant's support for the French Revolution in the light of his belief in the possibility of world peace.

6.731 —— 'Kant on authority', *Southern Journal of Philosophy*, 8, 1970, 157–63. Brief examination of his understanding of the relationship between authority, crisis and progress, focusing on his views of the French Revolution and religion.

6.732 **Bahr**, E., 'The pursuit of happiness in the political writings of Lessing and Kant', *Sts. Voltaire*, 151, 1976, 167–84.

6.733 **Baynes**, K., 'Kant on property and the social contract', *Monist*, 72, 1989, 433–53. Argues that he developed a theory of property rights based upon agreement between free and equal individuals.

6.734 **Beck**, L. W., 'Kant and the right of revolution', *J. Hist. Ideas*, 32, 1971, 411–22. His views on revolution are said to be contradictory, for though he was an enthusiastic supporter of the French and American Revolutions, his ethical and political ideas deny the right to revolt.

6.735 —— 'Kant's two conceptions of the will in their political context', in L. W. Beck, *Studies in the Philosophy of Kant*, Indianapolis, Ind., 1965, 215–9. Subtle argument that the apparent contradictions between his moral philosophy and political philosophy are based upon a false dichotomy between two concepts of will.

6.736 **Becker**, D., 'Kant's moral and political philosophy', in R. C. Solomon and K. M. Higgins, ed., *The Age of German Idealism*, 1993, 68–102. Examines the central status of the categorical imperative in Kant's moral philosophy, with particular attention to his conception of freedom and the role of the state in securing it.

6.737 **Booth**, W. J., *Interpreting the World: Kant's Philosophy of History and Politics*, Toronto, 1986. A dense and thoughtful analysis of the relationship between the three *Critiques* on the issue of how individual autonomy and political obedience can be reconciled.

6.738 **Bowie**, N. E., 'Aspects of Kant's philosophy of law', *Phil. Forum*, 2, 1971, 469–78. Examines this aspect of his thought in the context of natural law theory, legal positivism, and procedural justice.

6.739 **Brown**, S. M., 'Has Kant a philosophy of law?', *Phil. Rev.*, 71, 1962, 33–48. Argues that his moral and political philosophy founder upon the role he attributes to pure reason.

6.740 **Carnois**, B., *The Coherence of Kant's Doctrine of Freedom*, Chicago, Ill., 1987. Whilst largely a study in moral philosophy, the discussion on will in this text is important for an understanding of the relation between freedom and law in his political philosophy.

6.741 **Carr**, C. L., 'Kant's theory of political authority', *Hist. Pol. Thought*, 10, 1989, 719–31. Contends that his moralised version of the liberal argument avoids the traditional liberal tension between a commitment to individual freedom on the one hand and political authority on the other.

6.742 **Cavallar**, G., 'Kant's judgement on Frederick's enlightened absolutism', *Hist. Pol. Thought*, 14, 1993, 103–32. Argues that Kant's enthusiasm for the French Revolution can be better understood when viewed against his critique of Frederick's rule and of the idea of a 'philosopher-king'.

6.743 **Caygill**, H., *A Kant Dictionary*, 1993. An exhaustive guide to his key concepts, which stresses the reception his ideas received. Supplemented by a useful bibliography.

6.744 **Dahlstrom**, D., 'The natural right of equal opportunity in Kant's civil union', *Southern Journal of Philosophy*, 23, 1985, 295–303. In viewing Kant's treatment of equal opportunity as a natural right, Dahlstrom shows how his political philosophy is radically different from that of Rawls or Nozick, two thinkers strongly influenced by him.

6.745 **Delue**, S. M., 'Kant's politics as an expression of the need for his aesthetics', *Pol. Theory*, 13, 1985, 409–430. Argues that his ethics and political philosophy can be best understood through a reading of *The Critique of Judgement*.

6.746 **Doyle**, M. W., 'Kant, liberal legacies and foreign affairs', *Phil. & Pub. Affairs*, 12, 1983, 205–35 and 323–53. On the relevance of Kantian liberalism for international relations.

6.747 **Fischer**, N., 'The concept of community in Kant's architectonic', *Man World*, 11, 1978, 372–91. Scrutinises the relation between his conception of community in nature and a just political order.

6.748 **Gallie**, W. B., 'Kant on perpetual peace', in *Philosophers of Peace and War: Kant, Clausewitz, Marx, Engels and Tolstoy*, 1978, 8–36. Reconstructs the political context of his pamphlet on this subject in 1794, suggesting that its neglect has obscured his contribution to international relations theory.

6.749 —— 'Kant's view of reason in politics', *Phil.*, 54, 1979, 19–33. Comparison of Kant and Hegel, arguing that their differing political theories stem from alternative conceptions of reason.

6.750 **Galston**, W. A., *Kant and the Problem of History*, Chicago, Ill., 1975. Thoughtful examination of the relationship between the historical and political in his thought, incorporating a stimulating comparison with Rousseau's idea of the relation of nature and freedom, and suggesting that Kant's reformulation of Rousseau underlay his deduction of political principles from morality. An important, unconventional study that throws light upon his concepts of nihilism, morality and politics.

6.751 **Ginsberg**, R., 'Kant and Hobbes on the social contract', *Southwestern J. Phil.*, 5, 1974, 115–19. Argues that for Kant the principles of equality, liberty and independence are the guidelines for conduct within the state.

6.752 **Goedecke**, R., 'Kant and the radical regrounding of the norms of politics', *Journal of Value Inquiry*, 7, 1973, 81–95. Contends that his political writings have been misunderstood because they have been read from the perspective of English empiricism.

6.753 **Goldmann**, L., *Immanuel Kant*, 1971. An impressive, Marxist reading of Kant.

6.754 **Grcic**, J., 'Kant on revolution and economic inequality', *Kantstudien*, 77, 1986, 447–57. Argues that his conception of revolution is inconsistent with his moral philosophy.

6.755 **Gregor**, M. J., 'Kant's approach to constitutionalism', in A. S. Rosenbaum, ed., *Constitutionalism: The Philosophical Dimension*, New York, 1988, 69–87.

6.756 —— 'Kant's theory of property', *Rev. Metaph.*, 41, 1988, 757–87. Analyses the significance of this theory for his political philosophy.

6.757 —— *Laws of Freedom: A Study of Kant's Method of Applying the Categorical Imperative in the Metaphysik der Sitten*, 1963. Briefly examines his legal and political theory, illustrating how it fits into his overall system of moral philosophy.

6.758 **Gulyga**, A., *Immanuel Kant: His Life and Thought*, Boston, 1987. Examines the central tenets of his philosophy, placing them in their historical context.

6.759 **Hancock**, R., 'Kant and civil disobedience', *Ideal Studies*, 5, 1975, 164–76.

6.760 —— 'Kant and the natural right theory', *Kantstudien*, 52, 1961, 440–7. Compares Kant with Hobbes and Rousseau, arguing that his doctrine of natural right is original because of his distinctive analytical method.

6.761 **Guyer**, P., ed., *The Cambridge Companion to Kant*, 1992. Includes F. Beiser on his intellectual development, J. Schneewind on his moral philosophy and W. Kersting on his political philosophy.

6.762 **Harris**, C. E., 'Kant, Nozick and the minimal state', *Southwestern J. Phil.*, 10, 1979, 179–88. Argues that Kant, unlike Nozick, wanted the state to play a benevolent and paternalistic role within society.

6.763 **Hopton**, T., 'Kant's two theories of law', *Hist. Pol. Thought*, 3, 1982, 51–76. Explores the tensions in his ethical, legal and political theory which resulted from his combination of legal positivism with natural law theory.

6.764 **Howard**, D., *From Marx to Kant*, Albany, N.Y., 1985. Contentious argument that Kant's political philosophy is more rigorous and satisfactory than that of Marx.

6.765 —— 'Kant's political theory: the virtue of his vices', *Rev. Metaph.*, 34, 1980, 325–50. Attacks the presentation of Kant evident in the work of the neo-Kantians at the end of the nineteenth century, reconstructing the theory of politics embedded in his commitment to the Greek ideal.

6.766 —— 'Kant's system and its politics', *Man World*, 18, 1985, 79–98. Analysis of his essay on 'perpetual peace'.

6.767 **Kain**, P. J., 'Kant's political theory and philosophy of history', *Clio*, 18, 1989, 325–45. Argues that Kant's philosophy of history renders his political thought far more radical than the political thinking of his day.

6.768 **Kelly**, G. A., 'The structure and spirit of legality in Kant', *J. Pol.*, 31, 1969, 513–27. Brilliant discussion of the 'tensions between the anthropological *human being* and the moral *person* in Kant's essentially legalist approach to politics'.

6.769 **Kersting**, W., 'Politics, freedom, and order: Kant's political philosophy', in P. Guyer, ed., *The Cambridge Companion to Kant*, 1992, 342–66. Excellent account of the principal themes of his political thought, including his justification of private property and critique of Locke's labour theory, his *a priori* principles of civil society, the connection between his prohibition of resistance with his principle of publicity and right-improving reformism, his theory of perpetual peace, and a comparison of his political ideas with those of Locke and Hobbes.

6.770 **Kneller**, J., 'Imaginative freedom and the German Enlightenment', *J. Hist. Ideas*, 51, 1990, 217–32. Investigates the important relation between Kant's conception of aesthetic judgement and the possibility of political and moral progress.

6.771 **Krieger**, L., 'Kant and the crisis of natural law', *J. Hist. Ideas*, 26, 1965, 191–210.

6.772 **Laursen**, J. C., 'Scepticism and intellectual freedom: the philosophical foundations of Kant's politics of publicity', *Hist. Pol. Thought*, 10, 1989, 439–55. Interpretation of Kant's politics against the background of his early philosophical development.

6.773 —— 'The subversive Kant: the vocabulary of "public" and "publicity" ', *Pol. Theory*, 14, 1986, 584–603. On the political context of his use of the vocabulary of 'publicity', whereby he placed his hopes for progressive Enlightenment and better government in a free press and the right of everyone to criticise the government in print.

6.774 **Ludwig**, B., 'The "right of a state" in Immanuel Kant's "Doctrine of Right" ', *J. Hist. Phil.*, 28, 1990. 403–15. On the republican ideal elaborated in a text that is often neglected by commentators.

6.775 **Meiklejohn**, D., 'Kantian formalism and civil liberty', *J. Phil.*, 51, 1954, 842–47. Argues that his formulation provides a firmer basis than more recent theories for the safeguarding of civil liberties.

6.776 **Mendus**, S., 'Kant: an honest but narrow-minded bourgeois?', in E. Kennedy and S. Mendus, ed., *Women in Western Political Philosophy*, 1987, 21–43. Explains why he believed that women should be excluded from the public sphere.

6.777 **Meyer**, M. J., 'Kant's concept of dignity in modern political thought', *Hist. Euro. Ideas*, 8, 1987, 319–32. A thorough account of Kant's understanding of human dignity and of the development of the concept during the French Revolution.

6.778 **Mulholland**, L. A., 'Kant on war and international justice', *Kantstudien*, 78, 1987, 25–41. Argues that he saw perpetual peace being dependent on republicanism because it places human rights above national self-interest.

6.779 —— *Kant's System of Rights*, New York, 1990. Examines his theory of rights and its relation to the idea of liberty.

6.780 **Murphy**, J. G., 'Hume and Kant on the social contract', *Phil. Sts.*, 33, 1978, 65–79.

6.781 —— *Kant: The Philosophy of Right*, 1970. Assessment of the ethical foundations of Kant's political thought.

6.782 **Nicholson**, P. P., 'Kant on the duty never to resist the sovereign', *Ethics*, 86, 1976, 214–30.

6.783 —— 'Recent studies in English of Kant's political philosophy', *Pol. Sts.*, 23, 1975, 88–94. A comprehensive review of the literature on this topic, which corrects the tendency to underplay this area of Kant's thought, arguing that his political ideas are intimately related to his more general philosophy.

6.784 **O'Neill**, O., 'Kantian politics: the public use of reason', *Pol. Theory*, 14, 1986, 523–51. Suggests that Kant's vindication of toleration, which for him is connected with the very grounding of reason, is firmer than in some versions of liberalism.

6.785 **Reiss**, H. S., 'Kant and the right of rebellion', *J. Hist. Ideas*, 17, 1956, 179–92. Examines why he welcomed the American and French Revolutions while denying the right to rebel against established authority.

6.786 **Rickman**, H. P., 'Kant's political philosophy', *Phil.*, 54, 1979, 548–51. Shows how his political philosophy is founded on his ethics and epistemology.

6.787 **Riedel**, M., 'Transcendental politics? Political legitimacy and the concept of civil society in Kant', *Social Res.*, 48, 588–613. Argues that the formal nature of his conception of the social contract legitimises real economic and social inequalities.

6.788 **Riley**, P., 'Kant on will, "moral causality", and the social contract', *Modern Scholar*, 54, 1977, 107–22. Views his conception of the will in relation to the question of political legitimacy.

6.789 —— *Kant's Political Philosophy*, Toronto, 1983. Scrutinises his conceptions of universal republicanism and 'perpetual peace', analysing these in the context of his understanding of a morally good will.

6.790 —— 'On Kant as the most adequate of the social contract theorists', *Pol. Theory*, 1, 1973, 450–71. Sets out the connections between his 'quasi-contractarian political philosophy' and his more important moral theory, concluding eulogistically that he 'raises to their highest pitch the ideals of the contractarian and voluntarist tradition which he inherited and transformed'.

6.791 —— 'On Susan Shell's "Kant's Theory of Property" ', *Pol. Theory*, 6, 1978, 91–9. Questions Shell's deployment of alienation in understanding Kant and her corresponding politicisation of his epistemology.

6.792 —— 'The "elements" of Kant's practical philosophy: the groundwork after 200 years (1785–1985)', *Pol. Theory*, 14, 1986, 552–83. Reviews recent interpretations of Kant and is especially critical of Rawls's reading of him as a constructivist moral thinker and Sandel's interpretation, which presents him as a deontologist.

6.793 **Sacksteder**, W., 'Kant's analysis of international relations', *J. Phil.*, 25, 1954, 848–55.

6.794 **Saner**, H., *Kant's Political Thought: Its Origins and Developments*, Chicago, Ill., 1973. Schematic presentation of Kant, emphasising 'thought forms' in his early work which were later given a political context, the connection between his notions of literary and political struggle, and the metaphysical commitment to peace in his work. An offputting volume.

6.795 **Schwarz**, W., 'Kant's philosophy of law and international peace', *Philos. & Phenom. Res.*, 23, 1962, 71–80. Examines the Kantian concepts of right, obligation and freedom in relation to the idea of international peace, with particular reference to the United Nations.

6.796 —— 'The right of resistance', *Ethics*, 74, 1963–64, 126–34. Contends that Kant, in drawing a clear distinction between resistance and revolution, provides a solid justification for resistance based on his principles of right and freedom.

6.797 **Seebohm**, T., 'Kant's theory of revolution', *Social Res.*, 48, 1981, 557–87. Debunks those criticisms of Kant which argue that his understanding of revolution contradicts his practical moral philosophy.

6.798 **Seidler**, V. J., *Kant, Respect and Injustice: The Limits of Liberal Moral Theory*, 1986.

6.799 **Shell**, S. M., 'Kant's theory of property', *Pol. Theory*, 6, 1978, 75–90. Shows that Kant's view of consciousness was essentially proprietary, so that the justification of property was, in his view, the task of critical philosophy.

6.800 —— 'The cancelled bond: dialectic and monetary form in Kant and Hegel', *Phil. &*

Soc. Crit., 6, 1979, 165–86.

6.801 —— *The Rights of Reason: A Study of Kant's Philosophy and Politics*, Toronto, 1980.

6.802 **Singh**, R., 'Kant: morality and the right of resistance', *South African Journal of Philosophy*, 6, 1987, 8–15.

6.803 **Steinkraus**, W. E., 'Kant and Rousseau on humanity', *Southern Journal of Philosophy*, 12, 1974, 265–70.

6.804 **Stern**, D. S., 'Autonomy and political obligation in Kant', *Southern Journal of Philosophy*, 29, 1991, 127–48.

6.805 **Sullivan**, R. J., *Immanuel Kant's Moral Theory*, 1989. Connects his moral theory to his political philosophy and philosophy of history.

6.806 **Taylor**, C., 'Kant's theory of freedom', in Z. Pelczynski and J. Gray, ed., *Conceptions of Liberty in Political Philosophy*, 1984, 100–22. Rigorous account of his understanding of freedom in relation to his conception of political authority.

6.807 **Teuber**, A., 'Kant's respect for persons', *Pol. Theory*, 11, 1983, 369–92. Interesting elaboration of this concept, arguing that it serves to fix his principle that an individual must be treated as an end, differentiating this interpretation from that of Rawls and Nozick.

6.808 **Van der Linden**, H., *Kantian Ethics and Socialism*, Indianapolis, Ind., 1988. A clear study of Kant's moral and political philosophy, which examines his influence on Austro-Marxism (especially Herman Cohen), and scrutinises the implications of his thought for contemporary socialism.

6.809 **Velkley**, R. C., *Freedom and the End of Reason: On the Moral Foundations of Kant's Critical Philosophy*, Chicago, Ill., 1989. Argues that his philosophy was more influenced by Rousseau than is usually acknowledged.

6.810 **Waltz**, K. N., 'Kant, liberalism and war', *Am. Pol. Sc. Rev.*, 56, 1962, 331–40.

6.811 **Weiler**, G., 'Kant's question "what is man?" ', *Phil. Soc. Scs.*, 10, 1980, 1–24. Teases out the moral and political implications of his reflections on what it is to be human.

6.812 **Welding**, S. O., 'On Kant's concept of duty', *Ratio*, 13, 1971, 166–94. A critical survey which probes his failure to distinguish duties from inclinations and his inability to establish grounds for the justification of duty.

6.813 **Wilkins**, B. T., 'Teleology in Kant's philosophy of history', *Hist. & Theory*, 5, 1966, 172–85. Examines his 'idea of a universal history from a cosmopolitan point of view' to suggest that he formulated a rigorous theory of progress.

6.814 **Williams**, H., ed., *Essays on Kant's Political Philosophy*, 1992. Important collection of new and previously published essays, including H. Williams on his social and political thought, O. O'Neill on the connection between reason and politics, S. Shell on his 'political cosmology', O. Höffe on natural justice, W. Kersting on his concept of the state, R. Scruton on 'contract, consent and exploitation' in his work, R. F. Atkinson on his moral and political thought, P. Nicholson on 'revolutions and history' in his theory, and P. Riley on Arendt on Kant. The most wide ranging survey of his political theory.

6.815 —— 'Kant's concept of property', *Phil. Q.*, 27, 1977, 32–40. Argues that a firmer understanding of the modern state may be gained through a careful study of his political philosophy, especially his notion of private property.

6.816 —— *Kant's Political Philosophy*, 1983. Excellent introduction to his political thinking which ranges from his general conception of justice in relation to external acts, through the ideas of property and punishment, to individual freedom and state authority – and the rights and wrongs of rebellion.

6.817 —— 'Politics and philosophy in Kant and Hegel', in J. Priest, ed., *Hegel's Critique of Kant*, 1987, 195–203.

6.818 **Williams**, M. C., 'Reason and Realpolitik: Kant's "Critique of International Politics" ', *Can. J. Pol. Sc.*, 25, 1992, 99–119.

6.819 **Wolf**, F. O., 'Kant and Hobbes concerning the foundations of political philosophy', in L. W. Beck, ed., *Proceedings of the 3rd International Kant Congress*, Dordrecht, 1972, 607–13.

Montesquieu

6.820 **Baum**, J. A., *Montesquieu and Social Theory*, 1979. Argues that he made a significant contribution to the methodological development of sociology.

6.821 **Berlin**, I., 'Montesquieu', *Procs. Brit.*

Acad., 41, 1956, 267–96. Elegant introduction to his thought.

6.822 **Boase**, A. M., 'The interpretation of the *Lettres Persanes*', in W. Moore, R. Sutherland, and E. Starkie, ed., *The French Mind: Studies in Honour of Gustave Rudler*, 1952, 152–69. Demonstrates that the *Persian Letters* contain a number of political themes which are more thoroughly analysed in the *Spirit of the Laws*.

6.823 **Carrithers**, D., 'Montesquieu's philosophy of history', *J. Hist. Ideas*, 47, 1986, 61–80.

6.824 **Cohler**, A. M., *Montesquieu's Comparative Politics and the Spirit of American Constitutionalism*, Lawrence, Kan., 1988. Contends that his concern with spirit and character, rather than law and principle, was profoundly to influence the Federalists and Tocqueville, suggesting that they acquired from their reading of Montesquieu an acute sense of their age, the difficulties of arriving at a democratic form of government, and the means of overcoming those difficulties.

6.825 **Courtney**, C. P., *Montesquieu and Burke*, 1963.

6.826 **Cox**, I., 'Montesquieu and the history of French laws', *Sts. Voltaire*, 218, 1983, 1–201. Assesses his work in the light of its contribution to French legal and political thought.

6.827 **Crisafulli**, A. S., 'The *Journal des Sçavans* and the *Lettres Persanes*', in C. G. S. Williams, ed., *Literature and History in the Age of Ideas*, Cleveland, Ohio, 1975, 59–66. A short, literary analysis of the *Journal des Sçavans* and the *Lettres Persanes*, which endeavours to reveal ancient republican principles in Montesquieu's thought.

6.828 **Desserud**, D. A., 'Virtue, commerce and moderation in the 'tale of the troglodytes': Montesquieu's *Persian Letters*', *Hist. Pol. Thought*, 12, 1991, 605–26. On Montesquieu's preference, in the 'tale' as well as in the *Spirit of the Laws*, for a moderate regime based upon commerce in which citizens would acquire the skills of practical politics.

6.829 **Drennon**, H., 'The Persian Letters: a glance at Montesquieu and his politics', *Mississippi Quarterly*, 11, 1958, 83–94.

6.830 **Ellis**, H. A., 'Montesquieu's modern politics: *The Spirit of the Laws* and the problem of modern monarchy in old régime France', *Hist. Pol. Thought*, 10, 1989, 665–700. Examines whether he was an aristocratic reactionary or liberal, arguing that his ambiguous modernism enshrines a basic disagreement in eighteenth-century political discourse about the nature of French society.

6.831 **Fletcher**, D., 'Montesquieu's conception of patriotism', *Sts. Voltaire*, 56, 1967, 541–55. Argues that the Roman republican idea of civic virtue was central to his notion of patriotism.

6.832 **Gearhart**, S., 'Reading "De l'Esprit des Lois": Montesquieu and the principles of history', *Yale French Studies*, 59, 1980, 175–200. An Althusserian analysis of his conception of history and its relation to idealism.

6.833 **Grimsley**, R., 'The idea of nature in the "Lettres Persanes" ', in *From Montesquieu to Laclos: Studies on the French Enlightenment*, Geneva, 1974, 3–14. Argues that the *Persian Letters* should be viewed as a social and political critique of eighteenth-century French society.

6.834 **Hampson**, N., *Will and Circumstance: Montesquieu, Rousseau and the French Revolution*, 1983.

6.835 **Hulliung**, M., *Montesquieu and the Old Regime*, Berkeley, Calif., 1976.

6.836 —— 'Montesquieu's interpreters: a polemical essay', *Studies in the Eighteenth Century*, 10, 1981, 327–45.

6.837 **Hundert**, E. J., 'Sexual politics and the allegory of identity in Montesquieu's *Persian Letters*', *The Eighteenth Century: Theory and Interpretation*, 31, 1990, 101–16.

6.838 **Keohane**, N. O., 'The President's English: Montesquieu in America, 1976', *Pol. Sc. Re-r*, 6, 1976, 355–87.

6.839 —— 'Virtuous republics and glorious monarchies: two models in Montesquieu's political thought', *Pol. Sts.*, 20, 1972, 383–96. Examines Montesquieu's conception of monarchial and republican governments as ideal types.

6.840 **Kettler**, D., 'Montesquieu on love: notes on the "Persian Letters" ', *Am. Pol. Sc. Rev.*, 58, 1964, 658–61. A research note on his idea of love and its relation to political and social institutions.

6.841 **Klosko**, G., 'Montesquieu's science of politics: absolute values and ethical relativism in *L'Esprit des Lois*', *Sts. Voltaire*, 189, 1980, 153–77. Portrays his

political theory as a scientific system by examining in detail his understanding of the nature of science.

6.842 **Lafrance**, G., 'Montesquieu and Rousseau on constitutional theory', in A. S. Rosenbaum, ed., *Constitutionalism: The Philosophical Dimension*, New York, 1988, 54–68.

6.843 **Levin**, L. M., *The Political Doctrine of Montesquieu's Esprit des Lois: Its Classical Background*, Westport, Conn., 1973.

6.844 **Lowenthal**, D., 'Book I of Montesquieu's The Spirit of the Laws', *Am. Pol. Sc. Rev.*, 53, 1959, 485–98.

6.845 —— 'Montesquieu', in J. Cropsey and L. Strauss, ed., *History of Political Philosophy*, Chicago, Ill., 1972, 487–508. A thorough introduction to *The Spirit of the Laws*.

6.846 —— 'The design of Montesquieu's *Considérations*: considerations on the cause of greatness of the Romans and their decline', *Interpretation*, 2, 1970, 144–68. Examines this work in the light of his republicanism.

6.847 **Loy**, J. R., *Montesquieu*, New York, 1968.

6.848 **Manicas**, P. T., 'Montesquieu and the eighteenth-century vision of the state', *Hist. Pol. Thought*, 2, 1981, 313–47. Contends that, due to his application of the comparative method and emphasis on the holistic character of civilisations and societies, Montesquieu's classification of governments is a remarkable effort to reconceptualise the fundamental categories of political theory.

6.849 **Mason**, S. M., *Montesquieu's Idea of Justice*, The Hague, 1975.

6.850 **Masterson**, M. P., 'Montesquieu's grand design: the political sociology of "Esprit des Lois" ', *Brit. J. Pol. Sc.*, 2, 1972, 283–318.

6.851 —— 'Rights, relativism, and religious faith in Montesquieu', *Pol. Sts.*, 29, 1981, 204–16. Discusses the normative and analytical aspects of his work, especially with regard to his conceptions of natural law and natural rights.

6.852 **Merry**, H. J., *Montesquieu's System of Natural Government*, West Lafayette, Ind., 1970. Stresses the coherence of the *Spirit of the Laws*, relating it to his other works.

6.853 **Morgan**, C., *The Liberty of Thought and the Separation of Powers: A Modern Problem Considered in the Context of Montesquieu*, 1948. Uses his vindication of freedom as a stick to beat totalitarianism.

6.854 **Morris**, G. C., 'Montesquieu and the varieties of political experience', in D. Thomson, ed., *Political Ideas*, 1969, 81–94.

6.855 **Oake**, R. B., 'De l'Esprit des Lois, Books XXVI–XXXI', *Modern Language Notes*, 63, 1948, 167–71.

6.856 —— 'Montesquieu's analysis of Roman history', *J. Hist. Ideas*, 16, 1955, 44–59. Examines Montesquieu's conception of Rome as a timocratic republic.

6.857 **Pangle**, T. L., *Montesquieu's Philosophy of Liberalism: A Commentary on The Spirit of the Laws*, Chicago, Ill., 1974. Charts the shift in liberal arguments from natural rights discourse to a new philosophy of history through an examination of his thought. Useful introduction to his liberal republicanism.

6.858 **Ranum**, O., 'Personality and politics in the "Persian Letters" ', *Pol. Sc. Q.*, 84, 1969, 606–27. Examines Montesquieu's writings as an attempt not only to address social and political issues, but primarily as a means to overcome his own inability 'to adapt well to his society'.

6.859 **Richter**, M., 'An essay on explanation by Montesquieu', *Pol. Theory*, 4, 1976, 132–62. Introduction to 'An essay on the causes that may affect men's minds and characters', demonstrating that it was a working paper for the composition of the *Spirit of the Laws*.

6.860 —— 'Comparative political analysis in Montesquieu and Tocqueville', *Comp. Pol.*, 1, 1969, 129–60.

6.861 —— 'Modernity and its distinctive threats to liberty: Montesquieu and Tocqueville on new forms of illegitimate domination', in M. Hereth and J. Höffken, ed., *Alexis de Tocqueville zur Politik in der Demokratie*, Baden-Baden, 1981, 61–80. On their contrasting theories of despotism.

6.862 —— 'Montesquieu, the politics of language, and the language of politics', *Hist. Pol. Thought*, 10, 1989, 71–88. Subtle account of his linguistic innovations, arguing that he 'devised his own rhetoric of Enlightenment, his distinctive strategy of persuasion'.

6.863 —— *The Political Theory of Montesquieu*, 1977. Selections from his writings prefaced by a long and perceptive introduction.

6.864 **Roscow**, S. J., 'Commerce, power, and justice: Montesquieu on international politics', *Rev. Pol.*, 46, 1984, 346–66.

6.865 **Shackleton**, R., *Montesquieu: A Critical Biography*, 1961. Remains a classic account of his life and ideas.

6.866 —— 'Montesquieu, Bolingbroke, and the separation of powers', *French Studies*, 3, 1949, 25–38. Discusses the sources of Montesquieu's doctrine of the separation of powers.

6.867 —— 'Montesquieu and Machiavelli: a reappraisal', *Comparative Literature Studies*, 1, 1964, 1–13. Shows how Montesquieu's reading of Machiavelli stimulated his reflections on the relation between history and politics.

6.868 **Shanley**, M. L., and **Stillman**, P. G., 'Political and marital despotism: Montesquieu's "Persian Letters" ', in J. B. Elshtain, ed., *The Family in Political Thought*, 1982, 66–79. Analysis of the *Persian Letters* as a critique of the patriarchal family and political despotism.

6.869 **Shklar**, J. N., *Montesquieu*, 1987. Clear and perceptive introduction to his life and ideas.

6.870 —— 'Montesquieu and the new republicanism', in G. Bock, Q. Skinner and M. Viroli, ed., *Machiavelli and Republicanism*, 1990, 265–79. Discusses the republican thought of Montesquieu, Rousseau, Hamilton, Madison and Publius, with particular attention to the differences between Montesquieu and Rousseau.

6.871 —— 'Virtue in a bad time: good men and good citizens in Montesquieu's "L'Esprit des Lois" ', in A. J. Bingham and V. W. Topazio, ed., *Enlightenment Studies in Honour of Lester G. Crocker*, 1979, 315–28. Examines his ideas on public and private virtues.

6.872 **Vartanian**, A., 'Eroticism and politics in the "Lettres Persanes" ', *Romanic Review*, 60, 1969, 23–33. Examines the relation between eroticism and politics by focusing upon the 'seraglio' fiction of the *Persian Letters* as a critique of political despotism.

6.873 **Waddicor**, M. H., *Montesquieu's Theory of Natural Law*, The Hague, 1970. Comprehensive examination of this concept in his thought, arguing that it inclined him towards a reforming liberalism.

6.874 **Wernick**, R., 'The godfather of the American constitution', *Smithonian*, 20, 1989, 183–96. Discusses the extent to which the *Spirit of the Laws* was a model for the American constitution.

6.875 **Wolfe** C., 'The confederate republic in Montesquieu', *Polity*, 9, 1977, 427–45.

6.876 **Young**, D. B., 'Libertarian demography: Montesquieu's essay on depopulation in the "Lettres Persanes" ', *J. Hist. Ideas*, 36, 1975, 669–82.

6.877 —— 'Montesquieu's view of despotism and his use of travel literature', *Rev. Pol.*, 40, 1978, 392–405. Elucidates his typology of political regimes by examining his account of the Near East.

Rousseau

6.878 **Ake**, C., 'Right, utility, and Rousseau', *West. Pol. Q.*, 20, 1967, 5–14.

6.879 **Allers**, U. S., 'Rousseau's second discourse', *Rev. Pol.*, 20, 1958, 91–120. Focuses on his conception of liberty and its relation to equality in his *Discourse on the Origins of Inequality among Men*.

6.880 **Althusser**, L., *Montesquieu, Rousseau, Marx: Politics and History*, 1972. A provocative and original analysis of Rousseau's political thought.

6.881 **Armstrong**, G. K., 'Borrowings and uses of history in Rousseau', *Sts. Burke & Time*, 16, 1974–75, 129–47.

6.882 **Babbitt**, I., *Rousseau and Romanticism*, Austin, Tex., 1977.

6.883 **Baczko**, B., 'Rousseau and social marginality', *Daedalus*, 107, 1978, 27–40. Examines both his personal experience and writings in an attempt to reveal his ideas on individual and social marginality.

6.884 **Barber**, B. R., 'Rousseau and the paradoxes of the dramatic imagination', *Daedalus*, 107, 1978, 79–92. Argues that the apparent contradiction between natural man as innocent and social man as corrupt can be better understood if viewed as a dialectical relation expressing real tensions within modernity.

6.885 **Barnard**, F. M., 'National culture and political legitimacy: Herder and Rousseau', *J. Hist. Ideas*, 44, 1983, 231–51. Transcends the dichotomy between the cultural nationalism of Herder and the political nationalism of Rousseau, suggesting that whilst they retain differing conceptions of the political, they share a concern for the establishment of political legitimacy via national self-understanding.

6.886 —— 'Rousseau's agonizing over political

accountability', *Sts. Pol. Thought*, 1, 1992, 3–17.

6.887 —— 'Will and political rationality in Rousseau', *Pol. Sts.*, 32, 1984, 369–84. Questions the coherence of his view of autonomous and accountable agency in politics because of his ambivalence over political rationality and despite his distinctive analogy between willing in nature and willing in society.

6.888 **Bellhouse**, M. L., 'On understanding Rousseau's praise of Robinson Crusoe', *Can. J. Pol. & Soc. Theory*, 6, 1982, 120–37. Argues that he recreates *Crusoe* in one way in *Émile* and in another in his personal writings.

6.889 **Benda**, H., 'Rousseau's early discourses', Part I, *Pol. Sc.*, 5, 1953, 13–20; Part II, *Pol. Sc.*, 6, 1954, 17–27. Rather superficial account of the first and second *Discourses*.

6.890 **Berman**, M., 'Liberal and totalitarian therapies in Rousseau: a response to James M. Glass' "Political philosophy as therapy" ', *Pol. Theory*, 4, 1976, 185–94. Argues that a psychoanalytic interpretation of Rousseau obscures the 'radical energy and nihilistic fury' of his thinking.

6.891 **Bien**, J., 'On nature and destiny in Jean-Jacques Rousseau's *Discourse on Inequality*', *Man and World*, 10, 1977, 466–73.

6.892 **Bloom**, A., 'Jean-Jacques Rousseau', in L. Strauss and J. Cropsey, ed., *History of Political Philosophy*, Chicago, Ill., 1963, 514–35. Historically sensitive and comprehensive introduction to his political thought.

6.893 —— 'The education of democratic man', *Daedalus*, 107, 1978, 135–57. Rigorous and stimulating analysis of *Émile* which focuses upon Rousseau's analysis of *amour de soi* and *amour-propre*.

6.894 **Blum**, C. K., *Rousseau and the Republic of Virtue: The Language of Politics in the French Revolution*, Ithaca, N.Y., 1986. Examines how his concept of virtue is expressed in French Revolutionary thought, and simplified in late eighteenth-century French popular culture.

6.895 —— 'Rousseau's concept of "virtue" and the French Revolution', in A. J. Bingham and V. W. Topazio, ed., *Enlightenment Studies in Honour of Lester G. Crocker*, 1979, 29–48. Examines his conception of virtue and its appropriation by Robespierre and Saint-Just.

6.896 **Brint**, M. E., 'Jean-Jacques Rousseau and Benjamin Constant: a dialogue on freedom and tyranny', *Rev. Pol.*, 47, 1985, 323–46. Compares Constant's modern, individualist conception of freedom with Rousseau's ambivalent, collective conception, and seeks to construct a Rousseaunian response to Constant's critique.

6.897 **Brooks**, R. A., 'Rousseau's antifeminism in the *Lettre à d'Alembert* and *Émile*', in C. G. S. Williams, ed., *Literature and History in the Age of Ideas: Essays on the French Enlightenment Presented to George R. Havens*, Columbus, Ohio, 1975, 209–27. A thorough and straightforward account of Rousseau's sexism.

6.898 **Broome**, J. H., *Rousseau: A Study of his Thought*, New York, 1963. Useful and sympathetic introduction to his ideas.

6.899 **Burns**, J. H., 'Du côté de chez Vaughan: Rousseau revisited', *Pol. Sts.*, 12, 1964, 229–34. Excellent short survey of some of the secondary literature on his political thought.

6.900 **Cameron**, D. R., 'Rousseau, Professor Derathé and natural law', *Pol. Sts.*, 20, 1972, 195–201. Rigorous critique of the thesis that Rousseau's political thought falls within the natural law tradition, focusing upon Robert Derathé's *Jean-Jacques Rousseau et la Science Politique de son Temps*.

6.901 —— 'The hero in Rousseau's political thought', *J. Hist. Ideas*, 45, 1984, 397–419. Considers his little known manuscript of 1751 on the virtue of heroes.

6.902 —— *The Social Thought of Rousseau and Burke. A Comparative Study*, 1973. Argues that for all their apparent differences, there are underlying similarities in the political ideas of Rousseau and Burke, especially with regard to their attitude to empiricism and rationalism.

6.903 **Campbell**, B., 'Montaigne and Rousseau's first *Discourse*', *West. Pol. Q.*, 28, 1975, 7–31. Argues that Montaigne's influence makes Rousseau's first discourse profoundly at odds with the optimistic vision of his later writings.

6.904 **Canovan**, M., 'Rousseau's two concepts of citizenship', in E. Kennedy and S. Mendus, ed., *Women in Western Political Philosophy*, 1987, 78–105. Stimulating interpretation which, whilst recognising that he explicitly excluded women from his vision of political society, nevertheless attempts to construct a Rousseaunian, gender-neutral conception of citizenship.

6.905 —— 'The limits of seriousness: Rousseau and the interpretation of political theory', *Eur. Sts. Rev.*, 2, 1972, 1–24.

6.906 **Carter**, R. B., 'Rousseau's Newtonian body politic', *Phil. & Soc. Crit.*, 7, 1980, 143–68.

6.907 **Cell**, H. R. and **MacAdam**, J. I., *Rousseau's Response to Hobbes*, New York, 1988. A thorough, though not entirely original, study of Hobbes's influence of Rousseau's political thought, focusing on their treatment of religion and property.

6.908 **Chapman**, J. W., *Rousseau, Totalitarian or Liberal?*, New York, 1956. Argues that his theory is essentially liberal, notwithstanding certain illiberal aspects.

6.909 **Charvet**, J., 'Rousseau and the ideal of community', *Hist. Pol. Thought*, 1, 1980, 69–80. Argues that Rousseau's apparent promise of earthly liberation is flawed, along the lines suggested by Marx, so that what is ultimately proffered is political rather than complete human emancipation.

6.910 —— *The Social Problem in the Philosophy of Rousseau*, 1974. Analyses the fundamental problem of the transformation of natural man to a social being in Rousseau's second *Discourse*, the *Social Contract* and *Émile*.

6.911 **Christenson**, R., 'Political theory of male chauvinism: J. J. Rousseau's paradigm', *Midwest Quarterly*, 13, 1972, 291–9. Crude exposé of Rousseau's sexism.

6.912 **Cobban**, A., 'New light on the political thought of Rousseau', *Pol. Sc. Q.*, 66, 1951, 272–84. Comprehensive analysis of R. Derathé's classic studies on Rousseau's political and social thought: *Le Rationalisme de J.-J. Rousseau*, and *Jean-Jacques Rousseau et la Science Politique de son Temps*.

6.913 —— *Rousseau and the Modern State*, 1964. Comprehensive account of his political thought, focusing on his understanding of the relationship between the individual, state and civil society.

6.914 **Cohen**, J., 'Reflections on Rousseau: autonomy and democracy', *Phil. & Pub. Affairs*, 15, 1986, 275–97. Carefully reviews recent critical literature and defends his institutional ideal that realises autonomy under conditions of interdependence.

6.915 **Cohler**, A. M., *Rousseau and Nationalism*, New York, 1970.

6.916 **Coleman**, P., *Rousseau's Political Imagination: Rule and Representation in the Lettre à d'Alembert*, Geneva, 1984. Engaging reading of this text as pivotal in his intellectual development, arguing that his ideas remain pertinent in a world where scepticism about rationality is commonplace and the public culture is in decline. Includes thoughtful discussion of his political rhetoric, conception of order and sexual politics.

6.917 **Colletti**, L., *From Rousseau to Lenin*, New York, 1972. Contains two important essays on Rousseau's political and social thought: the first, 'Rousseau as critic of "civil society" ', analyses the second *Discourse* and the *Social Contract* as radical critiques of society; the second, 'Mandeville, Rousseau and Smith', compares their ideas on the issues of economic and political progress and civil virtue.

6.918 **Combee**, J. and **Plax**, M., 'Rousseau's noble savage and European self-consciousness', *Modern Age*, 17, 1973, 173–82. Examination of Rousseau's characterisation of the 'noble savage', which was informed by his reading of European travellers' accounts of voyages of uncharted lands.

6.919 **Cook**, T. E., 'Rousseau: education and politics', *J. Pol.*, 37, 1975, 108–28. On his prescriptions for educating people in citizenship.

6.920 **Cranston**, M., *Jean-Jacques: The Early Life and Work of Jean-Jacques Rousseau, 1712–1754*, 1983. The first part of a thorough and subtle intellectual biography which places his early intellectual writings within their historical context.

6.921 —— *Jean-Jacques: The Noble Savage*, 1991. The second volume of an outstanding intellectual portrait of Rousseau, focusing on his *Letter to M. d'Alembert*, *Julie or the New Héloïse*, *Émile*, and *The Social Contract*.

6.922 —— 'Rousseau in England', *Hist. Today*, 11, 1961, 599–606. Account of Rousseau's exile in England, but with insight into his ideas.

6.923 —— and **Peters**, R. S., ed., *Hobbes and Rousseau*, Garden City, N.Y., 1972. Includes L. Strauss, 'On the intention of Rousseau', J. McManners, 'The Social Contract and Rousseau's revolt against

society', J. Shklar, 'Rousseau's images o authority', W. Pickles, 'The notion of tir in Rousseau's political thought', R. Masters, 'The structure of Rousseau's political thought', R. Grimsley, 'Rousse: and the problem of happiness', J. Charv 'Individual identity and social consciousness in Rousseau's philosophy' J. Plamenatz, 'On le forçera d'être libre' and B. de Jouvenel, 'Rousseau's theory the forms of government'.

6.924 **Crocker**, L. G., *Jean-Jacques Rousseau: The Quest (1712–1758)* and *The Prophet Voice (1758–1778)*, 1968 and 1973. Informative and enjoyable volumes, though eclipsed by subsequent work.

6.925 —— *Rousseau's 'Social Contract': An Interpretive Essay*, Cleveland, Ohio, 196 Unconvincing depiction of him as a totalitarian thinker.

6.926 —— 'The priority of justice or law', *Yal French Studies*, 28, 1961–62, 34–42. Argues that Rousseau's political thought was, within its historical context, fundamentally conventional because of t priority he gave to law over justice.

6.927 —— 'The relation of Rousseau's second discourse and the contrat social', *Roman Review*, 51, 1960, 33–44. Portrays him a an illiberal thinker.

6.928 **Dagger**, R., 'Understanding the general will', *West, Pol. Q.*, 34, 1981, 359–71. Argues that the distinction between *the a a* general will is essential to unravel Rousseau's meaning.

6.929 **De Beer**, G. R., *Jean-Jacques Rousseau a his World*, 1972.

6.930 **de Jouvenel**, B., 'Rousseau', in M. Cranston, ed., *Western Political Philosophers*, 1964, 64–79. Cogent introduction to his political and social thought.

6.931 **Della Volpe**, G., *Rousseau and Marx an Other Writings*, 1978. A rigorous Marxist critique of Rousseau's social and politica thought, arguing that Rousseaunian and socialist conceptions of equality are essentially similar.

6.932 **de Magnin**, P. K., 'Rousseau's politics c visibility', *Diacritics*, 5, 1975, 51–6.

6.933 **Dent**, N. J. H., *A Rousseau Dictionary*, 1992. Contains entries on all of the important concepts of Rousseau's though

6.934 —— *Rousseau*, 1989. Outline and vindication of his political philosophy.

6.935 —— 'Rousseau and respect for persons',

S. Mendus, ed., *Justifying Toleration*, 1988, 115–35. Argues that he develops a complex, yet highly cogent, conception of political and social toleration.

6.936 **Dodge**, G. H., *Jean-Jacques Rousseau: Authoritarian or Libertarian?*, Lexington, Mass., 1971. Selection from secondary sources (L. Crocker, J. Talmon, J. McDonald, J. Chapman and others) on the issue of whether his writings endorse freedom or despotism.

6.937 **Durant**, W. and **Durant**, A., *Rousseau and Revolution, the Story of Civilization*, New York, 1967.

6.938 **Echeverria**, D., 'The pre-revolutionary influence of Rousseau's *Contrat Social*', *J. Hist. Ideas*, 33, 1972, 543–60. Argues that the book had a broader impact before 1789 than is usually supposed.

6.939 **Einaudi**, M., *The Early Rousseau*, New York, 1967. Places his early work in its historical and political context.

6.940 **Ellenburg**, S., *Rousseau's Political Philosophy: An Interpretation from Within*, Ithaca, N.Y., 1976. Establishes the 'non-individualism' and radical egalitarianism at the heart of his political ideas in a somewhat laborious study which remains uneasy about the connection between this theory and liberalism.

6.941 **Ellison**, C. E., 'Jean-Jacques Rousseau on the physiognomy of the modern city', *Hist. Euro. Ideas*, 12, 1990, 479–502. Argues that he saw the modern city as undermining the values essential to virtuous republican government.

6.942 —— 'Rousseau and the modern city: the politics of speech and dress', *Pol. Theory*, 13, 1985, 497–533.

6.943 —— 'The moral economy of the modern city: reading Rousseau's *Discourse on Wealth*', *Hist. Pol. Thought*, 12, 1991, 253–61. On an unfinished work in which, as elsewhere, Rousseau deplores the absence of virtue in modern society.

6.944 **Emberley**, P., 'Rousseau and the domestication of virtue', *Can. J. Pol. Sc.*, 17, 1984, 731–53. Argues that his conception of virtue, though classical in inspiration, was no longer civic, but confined to the private spheres of labour and love.

6.945 **Featherstone**, J., 'Rousseau and modernity', *Daedalus*, 107, 1978, 167–92. Examines the significance of *Émile* for an understanding of romanticism and progress.

6.946 **Fetscher**, I., 'Rousseau's concepts of freedom in light of his philosophy of history', in K. Friedrich, ed., *Liberty: Nomos IV*, New York, 1962, 29–56. Argues that whilst Rousseau's critique of his age was inspired by Hobbes and Mandeville, he departed radically from their thinking on the questions of virtue and political sovereignty.

6.947 **Fireside**, H. F., 'The concept of legislator in Rousseau's social contract', *Rev. Pol.*, 32, 1970, 191–7.

6.948 **Fletcher**, D., 'Self-realization and human freedom: Rousseau and Nietzsche', *Research Studies*, 42, 1974, 104–11.

6.949 **Fourny**, D., 'Rousseau's civil religion reconsidered', *French Review*, 60, 1987, 485–96. Examines the chapter on 'civil religion' in the *Social Contract*.

6.950 **Fralin**, R., 'Rousseau and community: the role of *Moeurs* in social change', *Hist. Pol. Thought*, 7, 1986, 131–50. Discusses the relationship between his apparent utopianism and assessment of the requirements of human community.

6.951 —— *Rousseau and Representation: A Study of the Development of his Concept of Political Institutions*, New York, 1978. Contends that he was more ambivalent about both representation and direct citizen participation in the political process than is usually thought.

6.952 —— 'The evolution of Rousseau's view of representative government', *Pol. Theory*, 6, 1978, 517–36. Stresses his ambivalence towards representation by focusing upon his institutional preferences.

6.953 **Friedrich**, C. J., 'Law and dictatorship in the contrat social', *Annales de Philosophie Politique*, 5, 1965, 77–97. Strives to debunk the belief that Rousseau was a totalitarian thinker, arguing that his writings embody the basic principles of constitutionalism.

6.954 **Gardiner**, P., 'Rousseau on liberty', in Z. A. Pelczynski and J. Gray, ed., *Conceptions of Liberty*, 1984, 83–98. Focuses on the problematic relation between freedom as individual independence and political liberty as participation within the civic realm.

6.955 **Gildin**, H., 'Revolution and the formation of political society in the *Social Contract*', *Interpretation*, 5, 1976, 247–65.

6.956 —— *Rousseau's Social Contract: The Design*

of the Argument, Chicago, Ill., 1983. A Straussian interpretation which pays careful attention to the significance of natural right and law in his thinking.

6.957 **Ginsberg**, R., 'Rousseau's *Contrat Social* in current contexts', *Sts. Voltaire*, 190, 1980, 252–8. Useful introduction to twentieth-century literature on Rousseau.

6.958 **Glass**, J. M., 'Political philosophy as theory: Rousseau and the pre-social origins of consciousness', *Pol. Theory*, 4, 1976, 163–83. Uses psychiatric theory to argue that for Rousseau the task of philosophy is to provide a therapeutic vision capable of breaking through patterns of socialisation.

6.959 **Gossman**, L., 'Rousseau's idealism', *Romanic Review*, 52, 1961, 173–82. Contends that his moral idealism could lead to nothing but the most austere of societies.

6.960 —— 'The innocent art of confession and rêverie', *Daedalus*, 107, 1978, 59–78. Reveals the importance of Rousseau's autobiographical texts to his understanding of the individual and society.

6.961 —— 'Time and history in Rousseau', *Sts. Voltaire*, 30, 1964, 311–49. A thorough account of Rousseau's historical method, as well as his influence on romanticism.

6.962 **Graham**, G. J., 'Rousseau's concept of consensus', *Pol. Sc. Q.*, 85, 1970, 80–99. Analyses his conception of the individual, political order and public consensus.

6.963 —— 'Rousseau's sexism revolutionized', in P. Fritz and R. Morton, ed., *Women in the Eighteenth Century and Other Essays*, Toronto, 1976, 127–39.

6.964 **Green**, F. C., *Jean-Jacques Rousseau: A Critical Study of his Life and Writings*, 1955. An impressive intellectual biography, though weak in its treatment of his political thought.

6.965 —— *Rousseau and the Idea of Progress*, 1950. A very readable account, contending that for Rousseau moral and intellectual progress were disconnected.

6.966 **Grimsley**, R., *J.-J. Rousseau: A Study in Self-Awareness*, 1961. Offers insight into his understanding of alienation.

6.967 —— 'Rousseau and Kierkegaard', *Cambridge J.*, 7, 1954, 615–26. Draws attention to the notions of individual identity and the state of nature, especially in the thought of Rousseau, and to their understanding of God and organised religion, as well as the creation of an authentic personality.

6.968 —— *Rousseau and the Religious Quest*, 1968. Shows how his religiosity nourishe and was fed by his social, political, and philosophical thought.

6.969 —— *The Influence of Rousseau*, 1973. Comprehensive and clearly written introduction to his thinking.

6.970 **Guéhenno**, J., *Jean-Jacques Rousseau*, 1966. Thorough and suggestive biograph in two volumes.

6.971 **Hall**, J. C., *Rousseau: An Introduction to h Political Philosophy*, 1973. A sympatheti and meticulous analysis of his central concepts.

6.972 **Hamilton**, J. F., 'Literature and the "natural man" in Rousseau's *Émile*', in C. G. S. Williams, ed., *Literature and History in the Age of Ideas: Essays on the French Enlightenment Presented to George R. Havens*, Columbus, Ohio, 1975, 195–206.

6.973 —— 'Parallel interpretations, religious an political, of Rousseau's *Discours sur l'inégalité*', *Sts. Voltaire*, 94, 1972, 7–16. Argues that Rousseau's conceptions of history and the individual were quasi-religious in nature yet constituted a critique of the religious vindication of inequality and political authority.

6.974 **Hampson**, N., *Will and Circumstance: Montesquieu, Rousseau and the French Revolution*, 1983.

6.975 **Harvey**, S., **Hobson**, M., **Kelley**, D. R. and **Taylor**, S. S. B., ed., *Reappraisals o Rousseau: Studies in Honour of R. A. Leig* 1988. A collection of seventeen essays ranging from his romanticism, contribution to the *Encyclopédie*, writing the *Social Contract*, to his reflections on music.

6.976 **Hoffman**, S., 'Rousseau on war and peace', *Am. Pol. Sc. Rev.*, 57, 1963, 317–33. Seeks to piece together his variou remarks on war and peace in order to reconstruct his understanding of international relations.

6.977 **Horowitz**, A., ' "Laws and customs thru us back into infancy": Rousseau's historical anthropology', *Rev. Pol.*, 52, 1990, 215–41. Resurrects his historical anthropology against the recent reading him as a rational moralist.

6.978 —— *Rousseau, Nature and History*, Toronto, 1987.

6.979 **Howard**, D., 'Rousseau and the origin o

revolution', *Phil. & Soc. Crit.*, 6, 1979, 349–70.

6.980 **Howells**, R. J., 'The metaphysic of nature: basic values and their application in the social philosophy of Rousseau', *Sts. Voltaire*, 60, 1968, 109–200. Focuses on *Émile* and the *Social Contract*.

6.981 **Huizinga**, J. A., *The Making of a Saint: The Tragi-Comedy of Jean-Jacques Rousseau*, 1976. Blends a discussion of his life and ideas in a lively narrative, which criticises some of the antinomies within his thought.

6.982 **Ingersoll**, D. and **Matthews**, R., 'The therapist and the lawgiver: Rousseau's political vision', *Can. J. Pol. & Soc. Theory*, 4, 1980, 83–99. Rousseau, according to the authors, depicts the legislator as one who, in emulating the tutor in *Émile*, assists individuals in realising that their best, particular interests are embodied in the general will.

6.983 **Jack**, M., 'One state of nature: Mandeville and Rousseau', *J. Hist. Ideas*, 39, 1978, 119–24. Argues that though they differ in their assessment of eighteenth-century society they share a common view about the state of nature and social evolution.

6.984 **Jimack**, P. D., 'Homme and citoyen in Rousseau's *Émile*', *Romanic Review*, 56, 1965, 181–7. A short, though detailed, study of his conception of natural man and the ideal citizen.

6.985 —— 'Rousseau and the privacy of self', *Sts. Voltaire*, 32, 1965, 73–90. An interesting, though dated, analysis of his political ideas through a detailed study of his autobiographical works.

6.986 —— *Rousseau-Émile*, 1983. A useful introductory guide to *Émile*, placing it in the wider context of his political and social thought.

6.987 **Jones**, J. F., *La Nouvelle Héloïse: Rousseau and Utopia*, Geneva, 1977. Pays close attention to contradictory themes in *La Nouvelle Héloïse*, arguing that they constitute an integral part of his understanding of utopia.

6.988 **Jones**, W. T., 'Rousseau's general will and the problem of consent', *J. Hist. Phil.*, 25, 1987, 105–30. Argues that his conception of the general will is given a rigorous empirical formulation.

6.989 **Jordan**, R. J. P., 'A new look at Rousseau as educator', *Sts. Voltaire*, 182, 1979, 59–72. Assesses the importance of *Émile* as a political text.

6.990 **Kateb**, G., 'Aspects of Rousseau's political thought', *Pol. Sc. Q.*, 76, 1961, 519–43. Examines his understanding of the principles of justice, autonomy, and fair play.

6.991 **Kavanagh**, T. M., *Writing the Truth: Authority and Desire in Rousseau*, Berkeley, Calif., 1987. Focuses upon the importance that his literary and autobiographical works have for his political thought.

6.992 **Kelly**, G. A., 'Borrowings and uses of history in Rousseau', *Sts. Burke & Time*, 16, 1974–75, 129–47. Argues that his pessimistic conception of history strongly influenced his social and political thought.

6.993 —— 'Rousseau, Kant and history', *J. Hist. Ideas*, 29, 1968, 347–64. Demonstrates that while Kant's moral preoccupation owes much to the influence of Rousseau, his historical vision was more optimistic than the latter's.

6.994 **Keohane**, N. O., ' "The masterpiece of policy in our century": Rousseau on the morality of the Enlightenment', *Pol. Theory*, 6, 1978, 457–84. Outlines his observation of the immoral effects of the transformation from natural to civil man.

6.995 **Lange**, L., 'Rousseau and modern feminism', *Soc. Theory & Pract.*, 7, 1981, 245–77.

6.996 —— 'Rousseau: women and the general will', in L. Clark and L. Lange, ed., *The Sexism of Social and Political Theory*, Toronto, 1979, 41–52. Argues that his concept of the general will cannot be made genuinely egalitarian because of the weight of gender bias in his thought.

6.997 **Leigh**, R. A., 'Jean-Jacques Rousseau and the myth of antiquity in the eighteenth century', in R. R. Bolgar, ed., *Classical Influences on Western Thought, 1650–1870*, 1979, 155–68. Briefly examines the works of Plutarch, Livy, Tacitus, and Sallust in the creation of a myth about the early Roman and Greek republic, and demonstrates its influence on Rousseau and other eighteenth-century thinkers.

6.998 —— ed., *Rousseau after Two Hundred Years*, 1982. A collection of fourteen essays covering his social and political thought, along with his reflections on language, literature and music. Includes S. Ellenburg, 'Rousseau and Kant: principles of political right', and C. Frayling and R. Wokler, 'From orang-utan to the vampire: towards an anthropology of Rousseau.'

6.999 **Lemos**, R. M., 'Rousseau's adumbration of republican democracy', *Soc. Theory & Pract.*, 3, 1975, 367–77.

6.1000 —— *Rousseau's Political Philosophy: An Exposition and Interpretation*, Athens, Ga., 1977. Detailed study of the discourses on political economy and inequality, together with the *Social Contract*.

6.1001 **Levin**, M., 'Rousseau on independence', *Pol. Sts.*, 18, 1970, 496–513. Examines his conception of the state of nature, the city state and education in the light of the theme of independence.

6.1002 —— 'Uses of the social contract method: Vaughan's interpretation of Rousseau', *J. Hist. Ideas*, 28, 1967, 521–36. Interesting demonstration of how C. E. Vaughan, in his introduction to the standard edition of Rousseau's works (published in 1915), attempted to transform 'someone he described as a "collectivist" into a late XIXth-century liberal evolutionist'.

6.1003 **Levine**, A., *The Politics of Autonomy: A Kantian Reading of Rousseau's Social Contract*, Amherst, Mass., 1976. Focuses on the ideas of sovereignty, the nature of the social contract and the general will in order to reveal the contradictions underlying his thought.

6.1005 **Losco**, J., 'Rousseau on the political role of the family', *Hist. Pol. Thought*, 9, 1988, 91–111. Argues that Rousseau envisaged family life as providing a precarious middle road for most humans between the solitary life left behind in the state of nature and the denatured life of the virtuous citizen.

6.1006 **Lough**, J., 'The earliest refutation of Rousseau's *contrat social*', *French Studies*, 23, 1969, 23–34. A systematic account of some of the earliest critiques of Rousseau's *Social Contract*, focusing on the conservative condemnation of his ideas on human nature, political sovereignty and religion.

6.1007 **Lovejoy**, A. O., 'The supposed primitivism of Rousseau's *Discourse on Inequality*', in *Essays on the History of Ideas*, Baltimore, Md., 1948, 14–37. Challenges the then dominant view that Rousseau's characterisation of the state of nature entailed a doctrine of primitivism.

6.1008 **Luke**, T. W., 'On nature and society: Rousseau versus the Enlightenment', *Hist. Pol. Thought*, 5, 1984, 211–45. Argues that far from being a misguided utopian, he was a critic of progress, who was alive to the disenchantment that the spread of Enlightenment rationality could bring; his work therefore constitutes a penetrating appraisal of the alienation and anomie inherent in modern industrial life.

6.1009 **MacAdam**, J. I., 'The discourse on inequality and the social contract', *Phil.*, 47, 1972, 308–22. Attempts to clarify his concept of independence.

6.1010 —— 'Rousseau and the friends of despotism', *Ethics*, 74, 1963, 34–43. Explores the work of Rousseau, Grotius and Constant on the question of despotism, arguing that in stressing political rights Rousseau can label Grotius and Hobbes 'friends of despotism', whilst Constant, in valuing individual over political rights, can accuse Rousseau of endorsing despotism.

6.1011 —— 'What Rousseau meant by the general will', *Dialogue*, 5, 1967, 498–515.

6.1012 **MacArdle**, A. D., 'Rousseau on Rousseau: the individual and society', *Rev. Pol.*, 39, 1977, 250–79. Analyses his conception of 'natural man' and reveals its significance for his understanding of political society.

6.1013 **McDonald**, J., *Rousseau and the French Revolution, 1762–1791*, 1965. A sharp and persuasive analysis of the uses made of Rousseau's thought before and during the French Revolution.

6.1014 **McKenzie**, L. A., 'Rousseau's debate with Machiavelli in the Social Contract', *J. Hist. Ideas*, 43, 1982, 209–28. Examines Machiavelli's influence on Rousseau, contending that both were pessimistic about the resolution of the contradiction between common good and individual interests.

6.1015 **McManners**, J., *The Social Contract and Rousseau's Revolt against Society*, 1968. Seeks to address the tension between authority and freedom in Rousseau's political thought by examining his personal circumstances.

6.1016 **McNeil**, G. H., 'The anti-revolutionary Rousseau', *Am. Hist. Rev.*, 58, 1953, 808–23. Presents his political thought as conservative in tone.

6.1017 —— 'The cult of Rousseau and the French Revolution', *J. Hist. Ideas*, 6, 1945, 197–212. Argues that the *Social Contract* acquired cult status during the Revolution and examines how opposing factions used the text to further their political ends.

6.1018 **Malkin**, E. E., 'Rousseau and Epictetus', *Sts. Voltaire*, 106, 1973, 113–55. Debunks the standard view that Rousseau's favourable disposition to stoicism was due to the influence of Seneca.

6.1019 **Manuel**, F. E., 'A dream of Eupsychia', *Daedalus*, 107, 1978, 1–12. A thoughtful examination of Rousseau's utopianism.

6.1020 **Marini**, F., 'Popular sovereignty but representative government: the other Rousseau', *Midwest Journal of Political Science*, 11, 1967, 451–70.

6.1021 **Marshall**, T. E., 'Rousseau and Enlightenment', *Pol. Theory*, 6, 1978, 421–55. Concentrating upon his defence of ignorance against the Enlightenment, the author suggests that his real hostility to the latter emerges from his belief in republican liberty.

6.1022 **Mason**, J. H., 'Individuals in society: Rousseau's republican vision', *Hist. Pol. Thought*, 10, 1989, 89–112. Attempts to explain the apparently contradictory elements in his political thought by relating his notions of social evolution and embryonic sociology to his political ideas.

6.1023 —— 'Reading Rousseau's First Discourse', *Sts. Voltaire*, 249, 1986, 251–66.

6.1024 **Masters**, R. D., *The Political Philosophy of Rousseau*, Princeton, N.J., 1968. Detailed exegesis of *Émile*, the first and second discourses, and the *Social Contract*.

6.1025 **Melzer**, A. M., 'Rousseau and the problem of bourgeois society', *Am. Pol. Sc. Rev.*, 74, 1980, 1018–33. Explores his critique of bourgeois society on the basis of its fragmentation of human souls, and his argument that psychic and social unity are interdependent and must be fostered through patriotism and virtue.

6.1026 —— 'Rousseau's moral realism: replacing natural law with the general will', *Am. Pol. Sc. Rev.*, 77, 1983, 633–51. Analyses his conception of natural 'man', natural law, and his critique of social corruption.

6.1027 —— *The Natural Goodness of Man: On the System of Rousseau's Thought*, Chicago, Ill., 1990. Examines this idea in his thought, showing how it provides the basis for his conceptualisation of the social contract.

6.1028 **Meyer**, P. H., 'The individual and society in Rousseau's *Émile*', *Mod. Lang. Q.*, 19, 1958, 99–114.

6.1029 **Miller**, J., *Rousseau: Dreamer of Democracy*, New Haven, Conn., 1984. Claims, against the trend of recent interpretation, that his ideas were democratic and revolutionary.

6.1030 **Moore**, S., 'Rousseau on alienation and the rights of man', *Hist. Pol. Thought*, 12, 1991, 73–85. Argues that he was the precursor of democratic socialism.

6.1031 **Morphos**, P. P., 'Renaissance tradition in Rousseau's second discourse', *Mod. Lang. Q.*, 13, 1952, 81–9. Argues that Rousseau and other eighteenth-century French thinkers were strongly influenced by Renaissance thought.

6.1032 **Neumann**, H., 'Philosophy and freedom: an interpretation of Rousseau's state of nature', *J. Gen. Ed.*, 27, 1976, 301–7. Examines his supposed belief in the superiority of the pre-social individual.

6.1033 **Nisbet**, R., 'Rousseau and equality', *Encounter*, 43, 1974, 40–51. Provides a brief résumé of the first and second *Discourses*, and proceeds with a comparative analysis of his conceptions of power and equality.

6.1034 **Noble**, R., 'Freedom and sentiment in Rousseau's philosophical anthropology', *Hist. Pol. Thought*, 9, 1988, 263–83. Discusses his conception of liberty in relation to his account of the evolution from nature to society.

6.1035 **Noland**, A., 'Rousseau and nineteenth-century French socialism', *Sts. Voltaire*, 57, 1967, 1097–122. Assesses his influence on Fourier, Proudhon, Cabet, Saint-Simon, Louis Blanc and Leroux.

6.1036 **Noone**, J. B., *Rousseau's Social Contract: A Conceptual Analysis*, 1981.

6.1037 —— 'Rousseau's theory of natural law as conditional', *J. Hist. Ideas*, 33, 1972, 23–42. Argues that he did not regard natural law as irrelevant, but believed that its obligatory character depends on an inner faith in the existence of God.

6.1038 —— 'The social contract and the idea of sovereignty in Rousseau', *J. Pol.*, 32, 1970, 696–708. Interprets the social contract as informed by a definition of moral consent and made up of a detailed set of procedural rules.

6.1039 **O'Hagan**, T., 'On Rousseau's *Social Contract*: translation and exegesis', *Hist. Pol. Thought*, 3, 1982, 245–68. Analysis of the problems of translation and linguistic misinterpretation in political thought, focusing on the *Social Contract*.

6.1040 **Okin**, S. M., 'Rousseau's natural woman', *J. Pol.*, 41, 1979, 393–416. A feminist critique of his patriarchal assumptions.

6.1041 **O'Neal**, J. C., 'Rousseau's theory of wealth', *Hist. Euro. Ideas*, 7, 1986, 453–67.

6.1042 **Osborn**, A. M., *Rousseau and Burke: A Study of the Idea of Liberty in Eighteenth-Century Political Thought*, New York, 1964. Unusual and unconvincing comparison of these thinkers, attempting to synthesise their conclusions, so that 'Rousseau bequeathed to posterity the constructive principles upon which a free society must be based; while Burke gave warning of the dangers that surrounded a democratic constitution'.

6.1043 **Peled**, Y., 'Rousseau's inhibited radicalism: an analysis of his political thought in light of his economic ideas', *Am. Pol. Sc. Rev.*, 74, 1980, 1034–45. Focuses on the contradiction between his economic (especially his defence of private property) and his political ideas.

6.1044 **Perkins**, M. L., *Jean-Jacques Rousseau on the Individual and Society*, Lexington, Ky., 1974. Argues that for Rousseau the ideal society is one in which individuals can enjoy their liberties whilst accepting the constraints imposed by the common good.

6.1045 —— 'Liberty and the concept of legitimacy in the *Discours sur l'inégalité*', *Sts. Voltaire*, 89, 1972, 1293–304.

6.1046 —— 'Rousseau on history, liberty, and national survival', *Sts. Voltaire*, 53, 1967, 76–169. Detailed study of the influence of ancient thinkers such as Polybius, Sallust and Tacitus on Rousseau's conception of history.

6.1047 **Plamenatz**, J., 'Pascal and Rousseau', *Pol. Sts.*, 10, 1962, 248–63. Suggests that Rousseau's thought was fundamentally liberal, and reveals how he translated certain religious and social ideas familiar to Pascal into political terms.

6.1048 **Plattner**, M. F., *Rousseau's State of Nature: An Interpretation of the Discourse on Inequality*, Dekalb, Ill., 1979. Demonstrates that the tension between individualism and collectivism in his thought can be traced to the 'low or "primitive" view of human nature presented in the *Second Discourse*'.

6.1049 **Porter**, J. M., 'Rousseau: will and politics', in J. M. Porter and R. Vernon, ed., *Unity, Plurality and Politics*, 1986, 52–74. Through a reading of the *Social Contract* Porter reveals the importance of the concept of will in grounding his political project.

6.1050 **Rapaport**, E., 'On the future of love: Rousseau and the radical feminists', *Phil. Forum*, 5, 1973–74, 185–205.

6.1051 **Rempel**, H. D., 'On forcing people to be free', *Ethics*, 87, 1976–77, 18–34. Defend this notion as compatible with liberalism, arguing that Rousseau deployed the idea rhetorically to throw light upon the general will.

6.1052 **Riley**, P., 'A possible explanation of Rousseau's general will', *Am. Pol. Sc. Rev.*, 64, 1970, 86–97. Interprets the concept as originating from a combination of ancient emphases on cohesiveness and modern concerns for voluntarism.

6.1053 —— 'Rousseau's general will: freedom of a particular kind', *Pol. Sts.*, 39, 1991, 55–74. Compares his conception of the general will with Kant's idea of 'good will'.

6.1054 **Ritter**, G., 'Direct democracy and totalitarianism', *Diogenes*, 7, 1954, 59–67. An ideologically charged interpretation of Rousseau as a forerunner of twentieth-century totalitarianism.

6.1055 **Roche**, K. F., *Rousseau: Stoic and Romantic*, 1974. Argues that his principal ideas have a Stoic ancestry.

6.1056 **Roosevelt**, G. G., 'A reconstruction of Rousseau's fragments on the state of war', *Hist. Pol. Thought*, 8, 1987, 225–44. Translation of some of his unpublished writings on war and the power relations between states, prefaced by a brief introduction.

6.1057 **Rosenberg**, A., 'Rousseau's *Lévite d'Ephraïm* and the Golden Age', *Australian Journal of French Studies*, 15, 1978, 163–72.

6.1058 —— 'Rousseau's view of work and leisure in the community', *Australian Journal of French Studies*, 18, 1981, 3–12.

6.1059 **Rosenfeld**, D., 'Rousseau's unanimous contract and the doctrine of popular sovereignty', *Hist. Pol. Thought*, 8, 1987, 83–111. Questions his democratic credentials, stressing that he never advocated even universal adult male suffrage. Whilst he may have been the champion of popular sovereignty, his conception of what constituted the people was severely limited.

6.1060 **Rule**, J. C., 'Jean-Jacques Rousseau: democrat or totalitarian?', *Critical Issues in*

History, 4, 1967, 490–2.

6.1061 **Salkever**, S. G., 'Interpreting Rousseau's paradoxes', *Eighteenth-Cent. Sts.*, 11, 1977–78, 204–26. Argues that his work is fraught with contradictions.

6.1062 **Schwartz**, J., *The Sexual Politics of Jean-Jacques Rousseau*, Chicago, Ill., 1984.

6.1063 **Shklar**, J. N., 'Jean-Jacques Rousseau and equality', *Daedalus*, 107, 1978, 13–26.

6.1064 —— *Men and Citizens. A Study of Rousseau's Social Theory*, 1969. Powerful study of his political and social thought, depicting him as 'the last of the classical utopists'.

6.1065 —— 'Rousseau's images of authority', *Am. Pol. Sc. Rev.*, 58, 1964, 919–32. Focuses upon the bipolarity in his work between the spontaneous march to inequality and oppression in which all participate.

6.1066 —— 'Rousseau's two models: Sparta and the age of gold', *Pol. Sc. Q.*, 81, 1966, 25–51. A rigorous analysis of his ideas on justice and equality within the context of his historical models.

6.1067 **Silverthorne**, M. J., 'Rousseau's Plato', *Sts. Voltaire*, 116, 1973, 235–49. Through a careful reading of Rousseau's annotated version of Plato's work, the author demonstrates the influence of Plato on his political thinking, especially the *Laws* upon his image of political society.

6.1068 **Simon-Ingram**, J., 'Rousseau and the problem of community: nationalism, civic virtue, totalitarianism', *Hist. Euro. Ideas*, 16, 1993, 23–9.

6.1069 **Skillen**, A., 'Rousseau and the fall of social man', *Phil.*, 60, 1985, 105–21. Critique of other commentators for failing to convey his 'dialectic of despair, whereby in the very act of coming together in the fullest desire for community, human beings are impelled into a spinning decline with an "inequality and vice" marked by radical self-estrangement and misery as well as material squalor'.

6.1070 **Sorenson**, L. R., 'Rousseau's liberalism', *Hist. Pol. Thought*, 11, 1990, 443–66. Portrays his political thought as a revision of early liberalism, arguing that in criticising doctrines of natural law and natural right he left his own conception of freedom without foundation.

6.1071 **Spurlin**, P. M., 'Rousseau in America, 1760–1809', *French American Review*, 1, 1948, 8–16. Assesses the extent to which Americans were acquainted with his political ideas.

6.1072 **Starobinski**, J., 'Jean-Jacques Rousseau', *Procs. Brit. Acad.*, 62, 1976, 95–107. A survey of his critique of 'polite' society and belief in the natural individual.

6.1073 —— *Jean-Jacques Rousseau: Transparency and Obstruction*, Chicago, Ill., 1988. An informed analysis, showing how his ideas were shaped by his personal circumstances.

6.1074 —— 'The accuser and the accused', *Daedalus*, 107, 1978, 41–58. Examines the importance of rhetoric in Rousseau's writings.

6.1075 **Steinberg**, J., *Locke, Rousseau, and the Idea of Consent: An Inquiry into the Liberal-Democratic Theory of Political Obligation*, Westport, Conn., 1978. Thoughtful survey of the 'use of the consent theory of political obligation in the liberal-democratic tradition', juxtaposing Locke's 'non-consent theory' of obligation with Rousseau's use of consent thinking. Celebrates the latter's reconciliation of law and moral obligation via the autonomous individual against Locke's 'privatisation' of autonomy which has influenced the subsequent liberal tradition.

6.1076 **Strauss**, L., 'On the intention of Rousseau', *Social Res.*, 14, 1947, 455–87.

6.1077 **Strauss-Lipschutz**, S., 'Rousseau on moral autonomy and political participation', *Michigan Academician*, 5, 1972, 41–55.

6.1078 **Symcox**, G., 'The wild man's return: the enclosed vision of Rousseau's *Discourses*', in E. Dudley, *et al.*, ed., *The Wild Man Within. An Image in Western Thought from the Renaissance to Romanticism*, Pittsburgh, Penn., 1972, 223–47. Illustrates his rejection of the contemporary image of the rational savage in favour of an emotionally determined 'Wild Man' – a counterpoint to the corrupt and effete society in which he lived.

6.1079 **Tanner**, T., 'Julie and "La Maison Paternelle": another look at Rousseau's *La Nouvelle Héloïse*', in J. B. Elshtain, ed., *The Family in Political Thought*, 1982, 96–124. Examines his critique of bourgeois family life.

6.1080 **Taylor**, S. S. B., 'Rousseau's contemporary reputation in France', *Sts. Voltaire*, 27, 1963, 1545–74. Assesses the eighteenth-century reception of his literary, religious, political, and educational works.

6.1081 **Teichgraeber**, R., 'Rousseau's argument for property', *Hist. Euro. Ideas*, 2, 1981, 115–34.

6.1082 **Temmer**, M., *Time in Rousseau and Kant: An Essay on French Pre-Romanticism*, Geneva, 1958.

6.1083 **Thakurdas**, F., *Rousseau and the Concept of the General Will: The Pursuit of an Elusive Concept*, Calcutta, 1976. A straightforward account of this notion.

6.1084 **Thomas**, P., 'Jean-Jacques Rousseau, sexist?', *Feminist Studies*, 17, 1991, 195–218.

6.1085 **Topazio**, V. W., 'A re-evaluation of Rousseau's political doctrine', in C. G. S. Williams, ed., *Literature and History in the Age of Ideas: Essays on the French Enlightenment Presented to George R. Havens*, Columbus, Ohio, 1975, 179–92. Pays particular attention to the ideas of sovereignty and the general will.

6.1086 —— 'Rousseau and Pirandello: a quest for identity and dignity', *Sts. Voltaire*, 58, 1967, 1577–92.

6.1087 —— 'Rousseau: humanism and humanitarianism', *Kentucky Romance Quarterly*, 20, 1973, 403–13. Contends that because he distrusted individuals, and in consequence led a solitary existence, his writings can in no way be seen as humanitarian. Yet, he was a humanist, Topazio argues, since he believed in the fulfilment and enrichment of the individual.

6.1088 —— 'Rousseau, man of contradictions', *Sts. Voltaire*, 18, 1961, 77–93.

6.1089 **Vance**, C. M., 'Rousseau's autobiographical venture: a process of negation', *Genre*, 6, 1973, 98–114. Analyses his autobiographical writings with particular reference to the question of the rapport between the individual and the social.

6.1090 —— *The Extravagant Shepherd: A Study of the Pastoral Vision in Rousseau's 'Nouvelle Héloïse'*, 1973.

6.1091 **Viroli**, M., *Jean-Jacques Rousseau and the 'well-ordered society'*, 1988. Sharp, careful study which revises 'the image of Rousseau as a disciple of the school of natural law in order to see his political doctrine as one of the last stages in the long history of republicanism'.

6.1092 —— 'Republic and politics in Machiavelli and Rousseau', *Hist. Pol. Thought*, 10, 1989, 405–20. Compares their usage of the republican vocabulary, concluding that important differences separated them even though they both belonged to the civic republican tradition.

6.1093 —— 'The concept of ordre and the language of classical republicanism in Jean-Jacques Rousseau', in A. Pagden, ed., *The Language of Political Theory in Early-Modern Europe*, 1987, 159–78. Analyses the notion of 'political order' in his thought, and its connection with his belief in the rule of law within the Republic.

6.1094 **Waldmann**, T., 'Rousseau on the general will and the legislator', *Pol. Sts.*, 8, 1960, 221–30. His conception of the general will is here viewed in terms of law and public utility, with the legislator acting as a constitutional interpreter.

6.1095 **Watt**, E. D., 'Rousseau rechaufée: being obliged, consenting, participating and obeying only oneself', *J. Pol.*, 43, 1981, 707–19. Dismisses his theory of participatory democracy as a pipe-dream.

6.1096 **Weirich**, P., 'Rousseau on proportional majority rule', *Philos. & Phenom. Res.*, 47, 1986–87, 111–26. Argues that for Rousseau proportional majority rule is the best practical expression of the general will.

6.1097 **Weiss**, P., 'Rousseau, anti-feminism and woman's nature', *Pol. Theory*, 15, 1987, 81–98. Suggests that the differentiation between the sexes in his work was not based on a belief in natural sexual difference, but was politically motivated.

6.1098 —— and **Harper**, A., 'Rousseau's political defense of the sex-roled family', *Hypatia*, 5, 1990, 90–109. Demonstrates how he rejected both the aristocratic and bourgeois families as models for the ideal political régime, favouring instead a conception of the family designed to nurture virtuous citizens.

6.1099 **Wexler**, V. G., ' "Made for man's delight": Rousseau as antifeminist', *Am. Hist. Rev.*, 81, 1976, 266–91. Examines his misogyny in the full context of his life and work.

6.1100 **Wilkins**, B. T., 'The nature of Rousseau', *J. Pol.*, 21, 1959, 663–84.

6.1101 **Willhoite**, F. H., 'Rousseau's political religion', *Rev. Pol.*, 27, 1965, 501–15.

6.1102 **Winwar**, F., *J.-J. Rousseau, Conscience of an Era*, New York, 1961.

6.1103 **Wokler**, R., 'A reply to Charvet: Rousseau

and the perfectibility of man', *Hist. Pol. Thought*, 1, 1980, 81–90. Attacks Charvet's interpretation of the idea of pity in Rousseau's writings and his neglect of the totality of Rousseau's moral theory.

6.1104 —— 'Perfectible apes in decadent cultures: Rousseau's anthropology revisited', *Daedalus*, 107, 1978, 107–34. Examines his anthropology, especially his views on the individual, in an attempt to illuminate his political thought.

6.1105 —— 'Rousseau and Marx', in D. Miller and L. A. Siedentop, ed., *The Nature of Political Theory*, 1983, 219–46. Argues that Marx's knowledge of Rousseau is largely skewed, focusing on its revolutionary implications rather than attempting to arrive at a comprehensive understanding. Demonstrates that Marx's reading of Rousseau is derived largely from that of Hegel.

6.1106 —— 'Rousseau's perfectibilian libertarianism', in A. Ryan, ed., *The Idea of Freedom: Essays in Honour of Isaiah Berlin*, 1979, 233–52. Suggests that his conception of perfectibility cannot be seen as a doctrine of social progress.

6.1107 —— 'Rousseau's two concepts of liberty', in G. Feaver and F. Rosen, ed., *Lives, Liberties and the Public Good*, 1987, 61–100. His defence of liberty is highly illiberal according to this interpretation.

6.1108 —— *Social Thought of Jean-Jacques Rousseau*, New York, 1987. A thorough study of Rousseau's works from 1750–56, tracing the influence of Diderot on his thought, and arguing that the *First Discourse* is the 'most shallow and least original' of his texts.

6.1109 —— 'The influence of Diderot on the political theory of Rousseau: two aspects of a relationship', *Sts. Voltaire*, 132, 1975, 55–111. Argues that Diderot exercised a profound influence on Rousseau's political thought, especially upon his preliminary formulation of natural rights and general will.

6.1110 **Wood**, E. M., 'The state and popular sovereignty in French political thought: a genealogy of Rousseau's "general will" ', *Hist. Pol. Thought*, 4, 1983, 281–315. Argues that the contours of Rousseau's discourse must be set in the context of French early modern history, dominated by two dilemmas which never figured centrally in English history: a divided polity which could not overcome the corporate fragmentation of its feudal past; and a state conceived as a kind of *private property*, a resource for princes and officeholders.

Vico

6.1111 **Barnouw**, J., 'The critique of classical republicanism and the understanding of modern forms of polity in Vico's *New Science*', *Clio*, 9, 1980, 393–418.

6.1112 **Berlin**, I., *Vico and Herder: Two Studies in the History of Ideas*, 1976. Enlightening interpretation, emphasising the originality of his understanding of historical development.

6.1113 —— 'Vico and the idea of the Enlightenment', *Social Res.*, 43, 1976, 640–53. Suggests that for Vico the idea of attaining a perfect society was conceptually flawed, especially because of his view of Providence.

6.1114 **Burke**, P., *Vico*, 1985.

6.1115 **Costa**, G., 'Vico and ancient rhetoric', in R. R. Bolgar, ed., *Classical Influences on Western Thought, 1950–1870*, 1979, 247–62. Explores the significance of his *Institutiones Oratoriae* for his political thought.

6.1116 —— 'Vico's political thought in his time and ours', *Social Res.*, 43, 1976, 612–24. Outlines his generally neglected political principles, especially his critique of rationality.

6.1117 **Haddock**, B. A., *Vico's Political Thought*, 1986.

6.1118 **Hutton**, P., 'Vico's theory of history and the French Revolutionary tradition', *J. Hist. Ideas*, 37, 1976, 241–56.

6.1119 **Jacobitti**, E. E., 'Political thought and rhetoric in Vico', *New Vico Studies*, 4, 1986, 73–89.

6.1120 **Mali**, J., 'The poetics of politics: Vico's "philosophy of authority" ', *Hist. Pol. Thought*, 10, 1989, 41–69. Focusing on the question of political myths, the author suggests that Vico's concept of authority allowed him to theorise myths in a quasi-materialist manner.

6.1121 **Mantano**, R., 'Vico's opposition to Enlightenment', *Ital. Q.*, 17, 1974, 3–34.

6.1122 **Tagliacozzo**, G., *Giambattista Vico: An International Symposium*, Baltimore, Md., 1969. Includes D. Faucci, 'Vico and

Grotius: jurisconsults of mankind', E. Kamenka, 'Vico and Marxism', and S. Caramella, 'Vico, Tacitus, and reason of state'.

6.1123 —— with **Mooney**, M., and **Verene**, D. P., ed., *Vico and Contemporary Thought*, 1980. Includes G. Costa, 'Vico's political thought in his time and ours', R. Nisbet, 'Vico and the idea of progress', and I. Berlin, 'Vico and the ideal of enlightenment'.

6.1124 —— ed., *Vico and Marx: Affinities and Contrasts*, 1983. Includes A. Pons, 'Vico, Marx, utopia and history', J. Barnoum, 'Man making history: the role of the plebeians in Vico, the proletariat in Marx', J. O'Neill, 'Naturalism in Vico and Marx: a theory of the body politic'.

6.1125 —— and **Verene**, D. P., ed., *Giambattista Vico's Science of Humanity*, Baltimore, Md., 1976. A central argument of these 28 essays is that Vico's belief in history should be seen as complementing Enlightenment ideas on reason and universalism by furnishing them with a critical dimension.

6.1126 **Valcone**, J. L., 'Vico's human science: the paradox of consciousness and access to social action', *Southern Journal of Philosophy*, 18, 1980, 371–92. Clarifies his conception of history and theory of social action through an examination of his *New Science*.

6.1127 **Vaughan**, F., *The Political Philosophy of Giambattista Vico: An Introduction to La Scienza Nuova*, The Hague, 1972. Argues that he pretended to admire the orthodox Christian view of history, but in fact drew upon Bacon and Spinoza to undermine it.

Voltaire

6.1128 **Ayer**, A. J., *Voltaire*, 1986. An engaging and lively account of his historical, dramatic, religious and philosophical writings.

6.1129 **Besterman**, T., 'Voltaire, absolute monarchy, and the enlightened monarch', *Sts. Voltaire*, 32, 1965, 7–21. Suggests that his resolute opposition to rule by committee and belief that great things are only achieved through the wisdom of an individual led him to the 'conviction that the only possible system of government for France was an absolute monarchy'.

6.1130 **Brumfitt**, J. H., 'History and propaganda in Voltaire', *Sts. Voltaire*, 24, 1963, 271–87. A detailed examination of Voltaire's principal historical works from *La Philosophie de l'Histoire*, *Le Siècle de Louis XIV*, to the *Dictionnaire Philosophique*, concluding that his historical writings are marked by a tension between a distinct political aim, the desire to instruct and moralise, and the wish to provide an objective and reliable historical method.

6.1131 **Crocker**, L. G., 'Voltaire and the political philosophers', *Sts. Voltaire*, 219, 1983, 1–17. Rushes through Voltaire's reading of the principal thinkers in Western political thought, focusing briefly upon his understanding of natural law, political virtue and the state.

6.1132 —— 'Voltaire's struggle for humanism', *Sts. Voltaire*, 4, 1957, 137–69.

6.1133 **Gay**, P., 'Voltaire's *Idées Républicaines*: a study in bibliography and interpretation', *Sts. Voltaire*, 6, 1958, 67–105.

6.1134 —— *Voltaire's Politics: The Poet as Realist*, Princeton, N.J., 1959. Examines his ideas on intellectual and civil liberty and 'constitutional absolutism', teasing out a series of contradictions in his thought between individual liberty and political authority.

6.1135 **Gossman**, L., 'Voltaire's Heavenly City', *Eighteenth-Cent. Sts.*, 3, 1969, 67–82. Examines the relation between literature, philosophy and utopianism in his writings.

6.1136 **Matthews**, R. E., 'Political allusions in Voltaire's "Les lois de Minos" ', *Nottingham French Studies*, 12, 1973, 11–22. Sets out his portrayal of the relation between liberty and authority and church and state.

6.1137 **Meyer**, H., 'Voltaire on war and peace', *Sts. Voltaire*, 142, 1976, 9–202. Comprehensive account of his pacifism.

6.1138 **Perkins**, M. L., 'Voltaire's principles of political thought', *Mod. Lang. Q.*, 17, 1956, 289–300. A rigorous analysis revealing the consistent theoretical basis of his political thought.

6.1139 **Rowe**, C., *Voltaire and the State*, New York, 1955. While the first part is a biographical study, the second analyses his political ideas.

6.1140 **Tate**, R. S., 'Voltaire and the question of law and order in the eighteenth century: Locke against Hobbes', in J. H. Fox, M. H. Waddicor and D. A. Watts, ed.,

Studies in Eighteenth-Century French Literature, 1975, 269–85. Interesting discussion of his political theory, purporting to detect in it both liberal and conservative strands.

6.1141 **Thielemann**, L., 'Voltaire and Hobbism', *Sts. Voltaire*, 10, 1959, 237–58. Demonstrates how Voltaire's work was influenced by, yet challenged, the thought of Hobbes.

6.1142 **Todd**, C., *Voltaire: Dictionnaire Philosophique*, 1980. Straightforward presentation of the principal ideas elaborated in the *Dictionnaire*.

6.1143 **Topazio**, V. W., 'Voltaire and Rousseau: humanists and humanitarians in conflict', *Rice University Studies*, 59, 1973, 83–92.

6.1144 —— 'Voltaire: "king" of the *philosophes*', in A. J. Bingham and V. W. Topazio, ed., *Enlightenment Studies in Honour of Lester G. Crocker*, 1979, 337–48. Examines his political and philosophical ideas, emphasising the extent to which they differ from those of the other *philosophes*.

6.1145 **Wade**, I. O., *The Intellectual Development of Voltaire*, Princeton, N.J., 1969. Large intellectual biography.

6.1146 **Waldinger**, R., *Voltaire and Reform in the Light of the French Revolution*, Geneva, 1959. A lucid account of the development of his ideas on social reform.

6.1147 **Werner**, S., 'Voltaire and Seneca', *Sts. Voltaire*, 67, 1969, 29–44. Thorough analysis of Seneca's influence on Voltaire's thought.

Other thinkers

6.1148 **Aldridge**, A. O., 'Benjamin Franklin and the *philosophes*', *Sts. Voltaire*, 24, 1963, 43–65. Examines the relationship between Franklin and the *philosophes*, surveying their admiration for his ethical and political thought and scientific work.

6.1149 **Baker**, K. M., 'A script for a French Revolution: the political consciousness of the abbé Mably', *Eighteenth-Cen. Sts*, 14, 1981, 235–63. Close analysis of *Des droits et des devoirs du citoyen*.

6.1150 **Barclay**, L., 'Louis de Bonald, prophet of the past?', *Sts. Voltaire*, 55, 1967, 167–204. On a counter-revolutionary thinker who sought to discredit the political and ethical writings of Montesquieu, Rousseau and Condorcet.

6.1151 **Barnard**, F. M., *Herder's Social and Political Thought: From Enlightenment to Nationalism*, 1965. Analyses his ideas on the state, society, history and progress.

6.1152 **Bellamy**, R., ' "Da metafisico a mercatante" – Antonio Genovese and the development of a new language of commerce in eighteenth-century Naples', in A. Pagden, ed., *The Languages of Political Theory in Early-Modern Europe*, 1987, 277–99. Outlines Genovese's moral anthropology which he used to reconcile the claims of morality and commerce.

6.1153 **Berlin**, I., 'Herder and the Enlightenment', in E. R. Wasserman, ed., *Aspects of the Eighteenth Century*, Baltimore, Md., 1965, 47–104. Brilliant exploration of the three main ideas in Herder's thought which run against the current of the age – 'Populism, Expressionism, and Pluralism'.

6.1154 **Bingham**, A. J., 'Marie Joseph Chénier, ideologue and critic', *Sts. Voltaire*, 94, 1972, 219–76. Rigorous account of his principal ideas, focusing on his understanding of education as leading to the overthrow of intellectual and political despotism and the creation of a just political order.

6.1155 **Caplow**, T., 'St. Pierre and the project of perpetual peace', *Tocqueville Review*, 8, 1986–87, 111–23. Examines Charles Irenee Castel de Saint-Pierre's plan to establish peace in Europe.

6.1156 **Cavanaugh**, G. J., 'Turgot: the rejection of enlightened despotism', *French Historical Studies*, 6, 1969, 31–58. Argues that he was critical of the Physiocrat belief in absolutism, yet did not support mass political participation, favouring instead a prudent political régime moving a people 'to maturity and self-reliance'.

6.1157 **Chevallier**, J. J., 'The failure of Mirabeau's political ideas', *Rev. Pol.*, 13, 1951, 88–107. Explains why his proposed 'ministerial' system appealed to neither side in the French Revolution.

6.1158 **Cobban**, A., 'The fundamental ideas of Robespierre', *Eng. Hist. Rev.*, 63, 1948, 29–51. A clear and concise presentation of his political ideas, examining the influence of Rousseau on his thought, especially with regard to popular sovereignty.

6.1159 —— 'The political ideas of Maximilien Robespierre during the period of the Convention', *Eng. Hist. Rev.*, 61, 1946,

45–80. Examines his ideas on monarchy, oligarchy, political sovereignty and military dictatorship.

6.1160 **Cohen**, D. K., 'The Viscomte de Bonald's critique of industrialism', *J. Mod. Hist.*, 41, 1969, 475–84. Suggests that he 'applied to economic change a critical apparatus derived from a political conservatism which grew in part out of the experience of the French Revolution'.

6.1161 **Coward**, D., *The Philosophy of Restif de La Bretonne*, 1991. The first comprehensive account of his moral and political thought.

6.1162 **Fehér**, F., *The Frozen Revolution: An Essay on Jacobinism*, 1987. Sharp analysis of the political ideas of the Jacobin régime, including a substantial critique of earlier historiography.

6.1163 **Fink**, B. C., 'The case for a political system in Sade', *Sts. Voltaire*, 88, 1972, 493–512. Attempts to tease out those elements in Sade's thought that ground a coherent political project.

6.1164 **Forsyth**, M., *Reason and Revolution: The Political Thought of the Abbé Sieyès*, 1987. Argues that Sieyès, far from being an impractical and metaphysically inclined doctrinaire, was a pragmatic libertarian with concerns not far removed from the contemporary English radical movement.

6.1165 **Gallanar**, J., 'Argenson's "Platonic Republics" ', *Sts. Voltaire*, 56, 1967, 557–75. Provides an account of his political thought through a rigorous textual analysis of three editions of *Considérations sur le gouvernement ancien et présent de la France*, contending that it culminates in a utilitarian conception of enlightened monarchy.

6.1166 **Gat**, A., 'Clausewitz's political and ethical world view', *Pol. Sts.*, 37, 1989, 97–106. Argues for the coherence of Clausewitz's political and ethical beliefs, the character of which were affected by the changing terms of political debate and thought within Germany.

6.1167 **Head**, B. W., *Ideology and Social Science: Destutt de Tracy and French Liberalism*, Dordrecht, 1985. Examines the work of de Tracy in relation to the formation of the concept of ideology and social science.

6.1168 **Horowitz**, I. L., *Claude Helvétius: Philosopher of Democracy and Enlightenment*, New York, 1954. A Marxist interpretation of his ideas.

6.1169 **Kelly**, G. A., 'The political thought of Lamoignon de Malesherbes', *Pol. Theory* 7, 1979, 485–508. A full consideration of this exemplar of the eighteenth-century 'constitutionalist' tradition of French thought, whose reformist and cautious mentality made him enemies among the French revolutionaries.

6.1170 **Kennedy**, E., *A Philosophe in the Age of Revolution: Destutt de Tracy and the Origin of 'Ideology'*, Philadelphia, Penn., 1978. The first comprehensive study of the originator of the concept.

6.1171 **Kissinger**, H. A., 'The conservative dilemma: reflections on the political thought of Metternich', *Am. Pol. Sc. Rev.* 48, 1954, 1017–30. Suggests that Metternich, unlike Burke, chose the terrain of reason to combat contemporary radical ideas and viewed conservatism as necessary to limit the claims of power.

6.1172 **Klinck**, D. M., 'The strange relationship of Rousseau to the French counter-revolution as seen in the early works of Louis de Bonald', *The Consortium on Revolutionary Europe, 1750–1850: Proceedings 1980*, 1, 1980, Athens, Ga., 14–22.

6.1173 **Ladd**, E. C., 'Helvétius and d'Holbach: la moralisation de la politique', *J. Hist. Ideas* 23, 1962, 221–38. Compares their ideas on utilitarian ethics, social reform and constitutional, or enlightened, monarchy.

6.1174 **Lebrun**, R. A., 'Joseph de Maistre and Rousseau', *Sts. Voltaire*, 88, 1972, 881–98. Argues that whilst Maistre was initially sympathetic to the ideas expressed in Rousseau's first discourse, *Émile*, and the *Nouvelle Héloïse*, he reacted violently against his political ideas after the French Revolution.

6.1175 —— *Throne and Altar: The Political and Religious Thought of Joseph de Maistre*, Ottawa, 1965. One of the most thorough accounts to date of his life and work.

6.1176 **Levine**, A., 'Robespierre: critic of Rousseau', *Can. J. Phil.*, 8, 1978, 543–57. Examines Robespierre's political practice in the light of Rousseau's political philosophy.

6.1177 **Levy**, D., 'Despotism in Simon-Nicholas-Henri Linguet's science of society: theory and application', *Sts. Voltaire*, 191, 1980, 761–68. Portrays Linguet as an anti-*philosophe* and anti-liberal, focusing on his view of property as a justification for monarchial absolutism.

6.1178 —— *The Ideas and Careers of Simon-Nicholas-Henri Linguet: A Study in Eighteenth-Century French Politics*, Chicago, Ill., 1980.

6.1179 **McConnell**, A., 'Helvétius' Russian pupils', *J. Hist. Ideas*, 24, 1963, 373–86. Discusses Helvétius's influence on one of the founders of the Russian radical intelligentsia, Alexander Radishchev (1749–1802), and provides an account of Helvétius's views on despotism, anticlericalism, utilitarianism, and social reform.

6.1180 **McKenzie**, A. T., 'Giuseppe Baretti and the "republic of letters" in the eighteenth century', *Sts. Voltaire*, 193, 1980, 1813–22. Contends that 'the republic of letters' is distinct from the political republic as it was not concerned with the problems of foreign relations, armies, or power; nevertheless, the two were limited by the idea of 'the institutionalisation of civic virtue'.

6.1181 **Maestro**, M., *Gaetano Filangieri and his 'Science of Legislation'*, 1976. Short introduction to his political thought.

6.1182 **Matrat**, J., *Robespierre: The Tyranny of the Majority*, 1975.

6.1183 **Mead**, W., 'The Marquis de Sade: politics on a human scale', *Esprit Créateur*, 3, 1963, 188–98. Explores his idea of freedom.

6.1184 **Medlin**, D., 'André Morellet, translator of liberal thought', *Sts. Voltaire*, 174, 1978, 189–201. Examines the liberal foundations of his political and social thought.

6.1185 **Meyer**, P. H., 'The French Revolution and the legacy of the philosophes', *French Review*, 30, 1956–57, 429–34. Particular attention is devoted to Jean François de la Harpe's political and religious attacks upon the ideas of the Enlightenment.

6.1186 **Morgan**, M. L., 'Liberalism in Mendelssohn's *Jerusalem*', *Hist. Pol. Thought*, 10, 1989, 281–94. Suggests a dissonance within the conceptions of the self deployed by Mendelssohn in his most famous work.

6.1187 **Murray**, J. C., 'The political thought of Joseph de Maistre', *Rev. Pol.*, 11, 1949, 63–86.

6.1188 **Pappé**, H. O., 'Sismondi's system of liberty', *J. Hist. Ideas*, 40, 1979, 251–66. Examines his contribution to the eighteenth-century debate on the relation between the individual, the state, and society.

6.1189 **Payne**, H. C., *The 'Philosophes' and the People*, New Haven, Conn., 1976. Examines their attitude and relation to the people in the light of their stated objective of eliminating superstition upon which much of the power of the *ancien régime* rested.

6.1190 **Perkins**, M. L., 'Civil theology in the writings of the Abbé de Saint-Pierre', *J. Hist. Ideas*, 18, 1957, 242–53. Presents him as a civil theologian concerned with the articles of faith needed to sustain republican government.

6.1191 —— 'The Leviathan and Saint-Pierre's Projet de paix perpétuelle', *Procs. Am. Phil. Soc.*, 99, 1955, 259–67. Argues that Saint-Pierre's conception of the neo-European republic was an extension of the Hobbesian civil common wealth.

6.1192 —— *The Moral and Political Philosophy of the Abbé de Saint-Pierre*, Geneva, 1959. A thorough account of his political ideas.

6.1193 —— 'Voltaire and the abbé de Saint-Pierre on world peace', *Sts. Voltaire*, 18, 1961, 9–34. Compares their political and social ideas, particularly their view of human nature and how this relates to the rule of law and perpetual peace.

6.1194 **Perlmutter**, A., 'Carl von Clausewitz, Enlightenment philosopher: a comparative analysis', *Journal of Strategic Studies*, 11, 1988, 7–19. Compares Clauswitz's *On War* with Montesquieu's *The Spirit of the Laws* and Smith's *The Wealth of the Nations*, arguing that this work reveals Clauswitz as a genuinely Enlightenment writer.

6.1195 **Poster**, M., 'The concepts of sexual identity and life cycle in Restif la Bretonne's utopian thought', *Sts. Voltaire*, 73, 1970, 241–71. Examines his utopian thought, establishing its significance for understanding the utopian socialism of the nineteenth century.

6.1196 **Ranum**, O., 'D'Alembert, Tacitus and the political sociology of despotism', *Sts. Voltaire*, 191, 1980, 547–58. Examines the influence of Montesquieu's and the Abbé de Saint-Pierre's classical republican analyses of despotism on d'Alembert's thought.

6.1197 **Ravitch**, N., 'Liberalism, Catholicism, and the abbé Grégoire', *Church Hist.*, 36, 1967, 719–39.

6.1198 **Rose**, R. B., 'Babeuf and the class struggle', *Aust. J. Pol. & Hist.*, 22, 1976, 367–78.

6.1199 —— 'Babeuf, dictatorship and

democracy', *Historical Studies*, 15, 1972, 223–36.

6.1200 —— *Gracchus Babeuf: The First Revolutionary Communist*, Stanford, Cal. 1978. Charts the influence of Rousseau on Babeuf's revolutionary theories and practice.

6.1201 **Schmidt**, R. J., 'Cultural nationalism in Herder', *J. Hist. Ideas*, 17, 1957, 407–17. Contends that Herder, whilst viewing the cultural and historical specificity of each nation as crucial, did not advocate an absolute state as an expression of the nation.

6.1202 **Schwartz**, L., 'F. M. Grimm and the eighteenth-century debate on women', *French Review*, 58, 1984, 236–43. Suggests that Grimm, whilst maintaining a pro-feminine stance, especially in his criticisms of Rousseau and Restif la Bretonne, was less than enlightened about the social and political significance of the growing feminist movement in France.

6.1203 **Seltzer**, J., 'The French citizen's catechism: a *philosophe*'s moral vision in 1793', *Sts. Voltaire*, 216, 1983, 406–7. Survey of the principal ideas in de Volney's *Catechism of the French Citizen* (1793), touching on his view of political liberty and utilitarian ethics.

6.1204 —— 'Volney's science of political society: from observations to application', *Sts. Voltaire*, 191, 1980, 774–81. Examines Volney's method of political and social analysis and suggests that his proposals for radical reform derived from the influence of Montesquieu.

6.1205 **Sorkin**, D., 'Wilheim von Humboldt: the theory and practice of self-formation (Bildung), 1791–1810', *J. Hist. Ideas*, 44, 1983, 55–73. Examines his conception of *Bildung* within the context of the individual's relation to the state and civil society.

6.1206 **Stricklen**, C. G., 'The *philosophe*'s political mission: the creation of an idea, 1750–1789', *Sts. Voltaire*, 86, 1971, 137–228. Argues that the initial work of the *philosophes* was not expressly pre-occupied with issues of political theory, but that in the 1770s and 1780s these questions of political theory became crucial.

6.1207 **Suozz**, M., 'The Enlightenment in Italy: Gaetano Filangieri's *Scienza della legislazione*', *Sts. Voltaire*, 155, 1976, 2049–62. Endeavours to reveal how his

work differed from that of other Italian political thinkers of the period.

6.1208 —— 'The Coppet circle: literary criticism as political discourse', *Hist. Pol. Thought*, 1, 1980, 753–73. Examines the Coppet circle's contribution to the development of French liberalism, focusing upon the relationship between aesthetics and politics in their thought.

6.1209 **Triomphe**, R., *Joseph de Maistre*, Geneva, 1968.

6.1210 **Velema**, W. R. E., *Enlightenment and Conservatism in the Dutch Republic: The Political Thought of Elie Luzac (1721–1796)*, 1993. A thorough account of the development of his political thought from its moderate Enlightenment stance, in which the influence of Montesquieu was strong, to a form of conservatism.

6.1211 **Verweyen**, H. J., 'New perspectives on Fichte', *Ideal Studies*, 6, 1976, 118–59. Examines his system of thought and argues that the culmination of his political philosophy can be found in his 'Addresses to the German Nation'.

6.1212 **Vyverberg**, H., 'Limits of nonconformity in the Enlightenment: the case of Simon-Nicholas-Henri Linguet', *French Historical Studies*, 6, 1976, 474–92. Rigorous analysis of Linguet's social and political thought, revealing that, despite his conservatism, he was influenced by the *philosophes*.

6.1213 **Walter**, E. W., 'Politics of violence: from Montesquieu to the terrorists', in K. H. Wolff and B. Moore, ed., *The Critical Spirit: Essays in Honor of Herbert Marcuse*, Boston, 1970, 121–49. Examines the connection between terror and revolution in the works of Robespierre and Saint-Just, demonstrating how their conceptions of revolution were derived from Montesquieu's political sociology.

6.1214 **Watt**, E. D., ' "Locked in": De Maistre's critique of French Lockeanism', *J. Hist. Ideas*, 32, 1971, 129–32. Argues that he viewed Locke's epistemology and moral philosophy as undermining political order.

6.1215 **Wells**, G. A., *Herder and After: A Study in the Development of Sociology*, The Hague, 1959. Includes sections on his anthropology and history of civilisation.

6.1216 **Whelan**, F. G., 'Vattel's doctrine of the state', *Hist. Pol. Thought*, 9, 1988, 59–90. Scrutinises his conception of the state, as portrayed in *Law of Nations*, with regard to the problems of war and international justice.

6.1217 **Williams**, D., 'Boudier de Villemert: "philosopher of the fair sex" ', *Sts. Voltaire*, 193, 1980, 1899–1901. Examines his *L'Ami des Femmes* as representative of a potent genre of moral and political writing that would stifle French enlightenment feminism.

6.1218 —— 'The fate of French feminism: Boudier de Villemert's *Ami des Femmes*', *Eighteenth-Century Studies*, 14, 1980, 37–55. Examines the work of the popular anti-*philosophe* writer and thinker de Villemert, contending that his *Ami des Femmes* was instrumental in undermining eighteenth-century French feminism.

6.1219 **Wilson**, A. M., 'Why did the political theory of the encyclopedists not prevail? A suggestion', *French Historical Studies*, 1, 1960, 283–94. Argues that their political ideas were Lockean to the extent that they emphasised individual rights and liberties, whilst their penchant for a minimal state was at odds with historical circumstances.

6.1220 **Wright**, J. K., 'Conversations with Phocion: the political thought of Mably', *Hist. Pol. Thought*, 13, 1992, 391–415. On the thought of Gabriel Bonnot de Mably (1709–85), a writer now recognised as an exponent of classical republican ideas.

(d) NORTH AMERICA

General

6.1221 **Agresto**, J., 'Liberty, virtue, and republicanism, 1776–87', *Rev. Pol.*, 39, 1974, 473–504. Claims that within a decade of the Revolution, Americans had abandoned the classical republican ideal of virtuous citizenship, settling instead for a Lockean political discourse which legitimated individual rights against the state.

6.1222 **Allen**, W. B., 'Theory and practice in the founding of the republic', *Interpretation*, 4, 1977, 79–97.

6.1223 **Appleby**, J., *Capitalism and a New Social Order: The Republican Vision of the 1790s*, New York, 1984. Suggests that the language of liberal republicanism influenced American capitalism through its image of a 'social order of free and independent men'.

6.1224 —— 'Liberalism and the American Revolution', *New England Quarterly*, 49, 1976, 3–26. Traces the roots of American republicanism to the writings of Locke, Smith and others.

6.1225 —— 'Republicanism in the old and new contexts', *Wm. & Mary Q.*, 43, 1986, 20–34. Argues that American thought was marked by two distinct forms of republicanism: the classical version of Harrington and Montesquieu, which characterised federalist thought, and the liberal version of the Jeffersonians, with its origins in the work of Bacon, Newton, Locke and Smith.

6.1226 —— 'The social origins of American Revolutionary ideology', *Journal of American History*, 64, 1978, 935–58. Argues against J. G. A. Pocock and others that liberalism was the dominant mode of political discourse in the period.

6.1227 **Bailyn**, B., 'Political experience and Enlightenment ideas in eighteenth-century America', *Am. Hist. Rev.*, 67, 1962, 339–51. Examines how the American Revolution, in destroying traditional sources of public authority, was open to the political and social ideals of the Enlightenment.

6.1228 **Banning**, L., 'Republican ideology and the triumph of the constitution, 1789–1793', *Wm. & Mary Q.*, 31, 1974, 167–88. Skilfully argues that the anti-federalists readily accepted the Constitution because of their immersion in the ideas of classical republicanism.

6.1229 **Berens**, J., 'A "God of order not of confusion": the American loyalists and divine providence, 1774–1783', *Historical Magazine of the Protestant Episcopal Church*, 47, 1978, 211–19. On how the church was ideologically torn between those who embraced a doctrine of popular sovereignty and those who believed in divine right.

6.1230 **Bloch**, R., *Visionary Republic: Millenial Themes in American Thought, 1756–1800*, 1985. Stimulating discussion of the pervasiveness and complexity of these themes, highlighting their reciprocal relationship with the radical and revolutionary bodies of secular thought which emerged in this period.

6.1231 **Brown**, S. G., *The First Republicans: Political Philosophy and Public Policy in the Party of Jefferson and Madison*, Syracuse, N.Y., 1954.

6.1232 **Buell**, R., 'Democracy and the American Revolution: a frame of reference', *Wm. & Mary Q.*, 21, 1964, 165–90. Demonstrates how American revolutionaries drew upon the ideas of English dissent, particularly those of contract and resistance to arbitrary power.

6.1233 **Calhoon**, R. M., *The Loyalists in Revolutionary America, 1760–1781*, New York, 1973. A massive, if conceptually disappointing, account. The first 23 chapters are devoted to the political thought of writers such as Boucher, Chandler, Seabury and Cooper.

6.1234 **Canavan**, F. P., 'The relevance of the Burke–Paine controversy to American political thought', *Rev. Pol.*, 49, 1987, 163–76. Argues that, despite appearances, Burke's thought offers more to American political culture than that of Paine because of Burke's 'realistic' view of popular consent and his scepticism about the liberal contractarian model.

6.1235 **Carey**, G. W., 'Republicanism and the Federalist', *Pol. Sc. R-er*, 19, 1990, 107–43.

6.1236 **Chaudhuri**, J., ed., *The Non-Lockean Roots of American Democratic Thought*, Tucson, Ariz., 1977. Among thinkers considered are Madison, Adams, Jefferson, Paine and John Wise.

6.1237 **Cohen**, L. H., 'The American Revolution and natural law theory', *J. Hist. Ideas*, 39, 1978, 491–502. Focuses upon the ideological basis of the Declaration of Independence and its relation to the idea of just revolution.

6.1238 **Colbourn**, H. T., *The Lamp of Experience: Whig History and the Beginnings of the American Revolution*, Chapel Hill, N.C., 1965.

6.1239 **Cress**, L. D., 'Radical Whiggery on the role of the military: ideological roots of the American Revolutionary militia', *J. Hist. Ideas*, 40, 43–60. Considers the influence of English commonwealth political theory on the decision to mobilise the militia in 1774–75.

6.1240 **Diggins**, J. P., *The Lost Soul of American Politics: Virtue, Self-Interest, and the Foundations of Liberalism*, New York, 1984. Includes thoughtful and original essays on Jefferson, the ideas of the framers, Adams, Emerson, Thoreau and Tocqueville in this influential intervention in the debates about the nature of the liberal tradition.

6.1241 **Dion**, L., 'Natural law and manifest destiny in the era of the American Revolution', *Can. J. Econ. & Pol. Sc.*, 23, 1957, 27–47. Examines the influence of natural law on the founding of the American republic and the doctrine of 'manifest destiny'.

6.1242 **Durey**, M., 'Thomas Paine's apostles: radical emigrés and the triumph of Jeffersonian republicanism', *Wm. & Mary Q.*, 44, 1987, 661–88. Demonstrates that an important component of the Republican party in the 1790s consisted of political emigrés from Britain and Ireland who brought with them a stock of political ideas acquired in radical societies – ideas that were essentially Painite.

6.1243 **Dworetz**, S. M., *Unvarnished Doctrine: Locke, Liberalism and the American Revolution*, Durham, N.C., 1990. Examines the debate over the Lockean versus republican influences on early American Revolutionary thought.

6.1244 **Epstein**, D. F., *The Political Theory of the Federalist*, Chicago, Ill., 1984.

6.1245 **Gummere**, R., *The American Colonial Mind and the Classical Tradition*, Cambridge, Mass., 1963. Examines the impact of classical Greek and Roman ideas on Franklin, Jefferson and Adams.

6.1246 **Hatch**, N. O., *The Sacred Cause of Liberty: Republican Thought and the Millenium in Revolutionary New England*, New Haven, Conn., 1977.

6.1247 **Hill**, W. C., 'Contrasting themes in the political theories of Jefferson, Calhoun, and John Taylor of Caroline', *Publius*, 6, 1976, 73–92. Contrasts Taylor's 'philosophic rationalism' with the political thought of Jefferson and Calhoun.

6.1248 **Holmes**, D., 'The Episcopal Church and the American Revolution', *Historical Magazine of the Protestant Episcopal Church*, 47, 1978, 261–91. On how the Church was ideologically split between those who argued that political authority derived from popular sovereignty (which justified the Revolution) and those who believed that only rights granted by established governments could be enjoyed by subject peoples (which justified British rule).

6.1249 **Horne**, T. A., 'Bourgeois virtue, property and moral philosophy in America, 1750–1800', *Hist. Pol. Thought*, 4, 1983, 317–40. Examines the adventitious and natural law theories of property rights in the political economy and social theory of the period.

6.1250 **Howard**, D., *The Birth of American Political Thought, 1763–87*, 1990.

6.1251 **Howe**, J. R., ed., *The Role of Ideology in the American Revolution*, New York, 1970. Nine essays including E. S. Morgan, 'The Revolutionary era as an age of politics', P. Gay, 'Enlightenment thought and the American Revolution', R. R. Palmer, 'Republicanism as a revolutionary ideology' and G. S. Wood, 'The transforming radicalism of the Revolution'.

6.1252 **Jacob**, M. C. and **Jacob**, J., ed., *The Origins of Anglo-American Radicalism*, 1984. Includes J. Appleby, 'The radical *double-entendre* in the right to self-government' and R. J. Twomey, 'Jacobins and Jeffersonians: Anglo-American radical ideology, 1790–1810'.

6.1253 **Jacobson**, N., 'Political science and political education', *Am. Pol. Sc. Rev.*, 57, 1963, 561–9. Argues that the early republic was marked by two dominant forms of political thought: the first, inspired by the works of Thomas Paine, was expressed in the ideals of friendship, individual spontaneity and uniqueness, as well as a disdain for material wealth; the second, expressed in the works of Hamilton and Madison, focused on the importance of social order, procedural rationality, and the material bases of political association.

6.1254 **Kenyon**, C., 'Men of little faith: the anti-federalists on the nature of representative government', *Wm. & Mary Q.*, 12, 1955, 3–43.

6.1255 —— 'Republicanism and radicalism in the American Revolution: an old fashioned interpretation', *Wm. & Mary Q.*, 19, 1962, 153–82. Contends that whilst the Revolution started as a conservative protest, it was soon radicalised due to its subscription to republican government and the transformation of Lockean political philosophy.

6.1256 **Kerber**, L., 'The republican ideology of the revolutionary generation', *American Quarterly*, 37, 1985, 474–95.

6.1257 **Kloppenberg**, J. T., 'The virtues of liberalism: Christianity, republicanism and ethics in early American political discourse', *Journal of American History*, 74, 1987, 9–33. On how religious, republican and liberal themes intermingled in the late eighteenth century, giving particular meaning to the ideas of individual autonomy and popular sovereignty.

6.1258 **Koch**, A., 'Pragmatic wisdom and the American Enlightenment', *Wm. & Mary Q.*, 18, 1961, 313–29. Focuses on Jefferson and Franklin, including their political ideas.

6.1259 —— 'The contest of democracy and aristocracy in the American Enlightenment', *Sts. Voltaire*, 26, 1963, 999–1018. Challenges the view that eighteenth-century American political thought was wholly derivative of English and French Enlightenment thinking. Analyses the particularity of American conceptions of government by consent, religious freedom, and popular sovereignty.

6.1260 **Kramnick**, I., 'The "Great National Discussion": the discourse of politics in 1787', *Wm. & Mary Q.*, 45, 1988, 3–32. Detects four competing discourses in debates between federalists and anti-federalists: republicanism, Lockean liberalism, work-ethic Protestantism, and state-centred theories of sovereignty.

6.1261 **Lewis**, E., 'The contribution of medieval thought to the American political tradition', *Am. Pol. Sc. Rev.*, 50, 1956, 462–74. On the similarities and dissimilarities between medieval political ideas and those of the founding fathers.

6.1262 **Lienesch**, M., 'In defence of the antifederalists', *Hist. Pol. Thought*, 4, 1983, 65–87. Argues that they have been retrospectively criticised in harsh terms largely because their political position has been misunderstood. But on key issues, such as the founding and political fortune, they developed a coherent position.

6.1263 **Lokken**, R. N., 'The concept of democracy in colonial political thought', *Wm. & Mary Q.*, 16, 1963, 568–80. On why the colonists preferred an English-style mixed constitution to democracy.

6.1264 **Lutz**, D. S., *Popular Consent and Popular Control: Whig Political Theory in the Early State Constitutions*, Baton Rouge, La., 1980.

6.1265 —— 'The relative influence of European writers on late eighteenth-century American political thought', *Am. Pol. Sc. Rev.*, 78, 1984, 189–98. A quantitative analysis of some 916 texts.

6.1266 **Mace**, G., *Locke, Hobbes and 'The Federalist' Papers, An Essay on the Genesis of the American Political Heritage*, Carbondale, Ill., 1979.

6.1267 **Matson**, C. D. and **Onuf**, P. S., *A Union of Interests: Political and Economic Thought in Revolutionary America*, Kansas, 1990.

6.1268 **May**, H. F., *The Enlightenment in America*, 1976. Examines the influence of Bacon, Newton, Locke and the *philosophes* on the political thought of Washington, Franklin and Jefferson, among others.

6.1269 **Miller**, G. T., 'Fear God and honour the king: the failure of loyalist civil theology in the Revolutionary crisis', *Historical Magazine of the Protestant Episcopal Church*, 47, 1978, 221–42. On the divisions between those who believed in popular sovereignty and those who argued that political authority was divinely bestowed.

6.1270 **Norton**, M. B., 'The loyalists' critique of the Revolution', *Library of Congress Symposia on the American Revolution, I, The Development of a Revolution Mentality*, Washington, D.C., 1972, 127–48. Argues that they were 'in the mainstream of eighteenth-century Whiggery'.

6.1271 **Pangle**, T. L., *The Spirit of Modern Republicanism: The Moral Vision of the American Founders and the Philosophy of Locke*, Chicago, Ill., 1988. On how Locke's conceptions of liberty, personal security, property and prosperity influenced the political thought of the founding fathers.

6.1272 **Reck**, A., 'Philosophy in the debates at the United States constitutional convention', in A. S. Rosenbaum, ed., *Constitutionalism: The Philosophical Dimension*, New York, 1988, 113–24. Examines the political and philosophical underpinnings of the four principal plans that were presented during the constitutional convention of 1787 – the proposals of Edmund Randolph, Charles Pinckney, William Paterson and Alexander Hamilton.

6.1273 **Reinhold**, M., 'Eighteenth-century American political thought', in R. R. Bolgar, ed., *Classical Influences on Western Thought, 1650–1870*, 1979, 223–43. Demonstrates that American political thinkers' knowledge of the ancients derived largely from their reading of seventeenth- and eighteenth-century English and continental thinkers, rather than from a direct reading of ancient texts.

6.1274 **Ripley**, R. B., 'Adams, Burke, and eighteenth-century conservatism', *Pol. Sc. Q.*, 80, 1956, 216–35. Debunks the thesis of R. Kirk that their conservatism is identical.

6.1275 **Rossiter**, C. L., *Seedtime of the Republic: The Origin of the American Tradition of Political Liberty*, New York, 1953. Classic account of the political ideas of colonial and Revolutionary America, with chapters on John Wise, Jonathan Mayhew, Richard Bland and Franklin.

6.1276 **Sandoz**, E., *Government of Laws: Political Theory, Religion and the American Founding*, Baton Rouge, La., 1990.

6.1277 **Shalhope**, R. E., 'Republicanism and early American historiography', *Wm. & Mary Q.*, 39, 1982, 334–56. Survey of scholarship on political thought, showing the importance in recent historiography of a 'civic humanist' paradigm.

6.1278 —— *The Roots of Democracy: American Thought and Culture, 1760–1800*, Boston, Mass., 1990.

6.1279 —— 'Toward a republican synthesis: the emergence of an understanding of republicanism in American historiography', *Wm. & Mary Q.*, 29, 1972, 49–80. Excellent survey of the scholarship on late eighteenth-century political thought.

6.1280 **Sheps**, A., 'Ideological immigrants in Revolutionary America', in P. Fritz and D. Williams, ed., *City and Society in the Eighteenth-Century*, Toronto, 1973, 231–46. On the belief among English radicals that America was an ideological haven and their account of the American republic on their arrival. Thinkers discussed include John Binns, Thomas Cooper and Joseph Priestley.

6.1281 **Shoemaker**, R., ' "Democracy" and "republic" as understood in late eighteenth-century America', *American Speech*, 41, 1966, 83–95.

6.1282 **Sinopoli**, R., *The Foundations of American Citizenship: Liberalism, the Constitution, and Civic Virtue*, 1992.

6.1283 **Smith**, J. E., 'Philosophical ideas behind the "Declaration of Independence" ', *Revue Internationale de Philosophie*, 31,

1977, 360–76. Focuses upon the individualistic nature of the political thought of the founding fathers, their instrumental conceptions of government, and their belief that the establishment of liberty would lead to equality.

6.1284 **Spurlin**, P. M., *The French Enlightenment in America: Essays on the Times of the Founding Fathers*, Athens, Ga., 1984. Contends that whilst the *philosophes* had considerable influence in America, the founding fathers were particularly uncomfortable with the speculative and metaphysical quality of French Enlightenment thought.

6.1285 **Storing**, H. J., *What the Anti-Federalists Were For*, Chicago, Ill., 1981.

6.1286 **Tate**, T. W., 'The social contract in America, 1774–1787: revolutionary theory as a conservative instrument', *Wm. & Mary Q.*, 22, 1965, 375–91. Shows that having used contract to account for separation and to provide a constitutional basis for the new governments, American writers were not inclined to use the theory to advocate a radical political programme.

6.1287 **Trivers**, H., 'Universalism in the thought of the founding fathers', *Virginia Quarterly Review*, 52, 1976, 448–62. Contends that the founding fathers were fundamentally Enlightenment thinkers due to their adherence to universal principles in human affairs.

6.1288 **White**, M., *The Philosophy of the American Revolution*, 1978.

6.1289 **Wills**, G., *Explaining America: The Federalist*, 1981. Close textual exegesis, suggesting that Madison and Hamilton were influenced by the Scottish Enlightenment – particularly Hume's political essays.

6.1290 **Wisly**, B., 'John Locke and the spirit of '76', *Pol. Sc. Q.*, 73, 1958, 413–25. Examines the Lockean influence on the framing of the Declaration.

6.1291 **Wood**, G. S., *The Creation of the American Republic, 1776–1787*, 1969. Brilliant guide to the ideas of the American founding.

6.1292 —— *The Radicalism of the American Revolution*, New York, 1992. Includes some in-depth discussion of the influences of the thinkers of this period in this lengthy study of the social and political character of the Revolution.

6.1293 **Yarbrough**, J., 'Republicanism reconsidered: some thoughts on the foundation and preservation of the American republic', *Rev. Pol.*, 41, 1979, 61–95. Focuses upon the distinction made by Adams, Hamilton, Madison and Jefferson between republicanism and liberal, representative democracy.

6.1294 **Zvesper**, J., *Political Philosophy and Rhetoric: A Study of the Origins of American Party Politics*, 1977. Radical revision of conventional accounts of the origin of the party system, highlighting the 'principled side of American parties' – in particular the role of the Jeffersonian Republicans in developing an abstract set of ideals, from which they agreed a programme. Concludes with an interesting analysis of the role of 'principles and rhetoric in the critical elections of 1793–1800'.

6.1295 —— 'The American founders and classical political thought', *Hist. Pol. Thought*, 10, 1989, 701–18. Examines the ideology of the founding fathers from the perspective that they tried to fuse, however unconsciously, the communitarianism of classical republicanism with the individualism of modern liberalism.

Hamilton

6.1296 **Frisch**, M. J., *Alexander Hamilton and the Political Order: An Interpretation of his Political Thought and Practice*, 1991.

6.1297 —— 'Hamilton's report on manufactures and political philosophy', *Publius*, 8, 1978, 129–39.

6.1298 **Kenyon**, C., 'Alexander Hamilton: Rousseau of the right', *Pol. Sc. Q.*, 73, 1958, 161–78. Equates his belief in an overriding public interest with Rousseau's theory of the general will.

6.1299 **Rossiter**, C. L., *Alexander Hamilton and the Constitution*, New York, 1964. Suggests that he has been underestimated as a political thinker, and carefully disentangles the various influences upon his ideas.

6.1300 **Shklar**, J. N., 'Alexander Hamilton and the language of political science', in A. Pagden, ed., *The Languages of Political Theory in Early-Modern Europe*, 1987, 339–55. Argues for the unique connection in eighteenth-century America between representative democracy and the scientific ethos in terms of political discourse.

6.1301 **Stourzh**, G., *Alexander Hamilton and the*

Idea of Republican Government, Stanford, Calif., 1970.

Jefferson and the Jeffersonians

6.1302 **Appleby**, J., 'Jefferson: a political reappraisal', *Democracy*, 3, 1984, 139–45. Examines his conception of freedom and contends that it must be viewed in terms of liberation from all forms of social authority.

6.1303 —— 'What is still American in the political philosophy of Thomas Jefferson?', *Wm. & Mary Q.*, 39, 1982, 287–309. Traces the influence of Destutt de Tracy on Jefferson's thought with regard to agricultural and commercial expansion, and examines Jefferson's belief in individual, moral perfectibility in the light of the civic humanist tradition.

6.1304 **Ashworth**, J., 'The Jeffersonians: classical republicans or liberal capitalists?', *Journal of American Studies*, 18, 1984, 425–35. Review of J. Appleby, *Capitalism and a New Social Order*, in which Ashworth usefully reviews the controversy between Banning and others who identify the Jeffersonians as civic humanists and Appleby and others who characterise them as archetypal liberals anticipating 'capitalism and a new social order'.

6.1305 **Banning**, L., 'Jeffersonian ideology and the French Revolution: a question of liberticide at home', *Sts. Burke & Time*, 17, 1976, 5–26.

6.1306 —— 'Jeffersonian ideology revisited: liberal and classical ideas in the new American republic', *Wm. & Mary Q.*, 43, 1986, 3–19. Argues, in an attempt to bridge the gap between revisionist and anti-revisionist historiography, that Jeffersonian thought cannot be classified as either liberal or civic humanist – it combined elements of liberalism and republicanism.

6.1307 —— *The Jeffersonian Persuasion: Evolution of a Party Ideology*, Ithaca, N.Y., 1978. Contends that Jeffersonian republicanism can be best understood as a restatement of the English Country party's preoccupation with the mixed constitution, civic virtue and corruption, with its roots in the writings of Harrington, Sidney, Trenchard and Bolingbroke.

6.1308 **Barnouw**, J., 'The pursuit of happiness in Jefferson and its background in Bacon and Hobbes', *Interpretation*, 11, 1983, 225–48.

6.1309 **Beloff**, M., *Thomas Jefferson and American Democracy*, 1948. Intellectual biography focusing on his political creed.

6.1310 **Benson**, C. R., *Thomas Jefferson as Social Scientist*, Rutherford, N.J., 1971. Argues that Jefferson can be considered a proto-sociologist due to his understanding of social control and the socio-psychological dimensions of human behaviour. Contends that his thought was influenced by Locke's and Hume's theories on natural law and natural rights.

6.1311 **Brown**, S. G., 'The mind of Thomas Jefferson', *Ethics*, 73, 1963, 79–99. Traces the sources of Jefferson's scientific, moral, social and political ideas to Bacon, Newton and Locke.

6.1312 **Carrithers**, D. W., 'Montesquieu, Jefferson and the fundamentals of eighteenth-century republican theory', *French-American Review*, 6, 1982, 160–88. Examines Jefferson's notes on his readings of *Spirit of the Laws* to reveal Montesquieu's influence on his political thought.

6.1313 **Chaudhuri**, J., 'Possession, ownership and access: a Jeffersonian view of property', *Political Inquiry*, 1, 1973, 78–95. Argues that Jefferson's conception of property was very different from Locke's in that his linking of rights and consent exposes 'the social basis of property without legitimizing the doctrines of *laissez-faire* or social elitism'.

6.1314 **Colbourn**, H. T., 'Thomas Jefferson's use of the past', *Wm. & Mary Q.*, 15, 1958, 56–70. Focuses upon Jefferson's readings of Whig historians, especially Cornelius Tacitus and William Blackstone, in his formulation of a doctrine of just rule.

6.1315 **Commager**, H. S., *Jefferson, Nationalism, and the Enlightenment*, New York, 1975.

6.1316 —— 'Jefferson and the Enlightenment', in C. Weymouth, ed., *Thomas Jefferson: The Man . . . His World . . . His Influence*, New York, 1973, 39–67.

6.1317 **Cooke**, J. W., 'Jefferson on liberty', *J. Hist. Ideas*, 34, 1973, 563–77. Thorough account of his ideas.

6.1318 **Cunningham**, N. E., *In Pursuit of Reason The Life of Thomas Jefferson*, Baton Rouge La., 1987. Includes an account of his political thought.

6.1319 **Diggins**, J. P., 'Slavery, race, and equality

Jefferson and the pathos of the Enlightenment', *American Quarterly*, 28, 1976, 206–28.

6.1320 **Foshec**, A. W., 'Jeffersonian political economy and the classical tradition: Jefferson, Taylor, and the agrarian republic', *Hist. Pol. Econ.*, 17, 1985, 523–50. Contends that Jefferson's and John Taylor's conceptions of the agrarian political republic were inspired by the classical Greek and Roman republics.

6.1321 **Gaustad**, E. S., 'On Jeffersonian liberty', in J. C. Brauer, ed., *The Lively Experiment Continued*, Athens, Ga., 1987, 85–104. Examines his conception of political, religious and academic freedom, and contending that he advocated this ideal at the expense of equality.

6.1322 **Ginsberg**, R., 'Suppose that Jefferson's rough draft of the declaration of independence is a work of political philosophy', *The Eighteenth Century: Theory and Interpretation*, 25, 1984, 24–44. Analysis of Jefferson's rough draft of the declaration of independence in the light of the themes of equality, human rights, revolution, sovereignty, rule of law, just war and international order.

6.1323 **Griswold**, A. W., 'Jefferson's republic: the rediscovery of democratic philosophy', *Fortune*, 41, 1950, 126–42. Ideologically charged article that uses Jefferson to attack totalitarianism.

6.1324 —— 'The agrarian democracy of Thomas Jefferson', *Am. Pol. Sc. Rev.*, 40, 1946, 657–81. Argues that he derived his conception of agrarian democracy from Locke's *Second Treatise* and the works of Adam Smith, and not from the physiocrats.

6.1325 **Hamowy**, R., 'Jefferson and the Scottish Enlightenment: a critique of Garry Wills's *Inventing America: Jefferson's Declaration of Independence*', *Wm. & Mary Q.*, 36, 1979, 503–23. Argues against Wills that Jefferson was more influenced by Locke than Scottish Enlightenment thinkers in drafting the declaration of independence.

6.1326 **Hardesty**, K., 'Thomas Jefferson and the thought of the *Encyclopédie*', *Laurels*, 52, 1981, 19–31. Examines the affinities between Jefferson's thought and that of the Encyclopedists, arguing that they shared a common, ancient conception of the individual as virtuous and hence capable of right and just governance.

6.1327 **Hellenbrand**, H., *The Unfinished Revolution: Education and Politics in the Thought of Thomas Jefferson*, Newark, N.J., 1990. Argues that he saw education as crucial to the creation of an active citizenship which would promote individual and social independence and restrain the centralisation of state power.

6.1328 **Howe**, D. W., 'European sources of political ideas in Jeffersonian America', *Reviews in American History*, 10, 1982, 28–44.

6.1329 **Jones**, J. F., 'Montesquieu and Jefferson revisited: aspects of a legacy', *French Review*, 51, 1978, 577–85. Traces Montesquieu's influence on his political thought.

6.1330 **Kaplan**, L. S., *Jefferson and France: An Essay on Politics and Political Ideas*, New Haven, Conn., 1967. Analysis of French influences on Jefferson's political and social thought.

6.1331 **Kloman**, W., 'The Jefferson theory of revolution', *Cybernetica*, 21, 1978, 193–204.

6.1332 **Koch**, A., 'Power and morals and the founding fathers: Jefferson', *Rev. Pol.*, 15, 1953, 470–90. Examines his political thought in the light of Lockean moral theory, and how the quest for reason implies the cultivation of moral virtue, which acts as a check against the abuse of political power.

6.1333 —— *The Philosophy of Thomas Jefferson*, New York, 1957. A standard account of his political and philosophical ideas, though tends to concentrate on his thought after 1785, giving a disproportionate status to the influence of French Enlightenment thinking upon him.

6.1334 **Lehman**, K., *Thomas Jefferson: American Humanist*, 1947. Traditional celebration of Jefferson's deployment of Greek and Roman culture and thought. Inevitably hagiographical, given the author's contention that 'this book deals with the meeting between a genius and a great subject'.

6.1335 **Lence**, R., 'Jefferson and the declaration of independence: the power and the natural rights of a free people', *Pol. Sc. R-er*, 6, 1976, 1–34. Argues that Jefferson's reference to the rights of man should not be interpreted in individualist terms but rather, as it implies the majority of the population, should be conceived in terms of 'the rights of the political community in general'.

6.1336 **McAllister**, E., 'Condorcet and Jefferson on education', *Condorcet Studies*, 2, 1987, 87–117. Suggests that they shared a vision of an education that would promote equality, cosmopolitanism and freedom from arbitrary government.

6.1337 **Matthews**, R. K., *The Radical Politics of Thomas Jefferson: A Revisionist View*, Lawrence, Kan., 1984. Contends that he held a conception of radical democracy and communitarian anarchism radically at odds with market liberalism.

6.1338 **Meyer**, J. P., 'Jefferson as a reader of Bodin: suggestions for further studies', in J. P. Meyer, ed., *Fundamental Studies on Jean Bodin*, New York, 1979, 1–32. A suggestive study, arguing that Jefferson's reading of Bodin's *Les Six Livres* may have had an early influence on his conception of sovereignty as limited by natural and divine law.

6.1339 **Mirkin**, H. G., 'Rebellion, revolution and the constitution: Thomas Jefferson's theory of civil disobedience', *American Studies*, 13, 1972, 61–74.

6.1340 **Morgan**, R., ' "Time hath found us": the Jeffersonian revolutionary vision', *J. Pol.*, 38, 1976, 20–36. Argues that for Jefferson and the Jeffersonians the Revolution was political rather than social in nature.

6.1341 **Murrin**, J. M., 'Can liberals be patriots? Natural right, virtue, and moral sense in the America of George Mason and Thomas Jefferson', in R. P. Davidson, ed., *Natural Rights and Natural Law: The Legacy of George Mason*, Fairfax, Va., 1986, 35–66. Argues that whilst Mason was not strongly influenced by moral sense theory, Jefferson was and therefore embraced a form of civic humanism.

6.1342 **Patterson**, C. P., *The Constitutional Principles of Thomas Jefferson*, New York, 1971. Demonstrates convincingly that he favoured the decentralisation of political power.

6.1343 **Peterson**, M. D., 'Thomas Jefferson and the French Revolution', *Tocqueville Review*, 9, 1988, 15–25. Argues that he was an enthusiastic supporter of the French Revolution, and examines its significance for his political and social thought.

6.1344 **Phipps**, W. E., 'Jefferson on political obligation', *Journal of the West Virginia Philosophical Society*, 12, 1977, 1–6.

6.1345 **Post**, D. M., 'Jeffersonian revisions of Locke: education, property-rights and liberty', *J. Hist. Ideas*, 47, 1986, 147–57. Exposes sharp distinctions between Jefferson's conceptions of property, education and liberty and those of Locke, arguing that Jefferson was the more egalitarian thinker.

6.1346 **Quinby**, L., 'Thomas Jefferson: the virtue of aesthetics and the aesthetics of virtue', *Am. Hist. Rev.*, 87, 1982, 337–56. Examines his conception of aesthetic sentiment and its relation to public and private virtue.

6.1347 **Sandler**, S. G., 'Lockean ideas in Thomas Jefferson's *Bill for Establishing Religious Freedom*', *J. Hist. Ideas*, 21, 1960, 110–16. Endeavours to show the relationship between Jefferson's *Bill* and Locke's *Letter Concerning Toleration*.

6.1348 **Shalhope**, R. E., 'Thomas Jefferson's republican and antebellum southern thought', *Journal of Southern History*, 42, 1976, 529–56. Argues that his paradoxical adherence to republicanism and support of slavery were the products of his pastoral republican ideology.

6.1349 **Sheehan**, B. W., 'Paradise and the noble savage in Jeffersonian thought', *Wm. & Mary Q.*, 26, 1967, 327–59. On his paradisaic conception of the Indian.

6.1350 **Sheldon**, G. W., *The Political Philosophy of Thomas Jefferson*, Baltimore, Md., 1991. Argues that, in fearing of the centralisation of political power, he developed a complex and original conception of political democracy, loosely based on the Greek polis and New England township.

6.1351 **Walton**, C., 'Hume and Jefferson on the uses of history', in C. Walton and J. P. Anton, ed., *Philosophy and the Civilising Arts: Essays Presented to Herbert W. Schneider on his Eightieth Birthday*, Athens, Ohio, 1975. On why Jefferson attacked Hume's *The History of England*.

6.1352 **Weyant**, R. V., 'Helvetius and Jefferson: studies of human nature and government in the eighteenth-century', *Journal of the History of the Behavioral Sciences*, 9, 1973, 29–41. Argues that Helvetius's strongly individualistic conception of society was derived from Locke, whilst Jefferson's communitarian conception was influenced by the tradition of Shaftesbury and the Scottish moralists.

6.1353 **Wills**, G., *Inventing America: Jefferson's*

Declaration of Independence, New York, 1978. Brilliantly argued thesis that far from bearing the imprint of Lockean political theory the Declaration, as Jefferson originally intended it, can be properly understood only if analysed as a product of the Scottish Enlightenment, whilst his political views derive from Hume, Reid, Smith, Ferguson and Hutcheson.

6.1354 **Wilson**, D. L., 'Jefferson vs Hume', *Wm. & Mary Q.*, 46, 1989, 49–70. Examines Jefferson's critical reading of Hume's *The History of England*.

Madison

6.1355 **Adair**, D., ' "That politics may be reduced to a science": David Hume, James Madison, and the tenth *Federalist*', *Huntington Libr. Q.*, 20, 1957, 343–60. On the influence of Hume's 'Idea of a perfect commonwealth' on Madison's view of factions and the kind of political arrangements needed to avoid them.

6.1356 **Branson**, R., 'James Madison and the Scottish Enlightenment', *J. Hist. Ideas*, 40, 1979, 235–50. Argues that Hume, Smith, Ferguson and Millar all influenced his political ideas.

6.1357 **Brant**, I., *James Madison and American Nationalism*, Princeton, N.J., 1960.

6.1358 **Carter**, B. K. and **Kobylka**, J. F., 'The dialogic community: education, leadership and participation in James Madison's thought', *Rev. Pol.*, 52, 1990, 32–63. Defends Madison as a theorist–politician whose ideas were informed by liberal and republican traditions and who viewed community as an evolutionary and ongoing dialogue about the common ends of a diverse people attached to the values of self-rule.

6.1359 **Conniff**, J., 'On the obsolescence of the general will: Rousseau, Madison and the evolution of republican political thought', *West. Pol. Q.*, 28, 1975, 32–58. Argues that most of the central concerns of the American theorists of the constitutional period were derived from an attempt to apply the classical republican model to their situation, and that this is exemplified in the evolution of James Madison's thought prior to the writing of *Federalist No. 10*.

6.1360 —— 'The Enlightenment and American political thought: a study of the origins of Madison's *Federalist No. 10*', *Pol. Theory*, 8, 1980, 381–402. Challenges Adair's account of Madison, proposing that the latter was influenced by a number of traditions, including republicanism, monarchical thought, religious toleration and the Scottish Enlightenment.

6.1361 **Gibson**, A., 'Impartial representation and the extended republic: towards a comprehensive and balanced reading of the tenth *Federalist* paper', *Hist. Pol. Thought*, 12, 1991, 263–304. On the conflicting interpretations of Madison's political thought, arguing that it combined a Lockean conception of government as umpire with a republican concern that the state should promote the public good.

6.1362 **Morgan**, E., 'Safety in numbers: Madison, Hume, and the tenth *Federalist*', *Huntington Libr. Q.*, 49, 1986, 95–112. Challenges the argument of D. Adair and others that Madison was profoundly influenced by Hume.

6.1363 **McCoy**, D. R., *The Last of the Fathers: James Madison and the Republican Legacy*, 1989. Unusual study of the period between his retirement from office and death, suggesting that his career and ideas in the 1820s and 30s present 'a unique opportunity to enrich our understanding of some critical themes in American history between the Revolution and the Civil War'.

6.1364 **Morgan**, R., 'Madison's analysis of the sources of political authority', *Am. Pol. Sc. Rev.*, 75, 1981, 613–25. Suggests that for Madison both governmental authority and the restraints upon it derive from the same ultimate and penultimate causes – human nature and opinion.

6.1365 —— 'Madison's theory of representation in the tenth *Federalist*', *J. Pol.*, 37, 1974, 852–85. Argues that he sought to demonstrate that the durability of the American republic would depend primarily on a constitutional superstructure of representation flexible enough to control the struggle of opposing interests.

6.1366 **Rakove**, J., 'The Madisonian theory of rights', *William and Mary Law Review*, 31, 1990, 245–66. On the strain of natural rights liberalism in his thought.

6.1367 **Riemer**, N., *James Madison: Creating the American Constitution*, Washington, D.C., 1986.

6.1368 —— 'James Madison's theory of the self-destructive features of republican government', *Ethics*, 65, 1954, 34–43. Appraisal of his proposals to eliminate factions.

6.1369 —— 'The republicanism of James Madison', *Pol. Sc. Q.*, 69, 1954, 56–64.

6.1370 **Zvesper**, J., 'The Madisonian systems', *West. Pol. Q.*, 37, 1984, 236–56. On the apparent contradiction of his evolving political theory: 'The pluralism of Madison the Federalist favoured the multiplication of social and economic interests, in order to facilitate competent governmental control and direction of those interests. The party system of Madison the Republican displayed more confidence in the political competence of citizens outside government.'

Other thinkers

6.1371 **Avery**, M. E., 'Toryism in the age of the American Revolution: John Lind and John Shebbere', *Historical Studies*, 18, 1978, 24–36.

6.1372 **Bloom**, E. A. and **Bloom**, L. D., 'Joseph Addison and eighteenth-century "liberalism" ', *J. Hist. Ideas*, 12, 1952, 560–83.

6.1373 **Clark**, M. D., 'Jonathan Boucher: the mirror of reaction', *Huntington Libr. Q.*, 33, 1969, 19–32. On the Maryland loyalist who is portrayed here almost as an American Burke.

6.1374 **Haraszti**, Z., *John Adams and the Prophet of Progress*, Cambridge, Mass., 1952. Account of his political thought based on the original notes he made on the books of writers such as Bolingbroke, Rousseau, Voltaire, Turgot and Condorcet.

6.1375 **Howe**, J. R., *The Changing Political Thought of John Adams*, Princeton, N.J., 1956.

6.1376 **Paynter**, J., 'John Adams: on the principles of political science', *Pol. Sc. Re-r*, 1976, 35–72.

6.1377 **Pencak**, W., *America's Burke: The Mind of Thomas Hutchinson*, Washington, D.C., 1982. Careful study of his political ideas, claiming that he had worked out a consistent conservatism in advance of the American Revolution.

6.1378 **Schulz**, C. B., 'John Adams on "the best of all possible worlds" ', *J. Hist. Ideas*, 44, 1983, 561–77. Revives the optimistic side of Adams's political thought by focusing on notes he made on a number of Greek philosophers.

6.1379 **Shulim**, J. I., 'John Daly Burk: Irish revolutionist and American patriot', *Trans. Am. Phil. Soc.*, 54, 1964, pt. 6., 5–60. On United Irishman living in America in the 1790s who through his journalism used natural rights doctrine to attack John Adams and the federalists for their conservatism.

6.1380 **Zimmer**, A. Y., *Jonathan Boucher: Loyalist in Exile*, Detroit, Mich., 1978.

7

NINETEENTH
CENTURY

(a) GENERAL

7.1 **Francis**, M., 'The nineteenth-century theory of sovereignty and Thomas Hobbes', *Hist. Pol. Thought*, 1, 1980, 517–41. Polemically rebuts the view that the majority of nineteenth-century theorising on state and sovereignty adopted a liberal individualist stance.

7.2 **Fuller**, T., 'The spiritualization of politics and modern political philosophy', *Human Society*, 6, 1983, 109–26. Focuses on the appearance of a new religious zeal in politics, manifest in the ideas of Hegel, Mill, Maine and Weber.

7.3 **Goodwin**, B., *Social Science and Utopia: Nineteenth-Century Models of Social Harmony*, 1978. Based on an assessment of a number of utopian thinkers, Goodwin argues that utopias necessarily function as self-sufficient, integrated and conflict-free social systems which inspire analysts and reformers. She also explores the tensions in the relationship between utopianism and a nascent social science and the validity of utopias as models of conflict resolution.

7.4 **Larsson**, R., *Theories of Revolution: From Marx to the First Russian Revolution*, Stockholm, 1970.

7.5 **Löwith**, K., *From Hegel to Nietzsche: The Revolution in Nineteenth-Century Thought*, Garden City, N.Y., 1967.

7.6 **Neale**, R. S., *Class and Ideology in the Nineteenth Century*, 1973.

7.7 **Talmon**, J. L., *Political Messianism: The Romantic Phase*, 1960. Focuses upon the 'expectation of universal regeneration' which affected political thought in the first half of the nineteenth century. Whilst political and social realities constantly intrude, the Messianic characteristics of the different ideologies under examination are rehearsed repeatedly, playing down differences between them.

(b) BRITISH ISLES

General

7.8 **Barrow**, L., 'Socialism in eternity: the ideology of plebeian spiritualists, 1853–1913', *History Workshop*, 9, 1980, 337–69. Focuses upon plebeian spiritualism, which arrived from North America and combined with indigenous beliefs to produce new radical movements. Barrow discusses the complex relationship between religious currents and political ideology.

7.9 **Bellamy**, R., 'T. H. Green, J. S. Mill, and Isaiah Berlin on the nature of liberty and liberalism', in H. Gross and R. Harrison, ed., *Jurisprudence: Cambridge Essays*, 1992, 257–85. A critique of Berlin's representation of these thinkers as synonomous with negative (Mill) and positive liberty (Green). The central idea of *On Liberty* is a defence of individual autonomy which Berlin attacks, whilst Green is justified in presenting himself as part of the same tradition as Mill, not as his antithesis.

7.10 **Betts**, R., 'The allusion to Rome in British imperialist thought of the late nineteenth and early twentieth centuries', *Victorian Studies*, 15, 1971, 149–61.

7.11 **Bowle**, J., *Politics and Opinion in the Nineteenth Century*, 1954.

7.12 **Burrow**, J. W., *Whigs and Liberals: Continuity and Change in English Political Thought*, 1988. Subtly reveals the complexity of nineteenth-century Whiggism and liberalism, focusing upon ways in which the eighteenth-century concept of the balanced constitution was transformed into pluralist and other modes of thinking.

7.13 **Collini**, S., 'Political theory and the "science of society" in Victorian Britain', *Hist. J.*, 23, 1980, 203-31.

7.14 —— *Public Moralists: Political Thought and Intellectual Life in Britain 1850–1930*, 1991. Examination of British moral and cultural attitudes, which addresses the work of central thinkers (Spencer, Mill, Arnold, Bagehot, Green, Dicey) in this period.

7.15 —— 'The idea of "character" in Victorian political thought', *Trans. Royal Hist. Soc.*, 35, 1985, 29–50.

7.16 —— with **Winch**, D., and **Burrow**, J. W., *That Noble Science of Politics: A study in Nineteenth-century intellectual history*, 1983. Excellent analysis of a variety of writers and traditions (including Malthus, Mill and Sidgwick) which combined to re-orientate traditional understanding of the political sphere and uncovered the workings of a science of politics. Imaginative intellectual history which draws eclectically upon nineteenth-century thought in the fields of political economy, high politics, philosophy, political science, history and economics.

7.17 **Deane**, S., *The French Revolution and Enlightenment in England, 1789–1832*, Cambridge, Mass., 1988. On the intellectual relationships which English writers developed with their French predecessors, and also the English reaction to the Enlightenment and Revolution, with chapters on, for example, 'Coleridge and Rousseau: a philosophy for the nation', 'Hazlitt and the French: a Jacobin profile' and 'English Dissent and the philosophes: the exercise of reason'.

7.18 **Eastwood**, D., 'Robert Southey and the intellectual origins of romantic conservatism', *Eng. Hist. Rev.*, 104, 1989 308–31. Opposes the tendency to view early nineteenth-century conservatism as purely constitutional and parliamentary i its concerns, through an examination of th origins of romantic conservatism. Concludes that the typologies deployed t understand the political thought of this period need alteration.

7.19 **Francis**, M., 'A prolegomenon for the history of British political thought during the nineteenth century', *Pol. Sc.*, 38, 198 70–85. Critical response to Collini, Wincl and Burrows, *That Noble Science of Politics*, focusing on the gaps in their account and their flawed historical vision

7.20 **Halliday**, R. J., 'Social Darwinism: a definition', *Victorian Studies*, 14, 1971, 389–407.

7.21 **Hardman**, M., *Six Victorian Thinkers in Context: Carlyle, Ruskin, Taylor, Mill, Newman, Arnold*, 1991. Rescues six majo intellectuals from the dowdy image of the Victorian 'sage', revealing them to be livel and courageous critics of the state.

7.22 **Jones**, G., *Social Darwinism and English Thought: The Interaction between Biologica and Social Theory*, 1980. Focuses upon th ubiquity of Social Darwinism and the key ideas which sustained it. Lucid treatment of the difficult and ambiguous relationshi between Social Darwinism and political and social theory at the end of the nineteenth century.

7.23 **Kriegel**, A. D., 'Liberty and Whiggery i early nineteenth-century England', *J. Mod. Hist.*, 52, 1980, 253–78. Examines whether Whig appeals to liberty were 'specious, calculated to legitimise the ascendancy of a privileged political and social order', concluding that this group held to a coherent belief in the continuing extension of rational liberty within an ordered society dominated by men of honour.

7.24 **Moore**, D. C., 'Political morality in mid-nineteenth century England: concepts, norms, violations', *Victorian Studies*, 13, 1969, 5–36.

7.25 **Pearson**, R., and **Williams**, G. L., *Political Thought and Public Policy in the Nineteenth Century: An Introduction*, 1984. Develops the connection between the principal ideologies of this period and the changing face of public policy in Britain.

7.26 **Perkin**, H., 'Individualism versus collectivism in nineteenth-century Britain: a false antithesis', *J. Brit. Sts.*, 17, 1977, 105–18. Assessing the interaction between policy and ideology, he stresses the tensions between different versions of collectivism.

7.27 **Pierson**, S., *Marxism and the Origins of British Socialism: The Struggle for a New Consciousness*, 1973. Assesses the struggle to inculcate a socialist consciousness in Britain, at the end of the nineteenth century, illuminating the interaction between Marxist ideas and indigenous traditions, resulting in the proliferation of competing schools of socialist thought. Of these ethical socialism became the dominant strand, a process illuminated through some well-presented case studies of leading individuals and theorists.

7.28 **Poynter**, J. R., *Society and Pauperism: English Ideas on Poor Relief, 1795–1834*, 1969. A clear account of how Malthus, Bentham and other classical liberals proposed to deal with the poor.

7.29 **Roberts**, D., *Paternalism in Early Victorian Britain*, 1979. Account of Whig and Tory arguments for social hierarchy, focusing on figures such as S. T. Coleridge and Thomas Carlyle.

7.30 **Sargent**, L. T., 'English and American utopias: similarities and differences', *J. Gen. Ed.*, 28, 1976, 16-22. Stimulating comparison of the differing projects pursued under the utopian banner in these countries, illustrating a shift towards more political concerns.

7.31 **Searle**, G. R., *The Quest for National Efficiency: A Study in British Politics and British Political Thought 1889/1914*, 1971.

7.32 **Soffer**, R. N., *Ethics and Society in England: The Revolution in the Social Sciences 1870–1914*, Berkeley and Los Angeles, Calif., 1978. Account of the rise of new liberalism in relation to the social sciences.

7.33 —— 'The revolution in English social thought, 1880–1914', *Am. Hist. Rev.*, 65, 1970, 1938–64.

7.34 **Waterman**, A. M. C., *Revolution, Economics and Religion: Christian Political Economy, 1798–1833*, 1991. Analyses the intellectual defence against the French Revolution which combined political economy with Anglican theology, occupying a middle ground between

ultra-Tory politics and radical reform.

7.35 **Watson**, G., *The English Ideology: Studies in the language of Victorian politics*, 1973. Examines the dominant political discourse (chiefly the English idea of government and liberty expressed through parliamentary institutions) of the Victorian age, through a variety of sources – history, poetry and fiction. Lively, if traditional, analysis.

7.36 **Weinstein**, W. L., 'The concept of liberty in nineteenth-century English political thought', *Pol. Sts.*, 13, 1965, 145–62. Explores the meaning of positive and negative liberty, analysing the merits and defects in each and concluding that these different interpretations did not necessarily disagree about the meaning of liberty. In fact, they were not logically incompatible.

Idealism

GENERAL

7.37 **Collini**, S., 'Hobhouse, Bosanquet and the state: philosophical idealism and political argument in England 1880–1918', *Past & Pres.*, 72, 1976, 86–111. Attempts to resolve the paradox whereby philosophically Hobhouse is viewed as the major critic of idealism and statism and Bosanquet as a defender of the state, yet politically Hobhouse defended state intervention whilst Bosanquet valorised individualism. In fact, no simple correspondence exists between idealism and collectivism, though idealist arguments provided new categories in which the liberal conception of society, market and the state was expressed.

7.38 —— 'Idealism and "Cambridge idealism"', *Hist. J.*, 18, 1975, 171–7.

7.39 —— 'Sociology and idealism in Britain 1880–1920', *Archives Européenes de Sociologie*, 19, 1978, 3–50.

7.40 **Milne**, A. J. M., 'The idealist critique of utilitarian social philosophy', *Archives Européenes de Sociologie*, 8, 1967, 319–31.

7.41 —— *The Social Philosophy of English Idealism*, 1962. Important study of the rise of this philosophical tradition in the work of Green, Royce, Bradley and Bosanquet, including a clear reconstruction of their principal ideas and astute criticism of their metaphysical findings.

7.42 **Morrow**, J., 'Ancestors, legacies and traditions: British idealism in the history of political thought', *Hist. Pol. Thought*, 6, 1985, 491–517. Focuses on the literature concerning the relationship between Green and the idealists, the impact of political idealism on late nineteenth and early twentieth-century developments in liberal theory and on the political practices of turn-of-the-century liberals.

7.43 —— 'Liberalism and British idealist political philosophy: a reassessment', *Hist. Pol. Thought*, 5, 1984, 91–108. Stresses Green's distinctive conception of personality which kept him within the liberal tradition unlike other contemporary idealists such as Bosanquet and Ritchie.

7.44 **Nicholson**, P. P., *The Political Philosophy of the British Idealists*, 1990. Reassesses the worth of this school, especially Bradley, Bosanquet and Green, whose work contrasted sharply with the positivism and empiricism of their intellectual environment.

7.45 **Robbins**, P., *The British Hegelians 1875–1925*, New York, 1982. A study of the impact of Hegelianism upon social and political thought in British academic life with particular emphasis on the views of Bradley, Bosanquet, Green and McTaggart.

7.46 **Simhony**, A., 'Idealist organicism: beyond holism and individualism', *Hist. Pol. Thought*, 12, 1991, 515–35. Argues that the organic conception of society defended by the British idealists transcends the traditional dichotomy between holistic and individualist conceptions of society, with particular reference to Green, Bosanquet and Hobhouse.

7.47 **Vincent**, A., and **Plant**. R., *Philosophy, Politics and Citizenship: The Life and Thought of the British Idealists*, 1984. Philosophy here means the idealism of T. H. Green and his followers, whilst politics connotes the new liberalism which came to the fore between 1880 and 1914; citizenship provides the link between the two.

GREEN

7.48 **Anderson**, O., 'The feminism of T. H. Green: a late-Victorian success story', *Hist. Pol. Thought*, 12, 1991, 671–93. Draws attention to the inescapable implication of his ideas: that ethical fulfilment is the mission of each individual and that the life of active citizenship must be open to all. Wishes to reinsert his influence upon middle-class women in the story of the winning of female suffrage.

7.49 **Bellamy**, R., 'A Green revolution?: idealism, liberalism and the welfare state', *Bulletin of the Hegel Society of Great Britain*, 10, 1984, 34–9.

7.50 **Cacoullos**, A. R., *Thomas Hill Green: Philosopher of Rights*, New York, 1974. Suggests that his theory of rights provides the core of his political theory, in a historical juxtaposition of his ideas and contemporary 'rights talk'.

7.51 **Greengarten**, I. M., *Thomas Hill Green and the Development of Liberal-Democratic Thought*, Toronto, 1981. Critical and lucid study of his political thought which seeks to rectify Richter's interpretation and suggests that his political theory was precipitated by his desire to transcend possessive individualism within liberalism. For this he attempted, but failed, to distil a new theory of human nature.

7.52 **Hansen**, P., 'T. H. Green and the limits of liberalism: a response to Professor Lawless', *Can. J. Pol. & Soc. Theory*, 2, 1978, 156–8. Reiterates the importance of Green's view of human nature for a liberal interpretation of industrial society.

7.53 —— 'T. H. Green and the moralization of the market', *Can. J. Pol. & Soc. Theory*, 1, 1977, 91–117. Stressing his underlying ontological principles, the author expounds his sophisticated defence of liberal democracy which involved constructing a broader concept of the human essence than the utilitarians.

7.54 **Holloway**, H., 'Mill and Green on the modern welfare state', *West. Pol. Q.*, 13, 1960, 389–405. Explores the paradox whereby Mill, the self-proclaimed socialist, has been passed over for Green as the theoretical founder of the welfare state. Green's ideas allowed for collective provision whereas Mill's opposition to social regulation mediated against the principles of welfare. Dated argument.

7.55 **Hoover**, K. R., 'Liberalism and the idealist philosophy of Thomas Hill Green', *West. Pol. Q.*, 26, 1973, 550–65. Rehearses his philosophical principles, in particular his rejection of empiricism and utilitarianism, and stresses his understanding of consciousness as central to his conception of the state. Concludes that his most ardent belief lay in individual self-development through a common 'telos'.

7.56 **Lawless**, A., 'T. H. Green and the British liberal tradition', *Can. J. Pol. & Soc. Theory*, 2, 1978, 142–58. Challenging Hansen, the author presents Green as crude in his understanding of capitalism, incoherent in his political economy and obscure in his legacy to liberalism, especially concerning positive freedom.

7.57 **Lewis**, H. D., 'Individualism and collectivism: a study of T. H. Green', *Ethics*, 63, 1952, 44–63.

7.58 **Morrow**, J., 'Property and personal development: an interpretation of T. H. Green's political philosophy', *Politics: Journal of the Australian Political Science Association*, 18, 1983, 84–92.

7.59 **Munroe**, D. H., 'Green, Rousseau, and the culture pattern', *Phil.*, 26, 1951, 347–57. Examines the competing definitions of the 'General Will' which Rousseau elided and the consequent impact this ambiguity had on Green's thought.

7.60 **Nicholson**, P. P., 'A moral view of politics: T. H. Green and the British idealists', *Pol. Sts.*, 35, 1987, 116–22. Systematic review of recent literature on Green.

7.61 —— 'T. H. Green and state action: liquor legislation', *Hist. Pol. Thought.*, 6, 1985, 517–50. Examines the question of state-imposed limitations of alcohol availability to see how far general political principles were connected to practical issues for Green.

7.62 **Randall**, J. H., 'T. H. Green: the development of English thought from J. S. Mill to F. H. Bradley', *J. Hist. Ideas*, 27, 1966, 217–44. Argues that Green was both a Platonist and an Augustinian, eliminating particulars, or feelings, from philosophical discourse.

7.63 **Rich**, P., 'T. H. Green, Lord Scarman and the issue of ethnic minority rights in English liberal thought', *Ethnic and Racial Studies*, 10, 1987, 149–68. Imaginative assessment of Green's thought, tracing his putative impact on the Scarman inquiry of 1987, in particular its discussion of minority group rights.

7.64 **Richter**, M., ed., *The Political Theory of T. H. Green*, New York, 1964.

7.65 —— *The Politics of Conscience: T. H. Green and his Age*, 1964. Excellent account which presents him as attempting to provide political justification for obedience and duty. Arguing that Green's work should be understood as a reaction to the crisis of faith unleashed by rationality and science, the book is full of insight into the Victorian intellectual milieu.

7.66 —— 'T. H. Green and his audience: liberalism as a surrogate religion', *Rev. Pol.*, 18, 1956, 444–72.

7.67 **Roberts**, J., 'T. H. Green', in Z. A. Pelczynski and J. Gray, ed., *Conceptions of Liberty in Political Philosophy*, 1984, 243–62. Views his political theory as an attempt to replace the 'negative' concept of liberty by one which emphasised the duties of individuals to society.

7.68 **Rodman**, J., 'What is living and what is dead in the political philosophy of T. H. Green', *West. Pol. Q.*, 26, 1973, 566–86. A radical reading of Green as a critic of the social coercion lurking behind the facade of political freedom and as a failed philosophical humanist.

7.69 **Simhony**, A., 'On forcing individuals to be free: T. H. Green's liberal theory of positive freedom', *Pol. Sts.*, 39, 1991, 303–20. Defends him from Berlin's accusation of implicit totalitarianism, though suggests that positive freedom does highlight some of the major problems liberalism faces.

7.70 —— 'T. H. Green's theory of the morally justified society', *Hist. Pol. Thought*, 10, 1989, 481–98. Examines his central ethical commitments – self-realisation and the common good – and concludes that he possessed a coherent view of the morally justified society as one which enabled all to realise their capacities.

7.71 **Smith**, C. A., 'The individual and society in T. H. Green's theory of virtue', *Hist. Pol. Thought*, 2, 1981, 187–201. Asserts that as a profound optimist he thought that morally desirable consequences for society would follow if individuals could be made to reject utilitarianism and accept a metaphysical ethic.

7.72 **Vincent**, A., ed., *The Philosophy of T. H. Green*, 1986. A collection of essays which departs from the narrow image of Green as simply a political or moral philosopher and reflects upon the diversity of his thought, including Walsh on his critique of Hume, Milne on his notions of common good and rights, Nicholson on his views on state intervention, and Harris on his theory of political obligation and disobedience.

OTHER THINKERS

7.73 **Randall**, J. H., 'Idealistic social philosophy and Bernard Bosanquet', *Philos. & Phenom. Res.*, 26, 1966, 473–502. Clarifies the legacy of Green for Bosanquet, arguing that the latter's hostility to utilitarianism helped provide justification for the emergence of a welfare state.

7.74 **Weiner**, M., *Between Two Worlds: A Study of the Political Thought of Graham Wallas*, 1971.

Hobhouse

7.75 **Collini**, S., *Liberalism and Sociology: L. T. Hobhouse and Political Argument in England 1880–1914*, 1979. Excellent account of Hobhouse which bypasses the interpretations of political theorists and sociologists by placing his evolving ideas in their complex historical context. Illustrates the opposition between individualism and collectivism which provided the central principle of his work, the development of his political ideas, the importance of idealist concepts in his thought and his ambitious reformulation of the theoretical and historical case for progress.

7.76 **Ginsberg**, M., 'L. T. Hobhouse (1864–1929)', in T. Raison, ed., *The Founding Fathers of Social Science*, 1969, 154–61. Celebrates his view of sociology as an independent discipline, which arose from his recognition of the interdependence between scientific advance and law and morals.

7.77 **Griffin**, C. M., 'L. T. Hobhouse and the idea of harmony', *J. Hist. Ideas*, 35, 1974, 647–61. Bold argument that harmony is the organising theme of Hobhouse's work and remains essentially ambiguous as a political principle. Paradoxically, Hobson contributed to the revision, and ultimate demise, of classical liberalism, according to Griffin.

7.78 **MacRae**, D., 'Leonard Trelawny Hobhouse 1864–1929', *L. S. E. The Magazine of the London School of Economics*, 43, 1972, 9–10.

7.79 **Mariz**, G., 'L. T. Hobhouse as theoretical sociologist', *Albion*, 6, 1974, 307–19.

7.80 **Owen**, J. E., *L. T. Hobhouse, Sociologist*, 1974.

7.81 **Seaman**, J. W., 'L. T. Hobhouse and the theory of "social liberalism" ', *Can. J. Pol. Sc.*, 11, 1978, 777–801. Challenges the conventional picture of Hobhouse as a liberal socialist by focusing upon his attachment to the institutions of the capitalist market economy and commitment to classical liberal morality. His doctrine of social harmony was unable to contain these differing elements.

7.82 **Weiler**, P., 'The new liberalism of L. T. Hobhouse', *Victorian Studies*, 16, 1972, 141–61. Well argued assessment of the sources and composition of his liberalism. Despite his theoretical failures, Weiler suggests, he provided some of the intellectual foundations of the modern welfare state.

Morris

7.83 **Arnot**, R. P., *William Morris: The Man and the Myth*, 1964.

7.84 **Boos**, F. S., 'Morris's German romances as socialist history', *Victorian Studies*, 27, 1984, 321–42.

7.85 —— and **Boos**, W., 'The utopian communism of William Morris', *Hist. Pol. Thought*, 7, 1986, 489–510. Compares Morris's communalism with the ideas of a number of other thinkers (Marx, Kropotkin, Williams, Bahro, Schumacher), concluding that his conception of labour constituted an enlightened attempt to create a distinctive and libertarian ethic of work.

7.86 —— and **Silver**, C. G., ed. *Socialism and the Literary Artistry of William Morris*, Columbia, Miss., 1990. A collection which interweaves his aesthetic praxis with his political ideas. Includes essays on *News from Nowhere* (Donaldson), his relationship with anarchism (Sargent), Bellamy (MacDonald), and contemporary political conflicts (Holzman), as well as a study of his socialist poetry (Waters).

7.87 **Faulkner**, P., *Against the Age: An Introduction to William Morris*, Winchester, Mass., 1980.

7.88 **Frye**, N., 'The meeting of past and future in William Morris', *Studies in Romanticism*,

21, 1982, 303–18. Discussion of the political implications of his poetry and fiction.

7.89 **Goode**, J., 'William Morris and the dream of revolution', in J. Lucas, ed., *Literature and Politics of the Nineteenth Century*, 1971, 221–80.

7.90 **Grennan**, M., *William Morris: Medievalist and Revolutionary*, New York, 1970.

7.91 **Harvey**, C., and **Press**, J., *William Morris: Design and Enterprise in Victorian Britain*, 1991. His achievements as a writer, designer and political visionary are analysed in the context of his role as a distinguished and original man of business.

7.92 **Ingle**, S., 'Socialist man: William Morris and Bernard Shaw', in B. Parekh, ed., *The Concept of Socialism*, 1979, 72–94. Demonstrates how each based their egalitarian beliefs on a vision of the nature of socialist 'man'. Concludes, somewhat unflatteringly, that both based this vision on their own characteristics.

7.93 **Kumar**, K., 'News from nowhere: the renewal of utopia', *Hist. Pol. Thought*, 14, 1993, 133–43. Explores *News From Nowhere*, 'a utopia that recharged the utopian genre'.

7.94 **McCulloch**, C., 'The problem of fellowship in communitarian theory: William Morris and Peter Kropotkin', *Pol. Sts.*, 32, 1984, 437–50. Suggests that fellowship is a key theme within communitarian discourse, yet communitarians struggle to reconcile the moral demands of fellowship with its psychological implications.

7.95 **Meier**, P., *William Morris: The Marxist Dreamer*, Atlantic Highlands, N.J., 1978. Well researched, sympathetic exposition of his thought.

7.96 **Morris**, M., ed., *William Morris: Artist, Writer, Socialist*, New York, 1966.

7.97 **Nairne**, S., et al., ed., *William Morris Today*, 1984.

7.98 **Silver**, C. G., 'Eden and apocalypse: William Morris's Marxist vision in the 1880's', *University of Hartford Studies in Literature*, 13, 1981, 62–77.

7.99 **Thompson**, E. P., *William Morris: Romantic to Revolutionary*, 1955. Lengthy and comprehensive consideration of Morris's life and work, which focuses upon the sources of his ideas and the political perspective he consistently enunciated.

7.100 **Williams**, R., *William Morris Today*, 1984.

Owen

7.101 **Claeys**, G., 'Country, city, and 'community': ecology and the structure of moral space in British Owenite socialism, 1800–1850', *Zeitschrift für Anglistik und Amerikanistik*, 32, 1985, 331–40. Explores the communitarian ideal at the heart of Owenite theory and practice, suggesting that the ecological dimension of this ideology has been neglected, whilst the Owenite critique of the city entailed a series of moral and behavioural possibilities.

7.102 —— 'Paternalism and democracy in the politics of Robert Owen', *Int. Rev. Soc. Hist.*, 27, 1982, 161–207.

7.103 —— 'The early socialist critique of democracy in Britain', in D. McLellan and S. Sayers, ed., *Socialism and Democracy*, 1991, 106–18. Summary of the new political language developed by Owenite socialism, which encouraged a social critique of liberalism and radical parliamentary reformers.

7.104 **Cole**, M. I. P., *Robert Owen of New Lanark*, 1969.

7.105 **Harrison**, J. F. C., *Robert Owen and the Owenites in Britain and America: the Quest for the New Moral World*, 1969.

7.106 **Johnson**, O., *Robert Owen in the United States*, New York, 1970.

7.107 **Miliband**, R., 'The politics of Robert Owen', *J. Hist. Ideas*, 14, 1954, 233–45.

7.108 **Morton**, A. L., ed., *The Life and Ideas of Robert Owen*, 1969.

7.109 **Pollard**, S., and **Salt**, J., ed., *Robert Owen, Prophet of the Poor: Essays in Honour of the Two Hundredth Anniversary of his Birth*, 1971.

7.110 **Taylor**, B., *Eve and the New Jerusalem: Socialism and Feminism in the Nineteenth Century*, 1983. A stimulating and insightful account of the Owenite socialists and their interpretation of the socialist–feminist ideal, inspiring attempts to construct a new sexual culture. Concludes that the neglect of Owenite socialism has compounded the marginalisation of feminist strands within socialism.

Spencer

7.111 **Francis**, M., 'Herbert Spencer and the myth of laissez-faire', *J. Hist. Ideas*, 39, 1978, 317–38. Argues that more accurate discussion of nineteenth-century political theory would result if the myth of 'laissez-faire' were ignored, and attention was focused instead on a theory of the natural harmony of society, held by both Tories and radicals.

7.112 **Goldthorpe**, J. H., 'Herbert Spencer (1830–1903)', in T. Raison, ed., *The Founding Fathers of Social Science*, 1969, 76–83. Forceful argument that, like Durkheim and Weber, he should be regarded as a key figure for contemporary sociology.

7.113 **Gray**, J., 'Spencer on the ethics of liberty and the limits of state interference', *Hist. Pol. Thought*, 3, 1982, 465–81. Finds in his neglected writings a coherent doctrine of liberty, its moral foundations and implications for the limitations of state interference.

7.114 **Gray**, T. S., 'Herbert Spencer: individualist or organicist?', *Pol. Sts.*, 33, 1985. Defends him against criticisms that he fails to reconcile his individualistic conception of natural rights with his organicist social beliefs.

7.115 —— 'Herbert Spencer's social contract theory', *Sts. Pol. Thought*, 1, 1992, 33–45. Rehearses his analytical contractarianism, deployed to justify the minimal state; this position constitutes an intermediary perspective between classical (Hobbes, Locke, Rousseau) and revisionist contractarians (Rawls).

7.118 —— 'Herbert Spencer's theory of social justice – desert or entitlement?', *Hist. Pol. Thought*, 2, 1981, 161–86. Suggests that he produced an 'entitlement' theory of justice: social justice is satisfied when everyone receives that reward to which they are entitled under the rules laid down by the law of equal freedom.

7.119 —— 'Is Herbert Spencer's law of equal freedom a utilitarian or a rights-based theory of justice?', *J. Hist. Phil.*, 26, 1988, 259–78. Argues that his work should be read as an ingenious attempt to reconcile two sets of urgent moral demands – the good and the right.

7.120 **MacRae**, D., ed., *Herbert Spencer: The Man Versus the State with Four Essays on Politics and Society*, 1969.

7.121 **Miller**, W. L., 'Herbert Spencer's drift to conservatism', *Hist. Pol. Thought*, 3, 1982, 483–97. Views him as a subscriber to both radical and conservative beliefs, though his core position was that of a liberal who looked forward to a quasi-anarchical industrial society guided largely by ethical principles and market competition.

7.122 —— 'Herbert Spencer's theory of welfare and public policy', *Hist. Pol. Econ.*, 4, 1972, 207–31. Stresses the originality of his welfare theory, especially his distinction between the welfare of society in its corporate capacity and as the sum of the well-being of its individual members. Emphasis is also given to the relationship between Spencer's theory and Pareto's economics.

7.123 **Paul**, E. F., 'Herbert Spencer: second thoughts. A response to Michael Taylor', *Pol. Sts.*, 37, 1989, 443–8. Defends her argument that Spencer's relative neglect the product of his fundamental inconsistency and deterministic predilections.

7.124 —— 'Herbert Spencer: the historicist as failed prophet', *J. Hist. Ideas*, 44, 1983, 619–38. Expounds his historicist fallacy, suggesting that he failed to reconcile his holism and individualism, which account for his inability to forsee future political developments in Britain.

7.125 **Paul**, J., 'The socialism of Herbert Spencer', *Hist. Pol. Thought*, 3, 1982, 499–514. Concludes that his anti-collectivism is contradictory because his practical political commitment to radical individualism never led him to abandon his earlier theoretical commitment to land nationalisation.

7.126 **Peel**, J. D. Y., *Herbert Spencer: The Evolution of a Sociologist*, 1971.

7.127 **Simon**, W. M., 'Herbert Spencer and the "social organism" ', *J. Hist. Ideas*, 21, 1960, 294–9.

7.128 **Steiner**, H., 'Land, liberty and the early Herbert Spencer', *Hist. Pol. Thought*, 3, 1982, 515–33. Examination of Spencer's equal liberty principle – and the derivative equal rights to the earth doctrine – in terms of his position on the ownership of land.

7.129 **Taylor**, M., *Men Versus the State: Herbert Spencer and Late Victorian Individualism*, 1992. Complex survey of his political and philosophical thought and the intellectual context in which it emerged. Suggests that he represented a larger current of individualist liberal thought at the end of the nineteenth century but dissociates him from the 'Manchester School' of mid-Victorian radicals.

7.130 —— 'The errors of an evolutionist: a reply to Ellen Frankel Paul', *Pol. Sts.*, 37, 1989, 436–42. Refutes Paul's critique of Spencer as based on a false antithesis between individualism and organism and on the assumption that he could not account for the rise of socialism.

7.131 **Weinstein, D.**, 'Equal freedom, rights and utility in Spencer's moral philosophy', *Hist. Pol. Thought*, 11, 1990, 119–43. Examines his evolutionary moral psychology of equal freedom and assesses the plausibility of his attempts to accommodate moral rights with utility.

7.132 **Wiltshire, D.**, *The Social and Political Thought of Herbert Spencer*, 1978. Lucid survey.

Utilitarianism

GENERAL

7.133 **Albee, E.**, *A History of English Utilitarianism*, New York, 1962.

7.134 **Camic, C.**, 'The utilitarians revisited', *Am. J. Soc.*, 85, 1979, 516–50. Investigation of the social theory of the major English utilitarians, which challenges the hostile treatment of this tradition by later generations of sociologists.

7.135 **Capaldi, N.**, *Bentham, Mill and the Utilitarians*, New York, 1965.

7.136 **Crimmins, J. E.**, 'John Brown and the theological tradition of utilitarian ethics', *Hist. Pol. Thought*, 4, 1983, 523–50. Examines theological utilitarianism, a transitory stage prior to fully developed, secular and mature utilitarian theory. Argues that a distinctive thread of utilitarian ethics was religious in character, as is evident from Brown's theology.

7.137 **Kort, F.**, 'The issue of a science of politics in utilitarian thought', *Am. Pol. Sc. Rev.*, 46, 1952, 1140–52.

7.138 **Marsh, P.**, ed., *The Conscience of the Victorian State*, New York, 1979. A collection of essays which assess 'the ways in which a variety of Victorians combined the promptings of conscience with the pursuit of power and their fashioning of policies for the state to follow', including Hamburger on the Whigs, Roberts on the utilitarians, Schreuder on 'Gladstone and the conscience of the state', Helmstadter on 'the nonconformist conscience' and Marsh on conservatism.

7.139 **Plamenatz, J.**, *The English Utilitarians*, 1958. This sharply written study argues that utilitarianism has been the dominant strain within English political and philosophical thought. Plamenatz traces the origins of utilitarianism back to Hobbes and Locke, though he locates Hume as the founder of the tradition. Whilst historical circumstances are played down, some insightful criticisms of utilitarian ideas as well as a self-critical reflection on the first edition illuminate this book.

7.140 —— 'The legacy of philosophical radicalism', in M. Ginsberg, ed., *Law and Opinion in England in the Twentieth Century*, 1959, 27–41. Celebrates the precision and rigour of utilitarian thinkers and the influence they have exercised over contemporary liberalism.

7.141 **Roberts, D.**, *Victorian Origins of the Welfare State*, 1960. Scholarly intervention in the debate about the Victorian governmental revolution and the influence of utilitarianism on this process.

7.142 **Stokes, E.**, *The English Utilitarians and India*, 1959. Subtle and insightful analysis of 'the English political mind in the nineteenth century as it was to be found at work in the administration of India'. Elegant demonstration of tensions within utilitarianism between liberty and authority.

7.143 **Thomas, W.**, *The Philosophical Radicals: Nine Studies in Theory and Practice, 1817–1841*, 1979. Important historical study of the political and intellectual dimensions of their work, including essays on Bentham, James Mill, J. A. Roebuck, J. Parker, A. Forblanque, J. Durham and G. Grote.

7.144 **Viner, J.**, 'Bentham and J. S. Mill: the utilitarian background', in *The Long View and the Short: Studies in Economic Theory and policy*, Glencoe, Ill., 1958, 306–31. A summary of the ideas and influence of these thinkers. Many of Viner's impressions have been subjected to critical scrutiny by later commentators.

BENTHAM

7.145 **Bader, W. C.**, 'Jeremy Bentham: businessman or "philanthropist"?',

Albion, 7, 1975, 245–54. Challenges Himmelfarb's view of the Panopticon as an institution of economic exploitation.

7.146 **Bahmueller**, C. F., *The National Charity Company: Jeremy Bentham's Silent Revolution*, Berkley, Calif., 1981. Sees Bentham's social engineering as antithetical to liberty, as he shifted from principles associated with the humanitarianism and liberalism of the Enlightenment.

7.147 **Baumgardt**, D., *Bentham and the Ethics of Today*, Princeton, N.J., 1952. Lengthy attempt to restore Bentham's reputation as a serious moral thinker, based upon a reasonably exhaustive and chronological commentary on his writings. An offputting tome, best used selectively.

7.148 **Boralevi**, L. C., *Bentham and the Oppressed*, New York, 1984. A hagiographical account of Bentham, masquerading as a radically revisionist interpretation, though includes a comprehensive bibliography.

7.149 **Budge**, I., 'Jeremy Bentham: a re-evaluation in the context of empirical social science', *Pol. Sts.*, 19, 1971, 18–36. Interesting comparison of the ideas of Bentham and Lasswell, a contemporary social theorist, assessing Bentham's significance for modern political science. Budge makes suggestive points about the continued relevance of Bentham's empirical and moral framework for social science research.

7.150 **Burkholder**, L., 'Tarleton on Bentham's *Fragment on Government*', *Pol. Sts.*, 21, 1973, 523–6. Defends the view that this text was written to refute Blackstone on the nature of government.

7.151 **Burns**, J. H., 'Jeremy Bentham and the French Revolution', *Trans. Royal Hist. Soc.*, 16, 1966, 95–114. Chronicles the troubled personal and intellectual relationship between Bentham and leading figures in the French Revolution, which resulted in his condemnation of events in France.

7.152 —— 'Jeremy Bentham: from radical Enlightenment to philosophic radicalism', *Bentham Newsletter*, 8, 1984, 4–14.

7.153 **Coates**, W. H., 'Benthamism, laissez faire, and collectivism', *J. Hist. Ideas*, 11, 1950, 357–63. Asks whether his reliance upon state intervention differentiates him from 'laissez faire' thinkers.

7.154 **Conway**, S., 'Bentham versus Pitt: Jeremy Bentham and British foreign policy', *His. J.*, 30, 1987, 791–809.

7.155 **Crimmins**, J. E., 'Bentham on religion: atheism and the secular society', *J. Hist. Ideas*, 47, 1986, 95–110. Outlines the basis of Bentham's critique of religion, connecting this to Mill's critique of the spiritual and emotional impoverishment of his vision.

7.156 —— 'Religion, utility and politics: Bentham versus Paley', in J. E. Crimmins ed., *Religion, Secularization and Political Thought: Thomas Hobbes to J. S. Mill*, 1989, 130–52. Contrasts the religious and secular versions of utility current at the end of the eighteenth century, subtly highlighting the differences in their emphases upon individual autonomy.

7.157 —— *Secular Utilitarianism: social science and the critique of religion in the thought of Jeremy Bentham*, 1990. Argues against the conventional explanation of his hostility to religion, suggesting that his atheism developed gradually in his early life and was bound up with his metaphysical principles. A scholarly examination of the sources at hand.

7.158 **Cross**, R., 'Blackstone versus Bentham', *Law Q. Rev.*, 92, 1976, 516–27.

7.159 **Cumming**, I., *Useful Learning: Bentham's Chrestomathia with particular reference to the influence of James Mill on Bentham*, Auckland, 1959. Idiosyncratic presentation of their relationship, focusing upon the theme of education.

7.160 **Dinwiddy**, J. R., *Bentham*, 1989. Short, accessible introduction to his life and thought which stresses his moral philosophy as the basis for his political and economic observations. A useful 'further reading' section is appended.

7.161 —— 'Bentham on private ethics and the principle of utility', *Revue International de Philosophie*, 141, 1982, 278–300.

7.162 —— 'Bentham's transition to political radicalism, 1809–10', *J. Hist. Ideas*, 26, 1975, 683–700. Examines Bentham's conversion to universal suffrage through a consideration of the political context in which he operated.

7.163 **Evans**, R., *The Fabrication of Virtue*, 1982

7.164 **Everett**, C. W., *Jeremy Bentham*, 1966. A chronological and dated account of his life and thought, supplemented by selected passages from his major works.

7.165 —— 'The Constitutional Code of Jeremy Bentham', in *Jeremy Bentham Bicentenary Celebrations*, 1948, 14–15.

7.166 **Finer**, S. F., 'The transmission of Benthamite ideas 1820–50', in G. Sutherland, ed., *Studies in the Growth of Nineteenth-Century Government*, 1972, 11–32. Focuses on the process by which Bentham's ideas were disseminated to interested legislators.

7.167 **Fry**, G. K., 'Bentham and public administration', *Public Administration Bulletin*, 24, 1977, 32–40.

7.168 **Goldworth**, A., 'The meaning of Bentham's happiness principle', *J. Hist. Phil.*, 7, 1969, 315–21. Subtle examination of the variety of possible interpretations of this principle.

7.169 **Gunn**, J. A. W., 'Jeremy Bentham and the public interest', *Can. J. Pol. Sc.*, 1, 1968, 398–413. Reinterpretation of this concept in his thought, suggesting that interpretations of him as either quasi-anarchist or quasi-totalitarian misrepresent his ideas.

7.170 **Hamer**, J. L., *Bentham and Beyond*, 1950.

7.171 **Harrison**, R., *Bentham*, 1983. Analysis of his thought which takes his political, ethical and metaphysical writings as a whole. Argues that his overriding metaphysical principle was the belief in utility as a clarification of the ideas of good, right and absolute truth and that his political and legal concerns follow from this principle. An assured and impressive treatment.

7.172 **Hart**, H. L. A., 'Bentham on sovereignty', *Irish Jurist*, 2, 1967, 327–35.

7.173 —— *Essays on Bentham, Jurisprudence and Political Theory*, 1982.

7.174 **Henriques**, U., 'Jeremy Bentham and the machinery of social reform', in H. Hearder and H. R. Loyn, ed., *British Government and Administration: Studies Presented to S. B. Chrimes*, 1974, 169–86. Despite his view of select committees as a democratic means of securing informed legislation, the author suggests that his ideas were not influential upon these bodies and that the question of individual responsibility for reform is essentially complicated.

7.175 **Himmelfarb**, G., 'Bentham scholarship and the Bentham "problem" ', *J. Mod. Hist.*, 41, 1969, 189–206. Prompted by the new edition of his collected works Himmelfarb provides a useful overview of the state of Bentham scholarship and the principal debates within it.

7.176 —— 'Bentham's utopia: the National Charity Company', *J. Brit. Sts.*, 10, 1970, 80–125. Examines his influence upon social reform, in particular his schemes for pauper management which proved more progressive than the ideas of many of his contemporaries.

7.177 —— 'On reading Bentham seriously', *Sts. Burke & Time*, 14, 1972–73, 179–86. Introduces the reader to the convoluted nature of Bentham's texts and the importance of his correspondence.

7.178 —— 'The haunted house of Jeremy Bentham', in *Victorian Minds*, 1968, 32–81. Attempts to locate the Panopticon within his personal and intellectual development, suggesting that it played an important part in his transition to philosophical radicalism.

7.179 **Hume**, L. J., *Bentham and Bureaucracy*, 1981. A comprehensive study of his writings on the social functions of legislation, which elucidates both the liberal and authoritarian elements in his theories of law and government.

7.180 —— 'Bentham as a social and political theorist', *Pol. Sc.*, 40, 1988, 111–27. Defends him as an imaginative and systematic theorist, especially of power, who was prevented by his utilitarian and individualist premises from constructing a convincing theory of the modern state.

7.181 —— 'Jeremy Bentham and the nineteenth-century revolution in government', *Hist. J.*, 10, 1967, 361–75. Returns to his writings to clarify the question of the influence 'Benthamism' had upon the state. Suggests that his economic ideas cannot be deduced from the *Constitutional Code* and that he should not be characterised simply as a 'laissez faire' thinker.

7.182 —— 'Revisionism in Bentham studies', *Bentham Newsletter*, 1, 1978, 3–20. A useful examination of a number of studies which have combined to overturn Halévy's classic study of utilitarianism; Hume endorses criticisms of the notion of Bentham as an irredeemable egoist in his view of human psychology though he concludes that Halévy's account of Benthamite politics may still stand.

7.183 —— 'The political functions of Bentham's theory of factions', *Bentham Newsletter*, 3,

1979, 18–27.

7.184 **Itzkin**, E., 'Bentham's Chrestomathia: utilitarian legacy to English thought', *J. Hist. Ideas*, 39, 1978, 303–16. Describes the plan of schooling detailed in the *Chrestomathia*. The plan was based on earlier educational philosophies, including those of Locke, Ball and Lancaster.

7.185 **James**, M. H., 'Bentham's democratic theory at the time of the French Revolution', *Bentham Newsletter*, 10, 1986, 5–16.

7.186 —— 'Bentham's political writings, 1788–95', *Bentham Newsletter*, 4, 1980, 22–4.

7.187 —— 'Public interest and majority rule in Bentham's democratic theory', *Pol. Theory*, 9, 1981, 49–64. Reviews Mackintosh's claim that Bentham's majoritarianism undermines the institution of private property.

7.188 **Keeton**, G. W., and **Schwartzenberger**, G., ed., *Jeremy Bentham and the Law: A Symposium*, 1948. Includes Ayer on the principle of utility, Everett on his influence in Britain and America, Fitzgerald on parliamentary reform, Fry on penal reform, and Zagday on the poor law.

7.189 **Kelly**, P., *Utilitarianism and Distributive Justice: Jeremy Bentham and the Civil Law*, 1990. A lengthy exposition of his unique utilitarian theory of justice, which claims he was a moderate welfare-state liberal with egalitarian leanings.

7.190 **Larrabee**, H. A., ed., *Bentham's Handbook of Political Fallacies*, Baltimore, Md., 1952.

7.191 **Lawless**, A., 'The ontology of discipline: from Bentham to Mill', *Can. J. Pol. & Soc. Theory*, 4, 1980, 100–20. Examines whether the shift in ideas between these thinkers' work tells us much about the changing social fabric of England, concluding that the expansion of productive capacity in the 1830s and 1840s undermined the significance of Bentham's productivity/scarcity dichotomy.

7.192 **Lieberman**, D., 'Historiographical review: from Bentham to Benthamism', *Hist. J.*, 28, 1985, 199–224.

7.193 **Lomer**, G. R., 'Jeremy Bentham', *Queen's Quarterly*, 67, 1960, 28–40.

7.194 **Long**, D. G., *Bentham on Liberty: Jeremy Bentham's Idea of Liberty in Relation to his Utilitarianism*, Toronto, 1977. Focuses on the early writings, arguing that his approach to liberty was based on his enlightenment conception of social science.

7.195 —— 'Censorial jurisprudence and political radicalism: a reconsideration of the early Bentham', *Bentham Newsletter*, 12, 1988, 4–23.

7.196 **Lyons**, D., *In the Interests of the Governed: A Study in Bentham's Philosophy of Utility and Law*, 1973. Explains his use of the principle of utility and argues that his conception of law is not based on a simple command theory. Precise and detailed textual analysis.

7.197 **MacDonagh**, O., and **Parris**, H., 'Which Benthamite doctrine of the state?', in H. J. Schultz, ed., *English Liberalism and the State: Individualism or Collectivism?*, Lexington, Mass., and Toronto, 1972, 125–36. Excerpts from their articles on the nineteenth-century revolution in government (*Hist. J.*, 1 and 3, 1958 and 1960), framed as a debate over the moral and political contexts for interventionist legislation.

7.198 **Mack**, M. P., *Jeremy Bentham: An Odyssey of Ideas 1748–1792*, 1962. Roughly chronological biography which intertwines his life and ideas, arguing that he created a distinctive intellectual methodology, not just a different political theory.

7.199 **Manning**, D. J., *The Mind of Jeremy Bentham*, 1968. Straightforward and accessible (multiple short chapters) account of his political and philosophical beliefs. Particular emphasis is given to the liberal conditions within which his ideas about government, state and the individual were formulated. The book is somewhat flawed by its Oakeshottian mantle: Bentham's politics are rigorously separated from his metaphysics.

7.200 **Milo**, R., 'Bentham's principle', *Ethics*, 84, 1973–74, 128–39.

7.201 **Mitchell**, C. S., *Bentham, Q.C.*, 1955.

7.202 **Nyman**, M., *Bentham and Hooker*, 1973.

7.203 **Parekh**, B., 'Bentham's theory of equality', *Pol. Sts.*, 18, 1970, 478–95. Skilfully outlines his reorientation of Aristotelian discussions of equality through his notion of equalisation, but concludes that this concept clashes with the implications of the greatest happiness principle.

7.204 —— *Jeremy Bentham: Ten Critical Essays*, 1974. Contributors range from J. S. Mill and Whewell to modern commentators. As a whole the book is uneven, though some of the essays (Parekh, Mitchell) illuminate key themes within Bentham's thought.

7.205 **Peardon**, T. P., 'Bentham's ideal republic', *Can. J. Econ. & Pol. Sc.*, 17, 1951, 184–203.

7.206 **Pitkin**, H. F., 'Slippery Bentham. Some neglected cracks in the foundation of utilitarianism', *Pol. Theory*, 18, 1990, 104–31. Thoughtful examination of a number of slippages embedded within his theory of utility, which leave his thought open to a variety of interpretations.

7.207 **Postema**, G. J., *Bentham and the Common Law Tradition*, 1986. Provides an historical account of the intellectual context in which the science of legislation was developed, a jurisprudential interpretation of Bentham's views on the social function of the institution of law and an examination of the philosophical coherence of his science of legislation.

7.208 **Pratt**, R. C., 'The Benthamite theory of democracy', *Can. J. Econ. & Pol. Sc.*, 21, 1955, 20–9.

7.209 **Pringle**, H., 'Sovereignty and inconvenience – the significance of Bentham's exasperation', *Aust. J. Pol. Sc.*, 27, 1992, 306–18.

7.210 **Robbins**, L., *Bentham in the Twentieth Century*, 1965. A brief but lucid exposition of his ideas, as well as an assertion of their continuing relevance.

7.211 **Roberts**, D., 'Jeremy Bentham and the Victorian administrative state', *Victorian Studies*, 2, 1958–59, 193–210. Suggests that his blueprint for an administrative state, outlined in *The Constitutional Code*, was roughly implemented by the mid-1850s, though establishing a direct causal connection is problematic and complex.

7.212 **Roberts**, W., 'Behavioural factors in Bentham's conception of political change', *Pol. Sts.*, 10, 1962, 163–79.

7.213 —— 'Bentham's conception of political change: a liberal approach', *Pol. Sts.*, 9, 1961, 254–66. Argues that he was an individualist and empiricist rather than a determinist in his account of political change and that these features typify liberalism since the eighteenth century.

7.214 —— 'Bentham's poor law proposals', *Bentham Newsletter*, 3, 1979, 41–2.

7.215 **Rosen**, F., 'Bentham and Mill on liberty and justice', in G. Feaver and F. Rosen, ed., *Lives, Liberties and the Public Good*, 1987, 121–38.

7.216 —— *Bentham, Byron and Greece: Constitutionalism, Nationalism, and Early Liberal Political Thought*, 1992. Re-examines Bentham's activities and thought against the background of the London Greek Committee in the 1920s as part of a larger examination of British political ideas in the early nineteenth century. Concludes that his constitutional theory was derived from Montesquieu and that liberty played a key role in his thought.

7.217 —— 'Elie Halévy and Bentham's authoritarian liberalism', *Enlightenment and Dissent*, 6, 1987, 59–76.

7.218 —— 'Jeremy Bentham and democratic theory', *Bentham Newsletter*, 3, 1979, 46–61.

7.219 —— *Jeremy Bentham and Representative Democracy: A Study of the Constitutional Code*, 1983. Attempts to read this text as a utilitarian statement on representative democracy. Learned and thoughtful exposition of the components of his political and legal thinking, which locates these ideas within modern debates concerning democracy and political institutions.

7.220 —— 'Jeremy Bentham: recent interpretations', *Pol. Sts.*, 30, 1982, 575–81. Reviews the work of the Bentham project in bringing to light primary sources as well as secondary studies.

7.221 **Rosenblum**, N. L., 'Bentham's social psychology for legislators', *Pol. Theory*, 1, 1973, 171–185. Examination of Bentham's claim to have developed a 'logic of the will', which finds expression in his depiction of a social psychology of those who prefer the legal order of the modern state.

7.222 —— *Bentham's Theory of the State*, 1978.

7.223 **Schwartz**, P., 'Jeremy Bentham's democratic despotism', in R. D. Collison Black, ed., *Ideas in Economics*, 1986, 74–103.

7.224 **Stearns**, J. B., 'Bentham on public and private ethics', *Can. J. Phil.*, 5, 1975, 583–94.

7.225 **Steintrager**, J., *Bentham*, 1977. Short and lucid account of the development of his thought, incorporating Enlightenment rationalism, the influence of James Mill and the 'conversion' to democracy in 1809–10.

7.226 —— 'Language and politics: Bentham on religion', *Bentham Newsletter*, 4, 1980, 4–20.

7.227 **Stephen**, L., *The English Utilitarians: Vol. 1, Jeremy Bentham*, New York, 1950. Heavily biographical account of his thought.

7.228 **Tarlton**, C. D., 'The overlooked strategy of Bentham's *Fragment on Government*', *Pol. Sts.*, 20, 1972, 397–406. Innovative reading of this text, suggesting it attempts to subvert the authority of Blackstone so that the ruling powers would perceive the dangers which arose from bad governance.

7.229 **Taylor**, B., 'Jeremy Bentham, the Church of England, and the fraudulent activities of the National Schools Society', *Pedagogica*, 18, 1978, 375–85. Shows that for Bentham, the fraudulent activities of the Church of England and its exclusionary policies necessarily contravened the principle of utility.

7.230 **Waldron**, J., *Nonsense upon Stilts: Bentham, Burke and Marx on the Rights of Man*, New York, 1987.

7.231 **Williford**, M., 'Bentham on the rights of women', *J. Hist. Ideas*, 36, 1975, 167–76. Outlines his belief in the emancipation of women and influence on Mill in this area.

JOHN STUART MILL

7.232 **Alexander**, E., *Matthew Arnold and John Stuart Mill*, 1965. Rather rigid analysis which regards Arnold as an exemplar of humanism, and Mill of liberalism. Argues for a fusion of the two traditions in line with the wishes of both thinkers.

7.233 **Anderson**, B. A., 'Mill on Bentham: from ideology to humanized utilitarianism', *Hist. Pol. Thought*, 4, 1983, 341–57. Argues that Mill's post-Bentham utility principle ceased to be a classical aggregative (average utility) or a substantive moral principle imposing a duty to maximise happiness. Rather, it became a complex principle specifying happiness as valuable for its own sake.

7.234 **Annas**, J., 'Mill and the subjection of women', *Phil.*, 52, 1977, 179–94. Critique of his belief in equal opportunity for women as insufficiently radical.

7.235 **Anschutz**, R. P., *The Philosophy of J. S. Mill*, 1953.

7.236 **Arneson**, R. J., 'Democracy and liberty in Mill's theory of government', *J. Hist. Phil.*, 20, 1982, 43–64. Focuses upon a contradiction between his qualified opposition to majority rule, on paternalistic grounds, and the anti-paternalism evident in *On Liberty*, concluding that he was insufficiently individualistic to resolve this tension.

7.237 —— 'Mill versus paternalism', *Ethics*, 90, 1980, 470–89. Reasserts the validity of his argument in this area against contemporary critics who have widened and diluted the meaning of paternalism. Traces the implications of these views for contemporaries trying to understand autonomy and to connect rationality and voluntary activity.

7.238 **August**, E., *John Stuart Mill: A Mind at Large*, New York, 1975.

7.239 **Ball**, T., 'The feminist and his father – a true detective story', in W. P. Shively, ed., *The Research Process in British Science*, 1984, 92–110. Attempts to solve the 'mystery' surrounding Mill's feminism, pointing to his father as the source of these commitments.

7.240 **Berger**, F. R., *Happiness, Justice and Freedom: The Moral and Political Philosophy of John Stuart Mill*, Berkeley, Calif., 1984. An elaborate exposition and defence of his moral philosophy, which is critically dependent on his psychological theories, and its interaction with his political theory. Extensive treatment is given to the rules which define Mill's notion of justice and underpin the achievement of a well-ordered political society in which autonomy and liberty can be attained. A significant and lucid corrective to more critical accounts of his theory.

7.241 **Britton**, K., *John Stuart Mill*, New York, 1969.

7.242 **Broadbent**, J. E., 'The importance of class in the political theory of John Stuart Mill', *Can. J. Pol. Sc.*, 1, 1968, 270–87. Suggests that his views on class are characterised by a tension between his advocacy of capitalist economics and rejection of fundamental inequalities in capitalist society.

7.243 **Brown**, D. G., 'John Mill: John Rawls', *Dialogue*, 12, 1973, 1–3.

7.244 —— 'Mill on harm to others' interests', *Pol. Sts.*, 26, 1978, 395–9.

7.245 —— 'Mill on liberty and morality', *Phil. Rev.*, 81, 1972, 133–58. Argues that a tension exists between his understanding of freedom and belief in the enforceability of morals, criticising his resolution of this problem by suggesting that immoral conduct cannot be equated with harm to others. Mill, he concludes, is theoretically consistent but wrong.

7.246 —— 'Mill's act-utilitarianism', *Phil. Q.*, 24, 1974, 67–8.

7.247 —— 'What is Mill's principle of utility?', *Can. J. Phil.*, 3, 1973, 1–12.

7.248 **Burns**, J. H., 'J. S. Mill and democracy, 1829–61 – I and II', *Pol. Sts.*, 5, 1957, 158–75 and 281–94.

7.249 **Cameron**, B., 'Mill's treatment of women, workers and private property', *Can. J. Pol. Sc.*, 13, 1980, 775–83.

7.250 **Campbell**, T. D., 'John Stuart Mill and freedom of speech', *Il Pensiero*, 4, 1971, 443–50.

7.251 **Canavan** F. P., 'J. S. Mill on freedom of expression', *Modern Age*, 23, 1979, 362–9.

7.252 **Canovan**, M., 'The eloquence of John Stuart Mill', *Hist. Pol. Thought*, 8, 1987, 505–20. A distinctive reading of *On Liberty* in terms of its rhetorical structure, which brings out the terms of his collaboration with Harriet Taylor and illuminates his political ideas.

7.253 **Carlisle**, J., *John Stuart Mill and the Writing of Character*, Atlanta, Ga., 1991. This interdisciplinary study argues that the concept of 'character' was central to Mill's writings on politics, philosophy, science, literature, sociology and psychology.

7.254 **Chandler**, J. A., 'The liberal justification for local government: values and administrative expediency', *Pol. Sts.*, 37, 1989, 604–11. Attempts to develop, on the basis of Mill's thought, a justification for local government as a way of ensuring that decisions that affect a community are made by its members alone.

7.255 **Claeys**, G., 'Justice, independence and industrial democracy: the development of John Stuart Mill's views on socialism', *J. Pol.*, 49, 1987, 122–47.

7.256 **Clor**, H. M., 'Mill and Millians on liberty and moral character', *Rev. Pol.*, 47, 1983, 3–26.

7.257 **Cohen**, M., ed., *The Philosophy of John Stuart Mill*, 1961.

7.258 **Coleman**, J., 'John Stuart Mill on the French Revolution', *Hist. Pol. Thought*, 4, 1983, 89–111. Attempt to understand the intellectual crisis he underwent in the late 1820s and early 1830s by looking at his changing attitudes to the French Revolution.

7.259 **Cooper**, W., **Nielsen**, K., and **Patten**, S., ed., *New Essays on John Stuart Mill and Utilitarianism*, Ontario, 1979. The contributors relate his ideas to tensions within the utilitarian tradition, between rule and act utilitarianism (Harrison, Copp) and between individualism and altruism (Monro, Norman). Also includes more polemical interventions concerning the contemporary ideological status of Mill's thought (Duncan and Gray, Arneson).

7.260 **Cowling**, M., *Mill and Liberalism*, 1963. Polemical work suggesting that he was a 'totalitarian' masquerading as liberal because he wished to subject the majority to the tutelage of a moral and intellectual elite.

7.261 **Cumming**, R. D., 'Mill's history of his ideas', *J. Hist. Ideas*, 25, 1964, 235–56.

7.262 **Cupples**, B., 'A defence of the received interpretation of J. S. Mill', *Aust. J. Phil.*, 50, 1972, 131–7.

7.263 **Davis**, E. G., 'Mill, socialism and the English romantics: an interpretation', *Economica*, 52, 1985, 345–58. Demonstrates the influence of the romantics upon Mill, arguing unconvincingly that this led him away from socialism.

7.264 **Derry**, J. W., 'Mill's modification of liberalism', in H. J. Schultz, ed., *English Liberalism and the State: Individualism or Collectivism?*, Lexington, Mass., and Toronto, 1972, 22–32. Conventional presentation of Mill's theoretical evolution as embodying the transformation of liberalism, in particular his mature belief that political institutions must be rooted in a liberal social environment to survive.

7.265 **Donner**, W., *The Liberal Self: John Stuart Mill's Moral and Political Philosophy*, Ithaca, N.Y., 1991. Reconstructs his theory of the good, attempting to resolve a number of traditional paradoxes within his thought, and examining his method of measuring value (the preferential ranking of pleasures by knowledgeable judges) in the light of contemporary normative debates. In conclusion the author provides a convincing reply to Gray's libertarian interpretation of Mill, arguing that the latter's commitment to the liberty of self-development draws him to radical egalitarianism.

7.266 **Dryer**, J. P., 'Mill's utilitarianism', in J. M. Robson, ed., *Essays on Ethics, Religion and Society; Collected Works of John Stuart Mill*, Toronto, 1969, ixiii–cxiii. Dry, textually based exposition of Mill's moral theory.

7.267 **Duncan**, G., *Marx and Mill: Two views of social conflict and social harmony*, 1972. Highlights their similarities and differences, arguing against a simplistic opposition between their ideas and placing them in the context of recent social theories.

7.268 —— 'Mill and Marx', in R. Fitzgerald, ed., *Comparing Political Thinkers*, 1980, 245–61. Compares their theories of human nature and attitudes to existing institutional structures, suggesting they shared certain characteristics, for instance an overemphasis on the degree of rationality and community possible in large, complex societies.

7.269 **Dworkin**, G., 'Marx and Mill: a dialogue', *Philos. & Phenom. Res.*, 26, 1965–66, 403–14. A fictional conversation between these thinkers, imagining their reactions to latterday developments.

7.270 **Eisenach**, E. J., 'Mill's *Autobiography* as political theory', *Hist. Pol. Thought*, 8, 1987, 111–31. Suggests we can treat the *Autobiography* as an important part of Mill's political thought.

7.271 **Feuer**, L., 'John Stuart Mill and Marxian socialism', *J. Hist. Ideas*, 10, 1949, 297–304. Clarification of Mill's knowledge of Marx's work, exploring the former's rejection of the Marxian language of revolution and readiness to use violent methods.

7.272 **Flew**, A., 'J. S. Mill – socialist or libertarian?', in M. Ivens, ed., *Prophets of Freedom and Enterprise*, 1975, 21–7. Determined to appropriate Mill for the right, Flew presents his concern for individuality and freedom as incompatible with collectivist goals in this polemical and one-dimensional study.

7.273 **Friedman**, R. B., 'A new exploration of Mill's essay *On Liberty*', *Pol. Sts.*, 14, 1966, 281–304. Opposes the conventional emphasis on his ambiguity and the tension between social utility and individual liberty in his thought, arguing for a more historically informed and sympathetic reading of *On Liberty*. Liberty, for him, was a flexible concept which applied differently to the enlightened minority and the majority in society.

7.274 **Fukuhara**, G., 'John Stuart Mill and socialism', *Bulletin of University of Osaka Prefecture*, 3, 1957, 64–75.

7.275 **Garforth**, F. W., *Educative Democracy: John Stuart Mill on Education in Society*, New York, 1980.

7.276 **Gaus**, G. F., 'The convergence of rights and utility: the case of Rawls and Mill', *Ethics*, 92, 1981–82, 57–72. Contrasts rights-based and utilitarian political theories yet notes that both rely upon similar political presumptions regarding the bounds of individual liberty. Gaus demonstrates this by comparing Mill with Rawls, concluding that both share a psychological conception of human nature.

7.277 **Gibbins** J., 'J. S. Mill, liberalism, and progress', in R. Bellamy, ed., *Victorian Liberalism*, 1990, 91–110. Maintains that Mill's sense of the difficulties attendant upon the 'transitional' nature of English society as it entered the mass industrial age provides the key to understanding his politics.

7.278 **Gildin**, H., 'Mill's *On Liberty*', in J. Cropsey, ed., *Ancients and Moderns: Essays on the Tradition of Political philosophy in Honor of Leo Strauss*, New York, 1964, 288–303. Reviews his argument concerning individual liberty, social restraint and freedom of speech, suggesting that whilst we enjoy many of the liberties for which he argued, the content of his discussion is not relevant to contemporary debate.

7.279 **Golding**, M., 'Mill's attack on moral conservatism', *Midwest Studies in Philosophy*, 1, 1974, 61–7.

7.280 **Goldstein**, L. F., 'Mill, Marx and women's liberation', *J. Hist. Phil.*, 18, 1980, 319–40.

7.281 **Gorovitz**, S., ed., *Mill: Utilitarianism*, Indianapolis, Ind., 1971. Alongside Mill's text are critical essays by Margolis, Mandelbaum, Harrod, Hall, Melden and Harrison on his treatment of this tradition, Urmson on his moral philosophy, and Ten on his understanding of self-regarding actions.

7.282 —— *Utilitarianism: John Stuart Mill*, Indianapolis, Ind., 1971.

7.283 **Gray**, J., 'John Stuart Mill and the future of liberalism', *Contemp. Rev.*, 229, 1976,

138–45. Argues for the transhistorical importance of Mill's defence of the open society and his combined hostility to social injustice and desire to restrict personal liberty as little as possible. These principles are presented as anti-socialist and anti-collectivist.

7.284 —— 'John Stuart Mill on liberty, utility, and rights', *Nomos XIII*, 1981, 80–116. A provocative reply to commentators who emphasise the incommensurability between utilitarianism and theories of moral justification. Mill's thought is presented as an integrated whole, in which the concept of happiness allows him to combine aggregative logic with his commitment to liberty.

7.285 —— 'John Stuart Mill: traditional and revisionist interpretations', *Literature of Liberty*, 11, 1979, 7–37. Admirably clear bibliographical review of the different schools of thought about his work.

7.286 —— 'J. S. Mill on the theory of property', in A. J. Parel and T. Flanagan, ed., *Theories of Property: Aristotle to the Present*, Ontario, 1979, 257–80.

7.287 —— *Mill on Liberty: a Defence*, 1983. A sympathetic exposition of Mill's utilitarian principles, which explicitly rejects conventional emphasis on the impossibility of providing a utilitarian justification for liberty. Suggests he was a more sophisticated, indirect utilitarian in a brief and lucid account which provides a useful review of the existing literature.

7.288 —— 'Mill's and other liberalisms', in K. Haakonson, ed., *Traditions of Liberalism: Essays on John Locke, Adam Smith and John Stuart Mill*, St. Leonards, N.S.W., 1988, 117–41. Partisan critique of the dominant strands of Mill's liberalism, which are rejected for their 'proto-socialist' utopianism; they have exercised too much influence, according to Gray, over contemporary liberal thought. Generally hostile account of Mill.

7.289 —— and **Smith**, G. W., ed., *J. S. Mill's On Liberty in Focus*, 1991. Brings together *On Liberty* and a selection of influential essays by a number of eminent Mill scholars, including Berlin, Ryan, Rees, Ten and Wollheim.

7.290 **Hainds**, J. R., 'John Stuart Mill and the Saint Simonians', *J. Hist. Ideas*, 7, 1946, 103–12. Clarification of Mill's relationship with and interpretation of this school of thought.

7.291 **Halliday**, R. J., *John Stuart Mill*, 1976. An introduction to his thought which begins with his 'mental crisis', suggesting that key shifts in his psychological, political and epistemological reasoning followed. Concludes that he failed to resolve the central paradox between his aristocratic instincts and support for political participation.

7.292 —— 'John Stuart Mill's idea of politics', *Pol. Sts.*, 18, 1970, 461–77. Demonstrates his shift away from utilitarianism and positivism towards a notion of politics based on fundamental divisions between social education and rational knowledge, liberty and indifference and rules of personal conduct and scientific truth. These distinctions were more fundamental than the divisions between contemporary ideologies.

7.293 —— 'Some recent interpretations of John Stuart Mill', *Phil.*, 43, 1968, 1–17.

7.294 **Hamburger**, J., *Intellectuals in Politics: John Stuart Mill and the Philosophic Radicals*, Yale, New Haven, 1965. Historical account of the political fortunes of this coterie in the early nineteenth century, which overstresses their ideological coherence and plays down theoretical differences between James and J. S. Mill.

7.295 **Harris**, A. L., 'J. S. Mill on monopoly and socialism', *J. Pol. Econ.*, 67, 1959, 604–11.

7.296 **Himmelfarb**, G., *On Liberty and Liberalism: The Case of John Stuart Mill*, New York, 1974. Emphasises the distinction between the conception of liberty advanced in *On Liberty* and that which appears in the rest of his work. Mill is criticised from a conservative viewpoint for making an absolute of individual freedom at the expense of the values of the organic community.

7.297 **Hoag**, R. W., 'Happiness and freedom: recent work on John Stuart Mill', *Phil. & Pub. Affairs*, 15, 1986, 188–99. Argues that his utilitarian defence of liberty depends on a concept of happiness that is pluralistic and non-hedonistic.

7.298 **Hodson**, J. D., 'Mill, paternalism and slavery', *Analysis*, 41, 1981, 60–2.

7.299 **Hollis**, M., 'J. S. Mill's political philosophy of mind', *Phil.*, 47, 1972, 334–47. Analyses the contradictions within his shifting account of the self, tracing it back to Hobbes and Hume, and tying it to his understanding of political freedom. Concludes that liberals cannot rely upon empirical observations concerning human nature: they need a metaphysic for the needs of humans.

7.300 **Holloway**, H., 'Mill and Green on the modern welfare state', *West. Pol. Q.*, 13, 1960, 389–405. Dated analysis of the paradox whereby Mill, the self-proclaimed socialist, has been passed over for Green as the theoretical founder of the welfare state. Green's ideas allowed for collective provision whereas Mill's opposition to social regulation mediated against the principles of welfare.

7.301 **Holmes**, S., 'John Stuart Mill: fallibilism, expertise and the politics–science analogy', in M. Dascal and O. Gruengard, ed., *Knowledge and Politics: Case Studies in the Relationship Between Epistemology and Political Philosophy*, Boulder, Calif., 1989. Examines the intimate relationship between Mill's commitment to public learning within a liberal democracy and his theory of the growth of knowledge. A tension between an attachment to science and individualism is said to underlie his work.

7.302 **Honderich**, T., 'Mill on liberty', *Inquiry*, 10, 1967, 292–7.

7.303 —— 'On Liberty and morality-dependent harms', *Pol. Sts.*, 30, 1982, 504–14. Challenges Wollheim's and Ten's views of the given principles of liberty in *On Liberty*; Mill, in fact, included morality-dependent harms in his consideration of the legitimate grounds for interference by the state.

7.304 —— 'The worth of J. S. Mill on liberty', *Pol. Sts.*, 22, 1974, 463–70.

7.305 **Hughes**, P., 'The reality versus the ideal: J. S. Mill's treatment of women, workers and private property', *Can. J. Pol. Sc.*, 12, 1979, 523–42.

7.306 **Justman**, S., *The Hidden Text of Mill's Liberty*, Savage, Md., 1991. Rediscovers, and perhaps overstates, Mill's civic republicanism.

7.307 **Kern**, P. B., 'Universal suffrage without democracy. Thomas Hare and John Stuart Mill', *Rev. Pol.*, 34, 1972, 306–23.

7.308 **Kilcullen**, J., 'Mill on duty and liberty', *Aust. J. Phil.*, 59, 1980, 290–300.

7.309 **Knowles**, D. R., 'A reformulation of the harm principle', *Pol. Theory*, 6, 1978, 233–46. Reconstructs his principle without the notions of jeopardy or insecurity in his definition of harm.

7.310 **Kornberg**, J., 'Feminism and the liberal dialect: John Stuart Mill on women's rights', *Can. Hist. Assoc. Hist. Papers*, 1974, 37–63. Assesses the relation between Mill's liberalism and mid-late nineteenth-century arguments for women's rights.

7.311 **Kurer**, O., 'John Stuart Mill on government intervention', *Hist. Pol. Thought*, 10, 1989, 457–81. Contends that he put forward a coherent theory of government intervention which regards government policy as the bolstering of progress, justice and human improvement.

7.312 —— *John Stuart Mill: The Politics of Progress*, 1991. Examination of the relationship between his belief in individual liberty and social policy.

7.313 **La Selva**, S. V., ' "A single truth": Mill on harm, paternalism and good samaritanism', *Pol. Sts.*, 36, 1988, 486–96. Argues that recent critics have confused apparent paternalism in *On Liberty* with good samaritanism; both have been seen as incompatible with the harm principle. In fact, good samaritanism is a special application of the harm principle, whilst paternalism is consistently rejected by Mill.

7.314 —— 'Selling oneself into slavery: Mill and paternalism', *Pol. Sts.*, 35, 1987, 211–23. Defends Mill from accusations that he resorts to paternalism on this issue; in fact his anti-paternalistic argument depends upon the paradox of sovereignty (self-embracing sovereignty is overridden by continuing sovereignty). The author suggests that a similar paradox may lie at the heart of the concept of freedom.

7.315 **Lachs**, J., 'Mill and Constant: a neglected connection in the history of liberty', *Hist. Phil. Q.*, 9, 1992, 87–96.

7.316 **Ladenson**, R. F., 'Mill's conception of individuality', *Soc. Theory & Pract.*, 4, 1977, 167–82. Opposes the conventional dichotomy between Mill's utilitarianism and his belief in the virtues of individuality.

7.317 **Laine**, M., *Bibliography of Works on John Stuart Mill*, 1982.

7.318 —— ed., *The Cultivated Mind; Essays on J. S. Mill presented to John M. Robson*, Toronto, 1991. Includes Ryan on the complex development of his notion of self,

Hamburger on the covert call for the eradication of Christianity in *On Liberty*, Simcox on his influence on British thought, and Collini on the marked shift in attitudes to his work between his death and 1945.

7.319 **Lee**, S., 'On the justification of paternalism', *Soc. Theory & Pract.*, 7, 1981, 193–204.

7.320 **Levy**, M., 'Mill's stationary state and the transcendence of liberalism', *Polity*, 14, 1981, 273–93.

7.321 **Lewisohn**, D. H., 'Mill and Comte on the methods of social science', *J. Hist. Ideas*, 33, 1972, 315–24.

7.322 **Lichtman**, R., 'The surface and substance of Mill's defense of freedom', *Social Res.*, 30, 1963, 469–94. Defends him from accusations of inconsistency by arguing for a difference between the structure of his position as against his stated belief. Despite this unsatisfactory proposition, the author shows a keen awareness of the tensions within his liberalism and the problems of definition involved in concepts such as restraint and self-realisation.

7.323 **Lyndon**, S. M., 'Marital slavery and friendship: John Stuart Mill's *The Subjection of Women*', in S. M. Lyndon and C. Pateman, ed., *Feminist Interpretations and Political Theory*, 1991, 164–80.

7.324 **Lyons**, D., 'J. S. Mill's theory of morality', *Nous*, 10, 1976, 101–19.

7.325 —— 'Liberty and harm to others', *Can. J. Phil.*, supp. 5, 1979, 1–19.

7.326 —— 'Mill's theory of justice', in A. I. Goldman and J. Kim, ed., *Values and Morals*, Dordrecht, 1978, 1–20.

7.327 **Mabbot**, J., 'Interpretations of Mill's Utilitarianism', *Phil. Q.*, 6, 1956, 115–20.

7.328 **McCloskey**, H. J., *John Stuart Mill: A Critical Study*, 1971.

7.329 —— 'Mill's liberalism', *Phil. Q.*, 13, 1963, 143–56.

7.330 **Magid**, H. M., 'Mill and the problem of freedom of thought', *Social Res.*, 21, 1954, 43–61. Critique of his defence of liberty of thought and potential constraints on this liberty. Magid applies these ideas in the context of scientific thought.

7.331 **Mandelbaum**, M., 'On interpreting Mill's Utilitarianism', *J. Hist. Phil.*, 6, 1968, 35–46. Attends to the relatively neglected passages of this text, illuminating his critique of Bentham and analysis of the concept of virtue.

7.332 **de Marchi**, N. B. 'The success of Mill's principles', *Hist. Pol. Econ.*, 6, 1974, 119–57.

7.333 **Mazlish**, B., *James and John Stuart Mill: Father and Son in the Nineteenth Century*, 1975. A 'psychohistory' of the Mills which deploys the Oedipus complex to interpret their relations and development. Despite the author's claims, little is added to our understanding of the younger Mill's political and economic thought.

7.334 **Megill**, A. D., 'John Stuart Mill's religion of humanity and the second justification for the writing of *On Liberty*', *J. Pol.*, 34, 1972, 612–29.

7.335 **Mineka**, F. E., 'J. S. Mill and neo-Malthusianism', *Mill Newsletter*, 8, 1972, 3–10.

7.336 **Mueller**, I. W., *John Stuart Mill and French Thought*, Urbana, Ill., 1956. Presents the 1830 revolution in France as the key event in his break with utilitarianism, a shift reinforced by his affinity with the revolutions of 1848.

7.337 **Otlow**, R., 'Why John Stuart Mill called himself a socialist', *Hist. Euro. Ideas*, 17, 1993, 479–83. Brief historical explanation of his self-definition as socialist, stressing the hostile reaction from the English establishment to his views on property which forced him outside conventional labels.

7.338 **Packe**, M., St. J., *The life of John Stuart Mill*, 1954. Chronological biography which presents a clear, if eulogistic, picture of the development of his thought.

7.339 **Panichas**, G. E., 'Mill's flirtation with socialism', *Southwestern J. Phil.*, 21, 1983, 251–70.

7.340 **Pappé**, H. O., *John Stuart Mill and the Harriet Taylor Myth*, 1962.

7.341 —— 'Mill and Tocqueville', *J. Hist. Ideas*, 25, 1964, 217–34.

7.342 **Parsons**, J. E., 'J. S. Mill's conditional liberalism in perspective', *Polity*, 5, 1972, 147–69.

7.343 **Pateman**, T., 'Liberty, authority and the negative dialectics of J. S. Mill', *Rad. Phil.*, 32, 1982, 16–22. Traces the utilitarian theories of liberty and authority and his break from such ideas.

7.344 **Pedersen**, J. T., 'On the educational function of political participation: a comparative analysis of John Stuart Mill's theory and contemporary survey research findings', *Pol. Sts.*, 30, 1982, 557–68.

Focuses on the problems of measuring the possible educational benefits of political participation, particularly concerning electoral behaviour. Concludes sceptically because of the difficulty in balancing educative improvement with the necessary spontaneity which aids educational advance.

7.345 **Pettit**, P., 'Liberalism and its defence: a lesson from J. S. Mill', in K. Haakonssen, ed., *Traditions of Liberalism: Essays on John Locke, Adam Smith and John Stuart Mill*, 1988, 169–81. Reviews the contributions in the same collection made by Gray and Ten as part of an overview of the different evaluative bases which liberals deploy to root their conception of freedom.

7.346 **Phillips Griffiths**, A. ed., *Of Liberty*, 1983. A series of essays, taken from the Royal Institute of Philosophy Lecture Series, 1980–1, which examine problems with the concept of liberty in liberal political discourse, including Lively on problems with Mill's deployment of paternalism, and Ryan on property and liberty in Mill's thought.

7.347 **Powers**, R. H., 'John Stuart Mill: morality and inequality', *South Atlantic Quarterly*, 58, 1959, 206–12. Rehearses Mill's arguments during the late nineteenth-century debate about female suffrage, suggesting his defence of equality remains relevant to debates about racial equality.

7.348 **Qualter**, T. H., 'John Stuart Mill, disciple of de Tocqueville', *West. Pol. Q.*, 13, 1960, 1880–89. Argues that Mill's *On Liberty* is strongly influenced by Tocqueville's ideas about freedom as expounded in *Democracy in America*.

7.349 **Radcliffe**, P., ed., *Limits of Liberty: Studies of Mill's on Liberty*, 1966.

7.350 **Rees**, J. C., 'A phase in the development of Mill's ideas on liberty', *Pol. Sts.*, 6, 1958, 33–44.

7.351 —— 'A re-reading of Mill on liberty', *Pol. Sts.*, 8, 1960, 113–29.

7.352 —— *John Stuart Mill's On Liberty*, 1985. Posthumously collected essays which provide a lucid exposition of his conception of freedom. Argues for the essential consistency of his political thought, and against the idea of a fundamental tension between liberty and justice in his work.

7.353 —— *Mill and his Early Critics*, 1956.

7.354 —— 'The reaction to Cowling on Mill', *Mill Newsletter*, 1, 1964, 2–11.

7.355 —— 'The thesis of the two Mills', *Pol. Sts.*, 25, 1977, 369–82. Argues against readings of Mill which stress his abandonment of rigid utilitarianism and later hostility to rules for the conduct of scientific enquiry. Interesting engagement with Feyerabend's appropriation of *On Liberty*.

7.356 —— 'Was Mill for liberty?', *Pol. Sts.*, 14, 1966, 72–7.

7.357 **Riley**, J., *Liberal Utilitarianism: Social Choice Theory and J. S. Mill's Philosophy*, 1988. Combines social choice theory with a particular reading of his liberal version of utilitarianism in the search for a credible liberal conception of utility. Stimulating analysis, yet problematic in its emphasis on his coherence and definition of utilitarianism.

7.358 **Robson**, J. M., *The Improvement of Mankind: The Social and Political Thought of John Stuart Mill*, 1968. Emphatic about the underlying unity of his mature work, this study traces the sources of his thought and concludes that utilitarianism provided the core principle for his political ideas. Well researched but somewhat simplistic presentation.

7.359 —— and **Laine**, M. ed., *James and John Stuart Mill: Papers of the Centenary Conference*, Toronto, 1976. Contains essays by Schneewind on the contemporary reception of Mill's *Utilitarianism*, Hollander on the Ricardian assumptions in Mill's thought, and Hamburger on the similarities and differences between Mill's and Tocqueville's conceptions of liberty.

7.360 **Rosen**, F., 'Bentham and Mill on liberty and justice', in G. Feaver and F. Rosen, ed., *Lives, Liberties and the Public Good*, 1987, 121–38.

7.361 **Rossi**, A. S., ed., *J. S. Mill and Harriet Taylor: Essays on Sex Equality*, Chicago, Ill., 1970.

7.362 **Ryan**, A., 'John Stuart Mill (1806–73)', in T. Raison, ed., *The Founding Fathers of Social Science*, 1969, 43–50. Neat illustration of the implications of his ideas for later social scientists.

7.363 —— *J. S. Mill*, 1974. A sustained and accessible examination of his key texts and ideas, which adopts a chronological format yet provides an illuminating guide to the political and intellectual context. Masterful presentation of his political philosophy.

7.364 —— *Mill on Liberty: A Defence*, 1983.

7.365 —— ed., *Sense and Sensibility in Mill's Political Thought in a Cultivated Mind: Essays on J. S. Mill presented to John M. Robson*, Toronto, 1992. Argues that the *Autobiography* is of philosophical interest as a 'self-subverting' text: Mill offers it as an account of his education but also implies that he never stopped being educated by Harriet Taylor.

7.366 —— *The Philosophy of John Stuart Mill*, 1970. Insists on the systematic character of his philosophy: from the philosophy of mathematics to the defence of individual liberty, Mill attacked the prevailing 'intuitive' theories and replaced them with a subtle empiricism.

7.367 —— 'Two concepts of politics and democracy: James and John Stuart Mill', in M. Fleisher, ed., *Machiavelli and the Nature of Political Thought*, 1973, 76–113. Contrasts the economic understanding of political behaviour evident in James Mill's thought with the emphasis upon self-development and participation in J. S. Mill's work.

7.368 —— 'Utilitarianism and bureaucracy: the views of J. S. Mill', in G. Sutherland, ed., *Studies in the Growth of Nineteenth-Century Government*, 1972, 33–62. Assesses his view of the civil service as a case-study for a broader consideration of the relationship between traditions of thought associated with individuals and institutional practices. Teases out the ambiguities and inconsistencies of the utilitarian tradition.

7.369 **Sakai**, N., *J. S. Mill's Conception of Freedom*, Zürich, 1957.

7.370 **Sarvasy**, W., 'J. S. Mill's theory of democracy for a period of transition between capitalism and socialism', *Polity*, 16, 1984, 567–87. Problematic attempt to reconcile Mill's socialism with his theory of democracy by suggesting that he understood democratic development as the transition from capitalism to socialism.

7.371 **Scanlon**, J. P., 'J. S. Mill and the definition of freedom', *Ethics*, 68, 1968, 194–206.

7.372 —— *The New Political Economy of J. S. Mill*, 1968.

7.373 **Schneewind**, J. B., ed., *Mill*, 1969. Wide ranging collection, including Russell on his legacy, Anshutz on his utilitarian logic, Hall on the 'proof' of utility in Bentham and Mill, Urmson on his moral philosophy, Mandelbaum on the problems of his utilitarianism, Burns on his commitment to democracy, Cowling on his place in the liberal tradition, Halliday reviewing recent interpretations of his thought, and Friedman on his theory of authority.

7.374 **Schwartz**, P., 'J. S. Mill and socialism', *Mill Newsletter*, 4, 1968, 11–15.

7.375 **Semmel**, B., *John Stuart Mill and the Pursuit of Virtue*, 1984. A cogent account of his ideas which stresses his 'neo-radicalism', involving the choice of virtue over material interests, as the key organising principle for his ethical, philosophical and political ideas.

7.376 **Shanley**, M. L., 'Marital slavery and friendship in John Stuart Mill's *The Subjection of Women*', *Pol. Theory*, 9, 1981, 229–47. Rebuttal of contemporary feminist criticism of the limitations of his legal interpretation of sexual equality, focusing upon his belief that gender equality was essential to marital friendship and social progress, a position which stands in direct opposition to orthodox liberal individualism.

7.377 **Skorupski**, J., *John Stuart Mill*, 1989. Focuses on his philosophy, in particular his understanding of empiricism, language and the inductive method, concluding with an analysis of his distinctive liberalism and its foundations in his father's belief in the general good.

7.378 **Smart**, P., 'Mill and human nature', in I. Forbes and S. Smith, ed., *Politics and Human Nature*, 1983, 36–52. Breaks his theory into its component parts, stressing his reliance upon utilitarian psychology and attempt to develop a concept of free will.

7.379 —— *Mill and Marx: Individual Liberty and the Roads to Freedom: a proposal for a comparative critical reconstruction*, 1991. Compares their respective theories of liberty and its potential attainment.

7.380 **Smith**, G. W., 'J. S. Mill on Edger and Reville: an episode in the development of Mill's conception of freedom', *J. Hist. Ideas*, 41, 1980, 433–58.

7.381 —— 'J. S. Mill on freedom', in Z. A. Pelczynski and J. Gray, ed., *Conceptions of Liberty in Political Philosophy*, 1984, 188–200. A critical review of the literature, concluding that his notion of liberty remains complex and contradictory and is not illuminated by describing him as a proponent of negative liberty.

7.382 —— 'The logic of J. S. Mill on freedom', *Pol. Sts.*, 28, 1980, 238–52. Detailed analysis of a key passage in his *Logic*, emphasising inconsistencies and tensions in his attempt to reconcile the compatibilist interpretation of freedom with the belief that freedom equals complete virtue. Also points to differing conceptions of freedom circulating within Mill's texts.

7.383 —— 'Utility, paternalism and slavery', *Pol.*, 1, 1981, 15–18. Consideration of the principles on which Mill's ban on voluntary slavery is based.

7.384 **Smith**, J. M., and **Sosa**, E., ed., *Mill's Utilitarianism*, Belmont, Calif., 1969.

7.385 **Spafford**, D., 'Mill's majority principle', *Can. J. Pol. Sc.*, 18, 1985, 599–608. Examines his ideas on this question, suggesting that he believed strongly in the establishment of a popular mandate to govern as the basis for a representative democracy.

7.386 **Spitz**, D., ed., *On Liberty*, New York, 1975.

7.387 **Strawson**, P. F., 'Social morality and individual ideal', *Phil.*, 36, 1968, 1–17.

7.388 **Struhl**, P. R., 'Mill's notion of social responsibility', *J. Hist. Ideas*, 37, 1976, 155–62. Bold interpretation of Mill as a theorist concerned to balance liberty against authority, emphasising the role of social responsibility in cementing his vision of social relations infused by respect, co-operation and concern.

7.389 **Sullivan**, E. P., 'A note on the importance of class in the political theory of John Stuart Mill', *Pol. Theory*, 9, 1981, 248–56. Argues that he allotted an important role to classes in historical change as well as to ideas, by focusing upon his writing about the Liberal parties in England and France in the 1830s.

7.390 —— 'Liberalism and imperialism: J. S. Mill's defence of the British empire', *J. Hist. Ideas*, 44, 1983, 599–617. Argues that he played a crucial role in transforming liberalism into an ideology which defended empire, though simplifies his ideas and overstates his break from the liberal tradition which preceded him.

7.391 **Tatalovich**, A., 'John Stuart Mill – *The Subjection of Women*: an analysis', *Southern Quarterly*, 12, 1973, 87–105.

7.392 **Ten**, C. L., 'Mill and liberty', *J. Hist. Ideas*, 30, 1969, 47–68.

7.393 —— *Mill on Liberty*, 1980. An accessible interpretation of *On Liberty*, which also provides a critical survey of recent interpretations of his thought.

7.394 —— 'Mill's defence of liberty', in K. Haakonssen, ed., *Traditions of Liberalism: Essays on John Locke, Adam Smith and John Stuart Mill*, St. Leonards, N.S.W., 1988, 143–68. Useful survey of the varying interpretations of Mill's utilitarianism proffered by contemporary commentators, in which the author reiterates his non-utilitarian interpretation of his thought.

7.395 —— 'Paternalism and morality', *Ratio*, 13, 1971, 56–66.

7.396 —— 'Self-regarding conduct and utilitarianism', *Aust. J. Phil.*, 55, 1977, 105–13. Challenges the attempt (by Wollheim) to reconcile Mill's liberalism with utilitarianism through an analysis of the question of self-regarding actions.

7.397 —— 'The liberal theory of the open society', in D. Germino and K. von Beyme, ed., *The Open Society in Theory and Practice*, The Hague, 1974, 142–63. Defends *On Liberty* from conservative and radical critics, demonstrating how individuality furnishes a positive guide for political action.

7.398 **Thomas**, W., *Mill*, 1985. Brief biographical study; an excellent starting point for those not acquainted with the subject.

7.399 **Thompson**, D. F., *John Stuart Mill and Representative Government*, Princeton, N.J., 1976.

7.400 **Tullock**, G., *Mill and Sexual Equality*, 1989. Restatement of the case for interpreting Mill's writings on the 'woman question' as those of a liberal feminist.

7.401 **Turk**, C., *Coleridge and Mill: A Study of Influence*, 1988. Illuminating comparison.

7.402 **Van Holthoon**, F. C., *The Road to Utopia: A Study of J. S. Mill's Social Thought*, Assen, 1971.

7.403 **Vernon**, R., 'J. S. Mill and the religion of humanity', in J. E. Crimmins, ed., *Religion, Secularization and Political Thought: Thomas Hobbes to J. S. Mill*, 1989, 167–82. Distinguishes Mill from other nineteenth-century secular radicals who advocated atheism; his interest in secular religion provides an important background to *On Liberty* and illustrates the communitarian concerns central to his thought.

7.404 **von Hayek**, F. A., *John Stuart Mill and Harriet Taylor*, 1969.

7.405 **Waithe**, M. E., 'Why Mill was for paternalism', *International Journal of Law and Psychiatry*, 6, 1983, 102–3.

7.406 **West**, E. G., 'Liberty and education: John Stuart Mill's dilemma', *Phil.*, 40, 1965, 124–42.

7.407 **White**, R. J., 'John Stuart Mill', *Cambridge J.*, 5, 1951, 86–96.

7.408 **Williams**, G. L., 'Mill's principle of liberty', *Pol. Sts.*, 24, 1976, 132–40. Interprets this principle in terms of justice and rights; these concepts are removed, by Williams, from the more utilitarian framework of Mill's predecessors, whilst freedom is interpreted as individual independence, not just the absence of restraint.

7.409 **Wolff**, R. P., *The Poverty of Liberalism*, 1968. Hostile review of Mill's defence of liberty, which illuminates the inconsistencies which lie, according to this radical critic, at the heart of liberalism. Similar problems emerge from consideration of the treatment of tolerance and community in Mill's thought.

7.410 **Wollheim**, R., 'John Stuart Mill and Isaiah Berlin. The ends of life and the preliminaries of morality', in A. Ryan, ed., *The Idea of Freedom*, 1979, 253–69. Critique of Berlin's reading of Mill, which suggests that utility remained at the heart of his moral principles.

7.411 —— 'John Stuart Mill and the limits of state action', *Social Res.*, 40, 1973, 1–30. Defence of his notion of self-regarding actions.

7.412 **Woods**, T., *Poetry and Philosophy: A Study in the Thought of John Stuart Mill*, 1961.

7.413 **Zastoupil**, L., 'Moral government: J. S. Mill on Ireland', *Hist. J.*, 26, 1983, 707–17.

7.414 **Zimmer**, L. B., 'John Stuart Mill and democracy, 1866–7', *Mill Newsletter*, 11, 1976, 3–17. Choosing the period of Mill's career when he was an M.P., Zimmer demonstrates his commitment to democracy, as it was defined in his day.

7.415 —— 'The "negative argument" in J. S. Mill's utilitarianism', *J. Brit. Sts.*, 17, 1977, 119–37. Explores the foundational role of 'negative argument' in utilitarian thought.

JAMES MILL

7.416 **Bain**, A., *James Mill. A Biography*, New York, 1967.

7.417 **Ball**, T., 'Platonism and penology: James Mill's attempted synthesis', *Journal of the History of the Behavioural Sciences*, 18, 1982, 222–9.

7.418 —— 'Utilitarianism, feminism, and the franchise: James Mill and his critics', *Hist. Pol. Thought*, 1, 1980, 91–115. Rescues him from the criticism that he was a male supremacist, thereby challenging the conventional belief that his son derived his 'feminism' from the elder Mill's critics, especially Bentham. Suggests that James Mill's ambivalent ideas, and the work of William Thompson, were the sources for J. S. Mill's commitment to female equality.

7.419 **Burston**, W. H., *James Mill on Philosophy and Education*, 1973.

7.420 **Carr**, W. R., 'James Mill's politics: a final word', *Hist. J.*, 15, 1971, 315–20.

7.421 —— 'James Mill's politics reconsidered: parliamentary reform and the triumph of truth', *Hist. J.*, 14, 1971, 553–80.

7.422 **Dinwiddy**, J. R., 'James Mill on Burke's doctrine of prescription', *Sts. Burke & Time*, 18, 1977, 179–90.

7.423 **Fenn**, R. A., *James Mill's Political Thought*, New York, 1987. Emphasises his philosophical framework as the key to understanding his political principles.

7.424 **Forbes**, D., 'James Mill and India', *Cambridge J.*, 5, 1951, 19–53.

7.425 **Haakonssen**, K., 'James Mill and Scottish moral philosophy', *Pol. Sts.*, 33, 1985, 628–41. Focuses on the Scottish moral philosophy tradition and its influence on his idea of a conjectural history of moral institutions. Concludes that the moral philosophy of Stewart provided a bridge to his mature utilitarianism.

7.426 **Hamburger**, J., *James Mill and the Art of Revolution*, Yale, New Haven, 1963.

7.427 —— 'James Mill on universal suffrage and the middle class', *J. Pol.*, 24, 1962, 167–90. Presents Mill as a firm believer in universal suffrage who hid his radicalism behind eulogies about middle-class virtues.

7.428 **Lively**, J., and **Rees**, J. C., ed., *Utilitarian Logic and Politics: James Mill's Essay on Government; Macaulay's 'Critique' and the Ensuing Debate*, 1978.

7.429 **Thomas**, W., 'James Mill's politics: a rejoinder', *Hist. J.*, 14, 1971, 735–50.

7.430 —— 'James Mill's politics: the *Essay on Government* and the movement for reform', *Hist. J.*, 12, 1969, 249–84.

7.431 **Woodcock**, M. B., 'Educational principles and political thought: the case of James Mill', *Hist. Pol. Thought*, 1, 1980, 475–99. Argues against the conventional antithesis between utilitarian (economic/instrumentalist) and participatory (educational/expressive) accounts of human nature and political obligation in scholarship on James Mill.

Other thinkers

7.432 **Blake**, R., *Disraeli*, 1969. A major political biography which includes a reconstruction of his paternalist, one-nation Toryism.

7.433 **Brown**, K. D., ed., *Essays in Anti-Labour History: Responses to the Rise of Labour in Britain*, 1974. Includes a consideration of Mallock and other conservative thinkers at the end of the century.

7.434 **Cachin**, M-F., ' "Non-governmental society": Edward Carpenter's position in the British socialist movement', *Prose Studies*, 13, 1990, 58–73. General overview of Carpenter's socialism and his account of changes on the British left.

7.435 **Calleo**, D. P., *Coleridge and the Idea of the Modern State*, Yale, New Haven, 1966.

7.436 **Claeys**, G., 'A utopian Tory revolutionary at Cambridge: the political ideas and schemes of James Bernard, 1834–1839', *Hist. J.*, 25, 1982, 583–603. Reconstructs his ideas and career and explains the temporary alliance which he forged with Owenites and other radicals.

7.437 **Colmer**, J., *Coleridge, Critic of Society*, 1959.

7.438 **Cunliffe**, J., 'The neglected background of radical liberalism: P. E. Dove's theory of property', *Hist. Pol. Thought*, 11, 1990, 467–90. Exposition of the ideas of this neglected Scottish thinker concerning the need for a property regime in land consistent with the natural right to private property. His prescription for the joint ownership of land is convincingly presented as the precursor of Spencer's approach.

7.439 **Eastwood**, D., 'Robert Southey and the intellectual origins of romantic conservatism', *Eng. Hist. Rev.*, 104, 1989, 306–31. Sharp account of how Southey and other High Tories shaped their opposition to political economy into a coherent social theory.

7.440 **Fasnacht**, G. E., *Acton's Political Philosophy*, 1952.

7.441 **Hanzawa**, T., 'Samuel Taylor Coleridge and "the friend": the emergence of a political philosopher', *Hist. Euro. Ideas*, 9, 1988, 681–95.

7.442 **Harvard**, W. C., *Henry Sidgwick and Later Utilitarian Political Philosophy*, Gainesville, Fla., 1959. Account of the ideas of a late nineteenth-century representative of the creed derived from Jeremy Bentham and J. S. Mill, engaged in a desperate rearguard action – on Harvard's reading – against emerging anti-utilitarian doctrines.

7.443 **Hilton**, B., 'Gladstone's theological politics', in M. Bentley and J. Stevenson, ed., *High and Low Politics in Modern Britain: Ten Studies*, 1983, 28–57. Suggests that Gladstone became a Lockean as he began to construe liberty as the means whereby God's natural laws might be discovered.

7.444 **Himmelfarb**, G., *Lord Acton: A Study in Conscience and Politics*, 1952.

7.445 —— 'The American Revolution in the political theory of Lord Acton', *J. Mod. Hist.*, 21, 1949, 293–312.

7.446 **Hunt**, E. K., 'Utilitarianism and the labour theory of value: a critique of the ideas of William Thompson', *Hist. Pol. Econ.*, 11, 1979, 545–71.

7.447 **Jay**, R., *Joseph Chamberlain: A Political Study*, 1981. A critical and historically informed study of Chamberlain's political career, which throws light upon the ambiguities and contradictions in his achievements and political thought. His career illustrates the transition in conservatism at the turn of the century.

7.448 **Kenny**, T., *The Political Thought of John Henry Newman*, 1957. Outlines his conservatism which is immanent within his theological reflections, emphasising the influence of Romanticism, the Oxford movement and Burke on his intellectual development.

7.449 **Morris**, R. C., 'Whitehead and the new liberals on social progress', *J. Hist. Ideas*, 51, 1990, 75–92. Argues against previous, misleading interpretations of Whitehead by relating his metaphysical ideas of process and progress to his understanding of individuality and sociability.

7.450 **Morrow**, J., *Coleridge's Political Thought: Property, Morality and the Limits of Traditional Discourse*, 1990. Comprehensive and perceptive, tracing the evolution of his political thinking, with close attention to the historical context.

7.451 **Nicholls**, D., 'Gladstone on liberty and democracy', *Rev. Pol.*, 23, 1961, 30–42. Assesses his commitment to the principle of liberty and ambivalent usage of the term.

7.452 **Pierson**, S., 'Edward Carpenter, prophet of a socialist millennium', *Victorian Studies*, 13, 1970, 301–19.

7.453 **Rowbotham**, S., 'In search of Carpenter', *History Workshop*, 3, 1977, 121–33. Outlines the influence of Carpenter's sexual and political radicalism upon contemporaries, especially Morris and other socialists.

7.454 —— and **Weeks**, J., *Socialism and the New Life: The Personal and Sexual Politics of Edward Carpenter and Havelock Ellis*, 1977. Two careful historical reconstructions of the ideas of Carpenter (Rowbotham) and Ellis (Weeks); these essays complement each other in their examination of the broad agenda developed by elements of the late nineteenth-century socialist movement, encompassing sexual politics, cultural politics and the articulation of subjective experience.

7.455 **Spring**, D., 'Walter Bagehot and deference', *Am. Hist. Rev.*, 81, 1976, 524–31. Review of the role of deference within Bagehot's understanding of liberty.

7.456 **Tsuzuki**, C., *Edward Carpenter 1844–1929: Prophet of Human Fellowship*, 1980. Historically informed biography which stresses the relationship between his campaign for sexual reform and his socialism.

7.457 **Vincent**, J., *Disraeli*, 1990. A short survey which concentrates on Disraeli's ideas on race, Judaism, religion and politics, challenging simplistic appropriations of Disraeli by later schools within conservatism.

7.458 **Weiler**, P., 'William Clarke: the making and unmaking of a Fabian socialist', *J. Brit. Sts.*, 14, 1974, 77–108. Surveys the career and ideas of a Fabian who abandoned his ideas in the 1890s, illustrating the destructive combination of utopian and spiritual ideas which he embraced. Weiler concludes that Clarke's belief in the inevitability of political and religious change caused his disillusion with socialism.

(c) EUROPE

General

7.459 **Aron**, R., *Main Currents in Sociological Thought: I Montesquieu, Comte, Marx, Tocqueville, The Sociologists and the Revolution of 1848*, 1965. Attempts to explain the rise of two dominant schools of contemporary sociology – Marxist and 'American' (empirical and analytical) – through a study of the contribution of these four thinkers to the development of sociological thought. Concludes with an interesting comparison of their responses to the Revolution of 1848, 'which, more than any other episode in the history of the nineteenth century, resembles the political conflicts of the twentieth century'.

7.460 **Bowman**, F. P., 'Religion, politics and utopia in French Romanticism', *Australian Journal of French Studies*, 11, 1974, 307–24. On the religious dimension of the ideas of French romantic socialists such as St. Simon and Constant.

7.461 **Chadwick**, O., *The Secularization of the European Mind in the Nineteenth Century*, 1975. This somewhat idiosyncratic study distinguishes secularisation from the Enlightenment, looking at religiosity and the extent of the population which this affected. Includes a chapter on Marx, Engels and religion, and an account of Mill and the theory of a secular state.

7.462 **Charlton**, D. G., 'Utopia and the politics of balance: a theme in French Romantic thought, *Australian Journal of French Studies*, 11, 1974, 193–209. Argues that the feature common to Romantics from Chateaubriand to Vigny was to find a politics of the middle way between competing extremes.

7.463 **Dietrich**, D. J., 'Priests and political thought: theology and reform in central Europe, 1845–1855', *Cath. Hist. Rev.*, 71,

1985, 519–46. Analysis of the work of two German Catholic theologians (Hirscher and Gunther) who connected their religious beliefs with reflections on social and political change.

7.464 **Eyck**, F. G., 'English and French influences on German liberalism before 1848', *J. Hist. Ideas*, 18, 1957, 313–41. Challenges the conventional view that German liberals in the north gravitated towards English influences whilst those in the south and west were more attracted to France, in a historically thorough treatment of this topic.

7.465 **Gruner**, S. M., *Economic Materialism and Social Moralism: A Study in the History of Ideas in France from the Latter Part of the Eighteenth Century to the Middle of the Nineteenth Century*, The Hague, 1973.

7.466 **Hayward**, J., *After the French Revolution: Six Critics of Democracy and Nationalism*, 1991. Analyses the problems of coming to terms with the revolution in nineteenth-century politics through an analysis of six major thinkers (Maistre, Saint-Simon, Constant, Tocqueville, Proudhon, Blanqui). Each is placed in his intellectual and political context, whilst the author concludes that general features are manifest in the thought of all.

7.467 **Jennings**, J. R., 'Conceptions of England and its constitution in nineteenth-century French political thought', *Hist. J.*, 29, 1986, 65–85. Suggests that sections of the French intelligentsia viewed England as an example of stable, peaceful and successful government, but that this admiration prompted a debate about politics which related more to French than English political conditions.

7.468 **Kahan**, A., *Aristocratic Liberalism: The Social and Political Thought of Jacob Burckhardt, John Stuart Mill, and Alexis de Tocqueville*, 1992. Presents these thinkers as variants of this perspective, stressing the influence Tocqueville exerted on Mill. The latter is interpreted as the antithesis of the quasi-democratic, totalitarian who appears in most accounts.

7.469 **Kelly**, G. A., 'Liberalism and aristocracy in the French Restoration', *J. Hist. Ideas*, 26, 1965, 509–30. Examines the thought of Mme de Staël, Jean Denis Lajuinais, and Benjamin Constant, with reference to the Restoration project of securing the spirit of liberty that motivated the French Revolution.

7.470 —— 'Parnassian liberalism in nineteenth-century France: Tocqueville, Renan, Flaubert', *Hist. Pol. Thought*, 8, 1987, 475–503. Argues that the weakness of French liberalism from 1848 to the present was caused by the withdrawal of its major thinkers from active politics into art and literature.

7.471 —— *The Humane Comedy: Constant, Tocqueville and French Liberalism*, 1992. Detailed account of the political thought of key French liberals in the early nineteenth century, illustrating their differences and difficult political context.

7.472 **Logue**, W., *From Philosophy to Sociology: The Evolution of French Liberalism, 1870–1914*, De Kalb, Ill., 1983. This period witnessed the transformation of liberalism based on metaphysical philosophy to liberalism based on sociology; the cause of this shift was the advent of new liberalism, according to Logue. Traces the complex evolution of a new perception of state and society among French liberals, a process in which Durkheimian sociology played a crucial role.

7.473 **Mason**, H. T., and **Doyle**, W., ed., *The Impact of the French Revolution on European Consciousness*, 1989. The essays dealing with political ideas include R. Bolster, 'Chateaubriand and the French Revolution', N. Wilson, 'The poetry and politics of emancipation: the French-Jewish response to the Revolution', B. Hamnet, 'Spanish constitutionalism and the impact of the French Revolution, 1808–1814', and M. Braers, 'Revolution and Risorgimento: the heritage of the French Revolution in nineteenth century Italy'.

7.474 **Mattheisen**, D. J., '1848: theory and practice of the German "juste milieu" ', *Rev. Pol.*, 35, 1973, 180–93.

7.475 **Nicholls**, D., 'Positive liberty, 1880–1914', *Am. Pol. Sc. Rev.*, 57, 1962, 114–28. Traces the shift in European political philosophy to a conception of liberty which viewed state intervention in a more benign fashion. Thoughtful, intellectual history.

7.476 **Pankhurst**, R. K., *The Saint-Simonians, Mill and Carlyle*, 1957.

7.477 **Poggi**, G., *Images of Society: Essays on the Sociological Theories of Tocqueville, Marx* and Durkheim, 1972. Examines and compares their contribution to sociological thought, ignoring their political and historical context and stressing the coherence of their ideas at the expense of critical reflection.

7.478 **Scott**, J. A., *Republican Ideas and the Liberal Tradition in France, 1870–1914*, New York, 1966.

7.479 **Simon**, W. M., *European Positivism in the Nineteenth Century*, Kennikat, 1971.

7.480 **Soltau**, R. H., *French Political Thought in the Nineteenth Century*, New York, 1959.

7.481 **Starzinger**, V., *Middlingness: Juste Milieu Political Theory in France and England, 1815–48*, Charlottesville, Va., 1965. Analyses the theory of 'juste milieu' as it was developed in this period to justify middle-class rule, by Roger-Collard, Guizot, Brougham and Macaulay.

7.482 **Swart**, K. W., 'Individualism in the mid-nineteenth century (1826–1860)', *J. Hist. Ideas*, 23, 1962, 77–90. Careful exposition of the different interpretations of individualism when it first entered the political vocabulary in this period, illuminating its conflation with liberalism.

7.483 **Welch**, C. B., 'Jansenism and liberalism: the making of citizens in post-revolutionary France', *Hist. Pol. Thought*, 7, 1986, 151–66. Argues that the middle classes found in Jansenism a religious conception of the individual which promised to renew a sense of citizenship.

Bakunin

7.484 **Avrich**, P., 'Bakunin's 'God and the State', *Anarchy*, 115, 1970, 276–82.

7.485 —— 'The legacy of Bakunin', *Russ. Rev.*, 29, 1970, 129–42.

7.486 **Kelly**, A., *Mikhail Bakunin: A Study in the Psychology and Politics of Utopianism*, 1982. Downplays the significance of his political ideology in favour of his utopian psychology which allowed him to justify dictatorship in the search for liberty. A clear, if controversial, account.

7.487 **Mendel**, A. P., *Michael Bakunin: Roots of Apocalypse*, New York, 1981. Lengthy and implausible account of his life and thought which stresses the authoritarian core of his political thought and explains this tendency with reference to contemporary psychological theory.

7.488 **Pyziur**, E., *The Doctrine of Anarchism of Michael A. Bakunin*, Milwaukee, Wis., 1955. Clearly presented defence of his place within the anarchist theoretical tradition, though highlights a number of inconsistencies in his theory of revolution and the future anarchist order.

7.489 **Woodcock**, G., 'Bakunin. The destructive urge', *Hist. Today*, 11, 1961, 469–78.

Durkheim

7.490 **Coser**, L., 'Durkheim's conservatism and its implications for his sociological theory', in K. H. Wolff, ed., *Emile Durkheim 1858–1917*, 1960, 211–32.

7.491 **Fenton**, C. S., 'Race, class and politics in the work of Emile Durkheim', in UNESCO, *Sociological Theories: Race and Colonialism*, Paris, 1980, 143–81. Assessment of the validity of functionalist theories of race through a study of Durkheim.

7.492 **Filloux**, J. C., 'Durkheimianism and socialism', *The Review*, 5, 1963, 51–65.

7.493 **Giddens**, A., 'Durkheim's political sociology', in *Studies in Social and Political Theory*, 1977, 235–72. Reconstructs Durkheim's neglected theory of politics and the state as central to his sociology, arguing that to characterise him as conservative is misleading owing both to his sympathy for the abolition of the division of labour and the weakening of the collective conscience in the modern age. Includes a clear account of Durkheim's principles for a democratic polity.

7.494 **Hawkins**, M. J., 'Emile Durkheim on democracy and absolutism', *Hist. Pol. Thought*, 2, 1981, 369–90. Critically examines his political thought with particular reference to his analysis and classification of different types of state, concluding that he never developed a mature theory in this area.

7.495 **Horowitz**, I. L., 'Socialisation without politicization: Emile Durkheim's theory of the modern state', *Pol. Theory*, 10, 1982, 353–77. Reviews the competing readings of his politics, arguing that his most distinctive contribution to political theory comes from his theorisation of state power.

7.496 **Larrain**, J., 'Durkheim's concept of ideology', *Sociological Review*, 28, 1980, 129–39.

7.497 **Llobera**, J. R., 'Durkheim, the Durkheimians and their collective misrepresentation of Marx', *Social Science Information*, 19, 1980, 385–411. Argues that the rejection of historical materialism central to Durkheim involved the perpetuation of the vulgar image of Marxism which was applied to contemporary French Marxists.

7.498 **Lukes**, S., *Emile Durkheim: His Life and Work*, 1973.

7.499 **Nisbet**, R., *Emile Durkheim*, Englewood Cliffs, N.J., 1965.

7.500 **Pearce**, F., *The Radical Durkheim*, 1989. Deploying the tools of structuralist Marxism, Pearce interrogates his key concepts and compares him with Marx, concluding that socialists have much to learn from a synthesis of Durkheimian political theory and non-humanist Marxism. A stimulating account of the 'founder of discursivity'.

7.501 **Pels**, D., 'A fellow-traveller's dilemma: sociology and socialism in the writings of Durkheim', *Acta Polit.*, 3, 1984, 309–29. Casts doubt on his affiliation to socialism, suggesting that his predilections were closer to the 'revisionist' school of Marxism.

7.502 **Richter**, M., 'Durkheim's politics and political theory', in K. H. Wolff, ed., *Emile Durkheim, 1858–1917*, 1960, 170–210.

Engels

7.503 **Carlton**, G., *Friedrich Engels: The Shadow Prophet*, 1965.

7.504 **Carver**, T., *Engels*, 1991. Argues that despite the collapse of state communism in Eastern Europe, Engels's ideas about the abolition of poverty and the interpretation of the past are still valid in modern times.

7.505 —— 'Engels' feminism', *Hist. Pol. Thought*, 6, 1985, 479–89. Suggests that the feminist praise which has been heaped upon *Origins of the Family, Private Property and the State* is misleading: Engels accepted traditional ways of conceptualising both the public and the private and the political and non-political that were not gender neutral.

7.506 —— *Friedrich Engels: His Life and Thought*, 1989. Explores the personality, aspirations and politics of Engels, with particular emphasis on the importance of his youthful development for his later career, concluding that he influenced Marx's thought and that previous account of his secondary role and deterministic interpretation of dialectics are misleading

7.507 —— 'Marx, Engels and dialectics', *Pol. Sts.*, 28, 1980, 353–63. Critique of the proposition that Marx embraced the positivism and determinism of his times in his later years, concluding that the myth of the perfect intellectual partnership between Marx and Engels should not stand.

7.508 **Claeys**, G., 'Engels' *Outlines of a Critique of Political Economy* (1843) and the *Origins of the Marxist Critique of Capitalism*', *Hist. Pol. Econ.*, 16, 1984, 207–32.

7.509 —— 'The political ideas of the young Engels, 1842–1845: Owenism, Chartism, and the question of violent revolution in the transition from utopian to "scientific" socialism', *Hist. Pol. Thought*, 6, 1985, 455–78. A historically informed account of the development of the political thought of the young Engels, which stresses his 'discovery' of the proletariat as the historical subject of the creation of communism.

7.510 **Coulter**, J., 'Marxism and the Engels paradox', *Socialist Register*, 8, 1971, 129–5 Attempts to reconstruct an alternative, with Marxism, to Engels's dialectical view of the natural sciences, calling for the 'expunction of this [Engels's] schema from Marxist philosophy'.

7.511 **Delmar**, R., 'Looking again at Engels's *Origins of the Family, Private Property and the State*', in J. Mitchell and A. Oakley, ed., *The Rights and Wrongs of Women*, 1976, 271–87. Reconstructs, via Engels, a socialist analysis of women's oppression and the preconditions of women's emancipation.

7.512 **Hayes**, B., and **Horowitz**, I. L., 'For Marx/against Engels: dialectics revisited', *Social Praxis*, 7, 1980, 59–75.

7.513 **Henderson**, W. O., *The Life of Friedrich Engels*, 1976. Biography (two volumes) of Engels from a Marxist-Leninist prospective.

7.514 **Himmelfarb**, G., 'Engels in Manchester: inventing the proletariat', *Am. Scholar*, 1002, 1983, 479–96.

7.515 **Hodges**, D. C., 'Engels' contribution to Marxism', *Socialist Register*, 1965,

297–310. Challenges the conventional picture of the young Marx as the hero of Marx scholarship and the late Engels its villain by arguing that Engels's emphasis was intended to accommodate scientific intellectuals, not socialists, and that he 'did a disservice to the analytical and critical method of Marx in a misguided effort to make it universal in scope'.

7.516 **Hunley**, J. D., *The Life and Thought of Friedrich Engels: A Reinterpretation*, 1991. Challenges the view that Engels disagreed with or distorted Marx's views.

7.517 **McLellan**, D., *Engels*, 1977. A brief guide to his life and thought which reflects the reassessment of Marxism that occurred in the 1960s and 1970s. Engels's memoirs are 'mined' to great effect.

7.518 **Marcus**, S., *Engels, Manchester and the Working Class*, New York, 1974.

7.519 **Nova**, F., *Friedrich Engels: His Contributions to Political Theory*, 1967. Limited and short assessment of his intellectual contribution, surpassed by the work of later commentators.

7.520 **Parsons**, H. L. 'Engels's development from Christianity to communism', *Revolutionary World*, 22, 1977, 180–90. Traces the life of the young Engels and assesses the central influences on his thought.

7.521 **Rex**, J., 'Friedrich Engels (1820–95)', in T. Raison, ed., *The Founding Fathers of Social Science*, 1969, 68–75. Thoughtful assessment of his contribution to Marxist theory.

7.522 **Rubel**, M., 'The "Marx legend", or Engels, founder of Marxism', in J. O'Malley and K. Algozin, ed., *Rubel on Karl Marx*, 1981, 15–25. Attempts to influence the debate about their intellectual relationship in nine terse paragraphs.

7.523 **Sayers**, J., **Evans**, M., and **Redcliff**, N., ed., *Engels Revisited: New Feminist Essays*, 1987. This collection evaluates Engels's impact on a century of feminist thought and practice, including Sayers, Evans and Redclift, 'Engels, socialism, and feminism', Gimenez, 'Marxist and non-Marxist elements in Engels' views on the oppression of women', Evans, 'Engels: materialism and morality', and Maconachie, 'Engels, sexual divisions, and the family'.

7.524 **Schedler**, G., 'Justice in Marx, Engels and Lenin', *Studies in Soviet Thought*, 18, 1978, 223–33.

7.525 **Stedman Jones**, G. S., 'Engels and the end of classical German philosophy', *New Left Rev.*, 79, 1973, 17–36. Reconstructs his systematisation of Marx's thought, suggesting that at key points he deployed the Hegelian philosophy of his youth because of his inability to think through the novelty of historical materialism as a science.

7.526 —— 'Engels and the genesis of Marxism', *New Left Rev.*, 106, 1977, 79–104. Critique of the one-sided nature of the judgements Marxists have made of his work. In fact, Engels made a distinctive contribution to the development of Marxist theory particularly through his concrete account of proletarian life and aspirations in the mid-1840s.

7.527 —— 'Engels and the history of Marxism', in E. J. Hobsbawm, ed., *The History of Marxism*, 1, 1980, 290–326.

7.528 **Stern**, B. J., 'Engels on the family', *Sc. & Soc.*, 12, 1948, 42–64.

7.529 **Suvin**, D., ' "Utopian" and "scientific": two attributes for socialism from Engels', *Minnesota Review*, 6, 1976, 59–70.

7.530 **Welty**, G., 'Marx, Engels and 'Anti-Dühring'', *Pol. Sts.*, 31, 1983, 284–94. Detailed textual analysis which challenges Carver's reading of the Marx–Engels intellectual relationship, suggesting that they concurred in their conceptions of the subject matter and method of political economy.

Hegelianism

HEGEL

7.531 **Acton**, H. B., 'Hegel's conception of the study of human nature', in *The Proper Study: Royal Institute of Philosophy Lectures*, vol. 4, 1969–1970, 1971, 32–47. Clarifies the psychological thought from which Hegel drew for his conception of human nature, his notion of mind – the antithesis of nature, and the synthesis of these entities – absolute mind.

7.532 **Arato**, A., 'A reconstruction of Hegel's theory of civil society', *Cardozo Law Review*, 10, 1989, 1363–88.

7.533 **Arthur**, C. J., 'Hegel as lord and master', in S. Sayers and P. Osborne, ed., *Socialism, Feminism and Philosophy: A*

Radical Philosophy Reader, 1990, 27–45. Argues, against Easton, that he systematically relegated women to a secondary role in social life.

7.534 **Avineri**, S., *Hegel's Theory of the Modern State*, 1972. A classic exposition of his theory of the state and its relationship to his broader philosophical scheme. Includes a sharp assessment of his conception of historical change and the political implications of Hegelian discourse.

7.535 —— 'Labour, alienation, and social classes in Hegel's *Realphilosophie*', *Phil. & Pub. Affairs*, 1, 1971, 96–119.

7.536 —— 'The instrumentality of passion in the world of reason: Hegel and Marx', *Pol. Theory*, 1, 1973, 388–404. Focusing on the problem of the relationship between subjective will and historical outcome, the author demonstrates the influence of Hegel's strictures upon Marx as well as key differences concerning the immanence of the relationship between passion and reason (Hegel) and the transcendence of this relationship (Marx).

7.537 **Barber**, B. R., 'Spirit's phoenix and history's owl or the incoherence of dialectics in Hegel's account of women', *Pol. Theory*, 16, 1988, 5–28. Subtle presentation of the contradictory aspects of Hegel's discussion of women; these tensions are rooted, Barber argues, in the profound philosophical contradictions in his thought.

7.538 **Beck**, L. W., 'The Reformation, the revolution, and the Restoration in Hegel's political philosophy', *J. Hist. Phil.*, 14, 1976, 51–61. Reconstructs his evaluation of the French Revolution, showing how he explained the absence of revolution in Germany through the Reformation. Concludes that he became increasingly politically quietistic as his life progressed.

7.539 **Beiser**, F. C., *The Cambridge Companion to Hegel*, 1993. Includes H. S. Harris on his intellectual development to 1807, A. Wood on his ethics, K. Westphal on the intellectual and political background to and structure of the *Philosophy of Right*, Beiser on his historicism, J. Toews on the transformation of Hegelianism, 1805–1846, and A. Wood on Marxist appropriations and interpretations of his work.

7.540 **Bellamy**, R., 'Hegel and liberalism', *Hist. Euro. Ideas*, 8, 1987, 693–708.

7.541 —— 'Hegel's conception of the state and political philosophy in a post-Heglian world', *Pol. Sc.*, 38, 1986, 99–112.

7.542 **Bergman**, F., 'The purpose of Hegel's system', *J. Hist. Phil.*, 2, 1964, 189–204.

7.543 **Berki**, R. N., 'Political freedom and Hegelian metaphysics', *Pol. Sts.*, 16, 1968, 365–83. Analyses his metaphysics to show that he understood political freedom as diversity; this perspective is contrasted with the limitations of the contemporary case for negative liberty. Berki reiterates Hegel's conclusion that political freedom means freedom of the particular.

7.544 **Berry**, C. J., 'From Hume to Hegel: the case of the social contract', *J. Hist. Ideas*, 38, 1977, 691–703. Compares their rejection of the contractarian justification of political allegiance, the product of their differing views of human nature.

7.545 —— *Hume, Hegel and Human Nature*, The Hague, 1982.

7.546 —— 'Property and possession: two replies to Locke – Hume and Hegel', in J. R. Pennock and J. W. Chapman, ed., *Property*, New York, 1980, 89–100. Rehearses these thinkers' rejection of Lockean individualism with particular emphasis on Hegel's belief that the relationship between property and people is necessary.

7.547 **Bienenstock**, M., 'Hegel at Jena: nationalism or historical thought?', *Archiv für Geschichte der Philosophie*, 61, 1979, 175–95.

7.548 —— 'The logic of political life: Hegel's conception of political philosophy', in M. Dascal and O. Gruengard, ed., *Knowledge and Politics: Case Studies in the Relationship Between Epistemology and Political Philosophy*, Boulder, Calif., 1989, 67–92. Reinterprets the *Philosophy of Right* as an attempt to clarify the meaning of the key concepts in political life, not as normative political theory. Indeed, political philosophy for Hegel involved the transformation of the realm of conceptual representation.

7.549 **Bloom**, A., *Introduction to the Reading of Hegel*, New York, 1969.

7.550 **Brinkley**, A. B. et al., ed., *Studies in Hegel*, New Orleans, La., 1960.

7.551 **Brod**, H., *Hegel's Philosophy of Politics*, 1992. A distinctive interpretation of his political philosophy as manifested in his analysis of the state. Argues that his political outlook needs to be understood through specifically Hegelian categories, rendering inadequate categorisations of him as liberal, totalitarian or anti-modern.

7.552 —— 'The "spirit" of Hegelian politics: public opinion and legislative debate from Hegel to Habermas', in P. G. Stillman, ed., *Hegel's Philosophy of Spirit*, New York, 1987, 124–44. Challenges conventional emphases upon bureaucracy as the centrepiece of Hegelian politics, insisting that he was more concerned with the political consciousness and identity of citizens in the modern political world, in line with his philosophy of spirit.

7.553 **Browning**, G. K., 'Hegel's Plato: the owl of Minerva and a fading political tradition', *Pol. Sts.*, 36, 1988, 475–85. Citing his interpretation of the *Republic* as an imaginative reconstruction of a disintegrating political culture, the author suggests that Hegel misread Platonic beliefs because of his concern to see in previous eras the prefiguration of his own theoretical practice.

7.554 —— 'Night in which all cows are black: ethical absolutism in Plato and Hegel', *Hist. Pol. Thought*, 12, 1991, 391–404. Both are said to wish to preserve political cohesion by eliminating ethical diversity.

7.555 —— 'Plato and Hegel: reason, redemption and political theory', *Hist. Pol. Thought*, 8, 1987, 377–93. Outlines these thinkers' shared recognition of the importance of social life for the individual, their insistence on certain political communities as the best way of organising social life and their differing political prognoses, stemming from distinctive conceptions of reason.

7.556 —— *Plato and Hegel: Two Modes of Philosophising about Politics*, 1991.

7.557 **Brudner**, A., 'Constitutional monarchy as the divine regime; Hegel's theory of the just state', *Hist. Pol. Thought*, 2, 1981, 119–40. Elucidating his theory of constitutional monarchy, the author argues that Hegel attempted to synthesize a Christian receptivity to transcendence with the modern commitment to the autonomy of the individual.

7.558 **Butler**, C., 'Technological society and its counterculture: an Hegelian analysis', *Inquiry*, 18, 1975, 195–212.

7.559 **Colletti**, L., *Marxism and Hegel*, 1973. Examines Hegel through the writings of later Marxists and the categories of Hegelian Marxism. A stylishly written attempt to smooth the intellectual path between Hegel and Marx.

7.560 **Cooper**, B., *The End of History: An Essay on Modern Hegelianism*, Toronto, 1984. The first lengthy study of Kojève's interpretation of Hegel, justifying the former's stress on the end of history as pertinent to contemporary conditions.

7.561 **Cordna**, C., 'The rights of the individual in Hegel's state', *Dialogos*, 18, 1983, 41–50. Highlights a number of tensions between his account of individual rights and the ideals of modern individualist liberalism.

7.562 **Cornu**, A., 'Hegel, Marx and Engels', in R. W. Sellars, et al., ed., *Philosophy for the Future: the Quest of Modern Materialism*, New York, 1949, 41–60.

7.563 **Cristi**, F. R., 'Hegel and Roman liberalism', *Hist. Pol. Thought*, 12, 1984, 281–94. Views the *Philosophy of Right* as the first modern political treatise which explicitly rests upon the separation between state and civil society, the hallmark of liberal constitutionalism. Concludes that his formula for solving the crises of modern liberalism was drawn from Roman sources.

7.564 —— 'Hegel on possession and property', *Can. J. Pol. & Soc. Theory*, 2, 1978, 111–24.

7.565 —— 'Hegel's conservative liberalism', *Can. J. Pol. Sc.*, 22, 1989, 717–38.

7.567 —— 'The *Hegelsche Mitte* and Hegel's monarch', *Pol. Theory*, 11, 1983, 601–22. Criticises those who wish to distinguish his ideas from totalitarianism by emphasising his democratic commitments, suggesting that the conception of civil society provides the key to his contradictory political allegiances, as Marcuse has argued.

7.568 **Cullen**, B., *Hegel's Social and Political Thought: An Introduction*, 1979. Account of his ideas which focuses upon the *Philosophy of Right* and his concern with the dissolution of community ties in modern society.

7.569 —— ed., *Hegel Today*, 1988. Essays which illustrate the continued relevance of Hegelian thought, including Cullen on the mediating role of estates and corporations in his theory of representation, Vincent on ethics and the Hegelian state, and Pattman on the implications of Hegelian idealism for understanding Protestant theology.

7.570 **Desmond**, W., *Hegel and His Critics: Philosophy in the Aftermath of Hegel*, Albany, N.Y., 1989. A volume which includes accounts of his major critics and the competing philosophical traditions within which his work has been placed. Includes Kline on Nietzsche and Marx, Vaught on dialectical logic, Mulholland on Marx, Hegel and the human individual, Maher on Hegel's critique of Marx, Cullen on Hegel and Kierkegaard, Dulckeit on Hegel and Russell, Williams on Hegel and Heidegger, Flay on Hegel, Derrida and Bataille, Rockmore on Husserl's critique of Hegel, and Winfield on Hegel and contemporary philosophy.

7.571 **Dickey**, L., *Hegel: Religion, Economics and the Politics of Spirit, 1770–1807*, 1987. Stresses the complex world of Protestant politics and theology as the key context for understanding his early intellectual development. From 1794 onwards, he strove to square the concept of civil piety with his other theoretical commitments.

7.572 **Doull**, J., 'Hegel's critique of Hellenic virtue', *Dionysius*, 9, 1985, 13–7.

7.573 **Drydyk**, J., 'Hegel's politics: liberal or democratic?', *Can. J. Phil.*, 16, 1986, 99–122.

7.574 **Durán de Seade**, E., 'State and history in Hegel's concept of people', *J. Hist. Ideas*, 40, 1979, 369–84. Isolates different interpretations of the people in Hegel's thought, suggesting that these reveal the shifting interpretation of history and freedom manifest in his intellectual development.

7.575 **Easton**, S., 'Functionalism and feminism in Hegel's political thought', *Rad. Phil.*, 38, 1984, 2–8. Rejects his fundamentalist reading of the family and exclusion of women from the public sphere, yet argues that a feminist reappropriation of Hegel is possible.

7.576 **Elder**, P., *Appropriating Hegel*, 1981.

7.577 **Findlay**, J. N., *Hegel: A Re-Examination*, 1958. Refutation of the dominant approaches to Hegel, emphasising the continued relevance of his sensitivity to contingency, contradiction and contestation in political discourse. Clear and thematic exposition.

7.578 —— 'Some merits of Hegelianism', *Procs. Aris. Soc.*, 56, 1955–56, 1–24.

7.579 —— 'The contemporary relevance of Hegel', in *Language, Mind and Value*, 1963, 217–31. Reconstructing the Hegelian dialectic as a feasible philosophical method, the author explore the notions of internality and totality, and celebrates his proximity to the uneveness o the experiential. Hegelian thought is advocated as the most suitable system for understanding modern life.

7.580 **Flechtheim**, O., 'Hegel and the problem o punishment', *J. Hist. Ideas*, 8, 1947, 293–368.

7.581 **Friedrich**, C. J., 'The power of negation: Hegel's dialectic and totalitarian ideology' in D. C. Travis, ed., *Hegel Symposium*, Austin, Tex., 1962, 13–35.

7.582 **Fuchs**, J-A., P., 'On the war path and beyond: Hegel, Freud, and feminist theory', *Wom. Sts. Int. For.*, 6, 1983, 565–72.

7.583 **Germino**, D., 'Hegel as a political theorist', *J. Pol.*, 31, 1969, 885–912.

7.584 —— 'Hegel's theory of the state: humanis or totalitarian?', *Statsvetenskaping Tidskrift*, 19, 1970, 293–313.

7.585 **Gillespie**, M. A., 'Death and desire: war and bourgeoisification in the thought of Hegel', in C. H. Zuckert, ed., *Understanding the Political Spirit: Philosophical Investigations from Socrates t Nietzsche*, Yale, New Haven, 1988, 153–79.

7.586 **Goldstein**, L. J., 'The meaning of "state' in Hegel's philosophy of history', *Phil. Q.* 12, 1962, 60–72.

7.587 **Gottfried**, P., 'On the social implications and context of the Hegelian dialectic', *J. Hist. Ideas*, 40, 1979, 369–84. Assesses the political dimensions and implications of the Hegelian dialectic, arguing that it is incompatible with a call to revolution.

7.588 **Gray**, J., *Hegel and Greek Thought*, New York, 1968.

7.589 **Greene**, M., 'Psyche and polity in Hegel' *Man and World*, 5, 1971, 313–31.

7.590 **Haines**, N., 'Politics and protest. Hegel and social criticism', *Pol. Sc. Q.*, 86, 1971 406–28.

7.591 **Hardimon**, M., *The Project of Reconciliation: Hegel's Social Philosophy*, 1993.

7.592 **Harris**, H. S., 'Hegel and the French Revolution', *Clio*, 7, 1977, 5–18. Challenging the myth of Hegel the politica reactionary, Harris outlines his belief in the unfolding of political progress through the rational equilibrium of the classes; the

Prussian Constitution was merely one stage in this process.

7.593 —— *Hegel's Development: Night Thoughts (Jena, 1801–1806)*, 1983. Thorough account of his political and intellectual development, relying upon detailed textual exegesis. A useful reference guide.

7.594 —— *Hegel's Development: Toward the Sunlight 1770–1801*, 1972. First part of a chronological account of his intellectual career, which gives particular emphasis to his early experiences, the impact of the French Revolution and the hesitant progress towards philosophical clarity which he made in these years.

7.595 **Hayim**, G. J., 'Hegel's critical theory and feminist concerns', *Phil. & Soc. Crit.*, 16, 1990, 1–21. Attempts to construct an alternative, feminist self-consciousness by analysing the gender implications of Hegel's dialectic of need and desire.

7.596 **Hinchman**, L. P., *Hegel's Critique of the Enlightenment*, Tampa and Gainesville, Fla., 1984. Exposition of his definition and critique of the Enlightenment. In conclusion the author attempts to draw out the contemporary worth of his views in the light of recent critical theory.

7.597 **Hofstadter**, A., 'Ownness and identity: re-thinking Hegel', *Rev. Metaph.*, 28, 1975, 681–97. Argues for the continuing relevance of Hegel's speculative reason, though the author remains critical of his ontology of property ownership.

7.598 **Hook**, S., *From Hegel to Marx: Studies in the Intellectual Development of Karl Marx*, 1966. Explores Marx's early development through studies of his relationship with and critique of Hegel and the Young Hegelians. A compelling and thorough account of the political and intellectual context in which Marx first developed his thought.

7.599 **Hoy**, J. B., 'Hegel's critique of Rawls', *Clio*, 10, 1981, 407–22.

7.600 **Hudson**, W., 'Hegel and Nietzsche', in R. Fitzgerald, ed., *Comparing Political Thinkers*, 1980, 185–202. Beginning with an elucidation of their differences, Hudson proceeds to highlight their critiques of modernity and the implications of their positions for contemporary political thought.

7.601 **Hyppolite**, J., *Studies in Marx and Hegel*, 1969. A closely argued and influential exposition of the influence of Hegel upon Marx, which also contains important essays on Hegel's concepts of existence and alienation, the impact of the French Revolution on his thought, Marx's critique of the Hegelian conception of the state, and the philosophical presuppositions behind *Capital*.

7.602 **Inwood**, M. J., *A Hegel Dictionary*, 1992. Exhaustive guide to Hegelian terminology and concepts, supplemented by an account of his intellectual development.

7.603 —— *Hegel*, 1983. A lengthy exposition of his metaphysical principles, presenting him as often obscure and equivocal. Concludes with an examination of his ethical and political ideas.

7.604 —— ed., *Hegel*, 1985. Important set of interpretative essays, including Walsh on the philosophical origins of his thought, Soll questioning aspects of Taylor's interpretation, Acton's reconstruction of the Hegelian view of human nature, Parkinson on his concept of freedom, and O'Brien on his philosophy of history.

7.605 **Jack**, B., 'The rationality of Hegel's concept of monarchy', *Am. Pol. Sc. Rev.*, 74, 1980, 709–20.

7.606 **Kain**, P. J., 'Hegel's political theory and philosophy of history', *Clio*, 17, 1988, 345–68. Argues that his thought combined Rousseau's political theory and Kant's philosophy of history.

7.607 **Kaufmann**, W., *Hegel: A Reinterpretation*, New York, 1966.

7.608 —— ed., *Hegel's Political Philosophy*, New York, 1970. Includes debates on Hegel and Prussianism (Knox and Carritt), his contemporary significance (Hook and Avineri), as well as a separate essay by Avineri on Hegel and nationalism.

7.609 **Kay**, G., 'Political economy: Hegel versus Ricardo', *Critique*, 10–11, 1978–9, 92–102.

7.610 **Kelly**, G. A., 'Hegel and the present standpoint', *Pol. Theory*, 4, 1976, 45–63. Explains the continuing significance of his political thought and his impact on political thinking in the twentieth century.

7.611 —— 'Hegel's America', *Phil. & Pub. Affairs*, 2, 1972, 3–36.

7.612 —— *Hegel's Retreat from Eleusis: Studies in Political Thought*, Princeton, N.J., 1978. Analysis of his mature political ideas, in their historical context, organised around the relationship between philosophy, politics and history in Hegelian thought. A scholarly rebuttal of a number of political and ideological readings of his work.

7.613 —— *Idealism, Politics and History: Sources of Hegelian Thought*, 1969. Examines, in turn, the influence exercised by Rousseau, Kant and Fichte over Hegel as part of a larger reconstruction of the political and intellectual context of Hegelian thought. Subtle and insightful mixture of metaphysical and political analysis.

7.614 —— 'Notes on Hegel's "lordship and bondage" ', *Rev. Metaph.*, 19, 1966, 780–802.

7.615 —— 'Social understanding and social therapy in Schiller and Hegel', *Sts. Burke & Time*, 13, 1972, 2203–29.

7.616 **Kierans**, K., 'On the limits of contemporary reflection on freedom: an analysis of Marxist and existentialist responses to Hegel', *Dionysius*, 10, 1986, 85–128.

7.617 —— 'The concept of ethical life in Hegel's *Philosophy of Right*', *Hist. Pol. Thought*, 13, 1992, 417–35. Argues that Hegel transcended the tension between tradition and modern freedom, believing that both were antagonistic yet symbiotic.

7.618 **Knox**, T. M., 'Hegel's attitude to Kant's ethics', *Kant-Studien*, 49, 1957, 70–81.

7.619 **Kojève**, A., ed., *Introduction to the Reading of Hegel*, New York, 1969.

7.620 **Kucheman**, C. A., 'Abstract and concrete freedom: Hegelian perspectives on economic justice', *Owl of Minerva*, 15, 1983, 23–44.

7.621 **Lakeland**, P., *The Politics of Salvation: The Hegelian Idea of the State*, Albany, N.Y., 1989.

7.622 **Lamb**, D., ed., *Hegel and Modern Philosophy*, 1987. Includes Easton on the relevance of Hegelianism for feminist social and political philosophy, Arthur on political economy in *The Philosophy of Right*, George on the Hegelian core of Marxism, Sayers on the parallel between Hegel's and Marx's scientific methods, and McCarney on the importance of Marx's methodological debt to Hegel.

7.623 —— *Hegel: From Foundation to System*, The Hague, 1980.

7.624 **Landes**, J., 'Hegel's conception of the family', *Polity*, 14, 1981, 5–28. Interesting analysis of his sense of the overlap between familial and political life.

7.625 **Levin**, M., and **Williams**, H., 'Inherited power and popular representation: a tension in Hegel's political theory', *Pol.*

Sts., 35, 1987, 105–15. Focuses upon tensions in his celebration of constitutional monarchy and critique of popular representation.

7.626 **Lonzi**, C., 'Let's spit on Hegel', in P. Bono and S. Kemp, ed., *Italian Feminist Thought: A Reader*, 1991, 40–59.

7.627 **Lukács**, G., *The Young Hegel: Studies in the Relations Between Dialectics and Economics*, 1975. Dense and historically detailed reconstruction of the development of Hegel's thought, emphasising the central political events of his time and his role in the development of German philosophy. Argues that political economy provided a conduit for the emergence of a dialectical mode of thought, drawing on Marx's remarks in the *Paris Manuscripts*.

7.628 **Lutz**, R. R., 'The 'new left' of Restoration Germany', *J. Hist. Ideas*, 31, 1970, 235–52. A stimulating comparison between the young Hegelians and the new left in the 1960s, based upon their shared enthusiasm for Hegel's dialectic.

7.629 **McCumber**, J., 'Contradiction and resolution in the state: Hegel's covert view', *Clio*, 15, 1986, 379–90. Examining his writing on 'aesthetics', the author extracts some neglected passages on political philosophy in which he proves critical of the modern state. Suggests that these should be read alongside sections of the *Philosophy of Right* conventionally dismissed as obscure or anomalous.

7.630 **MacGregor**, D., *Hegel, Marx and the English State*, Boulder, Calif., 1992. Focuses upon Hegel more than Marx, arguing unconvincingly that the former's ideas are compatible with democratic socialism and feminism.

7.631 —— *The Communist Ideal in Hegel and Marx*, 1984. Suggests that the mature Marx became even closer to Hegel, and that Hegelian logic suited Marx because it already contained the unique elements that later appeared in his social theory, including the notions of surplus value and transition to communism.

7.632 **MacIntyre**, A., ed., *Hegel: A Collection of Critical Essays*, New York, 1972. Includes Findlay on his contemporary relevance, Kaufman deconstructing the 'Hegel myth', Soloman analysing the coherence and meaning of the concept of 'geist', Taylor on the conceptual view of experience developed in the *Phenomenology* *of Spirit*, Kelly on the master/slave relationship, Schacht comparing his notion of freedom with that of other political philosophers, and Avineri reviewing the different schools of thought about his work.

7.633 **Mah**, H., 'The French Revolution and the problem of German modernity: Hegel, Heine, and Marx', *New Germ. Crit.*, 50, 1990, 3–20.

7.634 **Maher**, W., ed., *Hegel on Economics and Freedom*, Macon, Ga., 1987.

7.635 **Maletz**, D. J., 'Hegel on right as actualized will', *Pol. Theory*, 17, 1989, 33–50. Explores his view of right as active, self-liberating autonomy.

7.636 **Mehta**, V. R., *Hegel and the Modern State: An Introduction to Hegel's Political Thought*, New Delhi, 1968.

7.637 **Mitias**, M. H., *The Moral Foundation of the State in Hegel's "Philosophy of Right": Anatomy of an Argument*, Amsterdam, 1981.

7.638 **Moellendorf**, O., 'Racism and rationality in Hegel's *Philosophy of Subjective Spirit*', *Hist. Pol. Thought*, 13, 1992, 243–55. Examination of the causal role he allotted in this text to race, though racism is contingent not necessary in Hegelian philosophy.

7.639 **Moran**, P., 'Hegel's étatisme', *Revolutionary World*, 26, 1978, 1–12.

7.640 **Mosher**, M. A., 'Civic identity in the juridical society: on Hegelianism as discipline for the romantic mind', *Pol. Theory*, 11, 1983, 117–32. Focuses on the implications of Hegel's notions of individual autonomy and community for romantic thinkers.

7.641 —— 'The particulars of a universal politics: Hegel's adaptation of Montesquieu's typology', *Am. Pol. Sc. Rev.*, 78, 1984, 179–88. Explores the influence that Montesquieu's typology of regimes exerted on Hegel's thought and the latter's ultimate rejection of Montesquieu's monarchial order.

7.642 **Munson**, T. N., 'An interpretation of Hegel's political thought', *Monist*, 48, 1964, 97–111. Examines key themes within his political thought: the individual and the state, the state as the embodiment of reason, and the concretisation of the dialectic. Concludes by comparing him with Wittgenstein, finding similarities and differences.

7.643 **Naven**, F., *Revolution, Idealism and Human Freedom: Schelling, Hölderlin and Hegel and the Crisis of Early German Idealism*, The Hague, 1971.

7.644 **Nicholson**, P. P., 'Hegel on crime', *Hist. Pol. Thought*, 3, 1982, 103–21. Suggests that he offers a distinctive analysis which connects freedom to the existence of crimes and criminals.

7.645 **Nicolin**, F., *Hegel, 1770–1970*, Stuttgart, 1970.

7.646 **O'Hagan**, T., 'On Hegel's critique of Kant's moral and political philosophy', in S. Priest, ed., *Hegel's Critique of Kant*, 1987, 135–59.

7.647 **O'Malley**, J., et al., ed., *The Legacy of Hegel: Proceedings of the Marquette Hegel Symposium*, The Hague, 1973. Includes Weiss on Hegel scholarship in English, 1962–9, Calvez on Hegel and Marx, Fackenheim on the relationship between Hegel and Judaism, Avinieri on labour, alienation and classes in Hegel's thought, and Doull on the implications of Hegel's thought for liberalism, anarchism and socialism.

7.648 **Parkinson**, G. H. R., 'Hegel's concept of freedom', *Royal Institute of Philosophy Lectures*, 5, 1970–71, 174–95.

7.649 **Pelczynski**, Z. A., 'Freedom in Hegel', in Z. Pelczynski and J. Gray, ed., *Conceptions of Liberty in Political Philosophy*, 1984, 150–81. Explores his rich, multi-dimensional notion of human freedom, the culmination of an ongoing dialectical process.

7.650 —— ed., *Hegel's Political Philosophy: Problems and Perspectives*, 1971. An important collection of essays which examines key themes in his political philosophy in some analytical detail, including Pelczynski on the state, Plamenatz and Riedel on freedom, Suter on the French Revolution, Ilting on the *Philosophy of Right*, Heiman on Hegel's corporate doctrine, and Verene on war. The book finishes with a provocative account of the Marxian critique of Hegel's theory (Berki), a comparison between Hegel's account of the individual and that developed by Marx and Stirner (Fleischman), and a concluding essay on Hegel's contemporary significance (Pelczynski).

7.651 —— 'Hegel's relevance today: culture, community and political power in the

Philosophy of Right (1821)', *Europa, A Journal of Interdisciplinary Studies*, 2, 1979, 7–19. Argues that his political theory existed independently of his metaphysical beliefs and consisted of an alternative to liberal and Marxist theories of state and society, organised around the market economy and the modern state as the mediation between civil society and the community.

7.652 —— ed., *The State and Civil Society: Studies in Hegel's Political Philosophy*, 1984. Important collection which includes Ilting on the limitations of Marx's critique of his work, Pelczynski on the selective appropriation of civil society and its implications for Marxist theories of rationality, Benhabib on his awareness of the complexity of the social and cultural world which fostered the development of modern, industrial society, Kortian on the weaknesses of his theory of civil society, Bernstein on the master–slave relationship, Inwood on his relation to the Greeks, Plant on legitimation, Walton on the continuing significance of his understanding of modern society, Westphal on the nature of ethical life in the state, Hartmann on a possible reformulation of civil society and the state in his thought, and Petry on his theory of praxis, exemplified by his analysis of the English Reform Bill.

7.653 **Peperzak**, A., *Philosophy and Politics: A Commentary on the Preface to Hegel's Philosophy of Right*, The Hague, 1987.

7.654 **Pinkard**, T., 'Freedom and social categories in Hegel's ethics', *Philos. & Phenom. Res.*, 47, 1986, 209–32.

7.655 **Piper**, A. M. S., 'Property and the limits of the self', *Pol. Theory*, 8, 1980, 39–64. Suggests that Hegel's inconsistency about the necessity of private property has its roots in his differing conceptions of the self.

7.656 **Pippin**, R. B., *Hegel's Idealism*, 1989.

7.657 —— 'Hegel's political argument and the problem of verwirklichung', *Pol. Theory*, 9, 1981, 509–32.

7.658 **Planic**, Z., 'Family and civil society in Hegel's *Philosophy of Right*', *Hist. Pol. Thought*, 12, 1991, 305–15. Illustrates the tension between his characterisation of civil society as a moment of ethical life emerging from the family and his interpretation of civil society's opposition to, and transformation of, the family. The

implications of this conflict for his political and normative outlook are expertly addressed.

7.659 **Plant**, R., *Hegel*, 1973. Attempts to relate his metaphysical ideals to his political thought, arguing that this philosophy is best understood as the pursuit of coherence: the effort to overcome human estrangement from the world and the fragmentation of experience through an understanding of rationality and necessity.

7.660 —— 'Hegel and political economy, I and II', *New Left Rev.*, 103 and 104, 1977, 79–92 and 103–13. Reconstructs his theory in this area, focusing on the ownership and consequences of property in civil society and the system of needs which he saw as the object of political economy.

7.661 **Priest**, S., ed., *Hegel's Critique of Kant*, 1987. Includes a comparison between Kantian antinomies and Hegel's dialectic (Llewelyn), an assessment of Hegel's critique of Kant's moral and political theory (O'Hagan), and a comparative view of these thinkers' deployment of theology (Lamb) and philosophical history (Pompa). Philosophical in tone, this collection provides a rigorous examination of the relationship between the two thinkers.

7.662 **Raveh**, L., 'Hegel, spirit, and politics', in R. C. Solomon and K. M. Higgins, ed., *The Age of German Idealism*, 1993, 254–89.

7.663 **Raven**, H. M., 'Has Hegel anything to say to feminists?', *Owl of Minerva*, 19, 1988, 149–68.

7.664 **Reidel**, M., *Between Tradition and Revolution: The Hegelian Transformation of Political Philosophy*, 1984. A series of essays by a German political philosopher whose extensive understanding of the social and intellectual contexts of his political and historical philosophy is superior to that of some English-language scholars. Includes provocative and scholarly analysis of the *Philosophy of Right* in the context of the classical tradition of political thought.

7.665 **Reyburn**, H. A., *The Ethical Theory of Hegel*, 1967.

7.666 **Riley**, P., 'Hegel on consent and social-contract theory: does he "cancel and preserve" the will?', *West. Pol. Q.*, 26, 1973, 130–62.

7.667 —— *Will and Political Legitimacy: A Critical Exposition of Social Contract Theory in Hobbes, Locke, Rousseau, Kant, and Hegel*, 1982.

7.668 **Ritter**, J., *Hegel and the French Revolution: Essays on the Philosophy of Right*, Cambridge, Mass., 1982. Introduced by Winfield who stresses Hegel's examination of the legitimacy of modernity, this text contains Ritter's important essays on Hegel's notion of justice and its relationship to freedom.

7.669 **Rosen**, S., *G. W. F. Hegel: An Introduction to the Science of Wisdom*, Yale, New Haven, 1974.

7.670 **Rosenthal**, J., 'Freedom's devices: the place of the individual in Hegel's *Philosophy of Right*', *Rad. Phil.*, 59, 1991, 27–32. Complex survey of a number of tensions embedded in his conception of the relationship between freedom and the individual.

7.671 **Schacht**, R. L., *Hegel and After*, Pittsburg, Penn., 1975.

7.672 **Schmidt**, J., 'A *paideia* for the "bürger als bourgeois": the concept of "civil society" in Hegel's political thought', *Hist. Pol. Thought*, 2, 1981, 469–95. Argues for the distinctiveness of his conception of civil society, in reply to commentators who stress parallels with other theorists or view his political thought as a response to the emergence of modern industrial society. For Hegel, the dehumanising effects of civil society were the prerequisite for the reconciliation of bourgeois, Christian and citizen.

7.673 —— 'Recent Hegel literature', *Telos*, 46, 1980–81, 113–47.

7.674 **Scruton**, R., 'G. W. F. Hegel', in R. Scruton, ed., *Conservative Thinkers: Essays from the Salisbury Review*, 1988, 135–54. Dubious appropriation of Hegel for the conservative tradition, which stresses his concern with the spiritual malaise engendered by modernity.

7.675 **Seade**, E. D. de, 'State and history in Hegel's concept of a people', *J. Hist. Ideas*, 40, 1979, 369–84.

7.676 **Seeberger**, W., 'The political significance of Hegel's concept of history', *Monist*, 48, 1964, 76–96.

7.677 **Serequeberhan**, T., 'The idea of colonialism in Hegel's *Philosophy of Right*', *Int. Phil. Q.*, 29, 1989, 301–18.

7.678 **Shanks**, A., *Hegel's Political Theology*, 1991. Attempts to grasp the contemporary relevance of his political theology, which Shanks interprets as a uniquely radical critique of every sort of religious authoritarianism.

7.679 **Shklar**, J. N., *Freedom and Independence: A Study of the Political Ideas of Hegel's 'Phenomenology of Mind'*, 1976.

7.680 **Simpson**, P. A., 'Tragic thought: romantic nationalism in the German tradition', *Hist. Euro. Ideas*, 16, 1993, 331–6. Explores Hegel's writing on art and the state to examine the relationship between German nationalism and romanticism. Brief and unconvincing.

7.681 **Singer**, P., *Hegel*, 1983. A brief but commendably accessible introduction to his thought; useful for students first approaching Hegel.

7.682 **Smith**, S. B., 'Hegel's critique of liberalism', *Am. Pol. Sc. Rev.*, 80, 1986, 121–39. Presents him as occupying a middle-ground between liberalism and communitarian critics, particularly through his view of intermediary associations as buffers against the market and civic virtue.

7.683 —— *Hegel's Critique of Liberalism: Right in Context*, Chicago, Ill., 1989. Views his critique of liberalism as occupying a middle-ground between Rawlsian and communitarian positions, especially because of his distinctive critique of liberal, natural rights theory.

7.684 —— 'Hegel's idea of a critical theory', *Pol. Theory*, 15, 1987, 99–126.

7.685 —— 'What is "right" in Hegel's *Philosophy of Right*?', *Am. Pol. Sc. Rev.*, 83, 1989, 3–18.

7.686 **Soll**, I., 'Charles Taylor's *Hegel*', *J. Phil.*, 73, 1976, 697–710.

7.687 **Solomon**, R. C., *In the Spirit of Hegel*, 1983.

7.688 **Stace**, W. T., *Hegel*, 1955.

7.689 **Steinberger**, P. J., 'Hegel as a social scientist', *Am. Pol. Sc. Rev.*, 71, 1977, 95–110.

7.690 —— 'Hegel on marriage and politics', *Pol. Sts.*, 34, 1986, 575–91. Behind Hegel's views on marriage lie his complex theory of the self, which is the centrepiece of the *Philosophy of Right*. The author remains sceptical only of his account of women's role within marriage.

7.691 —— 'Hegel's occasional writings: state and individual', *Rev. Pol.*, 45, 1983, 188–208. Demonstrates how he resolved the individual–social tension through his principle of transcendence, yet violated this principle in his political writings.

7.692 —— *Logic and Politics: Hegel's Philosophy of Right*, Yale, New Haven, 1988. Exposition of his thought around the themes of individual freedom and a rational political order. These are elucidated in a lucid discussion of key sites for the development of the concept of right – punishment, morality, marriage and the rational state.

7.693 **Stern**, R., 'Unity and difference in Hegel's political philosophy', *Ratio*, 2, 1989, 75–88. Outlines his celebration of the differentiation of individuals as the basis for a higher political unification, concluding that he conceived this pluralism too narrowly in modern society.

7.694 **Stillman**, P. G., 'Freedom as participation: the revolutionary theory of Hegel and Arendt', *American Behavioral Scientist*, 20, 1977, 477–92.

7.695 —— 'Hegel's analysis of property in the *Philosophy of Right*', *Cardozo Law Review*, 10, 1989, 1031–72.

7.696 —— 'Hegel's civil society: a locus of freedom', *Polity*, 12, 1980, 622–46. Important corrective to previous interpretation of his thought, stressing the subtlety and centrality of his conception of civil society.

7.697 —— 'Hegel's critique of liberal theories of right', *Am. Pol. Sc. Rev.*, 68, 1974, 1086–92. Rehearses his rejection of theories of natural rights.

7.698 —— 'Hegel's idea of the modern family', *Thought*, 56, 1981, 342–52.

7.699 —— 'Property, freedom and individuality in Hegel's and Marx's political thought', in J. R. Pennock and J. W. Chapman, ed., *Property*, New York, 1980, 130–67. Compares Hegel's understanding of property – its relation to individuality and tendency to leave the poor marginal within civil society – with Marx's critique of property for the constraints it places on individuality.

7.700 **Taylor**, C., *Hegel*, 1975. An impressive reconstruction and evaluation of his thought which stresses his intellectual context and the notion of logic as central to comprehension of his work. Provides a stimulating conclusion in which his philosophy is viewed as an essential part of the conflict of interpretations through which we try to understand ourselves in modern societies.

7.701 —— *Hegel and Modern Society*, 1979.

7.702 —— 'Hegel: history and politics', in M. J Sandel, ed., *Liberalism and Its Critics*, 1984, 177–99. Excellent survey of Hegel's concept of 'sittlichkeit', the moral obligations of an individual to his/her community, which he theorised as a response to the unfolding crisis of modernity.

7.703 —— 'Hegel's ambiguous legacy for modern liberalism', *Cardozo Law Review*, 10, 1989, 857–70.

7.704 **Teichgraeber**, R., 'Hegel on property and poverty', *J. Hist. Ideas*, 38, 1977, 47–64. Outlines his understanding of property as an important moment in the shift to rational discourse. In Hegel's scenario there is little room for the propertyless.

7.705 **Thakurdas**, F., 'Hegel's philosophical politics and its influence on Marx', *Journal of Political Studies*, 4, 1971, 3–13. Critical and idiosyncratic review of scholarship on Hegel, restating Marx's debt to him.

7.706 **Travis**, D. C., ed., *A Hegel Symposium*, Austin, Tex., 1962.

7.707 **Tucker**, R. C., 'The cunning of reason in Hegel and Marx', *Rev. Pol.*, 18, 1956, 269–95.

7.708 **Tunick**, M., 'Hegel's justification of hereditary monarchy', *Hist. Pol. Thought*, 12, 1991, 481–96. A vigorous interpretation of the *Philosophy of Right* as a political text, exemplified through his views on hereditary monarchy.

7.709 —— *Hegel's Political Philosophy: Interpreting the Practice of Legal Punishment*, Princeton, N.J., 1992. Focusing on his justification of punishment, the author reconstructs his approach to legal institutions and social practices. Boldly reads his political philosophy as critical theory.

7.710 **Uchida**, H., *Marx's 'Grundrisse' and Hegel's 'Logic'*, 1988. A thorough and impressive account of the close relationship between the structure and ideas of the *Grundrisse* and Hegel's *Science of Logic*, in particular the close intertwining of form and content which Marx employs.

7.711 **Verene**, D. P., ed., *Hegel's Social and Political Thought: The Philosophy of Objective Spirit*, 1980. A collection of papers from the fourth conference of the Hegel Society of America, 1976, including Rosen on theory and practice in his thought, Plant on the centrality of political economy within his philosophy, Ver Eecke on his interweaving of politics and economics, expressed in his anti-utopian view of political life, Stillman on property and civil society, Adelman on the non-rational development of self-consciousness, Harris on his understanding of sovereignty and international relations, and Paolucci on the pertinence of his thought on the nation–state system.

7.712 **Walsh**, W. H., *Hegelian Ethics*, 1969.

7.713 **Waszek**, N., 'A stage in the development of Hegel's theory of the modern state', *Hegel-Studien*, 20, 1985, 163–72.

7.714 —— *The Scottish Enlightenment and Hegel's Account of Civil Society*, Dordrecht, 1988. Focuses on how Hegel's conception of the market and the division of labour, and his peculiar brand of liberalism, were influenced by Scottish Enlightenment thought.

7.715 **West**, C., 'Hegel, hermeneutics, politics: a reply to Charles Taylor', *Cardozo Law Review*, 10, 1989, 871–5.

7.716 **Wood**, A. W., *Hegel's Ethical Thought*, 1990. Exposition of the ethical theory underlying his philosophy of society, politics and history, including a critical discussion of his treatment of other moral philosophers (Kant, Fichte).

7.717 **Yack**, B., 'The rationality of Hegel's concept of monarchy', *Am. Pol. Sc. Rev.*, 74, 1980, 709–20. Defends his view of the monarchy as part of a complete account of necessary political conditions for a rational state.

THE YOUNG HEGELIANS

7.718 **Avineri**, S., *Moses Hess: Prophet of Communism and Zionism*, New York, 1985. Comprehensive account of his thought, clarifying his intellectual relationship with Marx and Hegel, and examining his notions of nationality, socialism and religion.

7.719 —— 'Socialism and judaism in Moses Hess's *Holy History of Mankind*', *Rev. Pol.*, 45, 1983, 234–53. Attempts to trace his Zionism back to his early work, against the conventional opinion that he shifted from socialism to nationalism.

7.720 **Berlin**, I., *The Life and Opinions of Moses Hess*, 1959.

7.721 **Brazill**, W. J., *The Young Hegelians*, 1970.

7.722 **Breckman**, W., 'Ludwig Feuerbach and the political theology of restoration', *Hist. Pol. Thought*, 13, 1992, 437–62. Contrary to Marx's interpretation, Feuerbach was an acute social critic who integrated his theological beliefs with his political ideals. Breckman presents him as especially concerned with the troubled relationship between commerce and virtue; his belief in unmediated social union influenced Marx strongly.

7.723 **Carns**, P., 'Max Stirner, the predecessor of Nietzsche', *Monist*, 21, 1971, 376–97.

7.724 **Clark**, J. P., *Max Stirner's Egoism*, 1976. Focuses upon his egoistic ethics, in order to examine similarities between his thought and the anarchist tradition of social and political philosophy.

7.725 **Hellman**, R. J., *Berlin, the Red Room and White Beer, the 'Free' Hegelian Radicals in the 1840s*, Washington, D.C., 1990.

7.726 **Lawrence**, J. P., 'Schelling as post-Heglian and as Aristotelian', *International Political Quarterly*, 26, 1986, 315–30. Argues that Schelling's critique of Hegel's *Logic* was influential for Marx, Kierkegaard, and the young Hegelian movement, concluding that Schelling drew heavily upon Aristotle's political insight.

7.727 **Mackintosh**, R., *Hegel and Hegelianism*, 1990.

7.728 **Mah**, H., *The End of Philosophy, the Origin of "Ideology": Karl Marx and the Crisis of the Young Hegelians*, Berkeley, Calif., 1987. Suggests that the contemporary notion of ideology was developed in the 1840s, particularly in the work of the Prussian members of the young Hegelian movement. An interesting alternative to conventional accounts of the origin of ideology.

7.729 **Nola**, R., 'The young Hegelians, Feuerbach, and Marx', in R. C. Solomon and K. M. Higgins, ed., *The Age of German Idealism*, 1993, 210–29.

7.730 **Patterson**, R. W. K., *The Nihilist Egoist: Max Stirner*, 1971.

7.731 **Rosen**, Z., *Bruno Bauer and Karl Marx: The Influence of Bruno Bauer on Marx's Thought*, The Hague, 1977.

7.732 —— 'The attitude of Hess to French socialism and his plans for publishing a series of socialist writings with Marx and Engels', *Phil. Forum*, 8, 1977, 310–22.

7.733 —— 'The influence of Bruno Bauer on

Marx's concept of alienation', *Soc. Theory & Pract.*, 1, 1970, 56–69.

7.734 —— 'The radicalism of a young Hegelian, Bruno Bauer', *Rev. Pol.*, 33, 1971, 377–404. Argues that he interpreted society as caught in a conflict between religion and criticism; reason would eventually release human consciousness from the bondage of theology. An illuminating discussion of the political implications of this perspective.

7.735 **Sass**, H.-M., 'Bruno Bauer's critical theory', *Phil. Forum*, 8, 1977, 92–120.

7.736 **Stepelvich**, L. S., 'Max Stirner and Ludwig Feuerbach', *J. Hist. Ideas*, 39, 1978, 451–63. Outlines the nature and consequences of the debate between these thinkers. Hegel's legacy was expressed both in Stirner's concrete egoism and Feuerbach's universal altruism.

7.737 —— 'Max Stirner as Hegelian', *J. Hist. Ideas*, 46, 1985, 597–614.

7.738 —— 'The first Hegelians: an introduction', *Phil. Forum*, 8, 1978, 6–20. Traces the emergence of the young Hegelians and their focus on the restoration of metaphysics, speculative theology and conservative social and political theory.

7.739 —— 'The revival of Max Stirner', *J. Hist. Ideas*, 35, 1974, 323–8.

7.740 —— 'Young Hegelianism: a bibliography of general studies, 1930 to present', *Phil. Forum*, 8, 1978, 21–3.

7.741 **Taylor**, C., 'Feuerbach and the roots of materialism', *Pol. Sts.*, 26, 1978, 417–21.

7.742 **Thomas**, P., 'Karl Marx and Max Stirner', *Pol. Theory*, 3, 1975, 159–79.

7.743 **Toews**, J. E., *Hegelianism: The Path Toward Dialectical Humanism, 1805–1841*, 1980. Study of the Hegelian project which begins by placing his mature philosophy in its historical context, then assesses the reception of his philosophy by sympathisers in his lifetime to explain the conflicts which beset Hegelians in the 1830s and 1840s. A major contribution to our understanding of the intellectual climate in Germany in this period as well as the ambiguities within the Hegelian system.

7.744 **Wartofsky**, M. W., *Feuerbach*, 1977. Distinguished and enlightening account of the development of his political and philosophical thought.

Kropotkin

7.745 **Cahm**, C., *Peter Kropotkin and the Rise of Revolutionary Anarchism 1872–1886*, 1989. In the first major study of Kropotkin for over a decade, Cahm places him firmly in the context of the development of the European anarchist movement, and concludes that previous assumptions about his disregard of the revolutionary potential of the labour movement were inaccurate.

7.746 **Di Norcia**, V., 'Calvin and Kropotkin', in R. Fitzgerald, ed., *Comparing Political Thinkers*, 1980, 203–22. Presents these thinkers as polar opposites in their views of human capacities and potential. The value of the comparison is unclear.

7.747 **McCulloch**, C., 'The problem of fellowship in communitarian theory: William Morris and Peter Kropotkin', *Pol. Sts.*, 32, 1984, 437–50. Suggests that fellowship is a key theme within communitarian discourse, yet communitarians struggle to reconcile the moral demands of fellowship with its psychological implications.

7.748 **Miller**, M. A., *Kropotkin*, Chicago, Ill., 1976. A major biographical study which charts his break from socialism and provides a clear outline of his anarchist communism which was elaborated especially between 1880 and 1900. Concludes with a perceptive critique of his conception of social revolution.

7.749 **Punzo**, V. C., 'The modern state and the search for community: the anarchist critique of Peter Kropotkin', *International Philosophical Quarterly*, 16, 1976, 3–32.

7.750 **Woodcock**, G., and **Avakumovic**, I. *The Anarchist Prince: A Biographical Study of Peter Kropotkin*, 1950.

Marx

THE EARLY MARX

7.751 **Althusser**, L., 'Marx's relation to Hegel', in *Politics and History*, 1972, 161–86.

7.752 **Arthur**, C. J., *Dialectics of Labour: Marx and His Relation to Hegel*, 1986. A scholarly, though at times difficult, account of this central theme, which owes much to Mészáros and Lukács.

7.753 **Avineri**, S., 'Marx and Jewish emancipation', *J. Hist. Ideas*, 25, 1964,

445–50. Important reinterpretation of this text's significance, despite its anti-semitism.

7.754 —— 'The Hegelian origins of Marx's political thought', *Rev. Metaph.*, 21, 1967, 33–50. Stresses Marx's *Critique of Hegel's Philosophy of Right* as the point of origin for many of his later ideas, revising conventional views about the stages through which his thought progressed: the basic ingredients of his theory were, in fact, in place as early as 1843.

7.755 —— 'The instrumentality of passion in the world of reason: Hegel and Marx', *Pol. Theory*, 1, 1973, 388–404. Focusing on the problem of the relationship between subjective will and historical outcome, the author demonstrates the influence of Hegel's strictures upon Marx as well as key differences concerning the immanence of the relationship between passion and reason (Hegel) and the transcendence of this relationship (Marx).

7.756 **Berki**, R. N., 'Through and through Hegel: Marx's road to communism', *Pol. Sts.*, 38, 1990, 654–71. Analyses the transitional period within the thought of the early Marx (1842–44), showing that the differing positions he adopted remained within Hegelian foundations. Marx first embraced communism in *The Manuscripts* of 1844, though his interpretation of it remained strongly Hegelian.

7.757 **Berry**, C. J., 'Need and egoism in Marx's early writings', *Hist. Pol. Thought*, 8, 1987, 461–73. Illuminates his implicit reliance on a number of Hegelian assumptions which have not been specified in accounts of his early thought, in particular his use of the Hegelian conception of civil society before 1845. Ultimately he rejected this Hegelian schema because of its inability to realise truly human needs.

7.758 **Cornu**, A., 'Marx's critique of Ricardo's and Hegel's concepts in his 1844 MSS', *Revolutionary World*, 37, 1980, 68–85.

7.759 —— *The Origins of Marxian Thought*, Springfield, Ill, 1957.

7.760 **Delfgaauw**, B., *The Young Marx*, 1962. A brief exposition of his ideas, stressing their continuing relevance.

7.761 **Easton**, L. D., 'Alienation and history in early Marx', *Philos. & Phenom. Res.*, 22, 1961, 193–205. Examination of the concept of alienation in the context of its appropriation by new left and existential currents, illuminating the particular blend of influences Marx synthesised – Hegel, Feuerbach and the Hellenic image of community. This resulted in a theory which was more conducive to totalitarianism than libertarianism.

7.762 —— 'Alienation, empiricism, and democracy in the early Marx', in J. Somerville and H. L. Parsons, ed., *Dialogues on the Philosophy of Marxism: From the Proceedings of the Society for the Philosophical Study of Dialectical Materialism*, 1974, 312–24. Traces the concept of alienation in his early work, connecting it to his unfolding political vision, and illuminating the philosophical tensions within it.

7.763 **Feenberg**, A., 'New grounds for revolution. The early Marx in a Lukascian perspective', *Phil. Forum*, 8, 1978, 186–218. Compares the metatheories offered by the young Marx and Lukács, both of which attempted to derive original grounds for revolution. Marx's revision of the notions of reason and need are interpreted as vital in this project.

7.764 **Fenves**, P., 'Marx's doctoral thesis on two Greek atomists and the post-Kantian interpretation', *J. Hist. Ideas*, 37, 1986, 433–52. Thoughtful survey, teasing out the implications of this text, which ultimately dramatises a philosophical clash between Hegel and Kant, a conflict which Marx resolved in favour of the former.

7.765 **Fuss**, P., 'Theory and practice in Hegel and Marx: an unfinished dialogue', in T. Ball, ed., *Political Theory and Praxis: New Perspectives*, Minneapolis, Minn., 1977, 97–116.

7.766 **Gagern**, M., 'The puzzling pattern of the Marxist critique of Feuerbach', *Studies in Soviet Thought*, 11, 1971, 135–58. Suggests that an overreliance on Marx's critique of Feuerbach has led to a biased interpretation of the Marxist notion of praxis, an uncritical reliance on Marx's critique of Feuerbach's understanding of Hegel's dialectic, and a false interpretation of humanism.

7.767 **Gilbert**, A., *Marx's Politics: Communists and Citizens*, 1983. Account of Marx's and Engel's activities, 1843–52, setting them in the context of the ideas of other German socialists of the 1840s such as Weitling and Schapper. The book's more general discussion (for instance of the Marxian theory of the state) has been surpassed by the work of other commentators.

7.768 **Gregory**, D., 'The influence of French socialism on the thought of Karl Marx, 1843–45', *Proceedings of the Western Society for the Study of French History*, 7, 1978, 242–51. Strives to counter the 'over-emphasis' on the Hegelian sources of his thought, pointing to the 'continuity between French socialism under the July Monarchy and the earliest, quasi-Romantic formulation of Marxism in the mid-1840s'.

7.769 **Hammen**, O. J., 'The young Marx reconsidered', *J. Hist. Ideas*, 31, 1970, 109–20. Lucid presentation of the view that Marx's ideas changed little in his lifetime except when he was constrained by tactical necessities.

7.770 **Hodges**, D. C., 'The young Marx: a reappraisal', *Philos. & Phenom. Res.*, 27, 1966, 216–29. Challenges radical appropriations of the early Marx because these deny the economic content of his notion of alienation and neglect his later rejection of his earlier writings.

7.771 **Hook**, S., *From Hegel to Marx: Studies in the Intellectual Development of Karl Marx*, 1966. Explores Marx's early development through studies of his relationship with and critique of Hegel and the young Hegelians. A compelling and thorough account of the political and intellectual context in which Marx first developed his thought.

7.772 **Horowitz**, I. L., 'A symposium on the young Karl Marx', *Sc. & Soc.*, 27, 1963, 283–326.

7.773 **Johnson**, C., 'Philosophy and revolution in the young Marx', *Sc. & Soc.*, 47, 1983, 66–83. Discerns three broad stages in Marx's conception of philosophy: a Hegelian view of philosophy as social change, the philosophical critique of alienation, and philosophy realised by the proletariat.

7.774 **Kauder**, E., 'The intellectual sources of Karl Marx', *Kyklos*, 21, 1968, 269–87. Explores the intellectual influences upon his early conception of alienation, social interchange and the structure of capitalism.

7.775 **Kontopoulos**, K., *Knowledge and Determination: The Transition from Hegel to Marx*, Amsterdam, 1980.

7.776 **Langslet**, L. R., 'Young Marx and alienation in Western debate', *Inquiry*, 6, 1963, 3–17.

7.777 **Liebich**, A., 'Hegel, Marx, and Althusser', *Pol. & Soc.*, 9, 1979, 89–102. Re-examines and explains Althusser's claim that the young Marx was not a Hegelian, suggesting that this claim remains unchanged despite Althusser's apparent recantation in his auto-critique.

7.778 **Lobkowicz**, N., 'Karl Marx and Max Stirner', in F. J. Adelmann, ed., *Demythologizing Marxism: A Series of Studies on Marxism*, The Hague, 1969, 64–95. Argues that the *German Ideology* was written to rebut the influence of Stirner's philosophy of total disillusionment. Close intellectual history

7.779 **Löwith**, K., 'Man's self-alienation in the early writings of Marx', *Social Res.*, 21, 1954, 204–30. Presents his early writings as committed to the resolution of philosophical problems prior to his turn to political economy. The concept of self-alienation, according to Löwith, connects these two bodies of thought.

7.780 **Lubasz**, H., 'Marx's initial problematic: the problem of poverty', *Pol. Sts.*, 24, 1976, 24–42. Suggests that he broke from Hegel and Feuerbach in his treatment of this problem, especially in his insistence on the distinction between essential and existential differentiation.

7.781 **McGovern**, A. F., 'Karl Marx's first political writings: the Rheinische Zeitung 1842–1843', in F. J. Adelmann, ed., *Demythologizing Marxism: A Series of Studies on Marxism*, The Hague, 1969, 19–63. Assessment of Marx's rarely studied newspaper articles, revealing that as early as 1843 he supported the elimination of property and poverty.

7.782 —— 'The young Marx on the state', *Sc. & Soc.*, 34, 1970, 430–66. A detailed chronology of his developing theory of the state which concludes that a distinctive interpretation of the universal state pre-existed his materialist interpretation.

7.783 **McLellan**, D., *Marx Before Marxism*, 1970. An account of his early thought (up to the *Paris Manuscripts*) which illuminates the historical and intellectual context in which he wrote. Excellent introduction to his early work.

7.784 —— *The Young Hegelians and Karl Marx*, 1969. Accessible and historically informed account of the influence of the left Hegelians upon the genesis of Marxism.

7.785 **Maguire**, J., *Marx's Paris Writings: An*

Analysis, Dublin, 1972. Cogent analysis of these writings, demonstrating that he was preoccupied with economic questions from an early stage and that he developed a notion of praxis in the 1840s. A critical reply to those commentators who have perceived a clear break in the course of his intellectual development.

7.786 —— *Marx's Theory of Politics*, 1978. Focusing specifically on his reading of politics, Maguire reconstructs his understanding of bourgeois political power against the background of contemporary events in France and Germany. Concludes by relating his account of politics to his materialism, defending his distinction between government (found in all societies) and politics (government in class societies) against the criticism of latterday commentators.

7.787 **Mewes**, H., 'On the concept of politics in the early work of Karl Marx', *Social Res.*, 43, 1976, 276–94. Illustrates the early Marx's concern for the revival of the ancient supremacy of political life, arguing that this interest survived in his later writings through his critique of social divisions in civil society.

7.788 **Mins**, H. F., 'Marx's doctoral dissertation', *Sc. & Soc.*, 12, 1948, 157–69. Close analysis of the background to, and context of, this text.

7.789 **O'Neill**, J., 'The concept of estrangement in the early and later writings of Karl Marx', *Philos. & Phenom. Res.*, 25, 1964, 64–84. Precise description of the shift in his concept of alienation, illustrating its ethical content and inadequacy for social analysis.

7.790 **Rosen**, Z., *Bruno Bauer and Karl Marx: The Influence of Bruno Bauer on Marx's Thought*, The Hague, 1977.

7.791 **Sass**, H. M., 'The concept of revolution in Marx's dissertation (the non-Hegelian origin of Karl Marx's early concept of dialectics)', *Phil. Forum*, 8, 1978, 241–55. Suggests that he began to develop an antithetical (to Hegel) model of dialectical change in history as early as 1839–41. In this he was significantly influenced by the Feuerbachian and Bauerian positions.

7.792 **Sayer**, D., 'The critique of politics and political economy: capitalism, communism, and the state in Marx's writings of the mid-1840s', *Sociological Review*, 33, 1985, 221–53. Stimulating account of the historical sociology developed in these texts which have been misrepresented by later commentators.

7.793 **Schwarz**, J., 'Liberalism and the Jewish connection: a study of Spinoza and the young Marx', *Pol. Theory*, 13, 1985, 58–84.

7.794 **Sherova**, E., 'The virtue of poverty: Marx's transformation of Hegel's concept of the poor', *Can. J. Pol. & Soc. Theory*, 3, 1979, 53–66. Identifies a tension between Marx's early views of the poor and his later treatment of the proletariat.

7.795 **Smith**, G. W., 'Sinful science? Marx's theory of freedom from thesis to theses', *Hist. Pol. Thought*, 2, 1981, 141–59. Analyses his doctoral dissertation to throw light upon his theory of freedom and determinism. His understanding of freedom is said to be based upon a dubious idealist conceptualisation, though his final position was philosophically serviceable and empirically useful.

7.796 **Struik**, D. J., and **Chamberlain**, G. L., 'Symposium on the young Marx', *Sc. & Soc.*, 27, 1963, 283–320.

7.797 **Teeple**, G., *Marx's Critique of Politics, 1842–1847*, Toronto, 1984. Thorough analysis of his early writings.

7.798 —— 'The doctoral dissertation of Karl Marx', *Hist. Pol. Thought*, 11, 1990, 81–118. A systematic exposition of this text and evaluation of its relevance to his later intellectual achievements, concluding that he developed a materialist logic as early as this text.

7.799 **Therborn**, G., 'The working class and the birth of Marxism', *New Left Rev.*, 79, 1973, 3–15. Traces the geographical, historical and intellectual context within which historical materialism was developed in the late 1840s, suggesting reasons why Marx and Engels, unlike later radicals, remained loyal to the working-class movement.

7.800 **Wolfson**, M., 'The day Karl Marx grew up', *Hist. Pol. Econ.*, 3, 1971, 335–52. Assesses the 'transition' in his thought which occurred in 1845. Somewhat simplified presentation of his ideological development.

MARX AND ETHICS

7.801 **Allen**, D., 'Does Marx have an ethic of self-realization?', *Can. J. Phil.*, 10, 1980, 377–86.

7.802 —— 'The utilitarianism of Marx and Engels', *Am. Phil. Q.*, 10, 1973, 189–99. Presents the unlikely thesis that these thinkers' arguments are the kind used by utilitarians, though not expressed in their language. A technical argument, drawn from selective textual references.

7.803 **Altman**, A., 'Is Marxism utopian?', *Phil. & Soc. Crit.*, 8, 1981, 387–404.

7.804 **Andrew**, E., 'Inalienable right, alienable property and freedom of choice: Locke, Nozick and Marx on the alienability of labour', *Can. J. Pol. Sc.*, 18, 1985, 529–50. Focuses upon a tension in natural rights thinking between the inalienability of natural or human rights and the tendency to individualise our conceptions of these, making them potentially alienable, like property. Contrasts Nozick's belief that all rights can be sold against Marx's position.

7.805 **Arneson**, R. J., 'What's wrong with exploitation?', *Ethics*, 91, 1980–81, 202–27.

7.806 **Aronovitch**, H., 'Marxian morality', *Can. J. Phil.*, 10, 1980, 357–76.

7.807 **Ash**, W., *Marxism and Moral Concepts*, New York, 1964.

7.808 **Balbus**, I., *Marxism and Domination*, Princeton, N.J., 1982.

7.809 **Bay**, C., 'Human needs, wants and politics: Abraham Maslow meet Karl Marx', *Social Praxis*, 7, 1981, 233–52.

7.810 **Booth**, W. J., 'Gone fishing. Making sense of Marx's concept of communism', *Pol. Theory*, 17, 1989, 205–22. Emphasises the idea of domination by an autonomous economic process as Marx's central ethical principle in order to highlight his rejection of liberalism, which can only grasp one form of unfreedom – coercion, the arbitrary rule of one will over another. This sense of 'objective compulsion' provided the foundation for his understanding of the principles which would inform communist society.

7.811 **Bose**, A., 'Marx on value, capital, and exploitation', *Hist. Pol. Econ.*, 3, 1971, 298–334. Elaborates his theory of capitalist exploitation in an attempt to prove the continued relevance of Marxian economics for contemporary societies.

7.812 **Brenkert**, G. G., 'Freedom and private property in Marx', *Phil. & Pub. Affairs*, 8, 1979, 122–47.

7.813 —— 'Marx and utilitarianism', *Can. J. Phil.*, 5, 1975, 421–34. Debunks the argument that he was a utilitarian of any sort.

7.814 —— *Marx's Ethics of Freedom*, 1983.

7.815 **Buchanan**, A., 'Exploitation, alienation and injustice', *Can. J. Phil.*, 9, 1979, 121–39.

7.816 —— *Marx and Justice: the Radical Critique of Liberalism*, 1982.

7.817 —— 'Marx, morality and history: an assessment of recent analytical work on Marx', *Ethics*, 98, 1988, 104–36.

7.818 **Burke**, J. P., **Crocker**, L., and **Legters**, L. H., ed., *Marxism and the Good Society*, 1981. Includes De George on Marxism and the good society, Crocker on Marx, liberty and democracy, Fischer on Marx's early conception of democracy, Burke on determinism and revolutionary change, McLellan on differences between Marx and Engels in their view of the communist future, and Di Quattro on justice.

7.819 **Chandel**, B., 'Freedom and morality in Marxist philosophy', in V. K. Roy and R. C. Sarikwal, ed., *Marxian Sociology, Volume One*, 1979, 445–76. Lucid defence of Marx's conception of and reliance upon freedom, which illuminates the connection between his ethical and social outlook.

7.820 **Clarke**, D. H., 'Marxism, justice and the justice model', *Contemporary Crisis*, 2, 1978, 27–62.

7.821 **Clarke**, J. J., ' "The end of history": a reappraisal of Marx's views on alienation and human emancipation', *Can. J. Pol. Sc.*, 4, 1971, 367–80. Deploys his notion of alienation to elucidate his beliefs about the 'end of history', suggesting that he was motivated by the possibility of humans being fully autonomous moral beings.

7.822 **Cohen**, G. A., 'Marx's dialectic of labour', *Phil. & Pub. Affairs*, 3, 1974, 235–61. Reconstructs his assessment of the progressive aspects of capitalism, especially his belief that labour under capitalism shows signs of freedom which is lacking in earlier, craft labour. Concludes that he believed that true freedom lay beyond the economic sphere, and depended on the abolition of labour.

7.823 **Cohen**, M., **Nagel**, T., and **Scanlon**, T., ed., *Marx, Justice and History*, Princeton, N.J., 1980.

7.824 **Crocker**, L., 'Marx's concept of exploitation', *Journal of Social Issues*, 28, 1972, 201–15. Unconvincing attempt to return exploitation, understood as the undemocratic control of production, to the centre of interpretations of Marx.

7.825 **Cunningham**, A., 'Objectivity and human needs in Marxism', *New Blackfriars*, 55, 1974, 112–23.

7.826 **Duncan**, G., 'Mill and Marx', in R. Fitzgerald, ed., *Comparing Political Thinkers*, 1980, 245–61. Compares their theories of human nature and attitudes to existing institutional structures, suggesting they shared certain characteristics, for instance an overemphasis on the degree of rationality and community possible in large, complex societies.

7.827 **Dupré**, L., 'Marx's idea of alienation revisited', *Man and World*, 14, 1981, 387–410.

7.828 **Edgley**, R., 'Marxism, morality and Mr Lukes', in D. McLellan and S. Sayers, ed., *Socialism and Morality*, 1990, 21–41. Defence of Marx's essential consistency in this area, suggesting that he only opposed the idealistic elements of moral discourse, not its substantive principles.

7.829 **Elliott**, J. H., 'Continuity and change in the evolution of Marx's theory of alienation from the *Manuscripts* through the *Grundrisse* to *Capital*', *Hist. Pol. Econ.*, 11, 1979, 317–62.

7.830 **Fetscher**, I., 'Karl Marx on human nature', *Social Res.*, 40, 1973, 443–67.

7.831 **Forbes**, I., 'Marx and human nature', in I. Forbes and S. Smith, ed., *Politics and Human Nature*, 1983, 20–35. Locates his interpretation of human nature within the larger context of the history of political thought, suggesting that his developmental model provides insight into contemporary problems.

7.832 **Fritzhand**, M., 'The foundations of Marxian ethics', in V. K. Roy and R. C. Sarikwal, ed., *Marxian Sociology, Volume One*, 1979, 381–406. Meandering, conventional presentation of Marx's ethics of freedom.

7.833 **Fuchs**, W., 'The question of Marxist ethics', *Philosophical Forum (Boston)*, 7, 1976, 237–45.

7.834 **Geras**, N., *Marx and Human Nature: Refutation of a Legend*, 1983. A terse argument that Marx possessed a coherent view of human nature, focusing predominantly on the sixth of his *Theses on Feuerbach*.

7.835 —— 'Marxism and moral advocacy', in D. McLellan and S. Sayers, ed., *Socialism and Morality*, 1990, 5–20. Admitting to the existence of contradictory attitudes to morality within Marxism, Geras stresses the concepts of need and equality as central to the reconstruction of a Marxian morality.

7.836 —— 'The controversy about Marx and justice', *New Left Rev.*, 150, 1985, 47–85.

7.837 **Gilbert**, A., 'Historical theory and the structure of moral argument in Marx', *Pol. Theory*, 9, 1981, 173–205. Defends the belief that ethical arguments played an important part in historical materialism, suggesting that Marx viewed morals as context-dependent for their meaning.

7.838 **Gray**, J., 'Marxian freedom, individual liberty, and the end of alienation', in E. F. Paul, J. Paul, F. D. Miller and J. Ahrens, ed., *Marxism and Liberalism*, 1986, 160–87. Assesses the Marxian claim that capitalism renders the proletariat unfree, differentiating between Marx's argument that the source of this unfreedom lies in its subjection to unplanned economic forces and G. A. Cohen's thesis. The achievement of communism, the antithesis of the process Marx analyses, is epistemologically impossible, according to Gray.

7.839 **Green**, M., 'Marx, utility, and right', *Pol. Theory*, 11, 1983, 433–46. Reconstructs his advocacy of socialism and communism on the basis of his critique of utilitarian and right-based moralities.

7.840 **Gregor**, J. A., 'Marxism and ethics, a methodological inquiry', *Philos. & Phenom. Res.*, 28, 1967–68, 368–84.

7.841 **Hammen**, O. J., 'A note on the alienation motif in Marx', *Pol. Theory*, 8, 1980, 223–42. Reviews the critical literature on this concept in his work, suggesting that shifts in his understanding of alienation have been neglected.

7.842 **Hancock**, R., 'Marx's theory of justice', *Soc. Theory & Pract.*, 1, 1971, 65–71. Reconstructs his deployment of justice which supplanted alienation as the key ethical category in his later work.

7.843 **Harris**, A. L., 'Utopian elements in Marx's thought', *Ethics*, 60, 1950, 79–99.

7.844 **Harris**, J., 'The Marxist conception of violence', *Phil. & Pub. Affairs*, 3, 1974, 192–220. Outlines this conception, comparing it to other accounts of political violence and emphasising its concern with indirectly caused violence.

7.845 **Heller**, A., *The Theory of Need in Marx*, 1976. Influential analysis of this concept in his thought, stressing his understanding of the alienation of needs. Imaginative, if one-dimensional, reading of the utopian aspects of Marxism.

7.846 **Hirst**, P. Q., 'Marx and Engels on law, crime, and morality', *Economy and Society*, 1, 1972, 28–56.

7.847 **Hodges**, D. C., 'Marxist ethics and ethical theory', *Socialist Register*, 1964, 227–41. A reply to Kamenka's interpretation of Marxist ethical theory, arguing that Marxism is devoid of ethical foundation.

7.848 —— 'Marx's contribution to humanism', *Sc. & Soc.*, 29, 1965, 173–91. Sceptical examination of attempts to appropriate him as a humanist thinker, exaggerating his ambivalence about many key humanist goals and principles.

7.849 **Holstrom**, N., 'Marx and Cohen on exploitation and the labour theory of value', *Inquiry*, 26, 1983, 287–307.

7.850 **Husami**, Z. I., 'Marx on distributive justice', *Phil. & Pub. Affairs*, 8, 1978–79, 27–64.

7.851 **Kain**, P. J., *Marx and Ethics*, 1988. Traces the development of his thought on ethics, and shows how he sought to transcend a morality of burdensome obligation and constraint so as to realise a community built upon spontaneous bonds of solidarity.

7.852 **Kamenka**, E., *Marxism and Ethics*, 1969.

7.853 —— 'Marxism and ethics – a reconsideration', in S. Avineri, ed., *Varieties of Marxism*, The Hague, 1977, 119–46. Despite Marx's many insights and historical sense, the reconstruction of an ethically driven socialism will take place outside Marxism, according to Kamenka.

7.854 —— *The Ethical Foundations of Marxism*, 1962. A careful reconstruction of the shifting basis for Marx's ethical commitments, which contrasts these ideas with Soviet interpretations of socialist morality.

7.855 —— 'The primitive ethic of Karl Marx', *Aust. J. Phil.*, 35, 1957, 75–96.

7.856 **Kline**, G., 'Was Marx an ethical humanist?', *Studies in Soviet Thought*, 9, 1969, 91–103.

7.857 **Kocis**, R. A., 'An unresolved tension in Marx's critique of justice and rights', *Pol. Sts.*, 34, 1986, 406–22. Rejects his view of rights as detrimental to community by

focusing on the tension between the Kantian aspects of his thought, concerning the inviolability of persons, and his consequentialist ethical theory.

7.858 **Levine**, A., 'Toward a Marxian theory of justice', *Pol. & Soc.*, 11, 1982, 343–62. Reconstructs a Marxian theory of justice in line with Roemer's distributional interpretation of socialism. A valuable critique of standard Marxist arguments in this area.

7.859 **Lukes**, S., *Marxism and Morality*, 1985. Rigorous assessment of the tensions involved in the reconstruction of a Marxian morality.

7.860 **McBride**, W., 'The concept of justice in Marx, Engels, and others', *Ethics*, 85, 1975, 204–18.

7.861 **McCarthy**, G., 'Marx's social ethics and the critique of traditional morality', *Studies in Soviet Thought*, 29, 1985, 177–99.

7.862 **McLellan**, D., 'Marx and the whole man', in B. Parekh, ed., *The Concept of Socialism*, 1979, 62–71. Intervention in the debate on Marx and human nature, examining the *Paris Manuscripts, German Ideology* and the later economic writings. Explores the difficulties which the socialist tradition has experienced in its conception of the individual.

7.863 —— 'Marx's view of the unalienated society', *Rev. Pol.*, 31, 1969, 459–65. Challenges the thesis of the epistemological break, by tracing his remarks about future communist society and the central role of labour in human freedom.

7.864 **Mészáros**, I., *Marx's Theory of Alienation*, 1970. A difficult text containing some provocative and original ideas.

7.865 **Miller**, R. W., 'Marx and Aristotle: a kind of consequentialism', in K. Nielsen and S. C. Patten, ed., *Marx and Morality*, Guelph, 1981, 323–52.

7.866 **Mongar**, T., *Original Marxism*, 1991. Argues that the substantive Marxian problematic is alienation rather than exploitation, and that while exploitation-centred communism has failed, Marxism is still relevant because of the extent of alienation within modern production.

7.867 **Myers**, D. B., 'Ethics and political economy in Marx', *Phil. Forum (Boston)*, 7, 1976, 246–59.

7.868 **Nielsen**, K., 'Marxian ideology and moral philosophy', *Soc. Theory & Pract.*, 6, 1980, 53–68.

7.869 —— and **Patten**, S. C., ed., *Marx and Morality*, Ontario, 1981. A collection which critically examines the possibility and nature of a Marxist moral theory (Shaw, Paniachas, Peffer, Kellner, Collier and Skillen) and the importance of justice within Marxist discourse (Allen, Young, Buchanan, Reiman, Miller).

7.870 **Ollman**, B., *Alienation: Marx's Conception of Man in Capitalist Society*, 1971. Presents alienation as an explanatory social theory in Marx's thought, based upon his distinctive and unchanging conception of human nature. An engaging and lucid account, somewhat dated in its treatment of these topics.

7.871 —— 'Is there a Marxist ethic? The fact-value distinction', *Sc. & Soc.*, 35, 1971, 156–68.

7.872 **O'Malley**, J., 'History and "man's nature" in Marx', *Rev. Pol.*, 28, 1966, 508–27.

7.873 **O'Rourke**, J. J., *The Philosophy of Freedom in Marxist Thought*, 1974.

7.874 **Parekh**, B., 'Marx's theory of man', in B. Parekh, ed., *The Concept of Socialism*, 1975, 38–61. Illuminating discussion of Marx's attempt to combine humanism (Fichte, Hegel), and naturalism (Feuerbach) in a new, dialectical vision of human potential and needs.

7.875 **Peffer**, R. G., *Marxism, Morality, and Social Justice*, Princeton, N.J., 1990. Comprehensive survey of the debates about and dimensions of Marx's moral theory, informed by the attempt to develop an adequate Marxian moral theory on the basis of a theory of social justice. Clear and well organised.

7.876 **Phillips**, P., *Marx and Engels on Law and Morals*, 1981.

7.877 **Plamenatz**, J., *Karl Marx's Philosophy of Man*, 1975. Admirably clear outline of his conception of human nature and the nature of alienation under capitalism. In the book's third section, the author looks more generally at theoretical difficulties associated with attempts to delineate human nature and questions Marx's axiom that conflicts between differing social groups necessarily depend for their resolution on a drastic transformation of the established order. Influential and important engagement with Marxian theory.

7.878 **Press**, H., 'The existential basis of Marxism', *Philos. & Phenom. Res.*, 37, 1976–77, 331–44. Outlines his philosophical and economic understanding of production, concluding that the essence of Marxism lies in his utopian image of social consumption.

7.879 **Restuccia**, P., 'Marx on alienation and private property', *Praxis*, 6, 1970, 215–22.

7.880 **Ring**, J., 'On needing both Marx and Arendt. Alienation and the flight from inwardness', *Pol. Theory*, 17, 1989, 432–48. Thorough examination of Arendt's neglected theory of alienation, which explores the complementary dimensions of her and Marx's ideas on this theme.

7.881 **Roemer**, J., *A General Theory of Exploitation and Class*, Cambridge, Mass., 1982.

7.882 —— 'New directions in the Marxian theory of exploitation and class', *Pol. & Soc.*, 11, 1982, 81–113. Proposes a general theory of exploitation of which Marxian theory forms a part. Concludes that the Marxian theory of exploitation is best characterised in terms of property relations.

7.883 —— 'Property relations vs surplus value in Marxian exploitation', *Phil. Pub. Affairs*, 11, 1981, 281–313.

7.884 —— 'Should Marxists be interested in exploitation?', *Phil. & Pub. Affairs*, 14, 1985, 30–65.

7.885 **Ryan**, C. C., 'Socialist justice and the right to the labour product', *Pol. Theory*, 8, 1980, 503–24. Reconstructs Marx's critique of the concept of justice in classical political economy, arguing that the Marxist theory of justice is distinctive because it includes an historical appraisal of past arrangements and future possibilities.

7.886 **Schaff**, A., *Marxism and the Human Individual*, New York, 1970.

7.887 **Schedler**, G., 'Justice in Marx, Engels and Lenin', *Studies in Soviet Thought*, 18, 1978, 223–33.

7.888 **Shandro**, A. M., 'A Marxist theory of justice?', *Can. J. Pol. Sc.*, 22, 1989, 27–42.

7.889 **Sichel**, B. A., 'Karl Marx and the rights of man', *Philos. & Phenom. Res.*, 32, 1971–72, 355–60.

7.890 **Somerville**, J., and **Parsons**, H. L., ed., *Dialogues on the Philosophy of Marxism: From the Proceedings of the Society for the Philosophical Study of Dialectical Materialism*, 1974. A collection which includes a number of contributions to and

surveys of debates about Marxist
humanism (Schaff, Hodges, Markovic),
ethics (Somerville, McConnell), and
alienation (Gregor, Easton, Horowitz).

7.891 **Soper**, K., 'Marxism and morality', *New Left Rev.*, 163, 1987, 101–13.

7.892 **Sowell**, T., 'Karl Marx and the freedom of the individual', *Ethics*, 73, 1963, 119–25.

7.893 **Springborg**, P., 'Karl Marx on human needs', in R. Fitzgerald, ed., *Human Needs and Politics*, 1977, 157–73. Demonstrates the centrality of needs in his thought, despite his failure to prove their objectivity.

7.894 **Stojanovic**, S., 'The ethical potential of Marx's thought', in T. Bottomore, ed., *Modern Interpretations of Marx*, 1981, 170–87. Examines the reasons for the absence of a coherent Marxist ethic, placing some of the blame on Marx's own ambivalence. Summarises both sides of this debate clearly and accessibly.

7.895 **Turner**, D., 'Marx, ideology and morality', in D. McLellan and S. Sayers, ed., *Socialism and Morality*, 1990, 65–80. Unusual discussion of the Marx/morality question, bypassing the designation of Marxism as either moral or amoral, and arguing that this tradition is concerned with how the existence of morality is made possible.

7.896 **Van der Linden**, H., 'Marx and morality: an impossible synthesis?', *Theory & Soc.*, 13, 1984, 119–35. Review of recent contributions to this debate, concluding that a Marxist ethical position is only possible when Hegelian influences are purged from Marx's thought.

7.897 **Vandeveer**, P., 'Marx's view of justice', *Philos. & Phenom. Res.*, 33, 1972–73, 366–86.

7.898 **Venable**, V., *Human Nature: The Marxian View*, 1966. A sketchy reconstruction of the Marxist view of human nature, which concludes that Marx and Engels broke with all previous traditions of political thought in their theory of morality.

7.899 **Walicki**, A., 'The Marxian conception of freedom', in Z. A. Pelczynski and J. Gray, ed., *Conceptions of Liberty in Political Philosophy*, 1984, 217–42. Reasserts freedom as Marx's key ethical category, touching on his commitment to individual fulfilment.

7.900 **West**, C., *The Ethical Dimension of Marxist Thought*, New York, 1991. Appropriates Marx for the 'radical historicist' school of thought on ethics, proposing that Engels and other Marxists foolishly indulged in the philosophical quest for objectivity. Concludes unconvincingly with a categorical distinction between Marx and later Marxist philosophers.

7.901 **Wood**, A. W., 'Marx on right and justice: a reply to Husami', *Phil. & Pub. Affairs*, 8, 1978–79, 267–95.

7.902 —— 'The Marxian critique of justice', *Phil. & Pub. Affairs*, 1, 1972, 244–82.

7.903 **Young**, G., 'Justice and capitalist production: Marx and bourgeois ideology', *Can. J. Phil.*, 8, 1978, 421–54.

MARX AND HISTORICAL MATERIALISM

7.904 **Acton**, H. B., *The Illusion of the Epoch: Marxism-Leninism as a Philosophical Creed*, 1955. Influential critique of the tenets of historical materialism.

7.905 —— 'The materialist conception of history', *Procs. Aris. Soc.*, 52, 1951–52, 207–24. Sets out to prove that this methodology is 'a mixture of tautology, platitude, this-worldliness, speculative history and common sense'.

7.906 —— *What Marx Really Said*, 1967. Brief and critical account of historical materialism.

7.907 **Adamson**, W., 'Marx's four histories: an approach to his intellectual development', *Hist. & Theory*, 20, 1980, 379–402.

7.908 **Andrew**, E., 'Class in itself and class against capital: Karl Marx and his classifiers', *Can. J. Pol. Sc.*, 16, 1983, 577–84.

7.909 **Ballestrem**, K. G., 'Sources of the materialist conception of history in the history of ideas', *Studies in Soviet Thought*, 26, 1983, 3–9. Brief and stimulating comparison between Marx's theory of history and those of the Greeks and the Scottish political economists.

7.910 **Bober**, M. M., *Karl Marx's Interpretation of History*, Cambridge, Mass., 1962. A sympathetic account of his historical method.

7.911 —— *Karl Marx's Theory of History: A Defence*, Princeton, N.J., 1965.

7.912 **Carver**, T., 'Putting your money where your mouth is: the social construction of individuality in Marx's *Capital*', *Sts. Pol.*

Thought, 1, 1992, 19–41. Focuses on the overlap between rational choice Marxism and Marx's own work, revealing that he depended upon a conceptual individualism which rational choice theorists might deploy in their concern for preference-formation. Illuminating contribution to debates about rational choice Marxism.

7.913 **Chesnokov**, D. I., *Historical Materialism*, Moscow, 1969.

7.914 **Cocks**, J., 'Hegel's logic, Marx's science, rationalism's perils', *Pol. Sts.*, 31, 1983, 584–603. Views Marx as deploying Hegelian logic both in his teleological preferences and in his mature scientific analysis. Attempts to reconstruct his historical analysis in the light of this assessment.

7.915 **Cohen**, G. A., 'Historical inevitability and human agency in Marxism', in Sir J. Mason, ed., *Predictability in Science and Society*, 1986, 65–87.

7.916 —— *History, Labour, and Freedom: Themes from Marx*, 1988. Recapitulates his account of historical materialism, attempting to reconcile this with some of the insights of rational choice theory and accommodating his critics on several points, though refuting them on major questions. Concludes with his important essay, 'Freedom, justice and capitalism'.

7.917 —— *Karl Marx's Theory of History: A Defence*, 1978. Influential reconstruction of historical materialism, combining textual analysis with analytical rigour. Cohen's deployment of functional modes of explanation results in firm emphasis upon the primary causal role of the productive forces. These emphases fundamentally shifted the terms of debate.

7.918 —— 'On some criticisms of historical materialism', *Procs. Arist. Soc.*, supp. 44, 1970, 121–42.

7.919 —— 'Reconsidering historical materialism', in J. R. Pennock and J. W. Chapman, ed., *Marxism: Nomos XXVI*, 1983, 227–52.

7.920 —— 'Restricted and inclusive historical materialism', *Irish Philosophical Journal*, 1, 1984, 3–31.

7.921 —— and **Kymlicka**, W., 'Human nature and social change in the Marxist conception of history', *J. Phil.*, 85, 1988, 171–91.

7.922 **Elster**, J., 'Marxism and individualism', in M. Dascal and O. Gruengard, ed.,

Knowledge and Politics: Case Studies in the Relationship Between Epistemology and Political Philosophy, Boulder, Calif., 1989, 189–206. Relates the epistemological to the political dimensions of individualism in Marx's work, concluding that he was both a political and ethical individualist.

7.923 **Fleischer**, H., *Marxism and History*, 1973.

7.924 **Gandy**, D. R., *Marx and History: From Primitive Society to the Communist Future*, Austin, Tex., 1979.

7.925 **Glezerman**, G., et al., *Historical Materialism*, Moscow, 1959.

7.926 **Hillel-Ruben**, D., *Marxism and Materialism*, 1977.

7.927 **Hodges**, D. C., 'Historical materialism and ethics', *Philos. & Phenom. Res.*, 23, 1962–63, 1–22.

7.928 **Honderich**, T., 'Against teleological historical materialism', *Inquiry*, 25, 1982, 451–69. Refutes teleological defences of the theory of causality embodied in historical materialism. Marx, on this reading, rejected teleology.

7.929 **Larrain**, J., *A Reconstruction of Historical Materialism*, 1986. A clear discussion of the most relevant issues concerning historical materialism, and a cogent presentation of arguments in favour of reconstructing it as theoretical practice.

7.930 **Lefebvre**, H., *Dialectical Materialism*, 1974.

7.931 **McMurty**, J., *The Structure of Marx's World View*, Princeton, N.J., 1978. Vigorous defence of historical materialism as outlined in the 1859 *Preface* against latterday critics.

7.932 **Miller**, R. W., 'The consistency of historical materialism', *Phil. & Pub. Affairs*, 4, 1975, 390–409.

7.933 **Mitchell**, J., 'Women's liberation, Marxism and the socialist family', in B. Parekh, ed., *The Concept of Socialism*, 1979, 221–30. Examination of the analytical worth of historical materialism concerning the position of women, emphasising Engels's ideas on the family.

7.934 **Moore**, S., 'Marx and Lenin as historical materialists', *Phil. & Pub. Affairs*, 4, 1974–75, 171–94. Interprets the historical materialism of Marx as an unstable combination of two conflicting accounts of history – a dialectic of liberation and a sociology of change. It is the first of these which later inspired Leninism, leaving Marx open to Bakunin's charge of elitism.

7.935 **Prinz**, A. M., 'Background and ulterior motive of Marx's *Preface* of 1859', *J. Hist. Ideas*, 30, 1969, 437–50.

7.936 **Rader**, M., *Marx's Interpretation of History*, New York, 1979.

7.937 **Rigby**, S. H., *Marxism and History: A Critical Introduction*, 1987. Argues that Marx's social theories were profoundly contradictory and have proved most useful when seen as a source of questions, concepts and hypotheses rather than a philosophy of historical development.

7.938 **Sayers**, S., 'Marxism and the dialectical method. A critique of G. A. Cohen', in S. Sayers and P. Osborne, ed., *Socialism, Feminism and Philosophy: A Radical Philosophy Reader*, 1990, 140–68. A critique of Cohen's analytical approach to historical materialism, arguing that a dialectical method is central to Marx's theory.

7.939 **Shaw**, W. H., *Marx's Theory of History*, Stanford, Calif., 1978.

7.940 **Sprinzak**, E., 'Marx's historical conception of ideology and science', *Pol. & Soc.*, 5, 1975, 395–416.

7.941 **Suchting**, W. A., ' "Productive forces" and "relations of production" in Marx', *Analyse und Kritik*, 4, 1982, 159–81.

7.942 **Torrance**, J., 'Reproduction and development: a case for a 'Darwinian' mechanism in Marx's theory of history', *Pol. Sts.*, 33, 1985, 382–98. Defends Cohen's functional interpretation of Marx's theory of history, though provides a corrective to the absence of a causal mechanism in Cohen's account by suggesting that Marx developed a rudimentary 'Darwinian' mechanism of historical selection.

7.943 **Wolfe**, B. D., *Marxism: One Hundred years in the Life of a Doctrine*, New York, 1965. A critical survey of historical materialism which stresses Marx's authoritarian temperament.

MARX AND POLITICAL IDEAS

7.944 **Adamiak**, R., 'The "withering away" of the state: a reconsideration', *J. Pol.*, 32, 1970, 3–18. Argues that Marx and Engels held identical positions on this question, believing, despite their anarchist rhetoric, that the state was indispensable.

7.945 **Andrew**, E., 'Marx's theory of classes: science and ideology', *Can. J. Pol. Sc.*, 8, 1975, 454–66. Emphasises the consistency and coherence of his concept of class, undermining those, like Althusser, who stress the epistemological break in his thought.

7.946 **Arnold**, N. S., 'Marx, central planning and utopian socialism', in E. F. Paul, *et al.*, ed., *Socialism*, 1983, 160–99. Demonstrates Marx's conviction that post-capitalist society will involve central planning, exploring the problems this has bequeathed for latterday Marxists.

7.947 —— *Marx's Radical Critique of Capitalist Society: A Reconstruction and Critical Evaluation*, 1990. Argues that socialist society as envisaged by Marx can be shown to entail significant exploitation and alienation of workers, much as in capitalist society.

7.948 **Ashcraft**, R., 'Marx and Weber on liberalism as bourgeois ideology', *Comp. Sts. Soc. & Hist.*, 14, 1972, 130–68. Suggests that the difficulties of defining political theory in the abstract are related to the ability to provide an account of the interrelation of phenomena, such as religious, economic and political change. Ashcraft therefore compares these thinkers, concluding that it is necessary to adopt an approach distinct from theirs to devise a successful political theory.

7.949 **Avineri**, S., ed., *Karl Marx on Colonialism and Modernization*, New York, 1969.

7.950 —— *The Social and Political Thought of Karl Marx*, 1968. An influential attempt to understand his work in an integrated way rather than emphasise differences between his early and mature ideas. Particular stress is placed upon Marx's engagement with Hegel as the source of his materialist system.

7.951 **Balibar**, E., 'Marx, Engels, and the revolutionary party', *Marxist Perspectives*, 2, 1978, 124–43.

7.952 **Bender**, F. L., 'The ambiguities of Marx's concepts of "proletarian dictatorship" and "transition to communism" ', *Hist. Pol. Thought*, 2, 1981, 525–76. Demonstrates that his position on the relationship of the proletariat to the socialist economy and its dictatorship remained contradictory and inconsistent.

7.953 **Berki**, R. N., *Insight and Vision: The Problem of Communism in Marx's Thought*, 1983. Separating the substantive from the formal aspects of communism in Marx's thought, Berki attempts to supersede conventional dichotomies in the interpretation of his thought and to present communism as the master category for comprehending the unity of his ideas.

7.954 **Berland**, O., 'Radical chains: the Marxian concept of proletarian mission', *Studies on the Left*, 6, 1966, 27–51. Interesting though improbable attempt to separate his belief in the role of the proletariat from the rest of his thought.

7.955 **Bernstein**, J., 'Right, revolution and community: Marx's "On the Jewish Question" ', in P. Osborne, ed., *Socialism and the Limits of Liberalism*, 1991, 91–119. Interesting attempt to connect justice and revolution by suggesting an account of right immanent within this text, concluding that Marx was not wholly opposed to rights arguments.

7.956 **Bien**, J., 'Dewey and Marx: two notions of community', *Phil. Today*, 24, 1980, 318–24.

7.957 **Blackburn**, R., ed., *Ideology in Social Science: Readings in Critical Social Theory*, 1972. Includes Hobsbawm on the uses different generations of historians have made of Marx, Geras on the central role of 'fetishism' in his critique of political economy, Nicolaus on the framework for investigating the class forces at work in contemporary capitalism outlined in the *Grundrisse*, Godelier on the different kinds of contradiction contained in Capital, and Colletti on the symbiotic relationship between the scientific vocation of Marxism and its revolutionary aspirations.

7.958 —— 'Marxism: theory of proletarian revolution', *New Left Rev.*, 97, 1976, 3–36. Views Marx and Engels as primarily political theorists who discovered the proletariat, the force for universal social liberation. An accessible introduction to the major themes of their political thought.

7.959 —— 'The politics of Marx and Engels', *New Left Rev.*, 97, 1976, 3–35.

7.960 **Bloom**, S., 'The "withering away" of the state', *J. Hist. Ideas*, 7, 1946, 113–21.

7.961 **Bloomfield**, J., ed., *Papers on Class, Hegemony and Party*, 1977. Includes Gunn on the need to develop a more complete Marxist political theory for socialism to enhance its democratic potential, Hall on the problems and opportunities associated with the 'base and superstructure' metaphor, and Hindess on non-

reductionist readings of class in Marxist theory.

7.962 **Bobbio**, N., 'Is there a Marxist theory of the state?', *Telos*, 35, 1978, 5–16. Addresses the weaknesses of Marxist theory in this area by suggesting that the few relevant passages in his work have been systematically misrepresented.

7.963 **Braybrooke**, D., 'Marx on revolutionizing the mode of production', in C. J. Friedrich, ed., *Revolution: Nomos VIII*, New York, 1966, 240–6. Challenges Tucker's (in the same volume) definition of the essential aspects of Marx's theory of revolution, stressing his emphasis on a shift in the mode of production as a prerequisite for wider change.

7.964 **Brownstein**, L., 'The concept of counterrevolution in Marxian theory', *Studies in Soviet Thought*, 22, 1981, 175–92.

7.965 **Carver**, T., 'Communism for critical critics? *The German Ideology* and the problem of technology', *Hist. Pol. Thought*, 9, 1988, 129–136. Questions the consistency of Marx's views on the relationship between industrial technology and communist society, asserting that the famous hunting/fishing paragraph from the *German Ideology* was intended as a parody of the utopian socialists.

7.966 —— 'Marx – and Hegel's *Logic*', *Pol. Sts*, 24, 1976, 57–68. Attempts to specify which texts Marx used for the *Grundrisse*, stressing the methodological implications of Hegel's work rather than the idea that Hegel provides the key to Marxist critique.

7.967 —— *Marx's Social Theory*, 1982.

7.968 **Chang**, S. H. M., *The Marxian Theory of the State*, New York, 1965.

7.969 **Clark**, J., 'Marx, Bakunin and the problem of social transformation', *Telos*, 42, 1979–80, 80–97.

7.970 **Cleaver**, H., *Reading Capital Politically*, Austin, Tex., 1979.

7.971 **Cohen**, C., 'Bourgeois and proletarians', *J. Hist. Ideas*, 29, 1968, 211–30.

7.972 **Cohen**, J. L., *Class and Civil Society: The Limits of Marxian Critical Theory*, 1983.

7.973 **Conway**, D., *A Farewell to Marx: An Outline and Appraisal of his Theories*, 1987. A critical appraisal of his claims about capitalism and theory of history, which concludes with a defence of free market capitalism as more congruent with human nature than Marxism.

7.974 **Corcoran**, P., 'The bourgeois in Marxian

rhetoric', *Hist. Pol. Thought*, 1, 1980, 301–14. Argues that the use of the term bourgeois cannot be fully exempt from its 'noble' origins.

7.975 **Cunliffe**, J., 'Marx, Engels and the party', *Hist. Pol. Thought*, 2, 1980, 349–69. Argues that for Marx the class/party relationship was not seen as particularly problematic in so far as he consistently emphasised the class and its expression in diverse types of political party. This outlook stemmed from his consistent commitment to the self-emancipation of the class and rejection of sectarian modes of organisation.

7.976 —— 'Marx's politics – the tensions in *The Communist Manifesto*', *Pol. Sts.*, 30, 1982, 569–74. Defends his consistency in the application of his general theory to particular strategy in Germany, even though this general theory contained differing emphases.

7.977 **Dahl**, R., 'Marxism and free parties', *J. Pol.*, 10, 1948, 787–813.

7.978 **Davis**, H. B., *Nationalism and Socialism: Marxist and Labor Theories of Nationalism to 1917*, New York, 1967. Overconfident celebration of Marxism's capacity to theorise nationalism, suggesting that a coherent perspective on this theme was in place by 1917. Despite this thesis, Davis provides a useful and thorough assessment of the ideas of Marx and Engels, later German social democrats and East European Marxists on this question.

7.979 —— 'Nation, colonies, and social classes: the position of Marx and Engels', *Sc. & Soc.*, 29, 1965, 26–43.

7.980 **Draper**, H., *Karl Marx's Theory of Revolution: Vol. 1, State and Bureaucracy*, 1977. Focuses upon Marx's early intellectual development and his world-historical view of the state.

7.981 —— *Karl Marx's Theory of Revolution: Vol. II The Politics of Social Classes*, 1978. Reconstructs the theory of proletarian revolution emphasising Marx's belief in the transformation of socio-political relations, the revolution of 1848–9 as the proving ground for his ideas and Marx's analysis of revolutions under the influence of different classes. Includes exhaustive references to Marx's and Engel's texts.

7.982 —— 'Marx and Engels on women's liberation', in R. Salper, ed., *Female Liberation: History and Current Politics*, New York, 1972, 83–107. Traces the evolution of Marxist-feminist theory from Marx's earliest works until 1884.

7.983 —— 'Marx and the dictatorship of the proletariat', *Études de Marxologie*, 6, 1962, 5–73.

7.984 —— 'Marx on democratic forms of government', *Socialist Register*, 1974, 101–24. Traces the development of his belief in the fusion of socialism and democracy, whilst stressing his critique of the utilisation of democratic reforms to undermine class resistance.

7.985 —— 'The concept of the "Lumpenproletariat" in Marx and Engels' *Economies et Sociétés*, 6, 1972, 22–85. Painstakingly charts the usage and meaning of this term, highlighting its unflattering implication.

7.986 —— 'The death of the state in Marx and Engels', *Socialist Register*, 7, 1970, 281–307.

7.987 —— *The 'Dictatorship of the Proletariat' from Marx to Lenin*, New York, 1987.

7.988 —— 'The principle of self-emancipation in Marx and Engels', *Socialist Register*, 8, 1971, 81–110. Identifies this as the central theme within the political thought of Marxism, emerging out of Marx's rejection of elitist philosophical models.

7.989 **Drucker**, H. M., 'Marx's concept of ideology', *Phil.*, 47, 1972, 152–62.

7.990 **Dumont**, L., *From Mandeville to Marx: The Genesis and Triumph of Economic Ideology*, Chicago, Ill., 1977. Idiosyncratic interpretation of the development of modern ideology and its relationship with economic thought, focusing especially on Marx's ideas and his consistent individualism.

7.991 **Ehrenberg**, J., 'Dialectics of dictatorship: Marx and the proletarian state', *Social Praxis*, 7, 1980, 21–39.

7.992 —— *The Dictatorship of the Proletariat: Marxism's Theory of Socialist Democracy*, 1992. A controversial defence of the dictatorship of the proletariat as the viable centrepiece of Marxist political thought. The author traces the development of this concept in an illuminating manner, though his conclusions concerning its plausibility are less convincing.

7.993 **Ellison**, C. E., 'Marx and the modern city: public life and the problem of personality', *Rev. Pol.*, 45, 1983, 393–420. Intertwines Marx's political theory with his observations about urban life, through his conception of public and private life within the modern city.

7.994 **Feher**, R., 'The French Revolutions as models for Marx's conception of politics', *Thesis Eleven*, 8, 1984, 59–76. Explores his attraction to the uniqueness of French political history, assessing his ambivalence about the democratic aspects of these revolutions.

7.995 **Femia**, J. V., 'Marx, Marxism and the good society', *Hist. Pol. Thought*, 4, 1983, 553–75. A review of the literature on Marxist socio-economic and political thought, which confronts the question of why, after various debunkings, Marxism still exerts such fascination – especially among academic scholars.

7.996 **Fetscher**, I., *Marx and Marxism*, New York, 1971. Influenced by Lukács, the author examines the relationship between Hegel and Marxism in order to refute Soviet interpretations of Marxist principles.

7.997 **Fiddick**, T., 'Marx's theory and strategy of permanent revolution', *Soc. Theory & Pract.*, 5, 1978, 45–64.

7.998 **Fischer**, G., ' "... the state begins to wither away ...": notes on the interpretation of the Paris Commune by Bakunin, Marx, Engels and Lenin', *Aust. J. Pol. Hist.*, 25, 1979, 66–76.

7.999 **Forbes**, I., *Marx and the New Individual*, 1990. With specific reference to the role of the concepts of human nature and historical development in Marx's thought, Forbes examines whether the individual is a central feature of Marx's account of social existence.

7.1000 **Forster**, M., 'Marx on the communist state: a partial eclipse of political reality', *Can. J. Pol. & Soc. Theory*, 4, 1980, 103–18. Examines the tensions between the 'anarchist' and 'statist' Marx, arguing that he never resolved this contradiction.

7.1001 **Friedman**, D. J., 'Marx's perspective on the objective class structure', *Polity*, 6, 1974, 318–44. Rejects the claim of some commentators that his theory of objective class structure depends upon the polarisation of the classes, in a lucid and accessible discussion of a complex subject.

7.1002 **Giddens**, A., *Capitalism and Modern Social Theory: An Analysis of the Writings of Marx, Durkheim and Max Weber*, 1971.

7.1003 **Gilbert**, A., 'Social theory and revolutionary activity in Marx', *Am. Pol. Sc. Rev.*, 73, 1979, 521–38.

7.1004 —— 'The storming of heaven: politics and Marx's *Capital*', *Nomos XXIV*, 1984, 119–68. Challenges Wolin's reading of Marx, presenting a more complex picture of the development of his critique of capitalism through the specific intellectual and political contexts he experienced. Gilbert is especially impressive when tracing the political impact of *Capital* on Marx's contemporaries.

7.1005 **Girardin**, J-C., 'On the Marxist theory of the state', *Pol. & Soc.*, 4, 1974, 161–92.

7.1006 **Goldstein**, L. F., 'Mill, Marx and women's liberation', *J. Hist. Phil.*, 18, 1980, 319–40.

7.1007 **Gottlieb**, R., 'A Marxian concept of ideology', *Philosophical Forum (Boston)*, 6, 1974–75, 300–96.

7.1008 **Gould**, C., *Marx's Social Ontology: Individuality and Community in Marx's Theory of Social Reality*, 1980.

7.1009 **Graham**, K., *Karl Marx Our Contemporary: Social Theory for a Post-Leninist World*, 1992. An analytical evaluation of his central concepts, in particular his historical materialism and political theory; a useful alternative to rational choice interpretations of his thought, especially of his class analysis.

7.1010 **Grossman**, H., *The Law of Accumulation and Breakdown of the Capitalist System*, 1991. With an introduction by Kennedy, this is an abridged version of a classic work on Marx's theory of crisis, until now not readily available in English.

7.1011 **Grundmann**, R., *Marxism and Ecology*, 1991. A militant defence of anthropocentric discourse, examining Marx's conception of technology, science and historical materialism to elucidate his distinctive stance towards nature. This perspective is contrasted with ecocentric arguments, whilst much light is thrown upon recent debates concerning ethics, individualism and functionalism in his thought.

7.1012 **Hall**, S., 'The 'political' and the 'economic' in Marx's theory of classes', in A. Hunt, ed., *Class and Class Structure*, 1977, 15–60. Interrogates certain critical passages in Marx concerning classes and class struggle, stressing the inconsistencies within and development of his ideas, and rehabilitating a number of earlier 'transitional' texts.

7.1013 **Hammen**, O. J., 'Alienation, communism, and revolution in the Marx-Engels *Briefwechsel*', *J. Hist. Ideas*, 33, 1972, 77–100. Mines their correspondence to throw light upon the nature and key events of their collaboration.

7.1014 **Harris**, B., 'Alienation of the capitalist class: towards a more careful reading of Marx', *Social Praxis*, 7, 1980, 77–90.

7.1015 **Hegedus**, A., 'Marx's analysis of bureaucracy', in *Socialism and Bureaucracy*, 1976, 9–16.

7.1016 **Held**, V., 'Marx, sex, and the transformation of society', *Phil. Forum*, 5, 1973–4, 168–83.

7.1017 **Hirst**, P. Q., *Problems in the Marxist Theory of Ideology*, 1976.

7.1018 **Hook**, S., 'Myth and fact in the Marxist theory of revolution and violence', *J. Hist. Ideas*, 34, 1973, 271–80.

7.1019 —— 'The Enlightenment and Marxism', *J. Hist. Ideas*, 29, 1968, 93–108. Illustrates the influence of Enlightenment faith in reason and commitment to natural rights on Marx's thought, stressing his ambivalence towards both notions.

7.1020 **Howard**, M. C., and **King**, J. E., *The Political Economy of Marx*, 1975.

7.1021 **Hunt**, G., 'The development of the concept of civil society in Marx', *Hist. Pol. Thought*, 8, 1987, 263–76. Contends that there were three stages in the development of his critique of civil society: the early Feuerbachian inversion of Hegelianism, the transitional stage where 'civil society' means 'social relations' in general, and the mature stage reached in the *Grundrisse* where Marx distinguished labour-power from labour and viewed the mode of production as the means by which civil society was to be anatomised. Ignorance of this shifting interpretation is said to have affected later Marxist theorists who have conflated these different positions.

7.1022 **Hunt**, R. N., *The Political Ideas of Marx and Engels: Vol. I: Marxism and Totalitarian Democracy, 1818–1850*, 1974. Emphasises their continual belief in participatory democracy through a detailed reconstruction of their developing political thought in its historical and biographical context.

7.1023 —— *The Political Ideas of Marx and Engels: Vol II: Classical Marxism 1850–1895*, 1984. Particular emphasis is given to the belief in participatory democracy through representative institutions in this reconstruction of their political thought.

7.1024 **Isaac**, J. C., *Power and Marxist Theory: A Realistic View*, Ithaca, N.Y., 1987.

7.1025 **Israel**, J., 'Remarks concerning some problems of Marxist class theory', *Acta Sociologica*, 13, 1970, 11–29.

7.1026 **Jessop**, R., ed., 'Marx and Engels on the state', in S. Hibbin, ed., *Politics, Ideology and the State*, 1978, 40–68. Reviews the different strands embedded within the Marxist theory of the state, concluding that a unitary theory of the state does not exist.

7.1027 —— and **Malcolm-Brown**, C., ed., *Karl Marx's Social and Political Thought: Critical Assessments, Volume I: Marx's Life and Theoretical Development, Volume II: Social Class and Class Conflict, Volume III: The State, Politics, and Revolution, Volume IV: Civil Society, Ideology, Morals, and Ethics*, 1990. Collections of previously published essays on these themes, framed by excellent introductions by the editors to the themes which arise.

7.1028 **Johnson**, C., 'The problem of reformism and Marx's theory of fetishism', *New Left Rev.*, 119, 1980, 70–96.

7.1029 **Johnstone**, M., 'Marx and Engels and the concept of the party', *Socialist Register*, 4, 1967, 121–58. Important assessment of the evolution of a number of 'models' of the party in the minds of Marx and Engels, determined by historical and political circumstances. Possibly over-schematic in presentation, this study nevertheless advanced debate in this area.

7.1030 —— 'Marx, Blanqui, and majority rule', *Socialist Register*, 20, 1983, 296–318.

7.1031 —— 'The Paris Commune and Marx's conception of the dictatorship of the proletariat', *Massachusetts Review*, 12, 1971, 447–62.

7.1032 **Jordan**, Z. A., *Karl Marx: Economy, Class and Social Revolution*, 1971.

7.1033 **Kain**, P. J., 'Estrangement and the dictatorship of the proletariat', *Pol. Theory*, 7, 1979, 509–20.

7.1034 —— 'Marx's theory of ideas', *Hist. & Theory*, 20, 1981, 357–78.

7.1035 **Kamenka**, E., ' "The party of the proletariat": Marx and Engels in the revolution of 1848', in E. Kamenka and F. B. Smith, ed., *Intellectuals and Revolution: Socialism and the Experience of*

1848, 1979, 76–93. Presents 1848 as the culmination of the evolution of the ideas of the early Marx and Engels and the consummation of their careers as revolutionaries; their strategic ideas shifted from support for radical democratic forces to advocacy of proletarian revolution.

7.1036 **Kennedy**, E., ' "Ideology" from Destutt de Tracy to Marx', *J. Hist. Ideas*, 40, 1979, 353–68.

7.1037 **Klagge**, J., 'Marx's realms of "freedom" and "necessity" ', *Can. J. Phil.*, 16, 1986, 769–77.

7.1038 **Levin**, M., 'Deutschmarx: Marx, Engels and the German question', *Pol. Sts.*, 29, 1981, 537–54.

7.1039 —— 'Marx and Engels on the generalised class state', *Hist. Pol. Thought*, 6, 1985, 433–53. Argues that the first uncircumscribed definition of the 'Marxist', class state theory did not appear until Engels's *Anti-Dühring* of 1878; the thesis of the generalised class state must therefore be taken as a component part of twentieth-century Marxism.

7.1040 —— 'Marx and working-class consciousness', *Hist. Pol. Thought*, 1, 1980, 499–515. Criticises the topographical theory of consciousness developed by Marx as incompatible with his belief that the working class are susceptible to the distortions of bourgeois ideology. Notes distinct stages in his understanding of the problematic nature of proletarian consciousness.

7.1041 —— *Marx, Engels and Liberal Democracy*, 1989. A critical survey of the Marxist account of democracy, focusing upon Marx's conception of proletarian emancipation.

7.1042 **Lewin**, H., and **Morris**, J., 'Marx's concept of fetishism', *Sc. & Soc.*, 41, 1977, 172–90.

7.1043 **Lichtman**, R., 'Marx's theory of ideology', *Socialist Revolution*, 23, 1973, 45–76. Lucid discussion of his understanding of consciousness and alienation and the implications of these ideas for his theory of ideology. Includes an admirably clear exposition of some of the major themes of *Capital*.

7.1044 **Liebich**, A., 'On the origins of a Marxist theory of bureaucracy in the *Critique of Hegel's "Philosophy of Right"* ', *Pol. Theory*, 10, 1982, 77–93. Cites this text to disprove the idea that he opposed

bureaucracy in its modern sense; in fact the *Critique* was motivated by immediate political concerns, constituting a reflection on problems of representation, public opinion and constitutionalism.

7.1045 **Lieven**, M., 'Marx and Engels's account of political power: the case of British factory legislation', *Hist. Pol. Thought*, 9, 1988, 505–27. Examines the plausibility of their theories of political power and the state in capitalist society from their accounts of the passage of British factory legislation. Concludes that a modern Marxist theory of the state and politics must begin with the radical critique and reconstruction of Marx's ideas.

7.1046 **Lipset**, S. M. and **Bendix**, R., 'Karl Marx's theory of social classes', in S. M. Lipset and R. Bendix, ed., *Class, Status and Power: Social Classes in Comparative Perspective*, 1967, 6–11. Reconstructs this theory from a diverse range of sources, suggesting that no coherent 'position' with regard to social classes was distilled by Marx.

7.1047 **Lovell**, D. W., *Marx's Proletariat: The Making of a Myth*, 1988. Contends that the concept of the proletariat was not only a crucial element of his theory but a significant departure from the thought of his socialist rivals.

7.1048 **McCarthy**, T., *Marx and the Proletariat: A Study in Social Theory*, Westport, Conn., 1978.

7.1049 **Magri**, L., 'Problems of the Marxist theory of the revolutionary party', *New Left Rev.*, 60, 1970, 97–128.

7.1050 **Maguire**, J., 'Marx on ideology, power and force', *Theory and Decision*, 7, 1976, 315–29. Argues that he was increasingly compelled to think more deeply about the social structures of capitalist societies, and that his understanding of ideology, power and force remains pertinent for contemporary social theory.

7.1051 **Mansfield**, H. C., 'Marx on Aristotle: freedom, money, and politics', *Rev. Metaph.*, 34, 1980, 351–67. Argues that the labour theory of value depends on Marx's analysis of 'the money-form', leading him to engage with Aristotle's theory of forms, and, ultimately, to reproduce Aristotelian notions of the natural economy and the importance of politics.

7.1052 **Maravall**, J. M., 'The limits of reformism: parliamentary socialism and the Marxist theory of the state', *Brit. J. Soc.*, 30, 1979, 267–90.

7.1053 **Mayer**, H., 'Marx, Engels and the politics of the peasantry', *Études de Marxologie*, 3, 1960, 91–152.

7.1054 **Meister**, R., *Political Identity: Thinking Through Marx*, 1991. Analyses, in turn, his politics of subjectivity, theory of democracy and materialism. These ideas are measured against contemporary debates about political identity.

7.1055 **Mellos**, K., 'The concept of ideology in Marx', *Social Praxis*, 7, 1980, 5–19.

7.1056 **Miliband**, R., *Marxism and Politics*, 1977. Drawing principally on the work of Marx, Engels and Lenin, this text examines the relationship between Marxist thought and politics and the absence of a systematic account of the latter within classical Marxism. Concludes by developing such an account in a sharply written yet partisan manner.

7.1057 —— 'Marx on the state', *Socialist Register*, 1965, 278–96. Traces the development of his account and critique of the state, focusing upon his political writings of the 1850s. The author 'clears' Marx of the charges of latent authoritarianism or sympathy for bureaucracy.

7.1058 **Miller**, D., 'Marx, communism and markets', *Pol. Theory*, 15, 1987, 182–204. Argues that contrary to appearances certain of the principles Marx deploys count for market socialism and against communism, especially his opposition to romantic anti-capitalism.

7.1059 **Miller**, R. W., *Analyzing Marx: Morality, Power and History*, Princeton, N.J., 1984. Outlines his ethical, philosophical and historical ideas, emphasising the centrality of class within his thought.

7.1060 **Mills**, C. W., ' "Ideology" in Marx and Engels', *Phil. Forum*, 16, 1985, 327–46.

7.1061 **Mishra**, R., 'Technology and social structure in Marx's theory: an explanatory analysis', *Sc. & Soc.*, 43, 1979, 133–57.

7.1062 **Molyneux**, J., *Marxism and the Party*, 1978.

7.1063 **Moore**, S., *A Critique of Capitalist Democracy: An Introduction to the Theory of the State in Marx, Engels and Lenin*, New York, 1957.

7.1064 —— *Marx on the Choice Between Socialism and Communism*, Cambridge, Mass, 1980.

7.1065 **Moss**, B. H., 'Marx and Engels on French social democracy: historians or revolutionaries?', *J. Hist. Ideas*, 36, 1985, 409–30. Traces Marx's response to French political developments as a 'sectarian' activist, which informed his historical analysis of these years.

7.1066 **Nicolaus**, M., 'Proletariat and middle class in Marx: Hegelian choreography and the capitalist dialectic', *Studies on the Left*, 7, 1967, 22–49. Revival of Berland's argument that Marxism does not need to rely on the proletariat as its social agent, applying the notion of the 'surplus class' to contemporary capitalist reality.

7.1067 **Ollman**, B., 'Marxism and political science: prolegomenon to a debate on Marx's method', *Pol. & Soc.*, 5, 1973, 491–511.

7.1068 —— 'Marx's use of "class" ', *Am. J. Soc.*, 73, 1968, 573–80. Reconstructs and criticises his description of the complexities of class formation and division, concluding that his concept of class is meaningful only when considered as part of his philosophy.

7.1069 —— 'Marx's vision of communism: a reconstruction', *Critique*, 8, 1977, 7–41. Charts the development of Marx's picture of communist society, scattered throughout his writings from 1844 onwards, concluding that his greatest contribution here was to present communism as immanent within capitalism.

7.1070 **O'Neill**, J., 'Alienation, class struggle and Marxian anti-politics', *Rev. Metaph.*, 17, 1964, 462–71.

7.1071 **Paastela**, J., *Marx's and Engels's Concepts of the Parties and Political Organizations of the Working Class*, Tampere, 1985.

7.1072 **Parekh**, B., *Marx's Theory of Ideology*, 1982. Fresh interpretation of this aspect of his theory, outlining the logical structure and epistemological basis of his understanding of ideology. Useful assessment of his analyses of the process whereby theorists become the apologists of the social order.

7.1073 —— 'Marx's theory of the state. A historical perspective', in V. K. Roy and R. C. Sarikwal, ed., *Marxian Sociology, Volume Two*, 1979, 71–128. Wide-ranging examination of several dimensions (conceptual, historical, theoretical) of this aspect of Marx's theory, which concentrates upon elucidating his understanding of the state.

7.1074 **Parkin**, F., *Marxism and Class Theory: A Bourgeois Critique*, 1979. Sceptical assessment of the adequacy of the Marxian model for explaining the complexities of contemporary class formation and social conflict.

7.1075 **Perez-Diaz**, V. M., *State, Bureaucracy and Civil Society: A Critical Discussion of the Political Theory of Karl Marx*, 1978. Argues that he failed to develop a coherent interpretation of politics and bureaucracy under capitalism.

7.1076 **Perrin**, R. F., 'Marxism and the reification of politics', *Can. J. Pol. & Soc. Theory*, 3, 1979, 5–19.

7.1077 **Petrus**, J. A., 'Marx and Engels on the national question', *J. Pol.*, 33, 1971, 797–824.

7.1078 **Plamenatz**, J., *Man and Society, Vol. II*, 1963. A lucid and critical survey of his political thought.

7.1079 **Postone**, M., *Time, Labor, and Social Domination: A Reinterpretation of Marx's Critical Theory*, 1993. Attempts to appropriate Marx for a rejection of the industrial production process and all forms of labour as inherently alienating; Marx, on this reading, was moving towards the insights of critical theory in his mature work.

7.1080 **Pranger**, R. J., 'Marx and political theory', *Rev. Pol.*, 30, 1968, 191–208. Interprets him as a theorist of citizenship which, he believed, originated in the workplace. Idiosyncratic and unconvincing.

7.1081 **Rapoport**, E., 'Anarchism and authority in Marx's socialist politics', *Eur. J. Soc.*, 17, 1976, 333–43.

7.1082 **Rattansi**, A., *Marx and the Division of Labour*, 1982. Argues that at first he conflated the concepts of class and division of labour but in his more 'mature' writings implied that the eradication of class did not necessarily entail an end to occupational specialisation.

7.1083 **Redner**, H., 'Beyond Marx – Weber: a diversified and international approach to the state', *Pol. Sts.*, 38, 1990, 638–53. Suggests that a roughly coherent theory of the state, advocated by Marx and developed by Weber, predominated until after the Second World War.

7.1084 **Rossanda**, R., 'Class and party', *Socialist Register*, 7, 1970, 217–33.

7.1085 **Rouse**, D., 'Marx's materialist concept of democracy', *Philosophy Research Archives*, 2, 1976, 429–44. Interprets his materialism as a corrective to the formal determinism of Hegel.

7.1086 **Rubel**, M., 'Notes on Marx's conception of democracy', *New Pol.*, 2, 1962, 78–90.

7.1087 **Sanderson**, J., *An Interpretation of the Political Ideas of Marx and Engels*, 1969.

7.1088 —— 'Marx and Engels on the state', *West. Pol. Q.*, 16, 1963, 946–55. Argues for the persistence of two distinct and contradictory accounts of the state in their work: the state as a class instrument and as a parasite living off society. Somewhat simplistic presentation, superseded by later commentators.

7.1089 **Sayer**, D., *Capitalism and Modernity: an excursion on Marx and Weber*, 1990. Reassessment of the ideas of Marx and Weber on modernity, arguing that their sociologies of the modern condition overlap. Suggests that they produced a critique of the nature of both power and subjectivity in modern society.

7.1090 —— *Marx's Method: Ideology, Science and Critique in Capital*, 1978. Concise and illuminating account of his interpretation of the natural and eternal forms, and their relation to social and historical analysis.

7.1091 **Schaff**, A., 'Marxist theory on revolution and violence', *J. Hist. Ideas*, 34, 1973, 263–70.

7.1092 **Schonfeld**, W. R., 'The classical Marxist conception of liberal democracy', *Rev. Pol.*, 33, 1971, 377–405. Examines the Marxian thesis that the transition from capitalism to socialism will occur under the democratic rule of the petty bourgeoisie. Rather rigid discussion of Marxist political thought.

7.1093 **Schroyer**, T., 'Marx's theory of the crisis', *Telos*, 14, 1973, 106–25. Rescues his method of critique as well as his formulation of the contradiction of capitalist society from his theory of capitalist crisis.

7.1094 **Schwartz**, N. L., 'Distinction between public and private life. Marx on the *zoon politikon*', *Pol. Theory*, 7, 1979, 245–66. Argues against the view that Marx rejected politics by proving that he held to a broad notion of political life.

7.1095 **Seliger**, M., *The Marxist Conception of Ideology, A Critical Essay*, 1977.

7.1096 **Shanin**, T., 'Late Marx and the Russian "periphery of capitalism" ', *Monthly Review*, 35, June 1983, 10–24. Sharp discussion of his later work, illustrating the bold claim that Marx rejected the notion that he prescribed in Volume I of *Capital* an evolutionary path that all countries, including Russia, should follow.

7.1097 **Siriani**, C., 'Production and power in a classless society: a critical analysis of the utopian dimensions of Marxist theory', *Socialist Review*, 11, 1981, 33–82.

7.1098 **Sitton**, J. F., *Marx's Theory of the Transcendence of the State: A Reconstruction*, New York, 1989. Concentrates on the state as a form of alienation under capitalism and the abolition of its functions under communism. Clear and original.

7.1099 **Spencer**, M. E., 'Marx on the state: the events in France between 1848–1850', *Theory & Soc.*, 7, 1978, 167–98.

7.1100 **Springborg**, P., 'Karl Marx on democracy, participation, voting and equality', *Pol. Theory*, 12, 1984, 537–56. Rehearses his classical defence of democracy which does not fit with later Marxist interpretations.

7.1101 **Stevenson**, J., 'Marx's theory of ideology', *Radical Philosophers' News Journal*, 9, 1977, 14–34. Teases out the implications of his few remarks about ideology and ideologues.

7.1102 **Thomas**, P., *Karl Marx and the Anarchists*, 1985. Argues that the dispute between Marx and the anarchists (mainly Stirner, Proudhon and Bakunin) was not merely a question of differing opinions about revolutionary tactics, but of competing accounts of human nature and social organisation. Defends Marx's belief that some sort of political life would always exist for humanity.

7.1103 **Tucker**, R. C., 'The Marxian revolutionary idea', in C. J., Friedrich, ed., *Revolution: Nomos VIII*, New York, 1966, 217–39. Reconstructs his theory of revolution, examining in particular Kautsky's refinement of the Marxian conception of social revolution.

7.1104 —— *The Marxian Revolutionary Idea*, 1970. Distinguishes between Marxism as political theory and ideology, focusing upon his understanding of justice, the centrality of modernisation in his thought and his theory of revolution.

7.1105 **Veyne**, P., 'Ideology according to Marx and according to Nietzsche', *Diogenes*, 99, 1977, 80–102.

7.1106 **Voegelin**, E., 'The formation of the Marxian revolutionary idea', *Rev. Pol.*, 12, 1950, 275–302. Traces the philosophical sources of Marx's perspective, culminating in an assessment of *The Communist Manifesto*.

7.1107 **Wagner**, Y., and **Strauss**, M., 'The programme of the *Communist Manifesto* and its theoretical foundations', *Pol. Sts.*, 17, 1969, 470–84.

7.1108 **Walliman**, I., *Estrangement: Marx's Conception of Human Nature and the Division of Labour*, 1981.

7.1109 **Warren**, M., 'Liberal constitutionalism as ideology. Marx and Habermas', *Pol. Theory*, 17, 1989, 511–34. Assessment of liberal constitutionalism, via these theorists, which distinguishes its democratic possibilities from its harmful ideological effects.

7.1110 **Wells**, D., *Marxism and the Modern State*, 1981. Focuses particularly on Marx's concept of fetishism to elucidate his analysis of capitalism.

7.1111 **Werlin**, R. J., 'Marxist political analysis', *Sociol. Inq.*, 42, 1972, 157–83.

7.1112 **Westowoski**, W., 'Marx's theory of class domination (an attempt at systematization)', *Polish Round Table*, 1, 1967, 21–53. Rigorous examination of the typologies of domination condensed within Marx's theory of class rule.

7.1113 **Wetter**, G. A., 'The ambivalence of the Marxist concept of ideology', *Studies in Soviet Thought*, 9, 1969, 177–83.

7.1114 **Wilde**, L., *Marx and Contradiction*, 1989. Claims that his greatest contribution to socio-political thought is the idea of capitalism as a contradictory system. The various themes addressed in the book hang together with difficulty around this central problematic.

7.1115 **Wilson**, M. T., *Marx's Critical/Dialectical Procedure*, 1990. Argues that he undertook a radical critique of the theoretical/analytical method of his predecessors and contemporaries in the fields of political economy, philosophy and the natural sciences to justify a new conception of humans as collective, cultural and historical beings.

7.1116 **Wolfson**, M., 'Three stages in Marx's thought', *Hist. Pol. Econ.*, 11, 1979, 117–46.

7.1117 **Wright**, E. O., 'The status of the political in the concept of class structure', *Pol. & Soc.*, 11, 1982, 321–41. Stresses the political dimensions of class, tracing the implications of a non-economistic perspective in a number of areas of debate.

7.1118 —— 'Varieties of Marxist conceptions of class structure', *Pol. & Soc.*, 9, 1980, 323–70. Compares the way contemporary Marxists have conceptualised the class structure of advanced capitalism, highlighting weaknesses on this issue in the Marxist tradition.

7.1119 **Zeitlin**, I. M., *Marxism: A Re-Examination*, 1967. Robust, though dated, defence of Marx as a scientific critic of capitalism.

MARX: GENERAL

7.1120 **Adamson**, W., *Marx and the Disillusionment of Marxism*, Berkeley, Calif., 1985.

7.1121 **Althusser**, L., *For Marx*, 1967. Influential, structuralist interpretation which emphasises the dichotomy between his early and late work.

7.1122 **Andrew**, E., 'A note on the unity of theory and practice in Marx and Nietzsche', *Pol. Theory*, 3, 1975, 305–16. Argues for the essential similarity between their ideas, especially in terms of their commitment to the creation of the 'new man' through praxis.

7.1123 **Avineri**, S., 'Marx and Darwin. A reconsideration', *Pol. Theory*, 7, 1979, 469–83. Challenges the myth of a connection between the two, both historically and theoretically.

7.1124 —— ed., *Marx's Socialism*, 1971. Important collection including Avineri, 'The Hegelian origins of Marx's political thought', Hodges, Fetscher and Bell on the young Marx, O'Malley on human nature in his thought, Cohen, 'Bourgeois and proletarians', Tucker, 'Marx as a political theorist', and Miliband, 'Marx and the state'.

7.1125 —— and **Farr**, J., ed., *After Marx*, 1984. A largely philosophical collection of essays concerning the contemporary state of Marx scholarship, including Shaw on rationality and class struggle, Miller on the central and misleading role allotted to the 1859 preface by later commentators, Thomas on the public/private dichotomy, Macpherson on democracy, Ball on Engels's positivism, and Farr on Marx as a methodological pluralist opposed to a unitary conception of science.

7.1126 **Berki**, R. N., 'On the nature and origins of

Marx's concept of labour', *Pol. Theory*, 7, 1979, 35–56. Argues that his concept of labour leaves unresolved tensions because the synthesis he attempts is too one-sided. Marx is presented as being undecided as to whether communism meant liberation from labour or the liberation of labour.

7.1127 **Bernstein**, S., 'From utopianism to Marxism', *Sc. & Soc.*, 14, 1949–50, 58–67.

7.1128 **Bevan**, R. A., *Marx and Burke: A Revisionist View*, La Salle, Ill., 1973.

7.1129 **Blumenberg**, W., *Karl Marx*, 1972.

7.1130 **Booth**, W. J., 'Explaining capitalism: the method of Marx's political economy', *Pol. Sts.*, 37, 1989, 612–25. Suggests that his explanation of capitalism relied on determinist and functionalist presuppositions, thereby rendering his thought unsuitable for rational choice theory.

7.1131 **Bottomore**, T., et al., ed., *A Dictionary of Marxist Thought*, 1983. An invaluable guide to the central concepts and categories within the Marxist tradition, written by the leading scholars in the field.

7.1132 —— ed., *Interpretations of Marx*, 1988. Contains 'classic' essays on historical materialism (Berlin, Lichtheim), ethics (Stojanovic), needs (Heller), the proletariat (Avineri), the state (Miliband), and ideology (Kolakowski).

7.1133 —— *Karl Marx*, 1973.

7.1134 **Buchanan**, A., 'The Marxist conceptual framework and the origins of totalitarian socialism', in E. F. Paul, J. Paul, F. D. Miller and J. Ahrens, ed., *Marxism and Liberalism*, 1986, 127–44. Interesting parallel between the core features of totalitarian socialism and aspects of Marx's and Engels's ideas, despite Buchanan's excessively analytical terminology.

7.1135 **Callinicos**, A., *The Revolutionary Ideas of Marx*, 1983.

7.1136 **Carmichael**, J., *Karl Marx*, New York, 1970.

7.1137 **Carter**, A. B., *Marx: A Radical Critique*, 1988. Useful discussion of the various interpretations of his thought, arguing that he approached class in an economistic way and conceptualised both historical transition and the state in a problematic fashion. An ambitious attempt to define a radical alternative to Marx on these questions.

7.1138 **Carver**, T., *A Marx Dictionary*, 1987.

7.1139 —— 'Marx – and Engels's "Outlines of a

Critique of Political Economy" ', *Hist. Pol. Thought*, 4, 1983, 357–65. Discussion of Marx's reception of Engels's criticism, written in November 1843, of bourgeois political economy – hitherto unchartered terrain in the young Hegelian movement.

7.1140 —— *Marx and Engels: The Intellectual Relationship*, 1983. Assesses the differences and similarities in their thought and critically assesses Engels's drift from Marx's historical materialism.

7.1141 —— 'Marx, Engels and dialectics', *Pol. Sts.*, 28, 1980, 351–63. Questions the assumption that they concurred on major theoretical questions, suggesting that, unlike Engels, Marx did not embrace positivism and determinism in his latter years.

7.1142 —— 'Marx, Engels and scholarship', *Pol. Sts.*, 32, 1984, 249–56. Emphasises Marx's distaste for the materialist dialectics propounded by Engels, a position which challenges recent critics who have stressed their essential intellectual similarity.

7.1143 —— 'Marx's 1857 Introduction', *Econ. & Soc.*, 9, 1980, 197–203.

7.1144 —— ed., *The Cambridge Companion to Marx*, 1991. Contains a number of notable scholarly articles, including Miller on political theory, Ball on the philosophy of history, Reiman on moral philosophy, Hearn on gender, and Wilde on dialectical logic.

7.1145 —— 'The "guiding threads" of Marx and Darwin', *Pol. Theory*, 10, 1982, 307–13.

7.1146 **Cornu**, A., 'Hegel, Marx and Engels', in R. W. Sellars, et al., *Philosophy for the Future: the Quest of Modern Materialism*, New York, 1949, 41–60.

7.1147 **Cowling**, M., and **Wilde**, L., ed., *Approaches to Marx*, 1989. Collection encompassing a number of key recent debates concerning the work of Marx and Engels (Cowling, Wilde, Carver, McCarney and Cunliffe) and the troubled relationship between Marxism and liberalism (Towers, Smart, Berry, Forbes, Levin, Carling).

7.1148 **Della Volpe**, G., *Rousseau and Marx*, 1978.

7.1149 **Distefano**, C., 'Masculine Marx', in S. M. Lyndon, and C. Pateman, ed., *Feminist Interpretations and Political Theory*, 1991, 146–65.

7.1150 **Drucker**, H. M., 'The Marx industry today', *Pol. Sts.*, 5, 1973, 385–8.

7.1151 **Duncan**, G., *Marx and Mill: Two Views of Social Conflict and Social Harmony*, 1973. Comparison of these thinkers which highlights their similarities and differences, arguing against a simplistic opposition between their ideas and placing these in the context of recent social theories. A lucid and thoughtful introduction to both theorists.

7.1152 **Dupré**, L., 'Recent literature on Marx and Marxism', *J. Hist. Ideas*, 35, 1974, 703–14. Useful review of recent literature on Marxism, inspired by Hegel's work and including a survey of later commentators' analysis of alienation.

7.1153 **Dworkin**, G., 'Marx and Mill: a dialogue' *Philos. & Phenom. Res.*, 26, 1965–66, 403–14. A fictional conversation between these thinkers, imagining their reactions to latterday developments.

7.1154 **Echeverin**, R., 'The concrete and the abstract in Marx's method: a reply to Carver', *Econ. & Soc.*, 9, 1980, 204–17.

7.1155 **Elster**, J., *An Introduction to Karl Marx*, 1986. Provides a critical account of the central aspects of his thought.

7.1156 —— *Making Sense of Marx*, 1985. An astute analysis of Marx, with many penetrating insights, from an author who has developed his own theory of 'rational choice Marxism' by stressing the role that should be attributed to individual agents in the explanation of social phenomena.

7.1157 **Evans**, M., *Karl Marx*, 1975. Introduction to his social and political thought which painstakingly reconstructs his understanding of history and politics whilst clarifying his mature economic work.

7.1158 —— 'Marx studies', *Pol. Sts.*, 18, 1970, 528–35. Reviews a number of recent contributions to the interpretation of Marxism, critically assessing Avineri, *The Social and Political Thought of Karl Marx* and Althusser, *For Marx*.

7.1159 —— 'More Marx studies', *Pol. Sts.*, 22, 1974, 218–23. Useful observations on McLellan, *Karl Marx*, Ollman, *Alienation* and recent editions of various Marx texts.

7.1160 **Fay**, M. A., 'Marx and Darwin', *Monthly Review*, 31, 1980, 40–57.

7.1161 **Fetscher**, I., *Marx and Marxism*, New York, 1971.

7.1162 **Feuer**, L., *Marx and the Intellectuals*, New York, 1969.

7.1163 —— 'The influence of the American communist colonies on Engels and Marx' *West. Pol. Q.*, 19, 1966, 356–74.

7.1164 **Garaudy**, R., *Karl Marx: The Evolution of his Thought*, 1967. A sympathetic account of his intellectual development.

7.1165 **Gerratana** V., 'Marx and Darwin', *New Left Rev.*, 82, 1973, 60–82. Compares the work of these two thinkers and their letters to each other, suggesting that they were both affected by scientific advances and neo-positivist agnosticism.

7.1166 **Goldstein**, L. F., 'Mill, Marx, and women's liberation', *J. Hist. Phil.*, 18, 1980, 319–34.

7.1167 **Gottfried**, P., 'Marx, Hegel and the *Philosophy of Right*', *Modern Age*, 22, 1978, 177–81.

7.1168 **Gouldner**, A. W., *The Two Marxisms*, 1980.

7.1169 **Gregory**, D., 'Marx and Engels's knowledge of French socialism', *Historical Reflections*, 10, 1983, 143–93.

7.1170 **Hammen**, O. J., *The Red 48ers: Karl Marx and Friedrich Engels*, New York, 1969.

7.1171 **Harrington**, M., 'Marx versus Marx', *New Pol.*, 1, 1961, 112–23.

7.1172 **Hobsbawm**, E. J., ed., *The History of Marxism, Vol. 1: Marxism in Marx's Day*, 1982.

7.1173 **Hodges**, D. C., 'The unity of Marx's thought', *Sc. & Soc.*, 28, 1964, 316–21. Rejects the thesis of the 'two Marxes', emphasising the continuity of his understanding of the emancipation of labour.

7.1174 **Hoffman**, J., *Marxism and the Theory of Praxis*, 1975. Outlines a scientific interpretation of Marxism, which involves the rehabilitation of Engels's dialectic of nature.

7.1175 **Hook**, S., ed., *Marx and the Marxists: An Ambiguous Legacy*, Princeton, N.J., 1955.

7.1176 **Hunt**, E. K., 'The invention of new Marxes to debunk', *Hist. Pol. Econ.*, 11, 1979, 145–56.

7.1177 **Hyppolite**, J., *Studies on Marx and Hegel*, 1969. A closely argued and influential exposition of the influence of Hegel upon Marx, which also contains important essays on Marx's critique of the Hegelian conception of the state and the philosophical presuppositions behind *Capital*.

7.1178 **Kamenka**, E., *Marx*, 1971.

7.1179 **Kenafick**, K. J., *Michael Bakunin and Karl Marx*, Melbourne, 1948.

7.1180 **Kettle**, A., *Karl Marx: Founder of Marxist Communism*, 1963.

7.1181 **Layder**, D., 'Problems in accounting for the individual in Marxist rationalist theoretical discourse', *Brit. J. Soc.*, 30, 1979, 149–63.

7.1182 **Levin**, M., 'Marxism and romanticism: Marx's debt to German conservatism', *Pol. Sts.*, 22, 1974, 400–13. Unconventional examination of the influence of reactionary social thought upon Marx, questioning the idea that Marxism follows 'simply as a logical development or extension of the radical tradition of the Enlightenment and the supporters of the French Revolution'.

7.1183 **Levine**, G., *Dialogue within the Dialectic*, 1984. Concentrates on Engels's role as editor of Marx's manuscripts and the implications of the Marx-Engels relationship for later debates within Marxism.

7.1184 **Lichtheim**, G., 'Marx and Freud', *Socialist Revolution*, 6, 1976, 3–55. Reflects upon attempts (especially by the Frankfurt school) to integrate these theorists and suggests that aspects of Freud's therapeutic theories, as opposed to his general thesis, can be incorporated within Marxism.

7.1185 —— *Marxism: A Historical and Critical Survey*, 1961. A thorough, critical analysis of Marx and Marxism from the lucid, and often acerbic, Lichtheim, which ranges from the origins of the ideology through its most successful practitioners to its contemporary exponents.

7.1186 **Lichtman**, R., *From Marx to Hegel*, 1974.

7.1187 **Loewenstein**, J. I., *Marx Against Marxism*, 1980. Stresses the distinction between his later works and the dogmatism of Engels and other Marxist thinkers.

7.1188 **Lovell**, D. W., *From Marx to Lenin: An Evaluation of Marx's Responsibility for Soviet Authoritarianism*, 1984.

7.1189 **Löwy**, M., 'Marx and Engels: cosmopolites', *Critique*, 14, 1981, 5–12.

7.1190 **McCarthy**, G., ed., *Marx and Aristotle: Nineteenth Century German Social Theory and Classical Antiquity*, 1992. Collection of essays assessing the Hellenic influences on Marx, including Barovitch on the early Marx, Nussbaum, Kain and Booth on his individualism, Gilbert on moral realism, and McCarthy, Margolis and Rockmore on Aristotle's influence.

7.1191 **MacIntyre**, A., *Marxism: An Interpretation*, 1953. Analyses Marxism as a secular body of thought with its origins in the rationalist Christianity of the Enlightenment. Brief, elegant and somewhat idiosyncratic, this text prefigures MacIntyre's later interest in communitarian discourse.

7.1192 **McLellan**, D., *Karl Marx: His Life and Thought*, 1973. One of the best intellectual biographies of Marx.

7.1193 —— ed., *Marx: The First Hundred Years*, 1983. A collection of essays celebrating the interdisciplinary character of Marx's work, including R. Williams on Marx's cultural theory, Kiernan on history, and McLellan's lucid introduction to his political theory, including a comparison with recent Marxist debates in this area.

7.1194 **MacRae**, D., 'Karl Marx (1818–83)', in T. Raison, ed., *The Founding Fathers of Social Science*, 1969, 59–67. Somewhat crude presentation of the ambivalence of Marx as a social scientist.

7.1195 **Mansfield**, H. C., 'Marx on Aristotle; freedom, money and politics', *Rev. Metaph.*, 34, 351–67. Illustrates Aristotle's legacy within Marx's thought but concludes that Marx was forced to break from these precepts in his development of the labour theory of value.

7.1196 **Markovic**, M., *The Contemporary Marx: Essays in Humanist Communism*, 1974.

7.1197 **Matthews**, B., ed., *Marx: A Hundred Years On*, 1983. Includes some important contemporary theorists reflecting on aspects of Marxism, including G. Williams on the Eighteenth Brumaire, S. Hall on Marxism and ideology, A. Hunt on the absence of an account of representative democracy in his work, G. Cohen on forces and relations of production, D. McLellan on historical materialism, G. Therborn on class analysis, and J. Mitchell on Marxist-feminism.

7.1198 **Mattick**, P., *Marx and Keynes*, Boston, Mass., 1969.

7.1199 **Mazlish**, B., *The Meaning of Karl Marx*, 1989. Exploration of the romantic sources of his thought, focusing especially upon the influence of the young Hegelians.

7.1200 **Mehring**, F., *Karl Marx*, Ann Arbor, Mich., 1962.

7.1201 **Meyer**, A. G., *Marxism: The Unity of Theory and Practice*, Ann Arbor, Mich., 1963. Presented as a jargon-free introduction to Marx's thought, this text is one-dimensional in its appraisal of his and later Marxist thought.

7.1202 **Miller**, J., 'Nietzsche and Marx', *Telos*, 37, 1978, 22–41.

7.1203 —— 'Some implications of Nietzsche's thought for Marxism', *Telos*, 37, 1978, 22–41. Argues that Nietzsche's thought challenges Marx's account of immanent critique, interested human agency and history as a unitary process of development. Concludes that the attempts by Adorno and Habermas to refute such criticism fails.

7.1204 **Nicolaus**, M., 'The unknown Marx', *New Left Rev.*, 48, 1968, 41–63. Defends the *Grundrisse* as providing a framework for analysing the forces at work in contemporary capitalism.

7.1205 **Olsen**, R., *Karl Marx*, Boston, Mass., 1978.

7.1206 **O'Malley**, J., 'Marx's 'economics' and Hegel's *Philosophy of Right*: an essay on Marx's Hegelianism', *Pol. Sts.*, 24, 1976, 43–56. Asserts the centrality of Hegelian ideas within Marx's economic writings, stressing his appropriation of Hegel's notion of science.

7.1207 —— and **Algozin**, K., ed., *Rubel on Marx: Five Essays*, 1981. Rubel on ethics, Engels, political economy and Marxism in Russia.

7.1208 **O'Neill**, J., 'For Marx against Althusser', *Human Context*, 6, 1974, 385–98.

7.1209 **Parekh**, B., 'Marx and the Hegelian dialectic', in V. K. Roy and R. C. Sarikwal, ed., *Marxian Sociology, Volume One*, 1979, 83–104. Examines Marx's critique of Hegel's dialectic suggesting that the resulting Marxian dialectic incorporated a major modification of Hegel's beliefs.

7.1210 **Parkinson**, G. H. R., ed., *Marx and Marxisms*, 1982. A collection focusing on the debates which have arisen out of Marx's work, including Edgeley on the scientific status of historical materialism, Atkinson on the historical claims of Marxism, Gray on Marx's conflicting conceptions of human nature, Duncan on the inadequacy of the classical Marxist theory of the state, and Lukes on the problems involved in the development of a self-consistent Marxist view of morality.

7.1211 **Pennock**, J. R., and **Chapman**, J. W., ed., *Marxism: Nomos XXVI*, 1983. Wide-ranging collection of essays, including Stillman, Riley, Elster and Cohen on morality, politics and methodology.

7.1212 **Rattansi**, A., ed., *Ideology, Method and Marx: Essays from Economy and Society*,

1989. Collection which examines important controversies concerning Marx's texts, in particular his early writings, in the wake of arguments between Althusserian and other commentators. Includes Evans on the 1844 *Manuscripts*, Tribe and Mepham on the *Grundrisse*, and Rancière's celebrated commentary on Althusser, translated into English for the first time.

7.1213 **Rubel**, M., and **Manale**, M., *Marx Without Myth: A Chronological Study of His Life and Work*, 1975. Reconstruction of his life and work, which quotes extensively from his published and unpublished writings. A useful background reference book.

7.1214 **Ryan**, A., 'A new look at Professor Tucker's Marx', *Pol. Sts.*, 15, 1967, 201–10.

7.1215 **Schmitt**, R., *Introduction to Marx and Engels: A Critical Reconstruction*, 1987.

7.1216 **Seery**, J. E., 'Deviations: on the difference between Marx and Marxist theorists', *Hist. Pol. Thought*, 9, 1988, 303–25. Suggests that the main difficulties in theorising after Marx issue from a reading of his thought that is too 'Althusserian'; only if we return to the 'early' Marx can we discover a renewable Marxist theoretical agenda.

7.1217 **Singer**, P., *Marx*, 1980. A brief introduction to his life and work which focuses upon his Hegelian origins, the centrality of alienation and his critique of liberal conceptions of freedom.

7.1218 **Slaughter**, C., *Marx and Marxism*, 1985. Presents the development of Marxism in the light of Marx's original concepts.

7.1219 **Smith**, A. A., 'Hegelianism and Marx: a reply to Colletti', *Sc. & Soc.*, 50, 1986, 148–76.

7.1220 **Springborg**, P., 'Rousseau and Marx', in R. Fitzgerald, ed., *Comparing Political Thinkers*, 1980, 223–44. Suggests that overemphasis on the similarities of these thinkers obscures the stoic and Christian influences upon Rousseau who, unlike Marx, was pessimistic about the future.

7.1221 **Stanley** J. L., 'Marx, Engels and the administration of nature', *Hist. Pol. Thought*, 12, 1981, 647–70. Challenges the 'new orthodoxy' which attempts to locate the origins of Stalinism in Engels's thought; in fact, Marx was also a 'reluctant Promethean' who developed an 'ambiguous naturalism', linked to a science

of human nature.

7.1222 —— and **Zimmerman**, E., 'On the alleged differences between Marx and Engels', *Pol. Sts.*, 32, 1984, 226–48. The authors repudiate the conventional dichotomy between their ideas by stressing the similarities between their views of human nature, science and the dialectics of nature.

7.1223 **Suchting**, W. A., 'Marx and Hannah Arendt's *The Human Condition*', *Ethics*, 73, 1962, 47–55. Review of this text which flatly rejects Arendt's reading of Marx.

7.1224 —— *Marx: An Introduction*, 1983.

7.1225 **Thomas**, P., 'Karl Marx and Max Stirner', *Pol. Theory*, 3, 1975, 159–79. Argues that the significance of, and context for, Marx's attack on Stirner in the *German Ideology* have been misunderstood. Stirner, in fact, prompted Marx to clarify his ideas concerning communism and individuality.

7.1226 —— 'Marx and science', *Pol. Sts.*, 24, 1976, 1–23. Challenges Engels's claim that Marx was a scientific socialist by suggesting that the latter held to a distinction between abstract reasoning, usually scientific, and more concrete historical analysis.

7.1227 **Tucker**, D. F. B., *Marxism and Individualism*, 1980. Defends him as a methodological individualist whose ideas prefigured the emphasis of game theorists on devising institutional arrangements to which it would be rational for self-interested individuals to give consent.

7.1228 **Tucker**, R. C., 'The cunning of reason in Hegel and Marx', *Rev. Pol.*, 18, 1956, 269–95.

7.1229 **Walker**, A., *Marx: His Theory and Its Context*, 1978.

7.1230 **Walton**, P. A., and **Hall**, S., ed., *Situating Marx*, 1972. Responding to the upsurge of interest in Marxism and the translation into English of several key texts, the editors presented a number of important essays on Marx, including McLellan on the *Grundrisse*, Walton on the dialectics of labour, Sohn-Rethel on mental and manual labour, O'Neill on the sources of Marx's theoretical critique, and O'Malley on the prospects of recovering the 'total Marx'.

7.1231 **Wardell**, M. L., 'Marx and his method: a commentary', *Sociol. Q.*, 20, 1979, 425–36.

7.1232 **Warren**, M., 'Marx and methodological individualism', *Phil. Soc. Scs.*, 18, 1988, 451–4. Distinguishes between the methodological individualism of actions as objects of explanation, to which Marx subscribed, from a methodological individualism of subjects, which he did not espouse.

7.1233 **Welty**, G., 'Marx, Engels and "Anti-Dühring" ', *Pol. Sts.*, 31, 1983, 284–94. Examines the intellectual partnership between them, questioning Carver's emphasis upon their dissimilarity, through the suggestion that Marx was familiar with the drafts of *Anti-Dühring*.

7.1234 **Wood**, A. W., *Karl Marx*, 1981. Reconstructs his philosophy and often opaque and incoherent reflections on epistemology, ontology, history and human destiny. The book is organised around five themes – alienation, historical materialism, morality, philosophical materialism and dialectics.

7.1235 **Worsley**, P., *Marx and Marxism*, 1982.

7.1236 **Zeitlin**, I. M., *Marxism: A Re-Examination*, Princeton, N.J., 1967. Plays down the Hegelian sources of Marx's thought, stressing his social theory.

Nietzsche

7.1237 **Andrew**, E., 'A note on the unity of theory and practice in Marx and Nietzsche', *Pol. Theory*, 3, 1975, 305–16. Compares their belief in the overcoming of human nature and the creation of the 'new man', though says little about the implications of this parallel.

7.1238 **Ansell-Pearson**, K., ed., *Nietzsche and Modern German Thought*, 1991. A collection of essays which examine Nietzsche's relation to Kant and the post-Kantian tradition in modern German thought, including Walker on Nietzsche's appraisal of Kant's critique of metaphysics, Janaway on Nietzsche's critique of the idea of the self based on Schopenhauer's understanding of the will, Forbes on Marx's and Nietzsche's influence on Western perceptions of change in society, and Ansell-Pearson on Nietzsche's notion of will to power.

7.1239 —— *Nietzsche contra Rousseau: A Study of Nietzsche's Moral and Political Thought*, 1991. Rejecting conventional interpretations of his political theory as either impossibly individualistic or totalitarian, the author relates Nietzsche to modern traditions of political thought and traces the influence of Rousseau upon his understanding of modernity and its discontents.

7.1240 —— 'Nietzsche on autonomy and morality: the challenge to political theory', *Pol. Sts.*, 39, 1991, 270–87. Argues that h challenge to political theory lay in his attempt to historicise the key concerns of moral and political theory, a consequence of his claim that morality and autonomy ar mutually exclusive.

7.1241 **Conway**, D. W., 'Solving the problem of Socrates: Nietzsche's *Zarathustra* as political irony', *Pol. Theory*, 16, 1988, 257–80. Outlines what he meant by suggesting that Socrates lacked genuine political irony and indicates the light this sheds upon Nietzschean criticism of libera conceptions of autonomy.

7.1242 **Dannhauser**, W., 'Friedrich Nietzsche', in L. Strauss and J. Cropsey, ed., *The History of Political Philosophy*, Chicago, Ill., 1963, 724–45.

7.1243 **Detwiler**, B., *Nietzsche and the Politics of Aristocratic Radicalism*, Chicago, Ill., 1990 Presents his vision as essentially subversiv for European political traditions and neare to the concerns of the radical right becaus of his interest in an aesthetic alternative t Western morality.

7.1244 **Diprose**, R., 'Nietzsche, ethics and sexua difference', *Rad. Phil.*, 52, 1989, 27–33.

7.1245 **Eden**, R., *Political Leadership and Nihilism: A Study of Weber and Nietzsche*, Tampa, Fla., 1983. Careful reading of bot thinkers, arguing that Nietzschean nihilism highlights some of the weaknesse of Weber's political theory.

7.1246 **Hinton Thomas**, R., *Nietzsche in German Politics and Society, 1890–1918*. Demonstrates the hostility which conservatives in Germany reserved for Nietzsche, and the appropriation of his ideas at various times by anarchists, socialists and feminists.

7.1247 **Hudson**, W., 'Hegel and Nietzsche', in R Fitzgerald, ed., *Comparing Political Thinkers*, 1980, 185–202. Beginning with an elucidation of their differences, Hudso proceeds to highlight their critiques of modernity and the implications of their positions for contemporary political thought.

7.1248 **Hunt**, L. M., *Nietzsche and the Origin of Virtue*, 1990. Argues unconvincingly that he developed a cogent political philosoph including a theory of human rights and a novel view of experimentation as an ethica ideal.

7.1249 **Karel**, H., 'Nietzsche's preface to constitutionalism', *J. Pol.*, 25, 1963, 211–25.

7.1250 **Minogue**, K., 'Nietzsche and the ideological project', in N. K. O'Sullivan, ed., *The Structure of Modern Ideology: Critical perspectives on Social and Political Theory*, 1989, 27–53. Places his relationship with different ideologies in the philosophical context of the meanings attached to the concept of ideology since the seventeenth century.

7.1251 **Pangle**, T. L., 'The roots of contemporary nihilism and its political consequences according to Nietzsche', *Rev. Pol.*, 45, 1983, 45–70.

7.1252 **Patton**, P., ed., *Nietzsche, Feminism and Political Theory*, 1993. Collection of twelve essays including K. Ansell-Pearson, 'Nietzsche, woman and political theory', P. Patton, 'Politics and the concept of power in Hobbes and Nietzsche', P. Deutscher, 'Is it not remarkable that Nietzsche should have hated Rousseau?', and T. Sadler, 'The postmodern politicization of Nietzsche'.

7.1253 **Read**, J. H., 'Nietzsche: power as oppression', *Praxis International*, 9, 1989, 72–87.

7.1254 **Rie**, R., 'Nietzsche and after', *J. Hist. Ideas*, 13, 1952, 349–69. Celebration of his influence upon subsequent philosophical and political ideas, comparing his achievements with his contemporaries, especially Wagner.

7.1255 **Solomon**, R. C., ed., *Nietzsche: A Collection of Critical Essays*, New York, 1973.

7.1256 **Strong**, T. B., *Friedrich Nietzsche and the Politics of Transfiguration*, Berkeley, Calif., 1975.

7.1257 **Warren**, M., 'Nietzsche and political philosophy', *Pol. Theory*, 13, 1985, 183–212. Original argument that his political philosophy should be understood through his philosophy of power, not his overt political standpoint.

7.1258 —— *Nietzsche and Political Thought*, 1988. Locates a number of tensions within his political thought, especially between his interpretation of individuality and culture. Concludes that there is no cogent political framework in his theory though he does attend to the project of presenting a 'critically postmodern philosophy of power'.

7.1259 —— 'The politics of Nietzsche's philosophy: nihilism, culture and power', *Pol. Sts.*, 33, 1985, 418–38. Argues that his philosophy is intrinsically political, because of its concern for the possibility of human agency in a historical world. His analysis of the tensions between cultural development and agency has parallels in the work of Marx and Weber.

7.1260 **Williams**, H., 'Nietzsche and fascism', *Hist. Euro. Ideas*, 11, 1989, 893–9. Explains the parallels commentators have found between his ethical theories and the later development of fascism, by highlighting his reliance upon cultural criticism and contempt for the masses.

7.1261 **Zuckert**, C. H., 'Nietzsche's rereading of Plato', *Pol. Theory*, 13, 1985, 213–38. Suggests that this intellectual engagement raises a number of important questions about politics and philosophy, in particular concerning Plato's misleading account of the nature and object of philosophy.

Proudhon

7.1262 **Ansart** J. J., *Proudhon*, Milan, 1978.

7.1263 **Condit**, S., *Proudhonist Materialism and Revolutionary Doctrine*, 1982. Brief and sympathetic exposition of this revolutionary project.

7.1264 **de Lubac**, H., *The Un-Marxian Socialist* 1948. Stresses the coherence and consistency of Proudhon's social and political theory.

7.1265 **Harbold**, W. H., 'Justice in the thought of Pierre-Joseph Proudhon', *West. Pol. Q.*, 22, 1969, 723–41.

7.1266 **Hoffman**, R., *Revolutionary Justice: the Social and Political Thought of P.-J. Proudhon*, Champaign-Urbana, Ill., 1972.

7.1267 **Hyams**, E., *Pierre-Joseph Proudhon: His Revolutionary Life, Mind and Works*, 1979. Sympathetic account of his career and ideas, stressing his attempt to steer an intellectual course between bourgeois thought and 'scientific' communism.

7.1268 **King**, P., *Fear of Power: An Analysis of Anti-Statism in Three French Writers*, 1967. Taking three different theorists as representatives of three variants of anti-statism (Tocqueville and liberalism; Proudhon and federalism; and Sorel and syndicalism), King discerns a common element in their thought: the key to justice resides in the quantum of power wielded by the state.

7.1269 **Labardie**, L., *Proudhon and Max Stirner*, New York, 1979.

7.1270 **Noland**, A., 'Pierre-Joseph Proudhon. Socialist as social scientist', *Am. J. Econ.*, 26, 1967, 313–28.

7.1271 **Ritter**, A., 'Proudhon and the problem of community', *Rev. Pol.*, 29, 1967, 457–77. Argues that community for Proudhon involved the reconciliation of individual freedom with social place, a project that lay at the heart of his theoretical endeavours. According to Ritter, the distinctive combination of realism and radicalism which he employed in his analysis remains important for the anarchist tradition.

7.1272 —— *The Political Thought of Pierre-Joseph Proudhon*, Princeton, N.J., 1969. Reinterprets him as a realist and moralist as well as a radical, arguing that restraint was built into his conception of political life and complemented his libertarian commitments. A sophisticated reconstruction of his thought which rebuts earlier characterisations of him as reactionary or proto-anarchist.

7.1273 **Schapiro**, J. S., 'P.-J. Proudhon, harbinger of fascism', *Am. Hist. Rev.*, 50, 1945, 714–37.

7.1274 **Silberner**, E., 'Proudhon's judeophobia', *Historica Judaica*, 10, 1948, 61–80. Assesses and accounts for Proudhon's anti-semitism, suggesting he played a crucial role in legitimising and strengthening anti-Jewish feeling among radical French theorists.

7.1275 **Vernon**, R., 'Freedom and corruption: Proudhon's federal principle', *Can. J. Pol. Sc.*, 14, 1981, 775–96.

7.1276 **Watkins**, F. M., 'Proudhon and the theory of modern liberalism', *Can. J. Econ. Pol. Sc.*, 13, 1947, 429–35.

7.1277 **Woodcock**, G., *Pierre-Joseph Proudhon: A Biography*, 1956.

Saint-Simon

7.1278 **Bazard**, S. A., *The Doctrine of Saint-Simon: An Exposition, First Year, 1828–1829*, Boston, Mass., 1958.

7.1279 **Carlisle**, R. B., 'Saint-Simonian radicalism: a definition and a direction', *French Historical Studies*, 5, 1967–68, 430–45. Illustrates the misleading interpretation of the nature and development of their thought engendered by the traditions of intellectual and economic history. In fact, the Saint-Simonians generated a culture of 'initiative, risktaking, flexibility and expansion among French businessmen'.

7.1280 **Goldstein**, L. F., 'Early feminist themes in French utopian socialism: the St.-Simonians and Fourier', *J. Hist. Ideas*, 43, 1982, 91–108. Outline of these thinkers' commitment to equal rights for women, arguing that they played a key role in developing the ideology of women's liberation.

7.1281 **Hart**, D. K., 'Saint-Simon and the role of the elite', *West. Pol. Q.*, 17, 1964, 923–31.

7.1282 **Iggers**, G. G., *The Cult of Authority: The Political Philosophy of the Saint-Simonians*, The Hague, 1970.

7.1283 **Ionescu**, G., 'Saint-Simon and the politic of industrial societies', *Govt. & Oppos.*, 8, 1973, 24–47.

7.1284 **Lukes**, S., 'Saint-Simon (1760–1825)', in T. Raison, ed., *The Founding Fathers of Social Science*, 1969, 27–34. Brief account of his intellectual influence and legacy.

7.1285 **Manuel**, F. E., *The New World of Henri Saint-Simon*, Cambridge, Mass., 1956.

7.1286 **Markham**, F. M. H., 'Saint-Simon. A nineteenth-century prophet', *Hist. Today*, 4, 1954, 540–7. Useful introduction to the origins and content of his work.

7.1287 **Simon**, W. M., 'History for utopia. Saint Simon and the idea of progress', *J. Hist. Ideas*, 17, 1956, 311–31. Considers the significance of the philosophy of history outlined in his work, arguing that history and the notion of progress informed his utopian political outlook.

7.1288 **Wokler**, R., 'Saint-Simon and the passage from political to social science', in A. Pagden, ed., *The Languages of Political Theory in Early-Modern Europe*, 1987, 325–38. Attempts to revise Foucault's account of the invention of man as a subject of science at the end of the eighteenth century, concluding that Saint-Simon, a key thinker in this field, tended to cast aside, not invent, the sciences of man that had already been formed in the Enlightenment.

Sorel

7.1289 **Beetham**, D., 'Sorel and the left', *Govt. &*

Oppos., 4, 1969, 308–23.

7.1290 **Berlin**, I., 'Georges Sorel', in *Against the Current: Essays in the History of Ideas*, 1979, 296–332.

7.1291 **Curtis**, M., *Three Against the Republic: Sorel, Barrès, and Maurras*, Princeton, N. J., 1959.

7.1292 **Greil**, A. L., *Georges Sorel and the Sociology of Virtue*, Washington, D.C., 1981.

7.1293 **Hamilton**, J. J., 'Georges Sorel and the inconsistencies of a Bergsonian Marxism', *Pol. Theory*, 1, 1973, 329–40. Traces the influence of Bergson's metaphysics upon Sorel, though suggests that the latter's resulting doctrine of individual and social freedom was untenable.

7.1294 **Horowitz**, I. L., *Radicalism and the Revolt Against Reason: The Theories of Georges Sorel*, 1961.

7.1295 **Humphrey**, R., *Georges Sorel: Prophet Without Honor*, Cambridge, Mass., 1951.

7.1296 **Jennings**, J. R., *Georges Sorel: The Character and Development of his Thought*, 1985. Outlines his methodological and ethical pluralism as the key to his political thought, charting his shift from Marxism through syndicalism to monarchism. Clear and insightful introduction.

7.1297 —— 'Sorel's early Marxism and science', *Pol. Sts.*, 31, 1983, 224–38. Despite his scientific inclinations, his early Marxism should be read as a non-determinist system which he later abandoned.

7.1298 **King**, P., *Fear of Power: An Analysis of Anti-Statism in Three French Writers*, 1967. Taking three different theorists as representatives of three variants of anti-statism (Tocqueville and liberalism; Proudhon and federalism; and Sorel and syndicalism), King discerns a common element in their thought: the key to justice resides in the quantum of power wielded by the state.

7.1299 **McInnes**, N., 'Georges Sorel (1847–1922)', in T. Raison, ed., *The Founding Fathers of Social Science*, 1969, 100–18. Brief sketch of his theoretical interests.

7.1300 **Meisel**, J. H., *The Genesis of Georges Sorel*, Ann Arbor, Mich., 1951.

7.1301 **Nichols**, R., 'Cracking foundations: "mystique" vs "politics" in Sorel and Benda', *Hist. Pol. Thought*, 14, 1993, 145–64. Comparison of their response to the Dreyfus affair as part of a larger consideration of their reaction to the crisis of late modernity.

7.1302 **Nye**, R. A., 'Two paths to a psychology of social action, Gustave le Bon and Georges Sorel', *J. Mod. Hist.*, 45, 1973, 411–38.

7.1303 **Parmée**, D., 'Georges Sorel: a reconsideration', *Cambridge J.*, 5, 1952, 355–73.

7.1304 **Portis**, L., *Georges Sorel*, 1980. Lively interpretation from an explicitly Marxist perspective.

7.1305 **Roth**, J., 'Revolution and morale in modern French thought: Sorel and the Sorelians', *French Historical Studies*, 3, 1963, 205–23. Clear presentation of the evolution of Sorel's thought, charting the emergence of a political movement inspired by Sorelian beliefs in France.

7.1306 —— *The Cult of Violence: Sorel and the Sorelians*, Berkeley, Calif., 1980. Assessment of the sources of his work and the impact of his ideas upon a number of contemporary ideological traditions.

7.1307 **Stanley**, J. L., *From Georges Sorel: Essays in Socialism and Philosophy*, New York, 1976.

7.1308 —— 'Sorel and the social uncertainty principle', *Can. J. Pol. & Soc. Theory*, 3, 1979, 83–94.

7.1309 —— *The Sociology of Virtue: the Political and Social Theories of Georges Sorel*, Berkeley, Calif., 1981. Defends his theoretical system as a resource for the social scientist despite the shifting and inconsistent political positions he adopted throughout his career. Focusing especially on his critique of Marxist conceptions of totality, Stanley emphasises his distinctive reading of concrete institutions as mediating forces in social development.

7.1310 **Talmon**, J. L., 'The legacy of Georges Sorel', *Encounter*, 5, 1970, 47–61.

7.1311 **Vernon**, R., ' "Citizenship" in "industry": the case of Georges Sorel', *Am. Pol. Sc. Rev.*, 75, 1981, 17–28.

7.1312 —— *Commitment and Change: Georges Sorel and the Idea of Revolution*, Toronto, 1978. Brief and perceptive introduction.

7.1313 —— 'Rationalism and commitment in Sorel', *J. Hist. Ideas*, 34, 1973, 405–21.

7.1314 **Wilde**, L., 'Sorel and the French right', *Hist. Pol. Thought*, 7, 1986, 361–74. Analyses his overwhelmingly moralistic approach to politics and social thought which, allied to his abhorrence of representative democracy, could find expression in apparently contradictory political positions.

7.1315 **Wood**, N., 'Some reflections on Sorel and Machiavelli', *Pol. Sc. Q.*, 83, 1968, 76–91.

Tocqueville

7.1316 **Allen**, B., 'The spiral of silence and institutional design: Tocqueville's analysis of public opinion and democracy', *Polity*, 27, 1991, 243–67.

7.1317 **Amann**, P., 'Taine, Tocqueville and the paradox of the Ancien Régime', *Romantic Review*, 52, 1961, 183–195. Although Taine's thought was strongly influenced by Tocqueville, he reaches a radically different conclusion on the survivability of the ancien régime, according to Amann.

7.1318 **Ankersmit**, F., 'Tocqueville and the ambivalences of democracy', *Rationality and Society*, 3, 1991, 308–316.

7.1319 **Bathory**, P. D., 'Tocqueville's religion: an exchange. Tocqueville on citizenship and faith: a response to Cushing Strout', *Pol. Theory*, 8, 1980, 27–38. A critique of Strout's failure to address the relationship between democracy and authority in his thought.

7.1320 **Beloff**, M., 'Tocqueville and the Americans', *Fortnightly Review*, 170, 1951, 573–9. On his observations about American democracy.

7.1321 **Boesche**, R. C., 'The strange liberalism of Alexis de Tocqueville', *Hist. Pol. Thought*, 2, 1981, 495–524. Argues that his ideas about social atomisation, individualism, centralisation and the mediocre nature of democratic society place his thought at the outer margins of liberalism.

7.1322 —— *The Strange Liberalism of Alexis de Tocqueville*, Ithaca, N.Y., 1987. A rigorous account of his 'aristocratic liberalism'.

7.1323 —— 'Tocqueville and *Le Commerce*: a newspaper expressing his unusual liberalism', *J. Hist. Ideas*, 44, 1983, 277–92. Examines the period in which Tocqueville was the leading influence in this newspaper, and reveals how he developed a distinctive critique of manufacturing society that does not fit easily in one ideological tradition.

7.1324 —— 'Why could Tocqueville predict so well?', *Pol. Theory*, 11, 1983, 79–103.

7.1325 —— 'Why did Tocqueville fear abundance: or the tension between commerce and citizenship?', *Hist. Euro.*

Ideas, 9, 1988, 25–45. Argues that he feared the acquisitive ethic of bourgeois society because it would undermine the social mores and institutions necessary for democracy.

7.1326 **Brogan**, H., *Tocqueville*, 1973. Brief introduction to his thought.

7.1327 **Brunius**, T., *Alexis de Tocqueville, The Sociological Aesthetician*, Uppsala, 1960. Examines his sociological analysis of art and aesthetics.

7.1328 **Burrage**, M., 'On Tocqueville's notion of the irresistibility of democracy', *Archives Européenes de Sociologie*, 13, 1972, 151–75. Examines the political and social ramifications of industrialisation.

7.1329 **Costner**, H. L., 'De Tocqueville on equality: a discourse on intellectual style', *Pac. Soc. Rev.*, 19, 1976, 411–30. Summary of Tocqueville's views on the close relationship between equality and liberty.

7.1330 **Drescher**, S., *Dilemmas of Democracy: Tocqueville and Modernization*, Pittsburgh, Penn., 1965. A stimulating analysis that traces the effect of political and social events on the development of his thought.

7.1331 —— *Tocqueville and Beaumont on Social Reform*, New York, 1968.

7.1332 —— *Tocqueville and England*, Cambridge, Mass., 1964. Chronological examination of the influence of English thought and institutions on his work.

7.1333 —— 'Tocqueville's two "Democracies" ', *J. Hist. Ideas*, 25, 1964, 201–16. Between the publication of the first and second volumes of *Democracy in America* his views on majority rule, centralisation and industrialisation were transformed by his active career in politics, according to Drescher.

7.1334 **Eberts**, P. R., and **Witton**, R. A., 'Recall from anecdote: A. de Tocqueville and the morphogenesis of America', *Am. Soc. Rev.*, 35, 1970, 1081–97.

7.1335 **Eden**, R., 'Tocqueville and the problem of natural right', *Interpretation*, 17, 1990, 379–87.

7.1336 **Eisenstadt**, A. S., ed., *Reconsidering Tocqueville's Democracy in America*, New Brunswick, N.J., 1988.

7.1337 **Frohnen**, B., *Virtue and the Promise of Conservatism: The Legacy of Burke and Tocqueville*, Lawrence, Kan., 1993. Argues that both offered rigorous philosophical arguments for a conservative conception of the good life.

7.1338 **Furet**, F., 'The intellectual origins of Tocqueville's thought', *Tocqueville Review*, 7, 1985–86, 117–29. A useful study that endeavours to expose the wide range of influences on his thought.

7.1339 **Gargan**, E. T., *Alexis de Tocqueville: the Critical Years, 1848–51*, Washington, D.C., 1955. Examines how his political participation in these years influenced his views on the evolution of democratic societies and the appearance of class conflict.

7.1340 —— *De Tocqueville*, New York, 1965. Useful introduction.

7.1341 —— 'The formation of Tocqueville's historical thought', *Rev. Pol.*, 24, 1962, 48–61.

7.1342 —— 'The purpose of Tocqueville's democracy', *Tocqueville Review*, 7, 1985–86, 67–75. Examines his purpose in studying American democracy.

7.1343 —— 'Tocqueville and the problem of historical prognosis', *Am. Hist. Rev.*, 68, 1963, 332–45. Examines how democratic society evolves through the erosion of aristocratic society, yet this does not imply a rupture with historical continuity. Tocqueville was therefore able to sketch the principal traits of the future.

7.1344 **Girard**, R., 'Stendhal and Tocqueville', *American Society Legion Honor Magazine*, 31, 1960, 73–83. Demonstrates their shared views on democracy and liberty.

7.1345 **Goldstein**, D., 'Alexis de Tocqueville's concept of citizenship', *Procs. Am. Phil. Soc.*, 108, 1967, 34–53. Examines how he envisaged the preservation of republican virtue in the democratic age.

7.1346 —— *Trial of Faith, Religion and Politics in Tocqueville's Thought*, New York, 1975. Argues that he regarded Christianity as a guarantee of human liberty and social cohesion.

7.1347 **Graebner**, N. A., 'Christianity and democracy: Tocqueville's views of religion in America', *J. Rel.*, 56, 1976, 263–73. Shows why he believed that religion can be used to counter the tendency within democratic society for individuals to concentrate on wealth-making.

7.1348 **Hadari**, S. A., *Theory in Practice: Tocqueville's New Science of Politics*, Stamford, Conn., 1989. Thorough analysis of Tocqueville's method, with special emphasis on his use of formal models and

his reliance on an historical method that is conceived as hermeneutical.

7.1349 —— 'Unintended consequences in periods of transition: Tocqueville's "Recollections" revisited', *Am. J. Pol. Sc.*, 33, 1989, 136–149. Examines the presentation of social change in the *Recollections*.

7.1350 **Hancock**, R. C., 'Tocqueville on the good American federalism', *Publius*, 20, 1990, 89–108.

7.1351 —— 'Tocqueville on the theory and practice of American federalism', *Tocqueville Review*, 10, 1989–90, 207–227.

7.1352 **Hennis**, W., 'Tocqueville's perspective: *Democracy in America* in search of the "new science of politics" ', *Interpretation*, 16, 1988, 61–86.

7.1353 **Herr**, R., *Tocqueville and the Old Regime*, Princeton, N.J., 1962. Analysis of the themes of aristocracy, democracy, tyranny, liberty and equality in *L'Ancien Régime et la Revolution*.

7.1354 **Hinkley**, C. J., 'Tocqueville on religious truth and political necessity', *Polity*, 23, 1990, 39–52. Argues that he saw religion as countering individualism and materialism.

7.1355 **Hoffman**, R. J. S., 'Tocqueville and Burke', *Burke Newsletter*, 2, 1961, 44–47. Examines Burke's influence on Tocqueville.

7.1356 **Horwitz**, M., 'Tocqueville and the tyranny of the majority', *Rev. Pol.*, 28, 1966, 293–307. Examines the problem of political tyranny in relation to centralisation and the rule of the masses.

7.1357 **Jacobitti**, S. D., 'Individualism and political community: Arendt and Tocqueville on the current debate in liberalism', *Polity*, 23, 1991, 585–604. Compares their views on community, morality and civic virtue in connection with liberalism's emphasis on individual rights and liberty.

7.1358 **Jardin**, A. *Tocqueville: A Biography*, New York, 1988. The most thorough intellectual biography to date.

7.1359 **Kahan**, A., 'Tocqueville's two revolutions', *J. Hist. Ideas*, 46, 1985, 585–96. Analyses the revolutionary developments of the *ancien régime* – centralisation, changes in interests, ideas, language, and society – and how these interact with the central themes of the Revolution – liberty and equality.

7.1360 **Keeney**, J., 'Tocqueville and the new

politics', *New Pol.*, 1–3, 1962. Argues that the lack of rigorous economic analysis in Tocqueville's work leads him to be less critical of democracy than he should have been.

7.1361 **Kessler**, S., 'Tocqueville on civil religion and liberal democracy', *J. Pol.*, 37, 1977, 119–46. Study of his notion of the political utility of civil religion in liberal democracies.

7.1362 —— 'Tocqueville on sexual morality', *Interpretation*, 16, 1989, 765–80.

7.1363 **King**, P., *Fear of Power: An Analysis of Anti-Statism in Three French Writers*, 1967. Taking three different theorists as representatives of variants of anti-statism (Tocqueville and liberalism; Proudhon and federalism; and Sorel and syndicalism), King discerns a common element in their thought – the key to justice resides in the quantum of power wielded by the state.

7.1364 **Kinzier**, B. L., 'Tocqueville and his interpreters, J. S. Mill and Henry Reeve', *Mill News*, 13, 1978, 2–10. Examines their responses to *Democracy in America*.

7.1365 **Koritansky**, J., *Alexis de Tocqueville and the New Science of Politics*, Durham, N.C., 1986.

7.1366 **Kraynak**, R., 'Tocqueville's constitutionalism', *Am. Pol. Sc. Rev.*, 81, 1987, 1175–95. Argues that he combines ancient conceptions of constitutionalism, whereby régimes are classified and seen in terms of creating the virtuous citizen, with modern conceptions that are formulated in terms of checks and balances in order to secure individual rights.

7.1367 **Lakoff**, S., 'Liberty, equality, democracy', in G. Feaver, ed., *Lives, Liberties and the Public Good*, 1988, 101–20. Argues that Tocqueville departs from Rousseau by formulating a conception of pluralism that protects liberty whilst preserving the principle of equality.

7.1368 **Lamberti**, J. C., *Tocqueville and the Two Democracies*, New York, 1988. Considers his two main themes of democracy and revolution in the light of his early political activities and subsequent historical studies.

7.1369 **Lawler**, P. A., 'Was Tocqueville a philosopher?', *Interpretation*, 17, 1990, 404–17. Argues that he used aspects of philosophical thought to advance the liberal cause of liberty.

7.1370 **Lerner**, M., 'Culture and personality in Tocqueville's America', *Southern Review* 1, 1965, 590–605. Examines the central aspects of his thought – equality, freedom, revolution, power, history, tyranny and their relation to key dimensions of contemporary American culture, such as the family, education, religion, and wealth

7.1371 —— *Tocqueville on American Civilization*, New York, 1969. Close consideration of *Democracy in America*.

7.1372 —— 'Tocqueville's *Democracy in America* politics, law and the elite', *Antioch Review* 25, 1965–66, 543–63. A thorough analysis of *Democracy in America* with particular attention to the key ideas of democracy, revolution, history, and concepts such as liberty and equality.

7.1373 **Leroy**, M., 'Alexis de Tocqueville', in W Ebenstein, ed., *Political Thought in Perspective*, New York, 1957, 472–500.

7.1374 **Lewis**, P. W., 'De Tocqueville and democracy', *Sewanee Review*, 54, 1946, 557–75. Introductory survey.

7.1375 **Lively**, J., *The Social and Political Though of Alexis de Tocqueville*, 1962. Among the more comprehensive and readable studies of his work.

7.1376 **Lombardo**, P. A., 'Historic echoes: romantic emphasis in Tocqueville's "Democracy in America" ', *J. Thought*, 16, 1981, 67–80. Examines the influence o the romantic movement on his thinking.

7.1377 **Masuqui**, K., ed., *Interpreting Tocqueville's "Democracy in America"*, Savage, Md., 1991. Important collection, including essays on his political thought (Lamberti, Hennis, Smith, Lawler, Zuckert) and political commitments and legacy (West, Schleifer, Wettergreen, Banfield, Marini, Ceaser).

7.1378 **Meyer**, J. P., *Alexis de Tocqueville: a Biographical Study in Political Science*, New York, 1960. Survey that touches upon the relation between his life and work.

7.1379 **Mitchell**, H., 'Alexis de Tocqueville and the legacy of the French Revolution', *Social Res.*, 56, 1989, 127–159.

7.1380 —— 'The changing conditions of freedom Tocqueville in the light of Rousseau', *Hist Pol. Thought*, 9, 1988, 431-55. Argues tha he was influenced by Rousseau in his development of the notions of liberty and virtue.

7.1381 —— 'Tocqueville's mirage or reality? Political freedom from old regime to revolution', *J. Mod. Hist.*, 60, 1988, 28–57. Examines his considerations of political liberty.

7.1382 **Mondale**, C., 'With Tocqueville in mind', *National Forum*, 61, 1981, 16–17. Examines his thoughts on local civic participation.

7.1383 **Morton**, F. L., 'Sexual equality and the family in Tocqueville's *Democracy in America*', *Can. J. Pol. Sc.*, 17, 1984, 309–24.

7.1384 **Nisbet**, R., 'Many Tocquevilles', *Am. Scholar*, 46, 1976–77, 59–75. Uses his analysis of democracy to reflect on totalitarianism, liberty and equality.

7.1385 —— 'Tocqueville', *International Encyclopedia of Social Science*, 16, 1968, 90–95. Rigorous study of his thoughts on power, class and mass culture.

7.1386 **Palmer**, R. R., *The Two Tocquevilles, Father and Son: Hervé and Alexis de Tocqueville on the Coming of the French Revolution*, Princeton, N.J., 1987.

7.1387 **Pappé**, H. O., 'Mill and Tocqueville', *J. Hist. Ideas*, 25, 1964, 217–34. Argues that Tocqueville's influence on Mill was minimal and sporadic.

7.1388 **Pope**, W., and **Pope**, L., *Alexis de Tocqueville: His social and political theory*, 1986. Important survey of his thought.

7.1389 **Pranger**, R. J., 'Tocqueville and political ambivalence', *Studies in Romanticism*, 2, 1962–63, 129–34. Argues that his views are marked by his adherence both to an aristocracy of the past and a democracy of the future.

7.1390 **Resh**, R., 'Alexis de Tocqueville and the negro democracy in America reconsidered', *Journal of Negro History*, 48, 1963, 251–59. Argues that his thought was influenced by a certain number of racist ideas.

7.1391 **Richardson**, W. D. and **Fessele**, B. H., 'Tocqueville's observations on racial and sexual inequalities in America', *Southeastern Political Review*, 19, 1991, 248–277.

7.1392 **Richter**, M., 'Comparative political analysis in Montesquieu and Tocqueville', *Comp. Pol.*, 1, 1969, 129–60. Demonstrates how their studies of societies are based on a comparative analysis between ancient and modern civilisations.

7.1393 —— 'Debate on race, Tocqueville – Gobineau correspondence', *Commentary*, 25, 1958, 151–60. Their views on race are seen in the light of an acceptance or

rejection of the principles of the French revolution.

7.1394 —— 'Modernity and its distinctive threats to liberty: Montesquieu and Tocqueville on new forms of illegitimate domination', in M. Hereth and J. Höffken, ed., *Alexis de Tocqueville: Zur Politik in der Demokratie*, Baden-Baden, 1981, 61–80. Examines their views on modernity and its implications for liberty.

7.1395 —— 'The uses of theory: Tocqueville's adaptation of Montesquieu', in M. Richter, ed., *Essays in Theory and History: An Approach to the Social Sciences*, 1970, 74–102. Demonstrates how Tocqueville's analysis of American democracy is influenced by Montesquieu's method and use of ideal types.

7.1396 —— 'Tocqueville's contribution to the theory of revolution', in C. J. Friedrich, ed., *Revolution: Nomos VIII*, New York, 1966, 75–121. Thoughtful reconstruction of his theory of 'permanent revolution', assessing his conception of violence, ideas, interests and classes in revolutionary situations and sense of underlying sociological laws that determine the nature of political systems.

7.1397 **Schlaerth**, W. J., ed., *A Symposium on Alexis de Tocqueville's Democracy in America*, New York, 1975. Includes Einaudi on democracy and America, Hartnett on American federalism, Hoffman on his views on religion, Miller on his notions of egalitarianism and constitutional democracy, and Timasheff, 'Tocqueville in the light of contemporary sociology'.

7.1398 **Schleifer**, J. T., 'Images of America after the revolution: Alexis de Tocqueville and Gustave de Beaumont visit the early Republic', *Yale University Library Gazette*, 51, 1977, 125–44.

7.1399 —— *The Making of Tocqueville's Democracy in America*, Chapel Hill, N.C., 1980. A thorough analysis of the writing of *Democracy in America*.

7.1400 **Schneck**, S. F., 'Habits of the head: Tocqueville's America and jazz', *Pol. Theory*, 17, 1989, 638–62. Drawing on Foucault, the author argues that the America portrayed in Tocqueville's work was, in reality, a fabrication.

7.1401 **Sennett**, R., 'What Tocqueville feared', *Partisan Review*, 45, 1979, 406–18. As a utopian thinker, according to Sennett, he contended that once economic equality is achieved, the danger of political tyranny is posed with regard to marginal groups.

7.1402 **Solomon**, A., *In Praise of Enlightenment*, New York, 1963, 263–81. Includes chapters on Tocqueville's moral and democratic theory.

7.1403 —— 'Tocqueville 1959', *Social Res.*, 26, 1959, 449–70. Examines his sociological and historical method, especially with regard to political elites.

7.1404 **Strout**, C., 'Tocqueville and republican religion: revisiting the visitor', *Pol. Theory*, 8, 1980, 9–26. Reassesses his admiration for religion in America because of its moderating effect on political and civil life.

7.1405 —— 'Tocqueville's clarity: describing America and thinking of Europe', *American Quarterly*, 21, 1969, 87–99.

7.1406 **Thurston**, C. J., 'Alexis de Tocqueville in Russia', *J. Hist. Ideas*, 37, 1976, 289–306.

7.1407 **Virtanen**, R., 'Tocqueville and the romantics', *Symposium*, 13, 1959, 167–85. Argues that his knowledge of romantic literature and thought are revealed in many aspects of his work.

7.1408 **Wach**, J., 'The role of religion in the social philosophy of Alexis de Tocqueville', *J. Hist. Ideas*, 7, 1947, 74–90.

7.1409 **Wade**, L. L., 'Tocqueville and public choice', *Public Choice*, 47, 1985, 491–508.

7.1410 **Weitman**, S. R., 'The sociological theories of Tocqueville's "The old regime and the revolution" ', *Social Res.*, 33, 1966, 389–406. Argues that, in his view, the French revolution accentuated the trend towards social uniformity.

7.1411 **Westfall**, W., 'Tocqueville, Emerson, and the abolitionists', *J. Thought*, 19, 1984, 56–64. Views 'ante bellum' America as offering a cultural and intellectual milieu in which a dialogue can take place between Tocqueville's critical sociology and Emerson's speculative philosophy.

7.1412 **Winthrop**, D., 'Tocqueville's American woman and "the true conception" ', *Pol. Theory*, 14, 1986, 239–61. Rigorous critique of the traditional interpretation of his thought on women in America, arguing that they should be understood as provoking sober reflection on democratic society in its entirety.

7.1413 —— 'Tocqueville's "Old Regime": political history', *Rev. Pol.*, 43, 1981, 88–111. Examines his analysis of the origins of the French revolution, noting his

recognition of the accommodation of various aspects of the *ancien régime* in the new order.

7.1414 **Zeitlin**, I. M., *Liberty, Equality, and Revolution in Alexis de Tocqueville*, Boston, Mass., 1971. Analysis of the grand themes of Tocqueville's work, particularly the idea of class.

7.1415 **Zemach**, A., 'Alexis de Tocqueville on England', *Rev. Pol.*, 13, 1951, 319–43. Examines his reflections on how England would pass peacefully from aristocracy to democracy.

7.1416 **Zetterbaum**, M., *Tocqueville and the Problem of Democracy*, Stanford, Calif., 1967. Presents him as a partisan of democracy.

7.1417 —— 'Tocqueville: neutrality and the use of history', *Am. Pol. Sc. Rev.*, 58, 1964, 611–21.

Weber

7.1418 **Ashcraft**, R., 'Marx and Weber on liberalism as bourgeois ideology', *Comp. Sts. Soc. & Hist.*, 14, 1972, 130–68.

7.1419 **Axtmann**, R., 'The formation of the modern state: a reconstruction of Max Weber's arguments', *Hist. Pol. Thought*, 11, 1990, 295–311. Reconstructs his complex account of the relations between different kinds of social action in his analysis of structural change in Western Europe.

7.1420 **Baehr**, P., 'The "masses" in Weber's political sociology', *Economy and Society*, 19, 1990, 242–65.

7.1421 **Beetham**, D., 'Max Weber and the liberal political tradition', *Eur. J. Soc.*, 30, 1989, 311–23.

7.1422 —— *Max Weber and the Theory of Modern Politics*, 1974. A successful attempt to reinstate his political theory within his intellectual development, proposing that his political ideas compel a reconsideration of some of the key themes in his sociology Weber is presented as engaged in the reformation of liberalism in the collectivist atmosphere of contemporary politics.

7.1423 **Bendix**, R., *Max Weber: An Intellectual Portrait*, New York, 1960.

7.1424 **Brubaker**, R., *The Limits of Rationality: An Essay on the Social and Moral Thought of Max Weber*, 1984.

7.1425 **Bruun**, H. H., *Science, Values and Politics*

in Max Weber's Methodology, Copenhagen, 1972.

.1426 **Cohen**, I. J., 'The underemphasis on democracy in Marx and Weber', in R. J. Antonio and R. M. Glassman, ed., *A Weber-Marx Dialogue*, Lawrence, Kan., 1985, 274–99. Assesses the implications for democratic theory of key elements of their thought, suggesting a concurrence in their underestimation of the strengths of democracy.

.1427 **Collins**, R., 'Weber's last theory of capitalism: a systematization', *Am. Soc. Rev.*, 45, 1980, 925–44.

.1428 **Dibble**, V., 'Social science and political commitments in the young Max Weber', *Archives Européenes de Sociologie*, 9, 1968, 92–110.

.1429 **Dronberger**, I., *The Political Thought of Max Weber: In Quest of Statesmanship*, New York, 1971.

.1430 **Eden**, R., 'Doing without liberalism: Weber's régime politics', *Pol. Theory*, 10, 1983, 379–407. Evaluates his alternative to liberalism and the influence his 'régime politics' has exercised over later intellectuals.

.1431 —— *Political Leadership and Nihilism: A Study of Weber and Nietzsche*, Tampa, Fla., 1983. Careful reading of both thinkers, arguing that Nietzschean nihilism highlights some of the weaknesses of Weber's political theory.

.1432 **Esquith**, S. L., 'Politics and values in Marx and Weber', in R. J. Antonio and R. M. Glassman, ed., *A Weber-Marx Dialogue*, Lawrence, Kan., 1985, 300–18. Essay on the historicity of values, which draws upon their observations about the importance of work in their societies.

.1433 **Giddens**, A., 'Marx, Weber and the development of capitalism', in *Studies in Social and Political Theory*, 1977, 183–207. Challenges the simplistic belief that Weber developed a unitary critique of historical materialism, suggesting that his historical studies partly vindicate Marx against his own disciples. In conclusion, Giddens attempts to fuse socialist convictions with market relations, stressing the compatibility of these thinkers.

.1434 —— *Politics and Sociology in the Thought of Max Weber*, 1972. Brief, incisive evaluation of the connections between his political writings and more academic sociology, arguing that the differing aspects of his work were united by the attempt to analyse the conditions governing the expansion of industrial capitalism in Germany.

7.1435 **Glassman**, R., ed., *Max Weber's Political Sociology*, Westport, Conn., 1984.

7.1436 **Holton**, R. J., and **Turner**, B. S., *Max Weber on Economy and Society*, 1989. Perceptive attempt to apply his ideas to contemporary problems, presenting him as the bearer of a radical liberal alternative to socialism and the new right.

7.1437 **Käsler**, D., *Max Weber: An Introduction to his Life and Work*, 1988. Clearly presented and sympathetic summary of his ideas. A helpful book for the student encountering Weber for the first time.

7.1438 **Koch**, A. M., 'Rationality, romanticism and the individual: Max Weber's "modernism" and the confrontation with "modernity" ', *Can. J. Pol. Sc.*, 36, 1993, 123–44. Examines the influence of the tension between rationalism and romanticism in his thought, arguing that he failed to transcend this dichotomy due to the absence of a serious exploration of alternative criteria by which modernism might be evaluated.

7.1439 **Krygier**, M., 'Weber, Lenin and the reality of socialism', in E. Kamenka and M. Krygier, ed., *Bureaucracy: The Career of a Concept*, 1979, 61–82. Suggests certain similarities in these thinkers' concern for the post-revolutionary fate of bureaucracy, despite their obvious differences.

7.1440 **Levine**, D. N., 'Rationality and freedom: Weber and beyond', *Sociol. Inq.*, 51, 1981, 5–26.

7.1441 **Lowenstein**, K., *Max Weber's Political Ideas in the Perspective of our Time*, Amherst, Mass., 1966. A general account of his political ideas, examining their contemporary relevance.

7.1442 **Löwith**, K., *Max Weber and Karl Marx*, 1982. Reprint of Löwith's controversial assessment of their theoretical relationship.

7.1443 **Mayer**, J. P., *Max Weber and German Politics: A Study in Political Sociology*, 1956.

7.1444 **Merquior**, J. G., *Rousseau and Weber*, 1980.

7.1445 **Mommsen**, W. J., 'Capitalism and socialism: Weber's dialogue with Marx', in R. J. Antonio and R. M. Glassman, ed., *A Weber-Marx Dialogue*, Lawrence, Kan.,

1985, 234–61. A fascinating comparison of the origins and development of their approaches to industrial capitalism, which endorses Weber's critique of the Marxist emphasis on property relations as the central and constitutive 'problem' of the capitalist order.

7.1446 —— *Max Weber on Politics and Social Theory*, 1989. An influential reading of his political and social theory as an integrated whole, including an account of recent work on Weber.

7.1447 —— 'Max Weber's political sociology and his philosophy of moral history', *Int. Soc. Sc. J.*, 17, 1965, 23–45. Regards his political views as the product of his fear that the central dynamics of the individual were endangered by the ultimate victory of bureaucracy. These fears found their political expression in his aristocratic liberalism.

7.1448 —— *The Age of Bureaucracy: Perspectives on the Political Sociology of Max Weber*, 1974. Presents him as concerned to examine and counter the development of bureaucratic structures which were stifling liberalism and individualism. His sociology rests upon a liberal individualist view of history whilst his advocacy of democracy was designed as an anti-authoritarian version of charismatic domination.

7.1449 —— *The Political and Social Theory of Max Weber: Collected Essays*, 1989. A collection of the essays of this leading Weber scholar on politics and social theory, socialism and political radicalism, and the rediscovery of Weber.

7.1450 —— and **Osterhammel**, J., ed., *Max Weber and his Contemporaries*, 1987. A large collection of essays which includes a useful bibliographical introduction by Mommsen, essays comparing Weber with contemporary nineteenth-century thinkers (Mommsen on Michels, Beetham on Mosca and Pareto, Merquior on Sorel, Ryan on Mill, and Giddens on Durkheim) a section devoted to 'The Realm of Politics' in which Weber is compared with his contemporaries in the realm of political thought (Theiner on Naumann, Schulin on Rathenau, Hübunger on Streseman, Chickering on Schäfer, Breuilly on Bernstein, Geary on Kautsky, Dahlman on Toller, and Levy on Gramsci), and an important concluding essay by Dahrendorf

on Weber and modern social science.

7.1451 **Parkin**, F., *Max Weber*, 1982.

7.1452 **Portis**, E., *Max Weber and Political Commitment*, Philadelphia, Penn. , 1986.

7.1453 **Prager**, J., 'Moral integration and political inclusion: a comparison of Durkheim's and Weber's theories of democracy', *Social Forces*, 59, 1981, 918–50.

7.1454 **Rossides**, D., 'The legacy of Max Weber a non-metaphysical politics', *Sociol. Inq.*, 42, 1972, 183–211.

7.1455 **Roth**, G., 'Political critiques of Max Weber: some implications for political sociology', *Am. Soc. Rev.*, 30, 1965, 213–23. Brief survey of the principal political attacks upon Weber, all of which distort their subject.

7.1456 **Rudolph**, L. I., and **Rudolph**, S. H., 'Authority and power in bureaucratic and patrimonial administration: a revisionist interpretation of Weber on democracy', *World Politics*, 31, 1979, 195–227.

7.1457 **Scaff**, L. A., 'Fleeing the iron cage: politics and culture in the thought of Max Weber', *Am. Pol. Sc. Rev.*, 81, 1987, 737–55.

7.1458 —— 'Max Weber's politics and political education', *Am. Pol. Sc. Rev.*, 67, 1973, 128–41.

7.1459 **Thomas**, J. J. R., 'Weber and direct democracy', *Brit. J. Soc.*, 35, 1984, 216–46.

7.1460 **Turner**, C., *Modernity and Politics in the Work of Max Weber*, 1992. Reviewing a number of recent interpretations of Weber's political theory, Turner argues that these do inadequate justice to his concept of the political which was articulated alongside his appeal to the neo Kantian philosophy of his day.

7.1461 **Warren**, M., 'Max Weber's liberalism for a Nietzschean world', *Am. Pol. Sc. Rev.*, 82 1988, 32–50. Innovative presentation of Weber's ethical commitments as consistent with his theory of democracy yet incompatible with his assessment of political possibilities. Avoiding conventional criticism of his political thought, Warren reads his ideas as symptomatic of real challenges for democratic theory in the face of bureaucratic nihilism and the divergence between the promise and performance of liberal democracies.

7.1462 —— *Nietzsche and Political Thought*, Cambridge, Mass., 1988.

7.1463 **Wilson**, H. T., 'The impact of nationalist ideology on political philosophy: the case of Max Weber and Wilhelmine Germany', *Hist. Euro. Ideas*, 16, 1993, 545–50. Attempts to locate his ambivalence concerning nationalism in the tensions between his class position, liberal beliefs and conception of the nation state.

7.1464 **Wolin**, S. S., 'Max Weber: legitimation, method and the politics of theory', *Pol. Theory*, 9, 1981, 402–24.

7.1465 **Wrong**, D. H., *Max Weber*, Engelwood Cliffs, N.J., 1970.

Other thinkers

7.1466 **Aldridge**, A. O., 'Apostles of reason: Camille Henriquez and the French Enlightenment', *Sts. Voltaire*, 55, 1967, 65–87.

7.1467 **Asher**, A., *Pavel Axelrod and the Development of Menshevism*, Cambridge, Mass., 1972.

7.1468 **Baron**, S. H., *Plekhanov: the Father of Russian Marxism*, 1963. An intellectual biography charting his shift from populism to Marxism and providing a sympathetic account of his evolving political theory. 1917 represented the demise of Plekanovite Marxism, according to Baron.

7.1469 **Bell**, D., 'Charles Fourier: prophet of eupsychia', *Am. Scholar*, Fall, 1968, 41–58.

7.1470 **Berlin**, I., *Russian Thinkers*, 1978. A collection of essays on the Russian intelligentsia in the nineteenth century, including a reflection on Herzen and Bakunin on individual liberty, and a consideration of the political ideas of the populists.

7.1471 **Bernstein**, S., *Auguste Blanqui and the Art of Insurrection*, 1971.

7.1472 **Biddiss**, M. D., *Father of Racist Ideology: The Social and Political Thought of Count Gobineau*, 1970.

7.1473 **Bobbio**, N., *On Mosca and Pareto*, Geneva, 1972. Includes essays on Mosca's theory of the ruling class and Pareto's political sociology.

7.1474 **Bowles**, R. C., 'The reaction of Charles Fourier to the French Revolution', *French Historical Studies*, 1, 1958–60, 348–56.

7.1475 **Bridenthal**, R., 'The "greening" of Germany", 1848: Karl Grün's "true" socialism', *Sc. & Soc.*, 35, 1971, 439–62. Argues for the similarity between contemporary new left ideals and the school of "true" socialism which appeared in the mid-1840s, Grün among them. The latter's thought is especially significant as he was one of Marx's targets in the *Communist Manifesto*.

7.1476 **Campbell**, P., 'Achille Murat, a precursor of de Tocqueville', *Cambridge J.*, 7, 1954, 298–307. Systematic account of Murat's understanding of American society and democracy. Special attention is devoted to his views on slavery, the social mores of the American people, and the political institutions of American democracy.

7.1477 **Cunliffe**, J., 'The liberal rationale of "rational socialism" ', *Pol. Sts.*, 36, 1989, 653–62. Focuses on the Belgian theorist, Colins, in the 1830s, to throw light on contemporary debates concerning natural rights and property entitlements in liberal theory.

7.1478 **Denholm**, T., 'Louis August Blanqui: the Hamlet of revolutionary socialism?', in E. Kamenka and F. B. Smith, ed., *Intellectuals and Revolution: Socialism and the Experience of 1848*, 1979, 14–30. Review of his political and intellectual career, which traces the influence of the utopians on his ideas and compares his insurrectionist beliefs with Leninism.

7.1479 **Derfler**, L., *Paul Lafargue and the Founding of French Marxism, 1842–1882*, 1991. An important interpretation of Lafargue as a propagandist rather than a theorist. Unfortunately this biography ends in its subject's mid-life.

7.1480 **Evans**, R. J., 'Theory and practice in German Social Democracy 1880–1914: Clara Zetkin and the socialist theory of women's emancipation', *Hist. Pol. Thought*, 3, 1982, 285–304. Suggests that her Marxism developed in response to the exigencies of contemporary politics, especially the growth of the Social Democratic Women's Movement, and that her socialist principles cannot be simply counteropposed against her feminism.

7.1481 **Femia**, J. V., 'Antonio Labriola: a forgotten Marxist thinker', *Hist. Pol. Thought*, 7, 1981, 557–72. Introduction to a relatively neglected Marxist whose major theoretical contribution resided in his critique of the positivism of Second International Marxism.

7.1482 **Field**, G. G., *Evangelist of Race: The Germanic Vision of Houston Stewart*

Chamberlain, New York, 1981. Assesses the life, work and influence of Chamberlain, comparing his thought to Rosenberg, Kraus and the Social Darwinists.

7.1483 **Gay**, P., *The Dilemma of Democratic Socialism: Eduard Bernstein's Challenge to Marx*, New York, 1952. Major intellectual biography of Bernstein, expertly and sympathetically outlining the development of revisionism and its critical reception amongst Marxists.

7.1484 **Hoover**, J., 'The foundation of the communitarian state in the thought of Friedrich Schleiermacher', *Hist. Pol. Thought*, 10, 1989, 295–312. Resuscitates his historical, communitarian view of the state to prove that such an approach is not inherently anti-liberal.

7.1485 **Jacobitti**, E. E., 'Labriola, Croce and Italian Marxism (1845–1910)', *J. Hist. Ideas*, 36, 1975, 297–318. Assesses the credentials of each as the founding figures of contemporary Italian Marxism.

7.1486 **Johnson**, C. H., 'Étienne Cabet and the problem of class antagonism', *Int. Rev. Soc. Hist.*, 76, 1971, 642–89.

7.1487 —— *Utopian Communism in France: Cabet and the Icarians, 1839–1851*, New York, 1974.

7.1488 **Kapp**, Y., *Eleanor Marx*, 1972 and 1976. Historically detailed, yet illuminating, biography (two volumes).

7.1489 **Lovell**, D. W., 'Early French socialism and politics: the case of Victor Considérant', *Hist. Pol. Thought*, 13, 1992, 257–79. Unusual because of the attention he paid to political questions, Considérant viewed the autonomy of politics as important, though ultimately he privileged the resolution of social questions, as did other French socialists, according to Lovell.

7.1490 **Mirfin**, D., 'Pareto and pluto-democracy', *Am. Pol. Sc. Rev.*, 62, 1968, 440–50.

7.1491 **Mühlestein**, H., 'Marx and the utopian Wilhelm Weitling', *Sc. Soc.*, 12, 1948, 113–29.

7.1492 **Piccone**, P., 'Labriola and the roots of eurocommunism', *Berkeley J. Sociol.*, 22, 1977–78, 3–43.

7.1493 **Riasanovsky**, N. V., *The Teaching of Charles Fourier*, Berkeley, Calif., 1969.

7.1494 **Rose**, R. B., 'Louis Blanc: the collapse of a hero', in E. Kamenka and F. B. Smith, ed., *Intellectuals and Revolution: Socialism*

and the Experience of 1848, 1979, 31–42. Explains his failure in 1848 as the product of his belief in universal consensus and the reconciliation of antagonistic classes.

7.1495 **Rozoux**, J, 'The reaction of Charles Fourier to the French Revolution', *French Historical Studies*, 1, 1958, 348–56.

7.1496 **Rüsen**, J., 'Jacob Burckhardt: political standpoint and historical insight on the border of post-modernism', *Hist. & Theory*, 24, 1985, 235–46.

7.1497 **Samples**, J., 'Kant, Töennies and the liberal idea of community in early German sociology', *Hist. Pol. Thought*, 8, 1987, 245–62. Interesting exploration of Töennie's concept of community, charting his influence upon sociological thought in Germany and comparing his ideas with Kant.

7.1498 **Sax**, B. C., 'State and culture in the thought of Jacob Burckhardt', *Annals of Scholarship*, 3, 1985, 1–35.

7.1500 **Sheehan**, J. J., *The Career of Lujo Brentano: A Study of Liberalism and Social Reform in Imperial Germany*, Chicago, Ill., 1966.

7.1501 **Sigurdson**, R. F., 'Jacob Burckhardt's liberal-conservatism', *Hist. Pol. Thought*, 13, 1992, 487–513. Bold attempt to reconstruct a Burckhardtian political philosophy, discerning in his liberal commitments, scepticism about nationality and hostility to industrial society, a putative liberal-conservatism.

7.1502 —— 'Jacob Burckhardt: the cultural historian as political thinker', *Rev. Pol.*, 52, 1990, 417–40.

7.1503 **Spitzer**, A. B., *The Revolutionary Theories of Louis Auguste Blanqui*, New York, 1957.

7.1504 **Stuurman**, S., 'Samuel Van Houten and Dutch liberalism, 1860–90', *J. Hist. Ideas*, 50, 1989, 135–52. Recreates the political thought and context of Van Houten with particular emphasis on the need to refashion sexual and class relations.

7.1505 **Sweet**, P. R., *Wilhelm von Humboldt: a biography*, 1978–80.

7.1506 **Taylor**, K., *The Political ideas of the Utopian Socialists*, 1982. Outlines the vision of Saint-Simon and his followers (Owen, Fourier, Cabet and Weitling), arguing that their concern about the alienating effects of modern life remains pertinent. Taylor stresses the components of their vision of harmony: association, community and co-operation.

7.1507 **Tonnesson**, K. D., 'The Babouvists: from utopia to practical socialism', *Past & Pres.*, 22, 1962, 60–76.

7.1508 **Tudor**, H., *Bernstein: The Preconditions of Socialism*, 1992.

7.1509 **Vernon**, R., 'Auguste Comte and the withering-away of the state', *J. Hist. Ideas*, 45, 1984, 549–66. Assesses his regionalist outlook in the early 1850s when he became explicitly critical of the nation-state.

7.1510 **Vogel**, U., 'Liberty is beautiful: Von Humboldt's gift to liberalism', *Hist. Pol. Thought*, 3, 1982, 77–101. Argues that his support for individual liberty proceeds neither from the Kantian postulate of natural right nor from utilitarian conceptions of happiness, but from an aesthetic commitment to the ideal of individuality.

7.1511 **Wittke**, C., 'Marx and Weitling', in M. R. Konvitz and A. E. Murphy, ed., *Essays in Political Theory presented to George H. Sabine*, New York, 1948, 179–93.

7.1512 —— *The Utopian Communist: A Biography of Wilhelm Weitling, Nineteenth-Century Reformer*, Baton Rouge, La., 1950.

(d)   NORTH AMERICA

General

7.1513 **Egbert**, D. D., and **Parsons**, S., ed., *Socialism in the United States*, Princeton, N.J., 1952.

7.1514 **Fine**, S., *Laissez-Faire and the General Welfare State: A Study in Conflict in American Thought 1869–1901*, Michigan, Ala., 1956.

7.1515 **Herreshoff**, D., *The Origins of American Marxism: From the Transcendentalists to De Leon*, New York, 1967. Charts the arrival of Marxist ideas in America at the end of the nineteenth century, the growth of labour radicalism and the dissemination of the ideas of De Leon. Accessible introduction to the topic.

7.1516 **Koch**, A., 'Aftermath of the American Enlightenment', *Sts. Voltaire*, 50, 1967, 735–63.

7.1517 **Meier**, A., *Negro Thought in America,*

1880–1915: Racial Ideologies in the Age of Booker T. Washington, Michigan, Ala., 1988. A study of the heritage of reconstruction and the central role of Washington in institutionalising the concepts of self-help and racial solidarity.

7.1518 **Watson**, D., 'The neo-Hegelian tradition in America', *J. Am. Sts.*, 14, 1980, 219–34. Compared with England, the academic impact of new-Hegelianism was short-lived, according to Watson, whilst its cultural and institutional influence was more profound on America than Britain between 1860 and 1914.

Calhoun

7.1519 **Baskin**, D., 'The pluralist vision of John C. Calhoun', *Polity*, 2, 1969, 49–65.

7.1520 **Capers**, G. M., *John C. Calhoun – Opportunist: A Reappraisal*, Gainesville, Fla., 1960. Generally sceptical discussion of his career and thought, though highlights the importance of some of his key ideas, such as his theory of government and the importance of his political and historical background.

7.1521 **Coit**, M. L., *John C. Calhoun: American Portrait*, Boston, Mass., 1950. Racy biography, though with some insight into his political ideas.

7.1522 **Drucker**, P., 'A key to American politics: Calhoun's pluralism', *Rev. Pol.*, 10, 1948, 412–26.

7.1523 **Putterman**, T. L., 'Calhoun's realism?', *Hist. Pol. Thought*, 12, 1991, 107–24. Reconstructs the 'realist' approach to politics which Calhoun developed, demonstrating its inability to account for the past or to alter the future.

7.1524 **Rice**, D. H., 'John C. Calhoun', *Hist. Pol. Thought*, 12, 1991, 317–28. Challenges attempts to place his thought in the traditions of conservatism or liberalism. Insofar as he was a liberal, his hesitation over minority rights points to a central paradox within liberalism.

7.1525 **Steinberger**, P. J., 'Calhoun's concept of the public interest: a clarification', *Polity*, 13, 1981, 410–24.

Thoreau

7.1526 **Borst**, R. R., *Henry David Thoreau: A*

Descriptive Bibliography, Pittsburgh, Penn., 1982.

7.1527 **Broderick**, J. C., 'Thoreau's proposals for legislation', *American Quarterly*, 7, 1955, 285–90.

7.1528 **Drinnon**, R., 'Thoreau's politics of the upright man', *Anarchy*, 26, 1963, 117–28.

7.1529 **Ford**, N. A., 'Henry David Thoreau, absolutionist', *New England Quarterly*, 19, 1946, 359–71. Argues that if he was never a member of an organised antislavery movement, he was in effect an absolutionist.

7.1530 **Gayet**, C., *The Intellectual Development of Henry David Thoreau*, Uppsala, 1981. Disputes the view that Thoreau's social philosophy remained anchored in the transcendental idea of the regeneration of self, claiming that he did have a programme of social reform.

7.1531 **Glick**, W., ed., *The Recognition of Henry David Thoreau*, Ann Arbor, Mich., 1969.

7.1532 **Harding**, W., *A Thoreau Handbook*, New York, 1959. Schematic treatment of his life and work, though includes a chapter on his thought which compares him with Fourier and charts his conception of the division of labour.

7.1533 —— ed., *Henry David Thoreau, a Profile*, New York, 1971.

7.1534 **Howe**, D. W., *Henry David Thoreau on the Duty of Civil Disobedience*, 1991. A brief celebration of Thoreau's 1849 essay.

7.1535 **Krutch**, J. W., *Henry David Thoreau*, 1949. Chronological account of his political life and ideas, surpassed by later studies.

7.1536 **Meyer**, M., *Several More Lives to Live: Thoreau's Political Reputation in America*, Westport, Conn., 1977.

7.1537 **Morris**, T., 'Thoreau, America's gentle anarchist', *Religious Humanism*, 3, 1969, 62–5.

7.1538 **Nichols**, C. H., 'Thoreau on the citizen and his government', *Pylon*, 13, 1952, 19–24.

7.1539 **Rosenblum**, N. L., 'Thoreau's militant conscience', *Pol. Theory*, 9, 1981, 81–110.

7.1540 **Sanborn**, F. B., *Henry David Thoreau*, Ann Arbor, Mich., 1975.

7.1541 **Sayre**, R. F., *Thoreau*, Princeton, N.J., 1977.

7.1542 **Sherman**, P., *The Shores of America: Thoreau's Inward Exploration*, Urbana, Ill. 1972. Lengthy exposition of his thought, interweaving his political insight and philosophy of nature.

7.1543 **Stoller**, *After Walden: Thoreau's Changing Views on Economic Man*, Stanford, Calif., 1957.

Other thinkers

7.1544 **Barker**, C. A., *Henry George*, 1955.

7.1545 **Blau**, J. L., 'Taylor Lewis: true conservative', *J. Hist. Ideas*, 13, 1952, 218–33. Exploration of the political ideas o this leading American classicist.

7.1546 **Carlett**, W. S., 'The availability of Lincoln's political religion', *Pol. Theory*, 10, 1982, 520–40. Examines his development of the notion of political religion, a response to the problem of political participation.

7.1547 **Goetzmann**, *The American Hegelians: An Intellectual Episode in the History of Western America*, New York, 1973.

7.1548 **Martin**, J. J., *Men Against the State: The Expositors of Individualist Anarchism in America, 1827–1908*, De Kalb, Ill., 1953.

7.1549 **Sargent**, L. T., 'English and American utopias: similarities and differences', *J. Gen. Ed.*, 28, 1976, 16–22. Stimulating comparison of the differing projects pursued under the utopian banner in these countries, illustrating a general shift towards more political concerns.

7.1550 **Schwartzman**, J., 'Henry George and George Bernard Shaw: comparison and contrast: the two nineteenth-century intellectual leaders stood for ethical democracy vs. socialist statism', *Am. J. Econ. Soc.*, 49, 1990, 113–27. Despite obvious affinities, Schwartzman suggests somewhat simplistically that these thinkers' socialism took opposing paths: George was attracted to cooperative liberalism whilst Shaw came to believe in socialist dictatorship.

8

TWENTIETH
CENTURY

(a) GENERAL

8.1 **Barry**, N. P., *An Introduction to Modern Political Theory*, 1988. Introduces the main concepts and ideas of key contemporary theorists.

8.2 **Berlin**, I., 'Political ideas in the twentieth century', *Foreign Affairs*, 28, 1950, 351–85.

8.3 **Bernstein**, R. J., *The Restructuring of Social and Political Theory*, New York, 1976. Impressive survey of a broad range of literature on the social sciences, involving the exposition of the ideas of a number of important thinkers to provide a larger picture of competing intellectual traditions. Argues that a shift in social theory is taking place in the wake of the discoveries of critical theory.

8.4 **Brecht**, A., *Political Theory: The Foundations of Twentieth-Century Political Thought*, Princeton, N.J., 1959. Ambitious and lengthy attempt to ground political theory in a series of systematic, scientific postulates. Reads somewhat dryly.

8.5 **Bronner**, S. E., *Moments of Decision. Political History and the Crises of Radicalism*, 1992. Documents the successes and failures of radical thought in the twentieth century, interpreting political events through these paradigms.

8.6 **Kymlicka**, W., *Contemporary Political Philosophy, An Introduction*, 1990. A critical and perceptive introduction to the rapidly growing literature on theories of justice and community, comparing the work of the most influential contemporary

Anglo-American theorists. Each chapter covers a major school of thought: utilitarianism, liberal egalitarianism, libertarianism, Marxism, communitarianism, and Leninism.

8.7 **Zoll**, R. A., *Twentieth Century Political Philosophy*, Englewood Cliffs, N.J., 1974. Brief, idiosyncratic survey of some of the central themes and traditions in this century, including Freudianism, fascism, communism, popular democracy, conservatism, existentialism and 'futurism'.

(b) BRITISH ISLES

General

8.8 **Barker**, R., *Political Ideas in Modern Britain*, 1978. Comprehensive and suggestive review of political thought since the 1880s, ranging from Hobhouse, Mallock and the Webbs through G. D. H. Cole and H. Laski to E. P. Thompson, R. Williams and M. Oakeshott.

8.9 **Bellamy** C. A., and **Whitebrook**, M. F., 'Reform or reformation: the state and the theory of the state in Britain', *Can. J. Pol. Sc.*, 14, 1981, 725–43.

8.10 **Bernstein**, G. L., *Liberalism and Liberal Politics in Edwardian England*, 1986. Stresses the importance of understanding the dynamic relationship between national and local elements of the Liberal party and provides a broad interpretation of liberal ideology.

8.11   **Bond**, J. C., 'The critical reception of English neo-Hegelianism in Britain and America, 1914–1960', *Aust. J. Pol. & Hist.*, 26, 1980, 228–41. Informative survey of the changing interpretations of the work of the English idealist philosophers in Britain and America. Demonstrates that neo-Hegelianism has been appropriated as the source of a number of competing political perspectives.

8.12   **Catlin**, G. E. G., 'Contemporary British political thought', *Am. Pol. Sc. Rev.*, 46, 1952, 641–59.

8.13   **Clarke**, P., *Liberals and Social Democrats*, 1978. Examines the relationship between socialism and liberalism at the turn of the century in this study of intellectuals who were liberals and social democrats (Wallas, Hobhouse, Hobson and Hammond). An engaging, historically informed discussion, throwing light upon the emergence of Fabianism, new liberalism and the downturn of liberal fortunes after 1914.

8.14   **Inglis**, F., *Radical Earnestness: English Social Theory, 1880–1980*, 1982.

8.15   **Searle**, G. R., *The Quest for National Efficiency: A Study in British Politics and Political Thought, 1899–1914*, 1971. Subtle, historically sensitive consideration of the significance of this theme within political discourse and its effect upon policy formation and party ideology.

8.16   **Semmel**, B., *Imperialism and Social Reform: English Social–Imperial Thought, 1895–1914*, 1960.

Berlin

8.17   **Cohen**, M., 'Berlin and the liberal tradition', *Phil. Q.*, 10, 1960, 216–27. Sceptical discussion of his interpretation of negative liberty, focusing on a confusion over his distinction between negative and positive liberty and that between individual liberty and public authority.

8.18   **Galipeau**, C. J., *Isaiah Berlin's Liberalism*, 1994. Presents his principal political ideas through an assessment of the diverse range of his work (including music criticism and broadcasting), emphasising the role of moral pluralism and his understanding of Western society in the formation of his liberalism.

8.19   **Gray**, J., 'On negative and positive liberty', in Z. A. Pelczynski and J. Gray, ed., *Conceptions of Liberty in Political Philosophy*, 1984, 321–48. Consideration of the development of Berlin's definition and advocacy of negative liberty, concluding that some forms of positive libertarianism do not rely upon rationalism and are, therefore, permissible.

8.20   **Kocis**, R. A., 'Reason, development and the conflicts of human ends: Sir Isaiah Berlin's vision of politics', *Am. Pol. Sc. Rev.*, 74, 1980, 38–52.

8.21   **Loenen**, J. H. M. M., 'The concept of freedom in Berlin and others: an attempt at classification', *Journal of Value Inquiry*, 10, 1976, 279–85.

8.22   **MacCallum**, G. C., 'Berlin on the compatibility of values, ideals, and "ends" ', *Ethics*, 77, 1966–67, 139–45. Spirited defence of the idea that 'all the positive values in which men have believed must, in the end, be compatible', against Berlin's critique of this position.

8.23   **MacFarlane**, L. J., 'On two concepts of liberty', *Pol. Sts.*, 14, 1966, 77–81. Thoughtful review of *Two Concepts of Liberty*, highlighting the absence of any discussion of liberty in the context of group membership and the weaknesses of the presentation of positive liberty in this text.

8.24   **Parekh**, B., 'Isaiah Berlin', in *Contemporary Political Thinkers*, 1982, 22–47.

8.25   —— 'The political thought of Sir Isaiah Berlin', *Brit. J. Pol. Sc.*, 12, 1982, 201–26.

8.26   **Polanowska-Sygulska**, B., 'One voice more on Berlin's doctrine of liberty', *Pol. Sts.*, 37, 1989, 123–7. Reviews the debate surrounding his views of liberty and reiterates his critique of positive conceptions of freedom.

8.27   **Reed**, G. F., 'Berlin and the division of liberty', *Pol. Theory*, 8, 1980, 365–80. Rejecting Berlin's emphasis on two irreconcilable concepts of liberty, the author proposes that these are complementary aspects of a coherent whole.

8.28   **Taylor**, C., 'What's wrong with negative liberty', in A. Ryan, ed., *The Idea of Freedom*, 1979, 175–93. Subtle examination of the theoretical underpinnings of the negative and positive views of freedom, especially the importance of conceptions of and discrimination between purposes which Berlin, among others, neglects.

8.29 **Wollheim**, R., 'John Stuart Mill and Isaiah Berlin. The ends of life and the preliminaries of morality', in A. Ryan, ed., *The Idea of Freedom*, 1979, 253–69. A critique of Berlin's reading of Mill which suggests that utility remained at the heart of the latter's moral principles.

Connolly

8.30 **Allen**, K., *The Politics of James Connolly*, 1980. Writing from a revolutionary Marxist perspective, Allen situates Connolly within the framework of the Second International and shows how its theoretical inadequacies account for his ambiguities and failings.

8.31 **Bew**, P., **Gibbon**, P., and **Patterson**, H., 'Marxism and Ireland', in *The State in Northern Ireland, 1921–72: Political Forces and Social Classes*, 1979, 1–43. Influential 'revisionist' account of Marxism's record of analysing Ireland, focusing especially on weaknesses in Connolly's comprehension of the Ulster question. Breaking from his analysis, the authors claim that 'the great unfulfilled need of Irish Marxist politics is a scientific analysis of Irish society'.

8.32 **Edwards**, O. D., *The Mind of an Activist – James Connolly*, 1971.

8.33 **Edwards**, R. D., *James Connolly*, Dublin, 1981.

8.34 **Greaves**, C. D., 'Connolly and Easter week: a rejoinder to John Newsinger', *Sc. & Soc.*, 48, 1984, 220–3. Brief and sharp retort to Newsinger (Science and Society, 47, 1983) arguing for the affinity between Connolly's socialism and nationalism.

8.35 —— *The Life and Times of James Connolly*, 1961. A dated presentation of him as an innovative Marxist whose ideas prefigured the 'stages theory' of the later Communist International.

8.36 **Howell**, D., 'James Connolly', in *A Lost Left: Three Studies in Socialism and Nationalism*, 1986, 17–154. Careful reconstruction of his historical context, avoiding approaches which present him either as 'the subject of an historical idealisation' or as the perpetrator of

'socialist apostasy'; Connolly emerges as a more complex historical and theoretical figure, frequently forced to compromise his political beliefs.

8.37 **Levenson**, S., *James Connolly*, 1973.

8.38 **Morgan**, A., *James Connolly: A Political Biography*, 1988. Presents his nationalism and socialism as distinct and contradictory philosophies, concluding that his nationalist sympathies predominated by 1916 when he joined the Easter Rising.

8.39 **Newsinger**, J., 'Connolly and his biographers', *Irish Political Studies*, 5, 1990, 1–9. Informative overview of the principal interpretations of his life and thought.

8.40 —— 'James Connolly and the Easter Rising', *Sc. & Soc.*, 47, 1983, 152–77. Bold argument that by participating in this insurrection Connolly 'subordinated his socialist politics to the exigencies of a Republican putsch'.

8.41 **Ransom**, B., *Connolly's Marxism*, 1980.

8.42 **Ryan**, D., *James Connolly: Socialist and Nationalist*, Dublin, 1948.

Hobson

8.43 **Allett**, J., *New Liberalism: The Political Economy of J. A. Hobson*, Toronto, 1982. Account of the ideas of a principal advocate in Britain at the beginning of the twentieth century of greater economic planning and state provision of social welfare: Hobson anticipated the liberal arguments of Keynes for a mixed economy.

8.44 **Brailsford**, H. N., *The Life Work of J. A. Hobson*, 1948.

8.45 **Freeden**, M., 'J. A. Hobson as a new liberal theorist: some aspects of his social thought until 1914', *J. Hist. Ideas*, 43, 1973, 421–43. Reconstructs his social liberalism, especially his attempt to construct 'a comprehensive science of human welfare'. Both emerged from his combination of Hegelian idealism and socio-biological principles.

8.46 —— ed., *Reappraising J. A. Hobson: Humanism and Welfare*, 1990.

8.47 **Mitchell**, H., 'Hobson revisited', *J. Hist. Ideas*, 26, 1965, 397–416. Explores the political background to his analysis of imperialism, focusing especially on the non-economic aspects of his thesis.

8.48 **Townshend**, J., *J. A. Hobson*, 1991.

Demonstrates how his ideas foreshadowed many of the theories which have shaped interpretations of state and society in the twentieth century.

Oakeshott

8.49 **Annan**, N., 'Revulsion to the right', *Pol. Q.*, 26, 1955, 211–9.

8.50 **Archer**, J. R., 'Oakeshott on politics', *J. Pol.*, 41, 1979, 150–68. Discusses his political thought through the concepts of experience, rationalism, tradition and human conduct, suggesting that his political allegiances defy conventional categorisation.

8.51 **Ashford**, N., 'Michael Oakeshott and the conservative disposition', *Intercollegiate Review*, 25, 1990, 39–50.

8.52 **Asthana**, M., 'Michael Oakeshott against scientism in politics', *Modern Review* (Calcutta), 131, 1972, 409–14.

8.53 **Auspitz**, J. L., et al., 'A symposium on Michael Oakeshott', *Pol. Theory*, 4, 1976, 261–352. Includes contributions by Auspitz (the most enthusiastic and sympathetic), Pitkin, Wolin and Spitz; Oakeshott's reposte is printed.

8.54 —— 'Bibliographical note', *Pol. Theory*, 4, 1976, 295–300. A comprehensive bibliography of Oakeshott's work, supplemented by selected secondary materials since 1965.

8.55 —— 'Michael Oakeshott: 1901–1990', *Am. Scholar*, 60, 1990–91, 351–70.

8.56 **Barber**, B. R., 'Conserving politics: Michael Oakeshott and political theory', *Govt. & Oppos.*, 11, 1976, 446–63. A clear, chronological reconstruction of his thought which focuses upon his ambivalence towards ends, reason and persuasion in political life.

8.57 **Baumgarth**, W. P., 'Habit and discovery: the political philosophy of Michael Oakeshott', *Pol. Sc. Re-r*, 7, 1977, 273–323. Comprehensive and sympathetic, though not uncritical, survey of his ideas.

8.58 **Berki**, R. N., 'Oakeshott's conception of civil association: notes for a critical analysis', *Pol. Sts.*, 29, 1981, 570–85. A clear assessment of this central theme, with particular emphasis upon the quality of life and the state.

8.59 **Boucher**, D., 'Overlap and autonomy: the different worlds of Collingwood and Oakeshott', *Storia*, 4, 1989, 69–89.

8.60 —— 'Politics in a different mode: an appreciation of Michael Oakeshott – 1901–1990', *Hist. Pol. Thought*, 12, 1991, 717–28. A sympathetic appraisal, highlighting his choice of history as the most appropriate idiom for theorising human conduct.

8.61 —— 'The creation of the past: British idealism and Michael Oakeshott's philosophy of history', *Hist. & Theory*, 23, 1984, 193–214. Reconstructs his theory of the historical mode of understanding as an example of the philosophy of history developed by the British idealists.

8.62 **Coats**, W. J., 'Michael Oakeshott as liberal theorist', *Can. J. Pol. Sc.*, 18, 1985, 773–87. Views Oakeshott, somewhat surprisingly, as 'one of the pre-eminent political theorists of modern European individualism'.

8.63 —— 'Some correspondences between Oakeshott's "civil association" and the republican tradition', *Pol. Sc. Re-r*, 21, 1992, 99–115. Attempts to establish affinities between Oakeshott's account of the civil obligations of individuals and the republican tradition, concluding unconvincingly that he can be read as a classical liberal.

8.64 **Covell**, C., 'Practices and persons: Strawson and Oakeshott', *Cambridge Rev.*, 100, 1978, 167–72.

8.65 **Cranston**, M., 'Michael Oakeshott's politics', *Encounter*, 28, 1967, 82–6. A sympathetic review of Greenleaf's account of Oakeshott, endorsing the latter's separation of philosophy and politics.

8.66 —— 'Remembrances of Michael Oakeshott', *Pol. Theory*, 19, 1991, 323–6.

8.67 **Crick**, B., 'The ambiguity of Michael Oakeshott', *Cambridge Rev.*, 112, 1991, 120–4.

8.68 —— 'The world of Michael Oakeshott', *Encounter*, 20, 1963, 65–74. Assessment of Oakeshott's post-war ideas, teasing out ambiguities in his rejection of rationalism and dominant political ideas.

8.69 **Dowling**, R. E., 'Oakeshott's theory of reason, tradition and conservatism', *Aust. J. Pol. & Hist.*, 5, 1959, 51–63. Challenges the Oakeshottian dichotomy between rational action and tradition as analytically incoherent and inappropriate for conservatives.

8.70 **Eccleshall**, R. R., 'Michael Oakeshott and sceptical conservatism', in L. Tivey and A. Wright, ed., *Political Thought Since 1945: Philosophy, Science, Ideology*, 1992, 173–95. Outline of the central themes in his political thought, concluding with an assessment of his position in relation to contemporary schools of thought.

8.71 **Falck**, C., 'Romanticism in politics', *New Left Rev.*, 18, 1963, 60–72. Unusually sympathetic commentary from the left, which recognises the significance of Oakeshott's project.

8.72 **Feaver**, G., 'Michael Oakeshott and political education', *Studies in Comparative Communism*, 2, 1969, 156–75.

8.73 —— 'The enduring and elusive legacy of Michael Oakeshott', *Sts. Pol. Thought*, 1, 1992, 95–122. Largely biographical review of his career, which compares his influence on British conservatism with that of Green on British liberalism at the beginning of the century.

8.74 **Franco**, P., 'Michael Oakeshott as liberal theorist', *Pol. Theory*, 18, 1990, 411–36. Bold reading of him as a member of the liberal tradition. Not surprisingly, Franco finds that he does not fit into the contemporary schools of liberal thought.

8.75 —— *The Political Philosophy of Michael Oakeshott*, 1990. Detailed and sympathetic to its subject, the author's attempt to portray Oakeshott as a coherent liberal is unconvincing.

8.76 **Friedman**, R. B., 'Oakeshott on the authority of law', *Ratio Juris*, 2, 1989, 27–40. Outlines his conception of authority which is incompatible with rational choice thinking and abstract philosophical approaches to the rule of law.

8.77 **Fuller**, T., 'Authority and the individual in civil association: Oakeshott, Flathman, Yves Simon', in J. R. Pennock and J. W. Chapman, ed., *Authority Revisited*, 1987, 131–51. Compares the positive and affirming conceptions of authority in the work of Oakeshott and Simon with Flathman's scepticism about authority, suggesting that the former developed a more profound and pure theory of authority.

8.78 —— 'The work of Michael Oakeshott', *Pol. Theory*, 19, 1991, 326–33.

8.79 **Grant**, R. A. D., 'Conservative thinkers: Michael Oakeshott: the poet of practice', *Salisbury Rev.*, 1, 1983, 12–16.

8.80 —— 'Inside the hedge: Oakeshott's early life and work', *Cambridge Rev.*, 112, 1991, 166–9.

8.81 —— 'Michael Oakeshott', in R. Scruton, ed., *Conservative Thinkers: Essays from the Salisbury Review*, 1988, 275–94. Describing Oakeshott as the 'greatest living political philosopher', Grant paints a largely sympathetic picture of his thought, though he provides important criticisms of the latter's understanding of tradition and practice.

8.82 —— *Oakeshott*, 1990. Brief, accessible introduction, which concentrates on his more abstract foundations and remains firmly within an Oakeshottian framework.

8.83 **Gray**, J., 'Oakeshott as a liberal', *Salisbury Rev.*, 10, 1991, 22–5. Argues that his liberalism derives from the characterisation of a civil association.

8.84 **Greenleaf**, W. H., *Oakeshott's Philosophical Politics*, 1966. Lucid introduction to the idealist foundations of Oakeshott's thought.

8.85 **Hall**, D., and **Modood**, T., 'A reply to Liddington', *Pol. Sts.*, 30, 1982, 184–9. Reiterate their thesis, adding that Oakeshott (and Liddington) fail to separate philosophy and practice.

8.86 —— 'Oakeshott and the impossibility of philosophical politics', *Pol. Sts.*, 30, 1982, 157–76. Rehearses his belief in the incompatibility between practical life and philosophical thinking, only to challenge such a view, arguing for the practical dimension of philosophy.

8.87 **Hart**, J., 'Two paths home: Kendall and Oakeshott', *Triumph*, 2, 1987, 28–34.

8.88 **Himmelfarb**, G., 'The conservative imagination: Michael Oakeshott', *Am. Scholar*, 44, 1975, 405–20. Rehearses the key themes of *On Human Conduct*, concluding that he is out of tune with the spirit of the age and is ultimately a moral relativist.

8.89 **Holliday**, I., 'On Michael Oakeshott', *Govt. & Oppos.*, 27, 1992, 131–47.

8.90 **King**, P., and **Parekh**, B., ed., *Politics and Experience; Essays Presented to Michael Oakeshott on the Occasion of his Retirement*, 1968. Includes essays on his theory of history (Walsh, Dray), interpretation of Hobbes (Goldsmith), political theory (Greenleaf, Wolin, Parekh), and a number of related problems (Pocock on the nature of tradition, Minogue on revolution,

Krook on rationalism).

8.91 **Kolnai**, A., 'Rationalism in politics', *Phil.*, 40, 1965, 68–71.

8.92 **Liddington**, J., 'Hall and Modood on Oakeshott', *Pol. Sts.*, 30, 1982, 177–83. Emphasises the changing basis of Oakeshott's thought and opposes the reading of *Experience and its Modes* offered by these critics.

8.93 —— 'Oakeshott: freedom in a modern European state', in Z. A. Pelczynski and J. Gray, ed., *Conceptions of Liberty in Political Philosophy*, 1984, 289–320. Explains his conception of liberty through a clear exposition of his notions of civil and enterprise associations.

8.94 **Looker**, R. J., 'Is there a conflict between reason and tradition?', *Inquiry*, 8, 1965, 301–8.

8.95 **MacCormick**, N., 'Spontaneous order and the rule of law: some problems', *Ratio Juris*, 2, 1989, 41–54. Compares Oakeshott's and Hayek's theories of law, concluding that both wrongly infer conclusions from their ideas which are inimical to the welfare state.

8.96 **Manning**, D. J., 'Professor Michael Oakeshott's contribution to political thought', *Clare Market Review*, 1965, 27–34.

8.97 **Mapel**, D. R., 'Civil association and the idea of contingency', *Pol. Theory*, 18, 1990, 392–410. Connects Oakeshott's emphasis on contingency with his anti-foundational conception of authority.

8.98 **Mayer**, J. L., 'Managers, Machiavelli, and Oakeshott, M. – caveat', *Publius*, 6, 1976, 101–5.

8.99 **Minogue**, K., 'Michael Oakeshott: the boundless sea of politics', in A. de Crespigny and K. Minogue, ed., *Contemporary Political Philosophers*, 1976, 120–46. A sympathetic outline of his opposition to rationalism, belief in discrete modes of experience and conception of civil association.

8.100 **Modood**, T., 'Oakeshott's conceptions of philosophy', *Hist. Pol. Thought*, 1, 1980, 315–22. Discusses the relationship between his general philosophical perspective and theory of politics.

8.101 **Monro**, D. H., 'Godwin, Oakeshott, and Mrs Bloomer', *J. Hist. Ideas*, 35, 1974, 611–24. Original assessment of the relationship between rationalism and institutions through a consideration of the opposing views of Oakeshott and Godwin Developing Oakeshott's example of the inadequacy of rationalism - the case of Victorian dress for women cyclists – Monr skilfully challenges his belief that the rational reformer must obey the dictates o social taste and convention.

8.102 **Norman**, J., ed., *The Achievements of Michael Oakeshott*, 1993. A collection of retrospective essays on Oakeshott, including Minogue on his principal political ideas, Fuller on his conception of civil life, and O'Sullivan on his place in the traditions of Western political thought.

8.103 **Parekh**, B., 'Michael Oakeshott', in B. Parekh, ed., *Contemporary Political Thinkers*, 1982, 96–123. Sympathetic though dense exposition of his ideas.

8.104 —— 'The political philosophy of Michael Oakeshott', *Brit. J. Pol. Sc.*, 9, 1979, 481–506. Outlines his philosophical predilections and understanding of political philosophy.

8.105 **Peardon**, T. P., 'Two currents in contemporary English political theory', *Am. Pol. Sc. Rev.*, 49, 1955, 487–95. Explains why Oakeshott's ideas articulate the spirt of his age, particularly his scepticism about social optimism and planning.

8.106 **Pitkin**, H. F., 'Inhuman conduct and unpolitical theory: Michael Oakeshott's *On Human Conduct*', *Pol. Theory*, 4, 1976 301–20.

8.107 —— 'The roots of conservatism: Michael Oakeshott and the denial of politics', *Dissent*, 20, 1973, 496–525. Outlines his rejection of rationalism in politics, focusing upon his marginalisation of genuine political life. Clearly argued and stimulating.

8.108 **Postan**, M. M., 'Revulsion from thought', *Cambridge J.*, 1, 1947–48, 395–408. A socialist reply to Oakeshott's rejection of rationalism.

8.109 **Raphael**, D. D., 'Professor Oakeshott's *Rationalism in Politics*', *Pol. Sts.*, 12, 202–13. Sharp review of this text, challenging a number of his categories and his belief that philosophy cannot possess a practical aim.

8.110 **Rathore**, L. S., and **Bhati**, P. S., 'Political ideas of Michael Oakeshott', *Indian Journal of Political Studies*, 3–4, 1980, 254–64.

8.111 **Rayner**, J., 'The legend of Oakeshott's

conservatism: sceptical philosophy and limited politics', *Can. J. Pol. Sc.*, 18, 1985, 313–38. Aligns Oakeshott's thought with Hume's speculative moderation rather than Burke's rejection of general beliefs, concluding that his ideas constitute a critique of modern conservatism.

8.112 **Rees**, J. C., 'Professor Oakeshott on political education', *Mind*, 62, 1953, 68–74.

8.113 **Riley**, P., 'Michael Oakeshott, political philosopher', *Cambridge Rev.*, 112, 1991, 110–3.

8.114 **Sanderson**, J., 'Professor Oakeshott on history', *Aust. J. Phil.*, 44, 1966, 210–23. Reconstructs his idealist philosophy of history.

8.115 **Singh**, R., *Reason, Revolution and Political Theory; Notes on Oakeshott's Rationalism in Politics*, New Delhi, 1967.

8.116 **Spitz**, D., 'A rationalist "malgré lui": the perplexities of being Michael Oakeshott', *Pol. Theory*, 4, 1976, 335–52.

8.117 **Thompson**, M. P., 'Michael Oakeshott: notes on "political thought" and "political theory" in the history of political thought 1966–1969', *Politisches Denken*, 1, 1992, 247–50.

8.118 **Varma**, V. P., 'Michael Oakeshott as a political philosopher', *Indian Journal of Political Science*, 36, 1975, 241–58.

8.119 **Watkins**, J. W. N., 'Political tradition and political theory: an examination of Professor Oakeshott's political philosophy', *Phil. Q.*, 2, 1952, 323–37. Close summary of his views, celebrating his understanding of partial knowledge and ability, displaying reservations, however, about his hostility to ideological politics.

8.120 **Williams**, H., *Concepts of Ideology*, New York, 1988. Compares the concepts of ideology advanced by Marx, Mannheim and Oakeshott, with particular reference to the light their ideas shed upon the rise of fascism in the 1930s.

8.121 **Williams**, K., 'The dilemmas of Michael Oakeshott: Oakeshott's treatment of equality of opportunity in education and his political philosophy', *Journal of the Philosophy of Education*, 23, 1989, 223–40. Despite his conservatism, Oakeshott's view of education is not elitist, according to Williams. His notion of civil life, however, disqualifies the redistribution of resources necessary to realise genuine equality of opportunity.

8.122 **Wood**, N., 'A guide to the classics: the scepticism of Professor Oakeshott', *J. Pol.*, 21, 1959, 647–62. An early assessment of Oakeshott, emphasising his sceptical conception of philosophy and pessimistic account of human nature.

Shaw

8.123 **Bevir**, M., 'The Marxism of George Bernard Shaw, 1883–1889', *Hist. Pol. Thought*, 13, 1992, 299–318. Traces the influence of Marxism upon Shaw in the 1880s, even when he turned to 'marginalist' economic theory; in this sense, Shaw needs to be distinguished from the other Fabians.

8.124 **Dunn**, D., 'A good Fabian fallen among the Stalinists', *Survey*, 28, 1984, 15–37. Explains Shaw's shift from Fabianism to Stalinism as the product of his disillusionment with the British political process and intellectualisation of Soviet purges and collectivisation.

8.125 **Griffith**, G., 'George Bernard Shaw's argument for equality of income', *Hist. Pol. Thought*, 6, 1985, 551–74. Whilst Shaw may not have been an original theorist, his enthusiasm for the issue of equality of income illustrates the open dialogue he attempted to incorporate within socialist discourse about thought and experience.

8.126 —— *Socialism and Superior Brains: The Political Thought of George Bernard Shaw*, 1992. A masterly and comprehensive survey of his neglected political theory which interprets his admiration for some aspects of Mussolini, Stalin and Hitler's programmes as based on little understanding of their real actions.

8.127 **Hubenka.**, L. J., ed., *Bernard Shaw and Practical Politics: Twentieth-Century Views on Politics and Economics*, 1976.

8.128 **Hummert**, P., *Bernard Shaw's Marxian Romance*, 1973. Problematic attempt to read him as a Marxist.

8.129 **Schwartzman**, J., 'Henry George and George Bernard Shaw: comparison and contrast: the two nineteenth-century intellectual leaders stood for ethical democracy vs. socialist statism', *Am. J. Econ. & Soc.*, 49, 1990, 113–27. Despite their obvious affinities Schwartzman suggests that their socialism developed in opposing directions: George was attracted to co-operative liberalism whilst Shaw came to believe in socialist dictatorship.

Other thinkers

8.130 **Atkinson**, C., and **Hughes**, J., 'Russell's critique of socialist theory and practice', in K. Coates, ed., *Essays on Socialist Humanism in Honour of the Centenary of Bertrand Russell 1872–1970*, 1972, 13–31. Clear introduction to these ideas, stressing their continued relevance.

8.131 **Barber**, B. R., 'Solipsistic politics: Russell's empiricist liberalism', *Pol. Sts.*, 23, 1975, 12–28. A bold reconstruction of his political thought which locates his liberal principles within his empiricist philosophy.

8.132 **Bernstein**, G. L., 'The limitations of the new liberalism: the politics and political thought of John Clifford', *Albion*, 16, 1984, 21–39. Assesses the politics and ideas of Clifford, Baptist minister and religious liberal, and explains the attraction for him of the new liberalism. Ultimately, however, his political priorities changed little, which suggests that new liberalism had less impact upon working-class politics than is often imagined.

8.133 **Boucher**, D., *The Social and Political Thought of R. G. Collingwood*, 1989. Uncritical exposition of his integration of philosophical, historical and political theorising in his advocacy of politics as a developed form of experience in which the liberal values of politics and civility are central.

8.134 —— 'The two Leviathans: R. G. Collingwood and Thomas Hobbes', *Pol. Sts.*, 35, 1987, 443–60. Examines the importance of Hobbes for Collingwood.

8.135 **Carpenter**, L. P., *G. D. H. Cole: An Intellectual Biography*, 1973.

8.136 **Cole**, M. I. P., 'The Webbs and social theory', *Brit. J. Soc.*, 12, 1961, 93–105.

8.137 **Cranston**, M., 'Keynes: his political ideas and their influence', in A. P. Thirlwall, ed., *Keynes and Laissez-Faire*, 1978, 101–15. Clarifies his status as a coherent liberal, despite accusations of pacifist and socialist predilections.

8.138 **Earle**, E. M., 'H. G. Wells, British patriot in search of a world state', in E. M. Earle, ed., *Nationalism and Internationalism:*

Essays Inscribed to Carlton J. H. Hayes, New York, 1950, 79–121. Finds in his fiction the vision of a new, peaceful international order in which national differences would be retained and encouraged.

8.139 **Gilbert**, M., *Churchill's Political Philosophy*, 1981. Important assessment of Churchillian thought by this leading authority.

8.140 **Greenleaf**, W. H., 'Laski and British socialism', *Hist. Pol. Thought*, 2, 1981, 573–91. Contrasts his libertarianism with the perspective of those advocating central planning within this tradition.

8.141 **Houseman**, G. L., *G. D. H. Cole*, Boston, Mass., 1979.

8.142 **Hyde**, W. J., 'The socialism of H. G. Wells in the early twentieth century', *J. Hist. Ideas*, 17, 1956, 217–34. Presents his socialism in the context of the ideology's rapid advance at this time, detailing his failed attempt to transform the Fabian society into a large, propagandist organisation.

8.143 **Kaye**, H. et al., *E. P. Thompson: Critical Perspectives*, 1990. Collection of articles looking at the central themes in the work of Thompson and his impact on contemporary thought; two commentators attempt to resuscitate his Marxism (Meiksens Wood, Soper).

8.144 **Newman**, M., *Harold Laski: A Political Biography*, 1993. Sympathetic and skilful reconstruction of his political thought.

8.145 **O'Sullivan**, N. K., 'Irrationalism in politics: a critique of R. G. Collingwood's *New Leviathan*', *Pol. Sts.*, 20, 141–51. Exposition and critique of his political theory, outlined in opposition to philosophical 'realism': Collingwood placed the struggle between rationalism and irrationalism at the heart of the history of political thought.

8.146 **Parsons**, W., 'Keynes and the politics of ideas', *Hist. Pol. Thought*, 4, 1983, 367–92. An examination of the neglected political dimensions of his thought, premised on the argument that political theorists have been remarkably reluctant to examine the impact of ideas in concrete social situations.

8.147 **Redner**, W. S., 'Conservatism, resistance and Lord Hugh Cecil', *Hist. Pol. Thought*, 9, 1988, 529–51. Outlines the theory of justifiable resistance to constituted authority as a central motif within the unsettled conservatism of the late-Edwardian period, and reveals how this was tempered by another conservative doctrine – a profound sense of civil and personal responsibility for one's behaviour.

8.148 **Rempel**, R. A., 'Conflicts and change in liberal theory and practice, 1890–1918: the case of Bertrand Russell', in P. J. Waller, ed., *Politics and Social Change in Modern Britain*, 1987, 117–39.

8.149 **Sarma**, G. N., *The Political Thought of Harold J. Laski*, 1968.

8.150 **Schneer**, J., *George Lansbury*, 1990. Draws on a range of previously unused sources to paint a sharp picture of his intellectual development.

8.151 **Terrill**, R., *R. H. Tawney and His Times: Socialism as Fellowship*, Cambridge, Mass., 1973.

8.152 **Weiler**, P., 'William Clarke: the making and unmaking of a Fabian socialist', *J. Brit. Sts.*, 14, 1974, 77–108.

8.153 **Winter**, J. M., 'R. H. Tawney's early political thought', *Past & Pres.*, 42, 1970, 71–97.

8.154 **Wright**, A., *G. D. H. Cole and Socialist Democracy*, 1979. Places Cole's thought in the context of the history of the labour movement and illustrates the influence upon him of pre-socialist radical ideals.

8.155 —— *R. H. Tawney*, 1987.

8.156 **Zylstra**, B., *From Pluralism to Collectivism: the Development of Harold Laski's Political Thought*, Assen, 1968.

(c) EUROPE

General

8.157 **Gombin**, R., *The Radical Tradition: A Study in Modern Revolutionary Thought*, 1978. Reconstructs a tradition of anti-orthodox Marxism, from anarchists to council communists, as the precursor of new left anti-authoritarianism. Ahistorical and misleading.

8.158 **Krieger**, L., *The German Idea of Freedom: History of a Political Tradition*, Boston,

Mass., 1957.

8.159 **Pierce**, R., *Contemporary French Political Thought*, 1968. Examines the thought of Mourier, Weil, Camus, Sartre, Aron and de Jouvenel, comparing their critique of French political theory in the post-war period.

8.160 **Simmons**, E. J., ed., *Continuity and Change in Russian and Soviet Thought*, Cambridge, Mass., 1955. Includes Karpovich on early twentieth-century liberalism, Hammond on Leninist authoritarianism, prior to 1917, Ulam on the theoretical constitution of Stalinism, and Berlin comparing Herzen and Bakunin on individual liberty.

Althusser

8.161 **Assiter**, A., 'Althusser and structuralism', *Brit. J. Soc.*, 35, 1984, 272–96.

8.162 **Benton**, T., *The Rise and Fall of Structural Marxism: Althusser and His Influence*, 1984. A dispassionate re-evaluation of Althusser's Marxism, placed in the context of French intellectual traditions, leading to an insightful account of the new directions in political theory and analysis made possible by his thought. An excellent guide to this thinker and the complex debates he inspired.

8.163 **Callinicos**, A., *Althusser's Marxism*, 1976. Generally critical assessment of his contribution to Marxism, but a useful introductory guide which connects his philosophical development and political ambiguity.

8.164 **Chiari**, J., *Structuralism: Claude Levi-Strauss, Michel Foucault, Louis Althusser in Twentieth-Century French Thought*, 1975.

8.165 **Clarke**, S., 'Althusserian Marxism', in S. Clarke et al., *One-Dimensional Marxism: Althusser and the Politics of Culture*, 1980, 7–102. A polemical critique of Althusser's interpretation of Marx's theory of society, particularly the notion of the mode of production. A companion to E. P. Thompson's rebuttal of this intellectual current.

8.166 **Collier**, A., *Scientific Realism and Socialist Thought*, 1988. Through a critique of Althusser's structuralist Marxism, Collier argues the case for a 'scientific socialism'.

8.167 **Connell**, R. W., 'A critique of the Althusserian approach to class', *Theory &*

Soc., 8, 1979, 303–46.

8.168 **Cranston**, M., 'The ideology of Althusser', *Problems of Communism*, 22, 1973, 53–60.

8.169 **Dowling**, W., *Jameson, Althusser, Marx: An Introduction to the Political Unconscious*, New York, 1984.

8.170 **Elliott**, G., *Althusser: The Detour of Theory*, 1988. Detailed account of his place in contemporary Marxist thought and a detached assessment of his political theory.

8.171 **Fraser**, T., 'Louis Althusser on science, Marxism and politics', *Sc. & Soc.*, 40, 1976–77, 438–64.

8.172 **Geras**, N., 'Althusser's Marxism: an account and assessment', *New Left Rev.*, 71, 1972, 57–86. Clear exposition of his principal ideas, followed by a critical assessment of his epistemological and political representation of Marxist theory.

8.173 **Gerratana**, V., 'Althusser and Stalinism', *New Left Rev.*, 101–2, 1977, 111–21. Charts Althusser's attempts to theorise Stalinism, suggesting that his belief that the latter constituted an aberration within Marxism remains inadequate.

8.174 **Glucksmann**, A., 'A ventriloquist structuralism', *New Left Rev.*, 72, 1972, 68–92. Hostile reading of Althusser's work, which claims to locate a number of contradictions within this corpus, particularly concerning his concept of structural causality.

8.175 **Goldstick**, D., 'Reading Althusser', *Revolutionary World*, 23–25, 1977, 110–32.

8.176 **Hirst**, P. Q., 'Althusser and the theory of ideology', *Economy and Society*, 5, 1976, 385–412.

8.177 **Hook**, S., 'For Louis Althusser', *Encounter*, 5, October 1973, 86–92.

8.178 **James**, S., 'Louis Althusser', in Q. Skinner, ed., *The Return of Grand Theory in the Human Sciences*, 1985, 141–57. Explores and explains his influence upon European Marxism.

8.179 **Kelly**, M., 'Louis Althusser and Marxist theory', *Journal of European Studies*, 7, 1977, 189–203.

8.180 **Kimmel**, B., 'Althusser and Habermas', *Human Factors*, 13, 1975, 90–106.

8.181 **Kolakowski**, L., 'Althusser's Marx', *Socialist Register*, 1971, 111–28. Unremittingly hostile review of his interpretation of Marx, stressing his deployment of 'confusing' Marxist categories and historical ignorance.

8.182 **Levine**, A., 'Althusser's Marxism', *Economy and Society*, 10, 1981, 243–83. A clear summary of his ideas, concluding that they find their contemporary expression in debates around the philosophy of science.

8.183 **Lewis**, J., 'The Althusser case – parts 1 and 2', *Marxism Today*, 16, 1972, 23–8 and 43–8. A sympathetic and influential (on the British left) response to Althusser.

8.184 **O'Donnell**, P., 'Lucien Seve, Althusser and the contradictions of the PCF', *Critique*, 15, 1981, 7–29.

8.185 **O'Hagan**, T., 'Althusser: how to be a Marxist in philosophy', in G. H. R. Parkinson, ed., *Marx and Marxisms*, 1982, 243–64. Rehearses Althusser's claim to combine philosophical objectivity with a political commitment to class struggle.

8.186 **Parker**, A., 'Futures for Marxism: an appreciation of Althusser', *Diacritics*, 15, 1985, 57–72. Clear presentation of the fundamental divergence between Marxism and deconstruction through a consideration of the Marxist elements within Althusser's repertoire.

8.187 **Poster**, M., 'Althusser on history without man', *Pol. Theory*, 2, 1974, 393–409. Examines the implications of Althusserian theory for comprehending historical processes, and places these ideas in the context of debates within the French Communist Party in the 1960s.

8.188 **Rancière**, J., 'On the theory of ideology: the politics of Althusser', *Rad. Phil.*, 7, 1974, 2–10. Unsympathetic exposition of his conception of ideology.

8.189 **Smith**, S. B., *Reading Althusser: An Essay on Structural Marxism*, 1984. A clear exposition of his key ideas, arguing that he legitimated the claims of intellectuals to speak on behalf of the masses.

8.190 **Thompson**, E. P., 'The poverty of theory', in *The Poverty of Theory and Other Essays*, 1978, 1–210. Brilliantly written critique of Althusser, which attempts to defend a traditional historical methodology whilst pouring scorn upon his theoretical claims.

8.191 **Veltmeyer**, H., 'Towards an assessment of the structuralist interrogation of Marx: Claude Levi-Strauss and Louis Althusser', *Sc. & Soc.*, 38, 1974, 385–421. Examines the compatibility and tensions between Marxism and structuralism, exploring Althusser's distinctions between thought and reality and science and ideology.

Aron

8.192 **Ionescu**, G., 'Raymond Aron: a modern classicist', in A. de Crespigny and K. Minogue, ed, *Contemporary Political Philosophers*, 1976, 191–208. Charts Aron's shift from orthodox sociology to a recognition of the centrality of politics in industrial societies and his deployment of an essentially classicist methodology.

8.193 **Pierce**, R., 'Liberalism and democracy in the thought of Raymond Aron', *J. Pol.*, 25, 1963, 14–35.

8.194 **Richter**, M., 'Raymond Aron as political theorist', *Pol. Theory*, 12, 1984, 147–51. Argues that he followed the tradition of Montesquieu and Tocqueville in understanding liberty, and that his contribution to liberalism lies in his scepticism and pragmatism.

8.195 **Strong**, T. B., 'History of choices in the foundations of the political thought of Raymond Aron', *Hist. & Theory*, 11, 1972, 179–93. Suggests that the similarity between Aron and British/American liberals is superficial: his thought can be traced back to a number of European philosophical traditions.

Bukharin

8.196 **Cohen**, S. F., *Bukharin and the Bolshevik Revolution: A Political Biography*, 1974. Still the best English-language biography and assessment of Bukharin.

8.197 —— 'Bukharin, Lenin and the theoretical foundations of bolshevism', *Sov. Sts.*, 21, 1969–70, 436–57. Traces the development of Bukharin's early thought, stressing the 'break' in his ideas when he began to write on imperialism and state capitalism as well as his anti-statism which influenced the development of Bolshevik ideology.

8.198 —— 'Marxist theory and Bolshevik policy: the case of Bukharin's *Historical Materialism*', *Pol. Sc. Q.*, 85, 1970, 40–61.

8.199 **Day**, R. B., 'The blackmail of the single alternative: Bukharin, Trotsky and perestroika', *Studies in Soviet Thought*, 1990, 159–88. Views Bukharin as the predecessor of Gorbachev's 'scientific Stalinism' which is contrasted with Trotsky's project for democratic planning.

8.200 **Heitman**, S., 'The myth of Bukharin's anarchism', *Rocky Mountain Social Science*

Journal, 1, 1963, 39–53.

8.201 **Hodges**, D. C., 'Bukharin's controversy with Marx; an analysis of the tensions within modern socialism', *Am. J. Econ. & Soc.*, 19, 1960, 259–74.

8.202 **Kemp-Welch**, A., ed., *The Ideas of Nikolai Bukharin*, 1992. A collection examining Bukharin's thinking in the 1920s, including critical assessments of his approach to economic development (Nove, Ferdinand and Danilov), theory of the state (Harding), theory of the party (Biggart), and approach to the question of political culture (Bogdanov).

8.203 **Kozlov**, N. N., and **Weitz**, E., *Nikolai Ivanovich Bukharin: A Centenary Appraisal*, 1990. Examination of the thought and career of the Bolshevik revolutionary, rejecting the interpretation which views him as an intellectual antecedent of Gorbachev.

Foucault

8.204 **Aladjem**, T. K., 'The philosopher's prism: Foucault, feminism and critique', *Pol. Theory*, 19, 1991, 277–91. Connects his hostility to Enlightenment discourse with certain traditions within feminism.

8.205 **Chiari**, J., *Structuralism: Claude Levi-Strauss, Michel Foucault, Louis Althusser in Twentieth-Century French Thought*, 1975.

8.206 **Connolly**, W., 'Taylor, Foucault, and otherness', *Pol. Theory*, 13, 1985, 365–76. Challenges Taylor's reading of Foucault, suggesting he obscures the political implications of Foucault's ontology.

8.207 **Dews**, P., 'Power and subjectivity in Foucault', *New Left Rev.*, 144, 1984, 72–95. Clear introduction to and critique of his notion of power, explaining why his ideas prevent the emergence of collective, counter-hegemonic politics.

8.208 **Dreyfus**, H. L. and **Rabinow**, P., *Michel Foucault: Beyond Structuralism and Hermeneutics*, Chicago, Ill., 1982. Argues that during the 1970s Foucault overcame the deficiencies of his earlier work with a new methodology, combining a type of archaeological analysis which preserves the distancing effect of structuralism and an interpretative dimension which develops the hermeneutic insight that the investigator is always situated and must understand the meaning of cultural practices from within their discourses.

8.209 **Dunn**, T. L., 'The politics of post-modern aesthetics: Habermas contra Foucault', *Pol. Theory*, 16, 1988, 209–28. A postmodernist celebration of Foucauldian ideas and their political implications against the Habermasian view.

8.210 **Fraser**, N., 'Foucault on modern power: empirical insights and normative confusions', *Praxis International*, 1, 1981, 272–87.

8.211 —— 'Foucault's body-language: a post-humanist political rhetoric?', *Salmagundi*, 61, 1983, 55–70.

8.212 —— 'Michel Foucault – a "young conservative?" ', *Ethics*, 96, 1985, 165–84. Suggests that Habermas's rejection of Foucault's critique of modernity is misplaced: Foucault rejects the discourse of humanism within modernity, but his ideas are more ambiguous here than Habermas suggests.

8.213 **Giddens**, A., 'From Marx to Nietzsche? Neo-conservatism, Foucault, and problems in contemporary political theory', in *Profiles and Critiques in Social Theory*, 1982, 215–30. Assesses Foucault's work as representative of a larger tradition of philosophical conservatism, criticising particularly his theories of power, discipline and surveillance.

8.214 **Hewitt**, M., 'Bio-politics and social policy: Foucault's account of welfare', *Theory, Culture and Society*, 2, 1983, 67–84. Lively extension of Foucauldian notions of the state regulation of the politics of life into the field of social policy. Illustrates especially the weaknesses of Marxist approaches to the political economy of welfare.

8.215 **Ingram**, D., 'Foucault and the Frankfurt school: a discourse on Nietzsche, power and knowledge', *Praxis International*, 6, 1986, 311–27. Exploration of the affinities between Foucault and the Frankfurt school, examining the Nietzschean roots of Adorno and Horkheimer and suggesting, unconventionally, that Foucault and Habermas share an emphasis upon communicative and aesthetic experience.

8.216 **Lemert**, C. C., and **Gillan**, G., *Michel Foucault: Social Theory as Transgression*, New York, 1982.

8.217 **McCarthy**, T., 'The critique of impure reason: Foucault and the Frankfurt School', *Pol. Theory*, 18, 1990, 437–69.

Describes a number of affinities between Foucault and critical theory, yet concludes that he errs in his wholesale critique of impure reason.

8.218 **Mirsen**, J., 'Strategies for socialists? Foucault's conceptions of power', *Econ. & Soc.*, 9, 1980, 1–43.

8.219 **Patton**, P., 'Taylor and Foucault on power and freedom', *Pol. Sts.*, 37, 1989, 260–76. Suggests the differences between these thinkers lie in their antithetical interpretations of power – Taylor representing the humanist and Foucault the anti-humanist standpoint. Clear summary of an important debate.

8.220 **Philip**, M., 'Foucault on power. A problem in radical translation?', *Pol. Theory*, 11, 1983, 29–52. Interprets his project as the replacement of classical liberal and Marxist formulations of politics, concluding that his conception of resistance is problematic.

8.221 —— 'Michel Foucault', in Q. Skinner, ed., *The Return of Grand Theory in the Human Sciences*, 1985, 65–82. Lucid and accessible guide to his philosophical and political ideas concerning power and rationality in modern societies.

8.222 **Poster**, M., *Foucault, Marxism and History: Mode of Production Versus Mode of Information*, 1984.

8.223 **Redner**, H., 'The infernal recurrence of the same: Nietzsche and Foucault on knowledge and power', in M. Dascal and O. Gruengard, ed., *Knowledge and Politics: Case-Studies in the Relationship Between Epistemology and Political Philosophy*, Boulder, Calif., 1989, 291–315. Explains the centrality of Nietzsche for postmodernist theorists, extending this influence to a parallel between Nietzsche's and Foucault's 'anarchistic' political sympathies, despite certain obvious differences between them.

8.224 **Sheridan** A., *Michel Foucault: The Will to Truth*, 1980.

8.225 **Smart**, B., *Foucault, Marxism and Critique*, 1983. Places his thought in the context of the Marxist tradition, stressing the latter's weaknesses in key areas of critical analysis.

8.226 —— *Michel Foucault*, 1985. Stresses his impact upon social science conceptions and analyses of power relations in a brief but enlightening overview.

8.227 **Taylor**, C., 'Foucault on freedom and truth', *Pol. Theory*, 12, 1984, 152–83. Assesses his repudiation of these goals, noting that this position raises fundamental questions about his own enterprise and Western philosophical thought more generally.

8.228 **White**, S. K., 'Foucault's challenge to critical theory', *Am. Pol. Sc. Rev.*, 80, 1986, 419–32. Suggests that unlike Habermas he fails to connect his notion of aesthetic subjectivity to his endorsement of new social movements.

8.229 **Wickham**, G., 'Power and power analysis: beyond Foucault?', *Economy and Society*, 72, 1984, 468–90.

Freud

8.230 **Abramson**, J. A., *Liberalism and its Limits: The Moral and Political Thought of Freud*, New York, 1984.

8.231 **Bocock**, R., *Freud and Modern Society*, 1976.

8.232 **Brunner**, J., *Freud's Politics: The Power and the Psyche*, 1991. Explores the social and scientific context of Freud's writings.

8.233 **Keat**, R., *The Politics of Social Theory: Habermas, Freud and the Critique of Positivism*, 1981. Assessment of critical theory's critique of positivist social theory through an analysis of Habermas's theory of knowledge – constitutive interests and psychoanalysis as models of social theory. Concludes with an in-depth analysis of the normative complexity of psychotherapeutic practices.

8.234 **Roazen**, P., *Freud: Political and Social Thought*, New York, 1969.

8.235 **Schorske**, C. E., 'Politics and patricide in Freud's *Interpretation of Dreams*', *Am. Hist. Rev.*, 5, 1973, 328–48.

8.236 **Turkle**, S., *Psychoanalytical Politics: Freud's French Revolution*, New York, 1978.

8.237 **Weinstein**, D., and **Weinstein**, M., 'Freud on the problem of order', *Diogenes*, 108, 1979, 39–56. Comparison of Freud's observations about the founding of social order with the social contract tradition, especially the work of Hobbes.

Gramsci

8.238 **Adamson**, W., 'Beyond "reform or revolution": notes on political education in Gramsci, Habermas, and Arendt', *Theory & Soc.*, 4, 1978, 429–60.

8.239 —— 'Gramsci and the politics of civil society', *Praxis International*, 7, 1987–88, 320–39.

8.240 —— 'Gramsci's interpretation of fascism', *J. Hist. Ideas*, 41, 1980, 615–34. Reconstructs his analysis, in prison, of the emergence of fascism, concluding that his sophisticated reading prefigured the later concerns of historians of this phenomenon.

8.241 —— *Hegemony and Revolution: A Study of Antonio Gramsci's Political and Cultural Theory*, Berkeley, Calif., 1980. An impressive survey, stressing the Hegelian-Marxist core of his ideas.

8.242 —— 'Towards the Prison Notebooks: the evolution of Gramsci's thinking on political organization, 1918–1926', *Polity*, 7, 1979, 38–64. Critique of interpretations which do not attend sufficiently to the dialectical nature of his ideas and the historical context in which he wrote.

8.243 **Adler**, F., 'Factory councils: Gramsci and the industrialists', *Telos*, 31, 1977, 67–90.

8.244 **Anderson**, P., 'Introduction to Antonio Gramsci, 1919–1921', *New Left Rev.*, 51, 1968, 22–7. A brief introduction to some of Gramsci's writings on the factory councils.

8.245 —— 'The antinomies of Antonio Gramsci', *New Left Rev.*, 100, 1976–77, 5–78. An influential critique of his concept of the war of position.

8.246 **Bates**, T. R., 'Antonio Gramsci and the Bolshevization of the PCI', *Journal of Contemporary History*, 11, 1976, 115–31. Charts the shift from his concern for workers' councils to his Bolshevik persuasions.

8.247 —— 'Antonio Gramsci and the Soviet experiment in Italy', *Societas*, 4, 1974, 39–54. Assesses Gramsci on workers' councils and his conception of the role of the party.

8.248 —— 'Gramsci and the theory of hegemony', *J. Hist. Ideas*, 36, 1975, 351–66. Reconstructs the theory of hegemony on the basis of his prison writings.

8.249 **Bellamy**, R., 'Gramsci, Croce and the Italian political tradition', *Hist. Pol. Thought*, 11, 1990, 313–39. Argues that despite his popularity among sections of the British left, Gramsci inherited from Croce, and the Italian political tradition generally, a political agenda and conception of politics particular to the

Italian situation.

8.250 **Bobbio**, N., 'Gramsci and the conception of civil society', in *Which Socialism?: Marxism, Socialism and Democracy*, 1987, 139–61. Presents his theory of the state as a break from previous conceptions which viewed the state as an end in itself, focusing on his understanding of civil society as a superstructural phenomenon, a position which distinguished him from classical Marxism.

8.251 **Boekelman**, M., 'On the political theory of Antonio Gramsci', *Alive Magazine*, 3, 1973, 37–52.

8.252 **Boggs**, C., 'Gramsci and eurocommunism', *Rad. Am.*, 14, 1980, 7–23. A critique of eurocommunist 'distortions' of Gramsci.

8.253 —— *Gramsci's Marxism*, 1976. A brief, lucid introduction, assessing the influence of other Marxists on him, though misrepresenting his concept of hegemony.

8.254 —— 'Gramsci's "Prison Notebooks" – parts 1 and 2', *Socialist Revolution*, 1 and 2, 1972, 29–56 and 79–118.

8.255 —— 'Gramsci's theory of the factory councils: nucleus of the socialist state', *Berkeley Journal of Sociology*, 19, 1974, 171–87.

8.256 —— *The Two Revolutions: Gramsci and the Dilemmas of Western Marxism*, Boston, Mass., 1984. Places more stress than previously on the different sides of Gramsci's thought – council democracy, Leninism and Western Marxism – and on the complex historical context in which he wrote. Boggs's interpretation of hegemony is consequently more sophisticated and rigorous than before.

8.257 **Buci-Glucksmann**, C., *Gramsci and the State*, 1980. A scholarly and masterful reading of the *Prison Notebooks*, centred around his shifting analysis of the state. These texts were informed by a continual dialogue with Leninism and are illuminated by constant reference to the history of the categories he deployed. The book's weakness is its reliance on Althusser and Lenin as sources of authority.

8.258 **Cain**, M., 'Gramsci, the state and the place of law', in D. Sugerman, ed., *Legality, Ideology, and the State*, 1983, 45–112.

8.259 **Calzolari**, A., 'Structure and superstructure in Gramsci', *Telos*, 2, 1969, 33–42.

8.260 **Cammett**, J., *Antonio Gramsci and the Origins of Italian Communism*, Stanford, Calif., 1967. Largely biographical consideration, examining his ideas during the two periods of his 'greatest creativity': as the leader of the 'Ordine Nuovo' movement, 1919–20, and as the key figure in Italian Communism in the 1920s. More useful for its historical detail than analytical insight, and easily surpassed by Femia's work.

8.261 **Cheal**, D. J., 'Hegemony, ideology and contradictory consciousness', *Sociol. Q.*, 20, 1979, 109–18. Tests Gramscian notions against opinion surveys of the British electorate.

8.262 **Colletti**, L., 'Antonio Gramsci and the Italian revolution', *New Left Rev.*, 65, 1971, 87–94.

8.263 **Cozens**, P., *Twenty years of Antonio Gramsci: A Bibliography of Gramsci and Gramsci Studies Published in English, 1957–1977*, 1977.

8.264 **Dahn**, B. L., 'Antonio Gramsci on reading Marx', *Quarterly Journal of Ideology*, 7, 1983, 43–8. Brief commentary upon his reconstruction of Marx's methodology.

8.265 **Davidson**, A., *Antonio Gramsci: The Man, His Ideas*, 1968. An intellectual biography which the author later surpassed.

8.266 —— *Antonio Gramsci: Towards an Intellectual Biography*, 1977. Deploying new evidence about Gramsci's early heterodoxy, and rejecting the approaches of Cammett and Fiori, this is a historically detailed account of his intellectual evolution.

8.267 —— 'Gramsci and Lenin 1917–1922', *Socialist Register*, 11, 1974, 125–50. Charts Gramsci's evolving Marxism with reference to the Russian revolution and his familiarity with Leninist doctrines. Concludes that Leninism and Gramscianism overlapped in theoretical terms.

8.268 —— 'Gramsci and reading Machiavelli', *Sc. & Soc.*, 37, 1973, 56–80. Argues for a reconsideration of Gramsci's interpretation of Machiavelli as a 'philosopher of praxis'.

8.269 —— *The Theory and Practice of Italian Communism*, 1982.

8.270 —— 'The varying seasons of Gramscian studies', *Pol. Sts.*, 20, 1972, 448–61. Traces the shifting evaluation of Gramsci by Italian commentators throughout the twentieth century, in accordance with the interests of the various sections of the

Italian left.

8.271 **Davis**, J. A., ed., *Gramsci and Italy's Passive Revolution*, 1979. A collection of essays connecting Italian history in the nineteenth century to his key concepts, especially passive revolution.

8.272 **Dimitrakos**, D. P., 'Gramsci and the contemporary debate on Marxism', *Phil. Soc. Scs.*, 16, 1986, 459–88. Explains the appeal and theoretical potency of Gramscian ideas for Western Marxists in the context of the crisis the left has undergone since the late 1960s.

8.273 **Eley**, G., 'Reading Gramsci in English: observations on the reception of Antonio Gramsci in the English speaking world 1957–82', *Eur. Hist. Q.*, 14, 1984, 441–78.

8.274 **Entwistle**, H., *Antonio Gramsci: Conservative Schooling for Radical Politics*, 1979.

8.275 **Evans**, G., 'Antonio Gramsci and Leninism', *Intervention*, 2, 1972, 74–94.

8.276 **Femia**, J. V., 'Gramsci: Marxism's saviour or false prophet?', *Pol. Sts.*, 37, 1989, 282–9. Sceptically reviews recent literature on him, concluding that for democratic socialists the choice between Lenin and Gramsci is an unsatisfactory one.

8.277 —— 'Gramsci's patrimony', *Brit. J. Pol. Sc.*, 13, 1983, 327–64. Returning to *The Prison Notebooks*, Femia stresses the gaps and discontinuities within Gramsci's thought, arguing that his legacy remains essentially ambiguous.

8.278 —— *Gramsci's Political Thought: Hegemony, Consciousness, and the Revolutionary Process*, 1981. An important assessment of the central aspects of his theory by a leading scholar in this field, who stresses the discontinuities within his intellectual evolution, specifying successive stages in this process. A powerful statement of the case that his work merits a historicist interpretation, in the course of which key themes in his thought stand out: the nature of power in capitalist societies, the methods of maintaining power, the character of the proletarian alternative and the relationship between the material and spiritual aspects of existence.

8.279 —— 'Gramsci, the "Via Italiana" and the classical Marxist-Leninist approach to revolution', *Govt. & Oppos.*, 14, 1979, 66–95. Reviews the competing political interpretations of Gramsci.

8.280 —— 'Hegemony and consciousness in the thought of Antonio Gramsci', *Pol. Sts.*, 23, 1975, 29–48. Focuses on his reformulation of the base and superstructure dichotomy through the concept of hegemony. Particular stress is given to his exposition of the winning of consent at the ideological level in modern societies.

8.281 —— 'The Gramsci phenomenon: some reflections', *Pol. Sts.*, 27, 1979, 472–83.

8.282 **Ferravotti**, F., 'Civil society and state structures in creative tension: Ferguson, Hegel, Gramsci', *State, Culture and Society*, 1, 1984, 3–25.

8.283 **Finocchiaro**, M., 'Gramsci. An alternative communism?', *Studies in Soviet Thought*, 27, 1984, 123–46.

8.284 —— *Gramsci and the History of Dialectical Thought*, 1989. A close, textual analysis of the *Prison Notebooks*, looking particularly at his critique of other thinkers. These criticisms are evaluated against Finocchiaro's account of these thinkers (Croce, Bukharin, Hegel).

8.285 —— 'Gramsci's Crocean Marxism', *Telos*, 41, 1979, 17–34. Presents Gramsci as essentially Crocean in all his writings.

8.286 —— 'Marxism, religion and science in Gramsci: recent trends in Italian scholarship', *Phil. Forum*, 17, 1985, 127–55.

8.287 —— 'Science and praxis in Gramsci's critique of Bukharin', *Phil. & Soc. Crit.*, 6, 1979, 25–56.

8.288 **Fiori**, G., *Antonio Gramsci: Life of a Revolutionary*, 1970. English translation of the best Italian study of Gramsci.

8.289 **Genovese**, E., 'On Antonio Gramsci', *Studies on the Left*, 7, 1971, 83–107. Creative application of his ideas to the American situation.

8.290 **Germino**, D., 'The radical as humanist. Gramsci, Croce and the "philosophy of praxis"', *Bucknell Review*, 20, 1972, 93–116.

8.291 **Giachetti**, R., 'Antonio Gramsci: the subjective revolution', in D. Howard and K. E. Klare, ed., *The Unknown Dimension: European Marxism since Lenin*, New York, 1972, 147–68. Outlines the total, trans-formatory view of revolution which he held.

8.292 **Ginsburg**, P., 'Gramsci and the era of "bourgeois" revolution in Italy', in J. A. Davis, ed., *Gramsci and Italy's Passive Revolution*, 1979, 31–66. Argues for a more rigorous and accurate elaboration of the

Marxist theory of bourgeois revolution, examining Gramsci's ideas in particular. Relies on exposition rather than evaluation.

8.293 **Hall**, S., **Lumley**, B., and **McLennan**, G., 'Politics and ideology: Gramsci', *Working Papers in Cultural Studies*, 10, 1977, 45–76. Exploration of his conception of ideology, which is compared with the ideas of Althusser and Poulantzas.

8.294 **Hallett**, F., 'Antonio Gramsci', *Political Affairs*, 36, 1958, 55–9.

8.295 **Harman**, C., *Gramsci versus Reformism*, 1983.

8.296 **Harvey**, J., 'Antonio Gramsci', *Marxism Today*, 11, 1967, 114–20. A brief introduction to his ideas for English readers, covering the main components of his thought.

8.297 **Hawley**, J. P., 'Antonio Gramsci's Marxism: class, state and work', *Social Problems*, 27, 1980, 584–600.

8.298 **Hearn** R., et al., 'Symposium on Gramsci and his views', *Australian Left Review*, 2, 1969, 60–7.

8.299 **Hobsbawm**, E. J., 'Gramsci and political theory', *Marxism Today*, 21, 1977, 205–13. A sympathetic evaluation of his Marxism.

8.300 **Hoffman**, J., *The Gramscian Challenge: Coercion and Consent in Marxist Political Theory*, 1984. Argues the unfashionable thesis that Gramsci saw consent as a mere supplement to coercion; the war of position is traced back to Bernstein and Kautsky, whilst Gramsci is roundly criticised for failing to recognise the inherently coercive nature of the dictatorship of the proletariat. Controversial and unconvincing.

8.301 —— 'The problem of coercion and consent in Marx and Gramsci', in M. Cowling and L. Wilde, ed., *Approaches to Marx*, 1989, 162–71. Reiterates his thesis that Gramsci was merely supplementing the classical Marxist view of politics, not supplanting it.

8.302 **Holub**, R. C., *Antonio Gramsci: Beyond Marxism and Postmodernism*, 1992. A detailed evaluation, situating his ideas in contemporary theoretical debates and providing an illuminating comparison with a number of twentieth-century Marxists, especially the Frankfurt school.

8.303 **Hunt**, G., 'Gramsci, civil society and bureaucracy', *Praxis International*, 6, 1986, 206–19. Harshly critical of Gramsci's theoretical rigour, Hunt concludes that civil society remains an essentially liberal

concept which has been appropriated too readily by currents such as eurocommunism.

8.304 —— 'Gramsci's Marxism and the concept of *homo oeconomicus*', *Int. Sts. Phil.*, 7, 1985, 11–23.

8.305 **Jacobitti**, E. E., 'Hegemony before Gramsci: the case of Benedetto Croce', *J. Mod. Hist.*, 52, 1980, 66–84. Argues that Gramsci drew upon the unhealthy influence of Croce over Italian intellectual life to formulate his notion of cultural hegemony. Jacobitti counters this misleading assessment of Croce's thought.

8.306 **Jessop**, R., 'The Gramsci debate', *Marxism Today*, 24, 1980, 23–5. Notes the diversity of contemporary interpretation and appropriation of his thought.

8.307 **Joll**, J., *Gramsci*, 1977. Introduces him as the most important twentieth-century Marxist theorist of the survival of capitalism in this lively, chronological account of the evolution of his thought.

8.308 **Kahn**, B. L., 'Antonio Gramsci on reading Marx', *Quarterly Journal of Ideology*, 7, 1983, 43–8.

8.309 **Kann**, M. E., 'Antonio Gramsci and modern Marxism', *Studies in Comparative Communism*, 13, 1980, 250–66.

8.310 **Karabel**, 'Revolutionary contradictions: Antonio Gramsci and the problem of intellectuals', *Pol. & Soc.*, 6, 1976, 123–72.

8.311 **Kaye**, H., 'Antonio Gramsci. An annotated bibliography of studies in English', *Pol. & Soc.*, 10, 1981, 335–53.

8.312 —— 'Political theory and history. Antonio Gramsci and the British Marxist historians', *Ital. Q.*, 25, 1984, 145–66. Compares the political theory embedded within the work of these historians with Gramsci's thought, especially through their work on class formation and contradictory consciousness.

8.313 **Kellner**, D., 'Ideology, Marxism and advanced capitalism', *Socialist Review*, 42, 1978, 37–55.

8.314 **Kertzer**, D. I., 'Gramsci's concept of hegemony: the Italian Church-communist struggle', *Dialectical Anthropology*, 4, 1979, 321–8.

8.315 **Kiernan**, V. G., 'The socialism of Antonio Gramsci', in K. Coates, ed., *Essays in Socialist Humanism*, 1972, 63–89. Bold reading of Gramsci as a socialist humanist.

8.316 **Kiros** T., *Towards the Construction of a*

Theory of Political Action: Antonio Gramsci. Consciousness, Participation and Hegemony, Lanham, Mass., 1985.

8.317 **McInnes**, N., 'Antonio Gramsci', *Survey: A Journal of Soviet and East European Studies*, 53, 1964, 3–15. Sympathetic and clear evaluation of his principal ideas.

8.318 **Maisels**, C. K., 'Gramsci between two internationals', *New Edinburgh Review*, 3, 1974, 25–9. A Leninist critique of Gramsci.

8.319 **Mancini**, G., *Worker Democracy and Political Party in Gramsci's Thinking*, SAIS-Bologna, 1973.

8.320 —— and **Galli**, G., 'Gramsci's presence', *Govt. & Oppos.*, 3, 1968, 325–38.

8.321 **Markovic**, M., 'Gramsci on the unity of philosophy and politics', *Praxis*, 3, 1967, 333–9. Suggests that he transcended classical Marxism and idealism in his philosophy.

8.322 **Marks**, L., 'Antonio Gramsci', *Marxist Quarterly*, 3, 1956, 225–38. The first English-language account of his thought.

8.323 **Martinelli**, A., 'In defence of the dialectic: Antonio Gramsci's theory of revolution', *Berkeley Journal of Sociology*, 13, 1968, 1–27. Sympathetic presentation of his transcendence of the traditions of neo-idealism and mechanical materialism. The dialectical method which he deployed should provide the basis of contemporary radical social theory, according to Martinelli.

8.324 **Mercer**, C., 'Culture and ideology in Gramsci', *Red Letters*, 8, 1978, 19–40. An Althusserian reading of his ideas.

8.325 **Merrington**, J., 'Theory and practice in Gramsci's Marxism', *Socialist Register*, 1968, 145–76. Clear, insightful account of his rejection of the dominant strains of contemporary Marxism, in particular through his more expansive and sophisticated understanding of the nature of power in modern societies.

8.326 **Morera**, E., 'Gramsci and democracy', *Can. J. Pol. Sc.*, 23, 1990, 23–37. Outlines some of the main elements in his prison work, which are the product of an implicitly held theory of democracy.

8.327 —— *Gramsci's Historicism: A Realist Interpretation*, 1990. Focusing upon his philosophy of historicism, Morera reinterprets some well-covered themes in Gramscian study and Marxist theory more generally, such as economic determinacy and the relative autonomy of politics. Sensible and thoughtful review of the various appropriations of his ideas.

8.328 **Moss**, H., *Gramsci and the Idea of Human Nature*, 1992. Discusses his thought with special reference to his ideas about and prescriptions for social change.

8.329 **Mouffe**, C., ed., *Gramsci and Marxist Theory*, 1979. An important collection of essays assessing the impact of Gramscian concepts upon debates within Western Marxism, including Mouffe on his contemporary significance, Bobbio on civil society, Texier on the Gramscian theorisation of the superstructure, Badaloni on his approach to revolution, Paggi on his distinctive Marxism, Mouffe's influential reconstruction of hegemony and ideology, Buci-Glucksmann on the state and passive revolution, Salvadori on the PCI's understanding of hegemony, and de Giovani comparing him with Lenin.

8.330 —— and **Sassoon**, A. S., 'Gramsci in France and Italy: a review of the literature', *Economy and Society*, 61, 1977, 31–68.

8.331 **Nemeth**, T., 'Gramsci's concept of constitution', *Phil. & Soc. Crit.*, 5, 1978, 295–318.

8.332 **Nield**, K., and **Seed**, J., 'Waiting for Gramsci', *Social History*, 6, 1981, 209–28. Intelligent and critical review of a number of recent studies, involving reflections upon the theoretical weakness of English intellectual life.

8.333 **Nowell-Smith**, G., 'Gramsci and the national popular', *Screen Education*, 22, 1977, 12–15. Translates this concept for an English audience because much of what Gramsci wrote on cultural questions has yet to appear in English.

8.334 **O'Connell**, G., 'Sources of Italian euro-communism: Gramsci, Italian culture and Catholicism', *Month*, 11, 1978, 383–8.

8.335 —— 'Sources of Italian euro-communism: the revolutionary strategy of Antonio Gramsci', *Month*, 11, 1978, 338–40.

8.336 —— 'The church and eurocommunism: formation of the communist mind in the thought of Antonio Gramsci', *Month*, 11, 1978, 257–61.

8.337 **Paggi**, L., 'Gramsci's general theory of Marxism', *Telos*, 33, 1977, 27–70. Examines his historicism and humanism as key concepts within his coherent political and philosophical universe.

8.338 **Pellicani**, L., *Gramsci: An Alternative*

Communism?, Stanford, Calif., 1981.

8.339 **Piccone**, P., 'From Spaventa to Gramsci', *Telos*, 31, 1977, 35–65. Cites Gramsci as the inheritor of the 'philosophy of praxis' tradition, which accounts for his belief that mankind was on the brink of a new epoch of true humanity and that Leninism constituted its realisation.

8.340 —— 'Gramsci's Hegelian Marxism', *Pol. Theory*, 2, 1974, 32–45. Contrasts Gramsci with Luxemburg, Lenin, Lukács and Korsch, all of whom failed to transcend a mechanical materialism.

8.341 —— 'Gramsci's Marxism. Beyond Lenin and Togliatti', *Theory & Soc.*, 3, 1976, 485–512. A rebuttal of the interpretation of Gramsci as a Leninist.

8.342 —— *Italian Marxism*, Berkeley, Calif., 1983. A sympathetic study of Gramsci's early thought.

8.343 **Pontusson**, J., 'Gramsci and eurocommunism. A comparative analysis of conceptions of class rule and socialist transition', *Berkeley J. Sociol.*, 25, 1980, 185–248.

8.344 **Pozzolini**, A., *Antonio Gramsci. An Introduction to his Thought*, 1970.

8.345 **Ramos**, V., 'The concepts of ideology, hegemony, and organic intellectuals in Gramsci's Marxism', *Theoretical Review*, 30, 1982, 8–34.

8.346 **Ransome**, P., *Antonio Gramsci: A New Introduction*, 1992. An accessible introduction to his thought, beginning with the social and political background in which he developed, and assessing key themes in his work – hegemony, ideology, politics and education.

8.347 **Richardson**, T., 'Science, ideology and commonsense: on Antonio Gramsci and Althusser', in S. Hibbin, ed., *Politics, Ideology and the State*, 1978, 99–122. Compares the ideas of these thinkers on the relationship between theory, ideology and political practice.

8.348 **Riva**, S., *An Introduction to Some Thoughts of Gramsci*, 1976.

8.349 **Rosengarten**, F., 'The Gramsci–Trotsky question (1922–1932)', *Sociological Text*, 4, 1984–85, 65–9.

8.350 **Rutigliano**, E., 'The ideology of labor and capitalist rationality in Gramsci', *Telos*, 31, 1977, 91–9. Views his thought as the expression of a particular stage of the production process.

8.351 **Salamini**, L., *The Sociology of Political Praxis: An Introduction to Gramsci's Theory*, 1981.

8.352 **Sallach**, D. L., 'Class domination and ideological hegemony', *Sociol. Q.*, 15, 1974, 38–50. Reads the notion of hegemony as a crucial contribution to a Marxist theory of social order.

8.353 —— 'The meaning of hegemony', *Australian Left Review*, August 1973, 32–7.

8.354 **Sarkar**, S., 'The thought of Gramsci', *Mainstream*, 7, 1968, 17–26.

8.355 **Sassoon**, A. S., ed., *Approaches to Gramsci*, 1982.

8.356 —— 'Gramsci's interpretation of fascism', *New Edinburgh Review*, 2, 1974, 4–7.

8.357 —— *Gramsci's Politics*, 1980. An assessment of his political theory as a coherent totality, in contrast to historicist readings, stressing the importance of developments in capitalist societies for proletarian theory and strategy. The Gramscian analysis of the party is presented as his central political principle.

8.358 —— 'Hegemony and political intervention' in S. Hibbin, ed., *Politics, Ideology and the State*, 1978, 9–39. A complex and important essay, charting the historical specificity of the concept of hegemony, the importance of prior revolutions for Gramsci's understanding of bourgeois revolution and his notion of the hegemony of a class as dependent upon its alliances.

8.359 **Schecter**, D., *Gramsci and the Theory of Industrial Democracy*, 1991. A theoretical assessment of his factory council writings, 1919–20, and their relation to his more mature work on the state–civil society relationship.

8.360 —— 'Gramsci, Gentile and the theory of the ethical state in Italy', *Hist. Pol. Thought*, 1989, 491–508. Suggests that despite the irreconcilable political differences between the fascist Gentile and the Marxist Gramsci, the desire to unite the state and civil society exists as an important common element in their ideas.

8.361 **Simon**, R., 'Gramsci's concept of hegemony', *Marxism Today*, 21, 1977, 78–86.

8.362 —— *Gramsci's Political Thought. An Introduction*, 1982. A brief account of his ideas, in particular his notion of hegemony which are counter-opposed to the dominant tradition of economism within the left's political thought.

8.363 **Stolz**, M. F., 'Gramsci's Machiavelli', *Human Society*, 4, 1981, 69–88.

8.364 **Thomson**, G., 'Gramsci: the first Italian Marxist', *Marxism Today*, 1, 1957, 61–2. One of the earliest English accounts, which briefly sketches his principal ideas.

8.365 **Todd**, N., 'Ideological superstructure in Gramsci and Mao Tse-Tung', *J. Hist. Ideas*, 35, 1974, 148–56. Compares their understanding of ideology and differing conceptions of the relationship between intellectuals and masses.

8.366 **White**, S., 'Gramsci and proletarian power', *New Edinburgh Review*, 3, 1974, 1–3.

8.367 —— 'Gramsci and the Italian Communist Party', *Govt. & Oppos.*, 2, 1972, 186–205. Presents the unconventional thesis of a complete discontinuity between Gramsci and Togliatti.

8.368 **Williams**, G., *Proletarian Order: Antonio Gramsci, Factory Councils and the Origin of Communism in Italy*, 1975. Lively account of the political events and relations of these years and their impact on Gramsci.

8.369 —— 'The concept of "egemonia" in the thought of Antonio Gramsci: some notes on interpretation', *J. Hist. Ideas*, 21, 1960, 586–99. Expounds his elaboration of and break with Marxist categories, concluding that a parallel exists between his ideas and the less theoretical concerns of the contemporary, British new left.

8.370 —— 'The making and unmaking of Antonio Gramsci', *New Edinburgh Review*, 3, 1974, 7–15.

8.371 **Woolcock**, J., 'Politics, ideology and hegemony in Gramsci's theory', *Social and Economic Studies*, 34, 1985, 199–210.

8.372 **Young**, J., 'Humanism of Antonio Gramsci and Rosa Luxemburg', *New Pol.*, 1, 1986, 243–58.

Habermas

8.373 **Adamson**, W., 'Beyond "reform or revolution"; notes on political education in Gramsci, Habermas, and Arendt', *Theory & Soc.*, 4, 1978, 429–60.

8.374 **Agger**, B., 'Work and authority in Marcuse and Habermas', *Human Studies*, 2, 1979, 191–208.

8.375 **Arnason**, T., et al., *Habermas Symposium*, 1977.

8.376 **Balbus**, I., 'Habermas and feminism. (Male) communication and the evolution of (patriarchal) society', *New Political Science*, 13, 1984, 27–47.

8.377 **Bernstein**, J., 'Fred Dallmayr's critique of Habermas', *Pol. Theory*, 16, 1988, 580–93. Critical review of Dallmayr's postmodernist 'misrepresentation' of Habermas in the same issue.

8.378 —— 'Habermas', in Z. A. Pelczynski and J. Gray, ed., *Conceptions of Liberty in Political Philosophy*, 1984, 397–425. Compares his critique of positivist conceptions of social theory with Berlin's ideas, suggesting that he rejected liberal notions of freedom without recourse to positive conceptions of liberty. A clear and accessible guide to his central ideas.

8.379 —— ed., *Habermas and Modernity*, 1985. A collection focusing upon the various traditions he synthesises, including Wellmer on his relation to Marx, Weber and Hegel, Jay and Whitebrook on his 'dilution' of the central tenets of critical theory, Giddens on the non-revolutionary nature of his thought, McCarthy and Rorty on the relationship between modernity and postmodernity in his work, and a reply by Habermas on these issues.

8.380 **Bohman**, J. F., 'Participating in enlightenment: Habermas' cognitivist interpretation of democracy', in M. Dascal and O. Gruengard, ed., *Knowledge and Politics: Case Studies in the Relationship Between Epistemology and Political Philosophy*, Boulder, Calif., 1989, 264–89. Explores his attempt to revise the insights of the Enlightenment through his social theory, with particular reference to the application of the concepts of knowledge and reason to politics. A clear introduction to his epistemological conception of democracy.

8.381 **Brand**, A., *The Force of Reason: An Introduction to the Work of Jürgen Habermas*, 1989.

8.382 **Calhoun**, C., ed., *Habermas and the Public Sphere*, 1992. Assessment of the historical and philosophical aspects of Habermas's theory, including McCarthy on the relationship between morality and politics, Benhabib on his intellectual relationship with Arendt, Baker on eighteenth-century France, and Zaret on religion and science in seventeenth-century England.

8.383 **Canovan**, M., 'A case of distorted communication. A note on Habermas and

Arendt', *Pol. Theory*, 11, 1983, 105–116. A critique of Habermas's misreading of Arendt's theory of political action, emphasising human originality as a neglected element in constraining communication.

8.384 **Cerutti**, F., 'Habermas and Marx', *Leviathan: Zeitschrift für Sozialwissenschaft*, 11, 1983, 352–75.

8.385 **Dallmayr**, F., 'Habermas and rationality', *Pol. Theory*, 16, 1988, 553–79. Immanent critique of his deployment of reason, which is derived from neo-Kantian and neo-positivist thought, and sits uneasily with his communicative ethics.

8.386 —— 'Reason and emancipation: notes on Habermas', *Man and World*, 5, 1984, 79–104. Admirably clear summary of his evolving conception of different cognitive pursuits and competing interests, which is followed by a critical review of the tension between his notion of an emancipatory interest and general political inclinations.

8.387 **Dumm**, T. L., 'The politics of post-modern aesthetics: Habermas contra Foucault', *Pol. Theory*, 16, 1988, 209–28. A postmodernist celebration of Foucauldian ideas and their political implications against the Habermasian view.

8.388 **Ealy**, S. D., *Communication, Speech and Politics: Habermas and Political Analysis*, Washington, D.C., 1981.

8.389 **Flay**, J. C., 'Habermas, eurocommunism and the theory of communication', in N. Fischer, et al., ed., *Continuity and Change in Marxism*, Atlantic Highlands, N.J., 1984, 131–43.

8.390 **Fleming**, M., 'Habermas, Marx and the question of ethics', in A. Honneth and A. Wellner, ed., *Die Frankfurter Schule und die Folgen*, Berlin and New York, 1986, 139–50.

8.391 **Flood**, T., 'Jürgen Habermas' critique of Marxism', *Sc. & Soc.*, 41, 1977–78, 448–64.

8.392 **Forester**, J., ed., *Critical Theory and Public Life*, Cambridge, Mass., 1985. Concerned with the interface between the ideas of critical theory and policy formation in different spheres, this volume includes two essays which deploy a Habermasian framework, including O'Neill on communicative competence, and Forester on the overlap between policy analysis and critical theory.

8.393 **Fraser**, N., 'Gender, citizenship and the public sphere: toward a feminist reconstruction of Habermas', in S. Sevenhuijsen, ed., *Feminism, Citizenship and Care*, Utrecht, 50–69.

8.394 —— 'What's critical about critical theory? The case of Habermas and gender', in S. Benhabib, et al., ed., *Feminism as Critique*, 1987, 31–55.

8.395 **Geuss**, R., *The Idea of a Critical Theory: Habermas and the Frankfurt School*, 1981.

8.396 **Giddens**, A., 'Habermas' critique of hermeneutics', in R. J. Bernstein, ed., *Studies in Social and Political Theory*, 1977, 135–64.

8.397 —— 'Habermas' social and political theory', in *Profiles and Critiques in Social Theory*, 1982, 82–99. Assesses the influence of the traditions of hermeneutics, psychoanalysis and critical theory on his thought. Useful introduction to the range of Habermasian discourse.

8.398 —— 'Jürgen Habermas', in Q. Skinner, ed., *The Return of Grand Theory in the Human Sciences*, 1985, 121–39. Brave attempt to distil his core ideas in an accessible fashion; an excellent starting point for those unfamiliar with Habermas.

8.399 **Held**, D., and **Larry**, S., 'Habermas' theory of crisis in late capitalism', *Radical Philosophers' News Journal*, 6, 1976, 1–19.

8.400 **Hohendahl**, P. U., 'Critical theory, public sphere, and culture: Jürgen Habermas and his critics', *New Germ. Crit.*, 16, 1979, 89–118.

8.401 —— 'The dialectics of enlightenment revisited: Habermas' critique of the Frankfurt School', *New Germ. Crit.*, 35, 1985, 3–26.

8.402 **Holton**, R. J., 'The idea of crisis in modern society', *Brit. J. Soc.*, 38, 1987, 502–20.

8.403 **Holub**, R. C., *Jürgen Habermas: Critic in the Public Sphere*, 1991. Shows how he has helped to shape the critical consciousness of post-war Germany, and gives a detailed account of the debates in which he has engaged since the early 1960s.

8.404 **Honneth**, A., and **Joas**, H., ed., *Communicative Action: Essays on Jürgen Habermas' The Theory of Communicative Action*, 1991. A collection which discusses specific aspects of this work as well as his overall contribution to social and political thought.

8.405 —— 'Moral evolution and domination of nature. Jürgen Habermas' theory of socio-cultural evolution', in *Social Action and Human Nature*, 1988, 151–67.

8.406 **How**, A., *The Gadamer-Habermas Debate: Hermeneutics Versus Critical Theory*, 1992. Presents the main features of a key debate from the 1970s which was concerned with the methodological and philosophical basis of the social sciences.

8.407 **Ingram**, D., *Habermas and the Dialectic of Reason*, New Haven, Conn., 1987. Stressing the aesthetic dimension of his concept of rationality, Ingram provides an introduction to the development of his thought and an important assessment of the extent to which Weber's conception of social rationalisation undermines the Habermasian theory of communicative action. Also questions his claim to have transcended first-generation critical theory and dissects his complex conception of the lifeworld. A difficult text which provides a comprehensive guide to his thought and the central theoretical debates in which he has been involved.

8.408 **James**, M., 'From Marx to incoherence: a critique of Habermas', *J. Soc. Phil.*, 12, 1981, 10–16. Bold critique of the Habermasian notion of 'human interests' which undermines the coherence of his ideal speech situation.

8.409 **Jay**, M., 'Habermas and modernism', in *Fin-de-Siècle Socialism and Other Essays*, 1988, 123–36. Sensitive exposition of his commitment to rationalist discourse though Jay remains sceptical about the nature of the aesthetic–practical rationality which Habermas proposes.

8.410 —— 'Habermas and post-modernism', in *Fin-De-Siècle Socialism and Other Essays*, 1988, 137–48. Defends Habermasian ideas as alternatives to the pessimism inherent in the endless search for difference.

8.411 **Keane**, J., 'Elements of a radical theory of public life: from Tönnies to Habermas and beyond', *Can. J. Pol. & Soc. Theory*, 6, 1982, 11–49. A survey of critical theory's traditional concern for public life, especially the ideas of Habermas. These are characterised by a tension between his advocacy of new forms of public life and the abstract-formal mode of argument he deploys.

8.412 —— 'Techné and praxis: the early Habermas' recovery of the concept of politics', in *Public Life and Late Capitalism*, 1984, 111–45. Sharp critique of

the young Habermas's deployment of this Aristotelian distinction in his critique of bureaucratic rationality, comparing his ideas with those of Arendt in this area.

8.413 **Keat**, R., *The Politics of Social Theory: Habermas, Freud and the Critique of Positivism*, 1981. Assessment of critical theory's critique of positivist social theory through an analysis of Habermas's theory of knowledge–constitutive interests and of psychoanalysis as a model of social theory. Concludes with an in-depth analysis of the normative complexity of psychotherapeutic practices.

8.414 **Kemp**, R., and **Cooke**, P., 'Repoliticising the "public sphere": a reconsideration of Habermas', *Social Praxis*, 8, 1981, 125–42.

8.415 **Kimmel**, B., 'Althusser and Habermas', *Human Factor*, 13, 1975, 90–106.

8.416 **Landes**, J. B., 'Jürgen Habermas' "The Structural Transformation of the Public Sphere": a feminist inquiry', *Praxis International*, 12, 1992, 106–27. Criticising his language-centred model, Landes emphasises the multiplicity of representation in human communication.

8.417 **Luban**, D., 'On Habermas on Arendt on power', *Phil. & Soc. Crit.*, 6, 1979, 79–92.

8.418 **McCarthy**, T., 'A theory of communicative competence', *Phil. Soc. Scs.*, 3, 1973, 135–56.

8.419 —— *The Critical Theory of Jürgen Habermas*, 1978. A systematic and comprehensive outline of his critique of the scientisation of politics and understanding of the 'cognitive interests' which help humans comprehend reality. Communication is here interpreted as his response to the problem of providing an enlarged conception of rationality.

8.420 **Mara**, G. M., 'After virtue, autonomy: Jürgen Habermas and Greek political theory', *J. Pol.*, 47, 1985, 1036–61.

8.421 **Miller**, J., 'Jürgen Habermas, legitimation crisis', *Telos*, 25, 1975, 210–20.

8.422 **Misgeld**, D., 'Modernity and social science: Habermas and Rorty', *Phil. Soc. Crit.*, 11, 1986, 355–70.

8.423 —— 'Science, hermeneutics and the utopian content of the liberal-democratic tradition: on Habermas' recent work', *New Germ. Crit.*, 22, 1981, 123–44.

8.424 **Murray**, J. P., 'Enlightenment roots of Habermas's critique of Marx', *Modern Schoolman*, 57, 1979, 1–24.

8.425 **O'Neill**, J., ed., *On Critical Theory*, 1976.

Includes Misgeld on the Habermas/ Gadamer debate, Weber on aesthetic experience and self-reflection with particular reference to Marcuse and Habermas, Wilson on Habermas's recent ideas on domination, communication and change, and Wellner on the 'linguistic turn' Habermas has imparted to critical theory.

8.426 **Outhwaite**, W., *Habermas*, 1986. An introduction to his thought which draws upon his early works on the public sphere and more recent studies of the philosophical discourse of modernity.

8.427 **Pettit**, P., 'Habermas on truth and justice', in G. H. R. Parkinson, ed., *Marx and Marxisms*, 1982, 207–28. Examines his consensus theory of justice, arguing that this is too readily conflated with a theory of truth.

8.428 **Pfeufer Kahn**, R., 'The problem of power in Habermas', *Human Studies*, 11, 1988, 361–87.

8.429 **Plant**, R., 'Hirsch, Hayek, and Habermas: dilemmas of distribution', in A. Ellis and K. Kumar, ed. *Dilemmas of Liberal Democracies: Studies in Fred Hirsch's Social Limits to Growth*, 1983, 45–64. Argues that these thinkers posit a similar diagnosis of the central problems of the capitalist welfare state, particularly in terms of the absence of an agreed morality in this system. Concludes that there are moral resources within a liberal state for securing ethical consensus.

8.430 —— 'Jürgen Habermas and the idea of legitimation crisis', *European Journal of Political Research*, 10, 1982, 341–52. A pertinent critique of his notion of undistorted communication as the foundation for a morally based political life.

8.431 **Pusey**, M., *Jürgen Habermas*, 1987.

8.432 **Raffel**, S., *Habermas, Lyotard and the Concept of Justice*, 1992. Regards the concept of justice as integral to their thought but suggests it is deployed by both only in constricted and unimaginative ways.

8.433 **Rasmussen**, D. M., 'Advanced capitalism and social theory: Habermas on the problem of legitimation', *Cultural Hermeneutics*, 3, 1976, 349–66.

8.434 —— *Reading Habermas*, 1990. Roots Habermasian discourse in the tradition of theorists wrestling with the dilemmas of

modernity, critically evaluating his theory of communicative action. Defends his essential consistency in steering a theoretical course between transcendental and empirical thought.

8.435 **Reid**, H. G., and **Yararella**, E. J., 'Critical political theory and moral development. On Kohlberg, Hampden-Turner and Habermas', *Theory & Soc.*, 4, 1977, 505–41.

8.436 **Riedmüller**, B., 'Crisis as crisis of legitimation: a critique of Jürgen Habermas's concept of a political crisis theory', *International Journal of Politics*, 7, 1977, 83–117.

8.437 **Rockmore**, T., 'Habermas and the reconstruction of historical materialism', *Journal of Value Inquiry*, 13, 1979, 195–206.

8.438 —— *Habermas on Historical Materialism*, Bloomington, Ill., Indianapolis, Ind., 1989.

8.439 **Roderick**, R., *Habermas and the Foundations of Critical Theory*, 1986.

8.440 **Rorty**, R., 'Habermas and Lyotard on post-modernity', *Praxis International*, 4, 1984, 32–44.

8.441 **Saiedi**, N., 'A critique of Habermas' *Theory of Practical Rationality*', *Studies in Soviet Thought*, 33, 1987, 251–65.

8.442 **Schroyer**, T., 'Marx and Habermas', *Continuum*, 8, 1970, 52–64. Perceptive study of Habermas's deployment of Marxist categories to refine critical theory, finding the origins of the Habermasian emphasis on the self-reflexivity of language in Marx's theory of the fetishism of the commodities.

8.443 —— 'The re-politicisation of the relations of production: an analytical interpretation of Jürgen Habermas's analytic theory of late capitalist society', *New Germ. Crit.*, 5, 1975, 105–28.

8.444 **Schwartz**, R. D., 'Habermas and the politics of discourse', *Can. J. Pol. & Soc. Theory*, 5, 1981, 45–68. A critical examination of the political dimensions of the Habermasian theory of language and communication, concluding that in prescriptive terms these ideas are tame.

8.445 **Sensat**, T., *Habermas and Marxism: An Appraisal*, Beverley Hills, Calif., 1979. An accessible outline of his social theory, which focuses upon his critique of Marxist political economy and historical materialism. Sensat rebuts his criticism.

8.446 —— 'Recasting Marxism: Habermas's proposals', in P. Bulzkowski and A. Klawiter, ed., *Theories of Ideology and Ideology of Theories*, Amsterdam, 1986, 123–46.

8.447 **Shapiro**, J. J., 'From Marcuse to Habermas', *Continuum*, 8, 1970, 65–76. Compares their development of the Kantian problematic, suggesting that Marcuse failed to provide a self-reflexive perspective on human liberation.

8.448 **Smith**, A., 'Ethics and politics in the work of Jürgen Habermas', *Interpretation*, 11, 1983, 333–51. Examination of the problem for political theory of the relationship of ethics to power, based on a consideration of Habermas's privileging of his communicative ethic over power. Despite this theoretical project, Smith concludes that power factors are not derivable from ethical beliefs.

8.449 —— 'Two theories of historical materialism. G. A. Cohen and Jürgen Habermas', *Theory & Soc.*, 13, 1984, 513–40. Compares their treatment of this theme, in particular their differing concepts of rationality, and suggests that Habermas sketches solutions to some of the problems within Cohen's account.

8.450 **Smith**, T., 'The scope of the social sciences in Weber and Habermas', *Phil. & Soc. Crit.*, 1, 1981, 69–83.

8.451 **Sumner**, C., 'Law, legitimation and the advanced capitalist state: the jurisprudence and social theory of Jürgen Habermas', in D. Sugerman, ed., *Legality, Ideology and the State*, 1983, 119–58.

8.452 **Therborn**, G., 'Jürgen Habermas: a new eclecticism', *New Left Rev.*, 67, 1971, 69–83. A clear exposition of his political epistemology, concluding that his break from Marxism is reinforced by the eclectic range of philosophical sources upon which he draws.

8.453 **Thompson**, J. B., *Critical Hermeneutics: A Study in the Thought of Paul Ricoeur and Jürgen Habermas*, 1981.

8.454 —— and **Held**, D., ed., *Habermas: Critical Debates*, 1982. An important collection, prefaced by a useful introduction to his work, including Heller on the complex relationship between him and Marxism, Bobner on his relation to critical theory, Hesse on recent reformulations of his epistemological views and the consequences of these for his theory of human action, Lukes on problems arising from the Habermasian attempt to provide rational grounds for judgements about morality and politics, Giddens on the 'absent core' of his thought – analysis of the mechanisms which sustain social interaction, Held on shortcomings in *Legitimation Crisis*, and Arato on the resources within this text for understanding Eastern European societies.

8.455 **Torpey**, J., 'Ethics and critical theory: from Horkheimer to Habermas', *Telos*, 69, 1986, 77–96.

8.456 **Warren**, M., 'Liberal constitutionalism as ideology. Marx and Habermas', *Pol. Theory*, 17, 1989, 511–34. Assessment of liberal constitutionalism, focusing on these theorists, which distinguishes its democratic possibilities from its harmful ideological effects.

8.457 **Watson**, S., 'Jürgen Habermas and Jean-François Lyotard: post-modernism and the crisis of rationality', *Phil. & Soc. Crit.*, 2, 1984, 1–24.

8.458 **White**, S., 'Habermas' communicative ethics and the development of moral consciousness', *Phil. & Soc. Crit.*, 2, 1984, 25–48.

8.459 —— 'Habermas on the foundations of ethics and political theory', in D. R. Sabia and J. Wallulis, ed., *Changing Social Science: Critical Theory and Other Critical Perspectives*, New York, 1983, 157–70.

8.460 —— 'Rationality and the foundations of political philosophy: an introduction to the recent work of Jürgen Habermas', *J. Pol.*, 41, 1979, 1156–71. Exposition of his rationalist and universalist theory of communicative ethics.

8.461 —— 'Reason and authority in Habermas: a critique of the critics', *Am. Pol. Sc. Rev.*, 74, 1980, 1007–17. Defends him against accusations of authoritarianism by outlining his conceptions of practical rationality and normative legitimacy.

8.462 —— *The Recent Work of Jürgen Habermas: Reason, Justice and Modernity*, 1988. A clear and reliable introduction to the work he produced in the 1970s and 1980s.

8.463 **Williams**, H., and **Fearon-Jones**, J., 'Jürgen Habermas and neo-Marxism', in L. Tivey and A. Wright, ed., *Political Thought Since 1945: Philosophy, Science, Ideology*, 1992, 115–132. Brief outline of his belief that the public realm established at the dawn of the modern age is increasingly under threat from instrumental rationality.

8.464 **Wood**, A., 'Habermas' defense of rationalism', *New Germ. Crit.*, 35, 1985, 145–64.

8.465 **Zimmerman**, R., 'Emancipation and rationality. Foundational problems in the theories of Marx and Habermas', *Ratio*, 26, 1984, 143–66. Compares the central ideas of both thinkers, arguing that Habermasian theory represents an advance over Marx in his introduction of a schema of personal socialisation, even though the consensus theory of truth which Habermas deploys is problematic.

Hayek

8.466 **Arnold**, R. A., 'Hayek and institutional evolution', *J. Liber. Sts.*, 4, 1980, 341–51.

8.467 **Barry**, N., 'F. A. Hayek and market liberalism', in L. Tivey and A. Wright, ed., *Political Thought Since 1945: Philosophy, Science, Ideology*, 1992, 133–50. Unashamedly sympathetic account of Hayek's thought which illustrates his ambiguous position within the liberal tradition.

8.468 —— 'Hayek on liberty', in Z. A. Pelczynski and J. Gray, ed., *Conceptions of Liberty in Political Philosophy*, 1984, 263–88. Assesses criticisms of his social philosophy whilst outlining his consequentialist justification of liberty.

8.469 —— *Hayek's Social and Economic Philosophy*, 1979. Roots his free-market liberalism in his broader metaphysical and philosophical framework; a lively celebration and advocacy of these ideas, supplemented by a discussion of his place within previous theoretical and ideological traditions.

8.470 **Baumgarth**, W. P., 'Hayek and political order: the rule of law', *J. Liber. Sts.*, 2, 1978, 11–28.

8.471 **Bay**, C., 'Hayek's liberalism: the constitution of perpetual privilege', *Pol. Sc. Rev.*, 1, 1971, 93–124. Accuses Hayek of representing the interests of a particular class and of Social Darwinist tendencies in a somewhat crude and polemical analysis.

8.472 **Brittan**, S., 'Hayek, the new right and the crisis of social democracy', *Encounter*, 54, 1980, 30–46. Outlines several themes in his thought, endorsing his opposition to

collectivism but remaining critical about some of his positions, for instance his opposition to the notion of social justice.

8.473 **Brough**, W. T., and **Naka**, S., 'Man, the market and the transfer state', in K. R. Leube and A. H. Zlabinger, ed., *The Political Economy of Freedom: Essays in Honor of F. A. Hayek*, 1984, 83–101. Celebrates his account of the natural tendency of humans to maximise wealth, a process mediated by social and political institutions.

8.474 **Burton**, J., ed., *Hayek's Serfdom Revisited* 1984.

8.475 **Butler**, E., *Hayek: His Contribution to the Political and Economic Thought of Our Time*, 1983. A useful introductory guide to the central themes of his work.

8.476 **Cody**, J. V., 'Bibliography of Friedrich A Hayek', *Literature of Liberty*, 5, 1982, 68–101.

8.477 **Connin**, L. J., 'Hayek, liberalism and social knowledge', *Can. J. Pol. Sc.*, 23, 1990, 297–315. Distinguishes his knowledge-based interpretation of liberalism from that of other thinkers, and defends him from accusations of extreme relativism.

8.478 **Cragg**, A. W., 'Hayek, justice and the market', *Can. J. Phil.*, 13, 1983, 563–8.

8.479 **Cristi**, F. R., 'Hayek and Schmitt on the rule of law', *Can. J. Pol. Sc.*, 17, 1984, 521–35.

8.480 **Crowley**, B. L., *The Self, the Individual, and the Community: Liberalism in the Political Thought of F. A. Hayek and Sidney and Beatrice Webb*, 1987. Contrasts these different exemplars of the liberal tradition but suggests that they share an anti-political outlook and function as mirror-images of each other. In conclusion, Crowley counters these perspectives with a community-orientated understanding of political life.

8.481 **Cunningham**, R. L., *Liberty and the Rule of Law*, 1979.

8.482 **Davenport**, J., 'An unrepentant old Whig', *Fortune*, March 1960, 134–5, 192, 194, 197–8. Outlines Hayek's philosophy on the occasion of the appearance of *The Constitution of Liberty*.

8.483 **de Crespigny**, A., 'F. A. Hayek: freedom for progress', in A. de Crespigny and K. Minogue, ed., *Contemporary Political Philosophers*, 1976, 49–66. Outline of his ontological liberalism, which questions the conherence of his opposition to state intervention in the economy.

8.484 **Diamond**, A. M., 'F. A. Hayek on construction and ethics', *J. Liber. Sts.*, 4, 1980, 353–66.

8.485 **Dietze**, G., 'From the Constitution of Liberty to its deconstitution by liberalist dissipation, disintegration, disassociation, disorder', in F. Keyer, ed., *Zur Verfassung der Freiheit, Festgube für Friedrich A. von Hayek. Zur Vollendung seines achtzigsten Lebensjahres*, Stuttgart, 1979, 177–97.

8.486 **Douglas**, J. D., 'The road to modernist slavery', in K. R. Leube and A. H. Zlabinger, ed., *The Political Economy of Freedom: Essays in Honor of F. A. Hayek*, 1984, 103–18. Rehearses Hayek's account of the repressive tendencies of modern states and societies, comparing his ideas with other theorists of totalitarianism such as Arendt.

8.487 **Durbin**, E. F. M., 'Professor Hayek on economic planning and political liberty', *Econ. J.*, 55, 1945, 357-70.

8.488 **Dyer**, P. W., and **Hickman**, R. H., 'American conservatism and F. A. Hayek', *Modern Age*, 23, 1979, 381–93.

8.489 **Finer**, H., *The Road to Reaction*, 1946. Polemical riposte to the *Road to Serfdom*.

8.490 **Forsyth**, M., 'Hayek's bizarre liberalism: a critique', *Pol. Sts.*, 36, 1988, 235–40. Explores the tension between his naturalist view of humans and liberal political views.

8.491 **Galeotti**, A. E., 'Individualism, social rules, tradition: the case of Friedrich A. Hayek', *Pol. Theory*, 15, 1987, 163–81. To prove that any political theory needs a notion of community, the author examines Hayek's individualistic thought, finding a communitarian motif at the heart of his theory of liberty.

8.492 **Gamble**, A., *Hayek and the Market Order*, 1993. Traces his intellectual development and influence on Austrian economics and English liberalism, surveying his central theories and assessing the coherence of his thought.

8.493 **Gissurarson**, H. H., *Hayek's Conservative Liberalism*, New York, 1987.

8.494 **Glasner**, D., 'Friedrich Hayek: an appreciation', *Intercollegiate Review*, 7, 1971, 251–5.

8.495 **Gordon**, S., 'The political economy of F. A. Hayek', *Can. J. Econ.*, 14, 1981, 470–87.

8.496 **Gray**, J., 'F. A. Hayek on liberty and tradition', *J. Liber. Sts.*, 4, 1980, 119–37. Teases out a number of unresolved tensions and ambiguities in his thought, highlighting especially the irreconcilability of his epistemological neo-Kantianism and evolutionary view of mind and society. Ultimately, for Gray, his thought does not amount to a satisfactory expression of liberalism.

8.497 —— 'F. A. von Hayek', in R. Scruton, ed., *Conservative Thinkers: Essays from the Salisbury Review*, 1988, 249–59. Spirited defence of him as a conservative because of his reconciliation of a modern sense of individuality with tradition.

8.498 —— 'Hayek and the rebirth of classical liberalism', *Literature of Liberty*, 5, 1982, 19–66.

8.499 —— *Hayek on Liberty*, 1984. A sympathetic account which stresses his intellectual cogency and the connection between his epistemological and economic beliefs. Includes an illuminating account of the centrality of his concept of a spontaneous social order, a provocative comparison with Mill and an endorsement of Hayek's opposition to rationalism in liberal discourse.

8.500 —— 'Hayek on liberty, rights and justice', *Ethics*, 92, 1981, 73–84. Analyses his attempted fusion of the rational and sceptical elements of modern political philosophy, suggesting that his failure reveals much about the contradictions within modern liberalism.

8.501 —— 'The road to serfdom: forty years on', in Institute of Economic Affairs, *Hayek's Serfdom Revisited*, 1984, 25–42.

8.502 **Hanowy**, R., 'Freedom and the rule of law in F. A. Hayek', *Il Politico*, 36, 1971, 349–77.

8.503 —— 'Hayek's concept of freedom: a critique', *New Individualist Review*, 1, 1961, 28–31.

8.504 —— 'Law and the liberal society: F. A. Hayek's *Constitution of Liberty*', *J. Liber. Sts.*, 2, 1978, 287–97.

8.505 —— 'The Hayekian model of government in an open society', *J. Liber. Sts.*, 6, 1982, 137–43.

8.506 **Harrod**, R., 'Professor Hayek on individualism', *Econ. J.*, 56, 1946, 435–42. Hostile review of his conception of individualism in social life.

8.507 **Heath**, E., 'How to understand liberalism as gardening: Galeotti on Hayek', *Pol.*

Theory, 17, 1989, 107–13. Refutes Galeotti's assertion of the dependency of Hayek's political theory on a communitarian social theory.

8.508 **Hoselitz**, B. F., 'Professor Hayek on German socialism', *Am. Econ. Rev.*, 35, 1945, 926–34.

8.509 **Hoy**, C. M., *A Philosophy of Individual Freedom: the Political Thought of F. A. Hayek*, Westport, Conn., 1984. Explores the connection between his philosophy of freedom and market economics. Largely sympathetic, though some critical comments are appended.

8.510 **Kirzner**, I. M., 'Entrepreneurship, choice and freedom', in F. W. Meyer, et al., ed., *Zur Verfassung der Freiheit: Festgabe für Friedrich A. von Hayek zur Vollendung seines achtzigsten Lebensjahres*, Stuttgart, 1979, 245–56.

8.511 **Kukathas**, C., *Hayek and Modern Liberalism*, 1989. Critique of his conception of liberalism, in particular its unstable Kantian foundations. Ultimately, for Kukathas, he is unable to reconcile the ideas of Kant and Hume, the former representing autonomy and rationality, the latter the historical nature of society and the artificial nature of morality. Concludes that liberalism can be defended around a richer, more plausible account of the self and society.

8.512 **Livingston**, D. W., 'Hayek as Humean', *Crit. Rev.*, 5, 1991, 159–77. Rescues him from the accusation that his Humean idiom contradicts his Kantian beliefs.

8.513 **MacCormick**, N., 'Spontaneous order and the rule of law: some problems', *Ratio Juris*, 2, 1989, 41–54. Compares Oakeshott's and Hayek's theories of law, concluding that both wrongly infer conclusions from their ideas which are inimical to the welfare state.

8.514 **Machlup**, F., ed., *Essays on Hayek*, 1977. A collection in honour of Hayek, including Roche on his contemporary relevance, Hartnell on the appeal of socialism to intellectuals via a study of *The Road to Serfdom*, Dietze on his analysis of the political structure requisite for a free society, and Letwin on his overall intellectual achievements.

8.515 —— 'Liberalism and the choice of freedoms', in E. Stressler, et al., ed., *Roads to Freedom: Essays in Honour of Friedrich A. von Hayek*, 1969, 117–46.

8.516 **Mack**, E., 'Hayek on justice and the market: a reply to MacLeod', *Can. J. Phil.*, 13, 1984, 569–74.

8.517 **MacLeod**, A., 'Hayek on justice and the market: a rejoinder to Cragg and Mack', *Can. J. Phil.*, 13, 1984, 575–84.

8.518 —— 'Justice and the market', *Can. J. Phil.*, 13, 1984, 551–62.

8.519 **Miller**, E. F., 'Hayek's critique of reason', *Modern Age*, 20, 1976, 383–94.

8.520 —— 'The cognitive basis of Hayek's political thought', in R. L. Cunningham, ed., *Liberty and the Rule of Law*, 1979, 242–67.

8.521 **Moss**, L. S., 'Reindustrialization and the rule of law', in K. R. Leube and A. H. Zlabinger, ed., *The Political Economy of Freedom: Essays in Honor of F. A. Hayek*, 1984, 119–36. Defends *The Road to Serfdom* as a pathbreaking text, arguing that much of Hayek's analysis remains pertinent to the contemporary debate about industrialisation in the United States.

8.522 **Nishiyama**, C., 'Anti-rationalism or critical rationalism', in F. W. Meyer, et al ed., *Zur Verfassung der Freiheit: Festgabe für Friedrich A. von Hayek zur Vollendung seines achtzigsten Lebensjahres*, Stuttgart, 1979, 21–42.

8.523 **O'Driscoll**, G. P., 'Spontaneous order and the co-ordination of economic activities', *J. Liber. Sts.*, 1, 1977, 137–51.

8.524 **Paul**, E. F., 'Liberalism, unintended orders and evolutionism', *Pol. Sts.*, 36, 1988, 251–72. A critique of liberalism grounded on evolutionary foundations, which reads Hayek as in many respects an evolutionary liberal, particularly in his development of the notion of spontaneous order.

8.525 **Plant**, A., 'A tribute to Hayek – the rational persuader', *Economic Age*, 2, 1970, 4–8.

8.526 **Plant**, R., 'Hirsch, Hayek, and Habermas dilemmas of distribution', in A. Ellis and K. Kumar, ed., *Dilemmas of Liberal Democracies: Studies in Fred Hirsch's Social Limits to Growth*, 1983, 45–64. Argues that these thinkers posit a similar diagnosis of the central problems of the capitalist welfare state, particularly in terms of the absence of an agreed morality in this system. Concludes that there are moral resources within a liberal state for securing ethical consensus.

8.527 **Raz**, J., 'The rule of law and its virtues', *Law Q. Rev.*, 93, 1977, 185–211.

8.528 **Rees**, J. C., 'Hayek on liberty', *Phil.*, 38, 1963, 346-60.

8.529 **Robbins**, L., 'Hayek on liberty', *Economica*, 28, 1961, 66–81.

8.530 **Rosenof**, T., 'Freedom, planning and totalitarianism: the reception of F. A. Hayek's *The Road to Serfdom*', *Canadian Review of American Studies*, 5, 1974, 149–65.

8.531 **Rothbard**, M. N., 'F. A. Hayek and the concept of coercion', in *The Ethics of Liberty*, Atlantic Highlands, N.J., 1982, 219–28. Criticises his 'woolly' concept of coercion, which renders the *Constitution of Liberty* unsuitable as a framework for individual liberty.

8.532 **Rowland**, B. M., 'Beyond Hayek's pessimism: reason, tradition and bounded constructivist rationalism', *Brit. J. Pol. Sc.*, 18, 1988, 221–41. Emphasises the inconsistency between his notions of traditionalism and constitutional design, locating this tension in his ambivalence about the proportions of reasoned choice and unreflective rule-following in human decisions.

8.533 —— *Ordered Liberty and the Constitutional Framework: the Political Thought of Friedrich A. Hayek*, Wesport, Conn., 1987. A critique of the ambiguity of the Hayekian concept of individual liberty, focusing upon the tension between his celebration of a natural, spontaneous order and his design for a new, democratic order. A persuasive account which revolves around the conflicting accounts of the self embedded in his work – the rational individual versus the social self.

8.534 **Scott**, G., 'The political economy of F. A. Hayek', *Can. J. Econ. & Pol. Sc.*, 14, 1981, 470–87.

8.535 **Seldon**, A., ed., *Agenda for a Free Society: Essays on Hayek's The Constitution of Liberty*, 1961. Includes Hutton on the tension between the individual and the social, Shenfield on the rule of law, and several essays charting the policy implications of his ideas (Morgan, Benham, Fogarty, Slesser, Nash).

8.536 —— 'Hayek on liberty and liberalism', *Contemp. Rev.*, 200, 1961, 399–406. Celebrates the main thrust of his political outlook, arguing that he proposes a fundamental reorientation of liberalism as an ideology.

8.537 **Shearmur**, J., 'The Austrian connection: Hayek's liberalism and the thought of Carl Menger', in B. Smith and W. Grassl, ed., *Austrian Economics: Philosophical and Historical Background*, 1986, 210–24.

8.538 —— 'The road to freedom: F. A. Hayek's intellectual journey', *Reason*, December 1984, 55–9.

8.539 **Shenfield**, A., 'F. A. Hayek, 1944, "60" ', *Modern Age*, 26, 1982, 245–8.

8.540 —— 'Law, legislation and liberty: Hayek's conceptual trilogy', *Modern Age*, 24, 1980, 142–9.

8.541 —— 'The new thought of F. A. Hayek', *Modern Age*, 26, 1982, 54–61.

8.542 **Tomlinson**, J., *Hayek and the Market*, 1990. Brief survey of his political and moral thought, including a useful section on the shifts in his political prognoses.

8.543 **Vanberg**, V., 'Spontaneous market order and social rules: a critical examination of F. A. Hayek's theory of cultural evolution', *Economics and Philosophy*, 2, 1986, 75–100.

8.544 **Vernon**, R., 'The "great society" and the "open society": liberalism in Hayek and Popper', *Can. J. Pol. Sc.*, 9, 1976, 261–76. Argues that the complexity of the liberal tradition has been undermined by the elision of concepts such as Popper's 'open society' and Hayek's 'great society'.

8.545 **Viner**, J., 'Hayek on freedom and coercion', *Southern Econ. J.*, 27, 1961, 230–6.

8.546 **Wilhelm**, M., 'The political thought of Friedrich A. Hayek', *Pol. Sts.*, 20, 1972, 169–84. Outlines his distinctive interpretation of liberalism and the centrality of the rule-of-law doctrine in his thought.

8.547 **Worsthorne**, P., 'F. A. Hayek: next construction for the giant', in M. Ivens, ed., *Prophets of Freedom and Enterprise*, 1975, 70–80. Appropriates Hayek for his own definition of freedom, criticising him only for the absence of a sustained examination of trade union power.

8.548 **Yaeger**, L. B., 'Utility, rights, and constraint: some reflections on Hayek's work', in K. R. Leube and A. H. Zlabinger, ed., *The Political Economy of Freedom: Essays in Honor of F. A. Hayek*, 1984, 61–80. Appropriates Hayek to justify the tendentious belief that utilitarianism provides the sole basis for successful policy formation.

Heidegger

8.549 **Bourdieu**, P., *The Political Ontology of Martin Heidegger*, 1991.

8.550 **Dauenhauer**, B. P., 'Renovating the problem of politics', *Rev. Metaph.*, 29, 1976, 626–41. Returns to the thought of Heidegger and Merleau-Ponty for a reconsideration of the nature of politics in the realms of speech and history.

8.551 **Edler**, F. H. W., 'Philosophy, language, and politics: Heidegger's attempt to steal the language of the revolution in 1933–4', *Soc. Res.*, 57, 1990, 197–238. An assessment of his relationship with national socialism and belief in the need to revolutionise political language.

8.552 **Fehér**, I. M., 'Fundamental ontology and political interlude: Heidegger as rector of the University of Freiburg', in M. Dascal and O. Gruengard, ed., *Knowledge and Politics: Case Studies in the Relationship Between Epistemology and Political Philosophy*, Boulder, Calif., 1989, 316–51. Connects Heidegger's tenure as rector, shortly after Hitler's rise to power, with his philosophical ideals, stressing the incompatibility between his idealism and the Nazi revolution.

8.553 **Harries**, K., 'Heidegger as a political thinker', *Rev. Metaph.*, 29, 1976, 642–69. Reconstructs his political philosophy in the 1930s to 'explain' his turn to national socialism.

8.554 **McCormick**, P., 'Heidegger, politics and the philosophy of history', *Phil. Sts. (Ireland)*, 27, 1980, 196–211.

8.555 **Zimmerman**, M. E., *Heidegger's Confrontation with Modernity, Technology, Politics and Art*, Indiana, Ind., 1990. Stimulating rereading of his critique of modernity, stressing the ecological dimension of his thought.

8.556 **Zuckert**, C. H., 'Martin Heidegger. His philosophy and his politics', *Pol. Theory*, 18, 1990, 51–79. Returns to his philosophical ideas to assess his controversial relationship to Nazi practice. Concludes that his philosophy prevented him from mounting a serious moral or political critique of fascism in Germany.

Kautsky

8.557 **Bronner**, S. E., 'Karl Kautsky and the

twilight of orthodoxy', *Pol. Theory*, 10, 1982, 580–605. Sympathetic reappraisal of Kantsky, assessing contemporary criticism of his work and his legacy for the tradition of social democracy.

8.558 **Geary**, D., *Karl Kautsky*, 1987. Clear and insightful account of his thought, stressing his production of a coherent and verifiable model of social development and proximity to Marx's thought in several areas.

8.559 **Salvadori**, M., *Karl Kautsky and the Socialist Revolution, 1880–1938*, 1979. Comprehensive account of the evolution of his thought and political context in which he operated, avoiding excessively hagiographic or hostile accounts of his life and thought and illuminating many areas of his work.

8.560 **Steensen**, G. P., *Karl Kautsky, 1854–1938: Marxism in the Classical Years*, Pittsburg, Pa., 1991. Outline of the development of his thought, illustrating in particular the role of Engels in influencing the orthodox Marxism he came to adopt.

8.561 **Townshend**, J., 'Reassessing Kautsky's Marxism', *Pol. Sts.*, 37, 1989, 659–64. Reviews and challenges the existing schools of thought concerning his notions of evolutionary change and the historical process.

Korsch

8.562 **Breines**, P., 'Korsch's "road to Marx"', *Telos*, 26, 1976, 42–56. Traces Korsch's intellectual development up to 1918.

8.563 **Ceppa**, L., 'Korsch's Marxism', *Telos*, 26, 1976, 94–119. Retraces his revision of Marxist theory, concluding that he retained a Marxian emancipatory framework.

8.564 **Goode**, P., *Karl Korsch: A Study in Western Marxism*, Atlantic Highlands, N.J., 1979.

8.565 **Jacoby**, R., 'The inception of Western Marxism: Karl Korsch and the politics of philosophy', *Can. J. Pol. & Soc. Theory*, 3, 1979, 5–34.

8.566 **Kellner**, D., 'Korsch's revolutionary historicism', *Telos*, 26, 1976, 70–93. Argues, unconventionally, that Korsch remained within a Leninist framework whilst criticising Soviet theory and practice.

8.567 **Negt**, O., 'Theory, empiricism and class struggle: on the problem of constitution in

Karl Korsch', *Telos*, 26, 1976, 120–42. Traces the political influences (including the English Fabians) on Korsch, arguing that his philosophical ideas developed in opposition to Marxism as a science of legitimation.

Lenin

8.568 **Barfield**, R., 'Lenin's utopianism: state and revolution', *Slavic Rev.*, 30, 1971, 45–56. Historically specific interpretation of *State and Revolution*, emphasising the timing of its writing, before the March revolution of 1917. Suggests that the libertarian ideas of this text were far more integral to Lenin's overall project than commentators who stress his 'deviation' in 1917 imagine.

8.569 **Beeching**, E., 'Lenin and the role of women', *Communist Viewpoint*, 2, 1970, 35–40.

8.570 **Besancon**, A., *The Rise of the Gulag: The Intellectual Origins of Leninism*, 1981.

8.571 **Bikkenin**, N. B., *Socialist Ideology*, Moscow, 1980.

8.572 **Bjarnason**, E., 'Lenin and state-monopoly capitalism', *Communist Viewpoint*, 2, 1970, 16–21.

8.573 **Claudin**, F., 'Democracy and dictatorship in Lenin and Kautsky', *New Left Rev.*, 106, 1977, 59–76. Assesses the political and theoretical conflict which emerged among them after 1917, concluding that their presentation of conflicting paths out of world capitalist crisis remains pertinent.

8.574 **Cliff**, T., *Lenin*, 1975–79. An historically informed, partisan interpretation of Lenin's life and work.

8.575 **Connor**, W., *The National Question in Marxist-Leninist Theory and Strategy*, Princeton, N.J., 1985.

8.576 **Currie** D., 'Lenin and the role of the party of scientific socialism', *Communist Viewpoint*, 2, 1970, 21–5.

8.577 **Daniels** R. V., 'The state and revolution: a case study in the transformation of Communist ideology', *American Slavic and East European Review*, 12, 1953, 22–43. Views *State and Revolution* as the product of Lenin's anarchist/utopian deviation in 1917; its ideals were supplanted by Stalinist conceptions of politics and the state.

8.578 **Davis** H. B., 'Lenin and nationalism: the redirection of the Marxist theory of nationalism, 1903–1917', *Sc. & Soc.*, 31, 1967, 164–85. Chronological assessment of his shifting position on the national question, presenting 1913 as a watershed when he began a thorough re-examination of nationalism and self-determination.

8.579 **Day**, R. B., 'Dialectical method in the political writings of Lenin and Bakunin', *Can. J. Pol. Sc.*, 9, 1976, 244–60. Reaffirms Lenin's critique of Bakunin's use of dialectics, concluding that the latter inadvertently helped negate the New Economic Policy which he supported.

8.580 **DeGrood**, D. H., 'The trial by fire of Marxism: the transition to Leninism', *Enquiry*, 3, 1971, 68–80.

8.581 **Dewhurst**, A., 'Lenin – peaceful co-existence and social progress', *Communist Viewpoint*, 2, 1970, 25–30.

8.582 **Draper**, H., *The 'Dictatorship of the Proletariat' from Marx to Lenin*, New York, 1987.

8.583 **Ehrenberg**, J., 'Communists and proletarians: Lenin on consciousness and spontaneity', *Studies in Soviet Thought*, 25, 1983, 285–306. Argues that Lenin valued spontaneous self-activity by workers.

8.584 —— 'Lenin and the politics of organisation', *Sc. & Soc.*, 43, 1979, 70–86.

8.585 —— 'Making the turn: the political roots of Lenin's theory of the party press', *Studies in Soviet Thought*, 21, 1980, 119–39. Clarifies the reasoning behind Lenin's theory of the press and the role he assigned to the party paper.

8.586 **Eissenstate**, B. W., ed., *Lenin and Leninism*, 1971. Seventeen essays including D. Hammer, 'The dictatorship of the proletariat', P. Schreiber, 'Lenin, Boganov, and the proletarian culture', L. Feuer, 'Between fantasy and reality: Lenin as a philosopher and social scientist', B. Ramundi, 'Leninism: rationale of party dictatorship', M. Pap, 'Lenin and the problem of self-determinism of nations', and J. Miller, 'Lenin and Soviet mythology'.

8.587 **Feuer**, L., 'Lenin's fantasy', *Encounter*, 5, 1970, 22–38.

8.588 **Florea**, E., 'Lenin on the concept of nation', *Revue Roumaine des Sciences Sociales, Serie de Philosophie et Logique*, 14, 1970, 31–6.

8.589 **Frankel**, B., 'The state of the state after Leninism', *Theory & Soc.*, 7, 1979,

199–242.

8.590 **Garvy**, G., 'The origins of Lenin's views on the role of banks in the socialist transformation of society', *Hist. Pol. Econ.*, 4, 1972, 252–63. Returns to Saint-Simon, Hobson, Parvus and Hilferding for the sources of Lenin's ideas on this question.

8.591 **Gerratana**, V., 'Stalin, Lenin and "Leninism"', *New Left Rev.*, 103, 1987, 59–77. Examines the possible connection between Stalinism and Leninism, concluding that Stalin's appropriation of the Leninist theoretical model prevented its further development for several decades.

8.592 **Glass**, S. T., 'The single-mindedness of Vladimir Illich Ulyanov', *Hist. Pol. Thought*, 8, 1987, 277–87. Suggests that Lenin's ideas remained essentially coherent until he became disillusioned with human nature.

8.593 **Gontraev**, G. A., 'The treatment of problems of Marxist ethics in the post-revolutionary works of Lenin', *Sov. Sts. Phil.*, 6, 1967, 34–41. An interesting topic treated peremptorily by the author who argues that immediately after 1917 'communist moral relationships were formed'.

8.594 **Gourfinkel**, N., *Portrait of Lenin*, New York, 1972.

8.595 **Harding**, N., 'Lenin and his critics: some problems of interpretation', *Eur. J. Soc.*, 13, 1976, 366–83.

8.596 —— 'Lenin's early writings – the problem of context', *Pol. Sts.*, 23, 1975, 442–58. Disparages the interpretation of Lenin as a Jacobin because of its misleading presentation of the political context in which he operated.

8.597 —— *Lenin's Political Thought*: Vol. I: *Theory and Practice in the Democratic Revolution*, 1977; Vol. II: *Theory and Practice in the Socialist Revolution*, 1981. Striking reinterpretation of Lenin's theory which rebuts those interpretations which stress his activism and downplay his theory, and corrects the notion that he was a dogmatic or opportunist thinker. Focuses on key themes within his political thought – revolution, imperialism, the party and the post-revolutionary state.

8.598 **Hegedus**, A., 'Lenin and the alternative types of socialist economy', in *Socialism and Bureaucracy*, 1976, 126–43. Outlines

his post-revolutionary articulation of a theory of administration in a socialist economy.

8.599 **Ionescu**, G., 'Lenin, the Commune and the state. Thoughts for a centenary', *Govt. & Oppos.*, 5, 1969–70, 131–65. Returns to Lenin's writings on the state to assess his role in the construction of, and later struggle against, the post-revolutionary state in USSR. Concludes critically that his theory of the state was developed from a misinterpretation of Marx's misunderstanding of the Commune.

8.600 **Jacoby**, R., 'Lenin and Luxemburg: negation in theory and praxis', *Rad. Am.*, 4, 1970, 21–31. Roots these thinkers' political differences in their theoretical divergence, stressing Luxemburg's emphasis on the unmediated dialectical interplay between Marxist theory and mass politics.

8.601 **Kashtan**, W., 'Lenin and contemporary imperialism', *Communist Viewpoint*, 2, 1970, 5–10.

8.602 **Katznelson**, I., 'Lenin or Weber? Choices in Marxist theories of politics', *Pol. Sts*, 29, 1981, 632–40. Assesses the relevance of their ideas for contemporary debates about bureaucracy.

8.603 **Khromuskin**, G. B., *Lenin on Modern Capitalism*, 1969.

8.604 **Kingston-Mann**, E., *Lenin and the Problem of the Marxist Peasant Revolution*, New York, 1983. Details the sources of his theory of peasant revolution.

8.605 **Kruger**, D. H., 'Hobson, Lenin, and Schumpeter on imperialism', *J. Hist. Ideas*, 16, 1955, 252–9.

8.606 **Krygier**, M., 'Weber, Lenin and the reality of socialism', in E. Kamenka and M. Krygier, ed., *Bureaucracy: The Career of a Concept*, 1979, 61–87. Suggests certain similarities in these thinkers' concern for the post-revolutionary fate of bureaucracy, despite their obvious differences.

8.607 **Kuvarkin**, V., 'Lenin's thought: towards understanding', *Revolutionary World*, 37–39, 1980, 99–128.

8.608 **Lane**, D., 'Leninism as an ideology of development', in G. de Kadt and G. Williams, ed., *Sociology and Development*, 1974, 23–37. Reads Leninism as a theoretical model of development, which provided the justification for a large-scale industrial system. After his death, in Lane's view, Leninism was interpreted selectively by Soviet policy makers who abandoned his more idealistic commitments concerning the future organisation of industrial society.

8.609 —— *Leninism: A Sociological Interpretation*, 1981. Analysis of Lenin's ideas and pronouncements as well as their transformation into an ideology after his death. Also tackles the question of the causal connection between Leninism and Stalinism.

8.610 —— 'Socialist revolutions?', *Pol. Sts.*, 30, 1982, 278–83. A critical, insightful review of recent interpretations of Lenin's and Trotsky's political theories.

8.611 **Le Blanc**, P., *Lenin and the Revolutionary Party*, 1989. Examining his conception of the revolutionary party and its place in Marxist thought, Le Blanc looks at his critics and adversaries and at the historical context which shaped his views.

8.612 **Lewin**, M., *Lenin's Last Struggle*, 1975. A vivid and important reinterpretation of the political and theoretical shifts he underwent towards the end of his life.

8.613 **Liebman**, M., *Leninism Under Lenin*, 1975. An historically informed consideration of the evolution of Leninism, stressing the development of his political thought, and steering a course between excessively hagiographic and hostile accounts of him. Concludes that Leninism ultimately failed, a judgement Liebman connects to a number of theoretical inadequacies on Lenin's part.

8.614 **Low**, A. D., *Lenin on the Question of Nationality*, New York, 1958.

8.615 **MacFarlane**, L. J., 'Marxist critiques of the state', in B. Parekh, ed., *The Concept of Socialism*, 1979, 167–91. Examination of the Kautsky-Lenin debate about the state in the light of recent interpretations of Marx's and Engels's writings on this question.

8.616 **MacIntyre**, A., 'How not to write about Lenin', in *Against the Self-images of the Age: Essays on Ideology and Philosophy*, 1971, 43–51. Points to the theoretical inconsistencies within Leninism and the limitations of his later protests against bureaucracy and Stalin which have been passed over by his more hagiographic commentators.

8.617 **Magnuson**, B., 'Lenin and workers' control', *Communist Viewpoint*, 2, 1970, 30–5.

8.618 **Mandel**, E., *The Leninist Theory of Organisation*, 1971.

8.619 **Melograni**, P., *Lenin and the Myth of World Revolution: Ideology and Reasons of State, 1917–1920*, 1989.

8.620 **Menasche**, L., 'How not to take Lenin seriously', *Sc. & Soc.*, 34, 1970, 331–42.

8.621 **Meyer**, A. G., *Leninism*, 1956. Clear, reliable and comprehensive account of Lenin's political ideas.

8.622 **Moran**, P., 'Leninism and the Enlightenment', *Studies in Soviet Thought*, 30, 1985, 109–30.

8.623 **Morgan**, M. C., *Lenin*, 1971.

8.624 **Page**, S. W., *Lenin and World Revolution*, New York, 1972.

8.625 —— ed., *Lenin: Dedicated Marxist, or Revolutionary Pragmatist?*, 1970.

8.626 —— *The Geopolitics of Leninism*, New York, 1982. Chronological study of his unfolding theory of European revolution from 1914, in which proletarian revolution in Germany played a central role. Lenin's ideas are closely interwoven with military and political events to illustrate the 'geopolitics of Leninism' – the notion of self-determination for nations. Unusual and problematic interpretation.

8.627 **Peled**, Y., 'Lenin on the Jewish question: the theoretical setting', *Pol. Sts.*, 35, 1987, 61–78. Argues against the view that he adopted a merely tactical approach to this question. The author traces his theory of nationality and reveals the crucial role of modernisation which would, in his view, eliminate ethnic conflict.

8.628 **Piccone**, P., 'Towards an understanding of Lenin's philosophy', *Rad. Am.*, 4, 1970, 3–20. Complex account of the shifting basis of his philosophy, intertwining political developments, theoretical debates among Marxists and the dominant philosophical traditions he encountered.

8.629 **Pipes**, R., 'The origins of Bolshevism: the intellectual evolution of young Lenin', in R. Pipes, ed., *Revolutionary Russia*, 1968, 26–52. Specifies four phases through which his ideas passed, from 1887–1899, after which he developed the 'undemocratic' doctrine of Bolshevism.

8.630 **Polan**, A. J., *Lenin and the End of Politics*, 1984. Lively analysis of the political forms and discourses of 'socialist' states in Eastern Europe through a consideration of the tension between the commune-state and the achievement of actual socialism.

Locates a subterranean authoritarianism in Lenin's conflation of political, institutional and constitutional forms with class relations, placing his writings in their political and theoretical context.

8.631 **Schapiro**, L., 'Lenin's heritage', *Encounter*, 5, 1970, 57–9.

8.632 —— and **Reddaway**, P., *Lenin: The Man, the Theorist, the Leader: A Reappraisal*, 1967.

8.633 **Schedler**, G., 'A defense of the Lenin-Engels view of dialectical materialism and class consciousness', *Revolutionary World*, 33, 1979, 55–70.

8.634 —— 'Justice in Marx, Engels and Lenin', *Studies in Soviet Thought*, 18, 1978, 223–33.

8.635 **Service**, R., *Lenin: A Political Life*, 1991–92. A three-volume work combining history and theory.

8.636 **Seth**, S., 'Lenin's reformation of Marxism: the colonial question as a national question', *Hist. Pol. Thought*, 13, 1992, 99–128. A bold attempt to explain the paradox whereby Marxism proved more successful in the former colonial countries of the East than the bourgeois societies of Western Europe, yet in the former region the national question, one of Marxism's theoretical failures, was salient. Lenin's reformulation of Marx is presented as crucial: his theory of imperialism brought the non-Western world into the ambit of Marxism yet he failed to theorise nationalism adequately.

8.637 **Shub**, D., 'Kropotkin and Lenin', *Russ. Rev.*, 12, 1953, 227–34.

8.638 —— *Lenin*, 1966.

8.639 **Shukman**, H., *Lenin and the Russian Revolution*, 1967. Outlines the course of events leading up to the revolution, illuminating his role within the party. Interprets Leninism as an opportunistic attitude towards power rather than an ideology.

8.640 **Sirianni**, C., 'Rereading Lenin', *Socialist Revolution*, 23, 1973, 77–106.

8.641 **Skilling**, H. G., 'Permanent or uninterrupted revolution: Lenin, Trotsky, and their successors in the transition to socialism', *Canadian Slavonic Papers*, 5, 1961, 3–30.

8.642 **Stewart**, W., 'Lenin – anarchism and the ultra-left', *Communist Viewpoint*, 2, 1970, 55–60.

8.643 **Sweezy**, P. M., and **Magdoff** H., ed., *Lenin Today: Eight Essays, on the Hundredth Anniversary of Lenin's Birth*, New York, 1970.

8.644 **Theen**, R. H. W., 'The idea of the revolutionary state: Tkachev, Trotsky, and Lenin', *Russ. Rev.*, 4, 1972, 383–98.

8.645 —— *V. I. Lenin: The Genesis and Development of a Revolutionary*, 1974.

8.646 **Topalian**, E., *Lenin*, 1984.

8.647 **Treadgold**, D., *Lenin and his Rivals*, 1955.

8.648 **Ulam**, A., *Lenin and the Bolsheviks*, 1966. Historical and biographical account of his political and intellectual role in the Russian Revolution.

8.649 —— 'Lenin: his legacy', *Foreign Affairs*, 48, 1970, 460–70.

8.650 **Wolfe**, B. D., *Lenin and the Twentieth Century*, Stanford, Calif., 1984.

8.651 **Woods**, A., *Lenin and Trotsky: what they really stood for: a reply to Monty Johnstone*, 1976.

Lukács

8.652 **Almasi**, M., 'Lukács on democracy', *New Hungarian Quarterly*, 26, 1985, 94–9.

8.653 **Arato**, A., 'Lukács' path to Marxism (1910–1923)', *Telos*, 7, 1971, 128–36. Stresses the influence of Simmel on his early intellectual formation.

8.654 —— and **Breines**, P., *The Young Lukács and the Origins of Western Marxism*, 1979. Outline of the central elements of his Marxism; these are contrasted with new left ideas and the development of orthodox Marxism.

8.655 **Baxandall**, L., 'George Lukács and the dangling man', *Phil. Forum*, 3, 1972, 498–511.

8.656 **Blakeley**, T., 'Lukács and the Frankfurt school in the Soviet Union', *Studies in Soviet Thought*, 31, 1986, 47–51.

8.657 **Breines**, P., 'Introduction to Lukács' *The Old Culture and the New Culture*', *Telos*, 5, 1970, 1–20.

8.658 —— 'Lukács, revolution and Marxism: 1885–1918', *Phil. Forum*, 34, 1972, 401–22.

8.659 —— 'Praxis and its theorists: the impact of Lukács and Korsch in the 1920s', *Telos*, 11, 1972, 67–203. A close consideration of the political and intellectual context in which the distinctive Marxism of these thinkers was developed and received.

8.660 **Buhr**, M., 'Georg Lukács and contemporary bourgeois ideology', *Sov.*

Sts. Phil., 25, 1987, 87–97.

8.661 **Cary**, W., 'An introduction to Georg Lukács', in *New Man or No Man*, Boston, Mass., 1969, 96–107.

8.662 **El-Hassan**, J., 'Consciousness and ideology. A critique of Lukács, Althusser and Poulantzas', *Dialectical Anthropology*, 11, 1986, 49–62.

8.663 **Esslin**, M., 'Solzhenitsyn and Lukács', *Encounter*, 5, March 1971, 47–51.

8.664 **Feenberg**, A., 'Lukács and the critique of 'orthodox' Marxism', *Phil. Forum*, 3, 1972, 422–68.

8.665 —— *Lukács, Marx and the Sources of Critical Theory*, Totowa, N. J., 1981. Comparative evaluation of *History and Class Consciousness* and Marx's *Economic and Philosophical Manuscripts*, charting these texts' impact upon the development of Marxist theory; particularly illuminating on the links between Lukács and the Frankfurt school, tracing the appropriation by later critical theorists of the concept of reification.

8.666 —— 'Reification and the antinomies of socialist thought', *Telos*, 92, 1971, 93–118. Celebrates Lukács's attempt to surmount the central antinomies within Marxist thought through his development of the concept of reification which allowed for a total understanding and critique of social relations.

8.667 **Fehér**, F., 'Lukács on Weimar', *Telos*, 39, 1979, 113–36.

8.668 **Heller**, A., 'Group interest, collective consciousness and the role of the intellectual in Lukács and Goldmann', *Social Praxis*, 6, 1979, 177–92.

8.669 **Jameson**, F., 'The case for Georg Lukács', *Salmagundi*, 13, 1970, 3–35.

8.670 **Jay**, M., 'The concept of totality in Lukács and Adorno', in S. Avineri, ed., *Varieties of Marxism*, The Hague, 1977, 147–74. Comparing their ideas on this score, Jay suggests that Adorno helped undermine the Lukácsian problematic in Western Marxism.

8.671 **Kadarkay**, A., *George Lukács: Life, Thought and Politics*, 1991. The only major biography in English of one of the most able and original thinkers to have worked within the Marxian tradition.

8.672 —— 'George Lukács's road to art and Marx', *Polity*, 13, 1980, 230–60.

8.673 **Kettler**, D., 'Culture and revolution: Lukács in the Hungarian revolution of 1918–19', *Telos*, 10, 1971, 35–92. Assesses the 'revolutionary culturism' developed by Lukács and his political associates in these years. Detailed intellectual history throwing light upon his influence on contemporaries such as Mannheim.

8.674 **Lapointe**, F., *Georg Lukács and his Critics: An International Bibliography with Annotations (1910–1982)*, Westport, Conn., 1983.

8.675 **Levi**, A., 'Humanism and the Marxist tradition. The young Marx, Lukács and the Yugoslavian school', in *Humanism and Politics. Studies in the Relation of Power and Value in the Western Tradition*, Bloomington, Ind., 1969, 397–445.

8.676 **Lichtheim**, G., *Lukács*, 1970. Brief introduction to and assessment of Lukács.

8.677 **Löwy**, M., *George Lukács: From Romanticism to Bolshevism*, 1979. Historically informed, chronological study of his intellectual development in the context of the radicalised intelligentsia of early twentieth-century Germany and Hungary. The book's insights are obscured rather than magnified by the constant references to a potential sociology of intellectuals.

8.678 —— 'Lukács and Stalinism', *New Left Rev.*, 91, 1975, 25–41. Assesses the break in Lukács's thought in the course of his identification with Stalinism after 1926.

8.679 **Lunn**, E., *Marxism and Modernism: An Historical Study of Lukács, Brecht, Benjamin, and Adorno*, 1985.

8.680 **Maier**, J., 'Georg Lukács and the Frankfurt School', *Sts. Sov. Thought*, 31, 1986, 53–7.

8.681 **Mészáros**, I., *Lukács's Concept of Dialectics*, 1971.

8.682 **Murphy**, P., *Writings By and About Georg Lukács: A Bibliography*, New York, 1976.

8.683 **Parkinson**, G. H. R., *George Lukács*, 1977. A chronological and uncritical exposition of his thought, stressing his contribution to and break from a number of contemporary cultural traditions.

8.684 **Piccone**, P., 'Dialectic and materialism in Lukács', *Telos*, 11, 1972, 105–35.

8.685 **Shue**, H. G., 'Lukács: notes on his originality', *J. Hist. Ideas*, 34, 1973, 645–52. Establishes that many of the writings of the early Marx were available to Lukács in the 1920s, arguing that commentators such as Lichtheim and MacIntyre overestimate his humanist intuition; in fact, he was well versed in these texts.

8.686 **Stedman Jones**, G., 'The Marxism of the early Lukács: an evaluation', *New Left Rev.*, 70, 1971, 27–64. A reassessment of Lukács, following the English translation of *History and Class Consciousness*, endorsing his belief in the scientific status of historical materialism.

8.687 **Stern**, L., 'George Lukács: an intellectual portrait', *Dissent*, Spring 1958, 162–73. Celebration of his distinctive thought, illustrating his concern for literary and social value, consciousness and reification; accessible overview of his various writings.

8.688 **Tertulian**, N., 'On the later Lukács', *Telos*, 40, 1979, 136–43.

8.689 **Truitt**, W. H., 'Ideology, expression and mediation in Marx, Raphael and Lukács', *Phil. Forum*, 3, 1972, 468-98.

8.690 **Witte**, B., 'Benjamin and Lukács. Historical notes on the relationship between their political and aesthetic theories', *New Germ. Crit.*, 5, 1975, 3–26.

8.691 **Zitta**, V., *Georg Lukács' Marxism: Alienation, Dialectics, Revolution. A Study in Utopia and Ideology*, The Hague, 1964. A lengthy and hostile treatment of his thought.

Luxemburg

8.692 **Basso**, L., *Rosa Luxemburg: A Reappraisal*, 1974. A sympathetic outline of her political theory, stressing her connection of proletarian experience to socialist goals.

8.693 —— 'Rosa Luxemburg: the dialectical method', *International Socialist Journal*, 16–17, 1966, 504–41.

8.694 **Cliff**, T., *Rosa Luxemburg*, 1968.

8.695 **Day**, R. B., 'Rosa Luxemburg and the accumulation of capital', *Critique*, 12, 1979–80, 81–96.

8.696 **Dunayevskaya**, R., *Rosa Luxemburg: Women's Liberation and Marx's Philosophy of Revolution*, 1983. An assessment of the revolutionary connection between Luxemburg and feminist consciousness, pointing to her philosophical shortcomings. Weakened somewhat by its excessively polemical tone.

8.697 **Eley**, G., 'The legacy of Rosa Luxemburg', *Critique*, 12, 1979–80, 139–49. Reasserts the complex historical context in which Luxemburg operated, against the ahistorical reading of Geras which, in Eley's view, glosses unevenness and contradictions in her political thought.

8.698 **Eltinger**, E., *Rosa Luxemburg: A Life*, 1986. A biography, using new Polish sources, which expresses the personal side of her life as well as her revolutionary Marxist theory and political activism.

8.699 **Frölich**, P., *Rosa Luxemburg: Ideas in Action*, 1972.

8.700 **Geras**, N., 'Rosa Luxemburg after 1905', *New Left Rev.*, 89, 1975, 3–46. Reconstructs her attitude towards the Russian revolution prior to 1917, illustrating how she differed from Trotsky and Lenin in this period yet arguing that with the outbreak of the revolution she came round to a position similar to Trotsky's.

8.701 —— 'Rosa Luxemburg: barbarism and the collapse of capitalism', *New Left Rev.*, 82, 1973, 17–38. Defends her against charges of economism and spontaneism on the basis of her belief in the need for political struggle and dialectical interpretation of the development and nature of capitalism.

8.702 —— *The Legacy of Rosa Luxemburg*, 1976. A series of essays on her political thought, including an assessment of the political implications of her economic theory of capitalist collapse, her contribution to the debate about the Russian revolution, her theory of the mass strike – viewed not as an irrational commitment to mass spontaneity but as part of a larger theory of the political pre-conditions for revolution – and an analysis of her differentiation between bourgeois and socialist democracy. A lucid reinterpretation of her ideas.

8.703 **Jacoby**, R., 'Lenin and Luxemburg: negation in theory and praxis', *Rad. Am.*, 4, 1970, 21–31. Roots these thinkers' political differences in their theoretical divergence, stressing Luxemburg's emphasis on the unmediated dialectical interplay between Marxist theory and mass politics.

8.704 **Kitschelt**, H., and **Wiesenthal**, H., 'Organisation and mass action in the political works of Rosa Luxemburg', *Pol. & Soc.*, 9, 1979, 153–202. Using several of Luxemburg's key ideas, the authors attempt to determine the structural conditions which make it possible for revolutionary action to lead to proletarian emancipation.

8.705 **Lee**, G., 'Rosa Luxemburg and the impact of imperialism', *Econ. J.*, 81, 1971, 847–62.

8.706 **Nettl**, J. P., *Rosa Luxemburg*, 1966. Heavyweight biography in two volumes, which includes specific consideration of her reply to the revisionists, her concept of the mass strike and the representation of 'Luxemburgism' by Stalinists. More valuable for its historical detail than theoretical insight.

8.707 **Vollrath**, E., 'Rosa Luxemburg's theory of revolution', *Soc. Res.*, 40, 1973, 83–109.

Merleau-Ponty

8.708 **Coole**, D., 'Phenomenology and ideology in the work of Merleau-Ponty', in N. K. O'Sullivan, ed., *The Structure of Modern Ideology: Critical Perspectives on Social and Political Theory*, 1989, 122–50. Lucid discussion of the significance of his work for a reconceptualisation of ideology because it challenges the epistemological and ontological dualisms which underpin Marxist approaches to this question.

8.709 **Dauenhauer**, B. P., 'Phases of Merleau-Ponty's political philosophy', *Rev. Pol.*, 51, 1989, 628–31.

8.710 —— 'Renovating the problem of politics', *Rev. Metaph.*, 29, 1976, 626–41. Returns to the thought of Heidegger and Merleau-Ponty for a reconsideration of the nature of politics in the realms of speech and history.

8.711 **Flynn**, B. C., 'The question of an ontology of the political: Arendt, Merleau-Ponty, Lefort', *Int. Sts. Phil.*, 16, 1984, 1–24. Contrasts Arendt's discursive 'style' of philosophising with that of Merleau-Ponty and Lefort as part of a broader consideration of the relationship between ontology and political philosophy. Philosophically and conceptually complex.

8.712 **Kruks**, S., 'Merleau-Ponty: a phenomenological critique of liberalism', *Phil. & Phenom. Res.*, 37, 1976–77, 394–407. Celebrates this thinker's sophisticated Marxist reading of liberalism, emphasising its ahistorical tendencies and inbuilt acceptance of inequality.

8.713 —— *The Political Philosophy of Merleau-Ponty*, 1981. Account of his political thought, stressing its roots in his general

philosophy in an analysis in which Kruks places him in his intellectual and political milieu and asks whether he followed his own methodological premises in his study of the political.

8.714 **Murungi**, J., 'Merleau-Ponty's perspective on politics', *Man and World*, 14, 1981, 141–52.

8.715 **Schmidt**, J., 'Lordship and bondage in Merleau-Ponty and Sartre', *Pol. Theory*, 7, 1979, 201–28. Confronts the problem of how they attempted to reconcile phenomenological and dialectical analyses of society, illuminating their reliance upon Hegel in particular.

8.716 **Whiteside**, K. H., *Merleau-Ponty and the Foundation of an Existential Politics*, Princeton, N.J., 1988. Reads his existentialisism as motivated by a rejection of idealist and empiricist traditions of interpreting the complexity of social and political life. Charts his disillusion with Sartrean Marxism and the incorporation, in the 1950s, of individualist liberal values into his thought.

Popper

8.717 **Feaver**, G., 'Popper and Marxism', *Studies in Comparative Communism*, 4, 1971, 3–25.

8.718 **Gray**, J., 'The liberalism of Karl Popper', *Govt. & Oppos.*, 11, 1976, 337–55. Establishes a link between Popper's philosophy of science and political philosophy through his pluralist ontology and libertarian account of human action.

8.719 **Lessnoff**, M., 'The political philosophy of Karl Popper', *Brit. J. Pol. Sc.*, 10, 1980, 99–126.

8.720 **Magee**, B., *Popper*, 1973. Though concerned primarily with his epistemology and philosophy, Magee includes a sharp discussion of the notion of the open society which serves as a 'philosophy of social democracy'.

8.721 **Parekh**, B., 'Karl Popper', in *Contemporary Political Thinkers*, 1982, 124–53.

8.722 **Quinton**, A., 'Karl Popper: politics without essences', in A. de Crespigny and K. Minogue, ed., *Contemporary Political Philosophers*, 1976, 147–67. Places Popper in the context of liberalism, based on his rejection of historicism and utopianism and 'correction' of Mill's theory of scientific knowledge.

8.723 **Sobolewski**, M., 'Marxism and the open society', in D. Germino and K. von Beyme, ed., *The Open Society in Theory and Practice*, The Hague, 1974, 204–16. Counters Popper's characterisation of Marxism, concluding that he theorises as a rational conservative.

Poulantzas

8.724 **Bridges**, A. B., 'Nicos Poulantzas and the Marxist theory of the state', *Pol. & Soc.*, 4, 1974, 161–90. Sets his theory of the state against the empirical and historical realities of capitalism, concluding that he successfully shifted Marxist theory to a 'focus on the organization and social reality' of the state.

8.725 **Caplan**, J., 'Theories of fascism: Nicos Poulantzas as historian', *History Workshop*, 3, 1977, 84–100.

8.726 **Clarke**, J., 'Marxism, sociology and Poulantzas' theory of the state', *Capital and Class*, 2, 1977, 1–31. Critique of Poulantzas for failing to transcend Marxist dogmatism and 'bourgeois' social science.

8.727 ——, with **Connell**, I., and **McDunough**, R., 'Misrecognising ideology in *Political Power and Social Classes*', *Cultural Studies*, 10, 1977, 106–22.

8.728 **Cutler**, A., 'Fascism and political theory', *Theoretical Practice*, 2, 1971, 5–15. Extended review of the strengths and weaknesses of Marxist theorisations of fascism, focusing especially on Poulantzas. Constrained by its dogmatic, Althusserian framework.

8.729 **Giner**, S., and **Salcedo**, J., 'The ideological practice of Nicos Poulantzas', *Archives Européenes de Sociologie*, 17, 1976, 344–65.

8.730 **Hall**, S., 'Nicos Poulantzas: state, power, socialism', *New Left Rev.*, 119, 1980, 60–9. Reappraisal of the distinctiveness of his theoretical work on the occasion of his death, assessing his revision of Marxism in a useful comparision with Foucault.

8.731 **Jessop**, R., *Nicos Poulantzas: Marxist Theory and Political Strategy*, 1985. Study of the origins and development of Poulantzas's thought.

8.732 **Lewis**, A., 'Nicos Poulantzas and the autonomy of the state', *Catalyst*, 20, 1980,

22–44.

8.733 **Miliband**, R., 'Poulantzas and the capitalist state', *New Left. Rev.*, 82, 1973, 83–92.

8.734 —— 'The capitalist state – reply to Poulantzas', *New Left Rev.*, 59, 1970, 53–60. Spirited defence of his text, *The State in Capitalist Society*, which forms an integral part of the much cited debate between these thinkers over the state and social power in capitalism.

8.735 **Plaut**, M., 'Positivism in Poulantzas', *Telos*, 1978, 159–67.

8.736 **Rabinach**, A. G., 'Poulantzas and the problem of fascism', *New Germ. Crit.*, 8, 1976, 157–70.

8.737 **Skotnes**, A., 'Structural determination of the proletariat and the petty bourgeoisie: a critique of Nicos Poulantzas', *Insurgent Sociologist*, 9, 1979, 34–54.

8.738 **Somerville**, J., 'Poulantzas, class and power: review of *State, Power, and Socialism*', *Ideology and Consciousness*, 7, 1980, 107–25.

Sartre

8.739 **Aronson**, R., *J. P. Sartre: The Politics of Imagination*, 1978.

8.740 —— 'Sartre and the dialectic: the purposes of *Critique, II*', *Yale French Studies*, 68, 1985, 85–107. Bold defence of the continuing relevance of his strictures on individual freedom; no attempt at critical evaluation is made.

8.741 —— 'The individualist social theory of Jean-Paul Sartre', in *Western Marxism: A Critical Reader*, 1977, 201–31. Charts the shift from individualist existentialism to a more collectivist and socialist political outlook in Sartre's work, though Aronson suggests that both dimensions remain in his thought.

8.742 **Barrow**, C. W., 'The historical problem of political organisation in Sartre's existential Marxism', *Hist. Pol. Thought*, 7, 1986, 527–36. Argues that it is possible to adopt a position which does justice to his existential self-understanding while remaining consistent with the presuppositions of a Marxist theory of ideology.

8.743 **Bondy**, F., 'Jean-Paul Sartre', in M. Cranston, ed., *The New Left: Six Critical Essays*, 1970, 51–82. Overview of his political career and affiliations, illustrating his shift from a revolutionist ethic under the pressure of scepticism and self-doubt.

8.744 **Caws**, P., *Sartre*, 1984. Illuminating introduction to the nature and style of his philosophical thought, encompassing the political and intellectual context of his work, and providing a sharp assessment of his concept of freedom and dialectical understanding of politics

8.745 **Chiodi**, P., *Sartre and Marxism*, 1976. Sensitive exploration of the nature of the fusion of Marxism and existentialism in his thought, emphasising his determination to break from scholastic Marxism and develop an 'authentic' strain.

8.746 **Cranston**, M., 'Jean-Paul Sartre: solitary man in a hostile universe', in A. de Crespigny and K. Minogue, ed., *Contemporary Political Philosophers*, 1976, 209–27. Outline of his political theory, a fusion of existentialism and Marxism, exploring the tensions which exist between these bodies of thought.

8.747 **Cumming**, R., 'This place of violence, obscurity and witchcraft', *Pol. Theory*, 7, 1979, 181–200. Discusses the thought of Sartre, focusing on the tensions between his Marxism and existentialism.

8.748 **Desan**, W., *The Marxism of Jean-Paul Sartre*, New York, 1966.

8.749 —— 'The significance of Jean-Paul Sartre', in J. Somerville and H. L. Parsons, ed., *Dialogues on the Philosophy of Marxism: From the Proceedings of the Society for the Philosophical Study of Dialectical Materialism*, 1974, 367–75. Traces the increasing appeal of Marxism for Sartre and the difficulties this raised for his existentialism.

8.750 **Dobson**, A., *Jean-Paul Sartre and the Politics of Reason: A Theory of History*, 1993. Distinctive interpretation of the central political motivations behind his philosophical development in a close study of his biographies of Baudelaire, Genet and Flaubert and secondary commentaries upon Volume II of the *Critique of Dialectical Reason*.

8.751 **Donos**, A., 'The notion of freedom in Sartre, Kolakowski, Markovic and Kosik', *Phil. Today*, 23, 1979, 133–57.

8.752 **Dufrenne**, M., 'Sartre and Merleau-Ponty', in H. J. Silverman and F. A. Elliston, ed., *Jean-Paul Sartre: Contemporary Approaches to his Philosophy*, Pittsburgh, Pa., 1980, 188–208. Thoughtful survey of their philosophical differences and particular relationships to Marxism.

8.753 **Flynn**, T. R., 'L'imagination au pouvoir. The evolution of Sartre's political and social thought', *Pol. Theory*, 7, 1979, 157–80. Stresses the foundational principles which allowed him to develop a distinctive political critique based upon the primacy of praxis.

8.754 **Glynn**, S., *Sartre: An Investigation of Some Major Themes*, 1987.

8.755 **Gorz**, A., 'Sartre and Marx', in *Western Marxism: A Critical Reader*, 1977, 176–200. Sympathetic presentation of Sartre's philosophical journey towards dialectical materialism, stressing the centrality of scarcity in his thought and his notion of the fused group in history. An important immanent critique.

8.756 **Greene**, N. N., *Jean-Paul Sartre: The Existentialist Ethic*, Ann Arbor, Mich., 1960. Accessible though flawed presentation of his philosophy and political thought, including a weak discussion of his relationship with Marxism.

8.757 **Kiernan**, R. E., 'The marriage of heaven and hell: an integrative study of the Marxism of Jean-Paul Sartre', *Studies in Soviet Thought*, 22, 1981, 111–46.

8.758 **Knecht**, I., 'Seriality: a ground for social alienation?', in H. J. Silverman and F. A. Elliston, ed., *Jean-Paul Sartre: Contemporary Approaches to his Philosophy*, Pittsburgh, Pa., 1980, 188–208. Complex but important application of the concept of seriality to Marx's notion of dialectical rationality, isolating the distinctiveness of the Sartrean account of alienation in his 'anthropological-structural' interpretation of this aspect of Marxism.

8.759 **McBride**, W. L., *Sartre's Political Theory*, Bloomington and Indianapolis, Ind., 1991. Reconstructs his thought around the themes of socialism and freedom, though overstates his significance as a political theorist.

8.760 **Odajnyk**, V. W., 'Sartre's dialectical reasoning on individual freedom', in J. Somerville and H. L. Parsons, ed., *Dialogues on the Philosophy of Marxism: From the Proceedings of the Society for the Philosophical Study of Dialectical Materialism*, 1974, 376–88. Focuses critically on his concept of individual freedom through which he tried to synthesise Marxism and existentialism; this project fails, according to Odajnyk, forcing him to abandon existentialism in *Critique of Dialectical Reason*.

8.761 **Peyre**, H. M., *Jean-Paul Sartre*, Columbia, Ohio, 1968.

8.762 **Poster**, M., *Sartre's Marxism*, 1979. Lucid and sympathetic introduction to the complexities of his Marxism.

8.763 **Sanyal**, G., 'Jean-Paul Sartre and Marxism', in V. K. Roy and R. C. Sarikwal, ed., *Marxian Sociology, Volume Two*, 1979, 147–89. Sympathetic exposition of Sartrean philosophy, and its proximity to Marxism, focusing especially on his distinction between philosophy and ideology and hostility to aspects of contemporary Marxism.

8.764 **Schmidt**, J., 'Lordship and bondage in Merleau-Ponty and Sartre', *Pol. Theory*, 7, 1979, 201–28. Confronts the problem of how they attempted to reconcile phenomenological and dialectical analyses of society, illustrating their reliance upon Hegel in particular.

8.765 **Thody**, P., *Sartre*, New York, 1971.

8.766 **Wood**, P. 'Sartre, Anglo-American Marxism, and the place of the subject in history', *Yale French Studies*, 68, 1985, 15–54. Compares Sartre's treatment of the dialectic of freedom and necessity in history with contemporary Marxist debates, featuring Althusser, Anderson and E. P. Thompson. Sartre, according to Wood, offers Marxism a new, potent discourse of the role of freedom in historical change.

8.767 —— 'The historical conditions of possibility of the rise and fall of Sartrean existentialism and existentialist Marxism', *University of Toronto Quarterly*, 59, 1990, 549–68. Thorough examination of the social and intellectual context within which Sartre's thought developed, emphasising the boldness and heterodoxy of Sartrean Marxism in its day.

8.768 **Yovel**, Y., 'Dialectic without mediation: on Sartre's variety of Marxism and dialectic', in S. Avineri, ed., *Varieties of Marxism*, The Hague, 1977, 175–93. Examination of the tensions in his existentialist treatment of the concepts of dialectic and reason, and their implications for existentialist Marxism.

Trotsky

8.769 **Anderson**, P., 'Trotsky's interpretation of Stalinism', *New Left Rev.*, 139, 1983, 49–58. An historically informed reconstruction of the fundamental tenets of Trotsky's theorisation of Stalinism, and an affirmation of their continuing relevance.

8.770 **Anin**, D. S., 'Lenin, Trotsky and Parvus', *Survey: A Journal of East and West Studies*, 1, 1979, 204–12.

8.771 **Averas**, D., 'Trotsky's Marxism – I and II', *International*, 2, 1976–77, 25–38 and 3, 1976–77, 33–48.

8.772 **Barnes**, J., 'Their Trotsky and ours', *New International*, 1, 1983, 9–89.

8.773 **Basmanov**, M., *The Nature of Contemporary Trotskyism*, Moscow, 1974. Orthodox Soviet critique.

8.774 **Beilharz**, P., 'The other Trotsky', *Thesis Eleven*, 3, 1981, 106–13.

8.775 —— 'Trotsky's Marxism – permanent involution?', *Pol. Theory*, 39, 1979, 137–52. Hostile and historically schematic reading of his theory of permanent revolution, which Beilharz contrasts with Lenin's thought.

8.776 —— *Trotsky, Trotskyism and the Transition to Socialism*, 1987. Introduction to the work of Trotsky and several later Trotskyists (James, Dunayevskaya, Mandel, Deutscher), identifying the importance of Soviet and Jacobin models within the Trotskyist political imagination, especially concerning the transition to socialism. Also provides a useful guide to Trotskyist ideas in the fields of historiography, political economy and philosophy.

8.777 **Bergman**, J., 'The perils of historical analogy: Leon Trotsky on the French revolution', *J. Hist. Ideas*, 48, 1987, 73–98.

8.778 **Buraway**, M., 'Two methods in search of science: Skockpol versus Trotsky', *Theory & Soc.*, 18, 1989, 759–806.

8.779 **Callinicos**, A., 'Their Trotskyism and ours', *International Socialism*, 22, 1984, 117–42.

8.780 —— *Trotskyism*, 1990. A brief and accessible account of Trotskyism as a political movement and body of thought in Britain and the United States. An excellent introduction to post-war writers in this tradition.

8.781 —— 'Trotsky's theory of permanent revolution and its relevance to the Third World today', *International Socialism*, 16, 1982, 98–112.

8.782 **Carmichael**, J., *Trotsky: An Appreciation of His Life*, 1975.

8.783 —— 'Trotsky's agony – I and II', *Encounter*, 5, May 1972, 30–45 and June 1972, 28–36. Lively survey of his career and principal political ideas, separating him from later Trotskyist currents and myths.

8.784 **Cliff**, T., *Permanent Revolution*, 1983.

8.785 —— *Trotsky: Towards October 1879–1917*, 1989. Claims to provide the most accurate account of Trotsky's career, relationship with Lenin and political ideas, in this chronological and didactic volume.

8.786 **Cox**, M., 'Perry Anderson and Leon Trotsky, or the revolutionary betrayed', *Critique*, 20–21, 1987, 151–64.

8.787 —— 'Trotsky and his interpreters; or, will the real Leon Trotsky please stand up?', *Russ. Rev.*, 51, 1992, 84–102. Guide to traditional Western interpretations of his thought alongside consideration of recent, historiographical developments in the Soviet Union.

8.788 **D'Agostino**, A., 'Ambiguities of Trotsky's Leninism', *Survey: A Journal of East and West Studies*, 24, 1979, 178–203.

8.789 **Day**, R. B., *Leon Trotsky and the Politics of Economic Isolation*, 1973. Idiosyncratic central argument that Stalin and Trotsky ultimately disagreed about integration into the world market.

8.790 **Deutscher** I., *The Prophet Armed: Trotsky 1879-1921*, 1954; *The Prophet Unarmed: Trotsky 1921–1929*, 1959; *The Prophet Outcast: Trotsky 1929–1940*, 1963. Outstanding historical account of his political career and ideas which has remained the dominant interpretation.

8.791 —— 'Trotsky in our time', in T. Deutscher, ed., *Marxism in Our Time*, 1972, 31–61. Celebration of the continuing significance of his 'socialism or barbarism' outlook and his maintenance of the essential spirit of Marxism.

8.792 —— 'Trotsky on Stalin', in *Heretics and Renegades and Other Essays*, 1969, 78–90.

8.793 **Dunayevskaya**, R., 'Leon Trotsky as man and theoretician', *Studies in Comparative Communism*, 1–2, 1977, 166–83.

8.794 **Geras**, N., 'Political participation in the revolutionary thought of Leon Trotsky', in G. Parry, ed., *Participation in Politics*, 1972, 151–68.

8.795 **Hallas** D., 'Trotsky's heritage', *International Socialism*, 40, 1988, 53–64.

8.796 —— *Trotsky's Marxism*, 1979. Brief and eulogistic introduction to his thought, outlining the development of the theory of permanent revolution, the impact of Stalinism and the relationship of class and party in his work.

8.797 **Hanson**, J., et al., *Leon Trotsky: The Man and His Work*, New York, 1969.

8.798 **Hobson**, C. Z., *Trotskyism and the Dilemma of Socialism*, 1988.

8.799 **Hodgson**, G., *Trotsky and Fatalistic Marxism*, 1975. Accuses Trotsky of 'active fatalism' in his conception of historical change.

8.800 **Howe** I., *Trotsky*, 1978. Lively and accessible introduction to his life and work, which contains some critical judgements about his political thought and concludes that he embodies the modern historical crisis.

8.801 **Johnstone**, M., 'Trotsky and the debate on socialism in one country', *New Left Rev.*, 50, 1968, 113–23.

8.802 —— *Trotsky and World Revolution*, 1977.

8.803 **Judd**, H., 'The relevance of Trotskyism: the great revolutionist's heritage: a discussion', *New International*, 15, 1949, 179–83.

8.804 **Kemp**, T., *Trotskyism, the Marxism of Today*, 1983.

8.805 **Kitchen**, M., 'Trotsky and fascism', *Social Praxis*, 2, 1975, 113–33. Review of this aspect of his theory, charting his break from Stalinist notions of social fascism and critically assessing his misunderstanding of Marx's theory of Bonapartism, which resulted in his inability to analyse the larger social crisis which engendered fascism.

8.806 **Knei-Paz**, B., *The Social and Political Thought of Leon Trotsky*, 1978. An important, though contested, assessment of the development of Trotsky's thought, arguing that his theory of revolution constituted the only sustained attempt to make Marxist principles relevant to the particular conditions of early twentieth-century Russia. Concludes that he was reluctant to adapt his theory to the changing realities engendered by Stalinism.

8.807 —— 'Trotsky, Marxism and the revolution of backwardness', in S. Avineri, ed.,

Varieties of Marxism, The Hague, 1977, 65–81. Subtle revision of the dominant academic approach which emphasises his internationalism to the detriment of his other theoretical insights. Knei-Paz therefore explores the intricacies of his investigation of 'backwardness' in capitalist development.

8.808 ——— 'Trotsky's cultural formation: an intellectual portrait', *Thesis Eleven*, 3, 1981, 89–105.

8.809 **Krassó**, N., 'Trotsky's Marxism', *New Left Rev.*, 44, 1967, 64–86. Critique of his failure to understand the role of the revolutionary party and associated belief that history was directly moulded by social forces. His theory thus tended towards 'sociologism' and voluntarism.

8.810 ——— ed., *Trotsky: The Great Debate Renewed*, St. Louis, 1972. A collection of articles taken from *New Left Rev.*, listed here under their individual authors.

8.811 **Krygier**, M., 'The revolution betrayed: from Trotsky to the new class', in E. Kamenka and M. Krygier, ed., *Bureaucracy: the Career of a Concept*, 1979, 88–111. Focuses on 'new class' theories of state socialist regimes, arguing that these may we added to the restricted range of categories theorised by Marxism.

8.812 **Law**, D., 'Studies on Trotsky', *Journal of Communist Studies*, 2, 1986, 83–90.

8.813 **Lichtheim**, G., 'Reflections on Trotsky', *Commentary*, Jan. 1964, 52–60.

8.814 **Lovell**, D. W., *Trotsky's Analysis of Soviet Bureaucatization*, 1985.

8.815 **Löwy**, M., *The Politics of Combined and Uneven Development: The Theory of Permanent Revolution*, 1981. Beginning with Marx and Engels, Löwy traces the development of this notion until its fully-fledged appearance in Trotsky's work.

8.816 **Lustig**, M. M., *Trotsky and Djilas: Critics of Communist Bureaucracy*, 1989.

8.817 **McNeal**, R. H., 'Trotskyist interpretations of Stalinism', in R. C. Tucker, ed., *Stalinism: Essays in Historical Interpretation*, New York, 1977, 30–52.

8.818 ——— 'Trotsky's interpretation of Stalin', *Canadian Slavonic Papers*, 5, 1961, 87–97.

8.819 **Maitan**, L., 'The theory of permanent revolution', in E. Mandel, ed., *The Theory of Permanent Revolution*, 1968, 50–69.

8.820 **Mandel**, E., 'Once again on the Trotskyist definition of the social nature of the Soviet Union', *Critique*, 12, 1979–80, 117–26.

8.821 ——— *Trotsky: A Study in the Dynamics of his Thought*, 1979. Ambitious presentation of his thought as 'an attempt to explain the twentieth century', highlighting his concept of proletarian democracy and opposition to Stalinism. Culminates, somewhat eulogistically, with the formation of the Fourth International.

8.822 ——— 'Trotsky's analysis of fascism', *International Socialist Review*, 32, 1971, 36–41.

8.823 ——— 'Trotsky's Marxism: an anti-critique', *New Left Rev.*, 47, 1968, 32–51. Spirited defence of Trotsky's coherent and consistent theoretical method against Krassó.

8.824 **Mavrakis**, K., *On Trotskyism: Problems of Theory and History*, 1976. A bizarre, Maoist reading of Trotsky.

8.825 **Michael**, L., *The Theory of Permanent Revolution: A Critique*, 1977.

8.826 **Molyneux**, J., *Leon Trotsky's Theory of Revolution*, 1981.

8.827 **Novack**, G., 'Liberal morality: the controversy between John Dewey and Leon Trotsky', *International Socialist Review*, 26, 1965, 118–24.

8.828 **Pablo**, M., 'Leon Trotsky and Rosa Luxemburg', in M. Raptis, ed., *Socialism, Democracy and Self-Management*, 1980, 106–18.

8.829 **Remington**, T., 'Trotsky, war, communism, and the origin of the NEP', *Studies in Comparative Communism*, 10, 1977, 44–59.

8.830 **Roberts**, G., 'Trotskyism and revolution', *International*, 4, 1977, 13–7.

8.831 **Rowney**, D. K., 'Development of Trotsky's theory of revolution, 1898–1907', *Studies in Comparative Communism*, 10, 1977, 18–33.

8.832 **Schachtman**, M., 'Trotsky's "Stalin": a critical evaluation', *New International*, 12, 1946, 229–36.

8.833 **Schurer**, H., 'The permanent revolution', *Survey*, 32, 1960, 68–73.

8.834 **Segal**, R., *The Tragedy of Leon Trotsky*, 1979. Stronger on biography than ideas.

8.835 **Seth**, R., *Lev Davidovitch Trotsky*, 1967.

8.836 **Sinclair**, L., *Leon Trotsky: A Bibliography*, Stanford, Calif., 1972.

8.837 **Skilling**, H. G., 'Permanent or uninterrupted revolution: Lenin, Trotsky, and their successors on the transition to socialism', *Canadian Slavonic Papers*, 5, 1961, 3–30.

8.838 **Stokes**, C., *The Evolution of Trotsky's Theory of Revolution*, Washington, D.C., 1982. Pinpoints four stages in the evolution of this concept, which are set against the background of other Marxist theories of revolution and his political career.

8.839 **Theen**, R. H. W., 'The idea of the revolutionary state: Tkachev, Trotsky, and Lenin', *Russ. Rev.*, 4, 1972, 383–98.

8.840 **Thompson**, P., and **Lewis**, G., *The Revolution Unfinished? A Critique of Trotskyism*, 1977.

8.841 **Van Houten**, G., 'Trotsky's permanent revolution – yesterday and today', *Communist Viewpoint*, 5, 1972, 34–45.

8.842 **Waiss**, P., *Trotsky in Exile*, 1971.

8.843 **Warth**, R., *Leon Trotsky*, Boston, Mass., 1977. Biography highlighting his personal defects and political errors, with scant attention to his political ideas.

8.844 **Wistrick**, R. S., 'Leon Trotsky's theory of fascism', *Journal of Contemporary History*, 11, 1976, 157–84. Argues that he provided one of the most sophisticated Marxist analyses of fascism but was constrained from a deeper understanding by his 'overconfidence concerning the revolutionary temper of the European working classes'.

8.845 **Woods**, A., *Lenin and Trotsky: What They Really Stood For: A Reply to Monty Johnstone*, 1976.

8.846 **Yepe**, R., 'Trotsky's Marxism', *New Left Rev.*, 51, 1968, 95–6.

Weil

8.847 **Blom**, L. A., and **Seidler**, V. J., *A Truer Liberty: Simone Weil and Marxism*, 1990. Demonstrates how she developed a penetrating critique of Marxism and a political philosophy which serves as an alternative to both liberalism and socialism.

8.848 **Dietz**, M., G., *Between the Human and the Divine: The Political Thought of Simone Weil*, 1988. Systematic and wide-ranging interpretation of Weil's ideas on labour, liberty, oppression, spirituality, patriotism and citizenship.

8.849 **McLellan**, D., *Simone Weil, Utopian Pessimist*, 1989. Excellent guide to her life and thought, including a sharp analysis of her critique of Marxism, supplemented by a useful bibliography.

8.850 **Rosen**, F., 'Labour and liberty: Simone Weil and the human condition', *Theoria to Theory*, 7, 1973, 33–47.

8.851 —— 'Marxism, mysticism, and liberty: the influence of Simone Weil on Albert Camus', *Pol. Theory*, 7, 1979, 301–19. Examines Weil's critique of Marxism which was adopted by Camus in *L'Homme Révolté*, and considers why Camus was drawn to Weil's mysticism.

Wittgenstein

8.852 **Danford**, J. W., *Wittgenstein and Political Philosophy: A Re-examination of the Foundations of Social Science*, Chicago, Ill., 1988.

8.853 **Griffiths**, A. P., ed., *Wittgenstein: Centenary Essays*, 1991. Fourteen contributors examine the relevance of his work for contemporary thought, and assess the effect of his work on the social sciences, in particular his contribution to current political thinking.

8.854 **Lugg**, A., 'Was Wittgenstein a conservative thinker?', *Southern Journal of Philosophy*, 23, 1985, 465–74.

8.855 **Nyiri**, J. C., 'Wittgenstein's later work in relation to conservatism', in B. McGuinness, ed., *Wittgenstein and His Times*, 1982, 44–60.

8.856 **Pitkin**, H. F., *Wittgenstein and Justice: On the Significance of Ludwig Wittgenstein for Social and Political Thought*, Berkeley, Calif., 1972. Following an exposition of his deployment of language, Pitkin traces the political implications of this philosophy, arguing that he allows us to grasp some of the central dilemmas of political life in the modern predicament. Stimulating and prescient.

8.857 **Tully**, J., 'Wittgenstein and political philosophy. Understanding practices of critical reflection', *Pol. Theory*, 17, 1989, 172–204. Critically surveys arguments that the free and rational nature of our political life is founded upon some form of critical reflection, deploying Wittgensteinian language-games to present critical reflection as a more open, pluralistic and self-reflexive activity.

Other thinkers

8.858 **Albertoni**, E. A., *Mosca and the Theory of Elitism*, 1987. Analysis of Mosca as an Italian liberal who developed elitist theories of government because of his fears that democracy would lead to the masses being corruptly led by demagogic tyrants.

8.859 —— ed., *Studies on the Political Thought of Gaetano Mosca: The Theory of the Ruling Class and its Development Abroad*, Milan, Montreal, 1982. Includes Albertoni on the evolution of his political thought, Ganci on a number of his intellectual contemporaries, and Ghiringhello surveying Italian scholarship on his social and political background.

8.860 **Ashcraft**, R., 'Political theory and political action in Karl Mannheim's thought: reflections upon *Ideology and Utopia* and its critics', *Comp. Sts. Soc. & Hist.*, 23, 1981, 23–50.

8.861 **Bair**, D., 'Simone de Beauvoir: politics, language, and feminist identity', *Yale French Studies*, 72, 1986, 149–62. Explains the lack of a developed political theory in her work as the product of her philosophical and feminist commitments, leading her to adopt language as her political weapon.

8.862 **Barker**, F., *Solzhenitsyn: Politics and Form*, 1977. Short but scholarly attempt to analyse his life and work.

8.863 **Baron**, S. H., 'Plekhanov's Russia: the impact of the West upon an "oriental" society', *J. Hist. Ideas*, 19, 1958, 388–404.

8.864 —— *Plekhanov, the Father of Russian Marxism*, 1963.

8.865 **Beetham**, D., 'From socialism to fascism: the relations between theory and practice in the work of Robert Michels – I and II', *Pol. Sts.*, 25, 1977, 3–24 and 161–81.

8.866 **Beilharz**, P., 'Isaac Deutscher: history and necessity', *Hist. Pol. Thought*, 7, 1986, 375–84. Focusing on his Trotskyist sense of history as theatre, Beilharz explores his affinity with Greek tragedy, Carlyle, Goethe, Shakespeare and Hegel.

8.867 **Bellamy**, R., 'From ethical to economic liberalism: the sociology of Pareto's politics', *Economy and Society*, 19, 1990, 431–55. Explains Pareto's apparent abandonment of liberalism for fascism through a consideration of Italian social conditions which forced him to reject the 'progressive' assumptions of English liberalism, leaving economic self-interest central in his thought.

8.868 —— 'Idealism and liberalism in an Italian "new liberal theorist": Guido de Ruggiero's *History of European Liberalism*', *Hist. J.*, 30, 1987, 191–200.

8.869 —— 'Liberalism and historicism: Benedetto Croce and the political role of idealism in Italy', in A. Moulakis, ed., *The Promise of History*, Berlin, New York, 1985, 69–119.

8.870 **Bendersky**, J. W., *Carl Schmitt: Theorist for the Rich*, Princeton, N.J., 1983. Rejects the traditional view that Schmitt's theories helped to undermine the Weimar republic and paved the way for the legalised, dictatorial authoritarianism of the Nazis.

8.871 **Bergman**, J., 'The political thought of Vera Zasulich', *Slavic Rev.*, 38, 1979, 243–58. Outline of her thought, including her polemical confrontations with Lenin and Plekhanov.

8.872 **Bobbio**, N., *On Mosca and Pareto*, Geneva, 1972. Includes essays on Mosca's theory of the ruling class and Pareto's political sociology.

8.873 **Caserta**, E. G., 'Croce and Marxism', *J. Hist. Ideas*, 44, 1982, 141–9. Re-examination of his brief philosophical engagement with, and critique of, Marx, suggesting that his ethico-political theory of history was formed in reaction to historical materialism.

8.874 **Chilcote**, R. H., *Amilcar Cabral's Revolutionary Theory and Practice: A Critical Guide*, 1990. A guide to Cabral's thought which deals with his writings on colonialism, nationalism, class struggle and the state.

8.875 **Dobson**, A., *An Introduction to the Politics and Philosophy of José Ortega y Gassett*, 1989. Clear introduction to this thinker's rejection of rationalism and attempt to construct a notion of vital reason in its place; these metaphysical ideas are connected to his political theory which is examined in the context of contemporary Spanish politics and ideas.

8.876 **Doerfel**, M., 'A prophet of democracy: Heinrich Mann, the political writer, 1905–1988', *Oxford German Studies*, 6, 1972, 93–111.

8.877 **Evans**, I., and **Ward**, L., *The Social and Political Philosophy of Jacques Maritain*, New York, 1955.

8.878 **Evans**, R. J., 'Theory and practice in

German social democracy 1880–1914: Clara Zetkin and the socialist theory of women's emancipation', *Hist. Pol. Thought*, 3, 1982, 285–304. Examines the influence of the contemporary political context on the development of socialist thought before 1914, using the example of Zetkin – the major theorist of women's emancipation in the SPD. Demonstrates that her thought evolved as the product of her engagement with new political and intellectual currents and that later commentators have simplified her ideas by overstressing either her feminism or socialism.

8.879 **Farrenkopf**, J., 'The early phase in Spengler's political philosophy', *Hist. Pol. Thought*, 13, 1992, 319–40. Argues that he was less anti-democratic before 1918 than later, contrary to the conventional emphasis on the coherence of his political ideas.

8.880 **Fishman**, W. J., 'Rudolf Rocker. Anarchist missionary (1873–1958)', *Hist. Today*, 16, 1966, 45–52.

8.881 **Fox**, R. W., 'Reinhold Niebuhr and the emergence of the liberal realist faith 1930–1945', *Rev. Pol.*, 38, 1976, 244–65. Reconstructs the mid-century thought of a distinctive liberal who supported the expansion of American power in the post-war world yet criticised its particular imperialist policies.

8.882 **Fraser**, J., *An Introduction to the Thought of Galvano della Volpe*, 1977.

8.883 **Geiman**, K. P., 'Lyotard's "Kantian socialism" ', *Phil. & Soc. Crit.*, 17, 1990, 23–37. Presents the lively thesis that Lyotard's 'search for dissensus' is based on Kant's doctrine of the 'highest good', the antithesis of practical reason.

8.884 **Germino**, D., 'Eric Voegelin: the in-between of human life', in A. de Crespigny and K. Minogue, ed., *Contemporary Political Philosophers*, 1976, 100–19. Outlines Voegelin's philosophy of consciousness, in which he characterises existence as irredeemably caught between the divine pull and the demonic counter-pull; this truth is obscured in modern political philosophy.

8.885 **Gottfried**, P. E., *Carl Schmitt: Politics and Theory*, 1990. Assessment of the work of this political philosopher and legal theorist, exploring his associations with Nazi ideas.

8.886 **Haimson**, L. H., *The Russian Marxists and the Origins of Bolshevism*, Harvard, Ill., 1955.

8.887 **Hannay**, A., 'Politics and Feyerabend's anarchist', in M. Dascal and O. Gruengard, ed., *Knowledge and Politics: Case Studies in the Relationship Between Epistemology and Political Philosophy*, Boulder, Calif., 1989, 241–63. Examination of the relationship between epistemological anarchism and the political sphere, arguing that Feyerabend maintains the connection though his belief in an ethos which connects personal dignity to the exercise of scientific judgements.

8.888 **Harris**, H. S., *The Social Philosophy of Giovani Gentile*, Urbana, Ill., 1960.

8.889 **Hillach**, A., 'The aesthetics of politics: Walter Benjamin's theories of German fascism', *New Germ. Crit.*, 17, 1979, 99–119.

8.890 **Hodder**, H. J., 'Political ideas of Thorstein Veblen', *Can. J. Econ. Pol. Sc.*, 22, 1956, 347–57.

8.891 **Howard**, M. C., and **King**, J. E., 'The political economy of Plekhanov and the development of backward capitalism', *Hist. Pol. Thought*, 10, 1989, 329–44. Argues that Plekhanov should be seen as a distinctive Marxist, not subsumed within the Second International, and that his understanding of the development of capitalism in Russia anticipated the difficulties which the Bolsheviks encountered.

8.892 **Jacobitti**, E. E., 'Hegemony before Gramsci: the case of Benedetto Croce', *J. Mod. Hist.*, 52, 1980, 66–84. Argues that Gramsci drew upon the unhealthy influence of Croce over Italian intellectual life to formulate his notion of cultural hegemony. Jacobitti counters this misleading assessment of Croce's thought.

8.893 —— 'Labriola, Croce and Italian Marxism (1895–1910)', *J. Hist. Ideas*, 36, 1975, 297–318. Assesses the credentials of each as the founding figures of contemporary Italian Marxism.

8.894 **Kennedy**, E., 'The politics of toleration in late Weimar: Hermann Heller's analysis of fascism and political culture', *Hist. Pol. Thought*, 5, 1984, 109–29. Analysis of his social democratic writings on fascism, produced on the eve of Hitler's accession to power: Heller saw fascism as part of a general crisis of democratic, rational culture in Europe.

8.895 **Kettler**, D., 'Political theory, ideology, sociology: the question of Karl Mannheim', *Cultural Hermeneutics*, 3, 1975, 69–80.

8.896 **Kitchen**, M., 'August Thalheimer's theory of fascism', *J. Hist. Ideas*, 34, 1973, 67–78. Critical assessment of his Marxist interpretation of fascism, stressing its anti-Stalinist implications.

8.897 **Kramm**, L., 'Gaining the open horizon: Eric Voegelin's search for order', *Hist. Pol. Thought*, 7, 1986, 311–76. Stresses the need to account for the rise of totalitarian ideologies as the central motif in Voegelin's thought. In the search for the foundational principles of political order, he reaches the 'open horizon': the realisation that no single truth underwrites political harmony.

8.898 **Löwy**, M., 'Revolution against "progress". Walter Benjamin's romantic anarchism', *New Left Rev.*, 152, 1985, 42–59.

8.899 **Maloney**, P., 'Anarchism and Bolshevism in the works of Boris Pilnyak', *Russ. Rev.*, 32, 1973, 43–53.

8.900 **Meisel**, J. H., *The Myth of the Ruling Class: Gaetano Mosca and the Elite*, Ann Arbor, Mich., 1962.

8.901 **Muller**, J. Z., 'Carl Schmitt, Hans Freyer and the radical conservative critique of liberal democracy in the Weimar Republic', *Hist. Pol. Thought*, 12, 1991, 695–715. Explores the critique of liberal democracy developed by two of the most important radical conservatives in German history and the process by which they became attracted to Nazi ideology.

8.902 **Niemeyer**, G., 'Conservatism and the new political theory', *Modern Age*, 23, 1979, 115–22. Presents Voegelin as an exemplar of the reorientation of contemporary conservatism.

8.903 **Odajnyk**, V. W., *Jung and Politics: The Political and Social Ideas of C. G. Jung*, New York, 1977. An account of his democratic and individualist predilections as part of a larger consideration of the role of psychology in political thinking.

8.904 **Olson**, A. M., 'Glasnost and enlightenment', *Phil. Today*, Summer 1990, 99–110. A critical reassessment of Karl Jasper's social and political philosophy, following recent developments in Eastern Europe, as the basis for a critique of Fukuyama's comments about the end of history and the victory of liberal democracy.

8.905 **Pontuso**, J. F., *Solzhenitsyn's Political Thought*, 1990. Analysis of his thought, especially his assessment of who was responsible for the terror in the Soviet Union.

8.906 **Radnoti**, S., 'Benjamin's politics', *Telos*, 37, 1978, 63–81.

8.907 **Riley**, P., 'Introduction to the reading of Alexandre Kojève', in M. Freeman and D. Robertson, ed., *The Frontiers of Political Theory: Essays in a Revitalised Discipline*, 1980, 233–84. Extensive assessment of his 'left Hegelianism', illustrating the theme of his mastery within his reading of Kant, Aristotle and Hegel, among others.

8.908 **Roberts**, D. D., 'Benedetto Croce and the dilemmas of liberal restoration', *Rev. Pol.*, 44, 1988, 214–41.

8.909 **Romm**, H., *The Marxism of Regis Debray: Between Lenin and Guevara*, Lawrence, Kan., 1978.

8.910 **Sandoz**, E., 'The foundations of Voegelin's political theory', *Pol. Sc. Re-r*, 5, 1971, 30–74.

8.912 **Schmidt**, J., 'Praxis and temporality: Karel Kosik's political theory', *Telos*, 33, 1977, 71–84.

8.915 **Singer**, B., 'The early Castoriadis: socialism, barbarism and the bureaucratic threat', *Can. J. Pol. & Soc. Theory*, 3, 1979, 35–56.

8.916 **Slevin**, C., 'Bertrand de Jouvenel: efficiency and amenity', in A. de Crespigny and K. Minogue, ed., *Contemporary Political Philosophers*, 1976, 168–90. Based on his belief in the duality of human nature – on the one hand a will to power and, on the other, a desire for security – de Jouvenel's ideas are presented as an important attempt to theorise the nature of political power and science.

8.917 **Sterling**, R. W., *Ethics in a World of Power: The Political Ideas of Friedrich Meinecke*, 1958. Traces the development of his ideas, from the notion of the nation as the ideal political community to his more general concern with political morality.

8.918 **Tilman**, R., 'Ideology and utopia in Milton Friedman', *Dissent*, 26, 1979, 69–76.

8.919 **Tribe**, K., 'Introduction to Neumann: law and socialist political theory', *Econ. & Soc.*, 10, 1981, 329–47.

8.920 **Van den Beld**, A., *Humanity: The Political and Social Philosophy of Thomas G. Masaryk*, The Hague, 1976.

8.921 **Willhoite**, F. H., *Beyond Nihilism: Albert Camus's Contribution to Political Thought*, Baton Rouge, La., 1969.

8.922 **Yates**, S., 'Feyerabend's "democratic relativism" ', *Inquiry*, 27, 1984, 137–42.

(d) NORTH AMERICA

General

8.923 **Abbott**, P., *Furious Fancies: American Political Thought in the Post-Liberal Era*, Westpoint, Conn., 1980. Overview of the dominant ideas of this period, arguing the unconventional view that liberalism is now defunct as an ideological paradigm.

8.924 —— 'The character of recent American political thought', *Can. J. Pol. Sc.*, 14, 1981, 377–96.

8.925 **Baskin**, D., 'American pluralism. Theory, practice, and ideology', *J. Pol.*, 32, 1970, 71–96.

8.926 **Birch**, A. H., 'Some reflections on American democratic theory', *Pol. Sts.*, 23, 1975, 103–9. Examines the argument that American political thought is unique and reviews the ideas of critics hostile to its democratic culture.

8.927 **Bond**, J. C., 'The critical reception of English neo-Hegelianism in Britain and America, 1914–1960', *Aust. J. Pol. & Hist.*, 26, 1980, 228–41. Informative survey of the changing interpretations of the work of the English idealist philosophers in Britain and America. Demonstrates that neo-Hegelianism has been appropriated as the source of a number of competing political perspectives.

8.928 **Ferkiss**, V., 'Technology and American political thought: the hidden variable and the coming crisis', *Rev. Pol.*, 42, 1980, 349–87.

8.929 **Fowler**, R. B., *The Dance with Community: The Contemporary Debate in American Political Thought*, Kansas City, Kan., 1991. Explores the centrality of community within American political discourse. Useful survey of the range of thought in American political life,

concluding that the upsurge of communitarian concern is the result of the crisis of modern liberalism.

8.930 **Lawler**, P. A., 'Pragmatism, existentialism and the crisis in American political thought', *Int. Phil. Q.*, 20, 1980, 327–38.

8.931 **Lustig**, R. J., *Corporate Liberalism: The Origins of Modern American Political Theory, 1890–1920*, Berkeley, Calif., 1982. Relates the formative years of industrial America to an underlying individualist liberalism, surveying the work of a number of key ideologues and theorists.

8.932 **Lynd**, S., *Intellectual Origins of American Radicalism*, New York, 1969.

8.933 **Skotheim**, R. A., *Totalitarianism and American Social Thought*, New York, 1971.

Arendt

8.934 **Adamson**, W., 'Beyond "reform or revolution": notes on political education in Gramsci, Habermas, and Arendt', *Theory & Soc.*, 4, 1978, 429–60.

8.935 **Allen**, W., 'Hannah Arendt. Existential phenomenology and political freedom', *Phil. & Soc. Crit.*, 9, 1982, 169–90.

8.936 **Barnard**, F., 'Infinity and finality: Hannah Arendt on politics and truth', *Can. J. Pol. & Soc. Theory*, 1, 1977, 29–57. Evaluation of Arendt's distinction between political action, which is essentially infinite in scope, and truth – the realm of finality.

8.937 **Beiner**, R., 'Action, natality and citizenship: Hannah Arendt's concept of freedom', in Z. A. Pelczynski and J. Gray, ed., *Conceptions of Liberty in Political Philosophy*, 1984, 349–75. Counterposes Arendt's notion of freedom against the individualist and liberal traditions within political thought.

8.938 —— 'Hannah Arendt and Leo Strauss: the uncommenced dialogue', *Pol. Theory*, 18, 1990, 238–54. Thoughtful comparison of these thinkers, suggesting that their critiques of modernity complement each other.

8.939 —— 'Hannah Arendt on capitalism and socialism', *Govt. & Oppos.*, 25, 1990, 359–70.

8.940 —— 'Judging in a world of appearances: a commentary on Hannah Arendt's unwritten finale', *Hist. Pol. Thought*, 1, 1980, 117–35. Reconstructs what Arendt would have written, had she lived, in Part Three of the *Life of the Mind*, on the basis of her lectures on Kant's political philosophy. Particular critical emphasis is given to her understanding of political judgement.

8.941 **Benhabib**, S., 'Hannah Arendt and the redemptive power of narrative', *Social Res.*, 57, 1990, 167–96. Explores some of the tensions within Arendt's thought, drawing especially on the critical ideas of Benjamin.

8.942 —— 'Judgement and the moral foundations of politics in Arendt's thought', *Pol. Theory*, 16, 1988, 29–51. Identifies tensions between the Aristotelian and Kantian sources for Arendt's conception of judgement, which constrain her attempt to develop a theory of judgement in the political realm.

8.943 **Bernauer**, J., ed., *Amor Mundi. Explorations in the Faith and Thought of Hannah Arendt*, Dordrecht, 1987.

8.944 —— 'On reading and mis-reading Hannah Arendt', *Phil. Soc. Crit.*, 11, 1985, 1–34.

8.945 **Bernstein**, R. J., 'Hannah Arendt: the ambiguities of theory and practice', in T. Ball, ed., *Political Theory and Praxis: New Perspectives*, Minneapolis, Minn., 1977, 141–58. Contrasts her theory of political action with Marxist conceptions of praxis, suggesting that her refusal to examine the social constraints upon political freedom remains problematic.

8.946 **Botstein**, L., 'Hannah Arendt', *Partisan Review*, 45, 1978, 368–80.

8.947 —— 'Liberating the pariah: politics, the Jews, and Hannah Arendt', *Salmagundi*, 60, 1983, 73–106. Relates Arendt's core principles to her understanding of the Jewish question as political rather than social in character.

8.948 —— 'The Jew as pariah. Hannah Arendt's political philosophy', *Dialectical Anthropology*, 8, 1983, 47–73.

8.949 **Bowen-Moore**, P., *Hannah Arendt's Philosophy of Natality*, 1989. Explores her thematisation and articulation of the profound dimensions of birth and beginnings in human existence.

8.950 **Bradshaw**, L., *Acting and Thinking: the Political Thought of Hannah Arendt*, Toronto, 1989. Central emphasis is given to her study of the relation between theory and practice of politics in this sympathetic and short account.

8.951 **Canovan**, M., 'A case of distorted communication. A note on Habermas and Arendt', *Pol. Theory*, 11, 1983, 105–16. A critique of Habermas's misreading of Arendt's theory of political action, emphasising human originality as a neglected element in constraining communication.

8.952 —— 'Arendt, Rousseau and human plurality in politics', *J. Pol.*, 45, 1983, 286–302. Despite similarities, these thinkers differ fundamentally on the question of plurality, Arendt arguing for a public realm filled by differentiated citizens and sustained by a culture of contingent agreements.

8.953 —— 'Hannah Arendt and the human condition', in L. Tivey and A. Wright, ed., *Political Thought Since 1945: Philosophy, Science, Ideology*, 1992, 72–90. An excellent guide to the development of Arendt's thought, supplemented by a useful overview of the criticism she has provoked.

8.954 —— *Hannah Arendt: A Reinterpretation of her Political Thought*, 1992. Scholarly interpretation, using a number of Arendt's unpublished writings to reveal the underappreciated originality of her political thought. Provides a distinctive reading of her theory of totalitarianism, an interpretation of her theory of action as the product of her work on totalitarianism, rather than a desire to return to the 'polis', an assessment of her moral and political ideas, the contemporary implications of her approach to authority, her opposition to epistemological foundations, and exploration of plurality in the modern context.

8.955 —— 'Hannah Arendt on ideology in totalitarianism', in N. K. O'Sullivan, ed., *The Structure of Modern Ideology: Critical Perspectives on Social and Political Theory*, 1989, 151–71. Focusing on the ambiguity in her thought concerning the ideological seriousness of totalitarian regimes, Canovan teases out her various observations on this question.

8.956 —— 'Politics as culture: Hannah Arendt and the public realm', *Hist. Pol. Thought*, 6, 1985, 617–42. Makes explicit an analogy between politics and high culture which has been implicit in her writings. For Arendt, the public realm was the arena where the affairs of the world and the actions of individuals are most starkly revealed.

8.957 —— 'Socrates or Heidegger? Hannah Arendt's reflections on philosophy and politics', *Social Res.*, 57, 1990, 135–65. Assesses the influence of these philosophers on Arendt's notion of democracy.

8.958 —— 'The contradictions of Hannah Arendt's political thought', *Pol. Theory*, 6, 1978, 5–26. Focuses on the tensions between Arendt's elitist and democratic emphases and her theoretical preferences and political practice. A clear and well organised guide to her major texts.

8.959 —— *The Political Thought of Hannah Arendt*, 1974. Brief introduction.

8.960 **Castoriadis**, C., 'The destinies of totalitarianism', *Salmagundi*, 60, 1983, 107–22. Appropriates Arendt's approach to totalitarianism as the basis for a more sophisticated interpretation of the Soviet Union.

8.961 **Cooper**, B., 'Action into nature: Hannah Arendt's reflections on technology', in R. B. Day, R. Beiner and J. Masciulli, ed., *Democratic Theory and Technological Society*, New York, 1988, 316–36.

8.962 **Cooper**, L. A., 'Hannah Arendt's political philosophy: an interpretation', *Telos*, 38, 145–76. Connects her emphasis upon participation in the political realm with her pluralistic theory of human activity and belief that certain ontological structures condition human existence.

8.963 **Crick**, B., 'On re-reading *The Origins of Totalitarianism*', *Social Res.*, 44, 1977, 106–26. Systematic review of her understanding of totalitarianism which reaches hack to her conception of human nature.

8.964 **D'Entrèves**, P., 'Agency, identity and culture: Hannah Arendt's conception of citizenship', *Praxis International*, 9, 1989, 1–24.

8.965 **Dietz**, M. G., 'Hannah Arendt and feminist politics', in S. M. Lyndon and C. Pateman, ed., *Feminist Interpretations and Political Theory*, 1991, 232–52.

8.966 **Dossa**, S., 'Hannah Arendt on Billy Budd and Robespierre: the public realm and the private self', *Phil. & Soc. Crit.*, 9, 1982, 306–18.

8.967 —— 'Human status and politics; Hannah Arendt on the holocaust', *Can. J. Pol. Sc.*, 13, 1980, 309–23.

8.968 —— *The Public Realm and the Public Self:*

The Political Theory of Hannah Arendt, Ontario, 1989.

8.969 **Flynn**, B. C., 'The question of an ontology of the political: Arendt, Merleau-Ponty, Lefort', *Int. Sts. Phil.*, 16, 1984, 1–24. Contrasts Arendt's discursive 'style' of philosophising with that of Merleau-Ponty and Lefort as part of a broader consideration of the relationship between ontology and political philosophy. Philosophically and conceptually complex.

8.970 **Forester**, J., 'Hannah Arendt and critical theory: a critical response', *J. Pol.*, 43, 1981, 196–202.

8.971 **Fuss**, P., 'Hannah Arendt's conception of political community', *Idealistic Studies*, 3, 1973, 252–65.

8.972 **Gray**, J. G., 'The winds of thought', *Social Res.*, 44, 1977, 44–62. Assesses moral considerations in the thought of Arendt.

8.973 **Habermas**, J., 'Hannah Arendt on the concept of power', in *Philosophical-Political Profiles*, 1983, 171–87.

8.974 —— 'Hannah Arendt's communications concept of power', *Social Res.*, 44, 1977, 3–24. Resuscitates this concept and extricates it from Arendt's Aristotelian theory of action, in contrast to other definitions of power.

8.975 —— 'Hannah Arendt's concept of power', *Merkur*, 30, 1976, 946–60.

8.976 **Hansen**, P., *Hannah Arendt: History, Politics and Citizenship*, 1993. Reassesses her thought, discussing her notions of history and action, distinction between the public and the private and views on totalitarianism.

8.977 **Heather**, G. P., and **Stolz**, M. F., 'Hannah Arendt and the problem of critical theory', *J. Pol.*, 41, 1979, 2–22. Counterposes the political theory of Arendt against the critical theorists' claim to fuse theory and praxis and rejection of the strategic dimensions of political analysis and action.

8.978 **Heller**, A., 'An imaginary preface to the 1984 edition of Hannah Arendt's *The Origins of Totalitarianism*', in F. Fehér and A. Heller, ed., *Eastern Left, Western Left: Totalitarianism, Freedom and Democracy*, 1987. Imaginative reconstruction of her thought in present circumstances, incorporating totalitarianism in the Soviet Union and the Third World, and its decline in the West.

8.979 —— 'Hannah Arendt on the "via contemplativa" ', *Phil. & Soc. Crit.*, 12,

1987, 281–96.

8.980 **Hill**, M., ed., *Hannah Arendt: The Recovery of the Public World*, New York, 1979. Important collection of essays by leading scholars on Arendt's political thought. Those not published elsewhere include Young-Bruehl on her intellectual career, Bakan on her conception of labour, Parekh on her critique of Marx, Frampton on *The Human Condition*, Hill on her image of freedom in the modern world, and Gray on freedom in her thought.

8.981 **Hinchman**, S. K., 'Common sense and political barbarism in the theory of Hannah Arendt', *Polity*, 17, 1984, 317–39. Expounds her thesis of the breakdown of 'common sense' – the development of views on public issues through discussion and debate – which she uses to explain the rise of totalitarianism in the 1920s and 1930s.

8.982 **Honig**, B., 'Arendt, identity and difference', *Pol. Theory*, 16, 1988, 77–98.

8.983 —— 'Declarations of independence: Arendt and Derrida on the problem of founding a republic', *Am. Pol. Sc. Rev.*, 85, 1991, 97–113.

8.984 **Honohan**, I., 'Hannah Arendt's concept of freedom', *Irish Philosophical Journal*, 4, 1987, 41–63.

8.985 **Ingram**, D., 'The postmodern Kantianism of Arendt and Lyotard', *Rev. Metaph.*, 42, 1988, 51–77.

8.986 **Isaac**, J. C., *Arendt, Camus, and Modern Rebellion*, 1992. Compares the ideas of these 'resistance' intellectuals who articulated a radical alternative beyond Marxism and liberalism.

8.987 —— 'Arendt, Camus, and postmodern politics', *Praxis International*, 9, 1989, 48–71.

8.988 **Jacobson**, N., 'Parable and paradox: in response to Arendt's *On Revolution*', *Salmagundi*, 60, 1983, 123–39.

8.989 **Jay**, M., 'Hannah Arendt: opposing views', *Partisan Review*, 45, 1978, 348–80.

8.990 **Jonas**, H., 'Acting, knowing, thinking: gleanings from Hannah Arendt's philosophical work', *Social Res.*, 44, 1977, 25–43. Thoughtful consideration of the philosophical influences upon Arendt and her translation of these ideals in the modern context.

8.991 **Kalla**, S., 'Hannah Arendt on civil disobedience', *Indian Philosophical Journal*, 13, 1986, 261–9.

8.992 **Kaplan**, G. T., and **Kessler**, C. S., ed., *Hannah Arendt: Thinking, Judging, Freedom*, 1990. Interdisciplinary collection of essays covering her major intellectual interests, which seeks to outline and investigate the unity of her life and work. Includes Adams's critique of her interpretation of totalitarianism, a more sympathetic exposition of this concept by Bittman, and Heller on the incomplete nature of her thought.

8.993 **Kateb**, G., 'Arendt and representative democracy', *Salmagundi*, 60, 1983, 20–59. Argues that despite her misgivings, representative democracy is essential to her conception of politics, because of the centrality of resistance in modern political life and the virtues it fosters.

8.994 —— 'Death and politics: Hannah Arendt's reflections on the American constitution', *Social Res.*, 54, 1987, 605–28.

8.995 —— 'Freedom and worldliness in the thought of Hannah Arendt', *Pol. Theory*, 5, 1977, 141–82. Reconstructs her view of political action as the sphere of freedom.

8.996 —— *Hannah Arendt: Politics, Conscience, Evil*, 1984. A critique which recognises the penetrating originality of many of Arendt's insights but rejects her more 'controversial' positions, such as her bifurcation of morality and politics, denigration of representative democracy and hostility to modern industrial life.

8.997 **King**, R. H., 'Endings and beginnings. Politics in Arendt's early thought', *Pol. Theory*, 12, 1984, 235–51. Assesses the disjunction between her analysis of totalitarianism and the theory of politics she came to enunciate.

8.998 **Knauer**, J. T., 'Motive and goal in Hannah Arendt's concept of political action', *Am. Pol. Sc. Rev.*, 74, 1980, 721–33. Defends her concept of political action against criticism that it is incapable of including strategic concerns, doing so through an examination of her belief in the relationship between instrumentality and meaning in political life.

8.999 **Kohn**, J., 'Thinking/acting', *Social Res.*, 57, 1990, 105–34. Connects her ethical, epistemological and political ideas, particularly in her analysis and advocacy of democratic forms.

8.1000 **Lane**, A., 'The feminism of Hannah Arendt', *Democracy*, 3, 1983, 107–17.

8.1001 **Lang**, B., 'Hannah Arendt and the politics

of evil', *Judaism*, 37, 1988, 264–75.

8.1002 **Levin**, M., 'On animal *laborans* and *homo politicus* in Hannah Arendt. A note', *Pol. Theory*, 7, 1979, 521–31. Argues that Arendt's dismissal of labour should not be read as hostility to the working class but is best understood as the antithesis of her concept of the political.

8.1003 **Luban**, D., 'Explaining dark times: Hannah Arendt's theory of theory', *Social Res.*, 50, 1983, 215–48. Outlines her understanding of the procedures of political explanation, suggesting that they would be of great use in mainstream political science.

8.1004 ——— 'On Habermas on Arendt on power', *Phil. & Soc. Crit.*, 6, 1979, 79–92.

8.1005 **McKenna**, G., 'Bannisterless politics: Hannah Arendt and her children', *Hist. Pol. Thought*, 5, 1984, 333–60. Categorises Arendt's politics as neither conservative nor liberal but as resigned pessimism: she regretted the loss of tradition while agreeing with the radical that the loss is irreversible. Her tragic outlook involved the abandonment of any hope for a collective solution to the 'crisis' of modernity.

8.1006 ——— 'On Hannah Arendt', in R. Boyers, ed., *The Legacy of the German Refugee Intellectuals*, New York, 1972, 104–22.

8.1007 ——— 'On Hannah Arendt: politics as it is, was, might be', *Salmagundi*, 10–11, 1969–70, 104–22.

8.1008 **Markus**, M., 'The "anti-feminism" of Hannah Arendt', *Thesis Eleven*, 17, 1987, 76–87.

8.1009 **May**, D., *Hannah Arendt*, New York, 1986.

8.1010 **Moors**, K. F., 'Modernity and human initiative in the structure of Hannah Arendt's *The Life of the Mind*', *Pol. Sc. Re-r*, 10, 1980, 189–230.

8.1011 **Morgenthau**, H., 'Hannah Arendt on totalitarianism and democracy', *Social Res.*, 44, 1977, 127–31. Outlines the break from the Western political tradition which her concept of totalitarianism entailed.

8.1012 **Nelson**, J. S., 'Politics and truth: Arendt's problematic', *Am. J. Pol. Sc.*, 22, 1978, 270–301.

8.1013 **Nisbet**, R., 'Hannah Arendt and the American Revolution', *Social Res.*, 44, 1977, 63–79. Despite broad approval the author contests minor points within Arendt's interpretation of this revolution,

especially concerning its social character.

8.1014 **O'Sullivan**, N. K., 'Hannah Arendt: hellenic nostalgia and industrial society', in A. de Crespigny and K. Minogue, ed., *Contemporary Political Philosophers*, 1979, 228–51. Rehearses her celebration of the public sphere which, she believes, should remain separate from the social realm, a modern phenomenon, and her interpretation of totalitarianism as an escape from loneliness into a world offering certainty and intelligibility.

8.1015 ——— 'Politics, totalitarianism and freedom: the political thought of Hannah Arendt', *Pol. Sts.*, 21, 1973, 183–98.

8.1016 **Parekh**, B., 'Hannah Arendt' in *Contemporary Political Thinkers*, 1982, 1–21.

8.1017 ——— *Hannah Arendt and the Search for a New Political Philosophy*, 1981. Particular stress is laid upon *The Life of Mind* as the author elucidates her critique of political philosophy.

8.1018 **Reshaur**, K., 'Concepts of solidarity in the political theory of Hannah Arendt', *Can. J. Pol. Sc.*, 25, 1992, 723–36.

8.1019 **Ricoeur**, P., 'Action, story and history on re-reading *The Human Condition*', *Salmagundi*, 60, 1983, 60–72.

8.1020 **Riley**, P., 'Hannah Arendt on Kant, truth and politics', *Pol. Sts.*, 35, 1987, 379–92. Approves of Arendt's choice of the *Critique of Judgement* as Kant's key political text, yet challenges her reconstruction of his politics.

8.1021 **Ring**, J., 'On needing both Marx and Arendt. Alienation and the flight from inwardness', *Pol. Theory*, 17, 1989, 432–48. Thorough examination of Arendt's neglected theory of alienation, which explores the complementary dimensions of her and Marx's ideas on this theme.

8.1022 ——— 'The pariah as hero. Hannah Arendt's political actor', *Pol. Theory*, 19, 1991, 433–52. Asserts the importance of a second model of political action in Arendt's thought, alongside the Greek 'hero': the pariah – history's outsider. Stimulating and original argument.

8.1023 **Schwartz**, B., 'The religion of politics. Reflections on the thought of Hannah Arendt', *Dissent*, 17, 1970, 144–61.

8.1024 **Shklar**, J. N., 'Hannah Arendt as pariah', *Partisan Review*, 50, 1983, 64–77.

8.1025 ——— 'Rethinking the past', *Social Res.*, 44,

1977, 80–90. Explores the notion of the 'monumental' history in the work of Arendt and applies this notion to her theory of revolutions.

8.1026 **Sitton**, J. F., 'Hannah Arendt's argument for council democracy', *Polity*, 20, 1987, 80–100.

8.1027 **Springborg**, P., 'Arendt, republicanism and patriarchalism', *Hist. Pol. Thought*, 10, 1989, 499–523. Argues, against Canovan, that the republican tradition which Arendt developed had its origins in nineteenth-century German thought.

8.1028 **Stern**, P., and **Yarborough**, J., 'Hannah Arendt', *Am. Scholar*, 47, 1978, 371–81.

8.1029 **Sternberger**, D., 'The sunken city: Hannah Arendt's idea of politics', *Social Res.*, 44, 1977, 132–46. Places her political thought in the tradition of the 'polis', suggesting that consultation, debate and decision animate her conception of the political sphere.

8.1030 **Stillman**, P. G., 'Freedom as participation: the revolutionary theory of Hegel and Arendt', *American Behavioural Scientist*, 20, 1977, 477–92.

8.1031 **Suchting**, W. A., 'Marx and Hannah Arendt's *The Human Condition*', *Ethics*, 73, 1962, 47–55. Assessment of this text which flatly rejects Arendt's reading of Marx.

8.1032 **Tiaba**, G., *Politics and Freedom: Human Will and Action in the Thought of Hannah Arendt*, Lanham, Md., 1987.

8.1033 **Tolle**, G., *Human Nature Under Fire: The Political Philosophy of Hannah Arendt*, Washington, D.C., 1982. A critique informed by an Aristotelian outlook.

8.1034 **Vollrath**, E., 'Hannah Arendt and the method of political thinking', *Social Res.*, 44, 1977, 166–82. Demonstrates the theoretical coherence of her work through her distinctive methodological approach and belief that social meaning relates to the communality of the world.

8.1035 **Whitfield**, S., *Into the Dark: Hannah Arendt and Totalitarianism*, Philadelphia, Pa., 1980.

8.1036 **Wolin**, S. S., 'Hannah Arendt and the ordinance of time', *Social Res.*, 44, 1973, 91–105. Defends her attempt to present political theory as relevant to the contemporary world and the product of reflection upon experience.

8.1037 —— 'Hannah Arendt: democracy and the political', *Salmagundi*, 60, 1983, 3–19. Reconstructs her belief that democracy undermines the distinction between the political and the social. Her belief in the essential diversity of political space explains her suspicion of democratic modes of thought.

8.1038 **Yarborough**, J., and **Stern**, P., '*Vita activa* and *vita contemplativa*: political thought in *The Life of the Mind*', *Rev. Pol.*, 43, 1981, 323–54.

8.1039 **Young-Bruehl**, E., *Hannah Arendt: For Love of the World*, Yale, New Haven, 1982. Detailed biographical study which elucidates the theoretical and political sources of her work.

8.1040 —— 'Reflections on Hannah Arendt's *The Life of the Mind*', *Pol. Theory*, 10, 1982, 277–305. Reconstruction of her complex argument in this text, celebrating her attempt to connect the workings of the mind with an account of the political conditions of freedom which render thought possible.

Dewey

8.1041 **Bednar**, C. S., 'Dewey's attempt to provide a metaphysical foundation for democracy', *W. Pol. Q.*, 24, 1971, 28–31. Examination of a moment in the development of American political thought when metaphysical ideas affected political discourse, focusing upon his rejection of natural rights theory.

8.1042 **Bernstein**, R. J., 'Dewey, democracy: the task ahead of us', in J. Rajchman and C. West, ed., *Post-Analytic Philosophy*, New York, 1985, 48–58. Assessment of the sources of his democratic perspective, emphasising the influence of Darwin. Concludes that he is best considered within the communitarian tradition.

8.1043 —— *John Dewey*, New York, 1966. One of the first comprehensive outlines of his thought, tracing his intellectual development which culminated in his theory of experience. This philosophical position provided, according to Bernstein, the organising principle for his ethical, aesthetic and political thought.

8.1044 —— 'One step forward, two steps backward: Richard Rorty on liberal democracy and philosophy', *Pol. Theory*, 15, 1987, 538–63. Criticises his self-definition as a Deweyan pragmatist mainly because, unlike Dewey, his liberalism amounts to a defence of the 'status quo'.

8.1045 **Cahm**, S. M., ed., *New Studies in the Philosophy of John Dewey*, Hanover, N.H., 1977. Includes Frankel, 'John Dewey's social philosophy', and Rorty, 'Dewey's metaphysics'.

8.1046 **Damico**, J., *Individuality and Community: The Social and Political Thought of John Dewey*, Gainesville, Fla., 1978. Presents him as a key democratic theorist, who advanced political realism yet retained a participatory interpretation of the political realm.

8.1047 **De Hann**, R., 'Kropotkin, Marx and Dewey', *Anarchy*, 55, 1965, 271–86.

8.1048 **Feuer**, L., 'John Dewey and the back-to-the-people movement in American thought', *J. Hist. Ideas*, 20, 1959, 545–68. An historical assessment of the influences upon his thought, stressing his infusion of the spirit of democratic socialism into epistemological debates.

8.1049 **Tiles**, J. E., *Dewey*, 1991. Thorough introduction to his political thought, examining his influence on later American ideas.

8.1050 **Wilkins**, B.T., 'James, Dewey and Hegelian idealism', *Hist. Pol. Thought*, 17, 1956, 332–46. Views William James and Dewey as symbolising the community – individual division among philosophical pragmatists, tracing these tensions back to Hegel.

Macpherson

8.1051 **Angus**, I. H., 'On Macpherson's developmental liberalism', *Can. J. Pol. Sc.*, 15, 1982, 145–50.

8.1052 **Dunn**, J., 'Democracy unretrieved, or the political theory of Professor Macpherson', *Brit. J. Pol. Sc.*, 4, 1974, 489–99. Insightful consideration of his impact upon debates within political theory.

8.1053 **Leiss**, W., *C. B. Macpherson. Dilemmas of Liberalism and Socialism*, 1988. Survey of his life and work, placing him in the context of North American politics and the political thinking of the twentieth century.

8.1054 **Miller**, D., 'The Macpherson version', *Pol. Sts.*, 30, 1982, 120–7. Survey of Macpherson's contribution to contemporary political theory, including some useful critical comments on his overall project and treatment of particular figures in the history of political thought.

8.1055 **Minogue**, K., 'Humanist democracy: the political thought of C. B. Macpherson', *Can. J. Pol. Sc.*, 9, 1976, 377–94. Suggests that he derives all the features of politics from a single principle – humanist democracy. Particular emphasis is given to the tension between communalism and individuality in his thought.

8.1056 **Panitch**, L., 'Liberal democracy and socialist democracy: the antinomies of C. B. Macpherson', *Socialist Register*, 18, 1981, 144–89.

8.1057 **Parekh**, B., 'C. B. Macpherson', in *Contemporary Political Thinkers*, 1982, 48–73. Clear exposition claiming that he was a liberal masquerading as a Marxist.

8.1058 **Seaman**, J. W., and **Lewis**, T. J., 'On retrieving Macpherson's liberalism', *Can. J. Pol. Sc.*, 17, 1984, 707–29. Dissection of the ethical foundations of his retrieval of liberal democracy, elucidating within it a liberal teleology of self-governance and an ontology of developmental human capacity. This latter position undermines the kind of political authority which he values in liberal democracies.

8.1059 **Svacek**, V., 'The elusive Marxism of C. B. Macpherson', *Can. J. Pol. Sc.*, 9, 1976, 395–430. Argues that his thought approximates to Marxism in a number of areas, though criticises his attachment to negative liberty and ambivalence about revolution.

8.1060 **Wand**, B., 'C. B. Macpherson's conceptual apparatus', *Can. J. Pol. Sc.*, 4, 1971, 526–40.

8.1061 **Weinstein**, M. A., 'C. B., Macpherson: the roots of democracy and liberalism', in A. de Crespigny and K. Minogue, ed., *Contemporary Political Philosophers*, 1976, 252–71. Outlines his concern for the moral foundations of democracy and, in particular, his enquiry into the limits and possibilities of liberal democracy, concluding that a number of tensions beset his proclamation of the ultimate morality of liberal democracy and condemnation of liberal society.

8.1062 **Wood**, E. M., 'C. B. Macpherson: liberalism and the task of socialist political theory', *Socialist Register*, 15, 1978, 215–40.

8.1063 **Wright**, A., 'C. B. Macpherson, democracy and possessive individualism', in L. Tivey and A. Wright, ed., *Political*

Thought since 1945: Philosophy, Science, Ideology, 1992, 151–72. A sensitive assessment of his critique and attempted reconstruction of the liberal democratic tradition, which displays an awareness of the limitations of his claim to establish a new structure for democratic theory and practice.

Marcuse

8.1064 **Agger** B., 'The growing relevance of Marcuse's dialectic of individual and class', *Dialectical Anthropology*, 4, 1979, 135–45.

8.1065 —— 'Work and authority in Marcuse and Habermas', *Human Studies*, 2, 1979, 191–208.

8.1066 **Andrew**, E., 'Work and freedom in Marcuse and Marx', *Can. J. Pol. Sc.*, 3, 1970, 241–56. Stresses the difference between these theorists, contrasting Marcuse's belief in the abolition of work with Marx's view that it constitutes a fundamental human need. Marx, Andrew concludes, did not shape Marcuse's notion of technological rationality.

8.1067 **Berki**, R. N., 'Marcuse and the crisis of the new radicalism: from politics to religion?', *J. Pol.*, 34, 1972, 56–92. Views Marcuse's work as riven by the tension between the 'political' and 'religious' strands within radical thought and as the culmination of the project of the left Hegelians.

8.1068 —— 'Notes on Marcuse and the idea of tolerance', in B. Parekh, ed., *Dissent and Disorder: Essays in Social History*, 1976, 53–9. Rehearses his theoretical critique of the notion of pure tolerance, endorsing his view that such an ethic is inherently liberal and that tolerance does not necessarily involve the promotion of diversity.

8.1069 **Bernstein**, R. T., 'Herbert Marcuse: an immanent critique', *Journal of Social Issues*, 27, 1971, 97–111. Critical analysis of his attempt to develop a genuine critical theory, suggesting that his later work degenerated analytically as a consequence.

8.1070 **Blakeley**, T. J., 'On Marcuse: the old and the new degeneration', *Studies in Soviet Thought*, 11, 1971, 196–7.

8.1071 **Breines**, P., ed., *Critical Interruptions: New Left Perspectives on Herbert Marcuse*, New York, 1972. A collection informed by its heady political context, including Weber on individuation as praxis, Leiss on

Marcuse's place within critical theory, and Ober on sexuality and politics in his work.

8.1072 **Bronner**, S. E., 'Art and utopia. The Marcusean perspective', *Pol. & Soc.*, 3, 1973, 129–63.

8.1073 **Bykhovskii**, B., 'Marcusism against Marxism – a critique of uncritical criticism', *Phil. & Phenom. Res.*, 30, 1969, 203–18. Rambling, simplistic attack upon Marcuse as an anti-Marxist.

8.1074 **Cerullo**, M., 'Marcuse and feminism', *New Germ. Crit.*, 18, 1980, 21–3.

8.1075 **Cohen**, J., 'Critical theory: the philosophy of Marcuse', *New Left Rev.*, 57, 1969, 35–51. An Althusserian critique of Marcuse, stressing his 'rejection' of Marxism.

8.1076 **Cranston**, M., 'Herbert Marcuse', *Encounter*, 32, March, 1969, 38–50. Examination of his hostility to liberalism, suggesting that he implicitly supports violence and intolerance.

8.1077 **Delaney**, P., 'Marcuse in the seventies', *Partisan Review*, 40, 1973, 455–60. Brief introduction to his thought in the context of the history of the new left.

8.1078 **Eccleshall**, R. R., 'Technology and liberation', *Rad. Phil.*, 11, 1975, 9–14. Accuses Marcuse of having a less satisfactory anthropology than Marx, and therefore of misunderstanding the productive base of post-capitalist society.

8.1079 **Eidelberg**, P., 'The temptation of Herbert Marcuse', *Rev. Pol.*, 31, 1969, 442–58. Simplistic critique of Marcuse's utopianism.

8.1080 **Fitzgerald**, R., 'Herbert Marcuse and Christian Bay', in R. Fitzgerald, ed., *Comparing Political Thinkers*, 1980, 262–84. Compares these thinkers as 'need theorists', noting Bay's critique of Marcuse's 'facile' distinction between real and false needs.

8.1081 **Franklin**, M., 'Dialectics of the beautiful soul of Herbert Marcuse', *Revolutionary World*, 23–25, 1977, 1–46.

8.1082 **Fry**, J., *Marcuse – Dilemma and Liberation; A Critical Analysis*, 1974. Rehearses his analysis of the present realities and long-range tendencies of North American society which, according to Fry, necessitate a fundamental shift in critical theory. Concludes critically by questioning the accuracy of Marcuse's reading of the long-term development of advanced capitalism.

8.1083 **Geoghegan**, V., *Reason and Eros: The Social Theory of Herbert Marcuse*, 1981. Clear, sympathetic exposition of Marcuse's ideas, stressing his continual concern for authentic existence and its recreation by humans. The development of his thought is explained by reference to his historical and political context.

8.1084 **Giddens**, A., 'The improbable guru: re-reading Marcuse', in *Profiles and Critique in Social Theory*, 1982, 144–63. Re-reading of *One-Dimensional Man* from a contemporary perspective, critically assessing the political implications of his project.

8.1085 **Goldmann**, L., 'Understanding Marcuse', *Partisan Review*, 38, 1971, 247–62. Traces his philosophical development in relation to Heidegger, Hegel, Marx and the Frankfurt school, illustrating his search for new agents of radical change.

8.1086 **Graubard**, A., 'One-dimensional pessimism: a critique of Herbert Marcuse's theories', *Dissent*, 15, 1968, 216–28.

8.1087 **Greeman**, R., 'A critical re-examination of Herbert Marcuse's works', *New Pol.*, 6, 1967, 12–23.

8.1088 **Herf**, J., 'The critical spirit of Herbert Marcuse', *New Germ. Crit.*, 18, 1979, 24–7.

8.1089 **Horowitz**, D., 'One-dimensional society?', *International Socialist Journal*, 4, 1967, 811–30. Sympathetic account of Marcuse's ideas by a leading new left writer.

8.1090 **Jay**, M., 'How utopian is Marcuse?', in G. Fischer, ed., *The Revival of American Socialism; Selected Papers of the Socialist Scholars Conference*, New York, 1971, 244–56. Examines his attempt to reintroduce a utopian dimension to socialist thought, especially through his stress on radical action and understanding of the unity of opposites – the true harmony of pacified existence.

8.1091 **Kateb**, G., 'The political thought of Herbert Marcuse', *Commentary*, 49, 1970, 48–63.

8.1092 **Katz**, B. M., *Herbert Marcuse and the Art of Liberation: An Intellectual Biography*, 1982. Deploys a number of unpublished manuscripts on aesthetic questions to reinforce his argument that Marcuse's work is best understood as an attempt to articulate the aesthetic as a realm of life where transcendent standards are operative. This position carries a number of political implications which the book outlines.

8.1093 —— 'Praxis and poiesis: toward an intellectual biography of Herbert Marcuse', *New Germ. Crit.*, 18, 1979, 12–28.

8.1094 **Kellner**, D., *Herbert Marcuse and the Crisis of Marxism*, 1984. Lengthy, comprehensive and sympathetic account.

8.1095 —— 'Introduction to *On the Philosophical Foundation of the Concept Labor*', *Telos*, 16, 1973, 2–8.

8.1096 **Kettler**, D., 'A note on the aesthetic dimension in Marcuse's social theory', *Pol. Theory*, 10, 1982, 267–75. Argues for the specificity of Marcuse's aesthetic conception of revolution, a neglected concept in later socialist theorising.

8.1097 —— 'Herbert Marcuse: the critique of bourgeois civilization and its transcendence', in A. de Crespigny and K. Minogue, ed., *Contemporary Political Philosophers*, 1979, 1–48. A sympathetic account of Marcuse's belief that proposals for moral and political survival through piecemeal management of the problems generated by industrial society are untenable because the advance of civilisation entails the complete loss of self. Critical review of his conception of revolution as the 'locus' for meaningful political practice.

8.1098 **Landes**, J. B., 'Marcuse's feminist dimension', *Telos*, 41, 1979, 158–65.

8.1099 **Lichtheim**, G., 'From Marx to Hegel: reflections on Georg Lukács, T. W., Adorno and Herbert Marcuse', *Triquarterly*, 12, 1968, 5–42. Compares these thinkers, stressing their differing historical and intellectual contexts and complementary ideas.

8.1100 **Lind**, P., *Marcuse and Freedom*, 1985.

8.1101 **Lipshires**, S., *Herbert Marcuse: From Marx to Freud and Beyond*, Cambridge, Mass., 1974. Stressing Marcuse's Hegelian Marxism, Lipshires explains his use of Freud as an attempt to avoid the mistake of critical theory – that of overstressing the role of the proletariat. Short, engaging exposition.

8.1102 **Livingston**, D. W., 'Burke, Marcuse and the historical justification for revolution', *Sts. Burke & Time*, 14, 1972–73, 119–33.

8.1103 **MacIntyre**, A., 'Herbert Marcuse: from Marxism to pessimism', *Survey*, 62, 1967,

38–44.

8.1104 ——— *Marcuse*, 1970. Hostile and inaccurate representation of Marcuse's thought from an old left perspective.

8.1105 **Malinovich**, M., 'Herbert Marcuse in 1978: an interview', *Social Res.*, 48, 1981, 362–94.

8.1106 **Marks**, R. W., *The Meaning of Marcuse*, New York, 1972. Brief, idiosyncratic interpretation.

8.1107 **Martineau**, A., *Herbert Marcuse's Utopia*, Montreal, 1986.

8.1108 **Mattick**, P., *Critique of Marcuse: One Dimensional Man in Class Society*, 1972.

8.1109 **Parekh**, B., 'Herbert Marcuse', in *Contemporary Political Thinkers*, 1982, 74–95. Careful though sharply critical exposition of his ideas.

8.1110 ——— 'Utopianism and Manicheanism: a critique of Marcuse's theory of revolution', *Social Res.*, 39, 1972, 621–51. Criticises his homogeneous characterisation of liberal society and exaggeration of the ideal society, concluding that these features hamper his development of a coherent view of revolution.

8.1111 **Peretz**, M., 'Herbert Marcuse: beyond technological reason', *Yale Review*, 57, 1968, 518-27.

8.1112 **Piccone**, P., and **Delfini**, A., 'Herbert Marcuse's Heideggerian Marxism', *Telos*, 6, 1970, 36–46.

8.1113 **Pippin**, R. B., **Feenberg**, A., and **Webel**, C. P., ed., *Marcuse: Critical Theory and the Promise of Utopia*, 1988. An impressive array of contributors reflect upon the implications of Marcuse's project (Habermas, Bernstein, Jay), the philosophical influences upon him (Schmidt, Pippin, Olafson), his political theory (Kellner, Lichtman), and theory of technology (Offe, Feenberg).

8.1114 **Rachlis**, C., 'Marcuse and the problem of happiness', *Can. J. Pol. & Soc. Theory*, 2, 1978, 63–88. Assesses his attempted reconciliation of Marx and Freud by analysing the problem of happiness in his thought.

8.1115 **Rhodes**, I. M., 'Pleasure and reason: Marcuse's idea of freedom', *Interpretation*, 2, 1971, 79–105.

8.1116 **Rickert**, J., 'The Fromm–Marcuse debate revisited', *Theory & Soc.*, 15, 1986, 351–400.

8.1117 **Robinson**, P. A., 'Herbert Marcuse', in *The Sexual Radicals: Reich, Roheim,*

Marcuse, 1972, 114–82. Traces the logic of Marcuse's evolution as a radical Freudian critic. An illuminating essay marred by its tendency to separate his pre-Freudian ideas from his later work.

8.1118 ——— *The Freudian Left: Wilhelm Reich, Géza Róheim, Herbert Marcuse*, New York, 1969.

8.1119 **Schoolman**, M., 'Further reflections on work, alienation, and freedom in Marcuse and Marx', *Can. J. Pol. Sc.*, 6, 1973, 295–302. Asserts that both these thinkers shared a belief in the abolition of work, against those critics who see work as part of the human essence. Draws a parallel between Marx's notion of labour and Marcuse's concept of play.

8.1120 ——— *The Imaginary Witness: The Critical Theory of Herbert Marcuse*, 1980. Detailed exposition of his thought, charting the impact of historical circumstances upon his shifting ideas. The book's central thesis is that his early work was animated by a radicalised liberalism sensitive to individual emancipation; with the advent of fascism this perspective disappeared from view.

8.1121 **Schreider**, C. D., 'Utopia and history: Herbert Marcuse and the logic of revolution', *Phil. Today*, 12, 1968, 236–45.

8.1122 **Sedgwick**, P., 'Natural science and human theory: a critique of Herbert Marcuse', *Socialist Register*, 3, 1966, 163–92.

8.1123 **Shapiro**, J. J., 'From Marcuse to Habermas', *Continuum*, 8, 1970, 65–76. Compares their development of the Kantian problematic, suggesting that Marcuse failed to provide a self-reflexive perspective on human liberalism.

8.1124 **Stevernagel**, G., *Radical Philosophy as Therapy: Marcuse Reconsidered*, Westport, Conn., 1979.

8.1125 **Velliamthadam**, T., *Tomorrow's Society: Marcuse and Freud on Civilization*, Kottayam, 1978.

8.1126 **Vivas**, E., *Contra Marcuse*, New York, 1971.

8.1127 **Walton**, P. A., 'From surplus value to surplus theories: Marx, Marcuse and MacIntyre', *Soc. Res.*, 37, 1970, 644–55. Stresses the importance for contemporary social and political theory of the rediscovery of Marx's concept of surplus value, via a consideration of Marcuse's claim that Marx failed to explain convincingly the absence of revolution in the West.

8.1128 —— 'Marx and Marcuse', *Human Context*, 3, 1971, 159–75.

8.1129 **Wiatr**, J. J., 'Herbert Marcuse: philosopher of a lost radicalism', *Sc. & Soc.*, 34, 1970, 319–30. A chronological account of the development of his thought in which the author expresses his disapproval of his shift from Marxism and hostility to communism in Eastern Europe.

8.1130 **Wolff**, K. H., and **Moore**, B., ed., *The Critical Spirit: Essays in Honor of Herbert Marcuse*, Boston, Mass., 1967.

8.1131 **Woolf**, R. P., 'Herbert Marcuse, 1898–1979: a personal reminiscence', *Pol. Theory*, 8, 1980, 5–8.

8.1132 **Zamoshkin**, A., and **Motroshilova**, N. V., 'Is Marcuse's critical theory of society critical?', *Soviet Review*, 11, 1970, 3–24.

Nozick

8.1133 **Andrew**, E., 'Inalienable right, alienable property and freedom of choice: Locke, Nozick and Marx on the alienability of labour', *Can. J. Pol. Sc.*, 18, 1985, 529–50. Focuses upon a tension in natural rights thinking between the inalienability of natural or human rights and the tendency to individualise our conceptions of these, making them potentially alienable, like property. Contrasts Nozick's belief that all rights can be sold with Marx's position.

8.1134 **Arrow**, K. J., 'Nozick's entitlement theory of justice', *Philosophia*, 7, 1978, 265–79. Attacks the logical basis of this theory, though concludes that his ideas reinforce the interpretation of economic life pioneered by a number of game theory and rational choice thinkers.

8.1135 **Barber**, B. R., 'Deconstituting Nozick: Robert Nozick and philosophical reductionism', *J. Pols.*, 39, 1977, 2–23. Views Nozick's ideas as lying somewhere between the utilitarian's statist, egalitarian ideas and anarchist, individualist and anti-statist views. Concludes that he lacks any sense of the public realm, hence the ambiguous stance he adopts towards politics.

8.1136 **Barnett**, R. E., 'Whither anarchy: has Robert Nozick justified the state?', *J. Liber. Sts.*, 1, 1977, 15–21.

8.1137 **Bell**, N. K., 'Nozick and the fairness principle', *Soc. Theory & Pract.*, 5, 1978, 654–74.

8.1138 **Blackstone**, W. T., 'The minimal state: an assessment of some of the philosophical grounds', *Personalist*, 59, 1978, 333–43.

8.1139 **Childs**, R. A., 'The invisible hand strikes back', *J. Liber. Sts.*, 1, 1977, 23–33.

8.1140 **Christie**, G. C., 'The moral legitimacy of the minimal state', *Arizona Law Review*, 19, 1978, 31–43.

8.1141 **Cohen**, G. A., 'Marxism and contemporary political philosophy, or why Nozick exercises some Marxists more than he does any egalitarian liberals', *Can. J. Phil.*, supp. 16, 1990, 363–87.

8.1142 —— 'Nozick on appropriation', *New Left Rev.*, 150, 1985, 89–105.

8.1143 —— 'Robert Nozick and Will Chamberlain. How patterns preserve liberty', in J. Arthur and W. H. Shaw, ed., *Justice and Economic Distribution*, Englewood Cliffs, N.J., 1978, 246–62. Refutes Nozick's objection to socialism, arguing that libertarians appropriate liberty for capitalist ends.

8.1144 **Danley**, J. R., 'Robert Nozick and the libertarian paradox', *Mind*, 88, 1979, 419–23.

8.1145 **Davis**, L., 'Comments on Nozick's entitlement theory', *J. Phil.*, 73, 1976, 836–44.

8.1146 **Davis**, M., 'Necessity and Nozick's theory of entitlement', *Pol. Theory*, 5, 1977, 219–32. Concurs with his refutation of anarchism yet criticises his defence of libertarianism on contractarian grounds.

8.1147 **Degregori**, T. E., 'Market morality – Robert Nozick and the question of economic-justice', *Am. J. Econ. & Sociol.*, 38, 1979, 17–30.

8.1148 **Drury**, S. B., 'Locke and Nozick on property', *Pol. Sts.*, 30, 1982, 28–41. Separates these thinkers' ideas regarding the foundation of private property because the accepted interpretation of Locke on this question is mistaken.

8.1149 —— 'Robert Nozick and the right to property', in A. J. Parel and T. Flanagan, ed., *Theories of Property: Aristotle to the Present*, Calgary, 1979.

8.1150 **Exdell**, J., 'Distributive justice: Nozick on property rights', *Ethics*, 87, 1976–77, 142–9. Argues that the Kantian imperative, which Nozick appropriates, does not provide justification for the private ownership of natural resources.

8.1151 **Fowler**, M., 'Self-ownership, mutual aid and mutual respect: some counter-examples to Nozick's libertarianism', *Soc. Theory & Pract.*, 6, 1980, 227–45.

8.1152 —— 'Stability and utopia: a critique of Nozick's framework', *Ethics*, 90, 1980, 550–63.

8.1153 **Goldman**, H. A., 'The entitlement theory of distributive justice', *J. Phil.*, 73, 1976, 823–35.

8.1154 **Goldsmith**, M. M., 'The entitlement theory of justice considered', *Pol. Sts.*, 27, 1979, 578–93. Perceptive examination of the principles underlying Nozick's theory of justice, stressing especially the need for an entitlement theory to provide rules for assigning specific rights.

8.1155 **Harris**, C. E., 'Kant, Nozick and the minimal state', *Southwestern J. Phil.*, 10, 1979, 179–88.

8.1156 **Held**, V., 'John Locke on Robert Nozick', *Social Res.*, 43, 1976, 169–95.

8.1157 **Henley**, K., 'Children and the individualism of Mill and Nozick', *Personalist*, 59, 1978, 415–9.

8.1158 **Hodson**, J. D., 'Nozick, libertarianism, and rights', *Arizona Law Review*, 8, 1978, 212–27.

8.1159 **Holmes**, R. L., 'Nozick on anarchism', *Pol. Theory*, 5, 1977, 247–56. Questions his justification of the minimal state, suggesting that this ultimately allows for the violation of human rights.

8.1160 **Jackson**, M. W., 'John Rawls and Robert Nozick', in R. Fitzgerald, ed., *Comparing Political Thinkers*, 1980, 285–302. Clear statement of their theoretical differences, suggesting that both present an unconvincing picture of human nature.

8.1161 **Johnson**, K., 'Government by insurance company: the anti-political philosophy of Robert Nozick', *West. Pol. Q.*, 29, 1976, 177–88.

8.1162 **Ladenson**, R. F., 'Nozick on law and the state: a critique', *Phil. Sts.*, 34, 1978, 437–44.

8.1163 **Litan**, R. E., 'On rectification in Nozick's minimal state', *Pol. Theory*, 5, 1977, 233–46. Argues that rectification (which will occur in Nozick's scenario when the principle of justice is violated) would be limited by his own 'minimal state' principles; in fact, a more egalitarian distribution of entitlements could be generated from Nozickian principles.

8.1164 **Machan**, T. R., 'Nozick and Rand on property rights', *Personalist*, 58, 1977, 192–5.

8.1165 **Martin**, M. W., 'Reason and utopianism in Wolff 's anarchism', *Southern Journal of Political and Social Theory*, 3, 1979, 46–9.

8.1166 **Nock**, C. J., 'Equal freedom and unequal property: a critique of Nozick's libertarian case', *Can. J. Pol. Sc.*, 25, 1992, 677–95.

8.1167 **O'Neil**, P., 'Inadequacy of contract theory in Robert Nozick, *Anarchy, State and Utopia*', *Personalist*, 60, 1979, 429–32.

8.1168 **O'Neill**, O., 'Nozick's entitlements', *Inquiry*, 19, 1976, 468–81.

8.1169 **Paul**, J., 'Nozick, anarchism and procedural rights', *J. Liber. Sts.*, 1, 1977, 337–40.

8.1170 —— ed., *Reading Nozick: Essays on Anarchy, State, and Utopia*, 1981. A large collection which begins with an overview of Nozick's text (Williams, Singer), proceeds to a consideration of his justification of the minimal state against anarchism (Holmes, Paul, Wolff), and critically assesses his conception of rights (Scanlon, Thomson, Scheffler, Mack, Nagel, Paul, Uyl and Rasmussen). Finally, a number of commentators reflect upon his entitlement theory of distributive justice (O'Neill, Ryan, Davis, Lyons, Steiner, Kirzner).

8.1171 **Pazner**, E. A., 'Entitlement principles and the original position: a Rawlsian interpretation of Nozick's approach to distributive justice', *Arizona Law Review*, 8, 1978, 169–79.

8.1172 **Postema**, G. J., 'Nozick on liberty, compensation and the individual's right to punish', *Soc. Theory & Pract.*, 6, 1980, 311–38.

8.1173 **Replogle**, R., 'Natural rights and distributive justice: Nozick and the classical contractarians', *Can. J. Pol. Sc.*, 17, 1984, 65–86.

8.1174 **Rodman**, J., 'Analysis and history – or, how the invisible hand works through Robert Nozick', *West. Pol. Q.*, 29, 1976, 197–201.

8.1175 **Rothbard**, M. N., 'Robert Nozick and the immaculate conception of the state', *J. Liber. Sts.*, 1, 1977, 45–57. Hostile and flawed attack upon his justification of the minimal state.

8.1176 **Ryan**, C. C., 'Yours, mine, and ours: property rights and individual liberty', *Ethics*, 87, 1976–77, 126-41. Rehearses Nozick's hostility to distributive justice, though suggests that his defence of the connection between property and individual liberty assumes private property rights, even though these may constrain the freedom of the majority.

8.1177 **Sampson**, G., 'Liberalism and Nozick's "minimal state" ', *Mind*, 87, 1978, 93–7.

8.1178 **Sanders**, J. T., 'The free market model versus government: a reply to Nozick', *J. Liber. Sts.*, 1, 1977, 35–44.

8.1179 **Scaff**, L. A., 'How not to do political theory: Nozick's apology for the minimal state', *Arizona Law Review*, 8, 1978, 193–211.

8.1180 **Scanlon**, T., 'Nozick on rights, liberty, and property', *Phil. Pub. Affairs*, 6, 1977, 3–25. Emphasises his distinctive emphasis on entitlement principles as the beginning and end of distributive justice and justifies his claim that economic liberty should be considered one of the conditions for the legitimacy of social institutions.

8.1181 **Singer**, P., 'Why Nozick is not so easy to refute', *West. Pol. Q.*, 29, 1976, 191–2.

8.1182 **Thigpen**, R. B., 'Two approaches to the principles of justice in recent American political philosophy: an essay review', *J. Thought*, 21, 1986, 118–26. Criticises both the 'imaginary situation approach' to justice of Rawls, Nozick and Ackerman, and the 'shared understandings approach' of Walzer. Concludes that both lack adequate principles which can only be provided by a concept of human nature.

8.1183 **Tucker**, D., 'Nozick's individualism', *Politics*, 14, 1979, 109–21.

8.1184 **Wolff**, J., *Robert Nozick: Property, Justice and the Minimal State*, 1991. Situates his libertarianism in the context of current debates, focusing on his doctrine of rights, derivation of the minimal state, and entitlement theory of justice.

8.1185 **Wood**, D., 'Nozick's justification of the minimal state', *Ethics*, 88, 1977–78, 260–2. Criticises the logical status of this argument.

8.1186 **Yanal**, R. J., 'Notes on the foundations of Nozick's theory of rights', *Personalist*, 60, 1979, 649–59.

Rawls

8.1187 **Abbott**, P., 'With equality and virtue for all. John Rawls and the liberal tradition', *Polity*, 8, 1976, 339–57.

8.1188 **Ake**, C., 'Justice as equality', *Phil. & Pub.*

Affairs, 5, 1975, 69–89.

8.1189 **Altham**, J. E. J., 'Rawls and power', *Cambridge Rev.*, 96, 1975, 106–8. Contrasts Rawls with Rousseau, suggesting that the former fails to understand the sense of liberty as autonomy.

8.1190 —— 'Rawls's difference principle', *Phil.*, 48, 1973, 75-8.

8.1191 **Amdur**, R., 'Rawls' theory of justice – domestic and international perspectives', *World Politics*, 29, 1977, 438–61.

8.1192 **Andelson**, R., 'Vive la difference: Rawls' "difference principle", and the fatal premises upon which it rests', *Personalist*, 56, 1975, 202–13.

8.1193 **Baier**, K., 'Justice and the aims of political philosophy', *Ethics*, 99, 1989, 771–90.

8.1194 **Barber**, B. R., 'Justifying justice: problems of psychology, measurement, and politics in Rawls', *Am. Pol. Sc. Rev.*, 69, 1975, 663–74. Asserts that his work is divorced from the historical and political realities which affect any theory of justice.

8.1195 **Barry**, B., 'John Rawls and the priority of liberty', *Phil. & Pub. Affairs*, 2, 1973, 274–90. Rigorous examination of Rawls's insistence on the priority of liberty with regard to wealth.

8.1196 —— 'Liberation and want-satisfaction: a critique of John Rawls', *Pol. Theory*, 1, 1973, 134–53. Incisive critique of a tension within liberal accounts of the value attributed to liberty through a study of Rawls. Concludes that liberals must logically stand by certain normative preferences despite their simultaneous desire for moral neutrality.

8.1197 —— 'On social justice', in R. E. Flathman, ed., *Concepts in Social and Political Philosophy*, 1973, 422–33. Elegant critique of Rawls's assumption that rational self-interest requires the adoption of a maximin policy, concluding that his two principles of justice cannot be deduced from his initial conditions.

8.1198 —— 'Reflections on justice as fairness', in H. A. Bedau, ed., *Justice and Equality*, Englewood Cliffs, N.J., 1971, 103–15.

8.1199 —— *The Liberal Theory of Justice: A Critical Examination of the Principal Doctrines in* A Theory of Justice *by John Rawls*, 1973. Influential critique supplemented by an 'apologia' in which the author expresses regret for his critical tone. Barry focuses critical fire on Rawls's derivation of the two theories of justice and 'anarchistic' liberalism.

8.1200 **Baumrin**, B. H., 'Autonomy in Rawls and Kant', *Midwest Studies in Philosophy*, 1, 1976, 55–7. Argues, against Johnson, for the essential continuity of their ideas.

8.1201 **Bedau**, H. A., 'Social justice and social institutions', *Midwest Studies in Philosophy*, 3, 1978, 159–75.

8.1202 **Bentley**, D. J., 'John Rawls: *A Theory of Justice*', *University of Pennsylvania Law Review*, 21, 1972–73, 1070–8.

8.1203 **Blocker**, H. G., and **Smith**, E. H., ed., *John Rawls' Theory of Social Justice: An Introduction*, Athens, Ga., 1980. A series of essays examining this theory, including Buchanan on the principles of justice, Katzner on the original position, Bowie on his notion of liberty, Beauchamp on the difference principle, and Schaar on equality. Also contains essays on the application of his principles to current political problems: Farrell on civil disobedience; Beitz on justice and international relations; Jones on discrimination; and Wicclair on the moral justification of intervention by one nation in the affairs of another. Finally, several commentators relate his work to broader philosophical traditions, including Darell on Kantian foundations, Goldman on utilitarianism, DeMarco on Marx, Goldman on the right, and Francis on the left. Nearly all these essays are commendably accessible and jargon-free.

8.1204 **Bloom**, A., 'Justice: John Rawls vs. the tradition of political philosophy', *Am. Pol. Sc. Rev.*, 69, 1975, 648–62. Reading of Rawls as a liberal democratic theorist concerned to undermine utilitarianism.

8.1205 **Bowie**, N. E., 'Some comments on Rawls' theory of justice', *Soc. Theory & Pract.*, 3, 1974, 65–74. Critical survey posing several key questions: who should participate in the formulation of principles of justice? can the equal liberty principle be successfully defended? are Rawls's two principles of justice compatible?

8.1206 **Braybrooke**, D., 'Utilitarianism with a difference: Rawls's position in ethics', *Can. J. Phil.*, 3, 1973, 303–31.

8.1207 **Brock**, D. W., 'John Rawls' theory of justice', *University of Chicago Law Review*, 40, 1973, 486–99.

8.1208 **Brown**, D. G., 'John Rawls: John Mill', *Dialogue*, 12, 1973, 477–9.

8.1209 **Buchanan**, J., 'A Hobbesian interpretation of the Rawlsian difference principle', *Kyklos*, 29, 1976, 5–25.

8.1210 —— 'Rawls on justice as fairness', *Public Choice*, 13, 1972, 123–8.

8.1211 **Caney**, S., 'Rawls, Sandel and the self ', *Int. Soc. Sc. J.*, 8, 1991, 161–71. Defends Rawls from Sandel's criticism of the asocial conception of the self at the heart of the former's work.

8.1212 **Care**, N. S., 'Contractualism and moral criticism', *Rev. Metaph.*, 23, 1969, 85–101. Attempts to clarify the nature of contractualism, concluding that it is incapable of providing a coherent basis for a moral theory, with particular reference to Rawls.

8.1213 **Chapman**, J. W., 'Rawls's theory of justice', *Am. Pol. Sc. Rev.*, 69, 1975, 588–93. Exploration of the sources of his theory – Hume, Kant and Rousseau.

8.1214 **Choptiany**, L., 'A critique of John Rawls's principles of justice', *Ethics*, 83, 1973, 146–50.

8.1215 **Clark**, B., and **Gintis**, H., 'Rawlsian justice and economic systems', *Phil. & Pub. Affairs*, 7, 1978, 302–25.

8.1216 **Copp**, D., 'Justice and the difference principle', *Can. J. Phil.*, 4, 1974, 229–40. Challenges Rawls's difference principle as conflicting with our considered judgements of what constitutes justice/injustice.

8.1217 **Corlett**, J. A., ed., *Equality and Liberty: Analysing Rawls and Nozick*, 1991.

8.1218 **Craig**, L. H., 'Contra contact: a brief against John Rawls' theory of justice', *Can. J. Pol. Sc.*, 8, 1975, 63–81. Challenges the foundations of the original position as well as the intuitive appeal of a contractarian approach.

8.1219 **Crocker**, L., 'Equality, solidarity and Rawls' maximin', *Phil. & Pub. Affairs*, 6, 1977, 262–6. Argues for a more egalitarian application of the 'maximin' principle to improve relative income differentials.

8.1220 **Daniels**, N. 'On liberty and equality in Rawls', *Soc. Theory & Pract.*, 3, 1974, 149–59. Doubts the compatibility of Rawls's belief in the equality of basic liberty and inequalities of wealth and power; this tension is traced back to the roots of liberal political theory.

8.1221 —— ed., *Reading Rawls: Critical Studies on Rawls' A Theory of Justice*, 1975. An important and much cited collection which assesses the worth and implications of his original position (Nagel, Dworkin, Fisk), examines his methodology (Hare, Feinberg, Dworkin, Lyons), assesses his concept of justice (Scanlon, Miller, Hart, Daniels), and examines the implications of these ideas for politics and policy (Sen, Barber, Michelman).

8.1222 **Darwall**, S. L., 'A defense of the Kantian interpretation', *Ethics*, 86, 1976, 164–70. Attempts to justify Rawls's Kantianism in the light of O. A. Johnson's criticisms in 'The Kantian interpretation', *Ethics*, 85, 1974, 58–66. Explores the relation between Rawls's conception of the original position and Kant's conception of autonomy and the categorical imperative.

8.1223 **Dasgupta**, P., 'On some problems arising from Professor Rawls' conception of distributive justice', *Theory and Decision*, 11, 1974, 325–44.

8.1224 **Delaney**, C. F., 'Rawls on justice', *Rev. Pol.*, 37, 1975, 104–11.

8.1225 **DeLue**, S. M., 'Aristotle, Kant and Rawls on moral motivations in a just society', *Am. Pol. Sc. Rev.*, 74, 1980, 385–93.

8.1226 **DeMarco**, J. P., 'Barry's critique of Rawls' liberalism', *Man and World*, 8, 1975, 454–60.

8.1227 —— 'Some problems in Rawls' theory of justice', *Philosophy in Context*, 2, 1973, 41–8.

8.1228 —— and **Richmond**, S. A., 'A note on the priority of liberty', *Ethics*, 87, 1976–77, 272–5. Analysis of Rawls's concept of liberty in the light of concrete examples which cast doubt on its applicability.

8.1229 **DiQuattro**, A., 'Rawls and left criticism', *Pol. Theory*, 11, 1983, 53–78. Argues against conventional left critics that Rawls's ideas are compatible with socialist ideas of social justice by elaborating the egalitarian implications of the difference principle.

8.1230 —— 'Rawls versus Hayek', *Pol. Theory*, 14, 1986, 307–10. Reviews debates about potentially socialist applications of Rawls's notions of distributive justice.

8.1231 **Doppelt**, G., 'Is Rawls's Kantian liberalism coherent and defensible?', *Ethics*, 99, 1989, 815–51. Sceptical assessment of whether the Kantian ideal of persons can successfully provide the sole basis for understanding the modern tradition or for a theory of justice. Contains a clear and farsighted account of Rawls's

ideas and theoretical weaknesses.

8.1232 —— 'Rawls' Kantian ideal and the viability of modern liberalism', *Inquiry*, 31, 1988, 413–49. Proposes that Rawlsian theory and liberal thought, more generally, lack a conception of moral reason adequate to comprehend and mediate the tensions and conflicts which make up Western political identity.

8.1233 —— 'Rawls' system of justice: a critique from the left', *Nous*, 14, 1980, 259–307. Sharp critique of his detachment of the 'concept of liberty from the organisation of daily economic life' and tendency to celebrate the social structure without paying heed to its undermining of autonomy.

8.1234 **Dworkin**, R., 'The original position', *University of Chicago Law Review*, 40, 1973, 500–33. Attempts to locate the presupposed deep theory which gives this position justificatory power, specifying the right of each individual to equal concern and respect. This is the ground, says Dworkin, on which Rawls can be challenged.

8.1235 **Escheté**, A., 'Contractarianism and the scope of justice', *Ethics*, 85, 1974, 38–49.

8.1236 **Feinberg**, J., 'Justice, fairness and rationality', *Yale Law Journal*, 81, 1972, 1004–31.

8.1237 **Fishkin**, J., 'Justice and rationality: some objections to the central arguments in Rawls's theory', *Am. Pol. Sc. Rev.*, 69, 1975, 615–29.

8.1238 **Flew**, A., 'A theory of social justice', in H. D. Lewis, ed., *Contemporary British Philosophy*, 1976, 69–85. Extensive review of Rawls, rehearsing the various criticisms made by other commentators.

8.1239 **Flynn**, J. J., and **Ruffinengo**, P., 'Distributive justice: some institutional implications of Rawls's *A Theory of Justice*', *Utah Law Review*, 1, 1975, 23–57.

8.1240 **Frankel**, C., 'Justice, utilitarianism and rights', *Soc. Theory & Pract.*, 3, 1974, 27–46. Rehearses Rawls's theory of justice, endorsing his critique of utilitarianism and questioning his conception of the proper objectives of human social intelligence.

8.1241 **Galston**, W. A., 'Moral personality and liberal theory: John Rawls's "Dewey Lectures" ', *Pol. Theory*, 10, 1982, 492–517. Commentary upon his recent extension of the sources of his argument which now includes a Kantian theory of individual motivation. Unwittingly, Galston suggests, Rawls throws into relief recent trends in American liberal politics and theory.

8.1242 **Gardner**, M., 'Rawls on the maximin rule and distributive justice', *Phil. Sts.*, 27, 1975, 255–70.

8.1243 **Gaus**, G. F., 'The convergence of rights and utility: the case of Rawls and Mill', *Ethics*, 92, 1981–82, 57–72. Contrasts right-based with utilitarian political theories yet notes that they produce similar political prescriptions regarding the bounds of individual liberty. He demonstrates this by comparing Mill with Rawls, concluding that both share a psychological conception of human nature.

8.1244 **Gauthier**, D., 'Justice and natural endowment: toward a critique of Rawls's ideological framework', *Soc. Theory & Pract.*, 3, 1974, 3–26. Examines his claim to combine rationality with morality, suggesting that an alternative conception of society needs to be proffered in accordance with the principles of justice. This alternative undermines the maximising conception of practical rationality at the heart of Rawls's theory.

8.1245 **Gibbard**, A., 'Disparate goods and Rawls' difference principle: a social choice theoretic treatment', *Theory and Decision*, 11, 1979, 267–88.

8.1246 **Gilbert**, A., 'Equality and social theory in Rawls's theory of justice', *Occasional Review*, 8–9, 1978, 95–117.

8.1247 **Gintis**, H., and **Clark**, B., 'Rawlsian justice and economic systems', *Phil. Pub. Affairs*, 7, 1977–78, 302–25.

8.1248 **Goldman**, A. H., 'Rawls's original position and the difference principle', *J. Phil.*, 73, 1976, 845–9.

8.1249 **Goodrum**, C., 'Rawls and egalitarianism', *Phil. & Phenom. Res.*, 37, 1976–77, 386–93. Rejects Rawls's argument that people would be prepared to accept inequalities in the original position.

8.1250 **Gordon**, S., 'John Rawls' difference principle, utilitarianism, and the optimum degree of inequality', *J. Phil.*, 70, 1973, 275–80.

8.1251 **Gorovitz**, S., 'John Rawls: a theory of justice', in A. de Crespigny and K. Minogue, ed., *Contemporary Political Philosophies*, 1976, 272–89. Rehearses his theory of justice, the conceptual foundation for a system of constraints on human interaction.

8.1252 **Gourevitch**, V., 'Rawls on justice', *Rev. Metaph.*, 28, 1975, 485–519. A critical review which takes issue with his emphasis on justice as a virtue of rules and institutions rather than a characteristic of the varied range of individuals. Complex and somewhat convoluted discussion.

8.1253 **Grcic**, J., 'Rawls and socialism', *Phil. & Soc. Crit.*, 7, 1980, 17–36.

8.1254 **Green**, K., 'Rawls, women and the priority of liberty', *Aust. J. Phil.*, supp. 64, 1986, 26–36.

8.1255 **Haksar**, V., 'Autonomy, justice and contractarianism', *Brit. J. Pol. Sc.*, 3, 1973, 487–509. Clear and stimulating review of the main ideas behind Rawls's theory of justice.

8.1256 —— *Civil Disobedience. Threats and Offers: Gandhi and Rawls*, 1987.

8.1257 —— 'Coercive proposals (Rawls and Gandhi)', *Pol. Theory*, 4, 1976, 65–79.

8.1258 —— 'Rawls and Gandhi on civil disobedience', *Inquiry*, 19, 1976, 151–92.

8.1259 —— 'Rawls' theory of justice', *Analysis*, 32, 1972, 149–53.

8.1260 **Hampton**, J., 'Should political philosophy be done without metaphysics?', *Ethics*, 99, 1989, 791–814. Explores the tension between his belief in the creation of public reason through an overlapping consensus and his universalist interpretation of freedom.

8.1261 **Hare**, R. M., 'Critical study. Rawls' theory of justice – I and II', *Phil. Q.*, 23, 1973, 144–55 and 241-52. Extended review which criticises his philosophical and ethical methodology, suggesting that his rational contractor theory does not save him from utilitarian conclusions.

8.1262 **Harsanyi**, J. C., 'Can the maximin principle serve as a basis for morality? A critique of John Rawls' theory', *Am. Pol. Sc. Rev.*, 69, 1975, 594–606. Outline of the Rawlsian deployment of the contractarian tradition (Locke, Kant, Rousseau) against utilitarianism.

8.1263 —— 'Sneed on Rawls' theory of social institutions', *Eskenntis*, 13, 1972, 34–9.

8.1264 **Hart**, H. L. A., 'Rawls on liberty and its priority', *University of Chicago Law Review*, 40, 1973, 534–55. Suggests he underestimates the problem of balancing conflicting liberties, and challenges the priority he accords to liberty.

8.1265 **Hedman**, C. G., 'Rawls' theory of justice

and "market socialism" ', *Rad. Phil.*, 28, 1981, 23–8. A reply to critics of market socialism, asserting that Rawls's individualism does not necessarily legitimate the problematic aspects of capitalist society.

8.1266 **Held**, V., 'On Rawls and self-interest', *Midwest Studies in Philosophy*, 1, 1976, 57–60.

8.1267 **Honderich**, T., 'The use of the basic proposition of a theory of justice', *Mind*, 84, 1975, 63–78.

8.1268 **Hoy**, J. B., 'Hegel's critique of Rawls', *Clio*, 10, 1981, 407–22.

8.1269 —— 'Three conceptions of autonomy in Rawls' theory of justice', *Phil. & Soc. Crit.*, 1, 1979, 59–78.

8.1270 **Hubin**, D. C., 'Justice and future generations', *Phil. Pub. Affairs*, 6, 1976, 70–83. Attempts to expand a moral principle concerning our behaviour towards the environment on behalf of future generations, based on Rawls's ideal contract model.

8.1271 **Jackson**, M. W., 'John Rawls and Robert Nozick', in R. Fitzgerald, ed., *Comparing Political Thinkers*, 1980, 285–302. Clear statement of their theoretical differences, suggesting that both present an unconvincing picture of human nature.

8.1272 —— 'The least advantaged class in Rawls's theory', *Can. J. Pol. Sc.*, 12, 1979, 727–46.

8.1273 **Jackson**, T. P., 'To bedlam and part way back: John Rawls and Christian justice', *Faith Philosophy*, 8, 1991, 423–47. Tracing the evolution of his theory of justice, the author argues that his ideas are incompatible with Christian doctrine.

8.1274 **Johnson**, O. A., 'Autonomy in Kant and Rawls: a reply to Stephen Darwall's *A Defense of the Kantian Interpretation*', *Ethics*, 87, 1977, 251–4. Defends his belief that aspects of Rawls are not consonant with Kantian ideas.

8.1275 —— 'Heteronomy and autonomy – Rawls and Kant', *Midwest Studies in Philosophy*, 2, 1977, 277–9. Reasserts his thesis of the incommensurability between Kantian conceptions of autonomy and Rawlsian theory.

8.1276 —— 'The Kantian interpretation', *Ethics*, 85, 1974, 58–66.

8.1277 **Kaye**, D. H., 'Playing games with justice: Rawls and the maximin rule', *Soc. Theory & Pract.*, 6, 1980, 33–51. Argues that the original position does not necessarily require the maximin rule over alternative decision-rules. Strays into mathematical and probability theory to elucidate this position.

8.1278 **Kukathas**, C., *Rawls: "A Theory of Justice" and Its Critics*, Stanford, Calif., 1990. Discusses central themes in his work, including moral individualism and contractarian theory, as well as his libertarian and communitarian critics.

8.1279 **Kymlicka**, W., 'Liberal individualism and liberal neutrality', *Ethics*, 99, 1989, 883–905. Examining several critiques of Rawls's individualist conception of neutrality, Kylicka concludes that individualism is not the central issue with regard to liberal claims to neutrality; rather, liberals need to consider whether the relevant relations for the development of individual values and autonomy are political ones.

8.1280 **Ladenson**, R. F., 'Rawls' principle of equal liberty', *Phil. Sts.*, 28, 1975, 49–54.

8.1281 **Lassman**, P., 'John Rawls, justice and a well-ordered society', in L. Tivey and A. Wright, ed., *Political Thought since 1945; Philosophy, Science, Ideology*, 1992, 196–218. Focuses on his combination of an older style of political philosophy, concerned with substantive problems, and the insights of the analytical movement in twentieth-century philosophy. Successfully hints at the complexity of Rawls's thought whilst clearly presenting his core principles.

8.1282 **Lessnoff**, M., 'Barry on Rawls' priority of liberty', *Phil. Pub. Affairs*, 4, 1974, 100–14. Criticises Barry's interpretation of Rawls, particularly the former's appropriation of standard economic techniques in an attempt to undermine Rawls's conception of liberty.

8.1283 —— 'John Rawls' theory of justice', *Pol. Sts.*, 19, 1971, 63–80.

8.1284 **Levine**, A., 'Beyond justice: Rousseau against Rawls', *Journal of Chinese Philosophy*, 4, 1977, 123–42.

8.1285 —— 'Rawls' Kantianism', *Soc. Theory & Pract.*, 3, 1974, 47–63. Argues against Rawls's claim to have broken completely with utilitarianism, suggesting that he is closer to this tradition than to Kant in his conception of rational agency, which is ultimately grounded in contingent assumptions about human nature.

Unusual, idiosyncratic interpretation.

8.1286 **Lloyd Thomas**, D. A., 'E pluribus unum', *Can. J. Phil.*, supp. 3, 1977, 49–70. Locates Rawls's 'thin' theory of the good within the liberal tradition, explaining the issues which arise from his attempt to bypass individual desires in his account of the principles of justice individuals rationally select in the original position.

8.1287 **Lyons**, D., 'Rawls versus utilitarianism', *J. Phil.*, 69, 1972, 535–45. Focuses upon his contract theory as the core of his justificatory power.

8.1288 **Lyons**, W., 'Liberalism and want-satisfaction: a critique of John Rawls', *Pol. Theory*, 1, 1973, 134–53. Deploys Rawls to illustrate a tension in liberalism between its commitment to a plurality of ethical beliefs and outcomes and attachment to certain ethical goals.

8.1289 **MacCormick**, N., 'Justice according to Rawls', *Law Q. Rev.*, 89, 1973, 393–417.

8.1290 **McDonald**, V., 'Rawlsian contractarianism: liberal equality or inequality?', *Can. J. Phil.*, supp. 3, 1977, 71–94. Hagiographic account of the *Theory of Justice* 'as the most coherent twentieth century restatement of the liberal egalitarian paradigm', stressing parallels between Rawlsian and Lockean contractarianism.

8.1291 **Macleod**, A., 'Critical notice: Rawls' theory of justice', *Dialogue: Canadian Philosophical Review*, 13, 1974, 139–59.

8.1292 **Macpherson**, C. B., 'Class, classlessness, and the critique of Rawls', *Pol. Theory*, 6, 1978, 209–11. Defends his own critique of Rawls's justification of inevitable inequalities.

8.1293 —— 'Rawls' models of man and society', *Phil. Soc. Sc.*, 3, 1973, 341–7. Sharp attack upon his justification of inegalitarian social relations and the tension between this and his vision of a well-ordered, harmonious social world.

8.1294 **Martin**, R., *Rawls and Rights*, Lawrence, Kan., 1985. Assesses the development of his thought over fifteen years, criticising him on the grounds that his theory might be better formulated with regard to rights.

8.1295 **Mason**, H., 'On the Kantian interpretation of Rawls' theory', *Midwest Studies in Philosophy*, 1, 1976, 47–55.

8.1296 **Masterson**, M. P., 'On being unfair to Rawls, Rousseau and Williams OR John Charvet and the incoherence of inequality', *Brit. J. Pol. Sc.*, 1, 1971, 209–23.

8.1297 **May**, T. G., 'Kant the liberal, Kant the anarchist: Rawls and Lyotard on Kantian justice', *Southern Journal of Philosophy*, 28, 1990, 525–38. Compares the return to Kant attempted by both Rawls and Lyotard, illustrating their contrasting attempts to root their theories of justice in his thought; concludes with the paradoxical view that Rawls is closer to the Kantian intention yet Lyotard is closer to his actual achievement in his 'investigations into Kant's multiple and irreducible ontological territories'.

8.1298 **Mendola**, J., 'On Rawls' basic structure: forms of justification and the subject matter of social philosophy', *Monist*, 71, 1988, 437–54. Following Rawls, the author stresses the importance of communities, understood as groups of agents who accept the same rational framework for action.

8.1299 **Merritt**, G., 'Justice as fairness: a commentary on Rawls' new theory of justice', *Vanderbilt Law Review*, 26, 1973, 665–96.

8.1300 **Michelman**, F. I., 'In pursuit of constitutional welfare rights: one view of Rawls' *Theory of Justice*', *University of Pennsylvania Law Review*, 121, 1973, 962-1019. Assesses the implications of this theory for constructing an adequate legal theory of welfare rights, suggesting that Rawls ignores needs-based claims.

8.1301 **Miller**, R. W., 'Rawls and Marxism', *Phil. Pub. Affairs*, 3, 1974, 167–91. Criticises his neglect of social conflict, suggesting that his ideas are no better than utilitarian ones in this area.

8.1302 —— 'Rawls, risk and utilitarianism', *Phil. Sts.*, 28, 1975, 55–61.

8.1303 **Mosher**, M. A., 'Boundary revisions: the deconstruction of moral personality in Rawls, Nozick, Sandel and Parfit', *Pol. Sts.*, 39, 1991, 287–302. Focusing upon the boundaries within and between selves in Rawlsian discourse, Mosher rehearses the critique of one of the intuitive certainties of liberal thought by showing that the impersonality required by a theory of justice pressurises every notion of personality within it.

8.1304 **Mueller**, D. C., **Tollison**, R. D., and **Willett**, T. D., 'The utilitarian contract: a generalization of Rawls' theory of justice', *Theory and Decisions*, 4, 1974, 345–65. Claim to offer a more general presentation of the theory of justice than Rawls, providing a bridge between utilitarian and social contract approaches.

8.1305 **Nagel**, T., 'Rawls on justice', *Phil. Rev.*, 82, 1973, 220–34. Locates bias within the original position, rendering it problematic as a fair device for selecting principles.

8.1306 **Narveson**, J. F., 'A puzzle about economic justice in Rawls' theory', *Soc. Theory & Pract.*, 4, 1976, 1–28. Critique of his apparent reconciliation of equality as a desirable goal and inequality as an accepted feature of capitalist society: Rawls fails to transcend these irreconcilable positions.

8.1307 —— 'Rawls on equal distribution of wealth', *Philosophia*, 7, 1978, 281–92. Examines his claim that equality is the benchmark of justice, concluding that this principle goes against intuition.

8.1308 **Nathan**, N. M. L., 'Some prerequisites for a political casuistry of justice', *Inquiry*, 13, 1970, 376–93.

8.1309 **Neal**, P., 'In the shadow of the general will: Rawls, Kant and Rousseau on the problem of political right', *Rev. Pol.*, 49, 1987, 389–409. Places Rawls's account of political right between Kant and Rousseau. More controversially, Neal makes the unlikely claim that Rawls's theoretical project – the desire to express politically the Kantian conception of autonomy – was, in fact, 'completed' by Rousseau.

8.1310 —— 'On the contradictions in John Rawls' *A Theory of Justice*', *Journal of the West Virginian Philosophical Society*, 12, 1977, 7–9.

8.1311 **Nickel**, J. W., 'Rawls on political community and principles of justice', *Law and Philosophy*, 9, 1990, 205–16. Criticises his interpretation of political community, suggesting that it exaggerates the role of political philosophy and the dangers of oppression resulting from stronger forms of community. Concludes that an overlapping consensus about a conception of justice is not a sufficient basis for a political community.

8.1312 **Nielsen**, K., 'Capitalism, socialism and justice: reflections on Rawls' theory of justice', *Social Praxis*, 7, 1981, 253–77.

8.1313 —— 'Equality, justice and class', *Dialectica*, 32, 1978, 126–33.

8.1314 —— 'Morality and ideology: some radical critiques', *Graduate Faculty Philosophy Journal*, 8, 1981–82, 189–254. Extremely useful summary of the 'radical' objections

to Rawls, centred upon the ideological status of his ideas. Extensive and clear.

8.1315 —— 'On the very possibility of a classless society. Rawls, Macpherson, and revisionist liberalism', *Pol. Theory*, 6, 1978, 191–208. Review of Macpherson's critique of Rawls's models of politics and society, assessing the former's claim that Rawls deploys a contradictory bourgeois model.

8.1316 —— 'Rawls and classist anarchism', *Mind*, 86, 1977, 19-30.

8.1317 —— 'Rawls and the left: some left critics of Rawls' principles of justice', *Analyse und Kritik*, 2, 1980, 74–97. Useful summary of left criticism, noting that this has generally been focused on the principles of justice.

8.1318 —— 'Rawls' defense of morality', *Personalist*, 59, 1977, 93–100.

8.1319 —— 'The choice between perfectionism and Rawlsian contractarianism', *Interpretation*, 6, 1977, 132–9.

8.1320 **Norton**, D. L., 'Rawls' theory of justice: a perfectionist's rejoinder', *Ethics*, 85, 1974, 50–7.

8.1321 **Nowell-Smith**, P. H., 'A theory of justice?', *Phil. Soc. Sc.*, 3, 1973, 315–29.

8.1322 **O'Connor**, J., 'Wolff, Rawls, and the principles of justice', *Phil. Sts.*, 19, 1968, 93–5.

8.1323 **Okin**, S. M., 'John Rawls: justice and fairness – for whom?', in S. M. Lyndon and C. Pateman, ed., *Feminist Interpretations and Political Theory*, 1991, 181–98.

8.1324 **Orr**, D., and **Ramm**, W., 'Rawls' justice and classical liberalism: ethics and welfare economics', *Economic Inquiry*, 85, 1974, 50–7.

8.1325 **Parekh**, B., 'John Rawls', in *Contemporary Political Thinkers*, 1982, 54–85.

8.1326 —— 'Reflections on Rawls' *Theory of Justice*', *Pol. Sts.*, 20, 1972, 478–83.

8.1327 **Paul**, J., 'Rawls on liberty', in Z. A. Pelczynski and J. Gray, ed., *Conceptions of Liberty in Political Philosophy*, 1984, 376–96. Outline of his interpretation of liberty, justification for its inclusion among the principles of justice and the implications of these ideas for public policy.

8.1328 **Pence**, G. E., 'Fair contracts and beautiful intuitions', *Can. J. Phil.*, supp. 3, 1977, 137–52. Clever critique of Rawls's attempt to extend contractarian thinking into the realm of ethics, questioning the claim that his veil of ignorance can guarantee impartiality through an assessment of the working of the principles of justice in medicine.

8.1329 **Pettit**, P., 'A theory of justice?', *Theory and Decision*, 4, 1974, 311–24.

8.1330 **Pogge**, T. W., *Realizing Rawls*, New York, 1989. A defence against criticisms tabled by Sandel and Nozick.

8.1331 **Pollock**, L., 'A dilemma for Rawls?', *Phil. Sts.*, 22, 1971, 37–43.

8.1332 **Proudfoot**, W., 'Rawls on the individual and the social', *Journal of Religious Ethics*, 2, 1974, 107–28.

8.1333 **Rapaport**, E., 'Classical liberalism and Rawlsian revisionism', *Can. J. Phil.*, supp. 3., 1977, 95–119. Interesting presentation of his revision of seventeenth-century contractarianism, raising important objections from the standpoint of liberalism to both versions of the social contract.

8.1334 **Raphael**, D. D., 'Critical notice: Rawls' theory of justice', *Mind*, 83, 1974, 118–27.

8.1335 **Rasmussen**, D. B., 'A critique of Rawls' theory of justice', *Personalist*, 55, 1974, 303–18.

8.1336 **Reiman**, J. H., 'A reply to Choptiany on Rawls on justice', *Ethics*, 84, 1974, 262–5.

8.1337 **Rostenstreich**, N., 'Public culture of a democratic society: comments on Professor Rawls' Dewey lectures', *Journal of Value Inquiry*, 17, 1983, 143–50. Focuses upon the relationship between moral and political theory in Kant's work and the bearing this has on Rawls.

8.1338 **Ryan**, A., 'John Rawls', in Q. Skinner, ed., *The Return of Grand Theory in the Human Sciences*, 1985, 101–19. Astute interpretation of his thought, focusing upon the enthusiastic reception his ideas have received in North America.

8.1339 **Scanlon**, T, M., 'Rawls' theory of justice', *University of Pennsylvania Law Review*, 121, 1973, 1020–78. Accessible introductory guide for the uninitiated.

8.1340 **Schaar**, J. H., 'Reflections on Rawls' theory of justice', *Soc. Theory & Pract.*, 3, 1974, 75–100. Following an outline of the original position, the author proves sceptical about the universality of Rawls's account of human nature, and the conflation of equality and justice which he encourages.

8.1341 **Schaefer**, D. L., 'A critique of Rawls' contract doctrine', *Rev. Metaph.*, 28, 1974,

89–115. Admirably clear discussion and critique of his derivation of morally obliging principles of justice from the original position, focusing on his failure to characterise adequately the parties to the original position.

8.1342 —— *Justice or Tyranny? A Critique of John Rawls's "Theory of Justice"*, New York, 1979. Sceptical discussion of these ideas, stressing his ideological commitments.

8.1343 —— 'The "sense" and non-sense of justice: an examination of John Rawls' *A Theory of Justice*', *Pol. Sc. Rev.*, 3, 1973, 1–41.

8.1344 **Schedler**, G., 'Rawls, Marx and the injustice of capitalism', *Revolutionary World*, 33, 1979, 85–97.

8.1345 **Schwarzenbach**, S. A., 'Rawls, Hegel, and communitarianism', *Pol. Theory*, 19, 1991, 539–71. Presents the unorthodox thesis that Hegel's influence is present in Rawls's work, rendering redundant the opposition between liberals and communitarians.

8.1346 **Schweitkart**, D., 'Should Rawls be a socialist? A comparison of his ideal capitalism with worker-controlled socialism', *Soc. Theory & Pract.*, 5, 1978, 1–27. Argument for a modified market socialism as superior to Rawls's idealised capitalism and more congruent with the latter's ethical commitments. Unusual and stimulating contribution to the debate about his work.

8.1347 **Scott**, G., 'John Rawls' difference principle, utilitarianism, and the optimum degree of inequality', *J. Phil.*, 70, 1973, 275–80.

8.1348 **Sen**, A., 'Rawls versus Bentham: an axiomatic examination of the pure distribution problem', *Theory and Decision*, 4, 1974, 301–9.

8.1349 **Sessions**, W. L., 'Rawls' concept and conception of the primary good', *Soc. Theory & Pract.*, 7, 1981, 303–24.

8.1350 **Shaw**, P., 'Rawls, the difference principle and equality', *Phil. Q.*, 42, 1992, 71–7. A critique of the difference principle from the standpoint of equality.

8.1351 **Shue**, H. G., 'The current fashions: trickle down by Arrow and close-knits by Rawls', *J. Phil.*, 71, 1974, 319–26.

8.1352 **Simson**, G. J., 'Another view of Rawls' theory of justice', *Emory Law Journal*, 23, 1974, 473–96.

8.1353 **Singer**, M. G., 'On Rawls on Mill on liberty and so on', *Journal of Value Inquiry*,

11, 1977, 141–8.

8.1354 **Slote**, M. A., 'Desert, content and justice', *Phil. Pub. Affairs*, 2, 1973, 323–47.

8.1355 **Snare**, F., 'John Rawls and the methods of ethics', *Phil. & Phenom. Res.*, 36, 1975, 100–12.

8.1356 **Sneed**, J. D., 'John Rawls and the liberal theory of society', *Erkenntis*, 10, 1976, 1–19.

8.1357 —— 'Political institutions as means to economic justice: a critique of Rawls' contractarianism', *Analyse und Kritik*, 1, 1979, 125–46.

8.1358 **Sterba**, J. P., 'In defense of Rawls against Arrow and Nozick', *Philosophia*, 7, 1978, 293–303. Defends Rawls's contractual alternative to utilitarian beliefs and rejects Nozick's criticism of the inadequacy of the Rawlsian conception of justice.

8.1359 —— 'Justice as desert', *Soc. Theory & Pract.*, 3, 1974, 101–16. Contests the particular conception of justice which, according to Rawls, would be adopted by those in the original position, arguing for an alternative whereby each person's contribution to economic production figures more prominently.

8.1360 **Strasnick**, S., 'Social choice and the derivation of Rawls's difference principle', *J. Phil.*, 73, 1976, 85–99.

8.1361 **Sumner**, L. W., 'Rawls and the contract theory of civil disobedience', *Can. J. Phil.*, supp. 3, 1977, 1–48. Clear and sharp assessment of his theory of political obligation, exemplified by the question of civil disobedience. Useful guide to the issues involved in the latter question as well as to this aspect of his theory.

8.1362 **Tattershall**, G., 'A Rawls bibliography', *Soc. Theory & Pract.*, 3, 1974, 123–7.

8.1363 **Taylor**, C., 'On social justice', *Can. J. Pol. & Soc. Theory*, 1, 1977, 89–96.

8.1364 **Thomas**, L. L., 'To *A Theory of Justice*: an epilogue', *Philosophical Forum*, 6, 1974–75, 244–53.

8.1365 **Van Dyke**, V., 'Justice as fairness: for groups', *Am. Pol. Sc. Rev.*, 69, 1975, 607–14. Stimulating assessment of the implications of the existence of interest groups for this theory of justice.

8.1366 **Wolff**, R. P., 'A refutation of Rawls' theorem on justice', *J. Phil.*, 63, 1966, 179–90.

8.1367 —— *Understanding Rawls: A Reconstruction and Critique of A Theory of Justice*, Princeton, N.J., 1977. A lively interpretation of this text as a 'multilayered record of at least twenty years of philosophical growth and development'; beginning with an assessment of the problems he faced when he first developed his theory, Wolff assesses the significance of his philosophy and the relationship between his work and Kant, concluding with his own critique.

8.1368 **Wright**, R. G., 'The high cost of Rawls' inegalitarianism', *West. Pol. Q.*, 30, 1977, 73–9.

8.1369 **Zamagni**, S., *Rawls Between Contractualism and Utilitarianism*, Bologna, 1981.

8.1370 **Zuckert**, M., 'Justice deserted: a critique of Rawls' *A Theory of Justice*', *Polity*, 13, 1981, 466–83. Hostile review, pointing to the inability of his principles to satisfy the criteria of justice he proffers.

Rorty

8.1371 **Bernstein**, R. J., 'One step forward, two steps backward: Richard Rorty on liberal democracy and philosophy', *Pol. Theory*, 15, 1987, 538–63. Criticises his self-definition as a Deweyan pragmatist mainly because, in contrast to Dewey, his liberalism amounts to a defence of the 'status quo'.

8.1372 —— 'Rorty's liberal utopia', *Social Res.*, 57, 1990, 31–72. Introduction to the key themes in his thought, assessing his impact on liberal democratic discourse.

8.1373 **Comay**, R., 'Interrupting the conversation: notes on Rorty', *Telos*, 69, 1986, 119–30.

8.1374 **Leland**, D., 'Rorty on the moral concern philosophy: a critique from a feminist point of view', *Praxis International*, 8, 1988, 273–83.

8.1375 **Wain**, K., 'Strong poets and utopia: Rorty's liberalism, Dewey and democracy', *Pol. Sts.*, 41, 1993, 394–407. Explores the tension between Rorty's increasingly political focus and the influence of his thought. Ultimately, for Wain, Rorty fails to synthesis Deweyan pragmatism and Nietzschean post-structuralism.

8.1376 **Weinstein**, M. A., 'Liberalism goes post-modern: Rorty's pragmatism', *Can. J. Pol. & Soc. Theory*, 10, 1986, 10–19. Sceptical assessment of the intellectual and political origins of his liberalism and the failures of his pragmatic philosophy.

Strauss

8.1377 **Anastaplo**, G., 'On Leo Strauss: a Yahrzeit remembrance', *University of Chicago Magazine*, 67, 1974, 30–8. Lively account of the excitement which his ideas generated.

8.1378 **Andrew**, E., 'Descent to the cave', *Rev. Pol.*, 45, 1983, 510–35. Challenges Strauss's appropriation of Plato's view of political philosophy as a transcendent realm beyond politics.

8.1379 **Beiner**, R., 'Hannah Arendt and Leo Strauss: the uncommenced dialogue', *Pol. Theory*, 18, 1990, 238–54. Thoughtful comparison of these thinkers, suggesting that their critiques of modernity complement each other.

8.1380 **Bernadette**, S., 'Leo Strauss's *The City and Man*', *Political Science Reviewer*, 8, 1978, 1–20. Views this text as an investigation of the conflict between nature and convention/law.

8.1381 **Berns**, L., 'Leo Strauss, 1899–1973', *Independent Journal of Philosophy*, 2, 1978, 1–3.

8.1382 **Bloom**, 'Leo Strauss: September 20, 1899 – October 18, 1973', *Pol. Theory*, 2, 1974, 372–92. Celebration of his life and work.

8.1383 **Cropsey**, J., 'A reply to Rothman', *Am. Pol. Sc. Rev.*, 56, 1962, 353–9. Defends Strauss against charges of elitism, arguing that his ideas emerge from the tradition of Platonic democracy.

8.1384 —— 'Leo Strauss: a bibliography and memorial, 1988–1973', *Interpretation*, 5, 1975, 133–47. Proposes the unlikely thesis that Strauss taught modesty.

8.1385 **Dallmayr**, F., 'Politics against philosophy: Strauss and Drury', *Pol. Theory*, 15, 1987, 326–37. Personal response to Strauss's complex political ideas, especially in the light of Drury's interpretation.

8.1386 **Drury**, S. B., 'Leo Strauss's classic natural right teaching', *Pol. Theory*, 15, 1987, 299–315. Specifies the natural right predilections of Strauss as the key to his political philosophy and, in particular, his critique of modernity. Unconventional and elitist interpretation of his thought.

8.1387 —— 'The esoteric philosophy of Leo Strauss', *Pol. Theory*, 13, 1985, 315–37.

Rehearses his commitment to the politically subversive nature of philosophical truth, concluding that his ideas are closer in meaning to Nietzsche than Plato.

8.1388 —— *The Esoteric Philosophy: The Political Ideas of Leo Strauss*, 1988. Presents him as a philosopher with a unique and disturbing set of ideas which he never states unambiguously. Attempting to avoid either hagiography or polemical criticism Drury focuses on his philosophical elitism and contempt for morality in political society.

8.1389 **Germino**, D., 'Second thoughts on Leo Strauss's Machiavelli', *J. Pol.*, 28, 1966, 794–817.

8.1390 **Gourevitch**, V., 'Philosophy and politics: I and II', *Rev. Metaph.*, 22, 1968, 58–84 and 281–328. Comprehensive account of Strauss's political thought, including an analysis of his account of love.

8.1391 **Gunnell**, J. G., 'Political theory and politics: the case of Leo Strauss', *Pol. Theory*, 13, 1985, 339–61. Stresses the rhetorical nature of his thought and suggests that his ideas throw into relief the problematic relationship between academic political theory and the realm of politics.

8.1392 —— 'The myth of the tradition', *Am. Pol. Sc. Rev.*, 72, 1978, 122–34. Places Strauss in the same genre of writing as Arendt and Voegelin, in that all attempt to use political theory to understand the modern predicament.

8.1393 **Jung**, H. J., 'Strauss's conception of political philosophy', *Rev. Pol.*, 29, 1967, 492–517. Critique of his view of political philosophy in the light of existential philosophy. Strauss, the author concludes, neglects the realm of political action.

8.1394 **Lampert**, L., 'The argument of Leo Strauss in *What is Political Philosophy*', *Modern Age*, 22, 1978, 38–46.

8.1395 **Lomenthal**, D., 'Leo Strauss's *Studies in Platonic Political Philosophy*', *Interpretation*, 13, 1985, 297–320.

8.1396 **McShea**, R. J., 'Leo Strauss on Machiavelli', *West. Pol. Q.*, 16, 1963, 782–97. Draws attention to the tension between the classical and biblical traditions deployed by Strauss.

8.1397 **Mansfield**, H. C., 'Strauss' Machiavelli', *Pol. Theory*, 3, 1975, 371–405.

8.1398 **Miller**, E. F., 'Leo Strauss: the recovery of

political philosophy', in A. de Crespigny and K. Minogue, ed., *Contemporary Political Philosophers*, 1976, 67–99. Rehearses his belief that political philosophy constitutes a sphere of knowledge as opposed to a realm of opinion, assessing his rehabilitation of the classical tradition in opposition to the modern.

8.1399 **Nicgorski**, W., 'Strauss and Christianity: reason, politics and Christian belief ', *Claremont Review*, 4, 1985, 18–21.

8.1400 **Niemeyer**, G., 'What is political knowledge?', *Rev. Pol.*, 23, 1961, 101–7. Criticises Strauss's view of the classics as 'closed' to the truths of revelation, rejecting his views on virtue and criticism of modernity.

8.1401 **Pippin**, R. B., 'The modern world of Leo Strauss', *Pol. Theory*, 20, 1992, 448–72.

8.1402 **Pocock**, J. G. A., 'Prophet and inquisitor', *Pol. Theory*, 3, 1975, 385–401. A response to Mansfield on Strauss.

8.1403 **Rothman**, S., 'The revival of classical political philosophy: a critique', *Am. Pol. Sc. Rev.*, 56, 1962, 341–52. Suggests that Strauss's classical theory of natural rights is dated and untenable.

8.1404 **Schaefer**, D. L., 'The legacy of Leo Strauss: a bibliographic introduction', *Intercollegiate Review*, 9, 1974, 139–48.

8.1405 **Steinberger**, J., 'Political philosophy, political theology and morality', *Thomist*, 32, 1968, 307–32. Focusing on Strauss's silences, the author provides a defence of his political thought against Christian critics.

8.1406 **Susser**, B., 'Leo Strauss: the ancient as modern', *Pol. Sts.*, 36, 1988, 497–514. Accounts for the influence of his critique of modern social science through his combination of pre-modern arguments with contemporary principles.

8.1407 **Tarcov**, N., 'Philosophy and history: tradition and interpretation in the work of Leo Strauss', *Polity*, 16, 1983, 5–29. Defends Straussian political theory, suggesting it is misleading to read him as a simple traditionalist; in fact, he developed a complex, historicist approach to the political thought of previous eras.

8.1408 **Ward**, J. F., 'Experience and political philosophy: notes on reading Leo Strauss', *Polity*, 13, 1981, 668–87. Outlines his refutation of historicism and belief in the essentially diverse nature of experience.

8.1409 **Warren**, S., *The Emergence of Dialectical Theory: Philosophy and Political Theory*, 1984. Approves of Strauss's critique of value-free social science but not his return to classical political philosophy.

Other thinkers

8.1410 **Coleman**, S., *Daniel de Leon*, 1990. Description of the ideas and political career of the most significant and influential American Marxist between 1890 and 1914.

8.1411 **Frankfurt**, H. G., 'The anarchism of Robert Paul Woolf ', *Pol. Theory*, 1, 1973, 405–14. Perceives a contradiction between Woolf 's apparent denial of the legitimacy of political authority and belief in the importance of consent within democracies, a recognition that amounts to the conventional and most widely accepted justification of constitutional political authority.

8.1412 **Heertje**, A., ed., *Schumpeter's Vision: Capitalism, Socialism and Democracy after 40 Years*, 1981. A collection commemorating this particular text (Samuelson, Haberles) and examining the accuracy of his predictions (Heilbroner, Lumbers, Smithies).

8.1413 **Kann**, M. E., 'Challenging Lockean liberalism in America. The case of Debs and Hillquit', *Pol. Theory*, 8, 1980, 203–22. Attempts to explain the absence of socialism in America through the 'Lockean preferences' of its people. The ideas of these early twentieth-century socialists are examined, revealing that their Marxism was propounded through Lockean language and ideas.

8.1414 **Miller**, E. F., 'David Easton's political theory', *Pol. Sc. Re-r*, 5, 1971, 184–236.

8.1415 **O'Brien**, J., 'American Leninism in the 1970s', *Rad. Am.*, 11–12, 1977–78, 27–62.

8.1416 **Polsby**, N. W., *Community Power and Political Theory*, New Haven, Conn., 1963. Sympathetic assessment of Dahl's project.

8.1417 **Reed**, A. L., 'W. E. B., DuBois: a perspective on the bases of his political thought', *Pol. Theory*, 13, 1985, 431–56. Counters the tendency to underplay his ideas by examining his views on inter-racialism, pan-Africanism and socialism. Concludes that collectivism and pluralism provided two of the central motifs in his thought.

8.1418 **Ricci**, D. M., 'Democracy attenuated: Schumpeter, the process theory, and American democratic thought', *J. Pols.*, 32, 1970, 239–68. Examines the process theory of democracy through an exposition of his critique of classical liberalism.

8.1419 **Salvatore**, N., *Eugene Debs: Citizen and Socialist*, Urbana, Ill., 1982.

8.1420 **Seretan**, L. G., *Daniel de Leon: The Odyssey of an American Marxist*, Cambridge, Mass., 1979.

8.1421 **Smith**, D., *The Chicago School: A Liberal Critique of Capitalism*, 1988. Explores the school's sociology and political economy from the premise that the tensions and weaknesses of their theories derived from contradictions within and between American capitalism and liberalism.

8.1422 **Steinkraus**, W. E., 'Martin Luther King's personalism and non-violence', *J. Hist. Ideas*, 34, 1973, 97–113.

8.1423 **Stuart**, J., 'William English Walling and the search for an American socialist theory', *Sc. & Soc.*, 35, 1971. Revives the early twentieth-century thought of Walling, significant for its revision of Marxist doctrines concerning the post-revolutionary period.

8.1424 **Tivey**, L., 'Robert Dahl and American pluralism', in L. Tivey and A. Wright, ed., *Political Thought Since 1945: Philosophy, Science, Ideology*, 1992, 91–114. Establishes the essential consistency in Dahl's work in this accessible introduction to the subject.

8.1425 **Walton**, H., *The Political Philosophy of Martin Luther King*, 1971.

8.1426 **Ware**, A., 'The concept of political equality: a post-Dahl analysis', *Pol. Sts.*, 29, 1981, 392–406.

8.1427 **Wilson**, K. D., 'Autonomy and Wolff's defence of anarchism', *Phil. Forum*, 8, 1976, 108–21. A critique of his notion of autonomy, which suggests that he should be more concerned with proving that political authority is logically inconsistent.

8.1428 **Young**, J., 'Daniel de Leon and Anglo-American socialism', *Labor History*, 17, 1976, 329–50. Differentiates him from Leninism by focusing upon his conception of the development of class consciousness among workers.

8.1429 ——— 'H. M. Hyndman and Daniel de Leon: the two souls of socialism', *Labor History*, 28, 1987, 534–6. Contrasts de Leon's popular vision of socialism with Hyndman's statism and centralism, celebrating the former's contribution to socialist thought.

INDEX